Interpreting

Interpreting Canada's Past

A PRE-CONFEDERATION READER

Volume One / Third Edition

Edited by

**J.M. Bumsted
and Len Kuffert**

OXFORD

UNIVERSITY PRESS

1904 🍁 2004

100 YEARS OF
CANADIAN PUBLISHING

OXFORD
UNIVERSITY PRESS

70 Wynford Drive, Don Mills, Ontario M3C 1J9
www.oup.com/ca

Oxford University Press is a department of the University of Oxford.
It furthers the University's objective of excellence in research, scholarship,
and education by publishing worldwide in

Oxford   New York
Auckland   Cape Town   Dar es Salaam   Hong Kong   Karachi
Kuala Lumpur   Madrid   Melbourne   Mexico City   Nairobi
New Delhi   Shanghai   Taipei   Toronto
With offices in
Argentina   Austria   Brazil   Chile   Czech Republic   France   Greece
Guatemala   Hungary   Italy   Japan   Poland   Portugal   Singapore
South Korea   Switzerland   Thailand   Turkey   Ukraine   Vietnam

Oxford is a trade mark of Oxford University Press
in the UK and in certain other countries

Published in Canada
by Oxford University Press

National Library of Canada Cataloguing in Publication

Interpreting Canada's Past/edited by
J.M. Bumstead and Len Kuffert. — 3rd ed.

Includes bibliographical references.
Contents: v. 1. Pre-Confederation
ISBN-10: 0-19-542017-9 (v.1)   ISBN-13: 978-0-19-542017-3

1. Canada—History—Textbooks.   2. Canada—History—Sources.
I. Bumstead, J.M., 1938–   II. Kuffert, L.B. (Leonard B.)

FC170.I57 2004   971   C2004-902342-X

Cover Design: Brett Miller

3 4 - 07 06 05
This book is printed on permanent (acid-free) paper ∞.
Printed in Canada

CONTENTS

Preface

■ As editors, we had several goals in mind in organizing and making the selections for these volumes of readings. One was to emphasize the continuities and discontinuities in the writing of Canadian history. A second goal was to illustrate the extent to which the interpretation of Canada's past is constantly evolving. A third goal was to draw attention to the writing of history—of Canada or anywhere—as an interpretive and imaginative act. To make these points, we have chosen a topical framework in which documents are mixed with secondary interpretations. The topics for the most part reflect the mainstream issues most often discussed in the introductory survey course in Canadian history. The primary documents are intended to allow readers and students of history to hear the voices of those who, if not direct participants in some of the events and processes considered here, nevertheless were contemporary players whose inflections and emphases on particular themes can help us better understand the priorities and assumptions of the past. Historians interpret the historical record from a distance, and primary sources can provide some relief to break up what otherwise might seem like a curiously featureless landscape. As for the interpretations of the historians, they have been chosen to represent a fairly broad time span and various points of view. Since historians' own surroundings and dispositions affect their work—just as these factors influence one's own life experience—so the student ought to be able to sense the imprint or the importance of the historians' own times on the interpretations included here. The selections have also been chosen to show how historians can approach a question or theme from many perspectives, ranging from chronological narrative to inventive case studies.

The topics in these volumes are presented in a rough chronological order, but need not be used by students in that order. Each topic is designed to be both self-contained and to relate to others. The topic is self-contained to the extent that it does not rely on other reading. It is linked to others in the sense that each topic touches upon some powerful common themes in history, like power, class, gender, and nation. Our short introductions to each topic are not meant to guide or limit the instructor or the student in their respective approaches to the material, but rather to point out some of the linkages we see within each subgroup of documents and readings, and to convey some sense of why we have chosen the material we have selected.

ONE

☐ The Origins of North Americans

Readings

PRIMARY DOCUMENTS

HISTORICAL INTERPRETATIONS

INTRODUCTION

■ Among the many fascinating questions for Europeans resulting from the realization that the Americas were indeed a 'New World' was that of the origins of the animals, plants, and human inhabitants to be found there. Europe had traditions extending back at least to the Greeks and to the Bible for explaining its own origins, but it was not clear whether those could be extended to the Americas, particularly given the fairly obvious presence of plants and animals previously unknown to Europeans. Especially fascinating was the matter of the human inhabitants. Were they a different species from those people previously known in Europe? Were they, indeed, human? This question was debated at some length in the early days, mostly in the context of determining whether the Americans were potential subjects of Christian missionary activity through possessing sentience, intelligence, and perhaps most importantly, souls. The determination that the American population was worthy of

Christianization did not, of course, solve the problem of where they had originated. The native inhabitants had their own origin myths, much as did the Christians in the Bible.

Many theories were advanced by Europeans in the sixteenth and seventeenth centuries to provide a rational explanation for the origins of America and of the Americans. One of the most interesting efforts was that made by Father José de Acosta in 1590 in a work entitled the *Natural and Moral History of the Indies*. Acosta considered his topic in the standard way developed over the centuries by Christian theologians. It consisted of posing questions, often as either/or alternatives, and then choosing answers on the basis of logical deduction backed by available information. By this process he determined that the Americans had migrated from elsewhere on the planet, probably by use of a land bridge. As more and more scientific work was done in the eighteenth and nineteenth centuries by all sorts of specialists, the notion of a land bridge became an increasingly popular theory to explain the origins of Americans. Like other scientific theories, it worked because it met the test of fitting most (if not quite all) of the available data. It also worked because those who propounded it insisted on extremely high standards for acceptable evidence, rejecting literary sources, hypothetical speculation, and extrapolation from other disciplines as basically unscientific. By the 1930s the theory had become fairly completely articulated, and by the 1980s it had achieved considerable sophistication and elaboration.

Like most scientific theories, the land bridge theory was subject to revision. Some of the revision occurred within the limits of the general theory itself, but there were also critics who complained that the theory did not fit perfectly with all the evidence. So long as there were only a few exceptions, the theory could still be regarded as sound. But by the end of the twentieth century increasing numbers of scholars thought there were far too many exceptions, perhaps even enough to render the theory suspect. Even the popular press began reporting on the suspicions that the theory had broken down.

Questions for consideration

1. Why was a land bridge between Asia and North America such an attractive concept?
2. What was the conventional scenario for the movement of people into North America?
3. In what ways did new evidence question the scenario?
4. Why is the subject of the origins of North Americans fraught with political contentiousness?

Suggestions for further reading

Nigel Davis, *Voyagers to the New World* (New York: William Morrow & Co., 1979). A sensible presentation of alternate scenarios of North American origins.

Elaine Dewar, *Bones: Discovering the First Americans* (Toronto: Random House Canada, 2001). A journalist explores the politics of the scientific issues of the origins debate.

E. James Dixon, *Bones, Boats & Bison: Archaeology and the First Colonization of Western North America* (Albuquerque: University of New Mexico Press, 1999). A good discussion of recent findings.

Brian M. Fagan, *Ancient North America: The Archaeology of a Continent*, 3rd edn (New York: Thames & Hudson, 2000). A useful summary of conventional wisdom.

PRIMARY DOCUMENTS

1 'Where the First People Came from', C. Douglas Ellis, ed., *Cree Legends from the West Coast of James Bay* (Winnipeg: University of Manitoba Press, 1995), 2–5.

So then, I shall tell another legend. I'll tell a story, the legend about ourselves, the people, as we are called. Also I shall tell the legend about where we came from and why we came . . . why we who are living now came to inhabit this land.

Now then, first I shall begin.

The other land was above, it is said. It was like this land which we dwell in, except that the life seems different; also it is different on account of its being cold and mild [here]. So then, this land where we are invariably tends to be cold.

So that is the land above which is talked about from which there came two people, one woman and one man . . . they dwelt in that land which was above. But it was certainly known that this world where we live was there.

Now then at one time someone spoke to them, while they were in that land of theirs where they were brought up. He said to them, 'Do you want to go see yonder land which is below?'

The very one about which they were spoken to is this one where we dwell.

'Yes', they said, 'we will go there.'

'The land', they were told, 'is different, appears different from this one where we dwell in, which you dwell in now during your lifetime. But you will find it different there, should you go to see that land. It is cold yonder. And sometimes it is hot.'

'It fluctuates considerably. If you wish to go there, however, you must go see the spider at the end of this land where you are. That is where he lives.'

The spider, as he is called, that is the one who is the net-maker, who never exhausts his twine—so they went to see him, who is called the spider.

Then he asked them, 'Where do you want to go? Do you want to go and see yonder land, the other one which is below?'

'Yes', they said.

'Very well', said the spider. 'I shall make a line so that I may lower you.'

So then, he made a line up to—working it around up to, up to the top.

'Not yet, not yet even half done', he said.

Then he spoke to them, telling them, better for him to let them down even before he finished it the length it should be.

Then he told them, 'That land which you want to go and see is cold and sometimes mild. But there will certainly be someone there who will teach you, where you will find a living once you have reached it. He, he will tell you every thing so you will get along well.'

So he made a place for them to sit as he lowered them, the man and the woman.

They got in together, into that thing which looked like a bag.

Then he instructed them what to do during their trip. 'Only one must look', he said to them. 'But one must not look until you have made contact with the earth. You may both look then.'

So, meanwhile they went along, one looked. At last he caught sight of the land.

The one told the other, 'Now the land is in sight.'

The one told the other, 'Now the rivers are in sight.'

They had been told however, that 'if one . . . if they both look together, before they come to the land, they will go into the great eagle-nest and they will never be able to get out and climb down from there.'

That's where they will be. That's what they were told.

Then the one told the other, 'Now the lakes are in sight. Now the grass.'

Then they both looked before they arrived, as they were right at the top of the trees. Then they went sideways for a short while, then they went into the great eagle-nest. That's where they went in, having violated their instructions. . . .

Then the bear arrived.

So he said to them . . . and they said to him, 'Come and help us.'

The bear didn't listen for long; but then he started to get up on his hind legs to go and see them. Also another one, the wolverine as he is called. They made one trip each as they brought them down.

But the bear was followed by those people.

That was the very thing which had been said to them, 'You will have someone there who will teach you to survive.'

This bear, he taught them everything about how to keep alive there.

It was there that these people began to multiply from one couple, the persons who had come from another land. They lived giving birth to their children generation after generation. That is us right up until today. That is why we are in this country.

And by-and-by the White People began to arrive as they began to reach us people, who live in this country.

That is as much as I shall tell.

2 From José de Acosta, *Historia Natural y Moral de las Indias*, vol. 1 (London: The Hakluyt Society, 1880 [1590]), 45–80.

CHAP XVI—*By what meanes the first men might come to the Indies, the which was not willingly, nor of set purpose*

Now it is time to make answer to such as say there are no Antipodes, and that this region where we live cannot bee inhabited. The huge greatnes of the Ocean did so amaze St. Augustine as he could not conceive how mankind could passe to this new-found world. But seeing on the one side wee know for certaine that many yeares agoe there were men inhabiting in these parts, so likewise we cannot deny but the scripture doth teaching us cleerely that all men are come from the first man, without doubt we shall be forced to believe and confesse that men have passed hither from Europe, Asia, or Affricke, yet must wee discover by what meanes they could passe. It is not likely that there was another Noes Arke by the which men might be transported into the Indies, and much lesse any Angell to carie the first man to this new world, holding him by the haire of the head, like to the Prophet Abacus; for we intrest not of the mightie power of God, but only of that which is conformable unto reason, and the order and disposition of humane things. Wherefore these two things ought to be held for wonderfull and worthie of admiration, yea, to bee numbred among the secrets of god. The one is, how men could passe so huge a passage by Sea and Lande; the other is, that there beeing such multitudes of people they have yet beene unknowne so many ages. For this cause I demaund, by what resolution, force or industrie, the Indians could passe so large a Sea, and who might be the Investor of so strange a passage? Truely I have often times considered thereof with my selfe, as many others have done, but never could I finde any thing to satisfie mee. Yet will I say what I have conceived, and what comes presently into my minde, seeing that testimonies faile men whom I might follow, suffering myselfe to be guided by the rule of reason, although it be very subtill. It is most certaine that the first men came to this land of Peru by one of these two meanes, either by land or by sea. If they came by sea, it was casually, and by chance, or willingly, and of purpose. I understand by chance being cast by force of some storme or tempest, as it happens in tempestuous times. I meane done of purpose, when they prepared fleetes to discover new lands. Besides these two meanes I see it is not possible to find out any other, if wee will follow the course of humane things and not devise fabulous and poetical fictions; for no man may thinke to fine another Eagle as that of Ganimede, or a flying Horse like unto Perseus, that should carie the Indians through the aire; or that peradventure these first men have used fishes, as Mirmaids, or the fish called a Nicholas, to pass them thither. But laying aside these imaginations and fopperies, let us examine these two meanes, the which will bee both pleasant and profitable. First, in my judgement, it were not farre from reason to say that the first and auncient people of these Indies have discovered and peopled after the same sort as wee do at this day, that is, by the Arts of Navigation and aide of Pilots, the which guide themselves by the height and knowledge of the heavens, and by their industrie in handling and changing of their sailes according to the season. Why might not this well be? Must we belieeve that we alone, and in this our age, have onely the Arts and knowledge to saile through the Ocean? Wee see even now that they cut through the Ocean to discover new lands, as not long since Alvaro Mendaria and his companions did, who parting from the Port of Lima came alongst the West to discover the land which lieth Eastward from Peru; and at the end of three moneths they discovered the Ilands which they call the Ilands of Salomon, which are many and very great, and by all likelehood they lie adioyning to new Guinnie, or else are very neere to some other firme land. . . . Seeing it is thus, why may we not suppose that the Ancients had the courage and resolution to travell by sea, with the same intent to discover the land, which they call Antiethon, opposite to theirs, and that, according to the discourse of their Philosophie, it should be with an intent not to rest untill they came in view of the landes they sought? . . . But to say the truth, I am of a contrary opinion, neither can I perswade my selfe that the first Indians came to this new world of purpose, by a determined voiage, neither will I yeeld, that the Ancients had knowledge in the Art of Navigation. . . . I conclude then, that it is likely the first that came to the Indies was by shipwracks and tempest of wether, but heereupon groweth a difficultie which troubleth me much. For, suppose wee grant that the first men came from farr Countries, and that the nations which we now see are issued from them and multiplied, yet can I not coniecture by what meanes brute beastes, whereof there is great aboundance, could come there, not being likely they should have bin imbarked and carried by sea. . . . I coniecture then, by the discourse I have made, that the new world, which we call Indies, is not altogether severed and disioyned from the other world; and to speake my opinion, I have long beleeved that the one and the other world are ioyned and continued one with another in some part, or at least are very neere. . . And I beleeve it is not many thousand yeeres past since men first inhabited this new world and West Infies, and that the first men that entred, were rather savage men and hunters; then bredde up in civil and well governed Common-weales; and that they came to this new world, having lost their owne land, or being in too great numbers, they were forced of necessitie to seeke some other habitations . . . .

HISTORICAL INTERPRETATIONS

3   From Diamond Jenness, ed., *The American Aborigines: Their Origins and Antiquity* (New York: Russell and Russell, 1933), 28–32.

The Bering Strait Land Connection

Many writers have assumed the former existence of a land area connecting Seward Peninsula in north-western Alaska and Siberia, and, indeed, a land bridge seems necessary in order to account for the migrations of plants and animals from one continent to the other. Some of the larger Quaternary mammals, such as the mammoth, bison, and horse, may have crossed on the ice which even today forms each winter across the strait, but it seems improbable, as Hay has pointed out,[1] that the numerous smaller animals would have followed this route. The question is of vital importance in any study of the routes and times of migration of early man, but appears not to have been considered from the geological standpoint. Extensive investigations by the United States Geological Survey in north-western Alaska, which have been admirably summarized in a recent bulletin,[2] throw some light on the problem and form the chief basis for the following discussion of the question.

A notable feature . . . of the coast region of north-western Alaska and Seward Peninsula, which at Cape Prince of Wales juts out into Bering Strait and lies only about fifty-five miles from East Cape on the Siberian side, is a coastal plain composed of unconsolidated sands, gravels, and clays. The plain is continuous along the coast except in a few places, such as Cape Prince of Wales, where highland areas of ancient solid rocks abut on the coast. The materials of the plain are Quaternary in age; they are in part marine, as is shown by the occurrence at a few places of marine fossils in some of the beds up to elevations of about 300 feet, but are dominantly alluvial stream deposits. They represent deposition during Pleistocene time by streams coming from the interior high plateau and mountainous regions, only the highest parts of which, in the Brooks Range, were glaciated. They thus probably include both glacial and interglacial beds, though the glacial deposits were not derived directly, but transported for some distance from the glaciated region in the interior. The beds contain in places numerous remains of mammoth, horse, bison, and musk-ox, together with well preserved logs of spruce which indicate a warmer climate at the time of deposition of some of the beds than the present, as no such trees now grow in the region. Probably the beds are interglacial in age, at least in part. The plain extends inland in places for sixty miles, and rises very gradually from the coast to an altitude of several hundred feet above the sea. The coast-line is characterized by sea-cliffs cut by wave action in the unconsolidated deposits, and by numerous barrier reefs, bars, and spits of sand formed by along-shore currents and by the rasping action of floating ice on the shallow bottom. The plain appears to continue below sea-level, except that the underneath part has been modified by marine erosion and deposition, for the sea-floor beneath the strait and over a large area to the north and south is nearly level and lies at a shallow depth. Uplift of the land or a lowering of sea-level of 180 feet would cause a land connection between the two continents.

The question of a former land connection obviously depends upon the relationship of sea and land in the region at different times during the Quaternary. In postglacial time the sea in the region of the strait appears to have stood no higher on the land than it does at present. No raised marine terraces have been noted in the vicinity of the strait. There are raised marine beaches up to sixty-five feet or somewhat more at Nome on the south side of Seward Peninsula, but these are Pleistocene or possibly, as is held by Dall,[3] Pliocene in age. Jenness[4] has pointed out that the development of the shore features at Cape Prince of Wales indicates a long period of time during which the sea has stood at the present level relatively to the land in this area. The extensive development of shore features along the coast to the north and south also shows this. The fact that sea-cliffs cut in the unconsolidated deposits occur north-west of Cape Prince of Wales shows that there has been some recession of the coast in this area; but there does not seem to be any evidence of recession of the coast in the strait itself. It is fairly certain, therefore, that there has been no land connection in postglacial time, at least during the past few thousand years, though the strait may have been deepened somewhat by the strong tidal currents that run through it, and have widened towards the north by recession of the coast.

During the Wisconsin stage of glaciation the general level of the sea must have been lower owing to the accumulation of ice on the land. The amount of lowering is generally estimated to have been at least 180 feet, so that a land bridge probably existed during the height of the last glaciation. The fact that the sea is cutting into the coastal plain in the region just north of the strait also suggests that this plain, which is in part alluvial, formerly extended above sea-level much farther to the north and west. During the waning of the last glaciation the sea gradually rose on the land, and this rise, together with erosion, may have opened the strait. The question is complicated by the possibility that there may have been uplift or depression of the land in the region of the strait as well as oscillations of sea-level, but so far as known the late-Pleistocene changes of level of the land affected only the glaciated regions and their borders, and the Bering Strait region is well outside of any large glaciated area. Marine beds in the coastal plain deposits prove that at times during the Pleistocene the sea stood higher on the land than it does now, so that instead of a land bridge there probably was a much wider and deeper strait. This may have occurred during an interglacial period; and it may account for the milder than present climate which appears to have prevailed in this region at one time during the Pleistocene, for freer access of Pacific waters into the Arctic may have caused milder conditions on the adjacent lands.

Thus the geological evidence, although it is not conclusive, strongly suggests that the strait has been open throughout postglacial time but has been widened and deepened; and that at certain times during the Pleistocene there was a land bridge and at other times a strait somewhat wider than the existing one.

NOTES

1. Hay, Oliver P. *The Pleistocene of North America and its vertebrated animals*, Carnegie Institute of Washington, p. 3, 1923.

2. Smith, Philip S. and Mertie, J.E., Jr. 'Geology and resources of north-western Alaska', United States Geological Survey, *Bulletin* 815, 1930.

3. Dall, W.H. *Pliocene and Pleistocene fossils from the Arctic coast of Alaska and the auriferous beaches of Nome*, Norton Sound, United States Geological Survey, Professional Paper 1250, 1921.

4. Jenness, Diamond. 'Little Diomede Island, Bering Strait', *American Geographical Review*, vol. 19, no. 1, pp. 78–86, 1929.

4   From K.R. Fladmark, 'Routes: Alternate Migration Corridors for Early Man in North America', *American Antiquity* 44 (1979): 55–8, 63.

Archaeologists concerned with the initial migration of man into North America seem satisfied with the concept of a mid-continental route for movement south of Beringia, despite lack of agreement over the age of such an event (e.g., Bandi 1969; Bryan 1965, 1969; Haynes 1966, 1969, 1971; Reeves 1971, 1973; Shutler 1971; Wendorf 1966). The possibility of a coastal migration route has not been seriously considered by New World specialists, who can accept that coastal adaptations developed from prior interior bases but are reluctant to consider the opposite alternative.

The intent of this paper is to examine and compare the feasibility of late Pleistocene coastal and interior routes for man entering southern North America from Beringia, in the light of recent geological and archaeological data. This will hopefully indicate that a chain of sea-level refugia along the North Pacific coast presents an attractive alternative to a mid-continental 'corridor' and that early coastal cultures may have been among the first to arrive south of the glaciated area of North America.

Despite protestations of faith to the contrary, there is still no firm evidence for man south of Canada prior to the onset of the Woodfordian substage of the Wisconsinan Glaciation (ca. 25–30,000 B.P.) and the majority of early sites postdate the climax of that stadial episode (e.g., Adovasio et al. 1975; Bada et al. 1974; Bedwell and Cressman 1971; Gruhn 1965; Haynes 1971; Irwin 1971; MacNeish 1971; Wormington 1971). The purpose of this observation is not to add to the debate about the age of the 'earliest'

early man in the New World, but merely to indicate that there is need to discuss his entry into southern North America *during* the last glacial period, when suitable routes were restricted by ice cover. If man spread south of the glaciated region during the mid-Wisconsinan interstadial, his choice of routes would have been nearly as varied as that presented by the modern geography of North America, with glaciers probably offering no significant barrier to most coastal, mountain, or plains-plateau areas. However, this possibility is not supported by available data.

The Mid-Continental 'Ice-Free Corridor'

The mechanism usually invoked to allow man south of the main ice front during or immediately following the climax of the last glacial episode is the so-called 'ice-free corridor', thought to have been formed by incomplete coalescence of Cordilleran and Laurentide glaciers along the eastern flanks of the Rocky Mountains. Opinions vary concerning the dating and extent of the corridor. In 1969, A.L. Bryan proposed that it was blocked by coalescent glaciers as late as 9000 BP, while Reeves (1971, 1973) employed essentially the same data to argue that the corridor remained largely unglaciated for about the last 55,000 years. Such conflicting interpretations reflect limited paleoenvironmental information from the critical central portion (between about 50° and 60° N), where Cordilleran and Laurentide ice fronts are most likely to have contacted.

The data are not greatly improved since

Reeves' 1973 review and the extent and duration of coalescence are still not clearly understood. In addition, the location and inhabitability of any ice-free terrain in the mid-continental area during a glacial period are highly dependent on whether eastern and western glaciers achieved a maximum extent synchronously or if, as has been suggested by Alley and Harris (1974), Cordilleran ice receded prior to the full extension of the continental ice sheet. The region is physiographically complex, and the suitability of a late Wisconsinan corridor for human occupation would be at least partially dependent on whether ice-free areas coincided with mountain, foothill, or plains-plateau terrain. However, present data are generally inadequate to indicate whether any mid-continental corridor existed during the Woodfordian substage, let alone whether it should be modelled as plains-plateau or mountain.

Merger of eastern and western 'Woodfordian' ice is indicated for the Athabasca River area, Alberta, where a Cordilleran ice flow may have been diverted hundreds of kilometres southward along the Laurentide ice front, depositing the Foothills Erratic Train (Roed 1975). Coalescence is also recognized for the Peace River district (W. Mathews, personal communication 1977). Such evidence indicates that Cordilleran and Laurentide ice fronts were, at least for a time, synchronously in close proximity, if not fully coalescent, throughout the mid-portion of the corridor. At best, these data imply only a narrow strip of ice-free terrain cut by occasional lobes of coalescent ice; at worst, the evidence in no way precludes complete ice coalescence between central Alberta and the Northwest Territories. Even assuming the best case—that is, a narrow unglaciated corridor—its basic inhabitability is by no means assured (cf. Morlan 1977; Haynes 1971; Reeves 1971).

During the late Pleistocene glaciation, Beringian grasslands were drained by unobstructed streams dominated then as now by the Yukon River. In contrast, the Laurentide ice front and isostatic depression completely blocked and reversed normal eastern and northern drainage in central Canada. During both advance and retreat phases, eastern ice acted as a mobile obstacle to drainage. Coupled with massive amounts of meltwater, it caused a complex of huge, shifting, sporadically interconnected glacial lakes to 'migrate' across the continent in time with the moving ice front. Virtually every part of the presumed corridor and the central plains-plateau of Canada is mantled with glacial lake sediments (Geological Survey of Canada 1968). Although these do not all result from synchronous pondages, the sheer size of some individual lakes must at times have presented obstacles to animal or human movement. With the onset of nonglacial climatic conditions, meltwater must have drowned all basins, creating a 'corridor' more closely resembling a canal than an inviting habitat for terrestrial hunters. Initially lacking fish, with unstable shorelines and fluctuating pondage levels, it is hard to see these lakes, particularly in early stages, as being anything but disadvantageous for human populations. Anybody living in central Canada during the late glacial and early postglacial periods had to cope with a largely lacustrine landscape wherever there was no ice— a landscape dominated by huge shallow pondages, ephemeral and shifting drainage patterns and massive seasonal surges of meltwater, and, more importantly, a landscape quite different from Beringia.

Reconstruction of the climate of the corridor during the climax and initial waning of the Woodfordian advance is hampered by short palynological sequences and by the absence of analogous situations elsewhere in the world. At present, the area is typified by severe winter temperatures, occasionally alleviated along the Rockies by warm westerly 'chinook' winds. Topographic depressions such as river valleys act as traps for dense cold air and have significantly cooler winter temperatures than surrounding plateau surfaces (cf. Farstad et al. 1965). During glacial episodes westerly circulation was probably diverted southward by the Laurentide icecap (Lamb and Woodroffe 1970) so that the ameliorating effect of chinook winds would have been lost or reduced in the central corridor area. In addition, any unglaciated land east of the Rockies would have been a major topographic low, trapping cold air flowing off surrounding higher ice surfaces. Even barring a severe katabatic wind, the proximity of major ice fronts suggests very low temperatures in the corridor, with cold air held below divides and between ice lobes, exacerbating the normal continental harshness of the region.

Among the few contenders for early archaeological sites in the corridor are two components at Fisherman Lake, Northwest Territories, containing pebble tools and retouched flakes, associated with a late stage of proglacial pondage and estimated to predate 11–12,000 BP (Millar 1968, 1972). The Taber burial, in southwestern Alberta, is stratigraphically estimated to predate 18,000 BP (Stalker 1969, 1977) and the Caribou Island site of east-central Alberta has yielded unifacial pebble tools in an estimated early postglacial context (Bryan 1968). The Bayrock site in southwestern Alberta has a single pebble tool associated with a bison skull dated about 11,000 BP (Wormington and Forbis 1965), and some charred bones from the Cochrane terraces near Calgary are also estimated to be about 11,000 years old (Churcher 1968). Surface finds of Clovis or Clovis-like fluted points have been recently reported from near Banff and Grande Cache, Alberta (B. Reeves, personal communication 1974; A.L. Bryan, personal communication 1975), and from Fort St John in northeastern British Columbia (Fladmark 1975). Similar finds were previously known from central and southern Alberta (Bryan 1968; Haynes 1971; Wormington and Forbis 1965). Dating of such materials by typological correlation to southern sites should be done with caution, but Clovis or Clovis-like points are the only recognizable archaeological complex with an areal distribution approximating the presumed limits of an early postglacial corridor (cf. Bryan 1968; Haynes 1971), although no fluted points are yet reported between Fort St John and the northwestern Yukon where a fragmentary specimen was found near Old Crow (Irving and Cinq-Mars 1974).

A wide range of data suggests that a mid-continental corridor was not an encouraging area for human occupation, if even basically inhabitable, during the climax and initial retreat of the Woodfordian ice. Extensive, perhaps even total glaciation of the central portion, huge meltwater pondages, and the general instability and primitiveness of a periglacial zone confined between fluctuating ice masses all strongly suggest that the biological productivity and carrying capacity of a Woodfordian corridor could have been at most only a feeble reflection of Beringia. So far, there is no evidence of significant biotic communities in the mid-portion of the corridor between 27,000 and about 11,500 BP. In central Alberta the oldest palynological sequence near the corridor shows a 'primitive' spruce forest by about 11,400 BP (Lichti-Federovich 1970) and a dated tusk from the Peace River area of British Columbia indicates that mammoths had reached that area by about 11,600 BP (Mathews 1963). These dates do not confirm that similar biota existed at the same time along the entire corridor, but they do suggest an approximate postglacial maximum age for the spread of major floral and faunal elements into the central portion.

No matter how interior migration corridors are reconstructed—during advance or retreat phases of glaciation, in the mountains or along the plains-plateau—one is still faced with the puzzling fact that the known distribution of early archaeological sites in the New World does not match that expected from an initial population spread by this route. Although this situation may change with better sampling, all definite pre-12,000 BP sites have been found far to the south of the glaciated area, most frequently within the Cordilleran and intermountain regions. However, if the initial population moved southward through a mid-continental corridor, one would expect that the oldest sites would occur closest to the southern ice margin, that there would be a perceptible temporal gradient from north to south, and that movement into peripheral areas such as intermountain plateaus and the Pacific coast would show a secondary temporal gradient with decreasing age from east to west. In fact the available evidence reflects no such gradients. The area directly along the southern margin of the Laurentide ice sheet appears relatively devoid of dated early sites. Furthermore, even in the central Yukon–Alaska refugium there are no acceptable sites dating to the period of the Woodfordian stade; Old Crow and nearby sites strongly indicate occupation of the area during the mid-Wisconsinan interstadial, but there are no known sites anywhere on the present land surface of Beringia dating between about 25,000 and 13,000 BP. Throughout North America only Clovis-like fluted points appear to suggest an early postglacial diffusion via a mid-continental route; available evidence is insufficient to show whether this reflects a north-to-south or south-to-north spread.

The Coastal Alternative

. . . Although it would seem eminently sensible to suppose that the relatively mild climate and rich resources of the Pacific coast of Beringia would have attracted full-time residents, many archaeologists persist in ignoring the maritime component of the Beringian environment and its implications for early cultural adaptations. Aigner (1976) argues effectively for the significance of maritime adaptations for Upper Paleolithic cultural evolution and observes that the early occupation of the Aleutians demonstrated at Anangula would not have been possible except by groups already full 'maritime' in orientation, possessing boats and sea-mammal hunting equipment. Aigner suggests that such an

adaptation has a long time-depth in Beringia and elsewhere. In this regard it is worth noting that at Terra Amata, France, there is evidence of a seashore camp with substantial dwellings and a rich cultural inventory, including the remains of marine molluscs and fish, left by occupants of the Riviera over 300,000 years ago (de Lumley 1969). People able to make pole-walled huts up to 15 m in length should have had no difficulty in manufacturing simple watercraft. Viable human populations reached Australia without the aid of a land bridge at least 30,000 years ago (Jones 1973), and by necessity their initial adaptation must have been littoral, if not fully maritime. In 1970, Johnson pointed out that an emergent land bridge was not an essential prerequisite for entering North America from Asia and that people have had the capability to cross Bering Strait by watercraft for at least 30,000 years. Some archaeologists have noted this observation, but none have taken the next step and suggested that instead of abandoning their boats on the American shore to run joyfully inland in search of 'big game', a few of these early voyagers may simply have continued southward along the Pacific coast of North America.

Given any kind of steerable watercraft, man's ability to reach the sea-level refugia of the North Pacific from Beringia seems undoubted. The only difficult area is the Pacific coast of the Alaska Peninsula west of Kodiak Island, where there is no direct evidence, as yet, of any unglaciated refugia. However, it is possible that outer islands such as the Shumagins or Chirikof Island remained unaffected by the last main glaciation or that floating ice shelves or seasonal sea ice provided inhabitable areas along the route. Once people reached the Kodiak refugium, intervening areas of ocean or ice separating the other refugia would have been relatively insignificant. The role of seasonal sea ice in aiding pedestrian travel along the coast may have been considerable, perhaps allowing caribou and other land mammals to become widely distributed. Glaciers filling inlets and straits may have aided travel between ice-free headlands, while the emergent low-relief terrain of the outer continental shelf would have produced a less irregular and

indented shoreline, with longer and more continuous strand flats and low-gradient beaches. . . .

REFERENCES

Adovasio, J.M., J.D. Gunn, J. Donahue, and R. Stuckenrath. 1975 'Excavations at Meadowcroft Rockshelter 1973–1974: a progress report', *Pennsylvania Archaeologist* 45(3):1–30.

Aigner, Jean. 1976 'Early Holocene evidence for the Aleut maritime adaptation', *Arctic Anthropology* 13(2):32–45.

Alley, N.F., and S.A. Harris. 1974 'Pleistocene glacial lake sequences in the foothills, southwestern Alberta, Canada', *Canadian Journal of Earth Sciences* 11:1220–35.

Bada, Jeffrey L., R.A. Schroeder, and G.F. Carte. 1974 'New evidence for the antiquity of man in North America deduced from aspartic acid racemization', *Science* 184:791–3.

Bandi, Hans-Georg. 1969. *Eskimo prehistory*. University of Alaska and University of Washington Press.

Bedwell, S.F., and L.S. Cressman. 1971 'Fort Rock report: prehistory and environment of the pluvial Fort Rock Lake area of south-central Oregon', *University of Oregon Anthropological Papers* 1:1–26.

Bryan, A.L.. 1965 'Paleo-American prehistory', *Occasional Papers Idaho State University Museum* 16.

———. 1968 'Early man in western Canada: a critical review', in *Early man in western North America*, edited by C. Irwin-Williams, pp. 70–7. *Eastern New Mexico University Contributions in Anthropology* 1(4).

———. 1969 'Early man in America and the late Pleistocene chronology of western Canada and Alaska', *Current Anthropology* 10:339–65.

Butzer, Karl W. 1971 *Environment and archaeology: an ecological approach to prehistory*. Aldine, Chicago.

Calder, J.A., and R.L. Taylor. 1968 *Flora of the Queen Charlotte Islands, part 1, systematics of the vascular plants*. Research Branch, Canada Department of Agriculture Monograph No. 4, Ottawa.

Churcher, C.S. 1968 'Pleistocene ungulates from the Bow River gravels at Cochrane, Alberta', *Canadian Journal of Earth Sciences* 5:1467–8.

Clague, J.J. 1975 'Late Quaternary sea-level fluctuations, Pacific coast of Canada and adjacent areas', *Geological Survey of Canada Paper* 75-1C:12–21.

Cowan, Ian M. 1941 'Fossil and subfossil mammals from the Quaternary of British Columbia', *Transactions of the Royal Society of Canada*, Section 4:39–50.

de Lumley, Henry. 1969 'A Paleolithic camp at Nice', *Scientific American* 220:42–59.

Dumand, D.E. 1974 'Remarks on the prehistory of the North Pacific: to lump or not to lump', in *Proceedings of the International Conference on the Prehistory and Paleoecology of the Western North American Arctic and Sub-arctic*, edited by S. Raymond and P. Schledermann, pp. 47–56. University of Calgary Archaeological Association.

Farstad, L., T.M. Lord, A.J. Green, and H.J. Hortie. 1965 'Soil survey of the Peace River area in British Columbia', *Report No. 8 of the British Columbia Soil Survey*. University of British Columbia and Research Branch. Canada Department of Agriculture.

Fladmark. K.R. 1975 'Peace past: a report on the archaeological reconnaissance of the Peace River basin, 1974 field season'. Unpublished report submitted to the Archaeological Sites Advisory Board of British Columbia, Victoria.

Florer, Linda F. 1972 'Quaternary paleoecology and stratigraphy of the sea cliffs, western Olympic Peninsula, Washington', *Quaternary Research* 2:202–16.

Geological Survey of Canada. 1968 *Glacial map of Canada*. Geological Survey of Canada, Map 1253A, Ottawa.

Gruhn, Ruth. 1965 'Two early radiocarbon dates from the lower levels of Wilson Butte Cave, south-central Idaho', *Tebiwa* 8(2):57.

Hansen, B.S., and D.J. Easterbrook. 1974 'Stratigraphy and palynology of late Quaternary sediments in the Puget lowland, Washington', *Geological Society of America Bulletin* 85:587–602.

Harington, C.R. 1975 'Pleistocene muskoxen (Symbos) from Alberta and British Columbia', *Canadian Journal of Earth Sciences* 12:903–19.

Haynes, C.V. 1966 'Elephant hunting in North America', *Scientific American* 214:104–12.

———. 1969 'The earliest Americans', *Science* 186:709–15.

———. 1971 'Time, environment and early man', *Arctic Anthropology* 8(2):3–14.

Herzer, R.H. 1971 'Bowie Seamount. A recently active, flat-topped seamount in the northeast Pacific Ocean', *Canadian Journal of Earth Sciences* 8:676–87.

Irving, William N., and J. Cinq-Mars. 1974 'A tentative archaeological sequence for Old Crow Flats, Yukon Territory', *Arctic Anthropology* 11 (supplement):65–81.

Irwin, Henry T. 1971 'Developments in early man studies in western North America, 1960–1970', *Arctic Anthropology* 8(2): 42–67.

Johnson, D.L. 1970 'The Bering bridge: not a prerequisite for late Pleistocene peopling of the New World', paper presented at the thirty-fifth annual meeting of the Society for American Archaeology, Mexico City.

Jones, Rhys. 1973 'Emerging picture of Pleistocene Australians', *Nature* 246:278–81.

Karlstrom, T.N.V. 1965 'Upper Cook inlet area and Matanuska River Valley', in *INQUA guidebook for field conference*, edited by F. Schultz and H. Smith, pp. 114–25. Lincoln.

———. 1969 'Regional setting and geology', in *The Kodiak Island refugium: its geology, flora, fauna and history*, edited by T.N.V. Karlstrom and G.E. Ball, pp. 20–55. Boreal Institute, University of Alberta, Ryerson Press.

Karlstrom, T.N.V., and G.E. Ball (editors). 1969 *The Kodiak Island refugium: its geology, flora, fauna and history*. Boreal Institute, University Alberta, Ryerson Press.

Klein, David R. 1965 'Postglacial distribution patterns of mammals in the southern coastal regions of Alaska', *Arctic* 18(1):7–20.

Lamb, H.H., and A. Woodroffe. 1970 'Atmospheric circulation during the late Ice Age', *Quaternary Research* 1:29–58.

Lichti-Federovich, S. 1970 'The pollen stratigraphy of a dated section of late Pleistocene lake sediment from central Alberta', *Canadian Journal of Earth Sciences* 7:938–45.

Macgowan, Kenneth, and J.A. Hester, Jr. 1962 *Early man in the New World*. Doubleday, New York.

MacNeish, R.S. 1971 'Early man in the Andes', *Scientific American* 224(4):36–46.

Mathewes, Rolf W. 1973 'A palynological study of postglacial vegetation changes in the University Research Forest, southwestern British Columbia', *Canadian Journal of Botany* 51:2085–2103.

Mathews, William H. 1963 'Quaternary stratigraphy and geomorphology of the Fort St. John area, northeastern British Columbia', *British Columbia Department of Mines and Petroleum Resources*, pp. 1–22.

Millar, J.F.V. 1968 'Archaeology of Fisherman's Lake area, western District of Mackenzie, Northwest Territories', Ph.D. dissertation, Department of Archaeology, University of Calgary.

———. 1972 'Western Canadian sub-arctic prehistory and the Dene', paper presented at the fifth annual meeting of the Canadian Archaeological Association, Burnaby.

Morlan, Richard. 1977 'Fluted point makers and extinction of the Arctic Steppe in eastern Beringia', paper presented at the tenth annual meeting of the Canadian Archaeological Association, Ottawa.

Reeves, B.O.K. 1971 'On the coalescence of the Laurentide and Cordilleran ice sheets in the western interior of North America with particular reference to the southern Alberta area', in *Aboriginal man and environments on the plateau of northwest America*, edited by A.H. Stryd and R.H. Smith, pp. 205–28. University of Calgary Archaeological Association.

———. 1973 'The nature and age of the contact between the Laurentide and Cordilleran ice-sheets in the western interior of North America', *Arctic and Alpine Research* 5:1–16.

Reid, John R. 1970 'Late Wisconsin and Neological history of the Martin River Glacier, Alaska', *Geological Society of America Bulletin* 81:3493–3604.

Roed, Murray A. 1975 'Cordilleran and Laurentide multiple glaciation west-central Alberta, Canada', *Canadian Journal of Earth Sciences* 12:1493–1515.

Schmoll, H.R., D.J. Szabo, M. Rubin, and E. Dobrovolny. 1972 'Radiometric dating of marine shells from the Bootlegger Cove clay, Anchorage area, Alaska', *Geological Society of America Bulletin* 83:1107–14.

Shutler, Richard. 1971 'Introduction to papers from a symposium on Early man in North America, new developments 1960–1970', *Arctic Anthropology* 8(2):1–2.

Stalker, A.M.S. 1969 'Geology and the age of the early man site at Taber, Alberta', *American Antiquity* 34:1425–1528.

———. 1977 'Indications of Wisconsin and earlier man from the southwest Canadian prairies', in *Amerinds and their paleoenvironments in northeastern North America*, edited by W.S. Newman and B. Salwen, pp. 119–36. New York Academy of Sciences, New York.

Terasmae, J., and J.G. Fyles. 1959 'Paleobotanical study of late glacial deposits from Vancouver Island, British Columbia', *Canadian Journal of Botany* 37:815–17.

Wagner, F.J.E. 1959 'Paleoecology of the marine Pleistocene faunas of southwestern British Columbia', *Geological Survey of Canada Bulletin* 52.

Wendorf, Fred. 1966 'Early man in the New World: problems of migration', *The American Naturalist* 100:253–70.

Wormington, H.M. 1971 'Comments on early man in North America 1960–1970', *Arctic Anthropology* 8(2):83–91.

Wormington, H.M., and R.G. Forbis 1965 'An introduction to the archaeology of Alberta, Canada', *Denver Museum of Natural History Proceedings* 11.

5   From J.M. Adovasio, 'The Ones that Will Not Go Away: A Biased View of Pre-Clovis Populations in the New World', in Olga Saffir and N.D. Praslov, eds, *From Kostenki to Clovis: Upper Paleolithic-PaleoIndian Adaptations* (New York and London: Plenum Press, 1993), 199–200, 202–7.

. . . The quest for evidence of the earliest inhabitants of the New World has absorbed the attentions of both professionals and interested laymen for a very long period of time. It can be said, however, that little tangible progress toward the achievement of this goal occurred much before the Folsom discoveries earlier in this century. As observed recently (Adovasio et al. 1988: 45), little progress has been made since that time.

For reasons that need not be reiterated here, the Folsom discoveries and, slightly later, the initial Clovis excavation at Blackwater Draw, New Mexico, represented a bona fide intellectual watershed in North American prehistory (Cotter 1937, 1938; Figgins 1927; Howard 1935). These revelations individually and collectively demonstrated without ambiguity the contemporaneity of man and certain now-extinct Ice Age fauna; hence, they established without any doubt a Late Pleistocene human presence in the New World. Since those protean discoveries—or at least since their widespread acceptance by the archaeological community—more than half a century has elapsed with the addition of very little substantive knowledge about the absolute date of the arrival or arrivals of the first Americans.

This is not to say, to be sure, that little research has been conducted, or that few papers and articles have been presented and published, or that a dearth of synthetic monographs have been generated. In fact, the reverse would seem closer to the mark. Virtually every year since Barnum Brown solemnly intoned (while dramatically clutching a fluted point to his breast!), 'I have the answer to the antiquity of man in the New World in my hand', one or another new locus is claimed by some scholar to be older (occasionally by many orders of magnitude!) than the semimystical 11,500-year benchmark provided by the first makers of fluted projectile points.

Indeed, since the early 1930s, a minimum of 300 sites from all over the Americas have been advanced, often forcefully and often with the appropriate media blitz, as proof positive that the fluted point makers were not, in fact, the primary occupants of the New World. While most of these sites have been deservedly forgotten after a brief Warholesque 15 minutes of fame, some few of them, to borrow the words of a cynical but grudgingly admiring skeptic, simply will not go away.

Before addressing these hardy survivors, it is worth noting that throughout the past five decades, much time and field and laboratory effort as well as large sums of money and thousands of published pages have been expended on issues alleged to be crucial to establishing the chronology of the arrival of the first Americans. These include the exposure (or non-exposure) and overall character of the Bering Land Bridge, the existence (or non-existence) of the so-called Ice-Free Corridor, and the age of the oldest archaeological sites in Siberia. Suffice it to note, while all these issues are indeed related to the central problem under discussion, none are critical to its ultimate resolution (cf. Fagan 1987, 1990; Grayson 1988). It now seems certain that for much of the last 60,000–70,000 years, humans could have passed dry-shod from the Old World to the New and, moreover, could have crossed via a now-submerged route that, climatologically, was neither Arctic desert nor ecologically as depauperate as such a characterization would

allow. What is more, once in the Americas, these first unwitting migrants could have moved into the interior, unhindered for most, if not all, of the Wisconsinan. Finally, while it is logical, germane, and eminently productive to examine the earliest Siberian settlements as they may reflect directly on the possible donor cultures, technologies, and populations for the first human percolations into this hemisphere, the absolute age of these Asian sites has no direct role in validating the antiquity of any site in the New World. . . .

The Sites That Will Not Go Away
THE BLUEFISH CAVE COMPLEX

The Bluefish site complex consists of a series of limestone rockshelters/caves located ca. 64.4 km (40 miles) southwest of Old Crow in the Keele Range of the Yukon Territory. Since the late 1970s, these sites, designated as Bluefish Caves I, II, and III, have been under investigation by Cinq-Mars and his associates of the Archaeological Survey of Canada (Cinq-Mars 1979, 1982, 1984; Cinq-Mars and Lauriol 1987; Morlan 1983; Morlan and Cinq-Mars 1982, 1989; Ritchie et al. 1982). Presently, these closed sites appear to contain the earliest indications of a human presence in the northern marches of the New World. The three Bluefish caves are situated within view of a series of glacial lakes and exhibit relatively straightforward macrostratigraphy but quite convoluted microstratigraphy. Above the bedrock in each cave is a layer of loess that varies in thickness from ca. 30 cm (11.8 inches) to 3 m (9.8 feet). Above the loess is a humus-laden lithosol with extensive exfoliation detritus.

According to Morlan (personal communication, 1989), the loess 'zone' within each site actually consists of hundreds, if not thousands, of discrete short-term depositional events that the excavator Cinq-Mars (1984) has correctly labelled a palimpsest. Though imperfectly understood at present, three separate cycles of loess accumulation punctuated by weathering episodes *may* be represented within the Bluefish Cave complex sites.

Organic preservation within caves I, II, and III is quite good with an excellent pollen record and an extensive faunal inventory. The pollen record appears to document a herbaceous tundra that grades into a shrub tundra and indicates a marked rise in birch (*Betula* spp.) from ca. 14,000–13,500 BP. The pollen record is paralleled at other northern localities and suggests the loess deposits are essentially undisturbed.

The faunal inventory at the sites includes mammoth (*Mammuthus primigenius*), horse (*Equus caballus*), bison (probably *Bison priscus*), elk (*Cervus canadensis*), and caribou (*Rangifer tarandus*), as well as a variety of smaller mammals, notably arctic (*Lepus arcticus*) and snowshoe (*Lepus americanus*) hares, ground squirrels (*Spermophilus* spp.), skunk (*Mephitis mephitis*), and a variety of microtines.

Twelve radiocarbon dates are currently available from the three Bluefish Caves that include both conventional radiocarbon and AMS (accelerator mass spectroscopy) assays run by three different laboratories. One date is on charcoal while the remainder are on bone collagen derived exclusively from cut, whittled, polished, or otherwise humanly modified bone. The oldest assay of ca. 23,500 BP, actually an average of two runs, was processed from a whittled and polished tibia from cave II. Other dates include a series of three runs on a butchered mammoth scapula from cave I ranging from ca. 20,000–15,500 BP and an assay of 12,950 ± 100 BP on a horse femur from the same site. The youngest collagen dates from the Bluefish Cave complex are on the order of 10,000 BP.

Although no hearths or other cultural features are represented at any of the three caves, according to Morlan (personal communication, 1989), all contain positive evidence of human occupation. Caves I and II produced unquestionable stone artifacts from the loess zones in general association with the faunal remains. These notably include wedge-shaped microblade cores, microblades, bifacial thinning flakes, a so-called 'graver or chiseloid', and other lithic reduction detritus. Interestingly, the loess samples extracted from caves I and II contain relatively abundant microdebitage in the form of tertiary finishing and/or rejuvenation flakes, which are notably abundant before the birch rise of ca. 14,000–13,500 BP. The microcore-microblade material is likewise more common before that time. All of the raw material is chert of non-local origin. Additionally, all of the Bluefish sites, including cave III, which heretofore was thought to be culturally sterile, have yielded an abundance of what the excavators deem to be cut, butchered, or otherwise modified bone, most of which does indeed seem to have resulted from human activity.

Although it is admittedly difficult to relate any stone artifact to a particular radiocarbon date, Cinq-Mars and his associates have effectively correlated the bone dates with the various Bluefish Cave macroloess levels and are confident that humans are present in this area no later than ca. 15,000–12,000 BP. The cut bones suggest an earlier occupation perhaps dating back to ca. 24,000–23,000 BP.

The Nenana Valley Site Complex

South and west of the Bluefish Caves, Powers and his associates have been intensively examining a series of open sites in the Nenana Valley of Alaska (Powers 1985, 1986; Powers and Hamilton 1978; Powers and Hoffecker 1985, 1989; Powers and Maxwell 1986; Powers et al. 1983). The study area lies ca. 100 km (62.1 miles) southwest of Fairbanks, Alaska, along a portion of the Nenana River, which flows northward out of the Alaska Range.

The geoarchaeology and paleoenvironment of the study area has been examined in some detail (see Powers and Hoffecker 1989). It appears that during the period between 14,000–10,000 BP, the Nenana Valley may have been part of a refugium for steppe-tundra biota that retreated there during the deterioration of Late Glacial environments. The presence of Dall sheep (*Ovis dalli*), elk, and steppe bison (*Bison priscus*) is documented for the Nenana Valley (Guthrie 1983) while a greater variety of pleniglacial forms are represented in adjacent areas (Guthrie 1968; Matthews 1982). If the Nenana Valley and surrounding localities were indeed part of a refugium, this situation may in turn have rendered the general area quite attractive for aboriginal settlement.

Since the early 1970s, a series of sites, many with circumscribed activity areas and features, have been recorded and subsequently excavated revealing what Powers and co-workers (1983) believe to be two distinctive Late Pleistocene-Early Holocene complexes. The earlier complex is represented at or near the base of the Nenana Valley loess sequence in the initial component (I) at three sites: Dry Creek, Moose Creek, and Walker Road. Tentatively labelled the Nenana Complex, this manifestation is securely dated by a series of radiocarbon assays to 12,000–11,000 BP (Powers and Hoffecker 1989: 270, Table 1).

Directly associated with these dates is an artifact inventory that includes unfluted lanceolate to triangular points, high frequencies of end unifaces (i.e., end 'scrapers'), other unifacial and bifacial forms, a few burins, and extensive lithic reduction detritus. Although wedge-shaped microcores, microblades, and microcore tablets are totally absent, generally small- to medium-sized blades, 'bladelets', and tools made on blades are illustrated from the complex (Powers and Hoffecker 1989: 278, Fig. 8).

The second and later complex recovered from the Nenana Valley is represented at Dry Creek (component II), Panguingue Creek (component II), Little Panguingue Creek (component II), and perhaps several other sites in the area. This complex is dominated by small wedge-shaped microcores, microblades, core tablets, and burins; it also includes a variety of other forms, notably bifacial lanceolate projectile points, a series of uniface types, assorted bifacial forms, so-called 'spokeshaves', and extensive

flaking debitage. Directly dated to 10,690 ± 750 BP at Dry Creek and somewhat later on Panguingue Creek, this second Nenana Valley manifestation is ascribed by the excavators to the Denali Complex initially defined by West (1967, 1975, 1981).

Although the relationship, if any, between the two Nenana Valley complexes is imperfectly understood at present, the earlier of these entities clearly documents yet another blade- and biface-producing population in place in the far north before 11,500 BP.

MONTE VERDE

More than 14,000 km (8,700 miles) south of the Nenana Valley is the open site of Monte Verde on the banks of Chinchihuapi Creek, a tributary of the Maullin River, some 33 air km (20.5 air miles) southwest of Puerto Mott in south-central Chile. The site is 15 km (9.3 miles) northwest of the Gulf of Ancud, an embayment of the Pacific Ocean. Since 1976, this extraordinary wetland locality has been under intensive scrutiny by a multidisciplinary, multinational group directed by Tom Dillehay, University of Illinois-University of Kentucky (Collins and Dillehay 1986; Dillehay 1984, 1986, 1987, 1989a, 1989b; Dillehay et al. 1983).

Two cultural components have been reported from Monte Verde, the earliest of which consists of three possible cultural features and 26 stone items including artifacts of unquestioned human manufacture in close association. Two of the features have yielded dates in the 34th millennium BP, which if correct, render this occupation the oldest directly dated manifestation of a human presence in the entire New World. Since the excavators themselves presently reserve judgment on the extent and character of the earlier Monte Verde occupation, I prefer to follow suit and concentrate, as they have, on the later component.

The second, later component at Monte Verde represents, in my view, the oldest definitive evidence of humans in South America and may well represent in terms of impact what one North American archaeoloeist calls the Folsom of that continent. . . . The settlement, which extends to both sides of the 4-m (13-foot) wide creek, comprises two clusters of apparently residential structures.

The first cluster is composed of logs and branches emplaced in broadly rectangular fashion forming 'rooms' with 1.8–2.1 m (6–7 foot) 'walls'. According to Dillehay (1987: 10), 'the logs apparently provided architectural stability for pole-frame huts draped with animal hides.' Additionally, Dillehay (1987: 10) notes the presence of two large hearths and a dozen smaller 'clay-lined braziers'.

The second cluster of structures, located downstream from the first activity area, is centred on a wishbone-shaped foundation that encompasses an area of ca. 5.9 m^2 (63 feet^2). The foundation was replete with the remnants of vertical posts that could well represent the remains of walls. The 'forecourt' of this structure included a small salt cache, perhaps used in hide tanning; clusters of mastodon (*Cuvieronius* spp.) bone and skin; extensive amounts of worked wood; other plant remains (apparently including medicinal species); and stone tools. This second activity area is interpreted by Dillehay (1987: 10) as, 'apparently a place where the prehistoric inhabitants prepared meat and animal hides, manufactured stone tools, and perhaps cured bodily ailments.'

The later Monte Verde component is securely dated by a series of over a dozen conventional radiocarbon and AMS assays to ca. 13,000 BP and appears to reflect, at the very least, a semi-sedentary utilization of an environmental setting not radically different from that evidenced in the area today. This utilization apparently included the year-round exploitation of small game, paleollama (*Paleolama* spp.), and mastodon, as well as a wide diversity of plants. Most interestingly, the tool kit is dominated by perishable artifacts with stone 'industry' that, while clearly of human origin, is truly depauperate and bears no resemblance to those discussed from any of the other sites in this paper.

MEADOWCROFT ROCKSHELTER AND RELATED CROSS CREEK SITES

Between the two extremes afforded by the Bluefish and Nenana sites in the far north and Monte Verde in the extreme south lies Meadowcroft Rockshelter. This site is a deeply stratified, south-facing sandstone rockshelter located 47 air km (29.2 air miles) southwest of Pittsburgh, Pennsylvania. Meadowcroft Rockshelter is situated within an unglaciated portion of the Allegheny Plateau on the north bank of Cross Creek, a minor west-flowing tributary of the Ohio River. Meadowcroft Rockshelter as well as the entire Cross Creek drainage has been under intensive multidisciplinary investigation by this writer and his associates since 1973.

Since the publication of the first radiocarbon sequence from Meadowcroft Rockshelter in 1974, this site has been unarguably one of the most controversial archaeological localities ever advanced for pre-Clovis candidacy. The reasons for this are relatively simple. Despite the fact that the final report has not yet appeared, Meadowcroft is the most intensively studied, most extensively written about, and most thoroughly dated of all the putative pre-Clovis sites known in the Americas.

Unlike many other allegedly early localities discussed and dismissed by Morlan (1988), Bryan (1986), or Fagan (1987), Meadowcroft demonstrates well-defined stratigraphy, artifacts of indisputable human manufacture, and clear stratigraphic associations between its 52 radiocarbon dates and its numerous artifacts and ecofacts. . . .

The 11 attritionally and/or colluvially emplaced strata at Meadowcroft currently afford the longest aboriginal occupational sequence available from the New World. The upper strata at the site (upper IIa–XI) span the entire Holocene while the lower strata (middle and lower IIa) extend well back into the late

Pleistocene. The validity of the 39 radiometric assays that postdate 12,800 BP have stirred little controversy but questions have been raised repeatedly about the reliability of the older dates from the site. Most of the criticisms of these older dates have revolved around the possibility of some form of contamination. Suffice it to note that after years of testing and retesting, there is absolutely no evidence whatsoever for particulate or non-particulate contamination at the site (for the most recent treatments of this issue, see Adovasio et al. 1988, 1989, 1990).

In view of this incontrovertible fact and applying the most conservative interpretation of the radiocarbon data, the excavators conclude that even if only the youngest date from the deepest culture-bearing level (upper middle stratum IIa) at Meadowcroft is considered, the minimum age for the presence of human populations within the state of Pennsylvania is ca. 11,300 BP. Furthermore, if the seven deepest dates associated with cultural material are averaged, then humans were definitely present in the Commonwealth by ca. 15,950 BP. . . .

REFERENCES

Adovasio, J.M., Gunn, J.D., Donahue, J, and Stuckenrath, R. 1977. 'Meadowcroft Rockshelter: Retrospect 1976', *Pennsylvania Archaeologist* 47:2–3.

———, Boldurian, A.T., and Carlisle, R.C. 1988. 'Who are those guys? Some biased thoughts on the initial peopling of the New World', in R.C. Carlisle, ed., *Americans before Columbus: Ice Age Origins*, pp. 45–61. Ethnology Monographs No. 12, Department of Anthropology, University of Pittsburgh.

———, Donahue, J., Stuckenrath, R., and Carlisle, R.C. 1989. 'Meadowcroft Rockshelter radiocarbon chronology: 1975-1989', paper presented at the First World Summit Conference on the Peopling of the Americas, Orono, Maine.

———, ———, and ———. 1990. 'The Meadowcroft radiocarbon chronology 1975-1990: Some ruminations', *American Antiquity* 55(2): 100–15.

Boldurian, A.T. 1985. 'Variability in Flintworking Technology at the Krajacic Site: Possible Relationships to the Pre-Clovis Paleo-Indian Occupation of the Cross Creek Drainage in Southwestern Pennsylvania', Ph.D. dissertation, University of Pittsburgh.

——— and Adovasio, J.M. 1986. 'Who Are Those Guys? An Examination of the Pre-Clovis Flintworking Complex from Meadowcroft Rockshelter and the Cross Creek Drainage', paper presented at the 51st annual meeting of the

Society for American Archaeology, New Orleans.

Bowler, J.M., Jones, R., Allen, H., and Thorne, A.G. 1970. 'Pleistocene human remains from Australia: A living site and cremation from Lake Mungo, Western N.S.W.', *World Archaeology* 2:39–60.

Bryan, A.L. 1986. 'Paleoamerican prehistory as seen from South America', in A.L. Bryan, ed., *New Evidence for the Pleistocene Peopling of the Americas*, pp. 1–14. Orono: Center for the Study of Early Man, University of Maine.

Cinq-Mars, J. 1979. 'Bluefish Cave I: A Late Pleistocene Eastern Beringian cave deposit in the Northern Yukon', *Canadian Journal of Archaeology* 3:1–32.

———. 1982. 'Les grottes du Poisson-Bleu', *GEOS* 11(1):19–21.

———. 1984. 'A Palimpsest in the Making: Taphonomic Note from the Bluefish Cave, Northern Yukon', paper presented at the First International Conference on Bone Modification, Carson City, Nevada.

——— and Lauriol, B. 1987. 'Notes de Recherches Interdisciplinaires: Les Grottes du Poisson-bleu et Quelques Autres Cavités Karstiques du Yukon Septentrional (Canada)', paper presented to the Twelfth International Congress, INQUA, Ottawa.

Collins, M.B., and Dillehay, T.D. 1986. 'The implications of the lithic assemblage from Monte Verde for early man studies', in A.L. Bryan, ed., *New*

Evidence for the Pleistocene Peopling of the Americas, pp. 339–55. Orono: Center for the Study of Early Man, University of Maine.

Cotter, J.L. 1937. 'The occurrence of flints and extinct animals in pluvial deposits near Clovis, New Mexico. Part IV. Report on the excavations at the gravel pit in 1936', *Proceedings of the Philadelphia Academy of Natural Sciences* 89:2–16.

———. 1938. 'The occurrence of flints and extinct animals in pluvial deposits near Clovis, New Mexico. Part VI. Report on the field season of 1937', *Proceedings of the Philadelphia Academy of Natural Sciences* 90:113–17.

Custer, J. 1984. *Delaware Prehistoric Archaeology: An Ecological Approach*. Dover: University of Delaware Press.

Dillehay, T.D. 1984. 'A late Ice Age settlement in Southern Chile', *Scientific American* 251(4):106–17.

———. 1986. 'The cultural relationships of Monte Verde: A Late Pleistocene settlement in the subantarctic forest of south-central Chile', in A.L. Bryan, ed., *New Evidence for the Pleistocene Peopling of the Americas*, pp. 319–37. Orono: Center for the Study of Early Man, University of Maine.

———. 1987. 'By the banks of the Chinchihuapi', *Natural History* 87(4):8–12.

———. 1989a. *Monte Verde: A Late Pleistocene Settlement in Chile*, Volume 1. Blue Ridge Summit, Pennsylvania: Smithsonian Institution Press.

———. 1989b. 'Pleistocene Peoples of Monte Verde, Chile', paper presented at the First World Summit Conference on the Peopling of the Americas, Orono, Maine.

———, Pino Q., M., Davis, E.M., Valastro, S., Jr., Varela, A.G., and Casimiquela, R. 1983. 'Monte Verde: Radiocarbon dates from an early man site in south-central Chile', *Journal of Field Archaeology* 9:547–9.

Fagan, B.F. 1987. *The Great Journey: The Peopling of Ancient America*. New York: Thames and Hudson.

———. 1990. 'Tracking the first Americans', *Archaeology* Nov./Dec.:14–20.

Figgins, J.D. 1927. 'The antiquity of man in America', *Natural History* 27(3):229–39.

Fitzgibbons, P.T. (with the assistance of J. Herbstritt, W.C. Johnson, and C. Robbins). 1982. 'Lithics artifacts from Meadowcroft Rockshelter and the Cross Creek drainage', in R.C. Carlisle and J.M. Adovasio, eds., *Meadowcroft: Collected Papers on the Archaeology of Meadowcroft Rockshelter and the Cross Creek Drainage*, pp. 91–111. Pittsburgh: Department of Anthropology, University of Pittsburgh.

Grayson, D.K. 1988. 'Americans before Columbus: Perspectives on the archaeology of the first Americans', in R.C. Carlisle, ed., *Americans before Columbus: Ice-Age Origins*, pp. 107–23. Ethnology Monographs 12. Department of Anthropology, University of Pittsburgh.

Guilday, J.E, Parmalee, P.W., and Wilson, R.C. 1980. 'Vertebrate faunal remains from Meadowcroft Rockshelter (36WH297), Washington County, Pennsylvania', manuscript on file, Department of Anthropology, University of Pittsburgh.

Guthrie, R.D. 1968. 'Paleoecology of the large mammal community in interior Alaska during the Late Pleistocene', *American Midland Naturalist* 79:346–63.

———. 1983. 'Paleoecology of the Dry Creek site and its implications for early hunters', in W.R. Powers, R.D. Guthrie, and J.F. Hoffecker, eds., *Dry Creek: Archeology and Paleoecology of a Late Pleistocene Alaskan Hunting Camp*, pp. 209–87. Submitted to the National Park Service, Washington, DC, Contract No. CX-9000-7-0047.

Haynes, C.V. 1987. 'Clovis origins update', *The Kiva* 52(12):83–93.

Howard, E.B. 1935. 'Evidence of early man in North America', *The Museum Journal* 24:2–3.

Matthews, J.V., Jr. 1982. 'East Beringia during Late Wisconsin Time: A review of the biotic evidence', in D.M. Hopkins, J.V. Matthews, Jr., C.E. Schweger, and S.B. Young, eds., *Paleoecology of Beringia*, pp. 127–50. New York: Academic Press.

Morlan, R.E. 1983. 'Counts and estimates of taxonomic abundance in faunal remains: Microtine rodents from Bluefish Cave I', *Canadian Journal of Archaeology* 7(1): 61–76.

———. 1988. 'Pre-Clovis people: Early discoveries of

America?', in R.C. Carlisle, ed., *Americans Before Columbus: Ice-Age Origins*, pp. 31-43. Ethnology Monographs No. 12, Department of Anthropology, University of Pittsburgh.

——— and Cinq-Mars, J. 1982. 'Ancient Beringians: Human occupation in the Late Pleistocene of Alaska and the Yukon Territory', in D.M. Hopkins, J.V. Matthews, Jr., C.E. Schweger, and S.B. Young, eds., *Paleoecology of Beringia*, pp. 353–81. New York: Academic Press.

——— and ———. 1989. 'The Peopling of the Americas as seen from Northern Yukon Territory', paper presented at the First World Summit Conference on the Peopling of the Americas, Orono, Maine.

Powers, W.R. 1985. 'North Alaska range early man project. *National Geographic Society Research Reports* 19:1–32.

———. 1986. *The Nenana Complex of the North Alaska Range and the Search for Clovis Origins*. Research Proposal to the National Science Foundation, Proposal No. BNS-8608012.

——— and Hamilton, T.D. 1978. 'Dry Creek: A Late Pleistocene human occupation in central Alaska', in A.L. Bryan, ed., *Early Man in America from a Circum-Pacific Perspective*, pp. 72–7. Occasional Papers No. 1. Department of Anthropology, University of Alberta, Edmonton.

——— and Hoffecker, J.F. 1985. *Nenana Valley*

Cultural Resources Survey 1984. Submitted to Alaska Division of Parks, Anchorage.

——— and ———. 1989. 'Late Pleistocene settlement in the Nenana Valley, central Alaska', *American Antiquity* 54(2):263–87.

——— and Maxwell, H.E. 1986. *Alaska Range Northern Foothills Cultural Resources Survey 1985*. Submitted to Alaska Division of Parks and Outdoor Recreation, Anchorage.

———, Guthrie, R.D., and Hoffecker, J.F. 1983. *Dry Creek: Archeology and Paleoecology of a Late Pleistocene Alaskan Hunting Camp*. Submitted to the National Park Service, Washington, DC, Contract No. CX-9000-7-0047.

Ritchie, J.C., Cinq-Mars, J., and Cwynar, L.C. 1982. 'L'environnement Tardiglaciaire du Yukon Septentrional, Canada', *Géographie Physique et Quaternaire* 36(1–2):241–50.

West, F.H. 1967. 'The Donnelly Ridge site and the definition of an early core and blade complex in central Alaska', *American Antiquity* 32:360–83.

———. 1975. 'Dating the Denali complex', *Arctic Anthropology* 12(1):76–81.

———. 1981. *The Archaeology of Beringia*. New York: Columbia University Press.

Yi, S., and Clark, G. 1985. 'The "Dyuktai culture" and New World origins', *Current Anthropology* 26(1):1–13, 19–20.

6 From E. James Dixon, 'Learning from Those Who Have Gone Before', *Bones, Boats & Bison: Archaeology and the First Colonization of Western North America* (Albuquerque: University of New Mexico Press, 1999), 111-15.

In recent years, the discovery, excavation, and analysis of Native American human remains has been controversial in the United States and to a lesser degree in Canada. Both Native and non-Native Americans are divided on the issue. The divisions are not strictly along racial or ethnic lines. Some people believe that all human remains should be reburied and not subject to scientific investigation. Others believe that the benefits of

scientific investigation are significant and that research on human remains can be conducted with respect and cultural sensitivity. Yet others feel that the antiquity of the remains makes a difference. While some people may object to recent (several hundred years old) human remains being the subject of study, they may have little or no objection to research conducted on skeletons that are thousands of years old.

For example, in the process of excavating and analyzing very old human skeletal material on Prince of Wales Island, Alaska, local Native people participated in the excavation, expressed a strong interest in their analysis, and believe the knowledge gained from archaeological research is important. In this case, scientists, Native people, and government agencies worked together in a spirit of co-operation and mutual respect. Yarrow Vaara, a member of the Tlingit tribe and student intern working at the site in 1997 and 1998, said that she regarded the human remains she was helping excavate as possibly those of her great uncle who was teaching her about her history. The Tlingit people are matrilineal, and uncles have an honoured role as mentors in the clan. Similar statements made by other Native people demonstrate that many recognize that this type of research can provide information that is important to them.

The Native American Graves Protection and Repatriation Act (NAGPRA), enacted by the United States Congress in 1990, requires archaeologists and governmental agencies to consult with Native American tribes prior to undertaking field research on federal lands or with federal support. Museums and other organizations that receive federal support are required to inventory and report human skeletal material, grave goods, and 'objects of cultural patrimony'. Objects in these categories must be returned to the appropriate Native American tribe upon their request following consultation with the museum or federal agency holding them.

It has been difficult to implement this law because it was passed without adequate financial support to enable Native Americans, government agencies, and museums to comply. In some instances, NAGPRA has polarized opinion, created resentments, and reduced co-operation. In other cases, it has resulted in better communication between Native Americans, federal agencies, and non-Native entities sponsoring archaeology and holding archaeological collections.

Although North American archaeologists recognize the study of ancient human remains is a sensitive issue for some people, most share the conviction that the knowledge gained from the study of human remains is extremely important. Furthermore, there is a vast amount of scientific information in the literature from the past century. This information provides important knowledge about human physical and cultural development, and human origins, as well as insight into the lives of ancient people.

During the late 1800s and early 1900s, scientists largely studied human remains by measuring human skeletons, particularly crania, and comparing measurements to define different groups of people. Since this rather simple beginning, scientists have developed a vast array of sophisticated technology and analysis that can be used to better understand our species and interpret the life history of individuals.

The human body is an encyclopedia of the events it has experienced. If an individual suffers a period of malnutrition, or even worse, starvation, the bones and teeth will record this event, particularly if the individual is young and still growing. Every time a person suffers from an infection or disease, the body produces and stores antibodies to fight the disease. Human DNA provides a record of an individual's ancestry. By examining and studying human remains, trained scientists can read a fascinating record that is unique for every individual.

Some non-destructive studies focus on the comparison of physical traits, such as bone structure, to determine the gender of skeletons. Studying dental patterns, the sequence of tooth eruption, and dental wear provides insight into an individual's relationship to other groups as well as an estimate of the age at the time of death, the diet, and other factors that were important while alive (Powell and Steele 1994; Smith 1984). Scientists can identify periods of malnutrition or famine, certain types of disease, injuries such as bone fractures, and other events recorded in the human skeleton as individuals develop, grow, and heal. By examining areas where muscles attach to bones, researchers can tell how muscular an individual may have been.

As science has progressed, the techniques for analysis have become increasingly refined and less destructive. Endoscopes (small fibre optic tubes) can be inserted into small spaces and enable examination and photography of interior regions of the skeleton, such as the brain case and marrow cavities in bones. Phytoliths (tiny growths of silica produced by plants that have distinct morphology for each plant species) can be removed from dental calculus, or plaque, and provide insight into the plants that may have been an important part of an individual's diet. Surface characteristics of bones and teeth can be analyzed and photographed under high magnification by using both conventional as well as scanning electron microscopes. Other non-invasive techniques include X-rays and computerized axial tomography (CAT) scans that provide three-dimensional views and pictures of the interior areas of the body. Many of these techniques are standard methods of examination used routinely on living individuals during medical and dental exams.

Contemporary analytical techniques include the extraction and replication of DNA that can be preserved in small amounts of bone. DNA provides a 'blueprint' of an individual's genetic makeup, the traits that make them unique and that they share with others as a member of a larger genetic group. DNA analyses are useful to objectively compare the genetic relationship of an individual to other individuals and groups of individuals. DNA analysis also can provide important cultural insight. For example, it is possible to determine whether individuals buried in the same locale, or even the same grave, were blood relatives. This type of evidence can help scientists interpret social structure, residence patterns, disease, and cultural practices of ancient people.

Probably the single most important breakthrough for Paleoindian archaeology in recent years has been the ability to reliably date bone by AMS ¹⁴C methods (Stafford et al. 1991; Taylor et al. 1985). Dating by this method can accurately determine when an individual died. Stable isotope analysis of carbon and nitrogen are measured from bone samples in conjunction with the same sample used for AMS dating. Isotope analysis can provide important insight into an individual's diet and can, for example, determine whether they subsisted largely on marine or terrestrial foods. These tests require only a few grams and in many cases, less than one gram of bone or other material. These analyses require no more material than might be extracted by a dentist when filling a tooth, trimming one's fingernails, or getting a haircut. Samples can be removed in a respectful manner and in ways that are virtually not detectable.

Another method for studying early human skeletal remains is facial reconstruction. These reconstructions are fascinating blends of art and science. Artists trained in human anatomy begin with casts of a human cranium and mandible and carefully reconstruct, or 'build', the facial characteristics of the individual from the cast outward. By adding muscle and other soft tissue to a cast of the skull and taking into consideration the gender and age of the individual, surprisingly accurate reconstructions of individuals can be made. Law enforcement officials have successfully used these techniques to help identify individuals from their remains. Computers are now employed to help recreate the physical appearance of ancient people. These reconstructions from human remains that are thousands of years old provide unique and moving portraits of people from the past.

Since the 1800s, there have been exaggerated claims of great antiquity attributed to human remains discovered in the Americas (Dickeson Exhibit Report 1846; Whitney 1867, 1880). More recently, careful geologic investigation and dating, particularly using AMS ¹⁴C techniques, have led to accurate age determinations of human bone. This research has clarified much of the ambiguity and confusion surrounding many of these early finds. . . .

REFERENCES

J.F. Powell and D.G. Steele, 'Diet and Health of Paleoindians: An Examination of Early Holocene Human Dental Remains', in Centre for Archaeological Investigations, Occasional Paper No. 22, edited by K. D. Sobolik, pp. 178–94. Southern Illinois University, Carbondale, 1994.

B.H. Smith, 'Patterns of Molar Wear in Hunter-Gatherers and Agriculturalists', *American Journal of Physical Anthropology* 69 (1984): 39–56.

T.W. Stafford et al., 'Accelerator Radiocarbon Dating at the Molecular Level', *Journal of Archaeological Science* 18 (1991): 35–72.

R.E. Taylor et al., 'Major Revisions in the Pleistocene Age Assignments for North American Human Skeletons by C-14 Accelerator Mass Spectrometry: None Older than 11,000 C-14 Years B.P.', *American Antiquity* 50 (1985): 136–40.

J.D. Whitney, 'Notice of a Human Skull, Recently Taken from a Shaft near Angel's, Calveras County, California', *California Academy of Natural Sciences Proceedings* 3 (1867): 277–8.

——, 'Auriferous gravels of the Sierra Nevada of California', *Contributions to American Geology*, Vol. 1. Memoir of the Museum of Comparative Zoology, 1880, 288321, Cambridge.

7   Anne McIlroy, 'Who were the first North Americans?', *Globe and Mail*, 6 Sept. 2003, F10.

For 50 years, the story of how people first came to North America was as simple as a tale written for children. Hunters from northern Asia walked across a land bridge between Siberia and Alaska about 11,500 years ago in search of big game like mastodons, mammoths and bison. They travelled south through a narrow corridor between the giant glaciers that engulfed the Rocky Mountains and the sheet of ice that covered much of Eastern Canada. As the ice receded, they prospered, populating much of North and South America, and were the ancestors of the modern native peoples.

That theory, now defended only by a handful of stubborn advocates, conflicts with evidence archaeologists began digging up in the late 1970s, and with new findings made from using modern techniques such as DNA analysis on skulls or other bones discovered years ago. But no simple narrative has taken its place.

Competing theories argue that the first North Americans may have been close relatives to ancient Australians, Japanese, Pacific Islanders, southern Asians or black Africans.

They may have crossed the Bering Strait, then travelled down the Pacific Coast by canoe or on foot. They may have floated here from the southern Pacific on rafts. They may have battled with later arrivals, or they may have had sex with them and produced offspring.

The story now reads like a mystery book, featuring competing detectives, with the final chapters missing. There are no satisfying conclusions, only intriguing clues that add heft to the idea that the ancestors of North American native peoples may not have been the first to settle here and certainly weren't the only early arrivals.

That idea is controversial, because some may see it as weakening the land claims of aboriginal people. 'If you want to see it that way, it undercuts this whole argument that they were here first', says University of Alberta archaeologist Ruth Gruhn, who is excavating a site in Baja California that she hopes will yield the bones of early migrants. 'No matter what, they were certainly here early enough and long enough to have a land claim.'

In hindsight, it seems hard to believe that the Northeast Asian theory stood unchallenged for so long. It was based on bits and pieces, the skull fragments of ancient North Americans and the beautifully carved stone spearheads they left wherever they settled. The so-called Clovis stone points, named after the town in New Mexico where they were first discovered in 1937, were later found in other parts of North America.

□ The Missionaries and the First Nations

Readings

PRIMARY DOCUMENTS

HISTORICAL INTERPRETATIONS

INTRODUCTION

■ Christianity was a missionary religion. It had begun in the land of the Jews and had spread rapidly outward, covering all of the Near East, North Africa, and Europe before the end of the eighth century. The Greeks, the Romans, the Gauls, and the Vikings—and many others—had all been convinced by a succession of great missionaries that Christianity represented a better set of spiritual teachings and beliefs than the ones they had previously accepted. Christianity had more difficulty with its missionary expansion after the great explorers opened up new areas of the world beginning in the fifteenth century. Not all peoples were as receptive of Christianity after 1500 as had been the residents of the Mediterranean region in the first centuries after the death of Christ.

Among the most controversial groups of missionaries were those belonging to the Society of Jesus, usually known as the Jesuits. The Society of Jesus was a religious order founded by the Spaniard Ignatius Loyola. Organized under tight military-like discipline, the members of the order took a special vow of obedience to the Pope. It was not originally intended to counter the spread of Protestantism, but rather to propagate and strengthen the Catholic faith throughout the world. Inevitably this led the Jesuits into missionary labours among non-Christians far from Europe and to leadership of the Counter-Reformation within Europe. The first Jesuits came to French America (Acadia) in 1611, and the early missionaries in Canada were forced to return to France after the English capture of Quebec in 1629. Returning in 1632, the Jesuits began a period of heroic missionary activity among the Huron, which produced a number of martyrs and ended with the virtual destruction of the Huron by their Iroquois enemies in 1649.

This period saw the beginning of the *Jesuit Relations,* a series of annual publications describing the work in North America of the missionaries, as well as extensive labour with the various aboriginal tongues. Jesuits also became well-known for their overland exploration activities. They were joined in French America by a number of female orders of nuns, of which the Ursulines were the most prominent. Modern scholars have often been highly critical of the French missionaries for their cultural ethnocentrism, seeing them as the leading edge of European imperialism in the New World.

Questions for consideration

1. In what ways were the missionaries ethnocentric?
2. How could they have better achieved their goals?

Suggestions for further reading

Carole Blackburn, *Harvest of Souls: The Jesuit Missions and Colonialism in North America, 1632–1650* (Montreal and Kingston: McGill-Queen's University Press, 2000). A recent critical study of the missionary thrust in early Canada.

J.H. Kennedy, *Jesuit and Savage in New France* (New Haven: Yale University Press, 1950). This is the standard modern account from the missionary perspective.

Francis Parkman, *The Jesuits in North America in the Seventeenth Century* (many editions). The classic nineteenth-century romantic story of the missionaries.

Reuben Gold Thwaites, ed., *The Jesuit Relations and Allied Documents: Travels and Explorations of the Jesuit Missionaries in New France 1610–1791*, 73 vols in 35 (New York: Pageant Books, 1959). The missionary case is presented in the words of the missionaries themselves.

Bruce G. Trigger, *Natives and Newcomers: Canada's 'Heroic Age' Reconsidered* (Montreal and Kingston: McGill-Queen's University Press, 1985).

PRIMARY DOCUMENTS

1 From George M. Wrong, ed., *The Long Journey to the Country of the Hurons/by Father Gabriel Sagard* (Toronto: Champlain Society, 1939), 167–70.

On the belief and faith of the savages in the Creator, and how they had recourse to our prayers in their necessities

Cicero has said, in speaking of the nature of the gods, that there is no people so savage, so brutal, or so barbarous that has not some instinctive notion about them. Now as there are diverse nations and countries of barbarians so also are there different opinions and beliefs because each of them fashions a god suitable to its place. Those who live near Miscou and Port Royal believe in a certain spirit they call *Cudoüagni*, and say that he often speaks to them and tells them what the weather is to be. They say that when he is angry with them he throws earth in their eyes. They believe also that when they die they go up to the stars, then enter beautiful green fields full of fine trees, flowers, and magnificent fruit.

The Souriquois, as I have learnt, actually believe in one God who has created everything, and say that after he had made all things he took a bundle of arrows and set them in the ground, and from these issued men and women, who have multiplied in the world up to the present time. In pursuing the subject a Frenchman asked a Sagamore if he did not believe in other than one God only. He replied that their belief was that there was one sole God, a Son, a Mother, and the Sun, which made four, that nevertheless God was above them all, but that the Son was good and also the Sun, because of the benefits they received from them, but that the Mother had no merit and ate them, and that the Father was not too good. Then he said: In former times there were five men who went towards the setting sun, and they met God, who asked them 'Where are you going?' They replied, 'We are going to look for our living.' God said to them, 'You will find it here.' They went on without heeding what God had said to them, so he took a stone and touched two of them and they were changed into stone. Then he again asked the other three, 'Where are you going?' and they replied as before. And God said to them again, 'Go no further, you will find it here'; but seeing that nothing came of it they went on, and God took two sticks and touched the first two with them, and they were changed into sticks, but the fifth man stopped, being unwilling to go further. And God again asked, 'Where are you going?' 'I am going to look for my living.' 'Stay, and you shall find it.' He stopped and went no further, and God gave him meat and he ate it. After having fared well he returned among the other savages and told them all the above story.

This Sagamore spoke and related also to this Frenchman another amusing tale, as follows. Once upon a time there was a man who had plenty of tobacco, and God spoke to the man and asked him where his pipe was. The man took it and gave it to God, who smoked for some time, and after having had a good smoke broke the pipe into fragments. The man asked him, 'Why have you broken my pipe? Surely you see that I have no other.' So God took one that he had and gave it to him saying, 'Here is one which I give you; take it to your grand Sagamore, let him keep it, and if he keeps it safe he will not be in want of anything whatever, nor any of his companions.' The man took the pipe and gave it to his grand Sagamore, and as long as he had it the savages lacked nothing in the world; but afterwards the Sagamore lost the pipe, and this was the cause of the severe famine they sometimes experience. For this reason they say that God is not too good; and they are right, since this demon who appears to them in the form of a god is an evil spirit, and is only concerned with their ruin and destruction.

The general belief of our Hurons (although they understand it themselves very imperfectly and speak of it in very different ways) is that the Creator who made the whole world is called Yoscaha, and in Canadian Ataouacan, and he has also a grandmother named Ataensiq. If you tell them that there is no likelihood that a God could have a grandmother, and that this is an inconsistency, they have no answer, as in regard to all the other details. They say that they [i.e., God and his grandmother] live far away, although they have no other sign or proof of it other than the story which they say was told them by an Attiuoindaron, who made them believe that he had seen him, as well as the print of his feet on a rock at the edge of a river, and that his house or lodge is made like theirs, with plenty of corn in it and everything else necessary to maintain human life. He sows corn, works, drinks, eats, and sleeps like others. All the animals on earth belong to him and are like servants of his. By nature he is very kind, and makes everything grow, and all he does is done well, and he gives us fine weather and everything else good and advantageous. But on the contrary his grandmother is spiteful, and she often spoils all the good her grandson has done. When Yoscaha grows old he renews his youth again in a moment and becomes like a young man of twenty-five or thirty, and thus he never dies but remains immortal, although he is somewhat at the mercy of bodily necessities like the rest of us.

Now it must be noted that when one begins to gainsay or dispute with them on these matters some make the excuse of ignorance, others desist for shame, and others who think of maintaining their position get confused immediately, and there is no consistency or likelihood in their assertions, as we have often seen and known by experience. This actually reveals that they do not really know and adore any divinity or God, of whom they could give some account and whom we could recognize; for though many speak in praise of their Yoscaha, we have heard others speak of him scornfully and irreverently.

They have, however, some respect for those spirits which they call Oki; but this word Oki means a great devil just as much as a great angel, a raging devilish disposition as well as a great, wise, understanding, or efficient intelligence, which does and knows something out of the ordinary. Thus they used often to call us so, because we knew and taught them things which were above their intelligence, according to their own words. They also give the name Oki to their medicine-men and magicians, indeed even to persons who are mad, infuriated, and possessed of the devil. Our Canadians and Montagnais call theirs Pirotois and Manitous, which mean the same thing as Oki does in the Huron tongue.

They believe also that there are certain spirits which bear rule over one place, and others over another, some over rivers, others over journeying, trading, warfare, feasts and diseases, and many other matters. Sometimes they offer them tobacco and make some kind of prayer and ritual observance to obtain from them what they desire. They also showed me many mighty rocks on the way to Quebec, in which they believed a spirit lived and ruled, and among others they showed me one, a hundred and fifty leagues from there which had something like a head and two upraised arms, and in the belly or middle of this mighty rock there was a deep cavern very difficult to approach. They tried to persuade me and make me believe absolutely, as they did, that this rock had been a mortal man like ourselves and that while lifting up his arms and hands he had been transformed into this stone, and in course of time had become a mighty rock, to which they pay respect and offer tobacco when passing it in their canoes, not always, but when they are in doubt of a successful issue to their journey. And as they offer the tobacco, which they throw into the water against the rock itself, they say to it, 'Here, take courage, and let us have a good journey', together with some other speech that I did not understand. The interpreter whom we mentioned in the preceding chapter assured us that he had once made a similar offering with them (for which we rebuked him sharply) and that that journey brought him more profit than any other he had ever made in those parts. Thus it is that the devil plays with them and holds them fast in his snares and subject to strange superstitions. . . .

2 From Joyce Marshall, ed., *Word from New France: The Selected Letters of Marie de l'Incarnation* (Toronto: Oxford University Press, 1967), 75-6.

[Marie de l'Incarnation was an Ursuline nun who worked closely with the Jesuits in the early days of the colony.]

It is a singular consolation to us to deprive ourselves of all that is most necessary in order to win souls to Jesus Christ, and we would prefer to lack everything rather than leave our girls in the unbearable filth they bring from their cabins. When they are given to us, they are naked as worms and must be washed from head to foot because of the grease their parents rub all over their bodies; and whatever diligence we use and however often their linen and clothing is changed, we cannot rid them for a long time of the vermin caused by this abundance of grease. A Sister employs part of each day at this. It is an office that everyone eagerly covets. Whoever obtains it considers herself rich in such a happy lot and those that are deprived of it consider themselves undeserving of it and dwell in humility. Madame our foundress performed this service almost all year; today it is Mother Marie de Saint-Joseph that enjoys this good fortune.

Besides the Savage women and girls, whom we receive in the house, the men visit us in the parlour, where we try to give them the same charity we do their women, and it is a very sensible consolation to us to take bread from our mouths to give it to these poor people, in order to inspire them with love for Our Lord and for his holy Faith.

But after all it is a very special providence of this great God that we are able to have girls after the great number of them that died last year. This malady, which is smallpox, being universal among the Savages, it spread to our seminary, which in a very few days resembled a hospital. All our girls suffered this malady three times and four of them died from it. We all expected to fall sick, because the malady was a veritable contagion, and also because we were day and night succouring them and the small space we had forced us to be continually together. But Our Lord aided us so powerfully that none of us was indisposed.

The Savages that are not Christians hold the delusion that it is baptism, instruction, and dwelling among the French that was the cause of this mortality, which made us believe we would not be given any more girls and that those we had would be taken from us. God's providence provided so benevolently against this that the Savages themselves begged us to take their daughters, so that if we had food and clothing we would be able to admit a very great number, though we are exceedingly pressed for buildings. If God touches the hearts of some saintly souls, so that they will help us build close to the Savages as we have the design to do, we will have a great many girls. We are longing for that hour to arrive, so that we will be more perfectly able to do the things for which Our Lord sent us to this blessed country. . . .

HISTORICAL INTERPRETATIONS

3   From Francis Parkman, *The Jesuits in North America in the Seventeenth Century*, vol. 1 (Toronto: George Morang & Company, 1900), 188–200.

Character of the Canadian Jesuits

Before pursuing farther these obscure, but noteworthy, scenes in the drama of human history, it will be well to indicate, so far as there are means of doing so, the distinctive traits of some of the chief actors. Mention has often been made of Brébeuf—that masculine apostle of the Faith—the Ajax of the mission. Nature had given him all the passions of a vigorous manhood, and religion had crushed them, curbed them, or tamed them to do her work—like a dammed-up torrent, sluiced and guided to grind and saw and weave for the good of man. Beside him, in strange contrast, stands his co-labourer, Charles Garnier. Both were of noble birth and gentle nurture; but here the parallel ends. Garnier's face was beardless, though he was above thirty years old. For this he was laughed at by his friends in Paris, but admired by the Indians, who thought him handsome.[1] His constitution, bodily or mental, was by no means robust. From boyhood, he had shown a delicate and sensitive nature, a tender conscience, and a proneness to religious emotion. He had never gone with his schoolmates to inns and other places of amusement, but kept his pocket-money to give to beggars. One of his brothers relates of him, that, seeing an obscene book, he bought and destroyed it, lest other boys should be injured by it. He had always wished to be a Jesuit, and, after a novitiate which is described as most edifying, he became a professed member of the Order. The Church, indeed, absorbed the greater part, if not the whole, of this pious family—one brother being a Carmelite, another a Capuchin, and a third a Jesuit, while there seems also to have been a fourth under vows. Of Charles Garnier there remain twenty-four letters, written at various times to his father and two of his brothers, chiefly during his missionary life among the Hurons. They breathe the deepest and most intense Roman Catholic piety, and a spirit enthusiastic, yet sad, as of one renouncing all the hopes and prizes of the world, and living for Heaven alone. The affections of his sensitive nature, severed from earthly objects, found relief in an ardent adoration of the Virgin Mary. With none of the bone and sinew of rugged manhood he entered, not only without hesitation, but with eagerness, on a life which would have tried the boldest; and, sustained by the spirit within him, he was more than equal to it. His fellow missionaries thought him a saint; and had he lived a century or two earlier, he would perhaps have been canonized: yet, while all his life was a willing martyrdom, one can discern, amid his admirable virtues, some slight lingerings of mortal vanity. Thus, in three several letters, he speaks of his great success in baptizing, and plainly intimates that he had sent more souls to Heaven than the other Jesuits.[2]

Next appears a young man of about twenty-seven years, Joseph Marie Chaumonot. Unlike Brébeuf and Garnier, he was of humble origin—

his father being a vine-dresser, and his mother the daughter of a poor village schoolmaster. At an early age they sent him to Châtillon on the Seine, where he lived with his uncle, a priest, who taught him to speak Latin, and awakened his religious susceptibilities, which were naturally strong. This did not prevent him from yielding to the persuasions of one of his companions to run off to Beaune, a town of Burgundy, where the fugitives proposed to study music under the Fathers of the Oratory. To provide funds for the journey, he stole a sum of about the value of a dollar from his uncle, the priest. This act, which seems to have been a mere peccadillo of boyish levity, determined his future career. Finding himself in total destitution at Beaune, he wrote to his mother for money, and received in reply an order from his father to come home. Stung with the thought of being posted as a thief in his native village, he resolved not to do so, but to set out forthwith on a pilgrimage to Rome; and accordingly, tattered and penniless, he took the road for the sacred city. Soon a conflict began within him between his misery and the pride which forbade him to beg. The pride was forced to succumb. He begged from door to door; slept under sheds by the wayside, or in haystacks; and now and then found lodging and a meal at a convent. Thus, sometimes alone, sometimes with vagabonds whom he met on the road, he made his way through Savoy and Lombardy in a pitiable condition of destitution, filth, and disease. At length he reached Ancona, when the thought occurred to him of visiting the Holy House of Loretto, and imploring the succour of the Virgin Mary. Nor were his hopes disappointed. He had reached that renowned shrine, knelt, paid his devotions, and offered his prayer, when, as he issued from the door of the chapel, he was accosted by a young man, whom he conjectures to have been an angel descended to his relief, and who was probably some penitent or devotee bent on works of charity or self-mortification. With a voice of the greatest kindness, he proffered his aid to the wretched boy, whose appearance was

alike fitted to awaken pity and disgust. The conquering of a natural repugnance to filth, in the interest of charity and humility, is a conspicuous virtue in most of the Roman Catholic saints; and whatever merit may attach to it was acquired in an extraordinary degree by the young man in question. Apparently, he was a physician; for he not only restored the miserable wanderer to a condition of comparative decency, but cured him of a grievous malady, the result of neglect. Chaumonot went on his way, thankful to his benefactor, and overflowing with an enthusiasm of gratitude to Our Lady of Loretto.[3]

As he journeyed towards Rome, an old burgher, at whose door he had begged, employed him as a servant. He soon became known to a Jesuit, to whom he had confessed himself in Latin; and as his acquirements were considerable for his years, he was eventually employed as teacher of a low class in one of the Jesuit schools. Nature had inclined him to a life of devotion. He would fain be a hermit, and, to that end, practised eating green ears of wheat; but finding he could not swallow them, conceived that he had mistaken his vocation. Then a strong desire grew up within him to become a Récollet, a Capuchin, or, above all, a Jesuit; and at length the wish of his heart was answered. At the age of twenty-one, he was admitted to the Jesuit novitiate.[4] Soon after its close, a small duodecimo volume was placed in his hands. It was a *Relation* of the Canadian mission, and contained one of those narratives of Brébeuf which have been often cited in the preceding pages. Its effect was immediate. Burning to share those glorious toils, the young priest asked to be sent to Canada; and his request was granted.

Before embarking, he set out with the Jesuit Poncet, who was also destined for Canada, on a pilgrimage from Rome to the shrine of Our Lady of Loretto. They journeyed on foot, begging alms by the way. Chaumonot was soon seized with a pain in the knee, so violent that it seemed impossible to proceed. At San Severino, where they lodged with the Barnabites, he bethought him of asking the intercession of a certain poor woman of that place, who had died some time before with the reputation of sanctity. Accordingly he addressed to her his prayer, promising to publish her fame on every possible occasion, if she would obtain his cure from God.[5] The intercession was accepted; the offending limb became sound again, and the two pilgrims pursued their journey. They reached Loretto, and kneeling before the Queen of Heaven, implored her favour and aid; while Chaumonot, overflowing with devotion to this celestial mistress of his heart, conceived the purpose of building in Canada a chapel to her honour, after the exact model of the Holy House of Loretto. They soon afterwards embarked together, and arrived among the Hurons early in the autumn of 1639.

Noël Chabanel came later to the mission; for he did not reach the Huron country until 1643. He detested the Indian life—the smoke, the vermin, the filthy food, the impossibility of privacy. He could not study by the smoky lodge-fire, among the noisy crowd of men and squaws, with their dogs, and their restless, screeching children. He had a natural inaptitude to learning the language, and laboured at it for five years with scarcely a sign of progress. The Devil whispered a suggestion into his ear: Let him procure his release from these barren and revolting toils, and return to France, where congenial and useful employments awaited him. Chabanel refused to listen; and when the temptation still beset him, he bound himself by a solemn vow to remain in Canada to the day of his death.[6]

Isaac Jogues was of a character not unlike Garnier. Nature had given him no especial force of intellect or constitutional energy, yet the man was indomitable and irrepressible, as his history will show.

We have but few means of characterizing the remaining priests of the mission otherwise than as their traits appear on the field of their labours. Theirs was no faith of abstractions and generalities. For them, heaven was very near to earth, touching and mingling with it at many points.

On high, God the Father sat enthroned; and, nearer to human sympathies, Divinity incarnate in the Son, with the benign form of his immaculate mother, and her spouse St Joseph, the chosen patron of New France. Interceding saints and departed friends bore to the throne of grace the petitions of those yet lingering in mortal bondage and formed an ascending chain from earth to heaven.

These priests lived in an atmosphere of supernaturalism. Every day had its miracle. Divine power declared itself in action immediate and direct, controlling, guiding, or reversing the laws of Nature. The missionaries did not reject the ordinary cures for disease or wounds; but they relied far more on a prayer to the Virgin, a vow to St Joseph, or the promise of a *neuvaine* or nine days' devotion to some other celestial personage; while the touch of a fragment of a tooth or bone of some departed saint was of sovereign efficacy to cure sickness, solace pain, or relieve a suffering squaw in the throes of childbirth. Once, Chaumonot, having a headache, remembered to have heard of a sick man who regained his health by commending his case to St Ignatius, and at the same time putting a medal stamped with his image into his mouth. Accordingly he tried a similar experiment, putting into his mouth a medal bearing a representation of the Holy Family, which was the object of his especial devotion. The next morning found him cured.[7]

The relation between this world and the next was sometimes of a nature curiously intimate. Thus, when Chaumonot heard of Garnier's death, he immediately addressed his departed colleague, and promised him the benefit of all the good works which he, Chaumonot, might perform during the next week, provided the defunct missionary would make him heir to his knowledge of the Huron tongue.[8] And he ascribed to the deceased Garnier's influence the mastery of that language which he afterwards acquired.

The efforts of the missionaries for the conversion of the savages were powerfully seconded from the other world, and the refractory subject who was deaf to human persuasions softened before the superhuman agencies which the priest invoked to his aid.[9]

It is scarcely necessary to add, that signs and voices from another world, visitations from Hell and visions from Heaven, were incidents of no rare occurrence in the lives of these ardent apostles. To Brébeuf, whose deep nature, like a furnace white hot, glowed with the still intensity of his enthusiasm, they were especially frequent. Demons in troops appeared before him, sometimes in the guise of men, sometimes as bears, wolves, or wild-cats. He called on God, and the apparitions vanished. Death, like a skeleton, sometimes menaced him, and once, as he faced it with an unquailing eye, it fell powerless at his feet. A demon, in the form of a woman, assailed him with the temptation which beset St Benedict among the rocks of Subiaco; but Brébeuf signed the cross, and the infernal siren melted into air. He saw the vision of a vast and gorgeous palace; and a miraculous voice assured him that such was to be the reward of those who dwelt in sav-

age hovels for the cause of God. Angels appeared to him; and more than once St Joseph and the Virgin were visibly present before his sight. Once, when he was among the Neutral Nation, in the winter of 1640, he beheld the ominous apparition of a great cross slowly approaching from the quarter where lay the country of the Iroquois. He told the vision to his comrades.

'What was it like? How large was it?' they eagerly demanded. 'Large enough', replied the priest, 'to crucify us all.'[10] To explain such phenomena is the province of psychology, and not of history. Their occurrence is no matter of surprise, and it would be superfluous to doubt that they were recounted in good faith, and with a full belief in their reality.

In these enthusiasts we shall find striking examples of one of the morbid forces of human nature; yet in candour let us do honour to what was genuine in them, that principle of self-abnegation which is the life of true religion, and which is vital no less to the highest forms of heroism.

NOTES

1. 'C'est pourquoi j'ai bien gagne à quitter la France, ou vous me fesiez la guerre de n'avoir point de barbe; car c'est ce qui me fait estimer beau des Sauvages.'—*Lettres de Garnier*, MSS.

2. The above sketch of Garnier is drawn from various sources. *Observations du P. Henri de St. Joseph Carme, sur son Frère le P. Charles Garnier*, MS.— *Abrégé de la Vie du R. Père Charles Garnier*, MS. This unpublished sketch bears the signature of the Jesuit Ragueneau, with the date 1652. For the opportunity of consulting it I am indebted to Rev. Felix Martin, S.J.—*Lettres du P. Charles Garnier*, MSS. These embrace his correspondence from the Huron country, and are exceedingly characteristic and striking. There is another letter in Carayon, *Première Mission*. Garnier's family was wealthy, as well as noble. Its members seem to have been strongly attached to each other, and the young

priest's father was greatly distressed at his departure for Canada.

3. 'Si la moindre dame m'avoit fait rendre ce service par le dernier de ses valets, n'aurois-je pas dus lui en rendre toutes les reconnoissances possibles? Et si après une telle charité ells s'étoit offerte à me servir toujours de mesme, comment aurois-je dû l'honorer, lui obéir, l'aimer toute ma vie! Pardon, Reine des Anges et des homes! pardon de ce qu'après avoir reçu de vous tant de marques, par lesquelles vous m'avez convaincu que vous m'avez adopté pour votre fils, j'ai eu l'ingratitude pendant des années entières de me comporter encore plutôt en esclave de Satan qu'en enfant d'une Mère Vierge. O que vous êtes bonne et charitable! puisque quelques obstacles que mes péchés ayent pu mettre à vos graces, vous n'avez jamais cessé de m'attirer au bien; jusque là que vous m'avez fait

admettre dans la Sainte Compagnie de Jésus, votre fils.'—Chaumonot, *Vie*, 20. The above is from the very curious autobiography written by Chaumonot, at the command of his superior, in 1688. The original manuscript is at the Hôtel Dieu of Quebec. Mr. Shea has printed it.

4. His age, when he left his uncle, the priest, is not mentioned. But he must have been a mere child; for at the end of his novitiate he had forgotten his native language, and was forced to learn it a second time.

'Jamais y out-il homme sur terre plus obligé que moi à la Sainte Famille de Jésus, de Marie et de Joseph! Marie en me guérissant de ma vilaine galle ou teigne, me délivra d'une infinité de peines et d'incommodités corporelles, que cette hideuse maladie qui me rongeoit m'avoit causé. Joseph m'ayant obtenu la grace d'être incorporé à un corps aussi saint qu'est celui des Jésuites, m'a preservé d'une infinité de misères spirituelles, de tentatious très dangereuses et de péchés très énormes. Jésus n'ayant pas permis que j'entrasse dans aucun autre ordre qu'en celui qu'il honore tout à la fois de son beau nom, de sa douce présence et de sa protection spéciale. O Jésus! O Marie! O Joseph! qui méritoit moins que moi vos divines faveurs, et envers qui avez vous été plus prodigue?'—Chaumonot, *Vie*, 37. Vol. I.–13

5. Je me recommandai à elle en lui promettant de la faire connoître dans toutes les occasions que j'en aurois jamais, si elle m'obtenoit de Dieu ma guérison.'—Chaumonot, *Vie*, 46.

6. *Abrégé de la Vie du Père Noël Chabanel*, MS. This anonymous paper bears the signature of Ragueneau, in attestation of its truth. See also Ragueneau, *Relation*, 1650, 17, 18. Chabanel's vow is here given *verbatim*.

7. Chaumonot, *Vie*, 73.

8. 'Je n'eus pas plutôt appris sa glorieuse mort, que je lui promis tout ce que je ferois de bien pendant huit jours, à condition qu'il me feroit son héritier dans la connoissance parfaite qu'il avoit du Huron.'—Chaumonot, *Vie*, 61.

9. As these may be supposed to be exploded ideas of the past, the writer may recall an incident of his youth, while spending a few days in the convent of the Passionists, near the Coliseum at Rome. These worthy monks, after using a variety of arguments for his conversion, expressed the hope that a miraculous interposition would be vouchsafed to that end, and that the Virgin would manifest herself to him in a nocturnal vision. To this end they gave him a small brass medal, stamped with her image, to be worn at his neck, while they were to repeat a certain number of *Aves* and *Paters*, in which he was urgently invited to join; as the result of which, it was hoped the Virgin would appear on the same night. No vision, however, occurred.

10. *Quelques Remarques sur la Vie du Père Jean de Brébeuf*, MS. On the margin of this paper, opposite several of the statements repeated above, are the words, signed by Ragueneau, '*Ex ipsius autographo*,' indicating that the statements were made in writing by Brébeuf himself.

Still other visions are recorded by Chaumonot as occurring to Brébeuf, when they were together in the Neutral country. See also the long notice of Brébeuf, written by his colleague, Ragueneau, in the *Relation* of 1649; and Tanner, *Societas Jesu Militans*, 533.

---

4 From J.H. Kennedy, *Jesuit and Savage in New France* (New Haven: Yale University Press, 1950), 97–108.

The Physical Aspects of Indian Life

Biard and Massé must have formed some idea about the Indians before they landed at Port Royal. Probably they had read of them; certainly they had heard talk about them on the docks of Dieppe or on shipboard. But with the sight of the Americans in the flesh, paddling out to meet them or waving a frantic welcome from the shore, they no longer needed to rely on second-hand accounts. From the very first they put their impressions down on paper; as long as the French ruled Canada, later missionaries imitated them.

Such accounts could not be absolutely objective, in view of the corporate and personal interests of the writers. Also, as Montaigne had remarked about travellers, 'your sophisticated men are more curious observers, and take in more things, but they glose them; to lend weight to their interpretations, and induce your belief, they cannot help altering their story a little. They never describe things as they really are, but bend them and mask them according to the point of view from which they see things.'[1] Even though the Jesuits tried honestly to write the truth, it was as they saw it; and Montaigne's warning is sound. If the modern reader approaches the writings of the Jesuits as their contemporaries did, he experiences little difficulty in plucking out the objective truth from their accounts. But the modern critic labours under a handicap: the Jesuits were more than simply Jesuitic; they reflected other ideas common to their times and country. Seventeenth-century Frenchmen, sharing the same ideas, could the more easily identify the peculiarly Jesuitic element in the *Relations* and thus, casting that element aside, regard only the facts about the Indians.

The inaccuracy and incompleteness of the *Relations* arose from the circumstances of missionary expansion. At first, in a rush to capture the essence of the Indian character, the Jesuits set down whatever they saw; without thought or discrimination they mingled bland generalizations about the whole race with precise comments about members of tribes whom they knew intimately. Biard, for example, attributed traits of the Acadian tribes to Indians in general. Later, as the missionaries ventured deeper into the forests and met other tribes, their observations became more exact. They rarely generalized, except to

contrast the distinguishing marks of one tribe with those of another that they already knew.[2] If the progress of the missions had followed the plan of Le Jeune and the paths laid out by nature, the *Relations* might have presented a systematic survey of the Indians, tribe by tribe. But many external factors, chiefly the temper and polity of the natives themselves, diverted the priests in their travels; as a result they knew few tribes well and some not at all. Where evidence was slight, as with the Sioux, the tendency to generalize persisted; then the *Relations* presented merely a blurred image. On the other hand, the *Relations* were packed with detail about tribes among whom the missionaries had long sojourned; here it was not vagueness but a profusion of facts, sometimes contradictory, that impeded accuracy.

As the missions spread, comments about individual traits took up more space in the reports. The relators sent home whatever facts they thought would inform or edify. In later years the novelty of recounting personal traits wore off. The missionaries devoted more space to native feasts, dances, and councils, which the early narrators had not considered very relevant to baptism and salvation. At a time when religious fervour was waning and secular curiosity was growing, pious authors needed the sharp spice of marvels and diversion to hold an audience. But even then missionaries professed interest in such external phenomena because they shed light upon the personality of the Indian.

As long as they remained ignorant of the local tongues, the missionaries depended upon their senses for impressions of the Indians. They could note physical appearances, but no more. Once the barrier of language was overcome, intimate contact allowed them to study the daily life and prejudices and ideas of the Indians and then to consider the best means of bringing them to baptism.

The misery and crudeness of the native culture struck Biard immediately. He had assumed, he confessed, that experience gained in the passage of time would have led these people to some stage of perfection in philosophy, the arts, and sciences; but he found them barren of all accomplishment. And he saw no indications of religion: they lacked doctrines, ceremonies, ritual, temples, and sacred edifices. He offered two explanations for such an abject condition; both became standard in the *Relations*. The simple, natural need to satisfy the pangs of hunger had forced the Indians to put aside intellectual development, literature, and medicine. Secondly, since they lived outside the grace of Christ and the way to eternal salvation, they could not share in the natural happiness that God contemplated for all His creatures.[3] With a complacency perhaps natural in a former professor of rhetoric, Biard was inclined to condemn the Indians for their barbarism. In later years Father Le Jeune also recognized this backwardness—which no one in fact denied—and deplored it. But he was far more tolerant; he never entertained the idea that such a condition would endure. The Germans, Spanish, or English, he wrote, were no more civilized before they became Christians. In his detailed account of the clothes and ornaments of the Montagnais, Le Jeune indulged in further reflections—as pertinent to Europeans as to Americans on the subject of progress:

> It was the opinion of Aristotle that the world had taken as it were three steps in order to arrive at the perfection which it possessed in his time. At the first, men contented themselves with life, seeking purely and simply the things just necessary and useful for its conservation. At the second they united the agreeable with the necessary, and civility with necessity. They found food first, then the seasoning; they covered themselves in the beginning against the rigour of the weather, and afterward they gave grace and charm to their dress; they made houses in the first ages simply to use, and afterward they made them to be seen. At the third step men of intellect, seeing that the world was enjoying the things which were necessary and pleasant for life, gave themselves to the contemplation of the things of nature and to the investi-

gation of the sciences, so that the great republic of men has perfected itself little by little, necessity marching ahead, civility and well-being coming after, and the sciences bringing up in the rear.

> Now I wish to say that our savages [both] the Montagnais and the nomads, are still only at the first stage of the three which I have just mentioned; they think only in order to keep alive; they eat so as not to die, they cover themselves to banish the cold, not for appearance; grace, civility, the knowledge of the arts, the natural sciences, and much less the supernatural truths, have as yet no dwelling in this hemisphere, at least in these countries. These people do not believe that there is any other science in the world than to live and eat, that is their whole philosophy. . . . In short they have nothing but life, yet they are not always sure of that, since famine very often kills them.[4]

On the other hand, the Jesuits found that the effects of barbarism were not all harmful. True, the Indians were ignorant; but as compensation they enjoyed 'the innocence of the first centuries'.[5] If the Americans did not know all the pleasures that their European contemporaries so avidly pursued, they were nevertheless content.[6] Jérôme Lallemant even blessed the poverty, suffering, cold, and hunger to which ignorance subjected the Indians: he felt that such hardships discouraged the sensual vices and allowed of little opportunity to sin.[7] If the relative freedom from sin did not approximate the state of nature, at least, according to Vimont, 'everything there has the freedom of the earliest times.'[8] One of Vimont's colleagues elaborated upon the pristine atmosphere of Canada. 'It seems that innocence, banished from the majority of the empires and kingdoms of the universe, retired into the great forests where these people live; their nature has something of the goodness of the terrestrial paradise before sin entered it; their customs have none of the luxury, ambition, avarice, or pleasures which corrupt our cities.'[9] 'Vice', another missionary observed, 'reigns in towns much more than in the woods . . . association with animals is not so harmful as that with men, and our savages live in . . . great innocence.'[10] As time passed the relators placed more emphasis upon the lesson to be drawn from such a condition of ignorant innocence, until what had originally been a consolation for the benighted heathen became a reproach to the civilized men of France. Father Charlevoix, who scolded his readers for abandoning the purity of the old faith, occasionally conveyed the impression that it was the Indians themselves, not the missionaries, who established the moral standards. Americans, he wrote, scorned French riches and conveniences because they wished to show that they were the true philosophers. But, he added honestly, they at least envied the French the abundance and delicacy of their food.[11]

Indian innocence encouraged the missionaries immensely, since it boded well for their task. 'The silence of the forests seems more fit to receive its influence [i.e., the gospel's] than the great bustle of Louvres and palaces.'[12] Certainly such opinions sprang rather from aspiration than from a stern regard for objectivity; but the missionaries grasped at every hopeful sign to buoy up their efforts.

The conviction that the Indians possessed a great potentiality for goodness, if not present innocence, sustained Father Le Jeune in his heroic struggle to entrench the missions solidly on Canadian soil. In 1654 he wrote that 'our savages are not so barbarous that they cannot be made children of God; I hope that where sin has reigned grace will triumph over it.'[13] Indeed, Le Jeune did not believe in their actual innocence; he knew them too well. But he did suspect that at one time the Hurons had had clearer and more natural knowledge of God, although later vice and low habits clouded even that knowledge. Thus he once wrote the equation, 'in barbarism, that is, in inconstancy'; and he reached the saddening conclusion that, no matter how diligently the Indians struggled to grasp the enlightenment of civilized Christianity, relics of their past condition clung to them and dragged them backward.[14] Had Le Jeune revisited Canada a century later, he would have found the retrogressive tendency still present. According to Charlevoix, even if the Indians were raised by the French from infancy, they nevertheless betrayed an inherited preference for the old ways.[15] Le Jeune and his contemporaries, more naively optimistic, would not have tolerated such an admission; they had always expected that inconstancy could be sloughed off, since they saw it as a mere consequence of paganism. But certainly by 1720 the missionary experience seemed to justify Charlevoix's conclusion. . . .

NOTES

1. Michel Eyquem de Montaigne, *Essays*, trans. E.J. Trechmann (New York, 1946), pp. 175–6.
2. Cf. 'Lettre du Père Charles l'Allemant', *Jesuit Relations*, IV, 211–13.
3. 'Relation de la Nouvelle France', III, 111, 115; 'Missio Canadensis', *Jesuit Relations*, II, 75.
4. 'Relation . . . 1632', V, 33; 'Relation . . . 1634', VII, 6–8.
5. 'Relation . . . 1651 & 1652', XXVII, 152.
6. 'Relation de la Nouvelle France', III, 135.
7. 'Relation . . . 1647', XXXI, 223–5.
8. 'Relation . . . 1644 & 1645', XXVII, 208.
9. 'Relation . . . 1647 & 1648', XXXII, 282.
10. 'Relation . . . 1661 & 1662', XLVII, 168.
11. Pierre F.X. Charlevoix, *Journal d'un voyage fait par l'ordre du roi dans l'Amérique Septentrionale* (Paris, 1744), VI, 32. Hereafter cited as *Journal*.
12. 'Relation . . . 1651 & 1652', XXXVII, 192.
13. 'Relation . . . 1634', VI, 140.
14. 'Relation . . . 1637', XII, 108; 'Relation . . . 1636', X, 125.
15. *Journal*, VI, 33.

5 From Denys Delâge and Jane Brierley, *Bitter Feast: Amerindians and Europeans in Northeastern North America, 1600–1664* (Vancouver: University of British Columbia Press, 1993), 191–4.

In 1642, Father Jérôme Lalemant wrote that 'the grace of baptism works powerfully in a heart.'[1] Looking at individual behaviour, one is indeed struck by the profound effect of baptism, and the sometimes radical personality change in certain converts. Like the social structure, personality structure was equally affected by Christianity, and this made interiorization of the new religious values all the more effective. The new religion was thrust upon a society already in the process of destructuration—that is, the disintegration of social and cultural patterns of thought. This was aggravated by the society itself, and it touched individuals whose sense of security had been deeply shaken and whose personalities were undergoing a similar process. It was as though this religion were reprogramming and restructuring profoundly traumatized human beings. One cannot help drawing a parallel, hypothetically at least, with the methods of modern religious sects for converting individuals who are either socially marginal or in a (temporary) state of psychological instability. We are familiar with the effects of personality restructuring resulting from membership in an institution that provides the double security of human and dogmatic support.

What stands out primarily is the intensity of religious practice. Huron converts and the Christian Algonkins of Quebec and Miscou displayed an uncommon degree of zeal and fervour.[2] According to Marie de l'Incarnation, it was beyond description.[3] The missionaries noted that there was nothing half-hearted about the Amerindians' faith, and neither cold nor ice nor distance could deter them.[4] The new Christians were proselytizers as well, and despite all opposition worked ardently to win over friends and relations. Often they had greater success than the missionaries.[5]

The more active the converts, the more they opposed tradition; the greater the aggressivity and hatred displayed by their traditionalist compatriots, the greater their own conviction about their role as 'public victims', martyrs to the faith.[6] Their self-image as members of the chosen few was strengthened by the many sufferings they were able to offer God as a passport to heaven.[7] By implication, pleasure was forbidden in this context of suffering. Take the case of the young girl who adopted a melancholy air in public in order to avoid 'the licence which the young men here assume . . . "When I go anywhere" (she said), "I alter my appearance; I keep my eyes cast down, and my forehead wrinkled, and I try to look sad so that no one is encouraged to accost me."'[8]

The new religion involved a highly negative self-image: that of the sinner who must redeem himself or herself. The following reply by an Attikamègue convert to Father Buteux offers convincing evidence of this: '*Question*: "What thoughts hast thou about thyself?" *Answer*: "That I am a dog, and less than a flea before God."'[9] The convert was afraid of himself, afraid of his thoughts and desires.[10]

In these circumstances, it comes as no surprise to find converts flogging themselves to expiate their sins,[11] rolling in the snow to escape the 'infernal flames' of temptation,[12] or scorching themselves with live coals.[13] It is true that traditional Huron civilization had forms of bodily discipline and self-repressive behaviour. Children were trained from a very young age, for example, to withstand the cold by being scantily clad.[14] Hurons (and Amerindians in general) were very hardy in this respect and always dressed less warmly than the French.[15] Boys were trained to hide their emotions. Men were expected to remain impassive in the face of pain or suffering,[16] to endure ritual fasting for a successful hunt, or to harden themselves to pain by applying brands to their bodies.[17] Such practices appear to have been the exception rather than the rule, however, and were intended to develop, rather than break down, bodily strength and resistance. Conversion, on the other hand, established conscious self-repression as a basic form of behaviour, accompanied by the massive introjection of the missionaries' directives.[18]

Guilt and self-conscious repression, combined with the ostentatious and proselytizing practice of their religion, epitomized the converts' behaviour. The evolution of the human animal to the human being (or *animal sapiens*) involves the conscious repression of basic instincts, beginning with a radical transformation of the original value system. According to Herbert Marcuse, this conversion of the pleasure principle to the reality principle can be defined as follows:[19]

FROM	TO
immediate satisfaction	delayed satisfaction
pleasure	restraint of pleasure
joy (play)	toil (work)
receptiveness	productiveness
absence of repression	security

Transformations within Huron society in the first half of the seventeenth century all resulted in the repression of the pleasure principle. Wars, disease, longer and more intensified labour, and finally the social division of labour, were all factors that brought new constraints and prepared the ground for establishing further controls that went beyond those traditionally required by Huron society. Christianity was to catalyze the need for an ideology and institutions to reinforce what Marcuse calls surplus repression. Theoretically, the inhibition of the pleasure principle in response to the imperatives of reality was aimed at guaranteeing greater individual security. The wars and epidemics that led to the disappearance of Huronia were accompanied by an observable inhibition of desire, a rise in surplus repression, and growing insecurity.

It is perhaps needless to add that constraints imposed in adulthood were not truly interiorized, the Huron superego having been formed in the context of the permissive upbringing characteristic of Amerindian civilizations.[20] However, the previously accepted instinctive tendencies were becoming increasingly incompatible with an ever more hostile reality. Although most constraints imposed on children were interiorized and belonged to the unconscious, among converts no prohibition imposed in adulthood could become an automatic, unconscious response. It could only give rise to a strong feeling of guilt accompanied by the need to adopt conspicuous forms of religious practice.

The concentration of religious capital in the hands of the missionaries brought about the correlative dispossession of the converted. The missionaries' conversion strategy aimed at removing the Amerindian's entire identity, so that 'being oneself' gave way to identification with another, to 'being like'.[21] The religious specialist's view of the convert established his or her identity. It was a view that both structured and destructured the personality. Unable to escape the eye of their religious mentors, the most credulous converts lived a life of pretense, mimicking the desired behaviour. They wore a mask and played a part. What the missionaries had once condemned, they now praised. Behaviour previously considered pagan was no longer associated with witchcraft. Thus the application of live brands to the body became a Christian purification practice—an act that, by the same token, embodied the recognition and legitimation of the missionary. Indeed, the influence of spells, associated with the privilege of being Christian, was now publicly recognized.

NOTES

1. *Jesuit Relations* [JR] (1642), 23:193.
2. JR (1647–8), 32:195–219; (1650–1), 37:51–61.
3. Marie de l'Incarnation, *Lettres historiques*, 35, 52, 55.
4. JR (1647), 31:155, 32:49–53.
5. JR (1639), 17:51. See also Marie de l'Incarnation, *Lettres historiques*, September 1639, 22.
6. JR (1645–6), 30:19–21; see also (1643–4), 26:217–57.
7. JR (1642), 23:109.
8. JR (1642), 23:73; see also (1638), 15:107; (1642), 23:63, 73, 193; (1643–4), 26:229; (1647–8), 32:215–19.
9. JR (1650–1), 37:59.
10. JR (1647–8), 32:217.
11. JR (1645–6), 29:75.
12. JR (1645–6), 30:39.
13. Idem.
14. Sagard, *Histoire du Canada*, 318; Sagard, *Le grand voyage du pays des Hurons*, 119 (171).
15. JR (1657–8), 44:281.
16. JR (1662–3), 48:169; (1645–6), 39:30.
17. JR (1637), 12:69–71.
18. Marcuse, *Eros and Civilization*, 16.
19. Ibid., 12, 38.
20. Ibid., 31–5.
21. Olivier, *Les enfants de Jocaste*, 67; see also 32, 65–72, 162–5, 176, 181.

6   From Carole Blackburn, *Harvest of Souls: The Jesuit Missions and Colonialism in North America*, 1632-1650 (Montreal and Kingston: McGill-Queen's University Press, 2000), 105-9.

Conversion and Conquest

> Why hast thou smitten us so that
> there is no healing for us?
> Jeremiah 14:19

> He delivers the afflicted by their
> affliction, and opens their ear
> by adversity.
> Job 36:15

The Jesuits hoped to promote the obedience and submission that was a necessary attribute of Christian life by reconfiguring Aboriginal social and political relationships. Conversion itself, however, and the Jesuits' ability to gain compliance most frequently occurred after a process of chastisement and humiliation that had been brought about by disease or the consequences of warfare. The Jesuits described the misfortunes that were increasingly experienced by Native people during the 1630s and 1640s as afflictions and crosses, and they wrote that these afflictions had an especially beneficial effect in inducing conversion and generating the humility and obedience that were appropriate to Christian behaviour. Le Jeune, for example, wrote that affliction 'opens the eyes of the understanding' (14:183). He and other Jesuits argued that suffering was necessary in order to reduce the pride and independence that kept people from recognizing the necessity of submission and their obligations to God and the Jesuits. This understanding was pointedly expressed in the *Relation* for the years 1642 and 1643, which stated: 'Humiliations are the harbingers that mark the dwellings of the great God; and tribulation attracts us more strongly and with much more certainty than does comfort. It is necessary to abase the pride and the haughtiness of these people, in order to give admission to the faith' (25:39).

The Hand That Smites Them

Shortly after the Jesuits arrived in Huron country, many of the villages were stricken with a disease of European origin. This was the first of a series of epidemics that further reduced the Huron population by almost half over a period of six years (Trigger 1987: 499). Although the Jesuits and other French also became ill during the initial epidemic, they recovered and remained relatively unaffected as the outbreaks of disease recurred. This was in sharp contrast to the inability of large numbers of Huron to withstand the diseases, and it suggested to many of them that the French had some effective means of prevention and cure. The Jesuits were accordingly asked to help stop the sickness—at which point, they took the opportunity to insist that all Huron pray and believe in God, presenting this as 'the true and only means of turning away this scourge of heaven' (13:159). While many people were initially prepared to adopt the Jesuits' terms, most did not realize the exclusive nature of the priests' demands, and they continued to seek other remedies, leaving the Jesuits to accuse them of hypocrisy and backsliding (13:165, 177).

As the diseases continued unabated, the Jesuits' proposed cures were soon discredited, though most Huron continued to believe that the priests had the power to protect themselves from the illnesses—a belief that was reinforced when the Huron observed the Jesuits spending so much time with the sick yet remaining 'full of life and health' (19:93). For the Huron, withholding assistance from someone who was ill violated community reciprocity, and as a sign of disregard for the welfare of others it could only be motivated by hostile intentions. Such behaviour was easily interpreted as a sign of complicity in a disease that had been caused by witchcraft, which was believed to be the most common cause of incurable illnesses and the most frequent expression of anti-social, hostile sentiments (Trigger 1987: 66–7). Although the residents of most Huron villages first sought to identify and eliminate possible witches among themselves, the majority came to the conclusion that the French, and particularly the Jesuits, were causing the diseases through sorcery.

This interpretation of the Jesuits as witches was encouraged by the priests' reputation as successful and potentially powerful supernatural practitioners. Evidence that the Jesuits possessed power had already been apparent in their success in praying for rain and their ability to predict lunar eclipses (15:139, 175), as well as by a number of the technologies they had brought from Europe. Brébeuf had been involved in a successful bid for rain during his first years with the Huron, before the English defeat of the French and the removal of the missionaries to France (10:43–9). This was not forgotten by those Huron who knew Brébeuf, and during the very dry spring and summer of 1635 they asked the Jesuits to pray for an end to the drought. The efforts of Huron *arendiwane* to do the same had been unsuccessful. One shaman in particular blamed the Jesuits for his failure and demanded, much to the chagrin of the priests, that they take down the cross they had erected in front of their cabin in Ihonatiria (10:37–43). The Jesuits not only refused to remove the cross but they twice enjoyed seeing their prayers and processions followed by a significant amount of rain, as well as by the admiration and respect of many people.

Suspicion about the Jesuits' involvement in the diseases also stemmed from the fact that most Huron did not completely understand the priests' intentions in wanting to live among them (17:125). While it was accepted that traders and warriors had occasion to live with allies or trading partners, the missionaries' evangelical purpose, based as it was on a universalist belief, had no precedent and consequently was open to local interpretation (Trigger 1987: 534). As the diseases spread, the Jesuits' teaching and habits were easily shaped into indisputable proof of hostile intentions and sinister activities, whose ultimate objective was the destruction of the Huron people.

This was particularly the case with behaviour that was culturally alien and either oddly inappropriate or more directly suggestive of the stinginess and uncooperative spirit which the Huron associated with witchcraft. The priests' habit of closing their door at certain times of the day for private meditation, for example, fell within the range of anti-social behaviour, and many Huron believed that the Jesuits needed this privacy in order to practise their sorcery (15:33). Their practice of speaking to those who were sick about death and the afterlife was similarly unusual and inappropriate (15:23, 69). Most people found the priests' continual references to death disturbing and morbid, and they suspected that the Jesuits were concerned not with an individual's recovery but solely with sending him or her to heaven. The Jesuits attempted to aid the sick as much as possible, hoping to advance the cause of Christianity by discrediting the cures offered by the shamans and setting an example of Christian charity (15:69). However, at the same time as they were diligently attempting to bring people some relief, their stern criticism of Native curing rites and their refusal to participate in them were viewed by most Huron as socially uncooperative behaviour and interpreted as further evidence that the priests actually wanted to prevent people from recovering. In this way, although the priests cast their behaviour in the benevolent idiom of Christian charity and sacrifice, the Huron interpreted it through the divergent idiom of harmful intent and sorcery. Some Huron even suggested that the Jesuits' wish to see them in heaven as soon as possible caused them to shorten the lives of those whom they felt were best prepared for the afterlife (19:241).

The unfamiliar material and technological features of the mission were similarly subject to interpretation by the Huron, who saw in them further evidence of the Jesuits' sorcery. The act of writing, especially, was subject to a variety of appropriations that challenged the Jesuits' own understanding and their expectation of its significance. Writing was the Jesuits' most potent technology, both as the source of their universal

truths and because Native people admired their ability to communicate silently through pieces of marked paper. The Jesuits based much of their faith in the truth of Christianity and its universal relevance on the authority of their written tradition. In their attempt to persuade people to convert, they lost no opportunity to assert the value of the Bible as a written document containing the authentic and undistorted Word of God. They argued that while oral traditions were subject to the fallibility of memory and the accumulation of lies and stories invented for the sake of entertainment, the basis of their own faith in the Word, not just spoken but recorded, was indisputable (11:153; 17:135). Le Jeune quickly identified the word used by the Montagnais to speak of the distant past, *nitatohokan*, as meaning 'I relate a fable, I am telling an old story invented for amusement' (6:157). By comparison, when some Huron asked Brébeuf how the Jesuits 'knew there was a Hell, and whence we obtained all that we told about the condition of the damned', he replied 'that we had indubitable proofs of it, that we possessed it through divine revelation; that the Holy Ghost himself had dictated these truths to certain persons, and to our Ancestors, who had left them to us in writing, and that we still carefully preserved the books containing them' (13:51–3).[1]

The Jesuits' faith in the Bible as a written document was deeply embedded in an assumption that all truth and knowledge was textually dependent (Mignolo 1992: 318). The proof of God himself could be 'read' in nature. As one of the priests explained, 'The reality of a God was . . . so clear that it was only necessary to open the eyes to see it written in large characters upon the faces of all creatures' (13:173). I have already noted that the Jesuits' mission in New France depended, in large part, on an oral practice and that the early history of Christianity was itself strongly oral, relying on an oral praxis of preaching and teaching the Word. However, the Jesuits came to North America after the Renaissance, when an ideology of the letter had emerged which emphasized the primacy of writing as well as the physical form of the book itself, both as the essential repository of knowledge and as its principal means of transmission (Mignolo 1992: 311, 318). While Christ himself was originally the Word of God embodied (11:169), the authority of this Word came to be the authority of the Book. Indeed, in an especially interesting gloss on Christ's physical embodiment of textual authority, Le Jeune referred to Christ as 'the living Book' (16:123). Writing, knowledge, and the material form of the book convened in an ideology and philosophy of writing that had considerable effect on interpretations of the New World and its peoples; the absence of a system of alphabetical writing quickly came to be interpreted as a sign of the absence of civilization and as evidence of the inferiority of New World peoples (Mignolo 1992: 317–18).

The priests knew that 'the art of inscribing upon paper matters that are beyond sight' (15:121) visibly impressed the people they were trying to convert. Notes sent between Jesuits from one village to another caused the Native people to think that the priests could predict the future and read minds at a distance, something that only shamans could similarly claim to do (Axtell 1988: 93). In 1635 Brébeuf wrote that the Huron admired the lodestone, prism, and joiner's tools, 'but above all . . . writing, for they could not conceive how, what one of us, being in the village, had said to them, and put down at the same time in writing, another, who meanwhile was in a house far away, could say readily on seeing the writing. I believe they have made a hundred trials of it' (8:113). He added: 'This serves to gain their affections, and to render them more docile when we introduce the admirable and incomprehensible mysteries of our Faith; for the belief they have in our intelligence and capacity causes them to accept without reply what we say to them' (8:113).

NOTES

[Editor's note: parenthetical references in the text are to volume and page number in Reuben Gold Thwaites, *Jesuit Relations and Allied Documents*, 73 vols (Cleveland: Burrows Bros, 1896–1901).]

1. In an especially interesting literal play on the Jesuits' insistence that the Bible was the unmediated, directly transmitted Word of God, Le Jeune reported: 'When I told them that we had a book which contained the words and teachings of God, they were very anxious to know how we could have gotten this book,—some of them believing that it had been let down from the Sky at the end of a rope, and that we had found it thus suspended in the air' (11:209).

REFERENCES

Axtell, James. 1988. *After Columbus: Essays in the Ethnohistory of Colonial North America*. New York and Oxford: Oxford University Press.

Mignolo, Walter D. 1992. 'On the colonization of Amerindian Languages and Memories: Renaissance Theories of Writing and the Discontinuity of the Classical Tradition', *Comparative Studies in Society and History* 34, 4: 301–30.

Trigger, Bruce. 1987. *The Children of Aataenstic: A History of the Huron People to 1660*, 2 vols. Montreal and Kingston: McGill-Queen's University Press.

THREE

☐ The Seigneurial System in Canada

Readings

PRIMARY DOCUMENTS

HISTORICAL INTERPRETATIONS

INTRODUCTION

■ From virtually the beginning of French settlement in North America, the role of the seigneurial regime in the socio-economic life of Canada has been a controversial one. Certainly at first glance, the establishment in the New World of a landholding system based on large landholders whose tenants stood in a dependent relationship to them seemed to recreate medieval institutions out of keeping with the 'free air' of North America. The nineteenth-century American historian, Francis Parkman, in his multi-volume study of the struggle between France and England/Britain for mastery of the North American continent, emphasized the great conflict as a clash between two very different societies. The English looked forward to the modern era, while the French faced back to the medieval period. According to Parkman, English America emphasized individualism, political liberty, material advancement, and freehold landholding, while New France stressed stability, order, tight political-religious controls, and a traditional relationship between landlord and tenant. The Company of New France made the first seigneurial concession in 1634 to Robert Giffard. This concession emphasized the mutual obligations of both seigneur and tenant, but also stipulated that any settlers on Giffard's grant would reduce the Company's obligation to supply settlers. This grant emphasized the relationship between the seigneurial system and land settlement, which it never really lost.

A number of major difficulties have faced those attempting to explain and interpret the seigneurial system in Canada. One is that the Crown continually made new regulations for the seigneuries. Another is that these new regulations were not necessarily carefully enforced. A third is that a number of the seigneuries were placed in or ended up in the hands of the Church, usually more likely to be a scrupulous administrator than private landholders. Finally, documentary evidence, especially for what was actually practised, is thin on the ground. What we do know is that by 1760 there were nearly 250 seigneuries in Canada, on which great variations in form and practice could exist.

Questions for consideration

1. What functions were served by the seigneurial system?
2. What did the seigneurial system not do?
3. Do any of the sources here regard the seigneurial system as truly feudal?

Suggestions for further reading

Louise Dechêne, *Habitants and Merchants in Seventeenth-Century Montreal* (Montreal and Kingston: McGill-Queen's University Press, 1992). Despite its title, a broad-ranging study of rural Canada, based on much research and quantitative data in the French *annales* tradition.

R. Cole Harris, *The Seigneurial System in Early Canada: A Geographical Study* (Madison: University of Wisconsin Press, 1966). This is the most influential modern study, by and large dubious of Old World origins.

William Bennett Munro, ed., *Documents relating to the Seigniorial Tenure in Canada, 1598–1854* (Toronto: Champlain Society, 1908). The best collection of printed documents, most of which are published only in the French originals.

——, *The Seigniorial System in Canada: A Study in French Colonial Policy* (New York: Longmans, 1907). The author's analysis of the documents he later reprinted.

PRIMARY DOCUMENTS

1 From *Edicts, Ordinances, Declarations and Decrees relative to the Seigniorial Tenure* (Quebec, 1852), 72.

DECREE OF THE KING DIRECTING THAT THE LANDS WHICH HAVE BEEN CONCEDED BE BROUGHT INTO CULTIVATION AND OCCUPIED BY INHABITANTS—JULY 6, 1711 [The Edict of Marly]

The King being informed that, among the tracts of land which His Majesty has been pleased to grant and concede in seigniory to his subjects in New France, there are some which have not been entirely settled, and others on which there are as yet no settlers to bring them into a state of cultivation, and on which also those to whom they have been conceded in seigniory have not yet commenced to make clearings for the purpose of establishing their domain thereon;

And His Majesty being also informed that there are some seigniors who refuse, under various pretexts, to concede lands to settlers who apply to them with the hope of being able to sell the same, and at the same time impose upon the purchasers the same dues as are paid by the inhabitants already settled on lands, which is entirely contrary to His Majesty's intentions, and to the clauses and conditions of the concessions, by which they are merely permitted to concede lands at an annual ground rent; whereby very great detriment is done to the new settlers, who find less land open to settlement in the places best adapted to commerce;

For remedy whereof His Majesty, being in his council, has ordained and ordains that, within one year at the farthest from the day on which the present decree shall be published, the inhabitants of New France to whom His Majesty has granted lands in seigniory, who have no domain cleared and who have no settlers on their grants, shall be held to bring them into cultivation and to place settlers thereon, in default of which it is His Majesty's will that the said lands be reunited to his domain after the lapse of the said period, at the diligence of the attorney general of the superior council of Quebec, and on the orders to be given in that behalf by the governor and lieutenant general of His Majesty, and the intendant in the said country;

And His Majesty ordains also, that all the seigniors in the said country of New France shall concede to the settlers the lots of land which they may demand of them in their seigniories, at a ground rent and without exacting from them any sum of money as a consideration for such concessions; otherwise, and in default of their so doing, His Majesty permits the said settlers to demand the said lots of land from them by a formal summons, and in case of their refusal, to make application to the governor and lieutenant general and intendant of the said country, whom His Majesty enjoins to concede to the said settlers the lands demanded by them, in the said seigniories, which dues shall be paid by the new settlers into the hands of the receiver of His Majesty's domain, in the city of Quebec, without its being in the power of the seigniors to claim from them any dues of any kind whatever.
. . .

2 'Report of General James Murray on the State of Canada under French Administration, 5 June 1762', in W.B. Munro, ed., *Documents relating to the Seigniorial Tenure in Canada* (Toronto: Champlain Society, 1908), 199–200.

The tenure of lands here is of two sorts:—

I. *The Fiefs or Seigneuries.* These lands are deemed noble; on the demise of the possessor, his eldest son inherits one-half, and shares with the other children in the remainder; if any of these die without posterity, the brothers share the portion of the deceased exclusive of their sisters. The purchaser of these fiefs enters into all the privileges and immunities of the same, but pays a fifth of the purchase-money to the sovereign, who is lord of the soil. By law the seigneur is restricted from selling any part of his land that is not cleared, and is likewise obliged (reserving a sufficiency for his own private domain) to concede the remainder to such of the inhabitants as require the same, at an annual rent, not exceeding one *sol*, or one halfpenny sterling, for each arpent in superficies. The seigneurs have had the right of *haute, moyenne, et basse justice*, in their several fiefs, but this was attended with so many abuses and inconveniences that the inferior jurisdictions were mostly disused.

II. *Terre en Roture*. The lands conceded by the seigneurs is the second sort of tenure, and these are called *terres en roture*. The property is entirely in the possessors, and the rent they pay can never be raised upon them. They can sell it as they please, but the purchaser is obliged to pay a twelfth part of the purchase-money to the seigneur. The children of both sexes share equally in the lands, but if upon a division, the several parts are found unequal to the subsistence of a family, they are obliged to sell to one another. By law, no man can build upon a piece of land of less extent than one arpent and a half in front, upon a depth of thirty or forty. This was done with a view to promote cultivation, and to oblige the inhabitants to spread; edicts have been published from time to time to reunite such lands to the Crown as were not settled within a term of years prescribed: the last of these was published in one thousand seven hundred and thirty-two.

HISTORICAL INTERPRETATIONS

3 From Francis Parkman, *The Old Regime in Canada*, vol. 2 (Toronto: George N. Morang & Co., 1899), 40–55.

Canadian Feudalism

Canadian society was beginning to form itself, and at its base was the feudal tenure. European feudalism was the indigenous and natural growth of political and social conditions which preceded it. Canadian feudalism was an offshoot of the feudalism of France, modified by the lapse of centuries, and further modified by the royal will.

In France, as in the rest of Europe, the system had lost its vitality. The warrior-nobles who placed Hugh Capet on the throne, and began the feudal monarchy, formed an aristocratic republic; and the King was one of their number, whom they chose to be their chief. But through the struggles and vicissitudes of many succeeding reigns royalty had waxed and oligarchy had waned. The fact had changed, and the theory had changed with it. The King, once powerless among a host of turbulent nobles, was now a king indeed. Once a chief, because his equals had made him so, he was now the anointed of the Lord. This triumph of royalty had culminated in Louis XIV. The stormy energies and bold individualism of the old feudal nobles had ceased to exist. They who had held his predecessors in awe had become his obsequious servants. He no longer feared his nobles: he prized them as gorgeous decorations of his court and satellites of his royal person.

It was Richelieu who first planted feudalism in Canada.[1] The King would preserve it there, because with its teeth drawn he was fond of it; and because, as the feudal tenure prevailed in Old France, it was natural that it should prevail also in the New. But he continued as Richelieu had begun, and moulded it to the form that pleased him. Nothing was left which could threaten his absolute and undivided authority over the colony. In France, a multitude of privileges and prescriptions still clung, despite its fall, about the ancient ruling class. Few of these were allowed to cross the Atlantic, while the old lingering abuses, which had made the system odious, were at the same time lopped away. Thus retrenched, Canadian feudalism was made to serve a double end—to produce a faint and harmless reflection of French aristocracy, and simply and practically to supply agencies for distributing land among the settlers.

The nature of the precautions which it was held to require appear in the plan of administration which Talon and Tracy laid before the minister. They urge that, in view of the distance from France, special care ought to be taken to prevent changes and revolutions, aristocratic or otherwise, in the colony, whereby in time sovereign jurisdictions might grow up, as formerly occurred in various parts of France.[2] And in respect to grants already made an inquiry was ordered to ascertain 'if seigniors in distributing lands to their vassals have exacted any conditions injurious to the rights of the Crown and the subjection due solely to the King.' In the same view the seignior was denied any voice whatever in the direction of government; and it is scarcely necessary to say that the essential feature of feudalism in the day of its vitality, the requirement of military service by the lord from the vassal, was utterly unknown in Canada. The royal governor called out the militia whenever he saw fit, and set over it what officers he pleased.

The seignior was usually the immediate vassal of the Crown, from which he had received his land gratuitously. In a few cases he made grants to other seigniors inferior in the feudal scale, and they, his vassals, granted in turn to their vassals—the *habitants*, or cultivators of the soil.[3] Sometimes the *habitant* held directly of the Crown, in which case there was no step between the highest and lowest degrees of the feudal scale. The seignior held by the tenure of faith and homage, the *habitant* by the inferior tenure

en censive. Faith and homage were rendered to the Crown or other feudal superior whenever the seigniory changed hands, or, in the case of seigniories held by corporations, after long stated intervals. The following is an example, drawn from the early days of the colony, of the performance of this ceremony by the owner of a fief to the seignior who had granted it to him. It is that of Jean Guion, vassal of Giffard, seignior of Beauport.

The act recounts how, in presence of a notary, Guion presented himself at the principal door of the manor-house of Beauport; how, having knocked, one Boullé, farmer of Giffard, opened the door, and in reply to Guion's question if the seignior was at home, replied that he was not, but that he, Boullé, was empowered to receive acknowledgements of faith and homage from the vassals in his name. 'After the which reply,' proceeds the act, 'the said Guion, being at the principal door, placed himself on his knees on the ground, with head bare, and without sword or spurs, and said three times these words: "Monsieur de Beauport, Monsieur de Beauport, Monsieur de Beauport! I bring you the faith and homage which I am bound to bring you on account of my fief Du Buisson, which I hold as a man of faith of your seigniory of Beauport, declaring that I offer to pay my seigniorial and feudal dues in their season, and demanding of you to accept me in faith and homage as aforesaid."'[4]

The following instance is the more common one of a seignior holding directly of the Crown. It is widely separated from the first in point of time, having occurred a year after the army of Wolfe entered Quebec.

Philippe Noël had lately died, and Jean Noël, his son, inherited his seigniory of Tilly and Bonsecours. To make the title good, faith and homage must be renewed. Jean Noël was under the bitter necessity of rendering this duty to General Murray, governor for the King of Great Britain. The form is the same as in the case of Guion, more than a century before. Noël repairs to the Government House at Quebec, and knocks at the door. A servant opens it. Noël asks if the governor is there. The servant replies that he is. Murray, informed of the visitor's object, comes to the door, and Noël then and there, 'without sword or spurs, with bare head, and one knee on the ground', repeats the acknowledgement of faith and homage for his seigniory. He was compelled, however, to add a detested innovation—the oath of fidelity to his Britannic Majesty, coupled with a pledge to keep his vassals in obedience to the new sovereign.[5]

The seignior was a proprietor holding that relation to the feudal superior which, in its pristine character, has been truly described as servile in form, proud and bold in spirit. But in Canada this bold spirit was very far from being strengthened by the changes which the policy of the Crown had introduced into the system. The reservation of mines and minerals, oaks for the royal navy, roadways, and a site (if needed) for royal forts and magazines, had in it nothing extraordinary. The great difference between the position of the Canadian seignior and that of the vassal proprietor of the Middle Ages lay in the extent and nature of the control which the Crown and its officers held over him. A decree of the King, an edict of the council, or an ordinance of the intendant, might at any moment change old conditions, impose new ones, interfere between the lord of the manor and his grantees, and modify or annul his bargains, past or present. He was never sure whether or not the government would let him alone; and against its most arbitrary intervention he had no remedy.

One condition was imposed on him which may be said to form the distinctive feature of Canadian feudalism—that of clearing his land within a limited time on pain of forfeiting it. The object was the excellent one of preventing the lands of the colony from lying waste. As the seignior was often the penniless owner of a domain three or four leagues wide and proportionately deep, he could not clear it all himself, and was therefore under the necessity of placing the greater part in the hands of those who could. But he was forbidden to sell any part of it which he had not cleared. He must grant it without price, on condition of a small perpetual rent; and this brings us to the cultivator of the soil, the *censitaire*, the broad base of the feudal pyramid.[6]

The tenure *en censive*, by which the *censitaire* held of the seignior, consisted in the obligation to make annual payments in money, produce, or both. In Canada these payments, known as *cens et rente*, were strangely diverse in amount and kind; but in all the early period of the colony they were almost ludicrously small. A common charge at Montreal was half a sou and half a pint of wheat for each arpent. The rate usually fluctuated in the early times between half a sou and two sous; so that a farm of a hundred and sixty arpents would pay from four to sixteen francs, of which a part would be in money and the rest in live capons, wheat, eggs, or all three together, in pursuance of contracts as amusing in their precision as they are bewildering in their variety. Live capons, estimated at twenty sous each, though sometimes not worth ten, form a conspicuous feature in these agreements; so that on payday the seignior's barnyard presented an animated scene. Later in the history of the colony grants were at somewhat higher rates. Payment was commonly made on St Martin's day, when there was a general muster of tenants at the seigniorial mansion, with a prodigious consumption of tobacco and a corresponding retail of neighbourhood gossip, joined to the outcries of the captive fowls bundled together for delivery, with legs tied, but throats at full liberty.

A more considerable but a very uncertain source of income to the seignior were the *lods et ventes*, or mutation fines. The land of the *censitaire* passed freely to his heirs; but if he sold it, a twelfth part of the purchase money must be paid to the seignior. The seignior, on his part, was equally liable to pay a mutation fine to his feudal superior if he sold his seigniory; and for him the amount was larger—being a *quint*, or a fifth of the price received, of which, however, the greater part was deducted for immediate payment. This heavy charge, constituting as it did a tax on all improvements, was a principal cause of the abolition of the feudal tenure in 1854.

The obligation of clearing his land and living on it was laid on seignior and *censitaire* alike; but the latter was under a variety of other obligations to the former, partly imposed by custom and partly established by agreement when the grant was made. To grind his grain at the seignior's mill, bake his bread in the seignior's oven, work for him one or more days in the year, and give him one fish in every eleven, for the privilege of fishing in the river before his farm—these were the most annoying of the conditions to which the *censitaire* was liable. Few of them were enforced with much regularity. That of baking in the seignior's oven was rarely carried into effect, though occasionally used for purposes of extortion. It is here that the royal government appears in its true character, so far as concerns its relations with Canada—that of a well-meaning despotism. It continually intervened between *censitaire* and seignior, on the principle that 'as his Majesty gives the land for nothing, he can make what conditions he pleases, and change them when he pleases.'[7]

These interventions were usually favourable to the *censitaire*. On one occasion an intendant reported to the minister, that in his opinion all rents ought to be reduced to one sou and one live capon for every arpent of front, equal in most cases to forty superficial arpents.[8] Everything, he remarks, ought to be brought down to the level of the first grants 'made in days of innocence'—a happy period which he does not attempt to define. The minister replies that the diversity of the rent is, in fact, vexatious, and that for his part he is disposed to abolish it altogether.[9] Neither he nor the intendant gives the slightest hint of any compensation to the seignior.

Though these radical measures were not executed, many changes were decreed from time to time in the relations between seignior and *censitaire*—sometimes as a simple act of sovereign

power, and sometimes on the ground that the grants had been made with conditions not recognized by the *Coutume de Paris*. This was the code of law assigned to Canada; but most of the contracts between seignior and *censitaire* had been agreed upon in good faith by men who knew as much of the *Coutume de Paris* as of the Capitularies of Charlemagne, and their conditions had remained in force unchallenged for generations. These interventions of government sometimes contradicted one another, and often proved a dead letter. They are more or less active through the whole period of the French rule.

The seignior had judicial powers, which, however, were carefully curbed and controlled. His jurisdiction, when exercised at all, extended in most cases only to trivial causes. He very rarely had a prison, and seems never to have abused it. The dignity of a seigniorial gallows with *high justice* or jurisdiction over heinous offences was granted only in three or four instances.[10]

Four arpents in front by forty in depth were the ordinary dimensions of a grant *en censive*. These ribbons of land, nearly a mile and a half long, with one end on the river and the other on the uplands behind, usually combined the advantages of meadows for cultivation, and forests for timber and firewood. So long as the *censitaire* brought in on Saint Martin's day his yearly capons and his yearly handful of copper, his title against the seignior was perfect. There are farms in Canada which have passed from father to son for two hundred years. The condition of the cultivator was incomparably better than that of the French peasant, crushed by taxes, and oppressed by feudal burdens far heavier than those of Canada. In fact, the Canadian settler scorned the name of peasant, and then, as now, was always called the *habitant*. The government held him in wardship, watched over him, interfered with him, but did not oppress him or allow others to oppress him. Canada was not governed to the profit of a class; and if the King wished to create a Canadian *noblesse*, he took care that it should not bear hard on the country.[11]

Under a genuine feudalism, the ownership of land conferred nobility; but all this was changed. The King and not the soil was now the parent of honour. France swarmed with landless nobles, while *roturier* land-holders grew daily more numerous. In Canada half the seigniories were in *roturier* or plebeian hands, and in course of time some of them came into possession of persons on very humble degrees of the social scale. A seigniory could be bought and sold, and a trader or a thrifty *habitant* might, and often did, become the buyer.[12]

Notes

1. By the charter of the Company of the Hundred Associates, 1627.
2. *Projet de Réglement fait par MM. de Tracy et Talon pour la justice et la distribution des terres du Canada,* Jan. 24, 1667.
3. Most of the seigniories of Canada were simple fiefs; but there were some exceptions. In 1671, the King, as a mark of honour to Talon, erected his seigniory Des Islets into a barony; and it was soon afterwards made an earldom, *comté.* In 1676, the seigniory of St Laurent, on the island of Orleans, once the property of Laval, and then belonging to François Berthelot, councillor of the King, was erected into an earldom. In 1681, the seigniory of Portneuf, belonging to Réné Robineau, chevalier, was made a barony. In 1700, three seigniories on the south side of the St Lawrence were united into the barony of Longueuil. (See Papers on the Feudal Tenure in Canada, Abstract of Titles.)
4. Ferland, *Notes sur les Registres de Notre Dame de Québec,* 65. This was a *fief en roture,* as distinguished from *fief noble,* to which judicial powers and other privileges were attached.
5. See the act in *Observations de Sir L.H. Lafontaine, Bart., sur la Tenure Seigneuriale,* 217, note.
6. The greater part of the grants made by the old Company of New France were resumed by the Crown for neglect to occupy and improve the land, which was granted out anew under the administration of Talon. The most remarkable of these forfeited grants is that of the vast domain of La Citière, large enough for a kingdom. Lauson, afterwards governor, had obtained it from the company, but had failed to improve it. Two or three sub-grants which he had made from it were held valid; the rest was reunited to the royal domain. On repeated occasions at later dates, negligent seigniors were threatened with the loss of half or the whole of their land, and various cases are recorded in which the threat took effect. In 1741, an ordinance of the governor and intendant reunited to the royal domain seventeen seigniories at one stroke; but the former owners were told that if within a year they cleared and settled a reasonable part of the forfeited estates, the titles should be restored to them. (*Édits et Ordonnances,* ii. 555.) In the case of the *habitant* or *censitaire,* forfeitures for neglect to improve the land and live on it are very numerous.
7. This doctrine is laid down in a letter of the Marquis de Beauharnois, governor, to the minister, 1734.
8. *Lettre de Raudot, père, au Ministre,* 10 Nov. 1707.
9. *Lettre de Ponchartrain à Raudot, père,* 13 Juin 1708. Vol. II—4.
10. Baronies and *comtés* were empowered to set up gallows and pillories, to which the arms of the owner were affixed. See, for example, the edict creating the Barony des Islets.
11. On the seigniorial tenure, I have examined the entire mass of papers printed at the time when the question of its abolition was under discussion. A great deal of legal research and learning was then devoted to the subject. The argument of Mr. Dunkin in behalf of the seigniors, and the observations of Judge Lafontaine are especially instructive, as is also the collected correspondence of the governors and intendants with the central government on matters relating to the seigniorial system.

12. In 1712, the engineer Catalogne made a very long and elaborate report on the condition of Canada, with a full account of all the seigniorial estates. Of ninety-one seigniories, fiefs, and baronies, described by him, ten belonged to merchants, twelve to husbandmen, and two to masters of small river craft. The rest belonged to religious corporations, members of the council, judges, officials of the Crown, widows, and discharged officers or their sons.

4   From Marcel Trudel, *The Seigneurial Regime* (Ottawa: Canadian Historical Association, 1971), 12-17.

The rights of the seigneur which were called *onereux,* because they were profitable, were also under the supervision of the state and the seigneur was not free to increase them.

The safeguard of the tenant lay in the Custom of Paris, enforced by the authorities: no obligation was recognized unless a title to it could be produced.

The first of these rights was the payment of 'rentes'. The usual rate was twenty sols per arpent of frontage. An average lot, having three arpents frontage, brought in sixty sols a year (about $3.00 in our currency—a small tax for land ceded free). The rate varied. At Les Eboulements ten sols and a capon were paid, while at La Durantaye six livres (about $6.00) was exacted. Whatever the rate it remained at the figure set in the contract.

The second right was known as 'lods et ventes'. It was similar to the *quint* in that it was a transfer tax paid by a person when he purchased a concession from a censitaire. It was about one-twelfth of the transfer price. As in the case of the *quint* it was aimed at discouraging mutation, since lands were ceded to the censitaire to cultivate them, not to speculate. The seigneur's interest in this tax was protected by the 'retrait', which could be invoked if a censitaire should sell his right too cheaply, thus reducing the mutation tax. In such cases a seigneur could reacquire the land at the price asked, provided he exercised this right within forty days.

Dating from an earlier period seigneurs in France had acquired various sources of revenue from activities on their seigneuries—from flour mills, from bake ovens, from the sale of wine or firewood or from hunting and fishing. These monopolies had taken the name of *banalités* from the word *ban,* meaning the right to command. The seigneur in New France also enjoyed a certain number of *banalités.* He had the exclusive right to build and operate a flour mill and he collected milling dues. Each time a censitaire went to the seigneur's mill to have his grain ground (and he was obliged to have it ground there) he gave the seigneur the fourteenth *minot.* At the very least these revenues allowed the seigneur to cover the cost of maintaining the mill and paying the miller.

At times, other rights were permitted. Such was the power to cut wood for building, or even for fuel, on the uncleared land of censitaires. State intervention reduced this right to one arpent out of each sixty. Eventually it was prohibited.

The seigneur might reserve the right to fish. In such cases the censitaire must, in accordance with the terms of his contract, purchase the right by surrendering about four barrels of eels, a tenth of the porpoises, and every twentieth, or even every eleventh fish.

Where a common for pasture had been given to the censitaires, dues might be exacted. At Boucherville, for instance, seven livres (about $7.00) and an eighth of a minot of wheat was the annual charge.

If a censitaire failed to put his land under cultivation, the seigneur might reunite it to the domain, but he could not do so except through the intervention of the intendant.[1]

The seigneur could impose 'corvées'. Many extravagant statements have been made on this subject by people who seem to have confused the seigneurial system with feudalism and so have come to believe that corvées could be imposed at will. In this country the right was governed by contract. Only three days, four at most, were exacted; one for seeding, a second for haying, a third for harvesting, and, if included in the contract, a fourth for the autumn ploughing. A censitaire could commute his service by paying forty sols per day, about $2.00 in our money. Three or four days were not much to give at that time, and it must be remembered that when a corvée was imposed for the highway, the seigneur was required to do his share of the work.

To sum up, the usual burdensome rights paid by censitaires in possession of an average lot (of three arpents by forty) were:

cens	6 sols ($0.30);
rentes	60 sols ($3.00);
milling tolls	14 minots out of 200;
corvée	3 days a year.

If the minot of wheat is valued at four livres, and a day's work at two livres, the total payment is $65.30. This sum represents the annual cost to the censitaire for the possession of a lot of three arpents by forty, the milling of his wheat and the security found within the seigneurial system.

IV. Duties of the Seigneur

The seigneury was not simply a gift from the state to recompense an individual. It was not given to the seigneur for the pleasure of making him a great landed proprietor. He who became a seigneur became a promoter of colonization and had to accept a whole series of duties which had been ordained for him.

A. DUTIES OF THE SEIGNEUR TOWARDS THE STATE

The seigneur had close ties to the state. His first duty on taking possession of his fief was to pay fealty and homage. To do so he went to the governor's chateau where, in the presence of the intendant, he took off his hat, laid down his weapons, knelt, and declared himself to be a vassal of the king. By this official act, a rite belonging to the feudal system, the state intended that he should proclaim himself a faithful subject and undertake in a solemn manner to honour his obligations as a seigneur.

Then, since the land was given that he might colonize it, the seigneur was bound, when called upon by the intendant, to present an 'aveu et dénombrement' of his fief. This document, prefaced by a declaration of title, contained an enumeration of each of the lots which he had ceded, a description of those lands, giving the names of the censitaires, the extent of the cultivated lands, and a statement of the sums levied for 'cens et rentes'. In short, the seigneur was subjected by the state to an extremely detailed inquiry into his affairs.

He also undertook to reserve for the king all oak growing on the seigneury. This precious wood was required for shipbuilding. When a seigneur discovered it, he notified the state and none might be cut for sale until it had been examined by the king's carpenters. He agreed to reserve all mines and minerals for the king. The soil belonged to the seigneur but the sub-soil was the property of the Crown.

Finally, the transmission of the seigneury except in direct succession was subject to the 'droit de quint'. Whoever bought a fief from a seigneur must pay this tax which was equivalent to one-fifth of the transfer value of that fief. This tax was paid to the state by the buyer, not, as is commonly held, by the seller. It was aimed against speculation and at ensuring that sales of seigneuries would be difficult. Those who wished to buy a seigneury worth 10,000 livres would hesitate when the tax would add 2,000 livres to the purchase price. The fief had been given to the seigneur to colonize it, not as a business venture.

B. DUTIES OF THE SEIGNEUR TOWARDS THE CENSITAIRES

The seigneur was under an obligation to the state: he made a solemn promise before the intendant to fulfill his obligations. He must prove that he populated his lands. He reserved oak, mines and minerals. If he wished to speculate with the seigneury, the purchaser must meet the 'droit de quint'. The obligations of the seigneur did not end here: there remained a series of duties towards the censitaires.

The first of these duties was 'tenir feu et lieu', that is to maintain a manorhouse as a residence within the seigneury. This did not mean that the seigneur must live there year-round. It was sufficient that the manorhouse should have a responsible tenant. Under the seigneurial system the censitaires are deemed to have need of the presence of a responsible person, for he who sets down a population should be present in his own person or by his deputy. Besides, the censitaires must pay their 'cens et rentes' at the manorhouse and nowhere else.

His second duty was to cede the lands. He might not sell woodlots unless they had first been ceded as part of the colonization duties of the seigneur. If someone applied for land, the seigneur could not refuse to accept him without sufficient cause. He was obliged to give the applicant a 'billet de concession', a temporary title which permitted him to prove his ability to bring the land into cultivation. Later, the applicant could obtain a 'contrat de concession', a contract drawn up in good and proper form. If the seigneur refused an applicant without a reason or without sufficient cause, the applicant could appeal to the intendant who had the power to overcome this manifestation of ill-will by ceding the land asked for. If the seigneur neglected to cede his lands, the fief could be reunited to the royal domain. By the edicts of Marly, in 1711, Louis XIV reminded colonial authorities that they must suppress all seigneuries in which the title-holder had neglected the development of his land. This was not an empty threat. Eighteen seigneuries were suppressed for cause in 1741 alone.

A third duty was to build and operate a flour mill. If he neglected to do so, the state could either authorize a censitaire to build it and to receive the toll as recompense, or it could itself build the mill, paying the cost from the toll which the seigneur had forfeited by neglecting his obligation.

If the seigneur had judicial rights, usually those of middle and low justice, he was bound to establish a seigneurial court and to pay the salaries of the court officers.

With regard to public charges, the seigneur was on the same footing as his censitaires. He was bound to subscribe to the cost of church and presbytery. If the intendant called for a 'corvée' for the highway, the seigneur must *work* on the road despite the fact that this work was supervised by the captain of militia, one of his own censitaires. In this respect a wide gulf separated the seigneurial system from feudalism.

V. Rights and Duties of the Censitaire

The rights of the censitaires are the counterpart of the duties of the seigneur. The advantages which the censitaires could demand of the seigneur were the presence of a responsible person in the manorhouse, concessions of lands, a mill, a court of justice, and subscription to the needs of the church. If the seigneur neglected to provide these advantages, the censitaires could appeal to the intendant. In return the censitaire must live up to his duties. He too must live on his land. He was bound to pay his dues at the manorhouse. The customary date for such payments was St Martin's Day, the eleventh of November. He must produce his title on demand, cultivate his land, give right-of-way to his neighbours, permit the building of communal roads on his concession, and pay 'lods et ventes' if he purchased another's concession. Failure to meet his obligations brought penalties which were imposed by the intendant. Between 1727 and 1730, Hocquart reunited two hundred lots to seigneurial domain for failure to reside. Non-payment of dues was punished by seizure of possessions or even a levy on the land. The intervention of the intendant was an important factor: it deterred the overhasty seigneur and overcame stubbornness on the part of a recalcitrant censitaire. It protected the one against the other.

VI. Characteristics of the System

A. THE SEIGNEURIAL SYSTEM WAS NOT FEUDAL

The seigneurial regime in New France in the seventeenth century was not a feudal system. In France itself the seigneurial system existed in an economic sense well before feudalism and after being integrated into the feudal system, had been transformed into a form of military organization. Beginning as an economic cell, the seigneury had become a military cell. It was at this time that the seigneurial system adopted feudal rites and feudal terminology. After the disappearance of feudalism the seigneurial system, became once more a land-granting system—an economic enterprise—while still retaining its feudal appearance, but except for this disguise the seigneurial system had nothing in common with feudalism.

Under this system an individual received a large grant of land with the title of seigneur but on the express condition that he concede lands to those who applied for them. His rights and duties were laid down by the state in minute detail. Nothing was left to the whim of either seigneur or censitaire. Every demand made by the seigneur was regulated by the state and every condition which the censitaire must accept was written into his contract when it was first drawn. State supervision was constant. The intendant intervened continually to see that both parties got their respective rights. If the censitaire failed in his duties, the state compelled him to perform them. If the seigneur neglected or refused to fulfill his function, the state could either take his place or reduce him to the rank of censitaire by reuniting his fief to the royal domain. Bound by contract to the state and to the censitaire, the seigneur bore no resemblance to his feudal counterpart. A society in which everyone enjoys equal protection from the state, and in which everyone is on the same footing with regard to public duties is not feudal. Even though the seigneurial system drew upon feudalism for some of its rites and part of its vocabulary, its essential content is not feudal.

NOTE

1. Under the Custom of Paris the seigneur could erect a communal oven which must be used by the censitaire who paid the due of one loaf in twenty-four. This right was not exercised in New France. The intendant Raudot asked that it should be abolished, merely from fear that some seigneur might try to exact it some day.

5   From Richard Colebrook Harris, *The Seigneurial System in Early Canada: A Geographical Study* (Madison: University of Wisconsin Press, 1966), 193–8.

With long, thin fields stretching away from the St Lawrence and straggling rows of farmhouses along either bank of the river for two hundred miles and more, the landscape of rural Canada towards the end of the French regime presented a unique face. Visitors commented on its distinctive charm, and scholars since have assumed that its distinctiveness reflected the influence of the seigneurial system. Yet . . . the seigneurial system was largely irrelevant to the early geography of Canada. The pattern of rotures was an important part of the geography of the colony, and the imprint of these early concessions is still preserved in the landscape of rural Quebec, although these patterns, the possible by-products of many methods of land-granting, were not in themselves the seigneurial system or even a reflection of it. Neither settlement patterns nor those of social and economic activity reflected the influence of the seigneurs. Seigneuries were indefinite units on the land, and seigneurial boundaries neither enclosed nor altered any of the principal patterns of human activity in the colony.

The seigneurial system could have shaped much of the geography of early Canada only if it had provided a mould first for settlement and then for the social and economic development of the colony, but there is little indication that during the French regime the system was ever such a mould. Few seigneurs profited from their concessions in a colony where seigneuries were often divided among many co-seigneurs, where seigneurial dues were low and, above all, where settlers were few and far between. In the seventeenth century, when there was only a handful of censitaires in their seigneuries and the land was a potential expense rather than a source of revenue, the seigneurs often neglected their holdings for years. Their censitaires often paid no dues, and may have forgotten their seigneurs' names. The censitaires, who often came to Canada with vivid memories of a seigneur's social and economic role in France and who quickly decided that illegal participation in the fur trade was the easiest road to wealth in the colony, sought to avoid most contacts with their seigneur. Their uneasiness about the seigneurs waned in the eighteenth century, to be replaced largely by indifference, and they settled into a way of life which was little influenced by him one way or the other. To be sure, in the last decades of the French regime land was becoming scarce in some seigneuries near Quebec, and the population in a number of seigneuries near either Quebec or Montreal had risen to the point where seigneurial revenues were substantial. Seigneurs took a more active interest in their concessions; without cheap land nearby, censitaires were increasingly tied to their own rotures. But Canadian seigneurs, always closely supervised by royal officials, found it difficult if not impossible to extend their influence over their censitaires, and even in these later years the seigneurial system remained in the background of Canadian life.

Certainly some seigneurs may have thought of their titles as status symbols even when the seigneuries which they controlled were wilderness tracts. Some may have viewed their titles as entrées for themselves or their sons to appointments in the army or civil service. These are matters on which the geographical evidence sheds no light, but which cannot alter the conclusion that the seigneurial system was largely irrelevant to the general and economic development of the colony.

In the years before the English conquest a French way of life had been recast in Canada. Canada and France were 3,000 miles apart, and the connection between them was a precarious voyage of several months' duration. Royal officials brought the king's authority to Canada and administered his laws as carefully as they could when the king's wishes were known often only after long delay, and often did not apply well to a Canadian situation. Frenchmen trickled across the Atlantic to settle in Canada, but the flow was so small that French ideas and customs were not replenished through immigration. The few who did come found a vastly different land. The colony was a ribbon of settlement in a wilderness of trees, rock and water. Land was everywhere, and it was free. The fur trade was open to all able-bodied men and offered, in addition to revenue from beaver pelts, complete independence from the traditional channels of authority. In these circumstances a French way of life had been transformed.

The principal change in Canada was towards more individual independence. Royal officials in Quebec and Montreal could regulate the commercial life of the towns and supervise the exports and imports which passed through Quebec, but exerted relatively little control over habitants who were spread out for more than two hundred miles along the banks of the St Lawrence, and who could vanish into the interior to escape any unwelcome pressure. The seigneurs found control expensive, and equally difficult to administer. The Church may have become the strongest of the traditional sources of authority, although its influence on the habitants is extremely difficult to assess. Certainly the habitants never quarrelled with its dogmas, but its controls and interdictions may have sat lightly on them. In later years an aged Philippe de Gaspé described the Canadian habitant as 'l'homme le plus independent du monde',[1] and if this was an exaggeration, there is no doubt that his independence was such that the seigneurial system, one of the sources of control in France, quickly disintegrated in Canada.

When Frederick Jackson Turner's frontier thesis was first vigorously challenged, ripples of the debate reached back to New France, and Turner himself wrote a short defence of the relevance of his ideas to an understanding of the French colony.[2] Turner knew little about New France, and his critics probably knew even less. Although the evidence in this study suggests that Turner was closer to the truth than were his critics, no one would want to reopen the argument along the earlier lines. There can be little doubt that in 1760 Canada was not an enclave of French civilization. Ideas and institutions, the way of life, had changed, and if it is helpful to consider a colony which had not moved westward in a hundred years a frontier, then the frontier was a seat of change, albeit one without a cutting edge where the metamorphic force of the wilderness reshaped European ways with particular alacrity.

Turner's contention that the change was related to the availability of free land to the west, to isolation, and to the safety valve is both shrewd and misleading when applied to Canada. Settlement in early Canada filled in a line between Quebec and Montreal; it did not expand westward. The fact that free land within seigneuries along the lower St Lawrence was more important than free land to the west meant that those aspects of a legal system which were designed to protect scarce land, and of the social hierarchy which were based on the control of scarce land, were superfluous. It also led to the development of a much more extensive agricultural system than was characteristic in northwestern France. In the sense that a French king and his ministers kept an interested if often poorly informed watch on Canada, and that his representatives in the colony maintained a closer vigilance, the colony was not isolated from France. And yet the very closeness of this contact inadvertently reinforced the collapse of a French institution; it must not be forgotten that the seigneurial system disintegrated in Canada in part because a French king reduced the prerogatives and the dues to which his Canadian seigneurs were entitled. When the conquest broke this French connection, seigneurial dues and seigneurial influence probably began to increase, and they might have done so long before if the seigneurs had been more isolated from French authority. There would not have been an explosion had safety valves in the direction of the Great Lakes or the American colonies not existed, but the alternative to farming and the ready escape from authority which they provided were fundamental ingredients in the Canadian situation.

And yet, Canada bore little resemblance to the unruly American settlements in the Appalachian valleys in the middle of the eighteenth century and, in the nineteenth century, in some areas farther west which had been settled before law and order were established. There were royal courts in Quebec, Trois-Rivières, and Montreal, as well as the intendant and Conseil Supérieur in Quebec, and the censitaire could appeal for justice to any one of them. When Canada was organized into parishes, a curé was seldom more than a few miles from any farm in his parish. Although a seigneur or co-seigneur was usually no farther away, the censitaire needed little from him. However, he went to mass, and may have taken many problems to his curé. The records of all the colony's courts attest to the use the censitaire made of them. The machinery of control had come to Canada, but its oppressive features were mitigated or atrophied from disuse because control was possible only to the degree that the censitaires would co-operate.

NOTES

1. Philippe A. de Gaspé, *Mémoires* (Quebec, 1885), p. 530.

2. F.J. Turner, 'The Rise and Fall of New France', *Minnesota History* 18 (Dec. 1937): 383–98.

6 From Morris Altman, 'Seigniorial Tenure in New France, 1688–1739: An Essay on Income Distribution and Retarded Economic Development', *Historical Reflections* 10, 2 (1983): 335–43.

Publications about the economic and social history of New France are legion; yet few scholars have studied the reasons for the colony's relatively retarded economic development. Jean Hamelin attributed economic stagnation in New France to a shortage of capital and labour—a view found to be seriously deficient.[1] Louise Dechêne thinks the failure to integrate agriculture into the international trade sector—a core/periphery dichotomy mirrored in New France itself—helped maintain a generally autarkic, stagnant agricultural sector.[2] W.J. Eccles argues that money to live in the style of Moliere's monsieur Jourdain diverted capital to the detriment economic development.[3] But no one discusses the impact of the seigniorial regime on the economy of New France. This paper shows that it modified the distribution of income, thereby changing the structure of effective demand, and thus the pattern of investment, probably reducing total output of the colony from what it otherwise might have been.

Specialists argue[4] that before the conquest of New France in 1763 the state, protecting the peasant from excessive seigniorial exactions,[5] made it possible for farmers to live largely free of economic constraints. The issue is specious, for the peasant needed no protection since he enjoyed a favourable bargaining position because of the colony's sparse population.[6] I argue that seigniorial institutions measurably reduced the favourable bargaining position of the peasant by imposing levies that retarded the economic development of the colony, even though—as an

analysis of the census data from 1688 to 1739[7] reveals—the peasants retained a rising portion of their economic surplus.[8]

In 1968 R.C. Harris argued that payments to the seignior were trivial, amounting to 5 to 10 per cent of the peasant family's annual income—a cheap price to pay for land, he insists.[9] Although Harris omitted the tithe from his calculation—3.8 per cent of the peasant's total grain production—some historians nevertheless use Harris as an authority to claim that the payments to the seignior and/or the church were trivial, amounting together to about 10 per cent of the peasant family's yearly income.[10] Louise Dechêne maintains, however, that the charges were burdensome.[11] This may well have been the case. But the issue remains to be clarified for Dechêne does not argue from a factual basis. She resorts to a hypothetical computation by Harris in order to revise the estimate of the payments of the censitaire—the peasant farmer of New France—to the seignior, arriving at a figure of 10 to 14 per cent. She goes on to argue that these charges consumed most of the peasant family's disposable income unless it produced more than fifty minots of wheat per annum.[12] Dechêne nowhere shows that the typical peasant family produced this or that quantity of wheat. The fifty minots of wheat is an imaginary figure, for Dechêne, like Harris, failed to consult the census material—the most reliable source from which to compute the level of wheat output.

Beyond the issue of computation and the reliability of sources lies the further problem of how much the state protected the censitaire against seigniorial exactions. Trudel, Harris, and Wallot maintain that the state exercised a stringent surveillance,[13] Wallot going on to explain that the abundance of land and the desire to attract immigrants induced colonial authorities to take special care to oversee seigniorial charges.[14] Dechêne insists the state never defended the censitaire's economic interests, allowing therefore the seignior to absorb a significant portion of the peasant family's disposable savings.[15] My analysis of the census records reveals that although the state did little to protect the censitaire, he was able to capture an increasing portion of the economic surplus over the period 1688–1739—probably as a result of the favourable bargaining position of the peasant family. The portion of peasant economic surplus absorbed by the seignior and the church proceeded partly from the seigniorial regime itself and partly from the services rendered to the peasant family by the seignior and the church.

Seigniorial Charges in New France: 1688–1739

Seigniorial charges must be described, however briefly, before discussing census material to measure their economic influence. The levies in New France include: the cens et rentes, the gristmill banalité, minor charges, the lods et ventes, and the tithe. They are discussed in light of the method of land concession. To obtain land a settler (the censitaire or the habitant) had to negotiate for the terms of a title-deed from a seignior—who received the land from the crown—paying a yearly rental to the seignior (cens et rentes).[16] The crown rarely granted wild land directly or freely to settlers; instead it granted en seigneurie territories conquered from the Indian nations helping, thereby, a select group (the seigniors) to live from the labour of an agricultural population. The crown could have introduced other forms of land tenure in New France; for example, settlers in some British North American colonies paid only a negligible fee for the land.[17] Since

seigniorial dues helped to pay neither for the colony's administration nor for its military protection[18] and since its establishment in New France was unnecessary—for much of North America flourished without it—it follows that fiscal and economic considerations do not explain why the crown imposed seigniorial tenure on its colonists.

The seigniors were under little pressure to make sub-grants. Therefore they could hoard land until they found censitaires with whom they could agree on terms for a title-deed. Only four seigniorial title-deeds—all issued after 1711—obliged seigniors to sub-grant land to potential settlers.[19] In general, colonial officials and even the crown defied its own decrees directed against land hoarding. Although the crown repeatedly passed ordinances to have uncleared and unsettled seigniorial land reunited to the royal domain—the arrêts of Marly of 6 July 1711 are the most well-known—the colonial authorities refused to enforce these decrees even when, in 1700, only 4 to 5 per cent of seigniorial land was cleared.[20] Indeed, the crown went on to approve decisions of the colonial authorities to increase the size of seigniories,[21] reuniting to the royal domain no more than one seigniory until 1741.[22] A similar inconsistency prevailed with respect to the number of seigniories created. Conferring no grants from 1714 to 1732, Versailles then went on to make fifty seigniorial concessions by 1760, the standard size of these grants being forty square miles—the largest made in the history of New France.[23] Meanwhile the crown issued legislation—like the arrêt de Versailles (1732)—decrying the illegal refusal of colonial authorities to reunite uncleared and unsettled seigniorial lands to the royal domain.[24] By 1763 the seigniors controlled 11,113,868 arpents (1 acre = 1.17869 arpents) of uncleared land, of which 9,313,888 were relatively fertile.[25] By 1739, I estimate that censitaires held only 802,530 arpents or 8.6 per cent of the available seigniorial land.[26] In sum, the seigniors presided over access to most of the colony's habitable land.[27]

The settler negotiated with the landlord, the seignior, who received in rent an amount that the two parties, bargaining freely, stipulated in the title-deed.[28] Since government rarely interfered in these negotiations, market and social forces largely determined the rental terms.[29] Payments consisted of a token homage, the censitaire's acknowledgement that land held in tenancy, *en censive*, could not be granted *en seigneurie*—and the rente, a genuine source of seigniorial revenue.[30] Throughout the French regime the cens et rentes together remained—with few exceptions after 1732—at one sol eight deniers per arpent (twelve deniers [d] = one sol [s]; twenty sols = one livre tournois [L]). Only in the Montreal region did the rate differ significantly, 2s ld per arpent, 20 per cent higher than elsewhere.[31] People paid in cash or in kind. Payments varied from cash plus one or more capons in the seventeenth century to cash plus wheat in the early eighteenth; by the end of the French regime most payments were in cash.[32]

The crown established another important seigniorial charge—the grist-mill banalité—when, in response to a petition from the seigniors in 1667, it decreed that censitaires must grind their grain at a seigniorial grist-mill, paying the fee of one-fourteenth of the grain ground. Prior to this date only a clause in a freely negotiated title-deed could compel a censitaire to grind the grain at the seigniorial mill.[33] But some confusion prevailed in this matter also. For almost twenty years later, in 1686, a royal arrêt ordered all seigniors in New France to construct banal-mills within one year of the arrêt. But this arrêt was published only in 1706 by the intendant Raudot who was somewhat mindful of the welfare of the censitaire.[34] The delay in publication may have resulted from an unwillingness of a colonial administration, staffed mainly by seigniors,[35] to impose the high cost of mill construction upon their brethren.[36]

The censitaire had to take to the banal-mill only the grain required for subsistence.[37] Were he to take it elsewhere, the seignior could seize both the grain and the vehicle used to transport it.[38] Moreover, a seignior who operated a mill could demolish all other grist-mills in his seigniory.[39] If the seigniorial mill produced a defective product, the censitaire could grind his wheat elsewhere.[40] He could also mill surplus grain anywhere, but the fee remained the same—one-fourteenth of the grain milled—within or outside his seigniory.

According to Article LXXI of the Custom of Paris, a cornerstone of the legal framework of New France since 1664, only a clause in the title-deed permitted a seignior to demand unpaid labour, the corvée, from his censitaire.[41] Since free bargaining determined the incidence of the corvée, it proved to be a minor and unusual charge in New France,[42] rarely exceeding six days per annum and even this service could be commuted for two livres by an arrêt of 1714.[43] In some cases the seignior could demand labour service, a species of paid corvée, whereby in exchange the censitaire enjoyed the use of the seigniorial commons and forest. Similarly a seignior occasionally compelled his censitaire to clear land for pasturage. The censitaire then would receive in return the right to the future use of that pasturage. But these paid corvées,[44] like payment for the right to fish in seigniorial waters, appear to have been infrequent.[45]

For every mutation in landownership—a sale, gift or inheritance other than in the line of direct succession—the censitaire had to pay a fine to the seignior within forty days. This fine, called lods et ventes, was fixed by the Custom of Paris at one-twelfth or 8.25 per cent of the mutation price. On failure to pay, the seignior could obtain a judgement from the intendant to seize the offending censitaire's property, including the *en censive* holding. The seignior could remit one-third of the lods et ventes to the censitaire, but he had no obligation to do so.[46]

The censitaire could conceal the de facto sale price from the seignior, trying to sell the land for a price higher than the seignior knew. But the seignior enjoyed a *droit de retrait*, the option to purchase land sold by the censitaire at the official sale price.[47] Thus, if the landlord believed that the censitaire declared a price below the actual sale price, he could buy the land at the price declared by the censitaire, cancelling thereby the censitaire's contract with a third party to sell the land for more money. Under these circumstances, the censitaire was predisposed to declare the actual sale price. Although the intendant Jacques Raudot complained in a dispatch to France in 1707 that the *droit de retrait* appears nowhere in the Custom of Paris, the intendant in 1714, Bégon, authorized seigniors to resort to this procedure.[48] In conjunction with the *droit de retrait* the lods et ventes imposed a burden on either the vendor or purchaser of a censive, depending upon whether the vendor could mark up the price sufficiently to cover the costs of the lods et ventes. R.C. Harris estimates that land

sold and bought by censitaires out of the line of direct succession brought to the seignior an average of L200 to L300 per annum for every 100 *en censive* holdings,[49] causing the censitaire to pay out, on average, two to three livres per annum in lods et ventes.

The church received one twenty-sixth or 3.8 per cent of the grain produced by the censitaire annually. In 1663, Bishop Laval had ordered a tithe of 7.7 per cent on all output produced, but censitaire protest prompted the bishop to agree to a tithe of 3.8 per cent of all output—a tithe approved by the crown in 1679. And by 1705 the colonial authorities ruled that the tithe could be levied only with respect to grain output, a decision approved by the crown in 1707. These laws remained unchanged for the balance of the French regime.[50]

NOTES

1. Jean Hamelin, *Economie et société en Nouvelle-France* (Québec: Les Presses de l'Université Laval, 1970), p. 123. Contrary to Hamelin, Denis Delâge, 'Les structures économiques de la Nouvelle-France et de la Nouvelle-York', *L'Actualité économique* 46 (1970–1):67–118, finds that labour scarcity posed no problem to the economic development of New France (p. 108). In *Les Bourgeois-gentishommes de la Nouvelle-France, 1729–1748* (Montreal: Fides, 1968), Cameron Nish shows the economic elite to have had ready access to disposable savings, that is, potential capital. Meanwhile, even among the peasantry I find considerable potential savings. Finally, Hamelin's notions about the crucial role of merchant capital find little scholarly acceptance. Authorities agree that not even in Europe was merchant capital a condition necessary for economic development. For example, see Charles Kindleberger, *Economic Response: Comparative Studies in Trade, Finance and Growth* (Cambridge, Mass.: Harvard University Press, 1978), pp. 135–66, and Paul Bairoch, *Révolution industrielle et sous-développement* (Paris: Mouton éditeur, 1974), pp. 45–70.

2. Louise Dechêne, *Habitants et marchands de Montréal au XVIIe siècle* (Paris: Librairie Plon, 1974), pp. 344–7, 482–6. Denis Delage, 'Les structures économiques', p. 117, argues that a dependence upon staple exports retarded economic development.

3. W.J. Eccles, *The Canadian Frontier, 1574–1760* (Hinsdale, Ill.: Dryden, 1969), especially pp. 70, 98 and W.J. Eccles, 'The Social, Economic and Political Significance of the Military Establishment in New France', *Canadian Historical Review* 52 (1971):11. Eccles also argues in *The Canadian Frontier*, p. 96, that reluctance to work hard made peasants less prosperous. Meanwhile merchants dissipated savings in conspicuous consumption. W.J. Eccles, 'The Social, Economic and Political Significance', p. 14.

4. Discussed generally by Fernand Ouellet, 'La formation d'une société dans la vallée du Saint-Laurent: d'une société sans classe à une société de classes', *Canadian Historical Review* 62 (1981): 407–50.

5. This essay does not discuss how fiscal and monetary policies affected the economic standing of

the peasant family; rather it measures the seigniorial régime's impact—within the framework of established fiscal and monetary policies—on the censitaire's retained earnings. See Guy Frégault, 'Essai sur les finances canadiennes', *Revue d'histoire de l'Amérique française* 12 (1958–1959): 307–22, 459–84; 13 (1959–1960):30–44, 157–82, for the fiscal and monetary aspects of state policy.

6. Evsey D. Domar, in 'The Causes of Slavery or Serfdom: A Hypothesis', *Journal of Economic History* 30 (1970):19, explains: When the scarce factor of production is not land but labour '. . . in the absence of specific governmental action to the contrary . . . the country will consist of family-size farms because hired labour, in any form, will be either unavailable or unprofitable: the wage of a hired man or the income of a tenant will have to be at least equal to what he can make on his own farm; if he receives that much, no surplus [rent] will be left to his employer. A non-working class of servitors or others could be supported by the government out of taxes levied [directly or indirectly] on the peasants, but it could not support itself from land rents.'

7. The last reliable census year for the pre-conquest period is 1739.

8. Economic surplus is defined as the output in excess of that required for consumption and the renewal of the cycle of production; it encompasses the 'normal' profit, the economic rent plus any 'disequilibrium' profit earned by the peasant family—its potential investment fund. Marvin Harris, 'The Economy Has No Surplus?', *American Anthropologist* 61 (1959):186–99, discusses the concept of economic surplus.

9. R.C. Harris, *The Seigneurial System in Early Canada: A Geographical Study* (Madison: University of Wisconsin Press, 1968), p. 81. Harris's method of calculation is not made explicit. More details are given on pp. 160–1. See note 12, below.

10. For example, W.J. Eccles, *The Canadian Frontier*, p. 67; W.J. Eccles, 'The Social, Economic and Political Significance', p. 15; J.-P. Wallot, 'Le régime seigneurial et son abolition au Canada',

Canadian Historical Review 50 (1969):373.

11. Louise Dechêne, 'L'évolution du régime seigneurial, le cas de Montréal aux XVIIe et XVIIIe siècles', *Recherches Sociographiques* 12 (1971):180.

12. Ibid. Dechêne cites R.C. Harris, *The Seigneurial System in Early Canada*, pp. 160–1, who argues that if a farm produced fifty minots of wheat, almost all of the economic surplus, or 16 per cent of wheat output, would be captured by the economic levies, the cens et rentes, the grist-mill banalité and the tithe.

13. Marcel Trudel, 'The Seigneurial Regime', *Canadian Historical Association Booklets* 6 (1971):12, 17, 20; R.C. Harris, *The Seigneurial System in Early Canada*, pp. 194, 197; J.-P. Wallot, 'Le régime seigneurial', pp. 371, 379, 380.

14. J.-P. Wallot, 'Le régime seigneurial', pp. 369, 373.

15. Louise Dechêne, 'L'évolution du régime seigneurial', p. 148.

16. W.B. Munro, *The Seigniorial System in Canada: A Study of French Colonial Policy* (New York: Longmans, Green, 1907), p. 76.

17. Ralph Davis, *The Rise of the Atlantic Economies* (London: Weidenfeld and Nicolson, 1977), pp. 276–8, discusses land acquisition in British North America. For more details see Marshall Harris, *The Origin of the Land Tenure System in the United States* (Ames: Iowa State College Press, 1953), especially pp. 116, 288 on New England.

18. For government subsidies to New France see Guy Frégault, 'Essai sur les finances canadiennes', 12 (1958–1959):460–1; 13 (1959–1960):175–7. See Ralph Davis, *The Rise of the Atlantic Economies*, pp. 286–7, and Douglass C. North, *Growth and Welfare in the American Past: A New Economic History* (Englewood Cliffs, NJ: Prentice-Hall), p. 54, for English subsidies to the North American colonies.

19. W.B. Munro, *The Seigniorial System in Canada*, p. 59.

20. On the arrêts of Marly see W.B. Munro, *Documents Related to the Seigniorial Tenure in Canada* (Toronto: The Champlain Society, 1908), pp. 91–3. Colonial authorities failed to enforce royal decrees published in 1672 and 1697 to annex

unsettled seigniorial lands to the royal domain. See W.B. Munro, *The Seigniorial System in Canada*, pp. 35, 36, 38; W.B. Munro, *Documents Related to the Seigniorial Tenure*, p. xxxviii; R.C. Harris, *The Seigneurial System in Early Canada*, p.31.

21. R.C. Harris, *The Seigneurial System in Early Canada*, p. 31. Many members of council in New France were seigniors—a fact explaining why colonial authorities showed special favour to the seigniors. See W.B. Munro, *The Seigniorial System in Canada*, p. 38.

22. R.C. Harris, *The Seigneurial System in Early Canada*, p. 36.

23. Ibid. Although, in 1741, the crown forced the colonial authorities to reunite to the royal domain twenty largely unsettled seigniories in the Lake Champlain–Richelieu River areas, these lands were nevertheless eventually reconceded to their original grantees. See W.B. Munro, *Documents Related to the Seigniorial Tenure*, p. lxxxii. In contrast seigniories annexed 460 censive holdings to their domain by 1732 for alleged violations of the arrêts of Marly, ibid., p. 176.

24. W.B. Munro, *Documents Related to the Seignioral Tenure*, pp. lxxvi–lxxxii.

25. Minutes of evidence taken before the Assistant Commissioner of Crown Lands and Emigration, the testimony of John Davidson, *Report on the Affairs of British North America from the Earl of Durham, with Appendices, The Colonies, Canada*, published in 1839 in *The British Parliamentary Papers* (Irish University Press, 1968), p. 41.

26. An estimate made by multiplying the average amount of land held by censitaires by the number of agricultural families. See Table 2, notes 2 and 8.

27. This land was the most accessible to river transportation, the only reliable mode of transportation at the time, unlike the Canadian Shield to the north and the Appalachian Highlands south of the St Lawrence and east of Lake Champlain.

28. R.C. Harris, *The Seigneurial System in Early Canada*, p. 66.

29. *The Report of the Commissioners Appointed to Inquire into the State of Laws and Other Circumstances Connected with the Seigniorial Tenure in* *Lower Canada and Appendix* (Kingston: Journals of the Legislative Assembly of the Province of Canada, 1844), 3.3, appendix F; R.C. Harris, *The Seigneurial System in Early Canada*, p. 64, concludes that there was no rent control in New France. Only the title-deed issued by the colonial authorities to the Seminary of Montreal in 1717 specified the rent to be paid to the seignior. See *The Report of the Commissioners*, p. 13. If the seignior refused to sub-grant at a rental payment *only* and the prospective tenant complained to the governor, the lieutenant-governor or the intendant, the government would sub-grant the seigniorial land at the rate prevailing for the seigniory in question, collecting the rental payments itself. W.B. Munro, *The Seigniorial System in Canada*, p. 59.

30. R.C. Harris, *The Seigneurial System in Early Canada*, pp. 63–9; W.B. Munro. *The Seigniorial System in Canada*, pp. 54, 76, 85–96.

31. *The Report of the Commissioners*, p. 4; R.C. Harris, *The Seigneurial System in Early Canada*, p. 67, confirms the Commissioners' findings that rents tended toward no increase in New France.

32. R.C. Harris, *The Seigneurial System in Early Canada*, p. 64.

33. W.B. Munro, *The Seigniorial System in Canada*, pp. 104, 108.

34. Ibid., p. 67; W.B. Munro, *Documents Related to the Seigniorial Tenure*, pp. 61, 106.

35. W.B. Munro, *The Seigniorial System in Canada*, p. 106.

36. R.C. Harris, *The Seigneurial System in Early Canada*, pp. 72–3, finds that to construct a small commercial grist-mill costs at least £2000.

37. Ibid., p. 117. Munro refers to Article LXXI of the Parlement of Paris.

38. Ibid., p. 110. According to a royal order of July 1675.

39. Ibid., p. 120; M.M. Lelièvre and Angers, eds., *Lower Canada Reports: Seigniorial Questions*, vol. A (Montreal: 1856), pp. 76a–79a.

40. W.B. Munro, *The Seigniorial System in Canada*, p. 112.

41. Ibid., p. 127.

42. Ibid.; R.C. Harris, *The Seigneurial System in Early Canada*, p. 70.

43. W.B. Munro, *The Seigniorial System in Canada*, pp. 129, 132.

44. R.C. Harris, *The Seigneurial System in Early Canada*, p. 70.

45. Ibid., p. 128; W.B. Munro, *Documents Related to the Seigniorial Tenure*, p. lxxviii.

46. W.B. Munro, *The Seigniorial System in Canada*, pp. 96–100.

47. W.B. Munro, *Documents Related to the Seigniorial Tenure*, p.74, notes 1 and 2.

48. W.B. Munro, *The Seigniorial System in Canada*, p. 99.

49. R.C. Harris, *The Seigneurial System in Early Canada*, p. 76, shows that the sale and purchase of land was a crucial part of the peasant farm economy during the French régime (pp. 140–6). See also, W.B. Munro, *The Seigniorial System in Canada*, p. 97; Louise Dechêne, 'L'évolution du régime seigneurial', p. 157.

50. W.B. Munro, *The Seigniorial System in Canada*, pp. 183–4.

☐ The Expulsion of the Acadians

INTRODUCTION

■ Canadian history certainly possesses its share of tragic events. The British expulsion of the French Acadians from Nova Scotia in 1755 is clearly one of the most important and durable of these unfortunate situations. The Acadian expulsion was one of the largest forcible migrations of Europeans carried out in North America in its early history. It was also the culmination of the first confrontation by the British with the problems involved in governing a French-speaking population in North America. Most of the 'facts' of the tragedy are not in dispute. The Acadian population of what became British Nova Scotia was transferred by the French Crown to the British by the Treaty of Utrecht in 1713. The transfer was carried out in Europe without consultation with the local population, which was given a year to remove from British territory or to make its peace with its new rulers, who had very limited power to enforce their rule on the Acadian majority that chose to remain. The symbol for the 'Acadian problem' was an unconditional oath of allegiance demanded (but seldom enforced) by the British and rejected by the Acadian population, which instead sought to be treated as neutrals in the ongoing wars between imperial France and imperial Britain in the Maritime region. By the conventions of international law the British clearly had a right to unconditional loyalty from the population under its rule. Most of the special circumstances involving the Acadians revolved around the matter of timing. The Acadian people could have been forced to a decision in 1714, but they were not required in that year to choose. Instead, the Acadian claims were allowed to continue, and when sporadic efforts were made by the British to enforce loyalty, special exemptions were usually granted to prevent the full force of the oath from taking effect.

By the 1750s, the Acadians had experienced several generations of practical forbearance by their British masters, and could well argue that they were not expecting a crisis. That crisis was brought about by British fears that the Acadians were a potential fifth column in Nova Scotia, and much ink has been spent arguing over the extent to which the Acadians actually represented a threat to the government. In the end, the British government moved swiftly and as ruthlessly as was within its power, not even consulting with neighbouring governments to which the Acadians were exiled. Interestingly enough, the British had to face the Acadians again in 1758, and again they decided on expulsion, although this later action has received much less attention from historians.

Questions for consideration

1. Why were the Acadians expelled?
2. What other policy or policies might have been pursued by the British to achieve the same ends?
3. What made the 1758 expulsions different from the 1755 ones?
4. Can modern ethics be used to judge events several centuries in the past?

Suggestions for further reading

Andrew Hill Clark, *Acadia: The Geography of Nova Scotia to 1760* (Madison: University of Wisconsin Press, 1981). A full study of the historical geography of Acadia.

Jean Daigle, ed., *The Acadians of the Maritimes: Thematic Studies* (Moncton: Centre d'études acadienne, 1982). A collection of essays on the history of the Acadians from the seventeenth century to the present.

Naomi Griffiths, *The Acadians: Creation of a People* (Toronto: McGraw-Hill Ryerson, 1969). Usually regarded as the standard account.

Geoffrey Plank, *An Unsettled Conquest: The British Campaign Against the Peoples of Acadia* (Philadelphia: University of Pennsylvania Press, 2001). A recent account by an American-based scholar.

PRIMARY DOCUMENTS

1 From 1755 council minutes, in Thomas B. Akins, ed., *Acadia and Nova Scotia: Documents Relating to the Acadian French and the First British Colonization of the Province 1714–1758* (Halifax, 1870), 247–57.

At a Council holden at the Governor's House in Halifax on
Thursday the 3rd July 1755.
PRESENT—
The Lieutenant Governor.
Councs.: Benj. Green, Jno. Collier, Willm. Cotterell, Jon^n. Belcher.

The Lieutenant Governor laid before the Council the two following Memorials, Signed by the Deputies and a number of the French Inhabitants of Minas and Pisiquid, and delivered to Capt. Murray the Commanding Officer there, by whom they had been transmitted to His Excellency.

[Translated from the French.]

'MINES June 10th. 1755.'

'To His Excellency CHARLES LAWRENCE, Governor of the province of Nova Scotia or Acadie, &c. &c.

'Sir,—

'We, the Inhabitants of Mines, Pisiquid, and the river Canard, take the liberty of approaching your Excellency for the purpose of testifying our sense of the care which the government exercises towards us.

'It appears, Sir, that your Excellency doubts the sincerity with which we have promised to be faithful to his Britannic Majesty.

'We most humbly beg your Excellency to consider our past conduct. You will see, that, very far from violating the oath we have taken, we have maintained it in its entirety, in spite of the solicitations and the dreadful threats of another power. We still entertain, Sir, the same pure and sincere disposition to prove under any circumstances, our unshaken fidelity to his Majesty, provided that His Majesty shall allow us the same liberty that he has granted us. We earnestly beg your Excellency to have the goodness to inform us of His Majesty's intentions on this subject, and to give us assurances on his part.

'Permit us, if you please, Sir, to make known the annoying circumstances in which we are placed, to the prejudice of the tranquillity we ought to enjoy. Under pretext that we are transporting our corn or other provisions to Beausejour, and the river St. John, we are no longer permitted to carry the least quantity of corn by water from one place to another. We beg your Excellency to be assured that we have never transported provisions to Beausejour, or to the river St. John. If some refugee inhabitants at the point have been seized, with cattle, we are not on that account, by any means guilty, in as much as the cattle belonged to them as private individuals, and they were driving them to their respective habitations. As to ourselves, Sir, we have never offended in that respect; consequently we ought not, in our opinion, to be punished; on the contrary, we hope that your Excellency will be pleased to restore to us the same liberty that we enjoyed formerly, in giving us the use of our canoes, either to transport our provisions from one river to the other, or for the purpose of fishing; thereby providing for our livelihood. This permission has never been taken from us except at the present time. We hope, Sir, that you will be pleased to restore it, especially in consideration of the number of poor inhabitants who would be very glad to support their families with the fish that they would be able to catch. Moreover, our guns, which we regard as our own personal property, have been taken from us, notwithstanding the fact that they are absolutely necessary to us, either to defend our cattle which are attacked by the wild beasts, or for the protection of our children, and of ourselves.

'Any inhabitant who may have his oxen in the woods, and who may need them for purposes of labour, would not dare to expose himself in going for them without being prepared to defend himself.

'It is certain, Sir, that since the savages have ceased frequenting our parts, the wild beasts have greatly increased, and that our cattle are devoured by them almost every day. Besides, the arms which have been taken from us are but a feeble guarantee of our fidelity. It is not the gun which an inhabitant possesses, that will induce him to revolt, nor the privation of the same gun that will make him more faithful; but his conscience alone must induce him to maintain his oath. An order has appeared in your Excellency's name, given at Fort Edward June 4th, 1755, and in the 28th year of his Majesty's reign, by which we are commanded to carry guns, pistols etc. to Fort Edward. It appears to us, Sir, that it would be dangerous for us to execute that order, before representing to you the danger to which this order exposes us. The savages may come and threaten and plunder us, reproaching us for having furnished arms to kill them. We hope, Sir, that you will be pleased, on the contrary, to order that those taken from us be restored to us. By so doing, you will afford us the means of preserving both ourselves and our cattle. In the last place, we are grieved, Sir, at seeing ourselves declared guilty without being aware of having disobeyed. One of our inhabitants of the river Canard, named Piere Melançon, was seized and arrested in charge of his boat, before having heard any order forbidding that sort of transport. We beg your Excellency, on this subject, to have the goodness to make known to us your good pleasure before confiscating our property and considering us in fault. This is the favour we expect from your Excellency's kindness, and we hope that you will do us the justice to believe that very far from violating our promises, we will maintain them, assuring you that we are very respectfully,

Sir,

Your very humble and obt. servants,'

Signed by twenty-five of the said inhabitants.

'MINES, June 24, 1755.

'To his Excellency CHARLES LAWRENCE, Esq., Governor of the province of Nova Scotia or Acadie.

Sir,—

'All the inhabitants of Mines, Pisiquid and the river Canard, beg your Excellency to believe that if, in the petition which they have had the honor to present to your Excellency, there shall be found any error or any want of respect towards the government, it is intirely contrary to their intention; and that in this case, the inhabitants who have signed it, are not more guilty than the others.

'If, sometimes, the inhabitants become embarrassed in your Excellency's presence, they humbly beg you to excuse their timidity; and if, contrary to our expectation, there is anything hard in the said petition, we beg your Excellency to do us the favour of allowing us to explain our intention.

We hope that your Excellency will be pleased to grant us this favour, begging you to believe that we are very respectfully,

> Sir,
> Your very humble and very obedient servants,'
> Signed by forty-four of the said inhabitants in the name of the whole.

The Lieutenant Governor at the same time acquainted the Council that Capt. Murray had informed him that for some time before the delivery of the first of the said memorials the French Inhabitants in general had behaved with greater Submission and Obedience to the Orders of the Government than usual, and had already delivered into him a considerable number of their Fire Arms, but that at the delivery of the said Memorial they treated him with great Indecency and Insolence, which gave him strong Suspicions, that they had obtained some Intelligence which we were then ignorant of, and which the Lieutenant Governor conceived might most probably be a Report that had been about that time spread amongst them of a French Fleet being then in the Bay of Fundy, it being very notorious that the said French Inhabitants have always discovered an insolent and inimical Disposition towards His Majesty's Government when they have had the least hopes of assistance from France.

The Lieutenant Governor likewise acquainted the Council that upon his receipt of the first Memorial, he had wrote to Captain Murray to order all those who had Signed the same, to repair forthwith to Halifax to attend him and the Council thereon, and that they were accordingly arrived and then in waiting without.

The Council having then taken the Contents of the said Memorials into Consideration, were unanimously of Opinion That the Memorial of the 10th of June is highly arrogant and insidious, an Insult upon His Majesty's Authority and Government, and deserved the highest Resentment, and that if the Memorialists had not submitted themselves by their subsequent Memorial, they ought to have been severely punished for their Presumption.

The Deputies were then called in and the Names of the Subscribers to the Memorial read over, and such of them as were present, ordered to Answer to their Names, which they did to the number of fifteen, the others being Sick, after which the Memorial itself was again read, and they were severely reprimanded for their Audacity in Subscribing and Presenting so impertinent a Paper, but in Compassion to their Weakness and Ignorance of the Nature of our Constitution, especially in Matters of Government, and as the Memorialists had presented a subsequent one, and had shewn an Appearance of Concern for their past behaviour therein, and had then presented themselves before the Council with great Submission and Repentance, The Council informed them they were still ready to treat them with Lenity, and in order to shew them the falsity as well as Impudence of the Contents of their Memorial, it was ordered to be read Paragraph by Paragraph, and the Truth of the several Allegations minutely discussed, and Remarks made by the Lieutenant Governor on each Paragraph, to the following Effect, vizt.

It was observed in Answer to this Paragraph of their Memorial of the 10th of June

'That they were affected with the Proceedings of the Government towards them.'

That they had been always treated by the Goverment with the greatest Lenity and Tenderness. That they had enjoyed more Privileges than English Subjects, and had been indulged in the free Excercise of their Religion. That they had at all times full Liberty to consult their Priests, and had been protected in their Trade and Fishery, and had been for many Years permitted to possess their Lands (part of the best Soil of the Province) tho' they had not complied with the Terms, on which the Lands were granted, by Taking the Oath of Allegiance to the Crown.

They were then asked whether they could produce an Instance that any Privilege was denied to them, or that any hardships, were ever imposed upon them by the Government.

They acknowledged the Justice and Lenity of the Government.

Upon the Paragraph where

'They desire their past Conduct might be considered.'

It was remarked to them that their past Conduct was considered, and that the Government were sorry to have occasion to say that their Conduct had been undutifull and very ungratefull for the Lenity shown to them. That they had no Returns of Loyalty to the Crown, or Respect to His Majesty's Government in the Province. That they had discovered a constant disposition to Assist His Majesty's Enemies, and to distress his Subjects. That they had not only furnished the Enemy with Provisions and Ammunition, but had refused to supply the Inhabitants, or Government, with Provisions, and when they did Supply, they have exacted three times the Price for which they were sold at other Markets. That they had been indolent and Idle on their Lands, had neglected Husbandry, and the Cultivation of the Soil, and had been of no use to the Province either in husbandry, Trade or Fishery, but had been rather an Obstruction to the King's Intentions in the Settlement.

They were then asked whether they could mention a single Instance of Service to the Government. To which they were incapable of making any Reply.

Upon reading this Paragraph,

'It seems that your Excellency is doubtfull of the Sincerity of those who have promised fidelity, That they had been so far from breaking 'their Oath, that they had kept it in spight of terrifying Menaces from another Power'

They were asked What gave them Occasion to suppose that the Government was doubtfull of their Sincerity? and were told, that it argued a Consciousness in them of insincerity and want of Attachment to the Interests of His Majesty and his Government. That as to taking their Arms, They had often urged that the Indians would annoy them if they did not Assist them, and that by taking their Arms by Act of Government, it was put out of the Power of the Indians to threaten or force them to their Assistance. That they had assisted the King's Enemies, and appeared too ready to Join with another Power, contrary to the Allegiance they were bound by their Oath to yield to His Majesty.

In Answer to this Paragraph,

'We are now in the same disposition, the purest and sincerest, to prove in every Circumstance Fidelity to His Majesty in the same manner as we have done, Provided that His Majesty will leave us the same Liberties which he has granted us'

They were told that it was hoped, they would hereafter give Proofs of more sincere and pure dispositions of Mind, in the Practice of Fidelity to His Majesty, and that they would forbear to Act in the manner they have done, in obstructing the Settlement of the Province, by Assisting the Indians and French to the distress and Annoyance of many of His Majesty's Subjects, and to the Loss of the Lives of several of the English Inhabitants. That it was not the Language of British Subjects to talk of Terms with the Crown, to Capitulate about their Fidelity and Allegiance, and that it was insolent to insert a *Proviso*, that they would prove their Fidelity *Provided* that His Majesty would give them Liberties.

All His Majesty's Subjects are protected in the Enjoyment of every Liberty, while they continue Loyal and faithfull to the Crown, and when they become false and disloyal they forfeit that Protection.

That they in particular, tho they had acted so insincerely on every Opportunity, had been left in the full Enjoyment of their Religion, Liberty and Properties, with an Indulgence beyond what would have been allowed to any British Subject, who could presume, as they have done, to join in the Measures of another Power.

They were told in answer to the Paragraph where,

'They desire their Canoes for carrying their Provisions from one River to another and for their Fishery'

That they wanted their Canoes for carrying Provisions to the Enemy, and not for their own use or the Fishery, That by a Law of this Province, All Persons are restrained from carrying Provisions from one Port to another, and every Vessel, Canoe or Bark found with Provisions is forfeited, and a Penalty is inflicted on the Owners.

They were also told in Answer to the following Paragraph,

'They Petition for their Guns as part of their Goods, that they may be restored to defend their Cattle from the Wild Beasts, and to preserve themselves and their Children, That since the Indians have quitted their Quarters, the Wild Beasts are greatly increased'

That Guns are no part of their Goods, as they have no Right to keep Arms. By the Laws of England, All Roman Catholicks are restrained from having Arms, and they are Subject to Penalties if Arms are found in their Houses.

That upon the Order from Captain Murray many of the Inhabitants voluntarily brought in their Arms, and none of them pretended that they wanted them for defence of their Cattle against Wild Beasts, and that the Wild Beasts had not increased since their Arms were surrendered. That they had some secret Inducement, at that time, for presuming to demand their Arms as part of their Goods and their Right, and that they had flattered themselves of being supported in their Insolence to the Government, on a Report that some french Ships of War were in the Bay of Fundy. That this daring Attempt plainly discovered the falsehood of their Professions of Fidelity to the King, and their readiness has been visible upon every Intimation of force or Assistance from France, to insult His Majesty's Government, and to join with his Enemies, contrary to their Oath of Fidelity.

Upon reading this Paragraph,

'Besides the Arms we carry are a feeble Surety for our Fidelity. It is not the Gun that an Inhabitant possesses, which will lead him to Revolt, nor the depriving him of that Gun that will make him more faithful, but his Conscience alone ought to engage him to maintain his Oath.'

They were asked, what Excuse they could make for their Presumption in this Paragraph, and treating the Government with such Indignity and Contempt as to Expound to them the nature of Fidelity, and to prescribe what would be the Security proper to be relied on by the Government for their Sincerity. That their Consciences ought indeed to engage them to Fidelity from their Oath of Allegiance to the King, and that if they were sincere in their Duty to the Crown, they would not be so anxious for their Arms, when it was the pleasure of the King's Government to demand them for His Majesty's Service. They were then informed that a very fair Opportunity now presented itself to them to Manifest the reality of their Obedience to the Government by immediately taking the Oath of Allegiance in the Common Form before the Council. Their Reply to this Proposal was, That they were not come pre- pared to resolve the Council on that head. They were then told that they very well knew these Six Years past, the same thing had been often proposed to them and had been as often evaded under various frivolous pretences, that they had often been informed that sometime or other it would be required of them and must be done, and that the Council did not doubt but they knew the Sentiments of the Inhabitants in general, and had fully considered and determined this point with regard to themselves before now, as they had been already indulged with Six Years to form a Resolution thereon. They then desired they might return home and consult the Body of the People upon this subject as they could not do otherwise than the Generality of the inhabitants should determine, for that they were desirous of either refusing or accepting the Oath in a Body, and could not possibly determine, till they knew the Sentiments of their Constituents.

Upon this so extraordinary a Reply they were informed they would not be permitted to Return for any such purpose, but that it was expected from them to declare on the Spot, for their own particular, as they might very well be expected to do after having had so long a time to consider upon that point. They then desired leave to retire to consult among them- selves, which they were permitted to do, when after near an hour's Recess, They returned with the same Answer, That they could not consent to take the Oath as prescribed without consulting the General Body, but that they were ready to take it as they had done before, to which they were answered, That His Majesty had disapproved of the manner of their taking the Oath before, That it was not consistent with his Honour to make any conditions, nor could the Council accept their taking the Oath in any other way than as all other His Majesty's Subjects were obliged by Law to do when called upon, and that it was now expected they should do so, which they still declining, they were allowed till the next Morning at Ten of the Clock to come to a Resolution. To which Time the Council then adjourned. . . .

The Council being met according to Adjournment, the french Deputies who were Yesterday Ordered to Attend the Council, were brought in, and, upon being asked what Resolution they were come to in regard to the Oath, They declared they could not consent to Take the Oath in the Form required without consulting the Body. They were then informed that as they had now for their own particulars, refused to Take the Oath as directed by Law, and thereby sufficiently evinced the Sincerity of their Inclination towards the Government, The Council could no longer look on them as Subjects to His Britannick Majesty, but as Subjects of the King of France, and as such they must hereafter be Treated; and they were Ordered to withdraw.

The Council after Consideration, were of Opinion That directions should be given to Captain Murray to order the French Inhabitants forthwith to Choose and send to Halifax, new Deputies with the General Resolution of the said Inhabitants in regard to taking the Oath, and that none of them should for the future be admitted to Take it after having once refused so to do, but that effectual Measures ought to be taken to remove all such Recusants out of the Province.

The Deputies were then called in again, and having been informed of this Resolution, and finding they could no longer avail themselves of the Disposition of the Government to ingage them to a Dutifull Behaviour by Lenity and perswasion, Offered to take the Oath, but were informed that as there was no reason to hope their proposed Compliance proceeded from an honest Mind, and could be esteemed only the Effect of Compulsion and Force, and is contrary to a clause in an Act of Parliament, I. Geo. 2. c 13. whereby Persons who have once refused to Take the Oaths cannot be afterwards permitted to Take them, but are considered as Popish Recusants; Therefore they would not now be indulged with such Permission; And they were thereupon ordered into Confinement.

2 Governor Lawrence to Board of Trade, 18 July 1755, in Akins, *Acadia and Nova Scotia*, 259–60.

Governor Lawrence to Board of Trade.

HALIFAX, 18th July, 1755.

MY LORDS,—

Since my last, of 28th of June 1755, sent express by Lieutenant Cunningham, the French have abandoned their Fort at St. John's River, and, as far as it was in their power, demolished it. As soon as the Forts upon the Isthmus were taken, Captain Rous sailed from thence with three twenty Gun Ships, and a Sloop, to look into St. John's River, where it was reported there were two French Ships of thirty-six Guns each; he anchored off the mouth of the River, and sent in his Boats to reconnoitre; they found no ships there, but, on their appearance, the French burst their Cannon, blew up their Magazine, burned everything they could, belonging to the Fort, and marched off. The next morning, the Indians invited Captain Rous on shore, gave him the strongest assurances of their desire to make peace with us, and pleaded in their behalf, that they had refused to assist the French upon this occasion, tho' earnestly pressed by them. I expect some of their Chiefs here in a very few days.

As the French Inhabitants of this Province have never yet, at any time, taken the oath of allegiance to His Majesty, unqualified, I thought it my duty to avail myself of the present occasion, to propose it to them; and, as the deputies of the different districts in Mines Basin, were attending in Town upon a very insolent Memorial, they had delivered to the Council, I was determined to begin with them. They were accordingly summoned to appear before the Council, and, after discussing the affair of the Memorial, article by article, the oath was proposed to them; they endeavoured, as much as possible, to evade it, and at last desired to return home and consult the rest of the Inhabitants, that they might either accept or refuse the Oath in a body; but they were informed that we expected every man upon this occasion to answer for himself, and as we would not use any compulsion or surprise, we gave them twenty four hours time to deliver in their answer; and, if they should then refuse, they must expect to be driven out of the country; and, tho' they should afterwards repent of their refusal, they would not be permitted to the oath. The next morning, they appeared and refused to take the oath without the old reserve of not being obliged to bear arms, upon which, they were acquainted, that as they refused to become English subjects, we could no longer look upon them in that light; that we should send them to France by the first opportunity, and till then, they were ordered to be kept prisoners at George's Island, where they were immediately conducted. They have since earnestly desired to be admitted to take the oath, but have not been admitted, nor will any answer be given them until we see how the rest of the Inhabitants are disposed.

I have ordered new Deputies to be elected, and sent hither immediately, and am determined to bring the Inhabitants to a compliance, or rid the province of such perfidious subjects. Your Lordships will see our proceedings in this case at large, as soon as it is possible to prepare the minutes of Council.

HISTORICAL INTERPRETATIONS

3   From C. Bruce Fergusson, 'The Expulsion of the Acadians', *Dalhousie Review* 35 (1955-6): 127-8.

Some observers have said that Germany's annexation of Alsace-Lorraine was worse than a crime—it was a blunder; others have seemed to say that the expulsion of the Acadians was not a blunder but rather a crime. However that may be, history caught up with the Acadians in 1755, when six thousand or more of them were uprooted from their beloved lands in Nova Scotia, placed on board ships and deported to British colonies to the south. Ninety-two years later, moreover, in a blend of fact and fancy, Longfellow caught them up in the lines of the poem *Evangeline*. Since that time, it seems, the warp of fact and the woof of imagination have been so interwoven by poetic licence in a memorable mosaic of sentimentality and suffering, that it is difficult to separate fact from fancy and to get at the sober truth of the matter. Yet even the most aloof observer must feel sympathy for any group of people who experience the testing of exile from their accustomed place, no matter whose the responsibility for the exile, and no matter whether that forced expatriation was deserved or undeserved. That being the case, the heart goes out to the Acadians of 1755, without any need for the head to appreciate anything of the circumstances, or for any question to be asked of the why or the wherefore. But the two hundredth anniversary of that event should provide the occasion for real attempts to understand what actually happened in 1755, and why and how it took place.

Was the expulsion of the Acadians a misfortune or was it a disaster? Were they the undeserved victims of misfortune, or did they reap disaster from their own folly? These are the salient questions which should be borne in mind whenever consideration is given to the fate of the Acadians in the year 1755. Their story, it is clear, is an admirable illustration of the relative strength of the ties that bind, and of the forces that influence, a people, as well as a supreme example of how a dramatic and colourful episode in the history of any people may be readily translated into the misty realm of romance, so that careful attention is needed for an adequate realization and a proper understanding. The story of the Acadians may be regarded as a tale that is told. But its versions differ, some of them are marred or distorted by emotion or bias, by artificial colouring or by unfounded judgments, and new appraisals are sometimes needed.

Centre or core of the Acadian problem was the oath of allegiance. One important factor was the fact that between the final capture of Port Royal by the British in 1710 and the fateful year 1755 most of the Acadians were unwilling to take the unconditional oath of allegiance. They refused to take the unqualified oath, insisted that they should not be required to take up arms in the event of war, and advanced the rather fantastic claim that they should be regarded as 'French Neutrals'.

Clearly the Acadian demand was an extraordinary one. It was the accepted conception then as now that the obligations incumbent upon those living within the bounds of the authority of a state included the taking of the oath of allegiance to that state. That was the case when New Sweden was obliged to submit to the New Netherlands in 1655, with those Swedes who desired to remain on the Delaware being expected to give an oath of unqualified allegiance to the new authority. That was also the case when the New Netherlands was obliged to submit to the English in 1664, and the Dutch about the Hudson and elsewhere were expected to do the same, if they remained beyond the period of a year. It was likewise the case, so far as France was concerned, when Frontenac received instructions respecting the expedition against New York, in the event of its capture, in 1689; and when the Duke d'Anville received instructions relating to his formidable but ill-fated expedition of 1746. Furthermore, this rule of broad international application was applied not only to the French in Canada after 1763, but also to those of Louisiana after 1803 when that territory became part of the United States, and to the Mexicans of northern Mexico after its cession to the United States in 1847. . . .

---

4 From Naomi Griffiths, *The Contexts of Acadian History 1686–1784* (Montreal and Kingston: McGill-Queen's University Press, 1992), 85–9.

We have a great deal of information on how Lawrence saw his own policy. There is no doubt that for him military matters were an understood priority. He shaped his policy for the colony accordingly. He wrote, at length, to Governor Shirley of Massachusetts, to other governors of British colonies in North America, and to the authorities in London.[1] Lawrence's policy resulted from the wish to make Nova Scotia a secure and flourishing outpost of the British

Empire in North America. He was convinced by 1753, when he was made lieutenant-governor of the colony, that the refusal of the Acadians to take an unqualified oath of loyalty to the British crown made them a major obstacle to the fulfilment of this ambition.[2] He held two completely different, but in his view interdependent, objectives: first, the preservation of British possessions in North America, and, second, the strengthening of Nova Scotia as a crucial and significant part of those possessions.

By the spring of 1755, Lawrence had become thoroughly convinced that his colony could not become a reliable outpost of the British Empire while the Acadians were among its people. Thus the best possible solution was to send them to be assimilated among the populations of the other British North American colonies. In the circular to the governors of these colonies quoted from earlier, this was made plain.[3] Lawrence informed his fellow governors of the unique opportunity now available: 'The success that has attended his Majesty's arms in driving the French from the Encroachments they had made in this province,' he wrote, 'furnished me with a favourable opportunity of reducing the French inhabitants of this Colony to a proper obedience to His Majesty's Government or forcing them to quit the country.' He went on to state that 'I offered such of them as had not been openly in arms against us, a continuance of the Possession of their lands, if they would take the Oath of Allegiance, unqualified with any Reservation whatsoever.' 'But this,' he also stated, 'they have most audaciously as well as unanimously refused.' Lawrence therefore turned to the council of the colony 'to consider by what means we could with the greatest security and effect rid ourselves of a set of people who would forever have been an obstruction to the intention of settling this Colony and that it was now from their refusal to the Oath absolutely incumbent upon us to remove.' The circular continued: 'As their numbers amount to near 7000 persons the driving them off with

leave to go whither they pleased would have doubtless strengthened Canada with so considerable a number of inhabitants; and as they have no cleared land to give them at present, such as able to bear arms must have been immediately employed in annoying this and neighbouring Colonies. To prevent such an inconvenience it was judged a necessary and the only practicable measure to divide them among the Colonies.'

Lawrence may have known what he was about and why, but the debate that has raged over the deportation of the Acadians ever since has been bitter and wide-ranging.[4] Whose influence ensured that the proposal of deportation became reality? Governor Shirley of Massachusetts?[5] What part did London play?[6] Was the determining factor the opinions of the British admirals Boscawen and Mostyn who arrived that spring? Can the whole episode really be summed up, as Guy Fregault believed, as an act of war, and be accepted in that context?[7]

For the Acadians in 1755 such questions must have been of considerably less importance than the events of the dispersion itself. Perhaps the only such matter that would have been argued among them would have concerned their own tactics. The crucial meetings between Acadian and English officials took place in early July, but these meetings were the culmination of an eventful spring. The incident that provided Nova Scotia with the opportunity to deport the Acadians, and to which Lawrence referred in his circular, was the fall of Beausejour, which had capitulated on 16 June 1755. While the campaign to capture the fort had been in progress, efforts had also been made to ensure that the Acadian population, as a whole, would remain quiet. In April and May orders were sent out to the Minas Acadians to surrender not only any weapons they might possess but also their boats.[8] A petition from the Acadians for the return of their possessions was written on 10 June and received in Halifax at the time when Lawrence received the news that Beausejour had fallen and that about 300

Acadians had been found in arms within the fort.[9]

A meeting of the Council, presided over by Lawrence, took place at the Governor's House on 3 July 1755.[10] The petition sent from Minas was discussed with a number of the signatories. The Council took the Acadians point by point through the petition and concluded by asking the Acadians to take an unqualified oath of loyalty to the King. It is obvious from the Minutes of this meeting that the Councillors found the petition 'an Insult upon His Majesty's Authority'. In it the Acadians had insisted that they had not only not violated their oaths but had kept faithful 'in spite of the solicitations and dreadful threats of another power'. They had affirmed their intentions of so keeping faith 'provided that His Majesty shall allow us the same liberty that we have enjoyed formerly.' In sum, the attitude of the Acadians was that they had proved their political neutrality to the government by their past actions and should now be rewarded. The Council was completely unpersuaded by the proofs offered and demanded further assurances. The Acadians, by such phrases as 'Permit us, if you please, Sir, to make known the annoying circumstances in which we are placed, to the prejudice of the tranquillity we ought to enjoy', showed that, in their own eyes, they had the right to argue with English officials. The Acadians had held this attitude from the time of Francoise Perrot in 1688. It was a point of view consistently repudiated by those sent from Europe to govern them. It was the attitude that was maintained by all of the Acadian delegates throughout the July meetings of 1755. Polite, unafraid, and obdurate the Acadians offered a qualified oath. The council minutes for 28 July conclude as follows:

> As it had been before determined to send all the French Inhabitants out of the Province if they refused to Take the Oaths, nothing now remained to be considered but what Measures should be Taken to send them away, and where they should be sent to.[11]

There is one indication that other tactics might have been considered among the Acadians. When finally convinced that exile was imminent, some of the delegates from the Minas basin did offer an unqualified oath of allegiance. The offer was made on 4 July 1744 only to be rejected by Lawrence and the Council on the grounds that 'there was no reason to hope their proposed compliance proceeded from an honest Mind and could be esteemed only the Effect of Compulsion and Force.'[12]

But such discussions among the Acadians in 1755 would have been overshadowed completely by the events of the deportation itself. . . .

NOTES

1. Almost all of this correspondence has been printed in Thomas B. Akins, ed., *Acadia and Nova Scotia: Documents Relating to the Acadian French and the First British Colonization of the Province 1714–1758* (Halifax, 1869; reprint, Cottonport, La.: Polyanthos, 1972), and *Report for 1905*.

2. 'Tho I would be very far from attempting such a step [imposing the unqualified oath] without Yourships approbation, yet I cannot help being of the opinion that it would be much better, if they refuse the oaths, that they were away.' In 'Lawrence to the Lords of Trade, August 1st, 1754', 55, p. 187 ff., and partially printed *Nova Scotia Archives* 1, 212–14.

3. 'Circular letter from Governor Lawrence to the Governors on the Continent', *Report for 1905*, 2: App. B., 15–16.

4. See the comments of the Abbé Raynal in his *Histoire philosophique et politique de l'établissement dans les deux Indes* (La Have, 1760), 360. A generation ago there were more than two hundred books and articles in print about the deportation

of the Acadians. See the bibliographic guides published by the Centre d'études Acadiennes, particularly Helene Harbec and Paulette Lévesque, eds, *Guide bibliographique de l'Acadie, 1976–1987* (Moncton, 1988).

5. While this has been a favourite conclusion of historians such as Brebner, George Rawlyk hotly contested this judgment in *Nova Scotia's Massachusetts*, 199 ff.

6. On this question see Placide Gaudet, *Le Grand Dérangement* (Ottawa, 1922).

7. 'La nouvelle écosse est en guerre et elle s'engage dans un mouvement de colonisation intensive. La

dispersion des Acadiens constitue un épisode de cette guerre et de ce mouvement.' *La Guerre de la Conquète* (Montreal, 1955), 272.

8. *Le Canada francais*, 1: 138–9.

9. On this episode and its impact on Lawrence, see J.B. Brebner, *New England's Outpost: Acadia before the Conquest of Canada* (New York, 1927), 199–202, 212–13.

10. Akins, *Nova Scotia Documents*, 247 ff.

11. 'Council Minutes', PANS, RG 5, vol. 187.

12. The issue is discussed extensively by Brebner, *New England's Outpost*, 216 ff.

5   From: Charles D. Mahaffie Jr, *A Land of Discord Always: Acadia from its Beginning to the Expulsion of its People 1604–1755* (Camden, Maine: Down East Books, 1995), 248–60.

The Beauséjour campaign was a huge success, and a cheap one. Robert Moncton's British-American force lost only twenty men killed and twenty wounded.[1] The French threat, for a time anyway, was ended, and Charles Lawrence was free to solve the problem of the Acadians.

He had no authority for what he was about to do—and he had told the Board of Trade that he would not do it without authority—but he was not going to put up with them any longer. Buoyed by a major victory—one for which he could claim much of the credit—he was ready to force the question of the oaths and drive into exile anyone who would not submit.

In June 1755, just before Louis Vergor surrendered Fort Beauséjour, the Acadian deputies from the Minas settlements had submitted a petition complaining about Alexander Murray's confiscation of the residents' boats and his order that they turn in their arms. Living in a watery wilderness, those were items they could hardly do without. Yet if the deputies' plea was reasonable, its reception at Halifax was not. Lawrence used it as an excuse to summon them to a meeting of the council, where he intended to force

them, as individuals, to swear unqualified oaths of allegiance, then and there.

They arrived on July 3, ready to explain why they needed boats and guns, only to hear a tongue-lashing and a litany of Acadian faults and misdeeds throughout forty years of British rule. They were called disloyal and impertinent, undutiful and ungrateful, indolent and idle, insincere and contemptuous. They had helped the king's enemies in the last war. Now they wanted boats so they could help them again. And as Catholics they had no right to guns in the first place. When they proclaimed their loyalty, they were told to prove it by swearing the same oath of allegiance as other British subjects, and they were to do it right away, on the spot.[2]

They were stunned. Not since Samuel Vetch had a governor treated Acadians so badly. Caulfeild, Doucett, Philipps, Mascarene, Cornwallis, Hopson, even Armstrong—all had made at least a show of reasoning with them. All had seemed to respect their neutrality, to accept their special status. This man would not.

The deputies pleaded for time to go home and consult their neighbours, but Lawrence was unyielding. They were given just that night to make up their minds, and when they came back the next morning with the same answer, the council formally ruled that they be deported.[3]

Hearing that, the deputies panicked. They offered to take the oath without qualification, but Lawrence announced that there would be no second chance. Having once refused, they were 'popish Recusants; Therefore they would not now be indulged with such Permission, And they were thereupon ordered into confinement.'[4]

By making an example of them, Lawrence sought to jar the rest, to break the Acadians' confidence that if they stood firm, all would be well. He ordered new deputies chosen to replace the men he had locked up, and he ordered that they and the deputies from Annapolis Royal bring in the final answer. In a letter to the Board of Trade—a letter delivered long after the fact—he explained what he was doing:

> As the French Inhabitants of this Province have never yet, at any time, taken the oath of allegiance to His Majesty, unqualified, I thought it my duty to avail myself of the present occasion, to propose it to them; and, as the deputies of the different districts in Mines Basin, were attending in Town upon a very insolent Memorial . . . I was determined to begin with them. . . . The oath was proposed to them; they endeavoured, as much as possible, to evade it, and at last desired to return home and consult the rest of the Inhabitants, that they might either accept or refuse the Oath in a body; but they were informed that we expected every man upon this occasion to answer for himself. . . . The next morning, they appeared and refused to take the oath without the old reserve of not being obliged to bear arms, upon which they were acquainted, that as they refused to become English subjects, we could no longer look upon them in that light; that we should send them to France by the first opportunity, and till then, they were ordered to be kept prisoners at George's Island, where they were immediately conducted. They have since earnestly desired to be admitted to take the oath, but have not been admitted, nor will any answer be given them until we see how the rest of the Inhabitants are disposed.
>
> I have ordered new Deputies to be elected, and sent hither immediately, and am determined to bring the Inhabitants to a compliance, or rid the province of such perfidious subjects.[5]

Probably he still thought he would have his way, that if he applied enough pressure, the body of the people would cave in. If they did not, he would take upon himself and the council the responsibility for the ultimate solution—the step the Board of Trade could never bring itself to approve.

Chief Justice Belcher prepared a written opinion. Short on legal reasoning but long on rhetoric, and filled with phrases like 'Rebels to His Majesty. . . . Perfidy and Treacheries. . . . Acts of Hostility. . . . inveterate enmity. . . . insolence and Hostilities', it held that deportation was justified by military necessity—or, as the learned justice put it, the 'Lex temporis'.[6] And Edward Boscawen's flagship was in Halifax. At Lawrence's request, the admiral and another senior officer, Admiral Savage Mostyn, attended a meeting of the council and 'gave it as their Opinion, That it was now the properest Time to oblige the said Inhabitants to Take the Oath of Allegiance to His Majesty, or to quit the Country.'[7]

Belcher's, though, was legal advice, and Boscawen and Mostyn's was military. Neither judge nor admirals had political authority, and the men who did would not have permitted the course Lawrence and the council chose to follow.

After the surrender of Fort Beauséjour, Lawrence had reported to the Board of Trade that some of the Acadians had helped the French defense and that he had 'given [Moncton] orders to drive them out of the Country.'[8] In a response that came too late to change events, Sir Thomas Robinson protested that the articles of capitulation called for a pardon. 'It cannot,' he said, 'be too much recommended to you, to use the greatest Caution and Prudence in your conduct towards these Neutrals, and to assure such of them, as may be trusted, especially upon their taking the Oaths to His Majesty . . . That they may remain in the quiet Possession of Their Settlements, under proper regulations.'[9] To make his point, Robinson sent along the text of the note British diplomats had just handed the French in which they objected even to the thought of Acadians leaving Nova Scotia.

The next year, when it was a fait accompli, the Board of Trade approved what Lawrence had done. 'As you represent it to have been indispensably necessary for the Security and Protection of the Province,' the board wrote, 'we doubt not but that your Conduct herein will meet with His Majesty's Approbation.'[10] Thus the policy of equivocation ended, but only after the question was moot. Had electronic communication existed in the eighteenth century, the expulsion of the Acadians would not have occurred.

Nor would it have occurred had the Acadians heeded unmistakable signals that the years of toleration were over. Even the deputies imprisoned on George's Island would have been released and left to live their lives if the Acadians had agreed to unqualified oaths of allegiance. But they would not. They must have argued long and prayed hard. Surely there were many who would have submitted. In the end, however, a rule of unity prevailed, and the Acadian response was unanimous. On Friday, July 25, and again on the following Monday, deputies from Annapolis Royal and new deputies from the Minas settlements arrived in Halifax with memorials and all the old arguments. On behalf of everyone, they refused the oath unless it were qualified by exemption from bearing arms.[11] It remained only for Lawrence and the council to decide how to deport them and where to send them.

In his letter to the Board of Trade, Lawrence had talked of exile to France. In the meantime, someone remembered the suggestion Peter Warren had made in 1745. If the Acadians were scattered among the different British colonies up and down the coast of North America, the king would not lose his subjects, the French would not be strengthened, and the unity of the Acadians would be broken forever. In the end, that was the plan adopted by Lawrence and the council, with Boscawen and Mostyn attending and agreeing, at a session held on July 28, 1755. The other councilmen—the men who took upon themselves the decision to exile a people—were the secretary of the province, William Cotterell; a New England merchant named Benjamin Green; Chief Justice Jonathan Belcher Jr.; a British settler named John Collier; and John Rous, a ship captain.[12]

Money was available, ships could be hired in Boston, and there were New Englanders still on hand from the Beauséjour campaign to do the dirty work. Lawrence laid it on in a torrent of paper. Orders were sent to Moncton at Fort Cumberland; to Captain John Handfield, the commander at Annapolis Royal; to Alexander Murray at Pisiquid; and to John Winslow, who with four companies of Americans would be in charge of depopulating and destroying Grand Pré and the farms around it.[13] The commanders were to use whatever stratagems they could devise to lure the men into confinement. When the ships came, and the men were aboard, the women and children would surely follow. The people's land, their livestock, and the grain they had harvested and stored for the winter was to be forfeited to the Crown. To discourage escape, homes and barns were to be burned. Not only would the land be emptied; it would be laid waste.

Passenger numbers and destinations were prescribed, and letters were prepared for the governors of the other colonies. Since the measures he was taking were necessary for the security of Nova Scotia, Lawrence was sure they would 'receive the inhabitants I now send and dispose of them in such manner as may best answer our design in preventing their reunion.' Dispersed, they would be no threat, and as 'most of them are healthy, strong people . . . they may become profitable and it is possible, in time, faithful subjects.'[14]

A note of urgency was added when word arrived of the Battle of the Monongahela and its terrible outcome. On August 8, Lawrence wrote Moncton to be on his guard, 'and use your utmost endeavours to prevent, as much as possible, this bad news reaching the ears of the French inhabitants.'[15] He hoped the roundup had begun, and indeed it had. Moncton's troops were ranging the countryside, taking prisoners and burning everything in sight. By August 11, they had already imprisoned 250 Acadians at Fort Cumberland.[16]

The operation at Chignecto did not, however, go smoothly. The French commander who had been forced from the Saint John showed up with his soldiers to help the Acadians fight back, and a guerrilla war began in the countryside behind the isthmus. On September 2, one of Moncton's detachments was surprised near the Petitcodiac River in the act of torching one of the refugee Acadians' little churches. Twenty-three soldiers were killed and seven were wounded—almost as many casualties as Moncton's whole army suffered in the siege of Fort Beauséjour. On October 1, eighty-six prisoners at Fort Lawrence escaped through a tunnel under the wall.[17]

Captain Handfield had nearly as much trouble at Annapolis Royal, although he faced no armed opposition and lost no men. The people of the Annapolis Valley had the closest ties to the British. Some had friends and kinsmen among those who would deport them, and Handfield's was not the ruthless sweep Lawrence wanted. He apparently even spared some on purpose. A British officer visiting Annapolis Royal two years after the expulsion reported being entertained by a grande dame 'of Romish Persuasion', an Acadian survivor.[18] She was Marie-Madeline Maisonnat, daughter of a privateer captain from the days of Villebon. She was also Handfield's mother-in-law.[19]

The roundup and embarkation were most efficient at the Minas settlements, where Winslow at Grand Pré and Murray at Pisiquid were in command. Since the greater numbers lived near Grand Pré, it fell to the American to be chief executioner.

Winslow was from Marshfield, near Plymouth, a great-grandson of one of the Pilgrim fathers and a well-respected soldier—stern when duty required, humane when duty allowed. Winslow did not like what he had to do at Grand Pré that summer and fall. His journal reveals a conscientious if not very well-lettered officer, one who would obey his orders, who shared Lawrence's fear of a populace whose sympathies lay with the enemy, but who knew that in ridding Nova Scotia of the Acadians he was ruining the lives of mostly innocent men, women, and children.[20] 'Altho it is a Disagreeable Part of Duty wee are Put Upon,' he wrote Lawrence, 'I am Sensible it is a Necessary one, And Shall Endeavor Strictly to Obey your Excellency's Orders [and] Do Everything in me to Remove the Neighbors About me to a Better Country.'[21]

He set up camp in the churchyard, and on September 2, he posted a summons requiring men and teenage boys to appear and hear the king's orders. Unsuspecting, they came. As they gathered, more than four hundred strong, they watched the soldiers close in. Then they heard Winslow deliver the awful verdict:

> Your Lands and Tennements, Cattle of all [kinds] and Live Stock of all Sortes are Forfitted to the Crown with all your other Effects Saving your Money and Household Goods and you your selves to be removed from this . . . Province.
>
> That it is Preremtorily his Majesty's orders That the whole French Inhabitants of these Districts, be removed, and I am Throh his Majesty's Goodness Directed to allow you Liberty to Carry of your money and Household Goods as Many as you Can without Discomemoading [discommoding] the Vessels you Go in. I shall do Everything in my Power that all Those Goods be Secured to you and that you are Not Molested in Carrying of them of and also that whole Familys Shall go in the Same Vessel, and make this remove which I am Sensable must give you a great Deal of

Trouble as Easy as his Majesty's Service will admit and hope that in what Ever part of the world you may Fall you may be Faithful Subjects, a Peasable and happy People.

I Must also inform you That it is his Majesty's Pleasure that you remain in Security under the Inspection and Direction of the Troops that I have the Honr. to Command.[22]

'Things', Winslow wrote later that day, 'are Now Very heavy on my harte and hands.'[23]

The people were frightened, bewildered, disbelieving. Winslow set a few men free to tell wives and children their fate, and there could be little doubt now that it was no bluff, that the British finally were serious. Still, they could not take it in. Winslow said later that they refused to accept what he told the men at the church. 'They did not then Nor to this Day do Imagine that they are Actually to be removed.' He could not, he said, 'Perswade the People I was in Earnest.'[24]

Yet there were some who knew, some who might have the will to resist. Winslow had to wait for provisions and more transports before he could ship the people away, but he detected a restiveness among his prisoners and decided to begin embarking them, to put those he thought might be the most troublesome on board the ships he already had. On September 10, he made the men gather in the churchyard, then ordered the youngest marched off. When they balked, he had his soldiers fix bayonets. He counted off twenty-four, the first to go, and gave one a shove. 'He obeyed and the rest followed, thoh Slowly, and went of Praying, Singing and Crying being Met by the women and Children all the way (which is ½ mile) with Great Lamentations upon their Knees, praying etc.' Before the day was over, 'the Ice being Broke', 230 young men were embarked. Thus, Winslow wrote, 'Ended this Troublesome Jobb, which was Scheen of Sorrow.'[25]

The job was just begun. It was not until the next month that enough ships were on hand to permit the loading of families. On October 8, the first of the women and children 'went of Very Solentarily and unwillingly, the women in Great Distress Carrying off Their Children In their arms. Others Carrying their Decript Parents in their Carts and all their Goods Moving in great Confussion and appeard a Sceen of woe and Distress.'[26] On October 13, Winslow issued sailing orders, and a few days later, nine transports weighed anchor in the Minas Basin with fifteen hundred Acadians bound for the Delaware and the Chesapeake—names most of them had never even heard. Some six hundred more would follow.

Winslow sent ships to take eleven hundred people Murray had rounded up at Pisiquid, and he sent troops to help Handfield scour the Annapolis Valley and embark sixteen hundred more at Annapolis Royal. He learned from Moncton that eleven hundred had been shipped from Chignecto. Meticulously, sadly, he recorded the buildings his men burned at Grand Pré and the farms nearby: 255 houses, 276 barns, 155 outhouses, 11 mills, and a church.[27] By December, the destruction was complete and the people were gone.

In all, nearly six thousand men, women, and children were torn from the homes they cherished and sent to exile in Massachusetts, Connecticut, New York, Pennsylvania, Maryland, Virginia, South Carolina, and Georgia. They were not by any means the whole of the population. When 1755 began, there had been between 11,000 and 12,500 Acadians living on the peninsula and on the Isthmus of Chignecto.[28] Some made their way out before the deportation started. Some escaped while it was going on. Perhaps two thousand—including nearly all the population of Cobequid—crossed Northumberland Strait to swell Acadian numbers on Isle St. Jean.[29] Others fled up the mainland coast to virgin land on what is now sometimes called the Acadian Peninsula of northeastern New Brunswick. Some made their way to Isle Royale, some to Quebec. Some vanished into the forests near home. A few, like Marie-

Madeline Maisonnat, were allowed to stay.

But even for those who escaped the soldiers, Lawrence's scheme to empty the land and his policy of scorched earth worked with terrible effect. When the burning was over, there were no homes, no farms, no churches, no settlements. There was no Acadia.

NOTES

1. Lawrence to the Board of Trade, 28 June 1755, Thomas B. Akins, ed., *Acadia and Nova Scotia: Documents Relating to the Acadian French and the First British Colonization of the Province 1714–1758* (Halifax, 1869; reprint, Cottonport, La: Polyanthos, 1972), 408–9. Hereafter *P.D.N.S.*

2. Meeting of the council, 3 July 1755, *P.D.N.S.*, 247–55.

3. Meeting of the council, 4 July 1755, *P.D.N.S.*, 255–6.

4. Ibid., 256.

5. Lawrence to the Board of Trade, 18 July 1755, *P.D.N.S.*, 259–60.

6. Opinion, 28 July 1755, Placide Gaudet, 'Acadian Genealogy and Notes', in *Concerning Canadian Archives for the Year 1905*, 3 vols (Ottawa: E.S. Dawson, 1906), II, App. A, Part 3, 63–5.

7. Meeting of the council, 15 July 1755, *P.D.N.S.*, 258.

8. Lawrence to the Board of Trade, 28 June 1755, *P.D.N.S.*, 409.

9. Robinson to Lawrence, 13 Aug. 1755, *P.D.N.S.*, 279.

10. Board of Trade to Lawrence, 25 Mar. 1756, *P.D.N.S.*, 298.

11. Meetings of the council, 25 and 28 July 1755, *P.D.N.S.*, 260–7.

12. Meeting of the council, 28 July 1755, *P.D.N.S.*, 263–7; John Bartlet Brebner, *New England's Outpost: Acadia before the Conquest of Canada* (New York, 1927; reprint, Hamden, Conn.: Archon Books, 1965), 222.

13. *P.D.N.S.*, 267–76.

14. Lawrence to the Governors on the Continent, 11 Aug. 1755, *P.D.N.S.*, 278.

15. Lawrence to Moncton, 8 Aug. 1755, *P.D.N.S.*, 269.

16. 'Diary of John Thomas', 391–2.

17. Ibid., 392–3.

18. Captain John Knox, *An Historical Journal of the Campaigns in North America For the Years 1757, 1758, 1759, and 1760*, ed. Arthur G. Doughty (Toronto: Champlain Society, 1914; reprint, New York: Greenwood Press, 1968), 94.

19. Hector J. Hébert, 'Marie-Madeline Maisonnat', in George W. Brown et al., eds, *Dictionary of Canadian Biography* (Toronto: University of Toronto Press, 1966), 3:421–2.

20. Winslow's journal, insofar as it relates to the expulsion of the Acadians, is in N.S.H.S. [Nova Scotia Historical Society], *Collections*, 3 (1882–3): 71–196. Extensive extracts are in Gaudet, 'Acadian Genealogy and Notes', 9–37.

21. Winslow to Lawrence, 30 Aug. 1755, Gaudet, ' Genealogy and Notes', 17.

22. Winslow's Journal, 5 Sept. 1755, Gaudet, 'Acadian Genealogy and Notes', 20.

23. Winslow to Murray, 5 Sept. 1755, Gaudet, 'Acadian Genealogy and Notes', 21.

24. Winslow to Lawrence, 17 Sept. 1755, Winslow's Journal, 6 Oct. 1755; Gaudet, 'Acadian Genealogy and Notes', 25, 29.

25. Winslow's Journal, 10 Sept. 1755, Gaudet, 'Acadian Genealogy and Notes', 23.

26. Winslow's Journal, 8 Oct. 1755, Gaudet, 'Acadian Genealogy and Notes', 29.

27. Extract from Winslow's Journal, Gaudet, 'Acadian Genealogy and Notes', 36.

28. Andrew Hill Clark, *Acadia: The Geography of Early Nova Scotia to 1760* (Madison: University of Wisconsin Press, 1968), 350.

29. D.C. Harvey, *The French Régime in Prince Edward Island* (New Haven: Yale University Press, 1926), 181.

6   From Earle Lockerby, 'The Deportation of the Acadians from Ile St-Jean, 1758',
Acadiensis 27 (Spring 1998): 45–94.

Deportation is a defining event in Acadian history and has played a profound role in shaping Acadian identity. For Acadians, deportation was a tragedy, resulting in the devastation of their society, the dispersal of close-knit families and the destruction of communities. At the same time, the travails of an uprooted pastoral people during deportation and its aftermath, and the extraordinary odyssey experienced by many of them, produced a shared heritage which has helped the Acadian community to re-establish itself. Acadian interpretations of deportation have provided a framework for the development of a rich, distinct, and undiminished sense of identity in the nineteenth and twentieth centuries.

The historiography of the deportation that has developed over the last two centuries is extensive and, like the events themselves, shaped by contesting perspectives. Most of what has been written focuses on the deportation of 1755 which resulted in the removal of 6000 to 7000 Acadians from the shores of the Bay of Fundy in Nova Scotia and adjacent areas. These people were sent into exile in British colonies from Massachusetts to Georgia. Longfellow's poem, *Evangeline*, played a major role in popularizing this deportation with Acadians and non-Acadians alike, and even imparted something of a romantic quality to the event. The second major deportation which occurred in 1758 in Prince Edward Island, then known to the French as Ile St-Jean, has received much less attention. It is not surprising that the deportation in Nova Scotia has overshadowed the smaller but equally traumatic and tragic one three years later involving settlers on Ile St-Jean, as most Maritime Acadians trace their ancestry to the first deportation. As well, the deportation from Ile St-Jean had a precedent, involved fewer people and has been less controversial. To a large degree, however, the two deportations affected one people. A significant portion of Ile St-Jean's population in 1758 was comprised of residents who had moved to the Island from Acadia (mainland Nova Scotia, including the isthmus of Chignecto) prior to the deportation of 1755, or shortly thereafter. Organized settlement by the French began on Ile St-Jean in 1720 and initially most settlers came from France. Over time, however, the population became increasingly Acadian as people moved to the Island from the mainland, particularly from 1750 to 1756.

Although a great deal has been published about the deportation of 1755, it attracted little historical attention during the first century after the event. In the second half of the nineteenth century and early part of the twentieth, as historical interest in the subject grew, writers tended to treat the subject as a matter for debate. Just as the deportation itself involved English-speaking Protestants on the one hand and French-speaking Catholics on the other, the writing in this period also reflected defensive and accusatory postures, depending upon the author's religious or racial background.[1] As the twentieth century has advanced, the historiography relating to Acadian deportation has become less partisan, though in the case of Ile St-Jean, not necessarily characterized by greater accuracy. The historiographies of both deportations reflect the early shaping influence of Catholic clerics who wrote history. This began in France in 1766 with Abbé Guillaume-Thomas-François Raynal's attack on British tyranny for the deportation of Acadians and continued in Canada, with Henri-Raymond Casgrain's late nineteenth-century works concerning the deportations. The 1758 deportation from Ile St-Jean received particular attention from clerical writers, as Casgrain's partisan contribution was reinforced early in the twentieth century by John C. MacMillan, and, again, well beyond the mid-point of this century, by J. Wilfred Pineau, both priests from Prince Edward Island. . . .

It is important to bear in mind that deportation of the Acadians was not an unparalleled or unprecedented event, as portrayed by some writers. Deportations have been occurring since Biblical times, if not before. The deportation of roughly 12,000 Acadians pales in comparison to a number of other deportations and expulsions.[2] The religious wars and persecution in France during the sixteenth and seventeenth centuries culminated in Louis XIV's expulsion of approximately 400,000 Huguenots, which virtually eliminated Protestantism in France.[3] In the twentieth century Stalin deported some 200,000 to 250,000 Crimean Tatars from the lands they had occupied for more than half a millennium. They were shipped to Central Asia, thousand of kilometres away, and it is estimated that between a quarter and a half of them perished. These events, in turn, are dwarfed by other deportations which occurred in Eastern Europe during the Second World War.[4] None of this of course diminishes the tragedy that deportation embodies for the Acadian people.

The deportation of 1755 has generated much more controversy than that of 1758. There are a number of reasons for this. During the former, France and Britain were not officially at war, while in the latter they were. Lawrence, who masterminded the deportation of 1755, has been condemned by many historians for his inhumanity, though he has also been judged as 'not a cruel man'.[5] Lawrence had relatively little influence on events in 1758; it was Amherst, Boscawen and Rollo who were responsible for the deportation of that year. Though resolute, they may have had more compassion than Lawrence. It is significant that even after he had been ordered to deport all of Ile St-Jean's population Rollo still permitted Biscaret and Cassiet to travel to Louisbourg to ask his superiors whether deportation orders might be overturned. Finally, the controversy surrounding the first deportation has to some degree diverted the attention of writers away from the second.

Although some have suggested that there was a deliberate policy of separating families in the deportation from Acadia, there has been no mention of this happening, even inadvertently, in the case of the deportation from Ile St-Jean and Ile Royale. The deportation from these islands seems to have been handled reasonably humanely, if such a thing is possible.[6] It is true that British miscalculation and delay may have led to more deaths among the deportees than would otherwise have been the case. By the time the main flotilla of transports arrived at Port-la-Joie it was already late in the year—some nine weeks after the capitulation of Louisbourg. Had authorities realized earlier the true size of the population on Ile St-Jean, a month's delay might have been avoided. The transports might then have crossed the Atlantic earlier in the fall, possibly missing the storms which are common later in the season. Not all of the delays, however, resulted from miscalculation. Bad weather accounted for a delay of one to two weeks during the passage of the 14 transports from Louisbourg to Port-la-Joie. Ironically, a further delay of at least a week may have been occasioned by Rollo's compassion or flexibility, as a week, perhaps more, was required for Biscaret and Cassiet to go to Louisbourg and return. Rollo, though, may have continued to carry out his plans during their absence.

The toll of disease aboard the transports carrying inhabitants of Ile St-Jean was appalling. Nevertheless, it was comparable to that experienced by those deported from Acadia in 1755, even though the voyage to the American colonies was much shorter than the trip across the Atlantic. Death tolls of 20 and 30 per cent were not uncommon on the transports which took Acadians to the American colonies. On the *Edward Cornwallis*, destined for South Carolina, slightly more than half the 417 passengers died.[7] Terrible as these losses were, they were not unusual. Shipboard conditions in the eighteenth century were generally dreadful. Those who sailed with the navy squadron under Admirals Boscawen and Mostyn, which arrived in Halifax on 28 June 1755, were so severely battered by scurvy, typhus and yellow fever that they could scarcely manoeuvre their ships into the harbour.[8] The condition of French soldiers and sailors arriving at Québec City in the 1750s was much the same.[9] One doctor wrote in the mid-eighteenth century that 'the number of seamen who died in time of war by shipwreck, capture, famine, fire or sword are but inconsiderable in respect to such as are destroyed by the ship diseases and the usual maladies of intemperate climates'.[10] Consider the fate of French sailors returning from Louisbourg to Brest in 1757.[11] Twenty-two vessels in Dubois de la Mott's squadron left Louisbourg at the end of October and 2000 men are said to have died during the three-week crossing or soon after the squadron's arrival.[12] Five thousand ill seamen landed and the typhus they carried spread into the civilian population at Brest where, according to one historian, 10,000 inhabitants of the town became victims of the epidemic. Civilian passengers of transoceanic transport vessels faced a risk of death due to disease comparable to that for seamen on military ships. Even in their own communities, French settlers were not immune to serious outbreaks of disease. Although not common, on occasion epidemics ravished the population of Ile St-Jean, Ile Royale and Acadia. In 1732/33 more than 150 people died of smallpox on Ile Royale. In 1755 French officials on Ile Royale reported that smallpox 'which has been greatly feared and usually makes great ravages in this climate' had broken out and was progressing rapidly.[13]

That some of the transports from Ile St-Jean made port in England, and French harbours other than St Malo, was not due to a plot, deception or treachery. Stormy weather may have blown some off course. The masters of other vessels, suffering damage to rigging or excessive hull leakage, may have deliberately sought English ports where they could more readily obtain repairs than in a country which was at war with Britain. Due to adverse weather, some transports took longer than usual to cross the Atlantic and consequently ran short of provisions. Certainly this was the case for the transports that put in at Boulogne. The masters of other transports running out of provisions may have felt it best to seek these in England rather than France. The diversions of transports were no doubt the result of improvisation in the face of difficult circumstances.

Despite Longfellow's characterization of Acadian life prior to the expulsion as one of peace, bliss and self-sufficiency, such depictions were far from the truth in Ile St-Jean during much of its 38 years as a French colony. The inhabitants did manage to establish a new settlement based largely on agriculture, where they could raise their families, practice their religion under the guidance of their priests, and live as French subjects. At the same time, however, the history of the settlers of Ile St-Jean prior to the expulsion includes extreme hardship. For almost every good harvest year it seems that there was one in which crops failed. In one or two instances widespread fires destroyed crops, livestock and farms. Famine and starvation were common and frequently occasioned desperate pleas for supplies from Louisbourg, Québec and even France itself. In 1756, famine on Ile St-Jean prompted authorities to relocate some families to Québec.[14] Many of the settlers the British deported were refugees from Acadia who had experienced severe destitution and deprivation on Ile St-Jean. By several accounts, including that of Abbé Girard, some newly arrived settlers lacked adequate clothing to conceal their nakedness.[15] Settlers had to contend with the political instability of the region, and could never rest assured that Ile St-Jean would provide the security they sought to live peaceful lives of loyalty to the French king. Indeed, the population of Ile St-Jean came within a hair of being deported to France in the mid-1740s following the first fall of Louisbourg. Some settlers retraced their steps back to Acadia then in anticipation of deportation.[16]

The troubles of French settlers on Ile St-Jean culminated with British occupation and orders for the deportation of the population. Slightly less than one-third of the 4700 residents reached France, a little more than one-third lost their lives through drowning and disease on the way to France, and about one-third managed to elude their captors. Most of the latter did so by fleeing the Island, though a few were able to remain. The people of Ile St-Jean, like their kin in Acadia, were unfortunately caught up in a global conflict which lasted close to two decades and affected not only North America, but also Europe, Africa and Asia. The Seven Years' War was its culmination. With the benefit of hindsight, and in the light of later events, the deportation can be regarded as militarily unnecessary. By today's terms the deportation of the inhabitants of Ile St-Jean was a harsh measure. A more humane approach might have achieved British objectives. The inhabitants might have become loyal subjects of the British crown, posing a threat to no one, and their communities might have remained intact. However, one cannot use twentieth-century ethics to judge events of almost two and a half centuries ago.

The Acadian expulsion is a gloomy chapter in the history of Nova Scotia and Prince Edward Island. On the Island, a community comprising five parishes was eradicated. Fortunately, it is but one chapter in the history of the French in Prince Edward Island. If any positive element can be discerned from the deportation experience, it is the role that it played in helping to foster determination among its survivors. Acadians responded to the tragedy of deportation by resolving to rebuild and to overcome close to a century of abandonment by their conquerors. The few who remained on the Island, together with those who returned there after 1763, formed the nucleus of a French population which has grown to more than 12,000, almost one-tenth of today's population. The British conquerors were unable to quell the Acadian spirit and will to triumph over adversity. It is these qualities which have enabled the Acadians of Prince Edward Island to establish themselves as a vibrant community with a rich culture, contributing in full measure to the quality of life and economic prosperity on Prince Edward Island.

Notes

*I refer to the deportation from Ile St-Jean as the 'deportation of 1758' although the deportation of that year included civilians, and administrative and military personnel from Ile Royale (Cape Breton) as well. The assistance of staff at the National Archives of Canada, Prince Edward Island Archives and Records Office, Harriet Irving Library at the University of New Brunswick and Centre d'études acadiennes at the Université de Moncton is gratefully acknowledged. The author is particularly indebted to Parks Canada staff of the archives at Fortress Louisbourg for providing access to documents held there.

1. See, for instance, Edouard Richard, *Acadia: Missing Links of a Lost Chapter in American History*, vol. II (Montreal, 1895) and the French version of this study as it appeared two decades later: *Acadie: Reconstitution d'un Chapitre Perdue de l'Histoire d'Amérique* (Québec, 1916–21). See too Casgrain, *Une Second Acadie* (Québec, 1894).

2. In addition to the two main deportations which occurred in 1755 and 1758, there were several other much smaller ones from Nova Scotia (including present-day New Brunswick) between 1755 and 1762.

3. The French government not only deported Huguenots but deliberately killed many. During the infamous St Bartholomew's Day massacre of 1572, which was authorized by the French king, tens of thousands of French Protestants were slaughtered. Estimates of the death toll vary

widely—from 30,000 to 100,000. See Alfred Sloan, *The Massacre of St. Bartholomew: Reappraisals and Documents* (The Hague, 1974), p. viii, and François Pierre Guillaume Guizot, *The History of France*, vol. 3 (New York, 1902), p. 302.

4. See Ann Sheehy, *The Crimean Tatars, Volga Germans and Meskhetians: Soviet Treatment of Some National Minorities* (London, 1971), pp. 10–11, 23–4, 31–2. Deported in 1944, the Crimean Tatars were crammed into cattle cars and many died of thirst, suffocation, and the stench of decomposing bodies. Estimates of the proportion who died within the first few months of reaching their destination range from 22 to 46 per cent. In 1915 some 50,000 Volga Germans, who had been in Russia for between 100 and 200 years, were deported to the east under such terrible conditions that the majority died. They were completely eliminated from their homeland in 1941–2 when 400,000 were deported to Siberia and northern Kazakhstan. In 1944 all of the estimated 200,000 Meskhetians were deported to Uzbekistan and Kazakhstan from their homeland of Meskhetia, a mountainous region on the border between Turkey and Georgia. Thirty thousand may have perished from hunger and cold in Uzbekistan alone. These deportations, in turn, were much smaller than those in Europe during the Second World War. The 1940s saw the violent expulsion of an estimated 12 to 15 million Germans from Poland, Czechoslovakia and Hungary. The death toll among them is estimated to be well in excess of one million. The most horrific mass exodus during the Second World War was of course related to the German attempt to eradicate Jewry from Europe by deporting an estimated six million of them to oblivion. For more on the deportation of Germans and Jews see Peter Steinberg, *Journey to Oblivion* (Toronto, 1991), pp. 3–5.

5. Dominick Graham, 'Charles Lawrence', *Dictionary of Canadian Biography (DCB)*, III, pp. 361–6.

6. John G. Reid, *Six Crucial Decades* (Halifax, 1987), p. 44, has described the deportation from Ile St-Jean as 'undoubtedly brutal' in comparison to the one from Acadia, citing the sinking of 'overloaded' transports conveying inhabitants of Ile St-Jean to France. The facts however would suggest that the deportation of 1758 was carried out more humanely than that of 1755. The loss of life by drowning which marked the deportation of the inhabitants of Ile St-Jean can hardly be said to have been caused by brutal treatment. Shipwrecks with the attendant loss of life were common in ocean and coastal travel during the eighteenth and nineteenth centuries.

7. 'Report of Edward Cornwallis', Andrew Sinclair, master, 17 November 1755, Council Records (Columbia, S.C.), p. 480, cited in Naomi E.S. Griffiths, *The Contexts of Acadian History 1686–1764* (Montreal and Kingston, 1992), p. 93.

8. Griffiths, *Contexts of Acadian History*, p. 92.

9. Regarding sickness of sailors arriving at Québec during the period 1755–9, see Gilles Proulx, *Between France and New France: Life Aboard the Tall Sailing Ships* (Toronto, 1984), p. 114.

10. Griffiths, *Contexts of Acadian History*, p. 92, n. 94.

11. President of the Navy Board to Prévost, 18 February 1758, Fonds des Colonies (FC), B, 107(2), p. 18, Archives Nationales, Paris; President of the Navy Board to Drucour and Prévost, 18 February 1758, FC, B, 107(2), p. 19; President of the Navy Board to Prévost, 10 March 1758, FC, B, 107(2), p. 27v. See also Etienne Taillemite, 'Emmanuel Augusta de Cahideuc, Comte Dubois de la Motte', *DCB*, III, p. 93.

12. Bona Arsenault, *Histoire et Généalogie des Acadiens*, vol. 5 (Ottawa, 1978), pp. 1762–3.

13. Le Normant to Minister, 30 June 1733, FC, C¹¹B, 14, pp. 132–4; Drucour and Prévost to Minister, 2 June 1755, FC, C¹¹B, 35, pp. 19–22. Both these references are cited in Linda M. Hoad, *Surgeons and Surgery in Ile Royale*, History and Archaeology, 6, National Historic Parks and Sites Branch, Parks Canada (Ottawa, 1976), p. 241.

14. Vaudreuil to Minister, 7 August 1756, FC, C¹¹A, 101, p. 84. For a printed transcript see Placide Gaudet, 'Acadian Genealogy and Notes', Appendix H: De L'Expulsion à la Prise de Québec, in

Report Concerning Canadian Archives for the Year 1905, vol. 2 (Ottawa, 1906), p. 183.

15. See Girard to Prévost, 24 October 1753, FC, C¹¹B, 33, pp. 288–9, and Vaudreuil to Minister, 18 April 1757, FC, C¹¹A, 102, p. 8. A printed transcription of the latter appears in Gaudet, 'Acadian Genealogy and Notes', Appendix H, p. 185. See also Drucour and Prévost to Minister, 25 November 1756, FC, C¹¹B, 36, p. 35.

16. A British prisoner of the French noted in his diary of 29 August 1746 that, while in the Chignecto area, he and his captors encountered 50 men, women and children on horses and mules, who had been 'routed from the Island of St. John's by [intended action of] Admiral Warren'. See Isabel M. Calder, *Colonial Captivities, Marches and Journeys* (New York, 1935), p. 23.

☐ The Quebec Act, 1774

INTRODUCTION

■ The Quebec Act was the first of a series of imperial legislative enactments that helped shape modern Canada by remaking the way in which the constitution of British North America (or provinces within it) operated. Constitutional history has become relatively unfashionable in the twenty-first century, but any study of the Quebec Act involves more than simply the recounting of the passage of a parliamentary statute. It suggests the many contradictory considerations that beset an Empire in the years after the successful completion of the Seven Years' War. That Empire was composed of a wide variety of people with different backgrounds and different histories whose contradictory interests could not easily be reconciled. On the surface, the Quebec Act was important because it sought to resolve a dozen years of uneasiness between the British governors of Quebec and the recently acquired bulk of the province's population, who were Roman Catholics speaking the French language and attempting to continue to enjoy their traditional laws and customs.

The British discovered that successfully governing a determined people required considerably more accommodation than had originally been intended or expected. Moreover, the question of accommodation came within a context that went far beyond the shores of the St Lawrence River and involved large grey areas in which virtually no evidence of public opinion existed then, or is available today. The British were forced to govern Quebec in the midst of a deteriorating relationship with their American colonies to the south and in terms of setting precedents within the British Isles themselves. The colonials to the south affected to regard concessions to the French Canadians as further evidence of the way in which Great Britain was prepared to abuse the rights and liberties of their American subjects. The Americans included the Quebec Act as one of the so-called 'Intolerable Acts' the British Parliament passed in 1774 in the wake of the Boston Tea Party. The British themselves feared that concessions to Catholics in Canada would have ultimate implications for Catholics closer to home, in Ireland and even in England itself. Further complicating matters, it was quite impossible to test public opinion on either side of the Atlantic. The British Parliament acted on the strength of extremely limited evidence of what the Canadians and Americans, among others, themselves really wanted, a situation typical of eighteenth-century politics.

Finally, there is the question of whether the British were motivated principally by views of justice and humanity or by the practical needs of an immediate political situation. Not to have satisfied the francophones in Quebec, after all, might have driven them into the arms of the already rambunctious Americans. Whether the legislation achieved its goal was another matter.

Questions for consideration

1. How was the Quebec Act received in Quebec?
2. What were the policy alternatives to that adopted in the 1774 legislation?
3. Were any of them really worth considering in 1774?

Suggestions for further reading

Alfred Leroy Burt, *The Old Province of Quebec* (Toronto: Ryerson Press, 1933). A very old study that has stood the test of time.

Hilda Neatby, *Quebec: The Revolutionary Age, 1760–1791* (Toronto: McClelland & Stewart, 1966). This work, while quite dated in some respects, remains the most judicious overall view of the Quebec Act in the context of the larger history of Quebec.

——, *The Quebec Act: Protest and Policy* (Scarborough, Ont.: Prentice-Hall of Canada, 1972). A useful compendium of historical writing on the Quebec Act.

PRIMARY DOCUMENTS

1   From 'The Quebec Act', in Adam Shortt and Arthur G. Doughty, eds, *Documents relating to the Constitutional History of Canada 1759–1791* (Ottawa: King's Printer, 1907), 403–5.

And, for the more perfect Security and Ease of the Minds of the Inhabitants of the said Province, it is hereby declared, That His Majesty's Subjects, professing the Religion of the Church of *Rome* of and in the said Province of Quebec, may have, hold, and enjoy, the free Exercise of the Religion of the Church of *Rome*, subject to the King's Supremacy, declared and established by an Act, made in the First Year of the Reign of Queen *Elizabeth*, over all the Dominions and Countries which then did, or thereafter should belong, to the Imperial Crown of this Realm; and that the Clergy of the said Church may hold, receive, and enjoy, their accustomed Dues and Rights, with respect to such Persons only as shall profess the said Religion.

Provided nevertheless, That it shall be lawful for His Majesty, His Heirs or Successors, to make such Provision out of the rest of the said accustomed Dues and Rights, for the Encouragement of the Protestant Religion, and for the Maintenance and Support of a Protestant Clergy within the said Province, as he or they shall, from Time to Time, think necessary and expedient.

Provided always, and be it enacted, That no Person, professing the Religion of the Church of *Rome*, and residing in the said Province, shall be obliged to take the Oath required by the said Statute passed in the First Year of the Reign of Queen *Elizabeth*, or any other Oaths substituted by any other Act in the Place thereof; but that every such Person who, by the said Statute is required to take the Oath therein mentioned, shall be obliged, and is hereby required, to take and subscribe the following Oath before the Governor, or such other Person in such Court of Record as His Majesty shall appoint, who are hereby authorized to administer the same; *videlicet,*

I A. B. do sincerely promise and swear, That I will be faithful, and bear true Allegiance to His Majesty King GEORGE, *and him will defend to the utmost of my Power, against all traitorous Conspiracies, and Attempts whatsoever, which shall be made against His Person, Crown and Dignity; and I will do my utmost Endeavour to disclose and make known to His Majesty, His Heirs and Successors, all Treasons, and traitorous Conspiracies, and Attempts, which I shall know to be against Him, or any of Them; and all this I do swear without any Equivocation, mental Evasion, or secret Reservation, and renouncing all Pardons and Dispensations from any Power or Person whomsoever to the Contrary.*

SO HELP ME GOD.

And every such Person, who shall neglect or refuse to take the said Oath before mentioned, shall incur and be liable to the same Penalties, Forfeitures, Disabilities, and Incapacities, as he would have incurred and been liable to for neglecting or refusing to take the Oath required by the said Statute passed in the First Year of the Reign of Queen *Elizabeth*.

And be it further enacted by the Authority aforesaid, That all His Majesty's Canadian Subjects, within the Province of Quebec, the religious Orders and Communities only excepted, may also hold and enjoy their Property and Possessions, together with all Customs and Usages relative thereto, and all other their Civil Rights, in as large, ample, and beneficial Manner, as if the said Proclamations, Commissions, Ordinances, and other Acts and Instruments, had not been made, and as may consist with their Allegiance to His Majesty; and Subjections to the Crown and Parliament of *Great Britain*; and that in all Matters of Controversy, relative to Property and Civil Rights, Resort shall be had to the Laws of *Canada*, as the Rule for the Decision of the same; and all Causes that shall hereafter be instituted in any of the Courts of Justice, to be appointed within and for the said Province, by His Majesty, His Heirs and Successors, shall, with respect to such Property and Rights, be determined agreeably to the said Laws and Customs of *Canada*, until they shall be varied or altered by any Ordinances, that shall, from Time to Time, be passed in the said Province by the Governor, Lieutenant Governor, or Commander in Chief, for the Time being, by and with the Advice and Consent of the Legislative Council of the same, to be appointed in Manner herein-after mentioned.

Provided always, That nothing in this Act contained shall extend, or be construed to extend, to any Lands that have been granted by His Majesty, or shall hereafter be granted by His Majesty, His Heirs and Successors, to be holden in free and common Soccage.

Provided also, That it shall and may be lawful to and for every Person that is Owner of any Lands, Goods, or Credits, in the said Province, and that has a Right to alienate the said Lands, Goods, or Credits, in his or her Life-time, by Deed of Sale, Gift or otherwise, to devise or bequeath the same at his or her Death, by his or her last Will and Testament; any Law, Usage, or Custom, heretofore or now prevailing in the Province, to the Contrary hereof in any-wise notwithstanding; such Will being executed, either according to the Laws of Canada, or according to the Forms prescribed by the Laws of *England*.

And whereas the Certainty and Lenity of the Criminal Law of *England*, and the Benefits and Advantages resulting from the Use of it, have been sensibly felt by the Inhabitants, from an Experience of more than Nine Years, during which it has been uniformly administered; be it therefore further enacted by the Authority aforesaid, That the same shall continue to be administered, and shall be observed as Law in the Province of *Quebec*, as well in the Description and Quality of the Offence as in the Method of Prosecution and Trial; and the Punishments and Forfeitures thereby inflicted to the Exclusion of every other Rule of Criminal Law, or Mode of Proceeding thereon, which did or might prevail in the said Province before the Year of our Lord One thousand seven hundred and sixty-four; any Thing in this Act to the Contrary thereof in any Respect notwithstanding; subject nevertheless to such Alterations and Amendments as the Governor, Lieutenant-governor, or Commander in Chief for the Time being, by and with the Advice and Consent of the legislative Council of the said Province, hereafter to be appointed, shall, from Time to Time, cause to be made therein, in Manner herein-after directed.

And whereas it may be necessary to ordain many Regulations for the future Welfare and good Government of the Province of *Quebec*, the Occasions of which cannot now be foreseen, nor, without much Delay and Inconvenience, be provided for, without intrusting that Authority, for a certain Time, and under proper Restrictions, to Persons resident there: And whereas it is at present inexpedient to call an Assembly; be it therefore enacted By the Authority aforesaid, That it shall and may be lawful for His Majesty, His Heirs and Successors, by Warrant under His or Their Signet or Sign Manual, and with the Advice of the Privy Council, to constitute and appoint a Council for the Affairs of the Province of *Quebec*, to consist of such Persons resident there, not exceeding Twenty-three, nor less than

Seventeen, as His Majesty, His Heirs and Successors, shall be pleased to appoint; and, upon the Death, Removal, or Absence of any of the Members of the said Council, in like Manner to constitute and appoint such major Part thereof, shall have Power and Authority to make Ordinances for the Peace, Welfare, and good Government, of the said Province, with the Consent of His Majesty's Governor, or, in his Absence, of the Lieutenant-governor, or Commander in Chief for the Time being.

Provided always, That nothing in this Act contained shall extend to authorize or impower the said legislative Council to lay any Taxes or Duties within the said Province, such Rates and Taxes only excepted as the Inhabitants of any Town or District within the said Province may be authorized by the said Council to assess, levy, and apply, within the said Town or District, for the Purpose of making Roads, erecting and repairing public Buildings, or for any other Purpose respecting the local Convenience and economy of such Town or District.

2   Guy Carleton to Lord Dorchester, 11 November 1774, in Shortt and Doughty, eds, *Documents*, 412–14.

CARLETON TO DARTMOUTH.[1]

QUEBEC 11th November 1774.

My Lord!—Soon after my Arrival here, I informed Your Lordship of the Gratefull Sense, The King's Canadian Subjects, in this Part of the Province entertained of the Acts of Parliament passed in their Favour during the last Session; those more remote have since, in all their Letters and Addresses, expressed the same Sentiments of Gratitude and Attachment to His Majesty's Royal Person and Government as well as to the British Interests.

The most respectable part of the English residing at this Place, notwithstanding many Letters received from Home, advising them to pursue a different Course, likewise presented an Address expressive of their Wish to see universal Harmony and a dutifull Submission to Government continue to be the Characteristic of the Inhabitants of this Province, and assuring me, that nothing should be wanting, upon their Parts, to promote so desirable an End; I believe, most of those, who signed this Address, were disposed to act up to their Declaration, which probably would have been followed by those, who did not, if their Brethren at Montreal had not adopted very different Measures.

Whether the minds of the latter are of a more turbulent Turn, or that they caught the Fire from some Colonists settled among them, or in reality Letters were received from the General Congress, as reported, I know not; Certain it is however, that shortly after the said Congress had published in all the American Papers their approbation of the Suffolk County Resolves[2] in the Massachusetts, a Report was spread at Montreal, that Letters of Importance had been received from the General Congress, all the British there flocked to the Coffee House to hear the News, Grievances were publicly talked of, and various Ways for obtaining Redress proposed, but that Government might not come to a true Knowledge of their Intentions, a Meeting was appointed at the House of a Person then absent, followed by several others at the same Place, and a Committee of four Named, consisting of Mr. Walker, Mr. Todd, Mr. Price, and Mr. Blake, to take Care of their Interests, and prepare Plans for Redress.

Mr. Walker, whose Warmth of Temper brought on him, some Time before my Appointment to this Command, the very cruel and every Way unjustifiable Revenge,[3] which made so much Noise, now takes the Lead, and is not unmindful of his Friend Mr. Maseres upon the Occasion.

Their Plans being prepared, and a Subscription commenced, the Committee set out for Quebec, attended in Form by their Secretary, a Nephew of Mr. Walker's, and by Profession a Lawyer; immediately upon their Arrival here, their Emissaries having prepared the Way, an Anonymous Summons was posted up in the Coffee House for all the British Subjects to meet at a particular Tavern, and a Messenger sent round with a verbal Notice to such as might not have seen the written Summons; At this first Meeting a Committee of seven, consisting of Mr. John Paterson, since gone to London, Mr. Zachariah Macaulay, Mr. John Lees Senior, said to intend going Home this Fall, Mr. John Altkin, their Treasurer, Mr. Randal Meredith, Mr. John Welles, and Mr. Peter Fargues, was appointed to prepare and adjust Matters with those of Montreal; several discreet People at this Place and Montreal declined attending those Meetings, as soon as they discovered what they aimed at.

There have been several Town meetings since, as they are pleased to stile them, and Meetings of the joint Committees, at which, 'tis said, they have resolved to write Letters of Thanks to the Lord Mayor and Corporation of London,[4] to some of the Merchants in the City, and to Mr. Maseres, for having taken the Province under their protection and praying a Continuance of their zealous Endeavours in so good a Cause; they intend a handsome Present in Cash to Mr. Maseres, with the Promise of a larger Sum, in Case he succeeds; Petitions are likewise to be presented to The King, to the Lords, and to the Commons,[5] but of all this I speak doubtfully, as they have taken uncommon Pains to keep their whole Proceedings from my knowledge.

This much however is Certain, that the Canadians feel some Uneasiness at these Proceedings; they are surprised that such Meetings and nocturnal Cabals should be suffered to exert all their Efforts to disturb the Minds of the People by false and seditious Reports, calculated to throw this Province into the same Disorders that reign in other Parts of this Continent; They express some Impatience and Indignation at being solicited to join in such Proceedings, and are not without their Fears, that some of their Countrymen, under the Awe of menacing Creditors, and others, from Ignorance, may have been induced to put their Hands to a Paper, which, they are assured, is intended to secure their Lands and Property, and take from the Governor the Power of seizing them to his own Use, or sending them and their Families up the Country among the Savages, or waging War, at his own Pleasure, upon the Bostonians; in short to relieve them from the Oppressions and Slavery imposed upon them by those Acts of Parliament; They are the more apprehensive these and such like Reports may have had Effect upon some weak and ignorant People, that from the Precision necessary, in the Translation, the Acts themselves have not as yet been promulgated.

I have assured the Canadians, that such Proceedings could never affect the late Measures taken in their Favor, nor did I believe, they ever would succeed with Government upon any Occasion, so that they might remain in perfect Tranquility upon that is to be established are well known, prejudices which popular Clamour has excited, will cease, and that His Majesty's Subjects of every description will see and be convinced of the Equity and good Policy of the Bill.

It will be your Care, Sir, at the same time you express to the King's new adopted Subjects His Majesty's gracious approbation of the Affection and Respect they have shown for His Government, to endeavour by every Argument which your own good sense will suggest to you, to persuade the natural born subjects of the justice & propriety of the present form of Government and of the attention that has been shewn to their Interests not only in the adoption of the English Laws, as far as it was consistent with what was due to the just Claims and moderate Wishes of the Canadian, but in the opening to the British Merchant, by an Extension of the Province, so many new Channels of important Commerce.

NOTES

1. Canadian Archives, Q 11, p. 11.
2. These were adopted on Sept. 9th, 1774.
3. The chief documents dealing with the Walker outrage are given in the 'Report on Canadian Archives' for 1888, p. 1.
4. 'On the 22nd of June, the Lord Mayor, attended by several aldermen, the recorder, and upwards of one hundred and fifty of the common council, went up with an address and petition to the King, supplicating his Majesty not to give his assent to the bill.' Cavendish's 'Debates' &c. Preface, p. IV.
5. These petitions were presented and are given [in Shortt and Doughty, eds, *Documents*] immediately following this despatch.

HISTORICAL INTERPRETATIONS

3 From Victor Coffin, *The Province of Quebec and the Early American Revolution* (Madison: University of Wisconsin Press, 1896), 480–6.

A. The Revolution in the Province of Quebec.

In the frequent extolling by British and Canadian writers of the *policy* of the Quebec Act, the reference is of course to the supposed effect of that Act in confirming the loyalty of the French Canadians at the revolutionary crisis, and thus in preserving the newly-acquired territories from the grasp of the revolutionary movement. If the conclusions of the last chapter be well taken, it will be seen that whatever the outcome of the measure, the inference as to policy is largely mistaken; that in other words, if the results were as stated, it would seem a rare and happy instance of immediate temporal reward for disinterested well-doing. It is not meant to deny that in the generally threatening conditions in America the firm attachment of the new subjects must have appeared to the home government as a very desirable thing; nor that the conviction of this desirability was probably a considerable factor in confirming the final conclusions as to their treatment. Such a motive would be of necessity strongly present in the case of such an unknown quantity as the new acquisition of a segment of another nationality; I have simply tried to show that it was not accentuated by the contemporary existence of other colonial problems to the extent of appreciably affecting the policy adopted toward the new subjects.

But further, I am obliged to take exception to the position of the upholders of the Act for other and stronger reasons. The credit for political sagacity assigned to the authors of that measure must be impugned not only on the ground that their work had little if any reference to the circumstances on which the credit is given, but also for the conclusive reason that the immediate results the Act were precisely the opposite of what had been anticipated and have ever since been assumed. It is the object of this chapter to show that not only was the Quebec Act not effectual in keeping the mass of the Canadians loyal, but that what effect it did have was in exactly the opposite direction. And before proceeding to this it should be noticed that in anticipating or extolling the results of the new settlement on the French Canadians there is curiously left out of sight by the upholders of the Act, any consideration of its effects either on the British in Canada or on the older colonies. Yet it is evident that for the true estimate of its policy, wisdom, or results there must be an accurate balancing. In view of the accompanying measures of the Government of the day in regard to the other colonies directly it is not surprising to find any thought of this entirely absent at the time. We however have no excuse for now neglecting it.

The question of the influence, direct or indirect, in general or in particular parts of the country, of the new settlement of Quebec affairs on revolutionary development in the other colonies, is one of an interest so great and so closely connected with my work that I can only express my regret at being unable at present to investigate it thoroughly. It must be left with a reference to the general classing of the Act with those of the same session in regard to Massachusetts Bay,[1] and to the emphasis so placed upon the measure in the early steps of the Continental Congress. One remarkable bit of private testimony in connection therewith might also be mentioned. In the Dartmouth Papers we find a letter from one Joseph Reed to the Earl of Dartmouth, Secretary of State, dated Philadelphia, Sept. 25, 1774, and giving an account of the alarming proceedings of the Congress then sitting there. The writer proceeds:—'But what shall I say to your Lordship of the appearances in this country; what seemed a little time since to be a spark which with prudence and wisdom might have been extinguished, is now a flame that threatens ruin both to parent and child. The spirit of the people gradually rose when it might have been expected to decline, till the Quebec Act added fuel to the fire; then all those deliberate measures of petitioning previous to any opposition was laid aside as inadequate to the apprehended danger and mischief, and now the people are generally ripe for the execution of any plan the Congress advises, should it be war itself.'[2] Without delaying further on the direct influence in the revolting colonies of the general feeling with regard to the Quebec settlement, it may be pointed out that the attitude of that section of the British party in the Province itself which I have above distinguished as closely in sympathy with what became the revolutionary element, is a fairly correct index to the general feeling. That element in Quebec had, in the circumstances of the province, no legitimate or immediate share in the general colonial quarrel; its grievance was the Quebec Act purely; yet we find this a grievance of strength sufficient to drive it almost immediately into secret and as soon as possible into open revolt.

In noting these consequences of the new settlement with regard to the English-speaking party in Quebec, we have first to observe its efficacy in openly separating the more advanced and more moderate section.[3] The first step of the party was the drawing up of protests against the Act; in which mild proceeding however all apparently did not take part. For Carleton writes Nov. 11, 1774 to Dartmouth, that the more respectable part of the English at Quebec, 'notwithstanding many letters received from home advising them to pursue a different course,' had presented a dutiful and submissive address; but that in Montreal, 'whether the minds of the latter are of a more turbulent turn, or that they caught the fire from some colonists settled among them, or in reality letters were received from the General Congress, as reported, I know not, certainly it is however that shortly after the said Congress had published in all the American papers their approbation of the Suffolk Co. resolves in the Massachusetts, a report was spread at Montreal that letters of importance had been received from the General Congress,' and public meetings were held by the British there for the consideration of grievances. Thence the infection had spread to Quebec where the same course was pursued, though 'several discrete persons' at both places had declined taking part. Since then there had been several 'town-meetings as they are pleased to style them;' though he speaks doubtfully, 'as have taken uncommon pains to keep their whole proceedings from my knowledge.' He describes these town meetings and reports as all 'breathing that same spirit, so plentifully gone forth through the neighbouring Provinces,' and speaks of the necessity of government guarding zealously 'against the consequences of an infection, daily, warmly recommended, and spread abroad by the Colonists here, and indeed by some from Europe, not less violent than the Americans.'[4]

The immediate outcome of these proceedings were numerously signed petitions against the Act, addressed to the King and to both Houses of Parliament. There can be no doubt that the leaders here and from this time on were constantly in more or less direct communication with the American Revolutionists and were aiming to keep as closely in touch with their efforts as possible. The letters spoken of above by Carleton undoubtedly did represent some such connection, and a few days later (Nov. 18, 1774)[5] Carleton transmits a copy of one which had fallen into his hands, and which probably was the communication referred to. And as it speaks of itself as being 'our first public correspondence with the town of Quebec,'[6] it will be worth while to refer more fully to it. It is dated Boston, Oct. 10, 1774, and is a moderate and dignified letter of thanks by one David Jeffries, on behalf of the 'Committee of Donations' of Boston, for a contribution (apparently of wheat)[7] 'to relieve the distressed poor of this oppressed town,' and is addressed to 'the Gentlemen of Quebec' through a trading firm named Minot, originally from Massachusetts. It speaks of the necessity of the union of all parts of the continent against oppression, and of the satisfaction afforded by the sympathy of the town of Quebec; refers to the policy of Great Britain in 'creating divisions amongst them and using them as engines to beat down and destroy the liberties of each other, that so all may be an easy prey to tyranny and despotic power,'—a policy to which 'the eyes of the colonists are opened;' and expresses the hope of the continued support of 'our friends in Canada,' with whom the writers will think themselves 'happy in keeping up a brotherly correspondence.' This letter is anterior to any action of Congress in regard to Canada, and the communication now opened was constantly kept up.[8] The American portion of the party together with a few of European birth, (nearly all apparently at Montreal), undoubtedly from this time became active partizans of the Revolutionary cause, which they publicly embraced on the appearance of the American invading force. January 12, 1775, Carleton writes that the British subjects are 'still exerting their utmost endeavors to kindle in the Canadians the spirit that reigns in the Province of the Massachusetts,'[9] and the following March 13,[10] that some of them 'continue suggesting into the minds of the Canadians an abhorrence for the form of government intended by the Act of last session,' and that they have translated the letter of Congress and actually imported 200 or 300 copies of it.

I need not go into details of the intrigues carried on and of the various methods of communication employed. The point of main interest here is that the final split in the party becomes now very evident. An attempt was made at Montreal to have delegates elected to the Congress of 1775, and notwithstanding Mr. John Brown's explanation of the cause of its failure,[11] there can be no doubt that the great body of the English were decidedly opposed to the step on general grounds, and that the leading American element found itself at this point finally separated from its former constituency. We find in short that the main body of the 'old subjects' remained, in spite of the Quebec Act, heartily loyal to English rule during this crisis; that their attitude was the same as that of the Tories, (the later United Empire Loyalists), in the other Provinces. They were probably willing to go farther in opposition to the government than their brethren in some of the other Provinces, for they were under more irritating conditions;[12] but they were not willing to go to the length of taking up arms.[13] . . .

NOTES

1. This has been universal among American writers. See *Roosevelt, Winning of the West*, I, for a more emphatic and recent position; and in connection the treatment above of Quebec boundaries, Chapter V, section B, a.

2. Hist. MSS. Commission, Report XI. Appendix, V. p. 362. I am indebted for the reference to the *Report for 1890* of the Canadian Archivist, p. XXI. It will be noticed that the writer selects from the various obnoxious measures of the late Parliamentary session, the Act in regard to Quebec, without any mention apparently of the more directly threatening ones concerning Massachusetts Bay. His thought may probably be more distinctly seen in a later horrified reference to 'The idea of bringing down the Canadians and savages upon the English Colonies.' Of the writer I know nothing surely; but he is possibly the same person to whom the Congressional *Diary* of Richard Smith makes reference March 1, 1776, as the 'Secretary to Gen. Washington.' and as having his salary then raised by Congress on account of important naval duties. (See *Amer. Hist. Review*, April, 1896, p. 507.)

3. See above c. 3, for analysis of the English party.

4. Can. Arch., Q. 11, p. 11.

5. Can. Arch., Q. 11, p. 103.

6. Ibid., Q. 11, p. 105. This expression does not by any means exclude, (rather indeed implies) previous correspondence with individuals.

7. Sent the previous 6th September. Congress had met for the first time at Philadelphia the day before.

8. In the following November we find the Massachusetts Provincial Congress appointing a committee (of which John Hancock and Samuel Adams are members), for the devising of means of keeping up a correspondence with Montreal and Quebec. John Brown was later appointed the agent of this committee.

9. Can. Arch., Q. 11, p. 110. See also anonymous letter from Montreal, Jan. 18, 1775. [4 *Amer. Arch.*, I, 1164].

10. Can. Arch., Q. 11, p. 129.

11. This was to the effect that the English in Quebec could not join the non-importation agreement, as in that case the French would immediately monopolize the Indian fur trade. (John Brown to Boston Com. of Correspondence, March 29, 1775, 4 *Amer. Arch.*, II, 243.

12. And hence did go to the verge of sedition, and at first probably were somewhat lukewarm in the defense of the Province.

13. Their attitude at Montreal is probably accurately represented by a paper in the *Hald. Coll.*, (*Rep. Can. Arch.*, 1888, p. 918,) which purports to be a proposal of terms of capitulation to Montgomery, and which is signed by English and French names. It stipulates for the free possession and enjoyment of rights and religion, non-interference of soldiers with the inhabitants, and *that they should not be obliged to take up arms against the mother country*. Accompanying this is another document, unsigned, which protests against the terms of the capitulation as a treaty between two enemies, (whereas it ought to be a fraternal union), and expresses a desire for such a union with the other colonies. There can be no doubt

that this latter is the voice of the few revolutionary sympathizers. Carleton writes Oct. 25, 1775, that on the attack on Montreal by the rebels a few of the inhabitants, 'mostly colonists,' had refused to take part in the defence. From which we are justified in concluding that the most of the English element had taken part.

4   From Hilda Neatby, *Quebec: The Revolutionary Age, 1760–1791* (Toronto: McClelland & Stewart, 1966), 125-7.

A More Effectual Provision: The Quebec Act

The Quebec Act, as the framers modestly claimed, was intended to make 'a more effectual provision for the province of Quebec.' The statement is accurate enough, but it needs interpretation. The Quebec Act applied to two areas: the narrow parallelogram along the St Lawrence defined as the province of Quebec by the Proclamation of 1763, and the much larger area about the Great Lakes and beyond, claimed by France and yielded to Britain by the Treaty of Paris, but until now no part of the province of Quebec.

The union of these areas in 1774 did two things. It introduced a new and controversial form of colonial government into the St Lawrence Valley and it laid down a new policy for the Ohio country, a subject of contention between Britain and the other American colonies for the past twenty years. These two things were done at a time when the taxation controversy with the American colonies was about to culminate in open rebellion. An act of such a kind, passed at such a time, and applying to such territory, could not be seen merely as the clearing away of unfinished business in the St Lawrence Valley. It was imperial legislation, dealing with a difficult imperial problem at a time of crisis in imperial relations. The act, moreover, was drafted in close consultation with Guy Carleton, in accordance with the plans formulated by him during his administration of Quebec—plans formulated quite frankly with a view to military action on the continent as well as to defence against a French invasion.

Apart from all imperial implications, however, provision for more effectual government of Quebec was long overdue. As has been seen, the British government had practically agreed on an important revision and clarification of the law in 1766. The plan was not executed, and from this time there had been repeated postponements as it became clear that an act of Parliament would be needed. Meanwhile, from the early opinion in June 1765 that the penal laws of Britain against Roman Catholics were not applicable in the American colonies, the views of legal experts slowly accumulated. In 1769, as the reports of Carleton, Maseres, and Hey were about to be brought home by Maurice Morgann, the Board of Trade, newly constituted under Hillsborough as Secretary of State for the American colonies, produced its own report on Quebec. Stimulated by renewed requests from merchants in London, Hillsborough and his board recommended an elected assembly so constituted as to be composed of a nearly equal number of seigneurs from country districts, presumed to be Roman Catholics, and merchants from the towns who would take the oath as Protestants. The law and the law courts were to be regulated according to the neglected plan of 1766. Detailed proposals were made for ecclesiastical arrangements, Protestant and Roman Catholic, and for raising a revenue. Hillsborough believed that this plan might be acted on during the winter of 1769–70. For this reason he declined to ask leave for Carleton to return to England in the fall of 1769 on the ground that he would be needed in Quebec to inaugurate the new constitution.[1]

Hillsborough had been too confident. His plan was set aside by his colleagues to wait for the arrival of Morgann early in 1770 with the Quebec reports. Later in that year Carleton reached London. Thereafter, while Cramahé in Quebec was repeatedly informed that the Quebec business was on the point of being settled, one year followed another and no action was taken. Not that ministers were exactly idle; they were adding to their collection of expert opinions the lengthy report of Wedderburn, the Solicitor General, Thurlow, the Attorney General, and Marriott, the Advocate General. By the end of 1773 His Majesty's ministers had at their disposal reports from no less than seven law officers, to say nothing of the amateur efforts of Carleton and Maurice Morgann. And still they hesitated.

It is possible to explain, if not to excuse, the fact that it took seven years to deal with a problem clearly stated in 1766. One reason was the weakness of the successive ministries until after 1770, when the advent of the North ministry gave a certain stability to administration. Once parliamentary legislation was determined on, however, any ministry would be reluctant to touch so contentious a matter as the government of Quebec. It would clearly be impolitic and unjust to satisfy all the wishes of the English mercantile minority, and yet, on the question of French laws and the Roman Catholic religion, popular prejudice would support the minority. Even apart from popular prejudice, the problem of devising a settlement for Quebec that would combine justice and some degree of satisfaction to new and old subjects without endangering the security of the state was indeed baffling. How could Roman Catholics be tolerated and conciliated and at the same time assimilated to Protestantism? What would be a good law for a former French community, cut off from France, united to England, a close neighbour of American colonies, and now infiltrated with Englishmen and Americans? This difficulty was exaggerated by the fact that the good lawyers who offered their expert opinions were, for the most part, too good to give their unqualified approval either to the French system, which they did not know well enough, or to the English, which they knew too well. As for the constitution, an English colony without an assembly seemed unthinkable, an assembly including Roman Catholics unreliable, and an assembly excluding Roman Catholics unjustifiable. It is not surprising if ministers found it easier to ask for reports than to make any use of them.

It is significant, however, that the lawyers' reports, with many individual differences, show a general agreement on the plan favoured by Maseres as the alternative to a code: a retention of English law as a basis with the Canadian law of land tenure, alienation, inheritance, and wills.[2]

For all this unanimity William Knox, the Under-Secretary for the Colonies, remarked '. . . after all the pains that had been taken to procure the best and ablest advice the ministers were, in a great measure, left to their own judgement.'[3] Nothing could have been more unjust than this suggestion that the government had been betrayed by its assistants. The differences between the reports were much less surprising than their substantial agreement on law, government, and religion. The ministers chose to walk by other lights, setting aside the reports, or rather, burying them. When the reports were asked for during the debate on the bill, the government refused to produce them, very naturally, for only Attorney General Thurlow's report gave any support to government policy.

The terms of the Quebec bill in its final form were based almost exclusively on the wishes of Canadians as interpreted by Guy Carleton. . . .

NOTES

1. P.A.C. [Public Archives of Canada], C.O. 42/29, 55.
2. Adam Shortt and Arthur G. Doughty, eds, *Documents relating to the Constitutional History of Canada 1759–1791* (Ottawa: King's Printer, 1907), pp. 327, 424, 437, 440; W.P.M. Kennedy and G. Lanctôt, eds, *Reports on the Laws of Quebec, 1767–70*, Public Archives of Canada, Publication No. 12 (Ottawa, 1931). The exception was Thurlow, Attorney General.
3. Shortt and Doughty, eds, *Documents*, p. 537 n.

5 From Gustav Lanctot, *Canada & the American Revolution, 1774-1784* (Toronto and Vancouver: Clarke, Irwin, 1967), 30-5.

The Campaign Against the Quebec Act

Two or three weeks after the adoption by the Continental Congress of the Suffolk County resolutions, with their condemnation of the Quebec Act, news of the adoption reached Montreal, where it created a sensation in the British colony, and especially among the American group. Carleton, who was immediately informed of the excitement, was not quite sure whether the Montrealers had 'caught the fire from some Colonists settled among them,' or whether 'in reality letters were received from the General Congress, as reported.' In any case, Britishers flocked to the Coffee House to hear the latest news. There, encouraged by the American protests, they discussed their own grievances and considered means of redress. A time was set for a later meeting but, in order that their activities might be less apparent to the government, it was agreed that subsequent gatherings should be held 'at the house of a person then absent' rather than at the Coffee House. Further meetings were held and a committee of action was set up. Three members of this committee, Thomas Walker, James Price, and John Blake were 'old subjects' from the British colonies; the fourth was Isaac Todd. Walker assumed a position of leadership and undertook to draw up a plan of reform and to raise subscriptions.[1]

Once the movement had been set on foot in Montreal, the committee moved to Quebec, where it summoned British citizens to meet at the tavern of Miles Prentice. A committee of seven was chosen and instructed to consult with the delegates from Montreal. Several American-style town meetings were held, open to all comers, as well as joint meetings of the committees. The committees decided to thank the mayor and the city of London for their help in the campaign to prevent passage of the Quebec Act. They also thanked the Colonists' adviser in London, Masères, and rewarded his services with a handsome honorarium. Finally a motion was adopted to address petitions to the King, the House of Lords, and the House of Commons.[2]

The petitions, dated November 12, 1774, were signed by 185 citizens. They protested against the substitution of French for British law, a substitution entailing the loss of habeas corpus and trial by jury. They pointed out that Canada's French population was no more than 75,000 and that the number of British settlers, which had now reached 3,000, was constantly increasing. They claimed that the petition presented in January, 1774 in the name of the Canadian people had been 'in a secret manner carried about and signed by a few of the seigneurs, chevaliers, advocates, and others in their confidence, at the suggestion and under the influence of their priests,' and that it had not been 'imparted to the inhabitants in general' who would have been 'alarmed' at such a step.[3] The British petitioners

could hardly have claimed accuracy for their figures since Masères himself had stated, some
years earlier, that an elected assembly 'would be
a representative only of the 600 new English settlers and an instrument in their hands of domi-
neering over 90,000 French citizens.'[4] The three
petitions for repeal of the Quebec Act were forwarded to Masères who delivered them in
January, 1775.[5]

Opponents of the Act did not include all
Britishers in Canada. A certain number of 'discreet persons' declined to enlist in the campaign.
The Canadians, for their part, were unanimous
in their refusal to co-operate with the committee.
Not only had they already expressed 'gratitude
and attachment' to England, but they were now
worried at the efforts of 'meetings and nocturnal
cabals to disturb the minds of people by false and
seditious reports.' For the adversaries of the Act,
urged on by Walker, had been actively engaged
in soliciting signatures among the different social
groups which they represented. The aim of the
petitions, as declared by these spokesmen, was to
protect Canadian lives and property, and to take
from the Governor the power to call Canadian
citizens to military service, to send them and
their families 'up the country among the savages,'
or, if he so chose, to dispatch them to wage war
against the New Englanders. In short, the one
aim of the petitions was to save Canadians from
the bondage into which they were being led by
laws made by the British Parliament.[6]

This propaganda, whose object was to create
an atmosphere of suspicion and alarm, derived a
certain force from the fact that it was dissemi-
nated by presumably faithful and loyal British
subjects. It was all the more dangerous since,
until the appearance of a translation on
December 8, four months after the publication of
the English text, most Canadians had no first-
hand knowledge of the Quebec Act. Leading
Canadian citizens expressed 'indignation and
impatience at being solicited to join in such proceedings.' They were also anxious lest 'some of
their countrymen, under the awe of menacing

creditors,' might have been induced to sign.[7]
While the Governor assured Canadians that
opposition and intrigue would not then or later
bring about any modification of their new privileges, he was also convinced that the government
could not guard 'too much or too soon against
the consequences of an infection, imported daily,
warmly recommended, and spread abroad by the
Colonists here and indeed by some from Europe,
not less violent than the Americans.'[8]

Events were following an inevitable course,
since political agitation was the only weapon
with which the Colonists, whether north or
south of the border, could fight the Quebec Act.
For the Americans, haunted by memories of devastating French raids,[9] and convinced that the
purpose of the new constitution was to mobilize
the people of Canada against the rebellious
colonies, the chief objective was to dissuade
their neighbours to the north from taking up
arms against them.[10] At the same time the protests of Congress and its 'Letter to the
Inhabitants of the Province of Quebec' gave fresh
impetus to the movement in favour of a representative assembly in Canada. Specifically, the
letter suggested a tactical line to be followed in
dealing with the French population, the line of
skilful diplomacy. Following this line, the
Colonists would present themselves as good
neighbours, desirous only of freeing their fellow
subjects from the alleged 'oppression and en-
slavement' which the laws of Parliament sought
to impose upon them.[11] During the last weeks of
1774 and the first months of 1775, the pro-rebel
forces maintained their unceasing efforts to kindle in the common people of Canada a spark of
the spirit that prevailed in the province of
Massachusetts.[12] By the middle of November, the
letter from Congress had been distributed from
one end of the province to the other. English
merchants ranged over the countryside and, on
the pretext of buying wheat from farmers, read
them the letter and incited them to rebellion,
while in the towns Britishers of every stripe
harped on the same theme.[13] Thus town and

country alike were subjected to constant political indoctrination and to an unremitting campaign of anti-English propaganda.[14]

Taking up the ideas of the congressional address, agents spread through the country elementary notions of political theory, and explained the advantages of a form of representative government in which the members, elected by the people, discuss and fix taxes. In short, the campaign constituted a complete social doctrine, illustrated by concrete examples drawn from the local and contemporary scene. To Canadians without experience in public affairs it revealed a whole world of new ideas tending to engender opposition to the Quebec Act and to any attempt to enrol them in the service of England against her rebellious colonies. The Anglo-American propagandists, playing on the theme of fear already introduced in the letter from Congress, repeated insistently that the new Act concentrated all power in the hands of the Governor, who could confiscate land, exile families, or, 'at his own pleasure,' send militiamen to war.[15] They even maintained that, under French law, Canadians would be led like slaves and that '*lettres de cachet* were to be brought into use again.'[16]

They also had recourse to the tax argument, always effective with farmers, and especially with Canadians who, throughout the period of French rule, had remained stubbornly averse to paying taxes of any sort. When the Quebec Act came into force, it was averred, the authorities would impose heavy taxes[17] in order to meet the expenses of the province and to pay the salaries of the Governor, judges, members of the new council, and other officials;[18] and of course they could not fail to increase the duties on wines and spirits.[19] As a last resort the 'Congressists,' as they were called, even attempted, by appealing to the pecuniary interests of the rural population, to foment opposition to the clergy and the seigneurs. Since the conquest, parishioners had frequently protested the rates at which tithes were fixed, and seigneurs had been unsuccessful in their schemes to increase rents. Now, however,

the new constitution would sanction higher rates for both rents and tithes. Thus the Quebec Act would subject Canadians once more to 'the despotism of their ancient masters.'[20]

This active and persistent propaganda made 'a deep impression on the minds of the country people.'[21] One contemporary reported that wicked Englishmen and Americans in the colony had poisoned the countryside and parts of the towns with their talk of some imaginary liberty.[22] For the first time Canadians could be heard discussing constitutional and political questions and talking of liberty and the rights of the people. Disturbed by the campaign of 'false and seditious reports' and the confusion it was creating in the minds of an ill-informed population, the country's leaders came to the defence of the charter and seized every opportunity to point out those articles in the Act which gave complete satisfaction to the aspirations of the Canadian people.[23] Their task was considerably facilitated by the publication of the Act, in French, in the *Quebec Gazette* of December 8.[24]

Shortly after the publication of the translation, a circular letter, signed *Le Canadien Patriote*, appeared in the same paper, and copies, transcribed by students at the Quebec seminary, were distributed throughout the province.[25] Refuting the allegations of the Colonists, the author pointed out that French law brought greater benefits to the Canadian people than did English law, and that it had nothing to do with *lettres de cachet*, prisons, war, taxes, or absolute power for the Governor. Furthermore, these benefits were guaranteed by the Quebec Act. One of the clauses of the Act, explained the *Patriote*, 'not only allows you the free exercise of the Roman Catholic religion but . . . lays open to you all the employments and places of trust in the province. This is the thing that shocks these Englishmen and makes them declare in the public newspapers that the said act of Parliament is a detestable and abominable act authorizing a bloody religion, which spreads around it, wherever it is propagated, impiety, murder and rebellion.

These violent expressions reveal the true character of their authors and show us how deeply they have been mortified at not having been able to obtain an assembly from which they had proposed to exclude you. . . . Should we not make ourselves perfectly ridiculous if we were now to express dislike of an act which grants us everything we had desired, the free exercise of our religion, the use of our ancient laws and the extension of the boundaries of our province? . . . To be sure, these laws do impose certain taxes on liquors. But were there not taxes of the same kind in the time of the French government? And are not the taxes laid upon such articles as are least necessary to our subsistence? As to the proposal of a Canadian regiment, would it not be to the advantage of the Canadians themselves to raise such a regiment?'[26]

NOTES

1. *Constitutional Documents*, Carleton to Dartmouth, 11 Nov. 1774, 586–8. Q. 11, Carleton to Dartmouth, 18 Nov. 1774, 103. Q. 13, List of the principal persons . . . , 1777, 105–6.
2. *Const. Docts.*, Carleton to Dartmouth, 11 Nov. 1774, 588.
3. Ibid., 'Petitions for the repeal of the Quebec Act, 12 Nov. 1774', 589–92.
4. Ibid., Baron Masères, 'Considerations on the expediency of procuring an act of Parliament for the settlement of the Province of Quebec', 257–69.
5. Francis Masères, *An Account of the Proceedings of the British and other Protestant Inhabitants of the Province of Quebec in North America, in order to obtain an House of Assembly in that Province* (London, 1775), 288.
6. *Const. Docts.*, Carleton to Dartmouth, 11 Nov. 1774, 588.
7. Ibid.
8. Ibid.
9. Ibid., Chief Justice Hey to the Lord Chancellor, 28 Aug. 1775, 668.
10. *Journals of the Continental Congress, 1784–1789*, ed. by W.C. Ford (Washington, 1904–1937), I, 105–14. Q. 11, Copy of Intelligence, 2 April 1775, 149.
11. *Const. Docts.*, Carleton to Dartmouth, 11 Nov. 1774, 588.
12. Q. 11, Carleton to Dartmouth, 12 Jan. 1775, 110.
13. Sanguinet, *Invasion du Canada*, 'Témoin oculaire de l'invasion du Canada par les Bastonnais', ed. by H.A. Verreau (Montréal, 1873).
14. *Const. Docts.*, Chief Justice Hey to the Lord Chancellor, 28 Aug. 1775, 668.
15. Ibid., 588.
16. Sanguinet, *Invasion*, 20. Masères, *Account of Proceedings* . . . , 'Le Canadien Patriote', 265. In pre-revolutionary France, the typical *lettre de cachet* was the instrument through which a subject was condemned to banishment or detention in a state prison. The sentence was pronounced and could be revoked 'at the King's pleasure.' It did not emanate from any court of justice and it was not subject to appeal.
17. Ibid.
18. Sanguinet, *Invasion*, 20.
19. Masères, *Account of Proceedings* . . . , 269.
20. *Const. Docts.*, Carleton to Gage, 4 Feb. 1775, 660.
21. Sanguinet, *Invasion*, 20; ibid., 'Journal de Badeaux', 164.
22. Dartmouth originals, A.V. to Mr. Tolver, 9 Dec. 1775, IV, fol. 1607.
23. *Const. Docts.*, Carleton to Dartmouth, 11 Nov. 1774, 588.
24. E Series, Quebec Council, C. II, 281.
25. Masères, *Account of Proceedings* . . . , 265–70.
26. Ibid., 168–9.

6 From Philip Lawson, *The Imperial Challenge: Quebec and Britain in the Age of the American Revolution* (Montreal and Kingston: McGill-Queen's University Press, 1989), 126-9.

The reaction of historians to the passage of the Quebec Act in 1774 has been as chequered as the genesis of the legislation itself. A myriad of analyses, interpretations, and judgments have characterized the writing on this event since the eighteenth century. Contemporary debate on the act has been reflected in scholarship right up to the present day. Opinions cover the gamut of late eighteenth-century feeling towards the legislation, from those in the American school who spelt out the act as the death-knell of liberty to those in England who wished to present the act as a piece of sublime imperial statesmanship and ending more latterly with scholars in Quebec favouring the decapitation theory when assessing the impact of the legislation.[1] In short, treatment of the act has been a reference point for some other historical purpose, whether to explain the flickering light of a democratic spirit in America or the growth of separatist movements in twentieth-century Quebec. The course of such scholarship has not always run true, but, overall, the results have been rewarding—not least in the emphasis placed on a piece of legislative activity by the British parliament that was both unique and crucial to the history of the old Atlantic empire. One facet of this oblique approach to the act that requires revision, however, is the English context to its passage. This theme has been touched upon in studies dealing specifically with Canadian history and the outbreak of the revolutionary war, but its broader significance has not really been appreciated.[2] It is not intended that this narrative will be repeated or reworked in the pages that follow. Instead, it is hoped that some of the mythology surrounding the government's motives during the passage of the act will be dispelled, allowing examination of how the challenge of Quebec obliged the British to think deeply about fundamental constitutional questions affecting their own lives. For if the struggle to formulate policy on Quebec had shown anything since 1760, it was that the domestic and imperial debate could not be separated.[3]

It is impossible to pinpoint a consensus amongst the ruling elites over the Quebec legislation, for, as could be seen in the debates from 1770 to 1773, none really existed. However, there was a genuine spirit of toleration and conciliation motivating those responsible for the legislation, a spirit reflecting a change in the political assumptions that were the legacy of the events of 1688. This shifting view was beautifully encapsulated in the confidence in the English constitution expressed by one member of the ruling classes at the time. To Sir John Eardley Wilmot, sometime chief justice of Common Pleas in the mid-eighteenth century, there was no challenge to which the English constitution could not adapt itself. When reflecting on this point in 1771, he told his son: 'whatever transient storms may arise here, there is an elastic spirit in our Constitution which will preserve it; and though many other climates are pleasanter, yet no part of the earth is, or ever was, blest with a Constitution so admirably fitted and adapted to securing the religious and civil rights of mankind.'[4] Of course, this 'elastic spirit' in the constitution would be stretched beyond breaking point over the next decade, but in terms of the immediate policy for Quebec in 1774, Wilmot's premise proved highly appropriate, and would do so again even after the loss of America. Indeed, this confidence lay at the heart of the government's case for supporting some unique clauses in the Quebec Act. When Lord North and other government spokesmen defended the legislation during May and June 1774, this underlying faith in the adaptability of British institutions and traditions carried the day. The retreat from the principles of religious exclusionism and political ascendancy that would not only secure Quebec's future under British rule but eventually recast the structure of society and politics at home found no clearer illustration than in the public and parliamentary debate on the Quebec Act.

The process began at a most unpropitious moment in relations between Britain and her American empire. After North's government had committed itself to doing something about Quebec's governance in the fall of 1773, news of events in Boston harbour intervened to dash any hopes of a quiet parliamentary session in the spring of 1774. Before the Tea Party it is known that the government intended to bring forward the Quebec legislation early in the new session. In the wake of the American crisis, and demands for a quick response, however, the timetable for the Quebec business obviously had to be rewritten. The affairs of the province were simply pushed down the ministerial list of priorities. This is an important point because it is so germane to controversies that have arisen over the sequential state of British policy in 1774, especially over the Quebec Bill. No new evidence has come to light to suggest that North meant to abandon the legislation for the province because of events in Boston, but he did have to postpone it until the tail end of the session. This postponement, however, became the subject of speculation, with many contemporary observers expressing the opinion that North intended a subterfuge. It was said that the premier had a hidden agenda in this controversial legislation, which he wished to slip through parliament in a period when few people remained at Westminster and criticism would be muted. John Dunning expressed this very fear in a Commons debate on 26 May, declaring that the legislation 'carries in its breast something that squints and looks dangerous to the other inhabitants of that country, our own colonies.'[5] There appeared to be weight in such opinions, because the facts seemed to support the argument. The legislation was passed late in the session with what seemed low attendances in a House containing MPs clearly ignorant of the issues involved. In addition, North also refused to lay all the relevant papers before the Commons when requested to do so by his critics. This defiance was then compounded in the eyes of the government's detractors by the displays of ministerial secrecy in debate. On one important debate over the religious clauses in the Quebec Act on 7 June, for example, the public were ejected from the Commons' gallery in order, it seemed, to restrict information about the question. Even the fact that the legislation originated in the Lords on 2 May has been interpreted as sinister evidence of secretiveness and a failure on the part of ministers and their supporters to deal fairly with the issues.

What can be said to refute such a strong case? The answer must be a great deal. Because of the recent invaluable publication of all the parliamentary debates on the Quebec legislation, it is practicable to revise some of the mythology surrounding this episode and reveal the proper context of the act. To deal with general issues first, attention must be paid to the question of timing. To accuse North of irregularity on this point presumes doubt about the first lord's sincerity in the fall of 1773. But no reason has ever been offered for questioning North's commitment to act on Quebec in 1774, and it is difficult to believe one will arise, for it was certainly not his style to promise something and not deliver.[6] The whole argument about wilful timing of the Quebec legislation assumes that action on this front was tangential, that the government was pushed into it because of the American crisis. Suddenly all the assurances of the summer and fall of 1773 about Quebec's governance meant nothing. Thus was the fallacy of the act as a coercive measure against America developed, with hybrids of that view constantly emerging before anyone who cared to look at the secondary literature on the topic. Even in Lord Donoughue's balanced account of the Quebec Act's passage through parliament, there appears the unsupportable, but characteristic, aside that 'the incipient colonial rebellion probably precipitated the timing of the Quebec Bill.'[7]

Related but more specific points about timing also require revision. Much has been made in studies of this period about the Quebec Act's introduction late in the parliamentary session, with low attendances and limited debate.[8] Yet much of this line of argument is erroneous in the full context of imperial issues in British politics at this time. There had actually been several precedents in recent years for discussing such matters well into June because of an ever-busy parliamentary schedule in the spring. Perhaps the best example was the East India Company business of 1767, on which debate ended on 25 June. The legislation passed in that month has certainly not received the attention that historians have reserved for the Quebec Act, and yet evidence from divisions that took place at Westminster in that session offers a sharp corrective to scholars keen to condemn North over timing.[9] In the Commons on 26 May 1767 a vote to reject government interference in East India Company affairs was lost by 151 votes to 84—anomalous numbers indeed if the equation between late session and low attendance is to be accepted as a hard and fast rule. The debates in the Upper House were more impressive, however. On 17 and 25 June 1767, divisions in the government's favour numbered 73 to 52 and 59 to 44 respectively. These attendances far outshine those in 1774 where, for instance, the Commons vote to pass the Quebec Act on 13 June numbered 56 votes to 20, and that in the Lords on 17 June produced a division of 26 votes to 7.[10] Thus the question is raised: why have historians commented so authoritatively on

the timing of the Quebec legislation and ignored parallel examples? The explanation lies in the fact that timing and low attendances are red herrings, fit only to be discounted by scholars interested in these events.

It is clear throughout this period that subject matter was the determining factor in attendance at Westminster, whether early or late in the session.[11] North himself recognized that lateness in the session could be a sensitive point and apologized for the circumstances that had forced him to introduce the Quebec legislation when he did. Nevertheless, it was not then the controversial issue it has since become for some historians. There were odd complaints over the four weeks or so that the bill was before parliament about lateness in the session and committee meetings, but they should not be taken too seriously. In actual parliamentary debating time the Quebec Bill received more attention than similar imperial legislation of the period. Indeed, several of those attending the sittings in June complained of interminable debate, not lack of it.[12] If MPs had wished to attend the discussions on Quebec, they could and would have done so. The low attendance should not be taken as implying a widespread lack of interest on the part of those at Westminster confronting Quebec's problems. Rather, it indicates that many of the politicians seeking an immediate response to the legislation as a whole faced a philosophical dilemma. They simply voted with their feet when the Quebec business came up.

NOTES

1. For a convenient summary of these historiographical debates, see P.W. Bennett and C.J. Jaenen, eds, *Emerging Identities: Selected Problems and Interpretations in Canadian History* (Scarborough, Ont.: Prentice-Hall, 1986), chapters 4–5.

2. The standard texts follow this pattern; see for example Hilda Neatby, *The Quebec Act: Protest and*

Policy (Scarborough, Ont.: Prentice-Hall, 1972); G. Lanctôt, *Le Canada et la Révolution Américaine, 1774–1783* (Montreal, 1965); and M. Brunet, *Les Canadiens après la conquête 1759–1775* (Montreal: Fides, 1969).

3. A more general exposition of this theme can be found in Lawson, 'The Missing Link: The Imperial Dimension in Understanding

Hanoverian Britain', *HJ* 29, no. 3 (1986): 747–51.

4. J. Wilmot, *Memoirs of the Life of the Right Honourable Sir John Eardley Wilmot, Knt., Late Lord Chief Justice of the Court of Common Pleas* (London, 1811), 166–7.

5. Cited in B. Donoughue, *British Politics and the American Revolution: The Path to War 1773–1775* (London: Macmillan, 1964), 122. For a similar view in the press at that time see the letter from Henry Middleton in the *Gentleman's Magazine* 44: 615–17.

6. The style and character of North's government is evocatively portrayed in P.D.G. Thomas, *Lord North* (London: Allen Lane, 1976), chapter 3.

7. Donoughue, *British Politics and the American Revolution*, 107. Similar sentiments can be found in Hilda Neatby, *Quebec: The Revolutionary Age 1760–1791* (Toronto: McClelland & Stewart, 1966), 140 and Burt, *The Old Province of Quebec*, 2nd edn (Toronto: McClelland & Stewart, 1968), I:169.

8. This trend has been encouraged by throwaway statements in contemporary diaries like Walpole. See A.F. Stuart, ed., *The Last Journals of Horace Walpole during the Reign of George III* (London: J. Lane, 1910), I:353, in which Walpole revealed: 'Much was said too on the production of the bill so late in the session, when some years have been taken to concoct it.'

9. For background see Lawson, 'Parliament and the First East India Inquiry, 1767', *Parliamentary History Yearbook* 1 (1982):99–114; and Bowen, 'British Politics and the East India Company, 1767–1773' (Ph.D., Wales, 1986).

10. *Parl. Hist.* 17:1400 and 1407.

11. This is well put in P.D.G. Thomas, *The House of Commons in the Eighteenth Century* (Oxford: Clarendon Press, 1971), chapter 6.

12. One observer commented on 14 June 1774 that 'ten nights the House of Commons was kept till one o'clock in the morning successively': cited in Donoughue, *British Politics and the American Revolution*, 125.

□ The Loyalists

INTRODUCTION

■ The American Revolution was a great civil war that pitted brother against brother and ultimately sundered the British Empire in America. Not only did the 13 rebellious colonies form the basis of the United States, but exiles or refugees from those colonies (usually called Loyalists) helped enable the British authorities to reconstitute the loyal provinces of what remained of British America as a revised imperial entity eventually to be known as British North America. The first exiles from the colonies were office-holders, wealthy merchants, and Anglican clergymen, driven out of America by the initial wave of hostility to the British.

But the war between the Americans and the British took six years, and ultimately forced large numbers of colonials representing a cross-section of the population to choose to remain with the Crown. That cross-section included many farmers, slaves and former slaves, First Nations allies of the British, and a wide variety of individuals of almost every European ethnic persuasion. These extremely diverse people were given land in the loyal provinces of British America—Quebec and Nova Scotia—and joined the resident populations of those territories (who, ironically enough, were usually not regarded as loyalists) in what became six distinct British colonies and eventually would become the Dominion of Canada.

A combination of Loyalist resettlement and imperial restructuring in the wake of the loss of the American colonies completely remade British North America between 1784 and 1791. The Loyalists provided the experienced anglophone settlers to populate the northern colonies and to be counterweights to the French Canadians in Quebec not available in the years immediately after 1763. A first round of imperial reorganization took place in 1784. Cape Breton was recognized as a separate colony, and both it and Île St-Jean (Prince Edward Island) were put under the authority of the governor of Nova Scotia. Controversy between Loyalist newcomers and the government of Nova Scotia resulted in the creation of New Brunswick as a separate colony in 1784, one that Loyalists could dominate and that could serve as a model of what could be wrought by men and women of loyalty and ability.

That loyal Britons made a reconstructed British North America both possible and viable cannot be disputed. What can be argued about is the influence of the newcomers. The Loyalist impact on constitutions and on the politics, economy, and institutions of British North America was obvious and easily documentable. Their effect on the values and culture of British North America has been more complex and problematic, particularly in later years.

Questions for consideration

1. What does Norman Knowles mean when he writes that the Loyalist tradition was 'invented'?
2. Does this imply that the Loyalists themselves were not historical figures?
3. Why does Loyalist 'diversity' somehow weaken their importance?

Suggestions for further reading

Wallace Brown and Hereward Senior, *Victorious in Defeat: The Loyalists in Canada* (Toronto: Methuen, 1984). Perhaps the best recent general synthesis.

Ann Gorman Condon, *The Envy of the American States: The Loyalist Dream for New Brunswick* (Fredericton: New Ireland Press, 1984). A study of the experiences of 20 members of the Loyalist elite in the new province of New Brunswick.

Barbara Graymont, *The Iroquois in the American Revolution* (Syracuse, NY: Syracuse University Press, 1972). Still the best study of how a number of Iroquois ended up as Loyalists in Canada.

Neil MacKinnon, *This Unfriendly Soil: The Loyalist Experience in Nova Scotia, 1781–1791* (Montreal and Kingston: McGill-Queen's University Press, 1986). A detailed study of the Loyalist settlement of Nova Scotia.

PRIMARY DOCUMENTS

1   The Petition of 55 Loyalists, 22 July 1783, in *Vindication of Governor Parr and his Council* (London, 1784).

The affairs at Nova Scotia and New York went on amicably among the Loyalists till August 1783, when it was discovered that the Rev. John Sayre, with fifty-four other persons, had privately presented to Sir Guy Carleton the following letter:

NEW-YORK, JULY 22, 1783.

SIR,

Your Excellency's kind attention and offers of your support to us demand our warmest thanks, which we beg the favour of you to accept.

The unhappy termination of the war obliges us, who have *ever been steady in our duty, as loyal subjects*, to leave our homes; and being desirous of continuing to enjoy the benefits of the British constitution, we mean to seek an asylum in the province of Nova Scotia.

Considering our several characters, and our former situation in life, we trust you will perceive that our circumstances will probably be the contrast to which they have been heretofore; especially as, from our respective occupations, we shall be unable *personally* to obtain the means of a tolerably decent support, unless your Excellency shall be pleased to countenance us by your recommendation in the following proposals; which are, with the utmost deference, submitted to your Excellency's consideration.

1. That a tract or tracts of land, free from disputed titles, be laid out for us in Nova Scotia, in such part of that province as one or more gentlemen, whom we propose to send forward for that purpose, being first approved of by your Excellency, shall pitch upon for us.

2. That this tract be sufficient to put us on the same footing with field-officers in his Majesty's army, with respect to the number of acres.

3. That, if possible, these lands may be exonerated of quit-rents.

4. That they be surveyed and divided at the expence of Government, and the deeds delivered to us as soon as possible, remitting the fees of office.

5. That, while we make this application to your Excellency, we wish not to be understood as soliciting a compensation for the losses we have sustained during the war, because we are humbly of opinion, that the settling of such a number of Loyalists of the most respectable characters, who have *constantly* had great influence in his Majesty's American dominions, will be highly advantageous in diffusing and supporting a spirit of attachment to the British constitution, as well as to his Majesty's royal person and family.

We have only to add our earnest request of your Excellency's aid and support in carrying this matter into execution, as soon as it shall comport with your leisure; and to assure your Excellency, that we are, with great respect, your Excellency's most humble and obedient servants,

Signed by, Addison, Henry (and 54 others). . . .

2   A Memorial of Samuel Hakes and 600 others, 15 August 1783, in *Vindication of Governor Parr and his Council.*

The Loyalists about this time (mid-August) discovered the art and designs of the Fifty-five: a meeting of them was held immediately; when they agreed upon . . . a Memorial to the Commander in Chief:

> The Memorial of the Subscribers,
> Humbly sheweth,
> That your Memorialists, having been deprived of very valuable landed estates, and considerable personal properties, without the lines, and being also obliged to abandon their possessions in this city, on account of their loyalty to their Sovereign, and attachment to the British constitution, and seeing no prospect of their being reinstated, had determined to remove with their families, and settle in his Majesty's province of Nova-Scotia, on the terms which they understood were held out *equally* to all his Majesty's persecuted subjects.
> That your Memorialists are much alarmed at an application which they are informed Fifty-five persons have joined in to your Excellency, soliciting a recommendation for tracts of land in that province, amounting together to *two hundred and seventy-five thousand acres*, and that they have dispatched forward Agents to survey the unlocated lands, and select the most fertile spots and desirable situations.
> That, chagrined as your Memorialists are at the manner in which the late contest has been terminated, and disappointed as they find themselves in being left to the lenity of their enemies, on the dubious recommendation of their leaders, they yet hoped to find an asylum under British protection, little suspecting there could be found, among their fellow-sufferers, persons ungenerous enough to attempt engrossing to themselves so disproportionate a share of what Government has allotted for their common benefit, and so different from the original proposals.
> That your Memorialists apprehend some misrepresentations have been used to procure such extraordinary recommendations, the applications for which have been most studiously concealed, until now that they boast its being too late to prevent the effect. Nor does it lessen your Memorialists surprize to observe, that the persons concerned (several of whom are said to be going to Britain) are most of them in easy circumstances, and, with some exceptions, more distinguished by the repeated favours of Government, than by either the greatness of their sufferings, or the importance of their services.
> That your Memorialists cannot but regard the grants in question, if carried into effect, as amounting nearly to a total exclusion of themselves and families, who, if they become settlers, must either content themselves with barren or remote lands, or submit to be tenants to those, most of whom they consider as their superiors in nothing but deeper art and keener policy.—Thus circumstanced,
> Your Memorialists humbly implore redress from your Excellency, and that enquiry may be made into their respective losses, services, situations, and sufferings; and if your Memorialists shall be found equally entitled to the favour and protection of Government with the former applicants, that they may be all put on an equal footing; but should those who first applied be found, on a fair and candid enquiry, more deserving than your Memorialists, then your Memorialists humbly request that the locating their extensive grants

may at least be postponed, until your Memorialists have taken up such small portions as may be allotted to them.

And your Memorialists, as in duty bound, shall ever pray, &c.

New-York, Aug. 15, 1783.

Signed by Samuel Hake,
and above 600 others.

3 The Diary of Sarah Frost, 1783, in Walter Bates, *Kingston and the Loyalists of the 'Spring Fleet' of 1783* (Fredericton: Non-Entity Press, 1980), 30-2.

Friday, June 6.—We are still lying at anchor waiting for other vessels of our fleet. My father will come on board in the morning if my husband can go and fetch him. I do so long to hear from my dear mother and my brothers and sisters. We have had a very bad storm this evening. Our ship tossed very much, and some of the people are quite sick, but I am in hopes the storm will soon abate. It grows late as I conclude for the night, hoping to see 'Daddy' in the morning.

Saturday, June 7.—My husband went on shore and brought father on board to breakfast. Soon after breakfast he returned on shore, for he expected to go home in the same boat he came down in, but hearing there was a vessel coming from Stamford today, he concluded to stay and return in it, so he came on board again to dine.

Sunday, June 8.—We are still lying at anchor in the North River. We expected to sail tomorrow for Nova Scotia, but I believe we shall remain at Staten Island or Sandy Hook for some days, or until our fleet is all got together.

Monday, June 9.—Our women, with their children, all came on board today, and there is great confusion in the cabin. We bear with it pretty well through the day, but as it grows towards night, one child cries in one place and one in another, whilst we are getting them to bed. I think sometimes I shall be crazy. There are so many of them, if they were as still as common there would be a great noise amongst them. I stay on deck tonight till nigh eleven o'clock, and now I think I will go down and retire for the night if I can find a place to sleep.

Tuesday June 10.—I got up early, not being able to sleep the whole night for the noise of the children. The wind blows very high. My little girl has been very sick all day, but grows better towards evening.

Wednesday, June 11.—We weighed anchor in the North River about six o'clock this morning, and sailed as far as Staten Island, where we came to anchor. I went on shore with Mr. Goreham and his wife, and Mr. Raymond and his wife, and my two children. We picked some gooseberries. We staid but a short time. In the afternoon I went ashore again with Mr. Frost and several others.

Thursday, June 12.—Nothing seems to be worth mentioning today. We are so thronged on board, I cannot set myself about any work. It is comfortable for nobody.

Friday, June 13.—It is now about half after three in the morning. I have got up, not being able to sleep for the heat, and am sitting in the entry-way of the cabin to write. It storms so I cannot go on deck. My husband and children are still sleeping. Through the day I am obliged to lie in my berth, being quite ill.

Saturday, June 14.—I am something better this morning. My husband brings me my breakfast, which I relish. We are still lying at Staten Island. We expected to sail this morning.

Sunday, June 15.—Our people seem cross and quarrelsome today, but I will not differ with any one, if I can help it. At half-past twelve our ship is getting under way—I suppose for Nova Scotia. I hope for a good passage. About five o'clock we come to anchor within six miles of the lighthouse at Sandy Hook. How long we shall lie here I don't know, but I hope not long. About six o'clock this evening we had a terrible thunder storm, and hail stones fell as big as ounce balls. About sunset there came another shower, and it hailed faster than before. Mr. Frost went out and gathered up a mugful of hail stones. Such an instance I never saw before on the 15th day of June.

Monday, June 16.—*Off at last!* We weighed anchor about half after five in the morning, with the wind north-nor'west, and it blows very fresh. We passed the lighthouse about half after seven. We have twelve ships belonging to our fleet besides our commodore's. Two hours later a signal was fired for the ships all to lie to for the *Bridgewater*, which seems to lag behind, I believe on account of some misfortune which happened to her yesterday. At 9 a.m. we have a signal fired to crowd sail. Again we are ordered to lie to. I don't know what it is for, as the *Bridgewater* has come up. It is now two o'clock, and we have again got under way. The mate tells me they have been waiting for a ship to come from New York, and she has overhauled us. We have now got all our fleet together: we have thirteen ships, two brigs, one frigate. The frigate is our commodore's. The wind dies away. It is now three o'clock, and the men are fishing for mackerel. Mr. Mills has caught the first one. I never saw a live one before. It is the handsomest fish I ever beheld. . . .

Monday, June 23.—It grows brighter towards noon, and the fog disappears rapidly. This afternoon we can see several of our fleet, and one of our ships came close alongside of us. Mr. Emslie says we are an hundred and forty miles from land now. The wind becomes more favorable, the fog seems to leave us and the sun looks very pleasant. Mr. Whitney and his wife, Mr. Frost and myself have been diverting ourselves with a few games of crib.

Tuesday, June 24.—The sun appears very pleasant this morning. Ten ships are in sight. The fog comes on, and they all disappear. We have been nearly becalmed for three days. A light breeze enables us to sail this evening two miles and a half an hour.

Wednesday, June 25.—Still foggy; the wind is fair, but we are obliged to lie to for the rest of the fleet. The commodore fires once an hour. The frigate is near us, and judging by the bells, we are not far from some of the other ships, but we can't see ten rods for the fog. We have *measles* very bad on board our ship.

Thursday, June 26.—This morning the sun appears very pleasant. The fog is gone to our great satisfaction. Ten of our ships are in sight. We are now nigh the banks of Cape Sable. At nine o'clock we begin to see land, at which we all rejoice. We have been nine days out of sight of land. At half after six we have twelve ships in sight. Our captain told me just now we should be in the Bay of Fundy before morning. He says it is about one day's sail after we get into the bay to Saint John's River. Oh, how I long to see that place, though a strange land. I am tired of being on board ship, though we have as kind a captain as ever need to live.

Friday, June 27.—I got up this morning very early to look out. I can see land on both sides of us. About ten o'clock we passed Annapolis; after that the wind all died away. Our people have got their lines out to catch codfish, and about half after five John Waterbury caught the first one for our ship.

Saturday, June 28.—Got up in the morning and found ourselves nigh to land on each side. It was up the river St. John's. At half after nine our captain fired a gun for a pilot; an hour later a pilot came on board, and at a quarter after one our ship anchored off against Fort Howe in St. John's River. Our people went on shore and brought on board spruce and gooseberries, and grass and pea vines with the blossoms on them, all of which grow wild here. They say this is to be our city. Our land is five and twenty miles up the river. We are to have here only a building place of forty feet in the front and a hundred feet back. Mr. Frost has now gone on shore in his whale boat to see how the place looks, and he says he will soon come back and take me on shore. I long to set my feet once more on land. He soon came on board again and brought a fine salmon.

Sunday, June 29.—This morning it looks very pleasant on the shore. I am just going ashore with my children to see how I like it. *Later*—It is now afternoon and I have been ashore. It is, I think, the roughest land I ever saw. It beats Short Rocks, indeed, I think, that is nothing in comparison; but this is to be *the city*, they say! We are to settle here, but are to have our land sixty miles farther up the river. We are all ordered to land to-morrow, and not a shelter to go under.

HISTORICAL INTERPRETATIONS

4 From Rev. Nathaniel Burwash, 'U.E. Loyalists, Founders of Our Institutions', United Empire Loyalist Association, *Annual Transactions*, 1904-1911, 35-43.

The beginnings of a nation or even of a colony are always important. They are as the first track made across a hitherto untravelled prairie; they give direction to all that follows. Improvements may be made afterwards. This crooked place may be made straight, or that rough place avoided, but the direction has been given by the man who opened up the way. The after history of a country lies largely in germ in the manner of life of its first settlers. If they have the capacity to construct a social organism, they will preserve all the good which they have themselves known and enjoyed in the past; they will adapt it to their new circumstances, and perchance even develop it in a new environment to a higher degree of perfection. If they have not that capacity, they will gradually relapse into barbarism. Forgetting or neglecting one after another of those habits and ways of life which make up civilization, their life will become more and more the life of the mere human beast. We have not a few examples

of this in the neighbouring Republic. In the mountain region of Kentucky and Tennessee, and in the upland region of Georgia and Alabama we have such. It appears again at least for a time on the frontiers of the west from Texas to Dakota. In such cases a force from without, either moral or physical, or both, becomes absolutely necessary for the re-establishment of civilized life.

In opposition to this tendency to degrade, we have two important social forces upon which both the preservation and advancement of society depend. The first is the conservative spirit. By this I do not mean a spirit of mere acquiescence, a lazy habit of merely doing as we have done, because we are too careless or spiritless to think of anything better; but the spirit which appreciates and reveres the good that has been handed down to us from the past; which is justly proud of its antiquity; which venerates the memory of those from whom we have received it; and which stands ready to devote both labour and suffering for its defence and maintenance. It is quite unnecessary to say that such a spirit our U.E. Loyalist forefathers possessed in a remarkable degree. It was indeed the inspiration of the great event of their lives. For it they sacrificed all material things. The other force is that genius for organization out of which all civilization springs. Some races have possessed this in remarkable measure. The Romans not only organized their own state and advanced it to a high perfection of civilization, but they established stable institutions and law and order over a vast extent of empire from the Persian Gulf to the Atlantic Ocean and from the Sahara to the frozen North. These institutions they not only planned and perfected, but they also put into and behind them the force which brought them into actual effect. Even after the force which made them effective was broken, the ideals of law, order, and justice were so perfect that they still persist in the states of Western and Southern Europe.

It may be remarked that this genius for organization is generally associated with great physical virility, strong will power, and a sense of order which makes lawlessness exceedingly distasteful and irritating. These are not always amiable qualities in the individual man, but they are of the highest importance in the strength of nations.

Perhaps no race has ever possessed these qualities in larger measure than the Anglo-Saxon. The physical virility of the race is obvious. The stubborn will power of John Bull is famous the world over. His sense of order is not so balanced and mechanical as that of the Celt, not so esthetic as that of Southern Europe, not so scientific, i.e., not so carefully brought out on intellectual lines, as that of the Germans. But it possesses a quality which gives it supremacy over all these. It is pre-eminently practical. It arranges things in such a way that they are convenient for use. It has an infinite capacity for the adaptation of its order to circumstances.

When our forefathers came to this land they came stripped of almost all the material adjuncts of civilization. Their houses were of the rudest and simplest construction; their furniture, primitive and scanty, their bill of fare not beyond one course of the most necessary things. The inbred gentility which could under such circumstances preserve a perfect propriety of manners without awkward embarrassment must command both admiration and respect. Yet such we have seen not only in the old patriarchs themselves, but also in the generation trained under their care. The piety which had no cathedral but the gothic arches of the great elms, no pastor or curate to lead in the devotions of the congregation, no organ to lead and sustain the anthem of praise, no church-going bell to remind the forgetful of the hour of prayer, but which always remembers the Sabbath Day and the morning and evening hours of prayer, is no mere outward ostentation. But such was the religion of thousands who laid the foundations of this Province.

The citizenship which does not wait for the appointment of police and magistrates, but anticipating the needs of society for the enforcement and maintenance of law and order, proceeds at once to make provision for that purpose, is something that springs out of the very heart of the people and indicates not only an advanced stage, but also the highest capacity of civilization. Today we are spending millions in providing for our new territories' Mounted Police and the machinery for the maintenance of law in establishing schools for the promotion of an intelligent and refined life, in supporting missionaries that the influence of religion may be exercised in the founding of the new provinces of the West and North. How was it a hundred years ago when the foundations were laid in Ontario by the U.E. Loyalists? Who sent them and maintained amongst them clergy and teachers, Governors and stipendiary magistrates and police to counteract the dangers of pioneer life? The answer is that very little was done for them; but wonderful things were accomplished by them for themselves. It is to this important historical fact that we wish to call attention. A volume might be filled with particulars. . . .

It would seem that the Loyalists who came from the north were more democratic and had imbibed some of the Puritan ideals; while those of the south, the Royal colonies of Virginia, Maryland and the Carolinas, were more aristocratic in their conception of the source of authority. The Bay country and the St Lawrence were largely settled by Palatines, who had been in New York State for a generation, in touch with the Dutch, and neighbours to the Puritans of Connecticut and Massachusetts, and here we have democratic appointment of the local officers needed for the preservation of good order even in advance of any organization of municipal government by the central authorities at Newark or York.

These two political forces, one from the throne across the seas and represented by the Supreme Officer in the Colony, and the other from the people, have moved forward through our history for more than a century, with many a conflict as to their respective boundaries of rights and authority. Gradually they have been defined, harmonized and united. Their harmonious unity has given us a form of political life thoroughly distinct from that of the people to the south of us. That unity has afforded the people the full enjoyment of citizen rights and the most satisfactory sense of free citizenship. It has at the same time maintained the dignity and authority of law and given to our public order a stability and an efficiency which is neither disturbed nor weakened by the sometimes stormy changes of political life. Such a unity and harmony has been possible because all the Loyalists whether more aristocratic or democratic in their proclivities and habits, were united in their common respect for law, in their love of good order, in their sense of the necessity in any community of such public regulations as will maintain the rights of all; and promote the common good. In a word, these people were a people with a genius for law and order. They had within themselves the elements which in all ages have created civilization. It was a moral impossibility that they should relapse into barbarism and lawlessness. For years crime was almost unknown among them; and when it did appear it was quietly and with dignity repressed, not by Judge Lynch, but by grave and orderly process of law. Very different were such men from those who in our own time and in various ages have escaped beyond the bounds of civilization that they may indulge their lawless proclivities and live in a state of anarchy worse than the lowest savage. These men in the early years of their lonely life passed through a test such as has broken down the steadfastness of the most highly civilized communities. If anything could put honesty and respect for the rights of property to the proof, it was the suffering of 'the Hungry Year.' And yet they passed through that not only with manly endurance, but with the kindly helpfulness of a Divine charity, sharing their last morsel with those who were more needy than themselves. The historian has already chronicled something of their simple yet wonderful story. Some day a Canadian poet will worthily celebrate their praises, or a great novelist will find in their lives the material for the most thrilling romance.

---

5 From Mary Beth Norton, 'Eighteenth-Century American Women in Peace and War: The Case of the Loyalists', *William and Mary Quarterly* 3rd ser., 33 (1976): 386–409.

In recent years historians have come to recognize the central role of the family in the shaping of American society. Especially in the eighteenth century, when 'household' and 'family' were synonymous terms, and when household manufactures constituted a major contribution to the economy, the person who ran the household—the wife and mother—occupied a position of crucial significance. Yet those who have studied eighteenth-century women have usually chosen to focus on a few outstanding, perhaps unrepresentative individuals, such as Eliza Lucas Pinckney, Abigail Smith Adams, and Mercy Otis Warren. They have also emphasized the activities of women outside the home and have concentrated on the prescriptive literature of the day. Little has been done to examine in depth the lives actually led by the majority of colonial women or to assess the impact of the Revolution upon them.[1]

Such a study can illuminate a number of important topics. Demographic scholars are beginning to discover the dimensions of eighteenth-century households, but a knowledge of size alone means little without a delineation of roles filled by husband and wife within those households.[2] Historians of nineteenth-century American women have analyzed the ideology which has been termed the 'cult of true womanhood' or the 'cult of domesticity', but the relationship of these ideas to the lives of women in the preceding century remains largely unexplored.[3] And although some historians of the Revolution now view the war as a socially disruptive phenomenon, they have not yet applied that insight specifically to the study of the family.[4]

Fortunately, at least one set of documents contains material relevant to an investigation of all these aspects of late eighteenth-century American family life: the 281 volumes of the loyalist claims, housed at the Public Record Office in London. Although these manuscripts have been used extensively for political and economic studies of loyalism, they have only once before been utilized for an examination of colonial society.[5] What makes the loyalist claims uniquely useful is the fact that they contain information . . . about the modes of life the war disrupted. . . .

Among the 3,225 loyalists who presented claims to the British government after the war were 468 American refugee women. The analysis that follows is based upon an examination of the documents—formal memorials, loss schedules, and private letters—submitted by these women

to the loyalist claims commission, and on the commission's nearly verbatim records of the women's personal appearances before them.[6] These women cannot be said to compose a statistically reliable sample of American womanhood. It is entirely possible that loyalist families differed demographically and economically, as well as politically, from their revolutionary neighbours, and it is highly probable that the refugee claimants did not accurately represent even the loyalist population, much less that of the colonies as a whole.[7] Nonetheless, the 468 claimants included white women of all descriptions, from every colony and all social and economic levels: they were educated and illiterate; married, widowed, single, and deserted; rural and urban; wealthy, middling, and poverty-stricken. Accordingly, used with care, the loyalist claims can tell us much about the varieties of female experience in America in the third quarter of the eighteenth century.[8] . . .

. . . [T]he fact that the women refugees displayed an intense awareness of their own femininity assumes a crucial significance. The phrases permeate the pages of the petitions from rich and poor alike: 'Though a Woman'; 'perhaps no Woman in America in equal Circumstances'; 'being done by a Woman'; 'being a poor lame and infirm Woman'. In short, in the female loyalists' minds their actions and abilities were to a certain extent defined by their sex. Femininity was the constant point of reference in measuring their achievements and making their self-assessments. Moreover, the fact of their womanhood was used in a deprecating sense. In their own eyes, they gained merit by not acting like women. Her services were 'allmost Matchless, (being done by a Woman)', wrote one 'tho' a Woman, she was the first that went out of the Gates to welcome the Royal Army,' declared another. Femininity also provided a ready and plausible excuse for failures of action or of knowledge. A South Carolinian said she had not signed the address to the king in Charleston in 1780 because 'it was not possible for a woman to come near the office.' A

Pennsylvanian apologized for any errors in her loss estimate with the comment, 'as far as a Woman can know, she believes the contents to be true.' A Nova Scotian said she had not submitted a claim by the deadline because of 'being a lone Woman in her Husband's Absence and not having any person to Advise with'. A Vermonter made the ultimate argument: 'had she been a man, Instead, of a poor helpless woman—should not have faild of being in the British Service.'[9]

The pervasive implication is one of perceived inferiority, and this implication is enhanced by the word women used most often to describe themselves: 'helpless.' 'Being a poor helpless Widow'; 'She is left a helpless Widow'; 'a helpless woman advanced in life'; 'being a helpless woman': such phrases appear again and again in the claims memorials.[10] Male loyalists might deem themselves 'very unhappy,' 'wretched,' 'extremely distressed,' or 'exceedingly embarrassed,' but *never* were they 'helpless.' For them, the most characteristic self-description was 'unfortunate,' a word that carried entirely different, even contrary, connotations.[11] Males loyalists can be said to have seen their circumstances as not of their own making, as even being reversible with luck. The condition of women, however, was inherent in themselves; nothing they could do could change their circumstances. By definition, indeed, they were incapable of helping themselves.

It should be stressed here that, although women commonly described themselves as 'helpless,' their use of that word did not necessarily mean that they were in fact helpless. It indicates rather that they perceived themselves thus, and that that perception in turn perhaps affected the way they acted (for example, in seeking charitable support instead of looking for work). Similarly, the fact that men failed to utilize the adjective 'helpless' to refer to themselves does not mean that they were not helpless, for some of them surely were; it merely shows that—however incorrectly—they did think that they could change their circumstances. These two words, with all their connotations, encapsulate much of

the divergence between male and female self-perceptions in late eighteenth-century America, even if they do not necessarily indicate much about the realities of male-female relationships in the colonies.[12]

There was, of course, more to the difference in sex roles than the sex-related ways in which colonial Americans looked at themselves. The claims documents also suggest that women and men placed varying emphases on familial ties. For women, such relationships seemed to take on a special order of magnitude. Specifically, men never said, as several women did, that after their spouses' deaths they were so 'inconsolable' that they were unable to function. One woman declared that after her husband's execution by the rebels she was 'bereft of her reason for near three months,' and another described herself as 'rendred almost totally incapable of Even writing my own Name or any assistance in any Shape that Could have the least Tendency to getting my Bread.'[13] Furthermore, although loyalist men expressed concern over the plight of the children they could not support adequately, women were much more emotionally involved in the fate of their offspring. 'Your goodness will easily conceive, what I must feel for My *Children*,' Alicia Young told a claims commissioner; 'for myself—I care not—Misfortunes and distress have long since made me totally indifferent to everything in the World but *Them*—they have no provision—no protector—but God—and me.' Women noted that their 'Sorrows' were increased by the knowledge that their children were 'Partners in this Scene of Indigence.' Margaret Draper, widow of a Boston printer, explained that although she had been ill and suffering from a 'disorderd Mind,' 'what adds to my affliction is, my fears for my Daughter, who may soon be left a Stranger and friendless.' In the same vein, a New Jersey woman commented that she had 'the inexpressible mortification of seeing my Children in want of many necessaries and conveniencies. . . . and what still more distresses me, is to think that I am obliged by partaking of it, to lessen even the small portion they have.'[14]

The women's emphasis on their families is entirely compatible with the earlier observation concerning the importance of their households in their lives. If their menfolk were preoccupied with the monetary consequences of adhering to the crown, the women were more aware of the human tragedy brought about by the war. They saw their plight and that of their children in much more personal terms than did their husbands. Likewise, they personalized the fact of their exile in a way that male loyalists did not, by almost invariably commenting that they were 'left friendless in a strange Country.' Refugee men, though they might call themselves 'strangers,' rarely noted a lack of friends, perhaps because of the coffeehouse networks. To women, by contrast, the fact that they were not surrounded by friends and neighbours seemed calamitous. 'I am without Friends or Money,' declared one; I am 'a friendless, forlorn Woman . . . a Stranger to this Country, and surrounded by evils,' said another. She is 'far from her native Country, and numerous Friends and Relations where she formerly lived, much respected,' wrote a third of her own condition.[15]

When the female refugees talked of settling elsewhere or of returning to the United States, they spoke chiefly of the friends and relatives they would find at their intended destinations. Indeed, it appears from the claims that at least six women went into exile solely because their friends and relatives did. A loyalist woman who remained in the United States after the war explained that she did so because she chose 'to reside near my relations [rather] than to carry my family to a strange Country where in case of my death they would be at the mercy of strangers.' And Mary Serjeant's description of her situation in America as it would have been had her hus-

band not been a loyalist carried the implication that she wished she too had stayed at home: 'His poor Children and disconsolate Widow would now have had a House of their own and some Land adjoining to it And instead of being almost destitute in a Land of Strangers would have remained among some Relatives.'[16]

In sum, evidence drawn from the loyalist claims strongly suggests that late eighteenth-century women had fully internalized the roles laid out for them in the polite literature of the day. Their experience was largely confined to their households, either because they chose that course or because they were forced into it. They perceived themselves as 'helpless'—even if at times their actions showed that they were not—and they strongly valued ties with family and friends. When the Revolution tore them from the familiar patterns of their lives in America, they felt abandoned and adrift, far more so than did their male relatives, for whom the human contacts cherished by the women seemed to mean less or at least were more easily replaced by those friendships that persisted into exile.

The picture of the late eighteenth-century woman that emerges from the loyalist claims, therefore, is of one who was almost wholly domestic, in the sense that that word would be used in the nineteenth-century United States. But at the same time the colonial woman's image of herself lacked the positive attributes with which her nineteenth-century counterpart could presumably console herself. The eighteenth-century American woman was primarily a wife and a mother, but America had not yet developed an ideology that would proclaim the social value of motherhood. That was to come with republicanism—and loyalist women, by a final irony, were excluded by their political allegiance from that republican assurance.[17]

NOTES

1. See, for example, such works as Mary Sumner Benson, *Women in Eighteenth-Century America: A* *Study of Opinion and Social Usage* (New York, 1935); Elisabeth Anthony Dexter, *Colonial Women*

of Affairs, 2nd edn (New York, 1931); and Joan Hoff Wilson, 'Dancing Dogs of the Colonial Period: Women Scientists', *Early American Literature* 7 (1973): 225–35. Notable exceptions are Julia Cherry Spruill, *Women's Life and Work in the Southern Colonies* (Chapel Hill, NC, 1938), and Eugenie Andruss Leonard, *The Dear-Bought Heritage* (Philadelphia, 1965). On the importance of the early American family see David Rothman, 'A Note on the Study of the Colonial Family', *William and Mary Quarterly* 3rd ser., 23 (1966): 627–34.

2. Two recent works that deal with family size, among other topics, are Robert V. Wells, 'Household Size and Composition in the British Colonies in America, 1675–1775', *Journal of Interdisciplinary History* 4 (1974): 543–70, and Daniel Scott Smith, 'Population, Family and Society in Hingham, Massachusetts, 1635–1880' (Ph.D. diss., University of California, Berkeley, 1973). Internal household relationships in seventeenth-century New England have been analyzed by Edmund S. Morgan, *The Puritan Family: Religion & Domestic Relations in Seventeenth-Century New England* (Boston, 1944), and John Demos, *A Little Commonwealth: Family Life in Plymouth Colony* (New York, 1970).

3. Barbara Welter, 'The Cult of True Womanhood, 1820–1860', *American Quarterly* 17 (1966): 151–74, was the first to outline the dimensions of this ideology. For writings dealing with some of the implications of the 'cult of domesticity' see Carroll Smith-Rosenberg, 'The Hysterical Woman: Sex Roles and Role Conflict in 19th-Century America', *Social Research* 39 (1972): 652–78; Ann Douglas Wood, 'Mrs. Sigourney and the Sensibility of the Inner Space', *New England Quarterly* 45 (1972), 163–81; Kathryn Kish Sklar, *Catharine Beecher: A Study in American Domesticity* (New Haven, Conn., 1973); and Nancy Falik Cott, 'In the Bonds of Womanhood: Perspectives on Female Experience and Consciousness in New England, 1780–1830' (Ph.D. diss., Brandeis University, 1974), esp. chap. 6. An explicit assertion that women were better off in

eighteenth-century America than they were later is found in Dexter, *Colonial Women of Affairs*, vii, 189–92, and in Page Smith, *Daughters of the Promised Land* (Boston, 1970), 37–76. But two European historians have appropriately warned that it may be dangerous to assume the existence of a 'golden, preindustrial age' for women, noting that the 'goldenness is seen almost exclusively in terms of women's work and its presumed relationship to family power, not in terms of other vital aspects of their lives, including the physical burdens of work and child bearing.' Patricia Branca and Peter N. Stearns, 'On the History of Modern Women, a Research Note', *AHA Newsletter* 12 (Sept. 1974): 6.

4. For example, John Shy, 'The American Revolution: The Military Conflict Considered as a Revolutionary War', in Stephen G. Kurtz and James H. Hutson, eds., *Essays on the American Revolution* (Chapel Hill, NC, 1973), 121–56; John Shy, 'The Loyalist Problem in the Lower Hudson Valley: The British Perspective', in Robert A. East and Jacob Judd, eds., *The Loyalist Americans: A Focus on Greater New York* (Tarrytown, NY, 1975), 3–13; and Ronald Hoffman, *A Spirit of Dissension: Economics, Politics, and the Revolution in Maryland* (Baltimore, 1973), esp. chaps. 6, 8.

5. Catherine S. Crary, 'The Humble Immigrant and the American Dream: Some Case Histories, 1746–1776', *Mississippi Valley Historical Review* 46 (1959): 46–66.

6. For a detailed examination of the claims process see Mary Beth Norton, *The British-Americans: The Loyalist Exiles in England, 1774–1789* (Boston, 1972), 185–222. More than 468 women appear in the claims documents; excluded from the sample selected for this article are all female children, all English women who never lived in America (but who were eligible for compensation as heirs of loyalists), and all American women who did not personally pursue a claim (that is, whose husbands took the entire responsibility for presenting the family's claims). In addition to those requesting reimbursement for property losses,

the sample includes a number of women— mostly the very poor, who had lost only a small amount of property, if any—who applied solely for the subsistence pensions which were also awarded by the claims commissioners. On the allowance system see ibid., 52–61, 111–21, and 225–9.

7. On the statistical biases of the loyalist claims see Eugene Fingerhut, 'Uses and Abuses of the American Loyalists' Claims: A Critique of Quantitative Analyses', *WMQ* 3rd ser., 25 (1968): 245–58.

8. This approach to women in the Revolutionary era differs from the traditional focus on their public contributions to the war effort. See, for example, Elizabeth F. Ellet, *The Women of the American Revolution* (New York, 1848–1850); Walter Hart Blumenthal, *Women Camp Followers of the American Revolution* (Philadelphia, 1952); Elizabeth Cometti, 'Women in the American Revolution', *NEQ* 20 (1947): 329–46; and Linda Grant DePauw, *Four Traditions: Women of New York during the American Revolution* (Albany, 1974).

9. The long quotations: Margaret Hutchinson, claims memorial, Feb. 23, 1784, A.O. 13/96, 601; Eleanor Lestor, claims memorial, n.d., A.O. 12/48, 359; Elizabeth Thompson to John Forster, Dec. 21, 1785, A.O. 13/136, 8; Mary Kearsley, testimony, Apr. 28, 1785, A.O. 12/38, 282; Mary Williams, affidavit, Dec. 21, 1785, A.O. 13/26, 535; Catherine Chilsom, claims memorial, Mar. 11, 1786, A.O. 13/24, 90. The shorter phrases: A.O. 13/16, 271, A.O. 13/24, 357, A.O. 13/26, 357.

10. A.O. 13/118, 488, A.O. 13/67, 234, A.O. 13/73, 586, A.O. 13/81, 59. Men also described women in the same terms; for examples see A.O. 13/28, 215, and A.O. 12/101, 235. The widows of Revolutionary soldiers also called themselves 'helpless'; see, for example, Papers of the Continental Congress, V, 16 (M-41), Roll 50, V. 37, 122 (M-42), Roll 55, National Archives.

11. T. 1/612, 157, A.O. 13/53, 62, A.O. 13/137, 574, A.O. 12/8, 124. For a few 'unfortunate' men see A.O. 12/46, 104, A.O. 12/51, 208, A.O. 12/13, 188, and A.O. 12/42, 132.

12. The women who were most definitely not helpless (for example, Susannah Marshall, Janet Cumming, and Sarah Troutbeck) did not use that word to describe themselves. Consequently, it appears that the term was not simply a formulaic one utilized by all women indiscriminately, but rather that it represented a real self-perception of those who did use it. At least one eighteenth-century woman recognized the sex-typed usage of the word 'helpless.' In her book of essays, Judith Sargent Murray noted that she hoped that 'the term, *helpless widow*, might be rendered as unfrequent and inapplicable as that of helpless widower.' See Judith Sargent Murray, *The Gleaner*, III (Boston, 1789), 223.

13. Isabella Logan, claims memorial, Feb. 17, 1784, A.O. 13/32, 126; Jane Hilding, claims memorial, July 30, 1788, A.O. 13/46, 315; Joyce Dawson to Lord Dunmore, July 24, 1781, A.O. 13/28, 220. Also of interest is Jane Constable to Lords of Treasury, n.d., A.O. 13/73, 374.

14. Alicia Young to Robert Mackenzie, June 6, 1789, A.O. 13/67, 643; Jane Roberts, claims memorial, Mar. 17, 1784, A.O. 13/71, 245; Margaret Draper to Lord —, Oct. 15, 1782, A.O. 13/44, 349; Elizabeth Skinner to commissioners, Aug. 28, 1786, A.O. 13/112, 61. Mrs. Draper lived to see her daughter well married (Margaret Draper to the Misses Byles, June 21, 1784, Byles Papers, 1, 134, Mass. Hist. Soc.). Cf. men's attitudes toward their children and other dependents in A.O. 13/75, 556, A.O. 12/105, 115, A.O. 13/131, 399, and A.O. 13/137, 2.

15. Elizabeth Putnam to Thomas Dundas, Nov. 7, 1789, A.O. 13/75, 309; Elizabeth Dumaresq to Lord Shelburne, Sept. 14, 1782, A.O. 13/44, 429; Elizabeth Barkesdale to commissioners, Nov. 24, 1786, A.O. 13/125, 402, Rachel Wetmore, claims memorial, Mar. 25, 1786, A.O. 13/16, 272. Other comments on neighbours and relatives may be found in A.O. 12/3, 231, A.O. 12/56, 339, A.O. 13/25, 275, A.O. 13/32, 595, A.O. 13/44, 345, A.O. 13/75, 544, 641, and A.O. 13/107, 271. Mr. and Mrs. James Parker had an interesting

exchange of letters on the subject of whether she would join him in England, in which her ties to her American friends figured strongly. 'Tho I would not hesitate one moment to go with you my Dearest friend to any place on earth, yet I cannot think of parting forever with my Dear and valuable friends on this side the atlantick, without many a heart felt sigh,' she wrote on July 24, 1783. His response (Mar. 5, 1784) recognized her concern: 'I realy sympathize with you on this trying scene of leaving of your Country and all our friends.' Parker Papers, Pt. VIII, nos. 26, 31, Liverpool Record Office.

16. Elizabeth Macnair to John Hamilton, Dec. 27, 1789, A.O. 13/131,400; Mary Serjeant to John Wilmot and Daniel P. Coke, Dec. 1, 1782, A.O. 13/49, pt. 1, 283. See also A.O. 13/34, 471, and A.O. 13/70B, 145, on resettlement. For women who followed friends and relatives into exile see A.O. 13/116, 468, A.O. 13/114, A.O. 12//102, 24, and A.O. 13/37, 3.

17. On the development of republican ideology pertaining to women see Linda K. Kerber, 'Daughters of Columbia: Educating Women for the Republic, 1787–1805', in Stanley Elkins and Eric McKitrick, eds., *The Hofstadter Aegis* (New York, 1974), 36–59.

---

6 From James W. St G. Walker, 'The Establishment of a Free Black Community in Nova Scotia, 1783-1840', in Martin L. Kilson and Robert Rotberg, eds, *The African Diaspora: Interpretive Readings* (Cambridge, Mass.: Harvard University Press, 1976), 207-15.

In November 1775 Lord Dunmore, the governor of Virginia, unwittingly committed the British forces to the cause of the American slave in the ensuing colonial rebellion. To enforce his declaration of martial law Dunmore offered freedom to any rebel-owned bondsman who would participate in 'speedily reducing this Colony to a proper sense of their duty, to his Majesty's crown and dignity.'[1] Although the British Empire was still determined to maintain the institution of slavery, and of course slaves owned by loyalists were not eligible to accept Dunmore's offer, yet the belief was born in slave society that a British victory would mean emancipation.[2] This belief was reinforced by Sir Henry Clinton's Philipsburg Proclamation of July 1779 in which he promised 'to every Negro who shall desert the Rebel Standard, full security to follow within these Lines, any Occupation which he shall think proper.'[3] Clinton also indicated that after the war the black troops would receive the same allowances of land and provisions as 'the Rest of the Disbanded Soldiers of His Majesty's Army.'[4]

Thousands of slaves were drawn to the British by the prospect of freedom, and their number was swelled by 'free Persons of Colour' who joined the British out of some motive other than a simple desire to leave a condition of servitude. Testimony given by black loyalists after the war revealed that the overriding motive of the escaping slaves, and one that was shared by the free blacks who became loyalists, was to achieve security in their freedom. In the confusion of war it was frequently easy to desert a master, and many thousands of escapees headed for Indian territory or established free 'maroon' communities in the wilderness. But the ideal of the black loyalist went beyond freedom: it was to become a small proprietor, self-sufficient upon land of his own and secured by British justice in his rights as a subject of the crown.[5]

The British, on the other hand, had no program for the blacks attracted to their ranks beyond their immediate value in putting down the 'unnatural rebellion' of the colonists. Britain's manpower needs were pressing, and, besides the mass of black recruits anticipated as a result of the proclamations, it was expected that the southern economy would break down as the workers deserted it and that slave owners would be forced to leave the war in order to protect their families from vengeful slaves.[6] In success the British command could afford to go without any explicit policy regarding the treatment and status of the black loyalists, but in defeat and retreat decisions had to be made. Arguing that 'an attention to Justice, and good faith, must plead strongly in behalf of the Negroes,' British officers evacuated some 10,000 black loyalists from Boston, Savannah, and Charleston as those cities fell to the American rebels.[7] After the signing of the provisional peace, and the evacuation of New York, a further 3,000 blacks were removed from the new American republic. Informed that 'their past services will engage the grateful attention of Government,' the blacks were carried to the West Indies, East Florida, and London, and about 3,500 were sent to Halifax in the loyalist province of Nova Scotia.[8]

With the free blacks who accompanied the main loyalist body to Nova Scotia in 1783 and 1784 went more than 1,200 slaves, owned by white loyalists and therefore unable to claim the protection of a magnanimous majesty.[9] Though it offered a haven to fleeing American slaves, Nova Scotia was itself no stranger to slavery. Slaves participated in the building of Halifax in 1749, and by the 1770s there were several hundred living in various parts of the province.[10] In a society conditioned to thinking of blacks as slaves, the claims of the free black loyalists for equality were not always to be taken seriously. Constituting over 10 per cent of the total loyalist influx, the free blacks were regarded more as the slaves whose race they shared than as the loyalists whose status they had earned. In the confusion surrounding the settlement of over 30,000 refugees, it was easy to overlook an insignificant group of former slaves.

According to imperial policy, all loyalists were to be placed upon free land in Nova Scotia, the amount depending on the rank and former holdings of the recipient. Ordinary soldiers and refugees were eligible to receive one hundred acres plus fifty acres for each family member. Priority was given to 'such as have suffered most' in the American war, that is, those who had lost the most in property or position.[11] Many whites of low station had to wait two or three years for their land, as Governor John Parr and his beleaguered officials strove to settle the officers and gentlemen, but at the lowest end of this system of priorities came the freed slaves who had lost no large estates or high positions. By the late 1780s less than one-third of the black families had been placed on lands. Even this fortunate minority had waited several years beyond the settlement of the whites; the farms they received, never more than fifty acres, averaged about one-quarter the size of those granted to their closest white neighbours; and they were usually located in the most isolated and least fertile regions of the province.[12]

The procedure established for administering loyalist grants called for disbanded troops from the same regiment, or civilian refugees from the same home district, to be settled together on one tract of land in Nova Scotia.[13] Out of this procedure grew three separate black communities and several smaller concentrations of black settlers on the fringes of white settlements. The largest was at Birchtown, near Shelburne, where over 1,500 free blacks were located by 1784. Of the 649 male heads of family, 184 received thirty-four acres each in 1788.[14] At Brindley Town, on the outskirts of Digby, one-acre town lots were laid out for the seventy-six black families settled there.[15] The third all-black settlement, Little Tracadie in Lower Sydney County (later Guysborough County), had seventy-four families each placed on a farm of forty acres in 1787.[16] Most important of the semi-integrated concentrations was Preston, on the eastern side of the harbour near Halifax, where fifty-one black families gained fifty-acre farms as part of several larger loyalist grants.[17] The newly created province of New Brunswick laid out 121 lots in three tracts for the blacks, but the land was so remote that only five farms were occupied and the other 100 or more families remained around the city of Saint John.[18] About 400 blacks remained in Halifax, and scattered families squatted on vacant lands or sought employment in a dozen other Nova Scotian settlements.[19] The physical circumstances, at least, were therefore present for the development of separate black communities in Birchtown, Brindley Town, Little Tracadie, Preston, Saint John, and Halifax.

The intention of the British government had been that no loyalist should be required to become a wage-labourer in order to survive. Provisions were promised to loyalists, partly as a reward for their loyalty and a compensation for their losses, but primarily to sustain them during their first few years in Nova Scotia until their new farms should become productive and enable them to support themselves.[20] The same confusion that surrounded land distribution, however, affected the granting of provisions. Poor whites were served last, blacks usually not at all. When black loyalists did receive provisions they were often required to earn them by labouring on public works, the supplies never lasted more than a few months, and the quality was inferior to that given the whites.[21] With neither land nor provisions, or at best an inadequate supply, the mass of free blacks was forced to seek some other means of support. Large numbers became tenant farmers, working the lands of white loyalist grantees under a share-cropping agreement. For others only indentured servitude provided a way to avoid starvation.[22] But in the larger centres, such as Shelburne, Halifax, Saint John, and Annapolis, a general shortage of labour created a demand for a pool of day workers. Those blacks settled on the outskirts of such towns were able to hire their skills or their labour by the day, and though at wage rates of eight pence to one shilling per day they were receiving only about one-quarter the prevailing rate for whites, at least they were able to sustain themselves or, if they had received lands, to supplement the produce of their inadequate farms.[23] With most people in the province pioneering their own farms or businesses, the blacks constituted the bulk of the free labour reserve that cleared the lands, laid the roads, and erected the public buildings of loyalist Nova Scotia.[24] Under such circumstances the black loyalists provided a valuable addition to the provincial economy.

Land, independence, and equality were denied the majority of black loyalists. So too was security. Tenant farmers could be moved arbitrarily to a virgin part of their landlord's estate, just after having cleared one area for planting.[25] Five-year indentures were forged to become thirty-nine-year terms, and indentured children were sold out of the province, in America or the West Indies, as outright slaves.[26] Some were reclaimed as slaves, through the courts, by loyalists who disputed the blacks' claims to have escaped from rebel masters, and others were simply kidnapped and sold back into slavery.[27] When economic depression and food shortage struck 'Nova Scarcity' in 1789, jobs disappeared and many more blacks had to opt for indentured servitude or face the prospect of starvation.[28]

Either as war veterans or as loyalists, the free blacks had a right to expect treatment as full citizens. On the one hand they were required to perform the duties of citizenship, on the other their rights fell far short of equality. Those with lands were obliged to pay taxes and serve in the militia, yet they were denied the vote and trial by jury.[29] In addition they often suffered restrictions in their private lives. The Shelburne magistrates issued orders 'forbidding Negro Dances and Negro Frolicks in this Town.' Contravention of the order meant being 'ordered out of their home for keeping a disorderly house.'[30] In Shelburne and Lower Sydney Counties blacks were whipped, mutilated, and even hanged for crimes that, when committed by whites, were often punished by the same magistrates with monetary fines.[31] During the eighteenth century no man or woman of low station could avoid the constant threat of physical suffering, yet it appears evident that for black Nova Scotians, as a group, the threat was greater and more frequently realized than for any others.

In many ways their life as freemen was not altogether different from the life of slavery they had left behind. As sharecroppers, indentured servants, or subsistence day-labourers they were still completely dependent upon white people and subject to the whims and prejudices of their employers. The law denied them equal privileges and services yet expected as much of them as any other resident, and when they strayed they were corrected with greater severity. There was no incentive for provincial officials to help or even allow the blacks to become self-sufficient, for to do so would be to deprive the province of a major pool of available labour.

While the economic climate in Nova Scotia created a peculiar position for the black loyalists, setting them apart from white society as a dependent and exploited class, the social environment of the 1780s set the conditions for their development as a distinct and separate community. Dominant among these social influences was a fundamentalist religious revival then sweeping the province. As slaves in the American colonies the blacks had been discouraged, and sometimes prevented, from embracing the religion of their owners. Most of them, therefore, though probably aware of Christian teachings, had never belonged to a formal congregation.[32] It is possible that this very prohibition, by associating Christianity with the status of freeman, made them anxious to exercise their new liberty by seeking baptism. They may also have been moved by the promise of equality of all men before a welcoming God. For whatever reason, it was the case that religious gatherings of any description—and the revival ensured that there were many—attracted free blacks in the hundreds.[33]

NOTES

1. Peter Force, ed., *American Archives: A Documentary History of the American Colonies* (Washington, 1837–1853), 4th ser., III, 1385.

2. Benjamin Quarles, *The Negro in the American Revolution* (Chapel Hill, 1961), 19–32; Herbert Aptheker, *The Negro in the American Revolution* (New York, 1940), 16–18.

3. New York Public Library (NYPL), Carleton Transcripts, doc. 2094.

4. Public Archives of Nova Scotia (PANS), vol. 359, doc. 65.

5. E.g., PANS, vol. 423, *passim*; PANS, Shelburne Records, Special Sessions, August 5, 1786; British Museum (BM) Add. Ms. 41262B, Clarkson Papers, II, 8–9.

6. Colonial Office (CO) 5/175: Dunmore to Germain, February 5, 1782; G.W. Williams, *History of the Negro Race in America from 1619 to 1880* (New York, 1882), I, 325; Quarles, *American Revolution*, 21, 112; Aptheker, *American Revolution*, 6.

7. Public Record Office (PRO) 30/11/2: Clarke to Cornwallis, July 10, 1780; PANS, Executive Council Minutes, 1777, 343; PRO 30/55/46: docs. 5268 (2) and (3); Quarles, *American Revolution*, 163–7; Aptheker, *American Revolution*, 19.

8. Public Archives of Canada (PAC), MG 23 A2, vol. 9, bundle 344; NYPL, Carleton Transcripts, doc. 10427, orders dated April 15 and May 22, 1783; PANS, vol. 423; PANS, vol. 369, doc. 198.

9. T. Watson Smith, 'The Slave in Canada', *Collections of the Nova Scotia Historical Society* 10 (1899): 23, 32.

10. Ibid., 9; Thomas Akins, 'History of Halifax City', *Collections of the Nova Scotia Historical Society* 8 (1895): 246; PANS, vol. 443, Poll Tax and Census Returns, 1767–1794; W.R. Riddell, 'Slavery in Canada', *Journal of Negro History* 5 (1920): 362.

11. PANS, vol. 349, doc. 33; PANS, vol. 369, doc. 6; PANS, vol. 32, doc. 78; PANS, vol. 33, doc. 3; CO 217/56: North to Parr, August 7, 1783.

12. PANS, Land Papers; PANS, vol. 371, List of Grantees of Land; PANS, vol. 394A, Abstracts of Surveys; PANS, vol. 459, Docket of Land Grants.

13. Margaret Ells, *Settling the Loyalists in Nova Scotia* (Ottawa, 1933), 105; PANS, vol. 346,

Proclamations, March 1 and June 22, 1784; PANS, vol. 369, doc. 6.

14. PAC, MG 9 B9-14, I, 'Muster Book of Free Blacks of Birch Town', 1784; PANS, Shelburne Records, 'A List of those Mustered at Shelburne in the Summer of 1784'; PANS, Land Papers, Raven, Joseph, and 182 others (sic), Shelburne, December 8, 1787; PANS, vol. 213, Council Minutes, February 28, 1788.

15. PANS, vol. 376, 'Return of Negroes and their families mustered in Annapolis County between May 28 and June 30, 1784'; CO 217/63; Bulkeley to Dundas, March 19, 1792, enclosing Millidge to Parr, March 1785; PANS, Nova Scotia Land Grants, Leonard, Joseph, and others, Digby Township, 1785.

16. PANS, Land Papers, Brownspriggs, Thomas, and 73 others, Tracadie, September 28, 1787; PANS, Box of Guysborough County Land Grants, folder 1, doc. 17.

17. PANS, Land Papers, Chamberlain, Theophilus, and 163 others, Preston Township, September 3, 1784, and Young, Thomas, and 34 others, Preston, December 5, 1787; PANS, vol. 370, Names of Original Grantees, February 1784, December 1784, March 1786, February 1787.

18. Public Archives of New Brunswick (PANB), Raymond Collection, 'Return of the Total Number of Men, Women and children of the Disbanded Loyalists Mustered on the River St. John', September 25, 1784; PANB, Colonial Correspondence, III, Carleton to Dundas, December 13, 1791; CO 217/63: 'The Humble Memorial and Petition of Thomas Peters, a Free Negro'.

19. Akins, 'History of Halifax', 103; Nova Scotia Archives Report (1934), Appendix B, 27–61; Society for the Propagation of the Gospel in Foreign Parts (SPG) Journal, XXV, 60–2, 71, 157, 308–9, 340, 358.

20. PANS, vol. 366, doc. 33.

21. PANS, Family Papers, Clarkson's Mission to America, 188; CO 217/63: Bulkeley to Dundas, March 19, 1792, enclosing 'Enquiry into the Complaint of Thomas Peters, a Black Man'; David George, 'An Account of the Life of Mr. David George', Baptist Annual Register 1 (1790–1793): 478; PANS, Halifax County Quarter Sessions, 1766–1801, June 7, 1791; James S. MacDonald, 'Memoir of Governor John Parr', Collections of the Nova Scotia Historical Society 14 (1910): 54.

22. BM, Clarkson Papers, II, 8–15; PANS, Clarkson's Mission, 66–7.

23. Akins, 'History of Halifax', 85; T.C. Haliburton, An Historical and Statistical Account of Nova Scotia (Halifax, 1829), II, 280; SPG, Dr. Bray's Associates, Unbound Papers, box 7, Canadian Papers, 1784–1836, Rowland to Associates, November 17, 1813; Boston King, 'Memoirs of the Life of Boston King, A Black Preacher', Arminian Magazine 21 (1798): 210; CO 217/63: 'List of the Blacks of Birch Town who gave in their Names for Sierra Leone', November 1791; C.B. Fergusson, ed., Diary of Simeon Perkins, 1790–1796 (Toronto, 1961), III, 194, 197–201, 344; PANS, Shelburne Records, General Sessions, September 2, 1784; CO 217/64: Proprietors of Lands to Dundas, May 16, 1793.

24. PANS, Clarkson's Mission, 73; CO 271/68: Howe to Quarrell, August 9, 1797; CO 217/63: Skinner to Dundas, n.d. (received April 1792); PANS, vol. 48, docs. 81, 87.

25. E.g., PANS, Bishop Charles Inglis, Journal, no. 2, book 5, 8.

26. BM, Clarkson Papers, II, 15, 19; PANS, Clarkson's Mission, 197–201; PANS, Shelburne Records, General Sessions, November 1, 2, 3, 1791.

27. BM, Clarkson Papers, II, 8, 22; PANS, Unpassed Bills, 1789, 'A Bill Intituled an Act for the Regulation and Relief of the free Negroes within the Province of Nova Scotia'; PANS, Shelburne Records, Special Sessions, August 25, 1785, August 5, 1786, General Sessions, April 12, 1786, April 5, July 8, 11, 19, 1791.

28. PANS vol. 346, doc. 115; PANS vol. 213, Council Minutes, July 9, 1789; MacDonald, 'John Parr', 51, 75; Akins, 'History of Halifax', 95; PANS, vol. 302, doc. 11; King, 'Memoirs', 209–10; PANS, Clarkson's Mission, 294–5; BM Add. Ms. 41262A, Clarkson Papers, I, Clarkson to

Hartshorne, December 13, 1791; SPG, Dr. Bray's Associates Minute Books, III, Millidge to Associates, October 13, 1788; George, 'Life', 499; PAC, MG 9 B9–14, III, 'From the Overseers of the Poor to the Magistrates of Shelburne', February 3, 1789.

29. FO 4/1: Peters to Grenville, n.d. (received December 26, 1790); BM, Clarkson Papers, II, 15, 21; PANS, vol. 444½, Poll Tax Returns, 1791–1796; SPG, Bray Minutes, IV, Stanser to Associates, November 18, 1811 and October 8, 1812; PANB, Colonial Correspondence, III, Carleton to Dundas, December 13, 1791.

30. PANS, Shelburne Records, Special Sessions, May 12, 19, 1785, General Sessions, July 3, 1799.

31. E.g., PANS, Quarter Sessions, Guysborough County, 1785–1800, October 10, 1787, August 12, 1789, February 8, March 31, August 11, 13, November 3, 1791; PANS, Shelburne Records, Special Sessions, February 24, June 7, 9, 1785, General Sessions, April 12, November 3, 1792; PANS, White Collection, VI, doc. 553.

32. See John Wesley, *The Works of John Wesley* (London, 1872), II, 337, 355; Wesley, *The Journal of the Rev. John Wesley* (London, 1909), I, 350–3; SPG, Bray Minutes, III, July 11, 1785; George, 'Life', 478.

33. George, 'Life', 478; King, 'Memoirs', 157–8.

---

7   From Norman Knowles, *Inventing the Loyalists: The Ontario Loyalist Tradition and the Creation of Usable Pasts* (Toronto: University of Toronto Press, 1997).

The Loyalist tradition occupied a prominent place in the social and political discourse of Upper Canada and Ontario in the nineteenth and early twentieth centuries. Most studies characterize the Loyalist tradition as a static body of beliefs and assumptions carried by the Loyalist pioneers and passed on to succeeding generations. The Loyalist tradition was in fact much more fluid. Shaped and reshaped by the political, social, and economic currents affecting successive generations, the Loyalist tradition evolved with changing concerns and conditions. This study has demonstrated the ways in which the Loyalist past was constructed and remade by various groups interested in the creation of usable pasts that spoke to present anxieties and interests. The multivocal nature of the Loyalist tradition challenges interpretations that portray the commemoration of the past as either an expression of popular consensus or an exercise in political and social hegemony. . . .

The Loyalist tradition was invented not inherited. The original Loyalist settlers of Ontario lacked a well-defined ideology or identity. Mixed motives, ethnic and religious diversity, preoccupation with the everyday work of surviving in the wilderness, frequent relocation, marriage into non-Loyalist families, and the influx of large numbers of American settlers combined to prevent the Loyalists from articulating a unified and distinctive message. All Loyalists, however, shared a common interest in land. It was land that attracted the Loyalists to Upper Canada in the first place or induced them to stay once they had arrived, and it was the right to acquire land that initially set the Loyalists apart as a distinct group. It was during the course of debates over government land policy and American immigration that the Loyalist tradition began to take shape. To defend their claims to such grants, Loyalists greatly exaggerated their losses, social status, and dedication to the Empire. The prolonged debate over the status of American settlers in the province divided the Loyalist population. Many Loyalists welcomed the Americans because of the speculative value they added to Loyalist land grants. Those within the governing elite, however, saw the Americans as a threat to their own power and privilege. The debate over the Alien Question witnessed the first attempt by members of the establishment to portray the province as an exclusive Loyalist preserve. The 'unquestioning' loyalty of the Loyalists became a useful weapon against their political opponents. As the demographic significance of the Loyalist population declined and the controversies surrounding U.E. Rights and the Alien Question resolved themselves, the province's Loyalist origins became increasingly irrelevant to the political discourse of the day. By the 1840s the Loyalists were a distant memory.

A renewed interest in the Loyalist past emerged at mid-century. Economic growth, expansionist ambitions, and sectional tensions combined to produce a growing national sentiment and a desire for a celebratory history of origins that would sanction future aspirations. At the same time, the growth of the state and the need to construct a public out of the province's diverse population contributed to official interest in the production of a unifying and future-oriented past. The anxiety produced by the passing of the last of the Loyalist pioneers, the vilifying treatment of Upper Canada's founders presented in contemporary American histories, and the filiopietism of Loyalist descendants ensured that much of this emergent historical consciousness was focused on the province's Loyalist origins. In 1859 the provincial legislature financially backed the first efforts to collect and preserve historical materials connected with the province's Loyalist founders. The memoirs and reminiscences collected at the time were distinguished by a focus on pioneer conditions, a profound sense of loss and degeneration, an idealization of the past, and repeated injunctions to the present generation to remain true to the legacy of their forefathers. State support for Loyalist history was withdrawn when it became evident that the nostalgic and idiosyncratic vernacular past contained in the reminiscences and memoirs of surviving Loyalists did not meet the needs of official history. A sense of filial obligation compelled Loyalist descendants such as William Canniff and Egerton Ryerson to persevere in their work.

Heavily influenced by the conventions of romance and the works of the American historian Lorenzo Sabine, Canniff and Ryerson produced an idealized version of the Loyalist past that greatly influenced the way in which the Loyalists were portrayed by publicists and promoters in later years. . . .

The popularity of the Loyalist tradition was not simply a product of its political utility. The unsettling change that accompanied urbanization and industrialization stimulated a nostalgic interest in the preservation of a simpler past among an anxious middle class. Concerned about their status and influence in the emerging industrial order, many professionals and white-collar workers turned to history and genealogy to affirm and defend their status, values, and beliefs. Some published filiopietistic family histories. Others joined exclusive hereditary and patriotic organizations such as the United Empire Loyalist Association. Still others sought to erect permanent memorials that attested to the enduring value of history and its lessons and provided a sense of rootedness and tradition at a time when urban growth, the collapse of old virtues, and the appearance of new vices raised serious questions about social order and community in the future.

Local boosterism and commercial considerations further contributed to the interest shown in the Loyalist past. Staging commemorative celebrations, erecting monuments, and publishing local histories became a popular means for communities to express local pride and to assert their place in the nation and its history. The use of history in this fashion often resulted in considerable competition and rivalry as communities promoted their historical pretensions. Much of the controversy surrounding the 1884 centennial celebrations centred on the appropriation of the Loyalist tradition by Toronto interests and the competing claims of centres such as Niagara-on-the-Lake. The past could also be profitable. Celebrations and monuments attracted visitors and tourists, who left money in the tills of local businesses. The proliferation of local and family histories at the end of the nineteenth century owed a great deal to the financial interest of enterprising publishers. As history became increasingly commercialized, the Loyalist past became a commodity marketed by promoters.

Most studies discuss the Loyalist tradition in terms of a single, coherent set of ideas. Although there was widespread consensus about the importance of the Loyalist past, there was little agreement about how the Loyalists should be remembered. The various official histories constructed by different interests to further a particular cause frequently were in conflict with each other and with a popular vernacular past of the pioneer. The controversy that surrounded the 1884 celebrations and the erection of Loyalist monuments and the divisions within the United Empire Loyalist Association highlight the degree to which the meaning of the past was contested throughout this period. The attempts by women and Natives to construct their own histories added to the difficulty of creating a unifying discourse. The very pluralism of the Ontario Loyalist tradition[s] demonstrates that the politics of commemoration are neither monolithic nor mechanistic but rather the product of the complex interaction of a wide range of social forces and conditions. Interests of class, gender, and race combined with local conditions and popular culture to create multiple understandings and uses of the Loyalist past. It is through understanding the power and influence of these 'limited identities' that the social and cultural significance of the Loyalist tradition becomes fully evident.

The Loyalist tradition experienced a significant decline following the First World War. The years after the war witnessed a substantial reduction in the publication of Loyalist history. Commemorative celebrations continued to be held and the occasional monument was still erected, but the events attracted much less attention than they had previously done. Membership in the United Empire Loyalist Association stagnated

and its activities became increasingly social. Canada's wartime experience effectively marginalized the Loyalist tradition. The First World War diluted the intense imperialist and anti-American sentiment that had come to dominate the Loyalist tradition. The horrors of war cooled Canadian enthusiasm for the Empire, increased nationalist sentiment, and resulted in demands for greater autonomy. At the same time, much of the hostility and mistrust of the Americans was eroded in the face of wartime association as allies and increasing economic, social, cultural, and political contact and exposure. Imperialist and anti-American sentiments became increasingly anachronistic as the political debates in which the Loyalist past had been a useful weapon faded into memory.[1]

By the 1920s the Loyalist tradition had lost much of its appeal to the middle class that had been at the forefront of the movements to commemorate the Loyalist centennial and erect monuments and that filled the ranks of the United Empire Loyalist Association. As their initial fears about the consequences of industrialization and urbanization were mollified, members of the middle class turned away from the past and embraced a faith in progress and materialism. Moreover, the utility of the Loyalist tradition as a badge of distinction had been seriously eroded. The transformation of history into a science practised by professionals trained in the critical use of sources undermined many of the assumptions about the Loyalists that had been invented over the past half-century. As the study of history became increasingly dominated by trained professionals preoccupied with the political and economic evolution of the nation, the history of the Loyalists came to be regarded as a peripheral pursuit best left to the antiquarian or filiopietistic genealogist.[2] Although the interest of professional historians in the Loyalist past declined, amateurs continued to do valuable research through local historical societies.

Unlike the legend of the founding fathers in the United States, the Loyalist tradition contained too many ambiguities to continue as a vital influence during the 1920s and beyond. Although the Loyalists were said to have laid the foundations of the province's material development, they were also associated with the reactionary forces that impeded the province's political progress. Moreover, the regional nature of the Loyalist past limited its ability to become the basis of a unifying national tradition. The exclusiveness of the tradition and the portrayal of the Loyalists as a superior, cultured, and an elevated elite further limited its appeal in an age of progressive reform and agrarian populism. The Anglophilia and racial assumptions of many Loyalist promoters alienated large elements within Canada's increasingly diverse and multiethnic population. Encumbered by social and racial pretensions, the Loyalist tradition became an embarrassing part of the nation's past for many Canadians. . . .

The years following the Second World War witnessed a resurgence of national sentiment in much of English Canada. Concerns with the growing economic and cultural influence of the United States resulted in a renewed effort to define and to defend Canada's cultural identity. In 1949 the federal government appointed Vincent Massey to chair the Royal Commission on National Development in the Arts, Letters and Sciences. Included in the commission's terms of reference was a statement of the desirability that 'the Canadian people should know as much as possible about their country, its history and traditions.' Recognizing the need for a unifying national history, the Massey commission recommended that more resources be committed to commemoration and the restoration and preservation of historic sites.[3] In the wake of the Massey report, federal, provincial, and local governments significantly increased their involvement in the heritage field. The celebration of the 100th anniversary of Confederation in 1967, continuing concerns about American domination, growth in the tourist industry, and the sense of discontinuity that accompanied rapid social

change sustained interest in the nation's past throughout the 1960s. As a result, the decades following the Second World War saw an unprecedented increase in the number of historic sites, monuments, local museums, and restoration projects. As Ontario's first pioneers, the Loyalists were well represented in the postwar heritage boom: parks and highways were dedicated to the Loyalists, local museums and plaques commemorated Loyalist settlement, and the homes of prominent Loyalists were restored and designated as historic sites. It needs to be stressed that the proliferation of Loyalist history did not represent a revival of the Loyalist tradition for its own sake but was a part of the larger heritage movement. The search for the elusive Canadian identity, the quest for stability and security during a period of social change and upheaval, and the commodification of the past by the tourist industry combined to maintain an active interest in Ontario's history by the state and the public during the postwar period.

In 1984 the province of Ontario officially celebrated its bicentennial. The 1984 celebrations, like those of a century before, were the subject of considerable controversy. It was argued by some that the whole affair was politically motivated—a costly ploy designed by the government of the day to spread generous grants around the province in a pre-election year.[4] Others questioned the date, insisting that 1791, the year the province was separated from Quebec, or 1867, the year the province entered Confederation, were more appropriate points from which to date the founding of the province. Franco-Ontarians and Natives pointed out that they had been present in the province long before the arrival of the Loyalists two hundred years ago.[5]

The bicentennial witnessed the appearance of a host of new publications hoping to cash in on the renewed interest in the Loyalists. The works were as much a product of their time as the publications of a century before had been. The imperialist rhetoric and preoccupation with social status that characterized the 1884 centennial were replaced by a celebration of the Loyalists' 'multi-ethnic heritage.' In the pluralistic Ontario of the late twentieth century, the Loyalists were reinvented as the nation's first refugees and the founders of multiculturalism. 'In their diversity and heterogeneity,' one writer asserted, 'we can find one origin of our "tossed salad" society with its stress on pluralism and tolerance, as opposed to the American melting pot.'[6] Significantly, such comparisons with American society were one of the few similarities between the 1884 and 1984 celebrations. The 1984 bicentennial confirmed the dynamic nature of the Loyalist tradition. The tradition continues to evolve as the past is reconstructed in the light of the conceptual needs of the present.

NOTES

1. On the eclipse of imperial and anti-American sentiment following the First World War see Robert Craig Brown and Ramsay Cook, *Canada, 1896–1921: A Nation Transformed* (Toronto: McClelland & Stewart, 1974), chap. 14

2. J.M. Bumsted, *Understanding the Loyalists* (Sackville, NB, 1986), 17.

3. On the impact of the Massey report see C.J. Taylor, *Negotiating the Past: The Making of Canada's National Historic Parks and Sites* (Montreal and Kingston: McGill-Queen's University Press, 1990), 131–41.

4. *Globe and Mail*, 12 June 1984, 23 June 1984.

5. *Globe and Mail*, 6 Oct. 1983, 12 Jan. 1984; *Toronto Star*, 8 Jan. 1984.

6. Bruce Wilson, *As She Began: An Illustrated Introduction to Loyalist Ontario* (Toronto: Dundurn, 1981), 10. Also see Phyliss R. Blakely and John N. Grant, eds, *Eleven Exiles: Accounts of Loyalists of the American Revolution* (Toronto, 1982); Wallace Brown and Hereward Senior, *Victorious in Defeat: The Loyalists in Canada* (Toronto, 1984); Joan Magee, ed., *Loyalist Mosaic: A Multi-Ethnic Heritage* (Toronto, 1984).

SEVEN

☐ The Western Fur Trade

Readings

PRIMARY DOCUMENTS

HISTORICAL INTERPRETATIONS

INTRODUCTION

■ The fur trade has received more attention from historians than any other single economic activity in Canadian history. Certainly the scholarly effort often appears disproportionate to the relative economic value of the trade itself. By comparison with the monetary importance of the fishery, or the timber industry, or even wheat production, the valuation of an annual export of furs to Europe was positively minuscule. But the fur trade was less important for its volume or financial value than for other factors. It required an active collaboration between First Nations and Europeans, for example, at the same time that it forced geographical expansion across North America as fresh sources of furs were sought in the interior of the North American continent. Certainly the fur trade was a critical component of the imperial struggle between France and Britain for the control of North America before 1760, and it subsequently played an important imperial role in keeping the northern part of the western half of the continent under British sovereignty.

The fur trade also provides a classic example of the progressive development of historical interpretation in Canadian history. Changes in interpretation are often not so much vertical as horizontal. They do not so much involve the total overturning and replacement of one line of argument and explanation with another as they involve adding new dimensions to the original approach. Economic analysis of the fur trade that dates back to its early nineteenth-century heyday remains just as valid today. What have been added over the years are considerations of other aspects of the trade besides the economic, as the readings here indicate.

Questions for consideration

1. What does the inventory of trade goods from a North West Company journal tell us about the trade?
2. How did Lord Selkirk analyze the western trade in 1815?
3. What was the role of the First Nations in the fur trade?
4. How did the nature of the fur trade change over time?

Suggestions for further reading

Jennifer S.H. Brown, *Strangers in Blood: Fur Trade Company Families in Indian Country* (Vancouver: University of British Columbia Press, 1980). An important study of the fur trade and its family structure.

D. Francis and Toby Morantz, *Furs: A History of the Fur Trade in Eastern James Bay, 1600–1870* (Montreal and Kingston: McGill-Queen's University Press, 1983). A history of the trade in one region sensitive to the First Nations involvement.

Donald Freeman and Arthur J. Ray, *'Give Us Good Measure': An Economic Analysis of Relations between the Indians and the Hudson's Bay Company before 1763* (Toronto: University of Toronto Press, 1978). An insightful analysis of the early fur trade on Hudson Bay.

John S. Galbraith, *The Hudson's Bay Company as an Imperial Factor, 1821–1869* (Toronto: University of Toronto Press, 1957). An institutional history that sees the fur trade in geopolitical terms.

PRIMARY DOCUMENTS

1   From Harry W. Duckworth, ed., *The English River Book: A North West Company Journal and Account Book of 1786* (Montreal and Kingston: McGill-Queen's University Press, 1990), 30, 101, 116–18.

page 60d
Inventory of Goods left at L'Isle a la Crosse in the Hands of
Mr Le Sieur—4 June 1786

5½ yds English Strouds
2½ yds Aurora[1]   do
14 yds Red Strouds
8½ yds blue   do
_____
30½
3 Chiefs Coats
1 Cased Capot[2]
4 Capots 3 Ells[3]
3   do   2½
9   do   2
2   do   1½
1   do   1
4 Mens white Shirts
1 Boys   do
2 Cased Hatts

14 p^r small Sleeves
2 p^r Moyen   do
9 Skaines Worsted
16 Rom as Hhdss[4]
4 p^s Gartering
15^{li} large Brass Wire
4^{li} small   do
1 doz: Japan'd Boxes wt
Glasses[5]
3 Spring Tobaco   do[6]
3 Bunches Beads
8½ Groce Thimbles
[blank] Hawks Bells[7]
7 doz: Gunworms
38 fire Steels
36 Gun flints

Continued

page 61
Inventory of Goods left at L'Isle a la Crosse con^d—

1 large Nattataned [?] Coleur[8]
1 small   do   do
1 pr Nons aprituss
7 doz: Box wood Combs
11 Horn Combs
1 doz Ivory Combs
10 doz large Knives
12 doz + 4 small   do
2 Cartouche   do
10 Buck handled knives
19 Doz: Rings
3 Pr Scizzars
1 doz: Stone Crosses[9]
8^{li} Vermillion
½^{li} Cotton Wick
1 Groce Awls

12 yds Lace
14 files (7 of which Damaged)
1 Round —
5 p^r Arm Bands
6 fine plain Dagues[10]
28 maces B Corn Beads[11]
2 Tin Basons
5 Plain Dags[12]
4 Battle Axes
1 Blkt 2½ Points
2   do   2 —
1   do   1 —
5 packs Cards —
1 Stock Lock —
1 Poudre Horn —

Continued

The Account Book
pages 47d–48

Dr Francois Raimond   Devant
1785

July 29	To Balance from last years Book	288
Augt 6	To Sund^{ies} at L. La Pluis P. Blotter	369
1786		
June	To Amt of your acct P A. Book	462
	To amunition & 1½ fath^m Tob° Isle a la Cross	50

	To Passage of your Woman	<u>100</u>
		<u>1269</u>
	To Balance due by you	341
Contra		
1786		
June 1	By so much to your Cr P Araba Bk	28
	By one years Wages	900
	By Balance due by you	<u>341</u>
	Lvs	1269

Pages 20d–21

Dr Francois Le Blan [Leblanc]   devant

1785		
July 29	To Balance from last years Book	182
Augt 6	To Sund^{ies} at Lac la Pluis p Blotter	347
	To 1 Tobacco Box at do	6
	To Sundries on the road p Blotter	62
1786		
May 30	To 2 Meas. Powder & Balls for Isle Crosse	24
	To 1 fath^m Tob°	20
	To amt of your acct at Lac La Ronge	78
June 1	To Balance due you	<u>81</u>
	Lvs	800
*July**	*To Francois Monette* *80*	
	To Balce *<u>1</u>*	
	81	
Contra		
1786		
June 1	By one years Wages	<u>800</u>
	Lvs	800
	By Balance due you	<u>81</u>
	By Balce	*<u>1</u>*

* Italicized entries were added later than the main entries, but in the same hand.

NOTES

1. Aurora, 'a rich orange colour, as of the sky at sunrise' (*OED*, noted 1791).
2. 'Cas'd' or 'cased', also used in connection with hats, may mean 'lined'; cf. 'cased cats', wildcat skins taken off the animal in such a way that the fur was inside. [Ed.: A 'capot' is 'a long coat with a hood, esp. (in Canada) tied with a colourful sash' (*Oxford Canadian Dictionary*).]
3. These would have been cloth. The ell (French *aune*) measured 45 inches in England (*OED*) and 1.188 metres or 46½ inches in France and French Canada, and *capots* varying from 4½ *aunes* to 1½ *aunes* appear in inventories. Although the width of these garments is not specified, the largest *capots* would have been very large indeed

and, like the Scotsman's plaid, useful when sleeping in the open air.

4. An uncertain reading, which could mean 'rum as hogsheads', although the amount of spirits implied is very large, and actual hogsheads (of 52½ imperial gallons) would never have been portaged. In another inventory 120 gallons of *double force* rum was contained in 14 barrels (Hudson's Bay Company Archives, F.4/1,3), for an average content of 8.57 gallons and weight of almost 86 pounds plus the keg—a typical 'piece' of ninety pounds.

5. Japanned boxes containing looking glasses (mirrors) or perhaps drinking tumblers.

6. Tobacco boxes presumably with spring-closed lids.

7. The smallest size of bells in the trade, and the commonest traded. The Hudson's Bay Company's Athabasca outfit for 1820–1 listed 2,000 hawks bells, and also 60 dogs bells and 58 horses bells.

8. This item defeats me. 'Nattataned' could just as easily be read 'Nallataned' or 'Nattalaned'; 'Coleur' is probably collar.

9. This may have been the North West Company's contribution to religion in the wilderness.

10. Probably *dag*, 'a kind of heavy pistol or hand-gun formerly in use' (*OED*), though it could also be for *dagger*.

11. These beads were the same as 'Beads barley corn', so called because of their size, which are listed in the Hudson's Bay Company's Moose Fort standard of trade for 1784, and in other inventories.

12. See note 10.

2 From Lord Selkirk, *A Sketch of the British Fur Trade* (1815), in J.M. Bumsted, ed., *The Collected Writings of Lord Selkirk 1810–1820*, vol. 2, *Writings and Papers of Thomas Douglas, Fifth Earl of Selkirk* (Winnipeg: Manitoba Record Society, 1987), 48–55.

I. Remarks on the respective systems adopted in Canada prior and subsequent to the Cession of that Colony to Great Britain.—General View of the Canadian Fur Trade.—Origin and Constitution of the North-West Company of Montreal.

The commercial benefits which were expected to accrue from the Fur Trade in Canada, formed the principal object in the original settlement of that colony.[1] For a long period that branch of trade furnished the chief employment of the colonists; but of late years the progress of population, and the increase of wealth, have given rise to other and more valuable branches of traffic.[2] The Fur Trade, however, still constitutes an important branch of Canadian commerce. An inquiry into the principles on which this trade has been conducted may be interesting, in many respects, not only to those who are connected with the colony, but to all who have turned their attention to the commercial resources, and colonial prosperity, of the British Empire: and the inquiry may be the more important, because the mode in which the Fur Trade is conducted does not appear to be generally understood, or justly appreciated, even in Canada.

While that province was in the possession of France, the Fur Trade was carried on under a system of exclusive privileges.[3] In each district of country, or nation of Indians, a licence was granted by the governor of the province, assigning to some favoured individuals the privilege of trading within the prescribed limits. The persons who obtained these privileges were generally officers of the army, or others of respectable family connection. Whatever were the motives in which this system originated, there can be no doubt that it contributed, in a very great degree, to the main object of the French government in their transactions with the Indian nations of America: *viz.* to establish and extend their political influence.[4] Whoever possessed the exclusive trade of a district was the only person to whom the Indians could apply for such articles as an intercourse with Europeans had introduced among them; and, independent of the ordinary transactions of barter, the natives had frequently occasion to solicit favours which they could only expect from the indulgence of the privileged traders. These were generally men of liberal education, who knew how to promote the views of government; and they had the greater anxiety on this head, as it was well known that if any of them abused their privileges, or otherwise failed in promoting the general objects expected from them, their exclusive rights would be withdrawn. The conduct of the traders was at the same time closely watched by the Missionaries, whose anxious attention was directed to prevent the abuses which had been found to arise from the sale of spirituous liquors among the savages; an object in which they appear to have been in general zealously seconded by the Provincial Government.[5]

This system appears to have been wisely adapted to increase the comforts, and improve the character, of the natives; as a proof of which, we need only compare the present state of the Indians in Canada, with that in which they stood immediately after the conquest of that province by Great Britain, at which period populous villages existed in many districts, where at present we meet only two or three wandering families, and these addicted to the most brutal excesses, and a prey to want and misery.

A few years after the conquest of Canada, the former system of traffic with the Indians was laid aside, as inconsistent with the received principles of freedom of trade; and, with the exception of one district, no more exclusive privileges were granted. After the trade was thrown open to the public, the first adventurers who arrived in the Indian country made very large profits, and this circumstance soon gave rise to a keen commercial competition, the result of which, however, was very different from that which would have taken place in a civilized country, where the effect of rivalship tends only to compel the trader to supply his customers with better goods, and on more reasonable terms.[6] Among the Indians it was found that a profuse supply of spirituous liquors was a shorter and more certain mode of obtaining a preference, than any difference in the quality or price of the goods offered for sale.[7] The ungovernable propensity of the Indians to intoxication is well known, and it is easy to imagine the disorders which would arise, when this propensity was fostered by unbounded temptation. But, to comprehend the full extent of the mischief, it must be recollected, that these rival traders were scattered over a country of immense extent, and at such a distance from all civil authority, as to lead them to believe that the commission of almost any crime would pass with impunity. In such a situation every art which malice could devise was exerted without restraint, and the intercourse of the traders with each other partook more of the style of the savages by whom they were surrounded, than of the country from which they had sprung. The only difference was that their ferocity was mixed with a greater portion of cunning. Direct personal violence was perhaps seldom resorted to, because it was more easy to succeed when the object was disguised, and effected through the agency of the Indians. Those of the natives who had formed a connection with one trader might be led by him to believe the most atrocious calumnies of another, and to credit the most absurd tales of his hostile and wicked designs; and, under the influence of continued intoxication, there was no pitch of fury to which an Indian might not be roused, nor any act of ferocity which he might not be impelled to commit. Mr. Henry, one of the first British subjects who engaged in the Canadian Fur Trade, in the very interesting account which he has published of his Travels and Adventures, observes, that on his arrival at the Grand Portage on Lake Superior, in the year 1775, 'he found the traders in a state of extreme reciprocal hostility, each pursuing his own interests in such a manner as might most injure his neighbour. The consequences,' he adds, 'were very hurtful to the morals of the Indians.' (*Page 239*).[8] The same facts are stated more at large by Sir Alexander M'Kenzie, who, in his Account of the Fur Trade, (prefixed to his Voyage through North America,) states, that 'this trade was carried on in a very distant country, out of the reach of legal restraint, and where there was a free scope given to any ways or means in attaining advantage. The consequence was, not only the loss of commercial benefit to the persons engaged in it, but of the good opinion of the natives, and the respect of their men, who were inclined to follow their example; so that with drinking, carousing, and quarrelling with the Indians along their route, and among themselves, they seldom reached their winter quarters; and if they did, it was generally by dragging their property upon sledges, as the navigation was closed up by the frost. When, at length, they were arrived, the object of each was to injure his rival traders in the opinion of the natives as much as was in their power, by misrepresentation and presents, for which the agents employed were peculiarly calculated. They considered the command of their employer as binding on them, and however wrong or irregular the transaction, the responsibility rested with the principal who directed them:—this is Indian law.' (*Page x.*)[9] The agents here alluded to, were the Coureurs des Bois, whom the Author had previously described, (*page ii.*) as French Canadians, who, by accompanying the natives on their hunting and trading excursions, had become so attached to the Indian mode of life, that they had lost all relish for their former habits, and native homes. Of these people the Author remarks, that they often brought home rich cargoes of furs, but that during the short time requisite to settle their accounts with the merchants, and procure fresh credit, they generally contrived to squander away all their gains. He adds, that 'this indifference about amassing property, and the pleasure of living free from all restraint, soon brought on a licentiousness of manners, which could not long escape the vigilant observation of the missionaries, who had much reason to complain of their being a disgrace to the christian religion, by not only swerving from its duties themselves, but by thus bringing it into disrepute with those of the natives who had become converts to it.' Sir Alexander M'Kenzie goes on to state, that from this conduct of the traders and their servants, the winter was passed among them in a continual scene of disagreement and quarrels; that the natives could entertain no respect for persons who conducted themselves with so much irregularity and deceit; that from the consequences of this licentious conduct, the traders were in continual alarm, and frequently laid under contribution by the Indians,—in short, that matters were daily becoming worse and worse, so that the merchants who furnished the traders with goods, and participated in their adventures, became disgusted with their ill success, and were with difficulty persuaded to continue their advances. The same Author specifies a few individuals, who, from greater precaution and good sense, were more successful than others, but observes, that these partial advantages 'could not prevent the people of Canada from seeing the improper conduct of some of their associates, which rendered it dangerous to remain any longer among the natives. Most of them who passed the winter at the Saskatchawan, got to the Eagle Hills, where, in the spring of the year 1780, a few days previous to their intended departure, a large band of Indians, being engaged in drinking about their houses, one of the traders, to ease himself of the troublesome importunities of a native, gave him a dose of laudanum in a glass of grog, which effectually prevented him from giving further trouble to any one, by setting him asleep for ever. This accident produced a fray, in which one of the traders and several of the men were killed, while the rest had no other means to save themselves but by a precipitate flight, abandoning a considerable quantity of goods, and near half the furs which they had collected during the winter and spring. About the same time, two of the establishments on the Assiniboin River were attacked with less justice, when several white men and a greater number of Indians were killed. In short, it appeared that the natives had formed a resolution to extirpate the traders; and, without entering into any further reasonings on the subject, it appears to be incontrovertible, that the irregularity pursued in carrying on the trade has brought it into its present forlorn situation.' (*Page xiii, xiv.*) 'The traders,' he adds, 'were saved from the indignation of the natives, only by the ravages of the small pox, which at this period spread among the Indians like a pestilence, and almost depopulated the country. By this calamity, the traders were rescued from personal danger, but the source of their profits was cut off, and very few peltries were to be obtained. Even such of the natives as escaped the contagion, were so alarmed at the surrounding destruction, that they were dispirited from hunting, except for their own subsistence.' In this deplorable state of things, it is not wonderful that the traders should have been (as the Author states) very much reduced in number, and that the merchants in Canada, who supported them, having foreseen that the continuance of such proceedings would be altogether fatal to their interests, should have been inclined to form a junction for carrying on the trade in partnership. Accordingly, during the winter 1783–4, these merchants formed an Association under the name of The North-West Company, in which the leading persons were Messrs. B. and J. Frobisher, and Mr. Simon M'Tavish, by whose influence chiefly the coalition had been brought about. The main principle of the arrangement was that the separate capitals of the several traders were to be thrown into a common stock, in consideration of which, each individual held a proportionable share of the combined adventure. In the arrangement of this co-partnership, difficulties were found, from the claims of some individuals (chiefly Messrs. Pangman and Gregory), who were not satisfied with the shares assigned to them, and who, refusing to concur in the coalition, continued to carry on a separate trade. This retarded for some time the formation of a general union, and, after that was effected, it was again dissolved by differences of a similar nature. This led, in the year 1798, to a great secession from the North-West Company, and to the formation of a New Company (known in Canada by the name of The X.Y. Company), which traded for some years in competition with the former establishment. A coalition, however, was at length effected between these rival bodies in the year 1805, at which time the North-West Company took its present shape.—The means by which this Association acquired a preponderance which has enabled the Company to secure to themselves so extensive and lucrative a trade, will be found well deserving of public attention.[10]

After the junction of the Old and New North-West Companies, the whole concern came to be divided into a hundred shares, of which a considerable proportion is held by the mercantile houses in London or Montreal, which had contributed the capital for the companies; and other shares are held by individuals who are termed *wintering partners,* and who take upon themselves the charge of managing the affairs of the Company in the interior. Of seventy-five shares assigned to the Old Company, thirty are held by one house at Montreal, the successors of those who planned the original coalition in 1783. Of twenty-five assigned to the New Company, eighteen or nineteen are appropriated to the different houses in Montreal or London, which had contributed a capital for the undertaking. All the remaining shares are distributed among the wintering partners, some of whom possess one share, and some two. The partners hold a general meeting every summer, at the rendezvous at Fort William, at the Grand Portage on Lake Superior, where all matters are decided by a majority of votes, every share giving one vote, and the absentees voting by proxy. At this meeting, the operations to be carried on during the succeeding year are arranged, and the station to be assigned to each individual is determined; the accounts of the former year are settled; and every partner brings a statement of the transactions of the department which has been under his charge.

When a wintering partner has served for a certain number of years, he is at liberty to retire from the concern; and, without doing any further duty, to receive not only his share of the capital of the Company, but also, for seven years, to draw one-half of the profits of the share which he had held. Upon his retiring, the vacancy is filled up by the election of a new partner. The candidates for this situation must have served the Company for a certain number of years as clerks, of whom a great number are employed under the direction of the wintering partners, and are entrusted with the command and immediate management of one or more trading posts situated in the interior. The election of a new partner is decided, like the other affairs of the Company, by the majority of votes at the general annual meeting of the partners: and, as the conduct of the new partner may affect in a material degree the personal interest of every one who has a right to vote in the election, it is not likely that the choice should fall upon a person destitute of those qualifications which are considered requisite for promoting the common interest. No candidate can have much chance of success, unless he be well acquainted with the nature of the trade, the character and manners of the Indians, and the mode of acquiring influence with them. He must also be of an active disposition, and likely to pursue with perseverance and vigour any object that can tend to promote the interest of the Company. The hope of obtaining the envied station of a partner, being kept alive among all the senior clerks, excites among them an activity and zeal for the general interests of the concern, hardly inferior to that of the partners themselves. They act under the immediate inspection of those who have a direct interest in the result of their management, and are sensible that all their ability must be exerted to secure the favour of their superiors. Every wintering partner watches closely the conduct of the clerks who are under his immediate command; he is excited to this vigilance, not merely by the common interest in which he participates as a partner, but also by feelings of personal responsibility. He comes to the general meeting to give an account of the transactions of his department; and the praise or the censure of his associates is dealt out to him, in proportion to the profit or loss which has occurred in the trade under his direction, and to the success, or failure, of the plans entrusted to his management.

Nothing certainly could be devised more admirably calculated than this system, to infuse activity into every department of so extensive a concern, and to direct that activity, in the most effectual manner, and with complete unity of purpose, towards the common interest. But however much this community of interest among all the partners, and the responsibility thus imposed upon each individual, tend to keep alive an active attention to the Company's affairs, it must be admitted that they are by no means calculated to produce much respect for the rights of others:—On the contrary, the very nature of the Association, and the extensive range which their operations embrace, cannot fail to produce an *esprit de corps* not very consistent with the feelings of propriety and justice.—This observation will be found particularly applicable to the wintering partners. In the common intercourse of civilized society the necessity of maintaining a fair character in the estimation of the public forms a continued check to that inordinate stimulus of self-interest which too often causes individuals to deviate from the principles of honour and honesty. But a wintering partner of the North-West Company is secluded from all society, except that of persons who have the same interests with himself; and if, in the pursuit of these, he should be induced to violate the rules of justice, he must feel that he is not likely to be judged with extreme rigour by the only persons for whose approbation he is solicitous. The civilized world is at so great a distance, that he cannot be very deeply affected by the chance of his conduct meeting with public reprobation; and he naturally flatters himself that his proceedings will never be investigated, or that if they should, there are so many persons to share in the responsibility, that it cannot fall very heavily on himself. In these remote situations, the restraints of law cannot operate as in the midst of a regular society.—When a plaintiff has to travel thousands of miles to find the court from which he is to seek redress, and when witnesses are to be brought from such a distance, at a vast expense, and to the total interruption of their ordinary pursuits, it must be a case of extraordinary importance, which would induce even a wealthy man to encounter the difficulty of obtaining it.[11] Every wintering partner, therefore, must naturally be aware of the extent of his power over individuals who are not rich enough to contend with the whole Association of which he is a member; and if under these circumstances, acts of injustice and oppression be committed against weaker neighbours, however greatly they are to be regretted, they cannot form a subject of much surprize.

Thus, from the very nature and organization of the Company, a conclusion may reasonably be drawn as to the line of conduct which they are most likely to pursue. That indeed may be varied in a certain degree by the personal character of the individuals at the head of the concern; but even supposing that these were men of the most honourable principles, and incapable of countenancing a systematic violation of justice, it would be with the greatest difficulty that they could restrain this tendency in others.

NOTES

Editor's note: The reference numbers in the text are Selkirk's page references to the original books.

1. Modern scholars might dispute Selkirk's assertion here; see, for example, Marcel Trudel, *The Beginnings of New France 1524–1663* (Toronto, 1973).

2. In general, see Fernand Ouellet, *Social and Economic History of Quebec, 1760–1850* (Toronto, 1980).

3. For a general description of the workings of the French fur trade, see Harold A. Innis, *The Fur Trade in Canada* (rev. ed., Toronto, 1956). But consult also William J. Eccles, 'A Belated Review of Harold Adams Innis's *The Fur Trade in Canada*', *Canadian Historical Review* 60 (1979): 419–44.

4. Most modern scholars would agree that Selkirk here overemphasizes the extent to which the French were able to exercise their monopoly through licensing.

5. Again, Selkirk overemphasizes the success of the government in controlling matters, especially in the so-called Brandy Trade. See, for example, J.E. Lunn, 'The Illegal Fur Trade Out of New France, 1713–1760', *Canadian Historical Association Annual Report* (1939): 61–76.

6. For modern scholarly accounts of the changes in the fur trade after 1763, consult E.E. Rich, *The Fur Trade and the Northwest to 1857* (Toronto, 1967), 130–85; Arthur J. Ray, *Indians in the Fur Trade: their role as hunters, trappers and middlemen in the lands southwest of Hudson Bay 1660–1870* (Toronto, 1974), 94 ff.

7. For recent analyses, see Ray, *Indians in the Fur Trade*, and Arthur J. Ray and Donald Freeman, *'Give Us Good Measure': An Economic Analysis of Relations between the Indians and the Hudson's Bay Company before 1763* (Toronto, 1978), 192–7.

8. Alexander Henry, *Travels and Adventures in Canada and the Indian Territories between the years 1760 and 1776* (New York, 1809).

9. Alexander Mackenzie, *Voyages from Montreal, on the River St. Laurence, through the Continent of North America, to the Frozen and Pacific Oceans; in the Years 1789 and 1793; With a Preliminary Account of the Rise, Progress, and Present State of the Fur Trade of that Country . . .* (London, 1801).

10. For the North West Company, see Marjorie Wilkins Campbell, *The North West Company* (Vancouver, 1983); Gordon Charles Davidson, *The North West Company* (New York, 1967); W. Stewart Wallace, ed., *Documents Relating to the North West Company* (Toronto, 1934); L.R. Masson, ed., *Les bourgeois de la Compagnie du Nord-Ouest . . .* (Quebec, 1889–1890).

11. The British government attempted to deal with these questions in 1803 with the passage of the so-called Canada Jurisdictions Act, which made the courts of Upper and Lower Canada responsible for the obtaining of justice in the western territories. This legislation, of course, became one of the major bones of contention between the Hudson's Bay Company (which denied that the act applied to territory in their charter) and the North West Company backed by the Canadian government (which insisted the act did apply). In general, see A.S. Morton, 'The Canada Jurisdiction Act and the North-West', *Transactions Royal Society of Canada* 3rd ser., 32 (1938): 121–38.

HISTORICAL INTERPRETATIONS

3 From Harold A. Innis, *The Fur Trade in Canada: An Introduction to Canadian Economic History* (New Haven: Yale University Press, 1930), 254–61.

Stress on the importance of the individual trader was accompanied by concentration in the external business of the company as conducted by the supply houses of Montreal and England shown in the growth of McTavish, Frobisher & Company. On April 15, 1787, Benjamin Frobisher of the firm of B. & J. Frobisher, died, and in the same month in a letter dated at Montreal, McTavish suggested[1] an arrangement by which the formation of a partnership would insure control over the Northwest trade and prevent opposition, especially from Gregory of the firm of Gregory & McLeod.

The partnership of McTavish, Frobisher &

Company was arranged on November 19, 1787. The firm controlled 7/16 of the trade. Mr. J. Hallowell was admitted to the new firm with 1 share on January 1, 1788. In the amalgamation of 1787 control of trade was assured. With these arrangements the firm of Dyer, Allan & Company in England, which had supported McTavish was given one half of the business and Brickwood, Pattle & Company the other half.

> J.F. to Messrs. Brickwood Pattle & Co.—Montreal, October 16, 1787.
>
> The cash which we will require in the course of the winter and to send our canoes away in the Spring may probably amount to 4 or £5,000 which we propose to draw for one half on your house and the other half on Messrs. Dyer, Allan & Co., you may be assured that we shall be as sparing and draw at as long a sight as possible.

In 1788 Dyer, Allan & Company proposed to retire and it was arranged that Phyn, Ellice & Inglis should take their share. In the new agreement[2] of 1790 at Grand Portage, McTavish, Frobisher & Company held 7/20 of the shares but one of the shares was given to Daniel Sutherland. In the agreement of 1802 the share of this Company was increased to 30/76 and the partnership was extended for twenty years. The union with the XY Company in 1804, with the Hudson's Bay Company in 1821, and the further extension of the agreement for twenty-one years demonstrated clearly the inevitable tendency with increasing capital toward cutthroat competition and monopoly. The influence of the Montreal and London supply houses became increasingly evident. Many of the old partners had died. The Beaver Club lost much of its importance. Alexander Henry alone had lived to see the whole trend of development from 1739 to 1824. Family influence became more important and the McGillivrays, nephews of Simon McTavish, and Ellice, came to hold key positions. It was possible for these interests to secure control over the Northwest Company as Selkirk had

acquired control of the Hudson's Bay Company. They were able to arrange for the final amalgamation with the Hudson's Bay Company to which the wintering partners exclaimed 'Amalgamation! This is not amalgamation but submersion! We are drowned men.'

The effect of these demands for large quantities of capital was shown also in the organization of the trade. The organization of the southern trade offered an important contrast. Smaller quantities of capital were necessary to carry on the trade and the geographic background made the control of any large organization difficult. For example the general store[3] formed at Michilimackinac on July 1, 1779, was of short duration and the agreement of 1785 was a failure. Whereas in this trade a large organization failed to achieve any permanent success the tendency in the trade to the Northwest was continually toward larger organizations. In the south the formation of large organizations was unsuccessful whereas in the north the formation of small competing organizations was unsuccessful.

The success of the large organization was the result of the necessity for close co-ordination and the demand for large quantities of capital. As already suggested the first evidence of co-operation among the traders was found in the penetration to the Saskatchewan in 1775 of traders who had been forced from the southern trade and from Albany as a result of the American Revolution. These traders brought with them substantial quantities of capital in the form of large boats on the lakes and they found it necessary in carrying on trade over such distances in the interior to co-operate. An appreciation of the necessity of close organization was shown at an early date partly as a result of the difficulties of the war. In 1776 the Northwest Company was accused[4] of sending a deputation to Congress.

> The North West Company are not better than they ought to be, their conduct in sending an Embassy to Congress in '76 may be traced now to matters

more detrimental. I hope the General will grant them no passes without insisting on their bringing the King's stores from the Portage.

In 1778 they combined to support Pond's expedition to Athabasca. The restricted number of passes was referred to as the cause of joint-stock operation in 1779. Difficulties with the Plains Indians at posts near Eagle Hills in the Saskatchewan in 1780 and the desolation caused by the smallpox were noted by Mackenzie as a cause of co-operation. After the Revolution a threatened encroachment from the United States on the boundary line from Lake Superior to Lake of the Woods was given as a reason for concerted action. 'Their first object was to prepare the necessary supplies and provide against any interruption to their business from the United States by discovering another passage from Lake Superior to the River Quinipigue.'[5] In 1784 Edward Umfreville was dispatched to discover a better route than that by Grand Portage. In these cases a common task presented itself and it could only be performed by co-operative effort.

In the later stages of development co-operation appears less important as a factor tending toward concentration, and the ruinous effects of competition under conditions of heavy overhead costs became a driving force in favour of amalgamation. Reference has been made to the competition of the small Montreal Company from 1785 to 1787, formed at the suggestion of Pangman, Ross, and Pond following disagreement with the 1784 arrangement under the auspices of Gregory, McLeod & Company. The competition of this small organization began with the outfit of 1785.[6] In that year the Northwest Company sent to Grand Portage and Detroit, 25 canoes and 4 bateaux with 260 men in canoes and 16 men in bateaux carrying 6,000 gal. of rum, 340 gal. of wine, 300 rifles, 8,000 lb. of powder, 120 cwt. of shot, all of which was valued at £20,500, whereas Gregory and McLeod sent 4 canoes with 50 men, 400 gal. of rum, 32 gal. of wine, 64 rifles, 1,700 lb. of powder and 20 cwt. of shot,

valued at £2,850, and Ross and Pangman took up the same number of canoes, 40 men, 350 gal. of rum, 32 gal. of wine, 36 rifles, 1,600 lb. of powder, 18 cwt. shot, valued at £2,775. In 1786 the Northwest Company increased their outfits to include 30 canoes and 300 men, 2 bateaux and 9 men, 3,000 gal. of rum, 500 gal. of wine, 500 rifles, 9,000 lb. of powder, 120 cwt. of shot, valued at £25,500, whereas Gregory and McLeod sent 8 canoes, 83 men, 1,600 gal. of rum, 64 gal. of wine, 104 rifles, 2,800 lb. of powder, 45 cwt. of shot, valued at £4,500. Finally, in the year of amalgamation, the Northwest Company sent 25 canoes and 250 men, 4 bateaux and 20 men, 5,300 gal. of rum, 786 gal. of wine, 500 rifles, 7,000 lb. of powder, 106 cwt. of shot, valued at £22,000, and Gregory and McLeod sent 9 canoes, 90 men, 1,600 gal. of rum, 54 gal. of wine, 150 rifles, 3,400 lb. of powder, 45 cwt. of shot valued at £4,700.

The small company in 1785 placed John Ross in charge of the Athabasca district, Alexander Mackenzie of English River, Peter Pangman of Fort des Prairies and Mr. Pollock, a clerk, of Red River. It was obliged to build new posts at Grand Portage and in the interior. The 'guides, commis, men and interpreters were few in number and not of the first quality.' The success of Pollock against Robert Grant and William McGillivray in the Red River department would probably not be important. Roderic Mackenzie describes the competition with Patrick Small and William McGillivray of the Northwest Company in the English River district in 1786 and the instructions[7] of Alexander Mackenzie who was in charge of the district are illuminating as to the character of the personnel. In the Athabasca district severe competition was the cause of the death of John Ross. In the summer of 1787 the union was arranged concerning which Alexander Mackenzie wrote, 'As we had already incurred a loss, this union was, in every respect, a desirable event to us, and was concluded in the month of July 1787.'[8] He wrote[9] to Roderic Mackenzie in a letter dated December 2, 1787:

After the experience you must have of the dreadful effect the late opposition has had upon those who were engaged in it and upon the country, I cannot believe you entertain any thought of a repetition on your own account. Could I, in four years of hard labour and anxiety, pay the debts I owe our concern in consequence, I should feel satisfied.

A new organization was under appreciable disadvantage having little knowledge of Indian habits, language, and economy. The best hunters were known and traded with by the old Company and Indians who were refused credit because of a bad reputation went to the new firm. A more serious difficulty was the lack of capital, but on the other hand in spite of the lack of capital competition was sufficiently ruinous to both companies to warrant an early amalgamation. Later competition brought out similar tendencies. After 1787 traders penetrated from Prairie du Chien on the Mississippi across the height of land to Red River, and from the rivers flowing into Lake Superior. In 1794 Beaubien and Laviolette came[10] into Red River from the south. According to John MacDonald an opposition appeared[11] apparently under David Grant at Sturgeon River in 1793 supported by Gregory and Robinson of Montreal and continued at that point and Nepawi the following year. Competition in Red River district meant surplus stocks of goods and ventures to more remote areas as in the Saskatchewan. In the winter of 1794–95 five different interests[12] were trading at La Souris. In 1799–1800 Alexander Henry (the younger) was opposed[13] at White Mud River by the T. Association from Montreal. In 1797 the larger interest became more important and according to Harmon established[14] a rival depot at Grand Portage. The interests concerned were apparently[15] those of John Mure of Quebec, Forsyth, Richardson and Company, Parker, Gerrard, Oglivy & Company, Phyn, Inglis and Company, and Leith, Jamieson & Company. Forsyth, Richardson & Company appear to have

been most active but the two firms of Forsyth and Ogilvy sent canoes to Fort Chipewyan in 1799. Simon McTavish wrote[16] in a letter dated Montreal, June 22, 1799, 'The threatened opposition have, this year made a serious attack on us, and I fear that a coalition of interests between the parties opposed to us may render them more formidable.' The amalgamation feared by McTavish which became known as the XY Company was formed in 1800 and was strengthened by the support of Sir Alexander Mackenzie. The effects of the opposition were shown in the Red River with special emphasis[17] beginning in 1801. In 1802 they had posts on the Saskatchewan;[18] in 1803 a post was built on Peace River above the Forks[19] and in the same year they had a post on Bear Lake.[20] In 1804 Harmon mentions[21] the XY fort at River Qu'appelle and also a winter post at Fishing Lake. In 1803 they built a post five miles above the Northwest post at Fort Alexandria in the Swan River country. The success of the XY interests is difficult to determine but it was not conspicuous. In the dispute over the ownership of land for the erection of buildings at Kaministiquia and at Sault Ste Marie following the removal of these posts to British territory the handicaps of the smaller Company were conspicuous. Alexander Henry in a letter dated Montreal, December 10, 1804, to John Askin, wrote, 'it is said the New Company lost £70,000 since their commencing the opposition, it will be some time before they bring up that sum.' On November 5, 1804, an agreement[22] of amalgamation was signed. The fur trade was singularly susceptible to ruin from competition and it was singularly dependent on the availability of large capital resources as well as skill and experience. Marked tendencies in the trade were the increasing importance of large quantities of capital and the increasing control which a smaller number of capitalists was able to exercise.

The weakness of the Company was a result of two conflicting tendencies incidental to the necessity for greater concentration of control and for greater reliance on the individual trader as competition increased. The internal trade as carried on by the wintering partners was conducted by men with strong personalities such as Peter Pond and Alexander Mackenzie who persisted in breaking from the organization and precipitating competition. In the agreement of 1804 Isaac Todd in a letter to the Lieutenant Colonel Green dated Montreal, October 25, 1804, wrote, 'Sir Alexander Mackenzie is excluded from any interference, with him and McGillivray there will, I fear, never be intimacy.' It is significant that Todd who was interested in the supply houses of Montreal should have been an influential negotiator for union.

NOTES

1. See R.H. Fleming, 'McTavish, Frobisher and Company', *Can. Hist. Rev.*, June, 1929.

2. For a description of the various early agreements of the Northwest Company see H.A. Innis, 'The Northwest Company', *Can. Hist. Rev.*, December, 1927.

3. See 'List of proprietors of the general store at Michilimackinac, the number of canoes each person has put in, their supposed value, and the present residence of each proprietor'—32 firms, 29½ canoes, and supposed value £488,750. *Report of the Pioneer Society of the State of Michigan*, IX, 658.

4. Extracts of letters from Lieutenant Governor Sinclair concerning the trade and traders to Michilimackinac and the Northwest, February 15, 1780, Can. Arch., Q, XVII, Pt. I, 256–7; see also Can. Arch., Haldimand Papers, B.217, p. 468.

5. Can. Arch., Haldimand Papers, B.217, p. 470; also Frobisher Letter Book, p. 60; see letters to the government on the subject of the boundary line, *Report on Canadian Archives*, 1888, pp. 68 f.; also petition of merchants, February 6, 1788, Can Arch., Shelburne MSS, LXXII, 288–93, and requests for exclusive privileges and charters, Memorial of the Northwest Company, Montreal, October 4, 1784; Benjamin and Joseph Frobisher to General Haldimand, Montreal, October 4, 1784, and Memorial of Peter Pond, Quebec, 18 April 1785, *Report on Canadian Archives*, 1890, pp. 48–54; *Nipigon to Winnipeg* (Ottawa, 1929).

6. L.R. Masson, *Les bourgeois de la Compagnie du Nord-Ouest: Récits de voyages, lettres et rapports inédits relatifs au Nord-Ouest canadien . . .* (Québec, 1889–90), I, 10.

7. Ibid., pp. 18 ff.

8. Alexander Mackenzie, *Voyages from Montreal through the continent of North America to the frozen and Pacific oceans in 1789 and 1793 with an account of the rise and state of the fur trade* (Toronto, n.d.), p. xiv.

9. Masson, *Les bourgeois*, I, 22.

10. Ibid., p. 290.

11. Ibid., II, 20.

12. Ibid., I, 294. Duncan McGillivray reports seven forts of the Northwest Company and 14 of the opponents in Red River in 1794–95. Peter Grant went with four canoes, the Hudson's Bay Company with five boats, and Michilimackinac interests, seventeen canoes.

13. Elliott Coues, ed., *New light on the early history of the greater Northwest: The manuscript journals of Alexander Henry* [the younger], *fur trader of the Northwest Company, and of David Thompson, official geographer and explorer of the same company, 1799–1814; exploration and adventure among the Indians on the Red, Saskatchewan, Missouri, and Columbia Rivers* (New York, 1897), I, 5.

14. Daniel Williams Harmon, *A journal of voyages and travels in the interior of North America . . . including an account of the principal occurrences, during a residence of nineteen years, in different parts of the country . . .* (Toronto, 1904), p. 15.

15. Masson, *Les bourgeois*, II, 498–9. For a valuable discussion see R.H. Fleming, 'The Origin of Sir Alexander Mackenzie and Company', *Can. Hist. Rev.*, June, 1928, pp. 137–55.

16. Masson, *Les bourgeois*, I, 47.
17. Coues, ed., *New light*, I. Alexander Henry does not mention XY competition until 1801.
18. Masson, *Les bourgeois*, II, 23 ff.
19. J.B. Tyrrell, ed., *David Thompson's Narrative of his Explorations in Western America, 1784–1812*

(Toronto, 1916), p. lxxxii.
20. Masson, *Les bourgeois*, II, 123.
21. Harmon, *A journal of voyages and travels*, pp. 75, 80.
22. Masson, *Les bourgeois*, II, 484.

4   From Elaine Allan Mitchell, 'The Scot in the Fur Trade', in W. Stanford Reid, ed., *The Scottish Tradition in Canada* (Toronto: McClelland & Stewart, 1976), 31–40.

Among Orkneymen who rose to prominence in the Hudson's Bay Company prior to its coalition with the North West Company in 1821 were Alexander Kennedy, Joseph Isbister and William Sinclair (the latter said to be descended from the old earls of Orkney). Another Orkneyman, William Tomison, the Company's dominant figure on the Saskatchewan for twenty years, is also remembered for his courage in caring for the Indians during the terrible smallpox epidemic of 1781–2. About 1826 the Company's agent in Orkney was John Rae, father of the famous Arctic explorer, Dr. John Rae, of whom we shall be hearing more later. Edward Clouston, a lawyer, took on the post in 1836, retaining it for almost thirty years. Gentle and kindly, he was affectionately remembered by many of the young men who passed through his hands. His two sons, Robert and James Stewart Clouston, became clerks in the service, Robert rising to the rank of chief trader before his premature death and James to that of chief factor. Both married into the Company's hierarchy. Robert's wife was Jessy Ross, daughter of Chief Factor Donald Ross of Norway House, and James's, Margaret Miles, whose father, Chief Factor Robert Miles, was his chief at Moose Factory. Jessy Clouston died from tuberculosis after a year of marriage and is buried in Playgreen cemetery at Norway House. James's eldest son, Edward Seaborn Clouston, had a distinguished career in Canada. Entering the Bank of Montreal at the age of sixteen, he became successively general manager and vice-president. He

was honoured with a baronetcy in 1908.

It was only after 1763 that other Scots, Highlanders in particular, but Lowlanders too, began to play an increasingly influential part in the Canadian fur trade. As in the Orkneys, the principal spur for emigration was poverty. But in the case of the Highlanders, the poverty was not only more immediate and acute but intensified by political and religious persecution and social decay. The erosion of the power of their chieftains and of the old system of land tenure, which culminated in the defeat of the clans at Culloden in 1745, left many young Highlanders with no prospects for the future and still others no choice but exile. North America received the larger share of this emigration. The West Indian islands offered vast sugar plantations and a thriving foreign trade, while in Canada, once the French had withdrawn from the northwest, the most rapidly expanding and profitable field for exploitation was the fur trade.

Beyond all these considerations, however, Scots, generally speaking, seem to have had a natural affinity for the trade. In the first place, partly no doubt as a result of early political and commercial ties with France, as well as a shared dislike (or envy) of the English, they got along well with the French in Canada, without whose help the Canadian trade could never have been revived so soon. It appears moreover that the Highlanders at least (perhaps because of the intricacies of their own Gaelic) possessed an innate linguistic ability, which enabled them to acquire quickly a fluency in French and in the Indian tongues of the districts to which they were posted. Isaac Cowie noticed this facility in 1867, remarking that the newly engaged Highlanders in his group were picking up both languages much more readily than their companions.[1]

Cowie observed, too, that the Highlanders were generally livelier and more active than the others, besides adapting themselves more rapidly to a new and alien environment. Their native climate, which could be harsh at times, probably fitted them better for a country with a decided winter, while their own hills were rugged enough to predispose them to a liking for the Rockies. With lands at home only partly suitable for cultivation and even when arable worked with difficulty, they were more inclined to accept the hardships of the northwest and to be less intimidated by its overpowering physical characteristics than men used to gentler and lusher landscapes.

Aggressive, enterprising, courageous, ambitious, determined and shrewd, the Scottish recruits were finally, because of their common school system, better educated on the whole than their English counterparts of the day. One must not, of course, rate them too highly. Other nationalities share these desirable traits and undoubtedly Scottish clannishness, as we shall see, played a major role in their eventually overwhelming predominance in the Montreal trade. But when every tendency to exaggerate is discounted, a sufficient core of truth remains to sustain our argument that the Scot fitted naturally into the fur trade world.

Like the Orkneymen, needless to say, the Highlanders exhibited the defects of their virtues. If they were lively and quick, their tempers were equally so; with generations of clan wars behind them, they were apt to be quarrelsome, while their daring frequently led them into untenable positions. Excessively proud and often conceited, they were as easily offended and, when their numbers gave them superiority, sometimes hard to handle. At their best, however, they made loyal, capable, brave and intelligent officers and servants.

Some of the Scots who came to Canada at the close of the Seven Years' War to pursue the fur trade were, like Simon McTavish, already engaged in the Albany trade and merely moved north to be closer to the centre of activity. Others, like Richard Dobie and his associate, William Grant of Three Rivers, came directly from the Old Country. They represented all classes and degrees. Dobie, a Lowlander from the neighbourhood of Edinburgh, had a sister married to a poor Gilmerton weaver and presumably came from the same milieu. Grant's father farmed a small Highland holding, Inverlochy, in Strathavon, upper Banffshire, but William's uncles, John and Francis Grant, owned large plantations in Jamaica and John was Chief Justice of the island from 1783–90. When he retired, John bought Kilgraston, a Perthshire estate, to which his brother succeeded in 1793. Other Grants in the fur trade were so numerous and their relationships so confusing that so far no one has been able to sort them out.

The sons of Scots settled in the English colonies before the Revolutionary War, and who later came to Canada as United Empire Loyalists, also figured largely in the Montreal trade. One of them was the famous Nor'Wester, Simon Fraser, explorer of the tempestuous river which bears his name, who was born in Bennington, New York, in 1776. Still others were the sons and grandsons of men attached to the Highland regiments disbanded after the Seven Years' War and again after the American Revolution, the best known being the 78th, or Fraser Highlanders, who settled about Murray Bay, Quebec, and the Glengarry Highlanders, who made homes for themselves in what is now Glengarry County, Ontario.

From the height of their own royally-chartered and century-old company the Hudson's Bay men referred to the early Canadian traders as 'pedlars.' Although intended as a term of opprobrium, that, in essence, was what they were— daring, resourceful and adventurous individuals, risking their own or borrowed capital, to say nothing of their lives, in an attempt to make their fortunes. Some of the earliest of them exploited fields relatively close to Montreal, Richard Dobie, for example, turning his attention to Timiskaming in 1764. William Grant of Three Rivers traded at Michilimackinac and in the Illinois country, while the Montreal firms of Todd, McGill & Co. and Forsyth, Richardson & Co. not only had extensive interests southwest of the Great Lakes but also secured a hold on Nipigon. James McGill, Thomas and John Forsyth, and John Richardson were all Scottish-born. Isaac Todd's birthplace is not known and he retired in England, but he was an active member of St Gabriel's Presbyterian Church in Montreal and presumably also a Scot.

The first trader on the Saskatchewan after 1763 appears to have been a Frenchman previously engaged in that trade, known as 'Franceway' (François). He wintered there in 1765 or 1766, probably outfitted by Isaac Todd and James McGill. James Finlay, Sr., a Scot trading on his own account, followed him in 1768. Another Scottish trader, Thomas Corry, spent the winters of 1771–2 and 1772–3 on the Saskatchewan and a measure of the profits to be made in those early days may be judged from the fact that he accumulated sufficient capital in the two seasons to allow him to retire from the trade.[2] But although two Scots were thus apparently the first to follow a Frenchman to the northwest, French, Swiss, English, Irish and American traders were all soon to be found there.

Almost from the beginning, because of the high capital risk and the extended credit necessary for trading over such great distances, individual 'pedlars' tended to combine forces. At first these unions were temporary, usually made for one year only and sometimes ending unhappily. Indeed it was hostilities among the various factions, climaxed by a murder in the interior, which led to the formation in 1783 of the first association of traders known as the North West Company. This amalgamation was primarily the work of Simon McTavish who, with the Frobisher

brothers, Benjamin and Joseph, held six of the sixteen shares in the concern. The Frobishers were Yorkshiremen, the only two Englishmen among the original partners, while of the remaining seven, McTavish and three others were Scots, with one Irishman, one Frenchman and one American comprising the rest.

The infant North West Company was strongly opposed by another influential Montreal firm, Gregory, McLeod & Co., which had been left out of the new arrangement. One of its founders in 1773 had been James Finlay, Sr., who retired ten years later and was replaced by Normand McLeod, a Detroit trader born in Skye. Young Alexander Mackenzie entered its service about 1779, to be followed by his cousin, Roderick, in 1784. The increasing bitterness between the rivals in the northwest culminated during the winter of 1786–7 with the murder in Athabasca of John Ross, a partner of Gregory, McLeod & Co. Roderick Mackenzie and Simon McTavish's nephew, William McGillivray, brought the news down to the central depot at Grand Portage in the summer of 1787 and their respective principals, fearing that Ross's death would lead to reprisals, immediately decided to unite their interests under the name of the North West Company. Shortly afterwards the newly formed firm of McTavish, Frobisher & Co., whose partners, Simon McTavish and Joseph Frobisher, held the dominant interest in the North West Company, became its Montreal agents.

Meanwhile, in their turn, the English on Hudson's Bay had been pushing inland. Apparently the opposition of French traders in the interior had never been serious enough to force them to alter their original mode of conducting their trade and for some years after 1763 they had continued to maintain large, impressive and well-stocked factories on the seacoast and to wait for the Indians to bring down their furs. But it was not long before it became clear that, with active Canadian traders swarming inland and intercepting their customers, they must try a new approach. Accordingly, in 1774 they built Cumberland House on the Saskatchewan and quickly established other posts in the interior to enable them to meet the Indians on their own lands. It was now that the disadvantages of a long residence on the Bay, as well as the drawbacks of their Orkney servants, became glaringly evident and their situation was even more serious, of course, when the independent Canadian traders combined to form the North West Company.

To begin with, there was the vexing problem of transporting goods and servants inland. On the larger rivers, where boats could be used, the Orkneymen fared well enough, being accustomed to handling them from childhood. Indeed the development of the famed York boat, which was to be the Company's standby in the northwest until modern transportation reached the area, was directly due to Orkney knowledge and skill. Unfortunately, most of the rivers on the Laurentian Shield, which forms a vast collar about the Bay, were not only tortuous, but shallow during most of the summer and broken by falls. On them only canoes would answer.

The English suffered from grave disadvantages even in the matter of obtaining canoes. There was no suitable birch bark within a considerable distance of Hudson's Bay and they had therefore to depend largely on the inland Indians to supply them. But many of these Indians were strongly attached to the Canadian traders, or afraid of offending them, and when it suited their purpose, the Canadians did not scruple to pre-empt canoes which the English had ordered or, if necessary, take them from the Indians by force. Since the Orkney servants were unfamiliar with such unsteady craft, the Hudson's Bay Company had to rely for crews on its homeguard Indians (those about the Bay) and run the risk of having them 'enticed' by the Canadians in the interior. Even if a few Orkneymen did become accustomed to handling canoes during the period of their contracts, they often left the country for good at their expiry, to be replaced by inexperienced hands. Moreover, hardy

though they were and patient under hardships, the Orkneymen were slow in acquiring wilderness skills, many of them being intimidated by the prospect of living and travelling in the forests of the Shield. Worse still, they were neither as active nor as aggressive in the pursuit of furs as were the Canadian traders and their French and Scottish servants. All these handicaps took years to overcome and even up to the time of the union in 1821, as several Hudson's Bay officers frankly admitted, their own men rarely attained the standard of their opponents.

In these circumstances, the London Committee recommended hiring Canadians, who would not only be useful themselves but serve as examples and teachers for the Orkneymen. The officers in the interior did manage to entice a few from the opposition but this solution (again with some exceptions) proved unsatisfactory. Few Canadians would accept the salaries offered, and those who did frequently turned out to be not only untrustworthy but undisciplined, perhaps the most heinous of sins in a semi-militaristic organization like the Hudson's Bay Company. As N.M.W.J. McKenzie was later to remark of his chief factor at Fort Ellice, Archibald MacDonald, 'you might break all the ten commandments in one clatter, but to break any of the rules and regulations of the service, that was quite another thing.'[3] On the whole, it would seem, deserters on both sides generally tended to be misfits or malcontents, unlikely to make good servants for either company.

During these same years changes were also taking place in the Canadian trade, and in the process the French in the country were losing out to the Scots. The partners of the various interested firms were bringing in needy, or deserving, relatives and friends as apprentice clerks and these newcomers were gradually replacing the French masters inland. It was not always, however, a case of nepotism or greed. Often the French servants or clerks, like Panneton, master of Fort Abitibi until 1776, were men of little or no education. Although they had grown up in the country and were at home with the Indians, they were probably not the organized and efficient managers which an increasingly complex and competitive trade was coming to need. Where the French were qualified, they appear to have held their own, but when they retired, as they were more and more often replaced by Scots, the general trend was unmistakable.

Even when there were no relatives or friends to consider, the North West Company apparently favoured Scottish clerks and servants. In October, 1798, McTavish, Frobisher & Co. requested Aneas Cameron of Fort Timiskaming, who was returning to Scotland on leave, to engage 'four or five decent young men from the Age of 18 upwards, of good character &

Sufficient Education as Apprentices or Clerks to the Concern, for 5, 6, or 7 years' on very favourable terms indeed. The agents also directed Cameron to write to a gentleman in the Orkneys, who was known to them, and to assist him in getting any servants he might be able to hire for them to Greenock. Should the gentleman fail to secure any, the agents added, Cameron himself should search out and engage an equal number of seamen from any other part of Scotland, as well as two or three good ship's carpenters, able to navigate the Company's small vessels on the Great Lakes and willing to double as seamen. To the latter he might offer from £50 to £100 a year, provided they had sufficient education to keep their cargo accounts.[4]

NOTES

1. Isaac Cowie, *The Company of Adventurers* (Toronto: William Briggs, 1913), p. 123.
2. *Documents Relating to the North West Company* W. Stewart Wallace, ed. (Toronto: The Champlain Society, 1934), pp. 3, 434.
3. N.M.W.J. McKenzie, *The Men of the Hudson's Bay Company, 1670 A.D.–1920 A.D.* (Fort William, Ont.: Times-Journal Presses, 1921), pp. 7ff.
4. Wallace, pp. 3, 434.

---

5   From Arthur J. Ray, *Indians in the Fur Trade: Their Role as Trappers, Hunters, and Middlemen in the Lands Southwest of Hudson Bay 1660–1870* (Toronto: University of Toronto Press, 1974), 51–65.

During the early years of the fur trade in western Canada, competition between the English and the French was largely centred on Hudson Bay, and certain key posts such as York Factory changed hands several times. This period of instability ended in 1713 with the signing of the Treaty of Utrecht which gave the English permanent control of the Bay. As the English fur trade was re-established in the postwar years under the direction of the Hudson's Bay Company, two posts quickly emerged as the leading centres of trade for the western interior of Canada—York Factory and Fort Albany. Of the two, York

Factory was more important in terms of its volume of trade . . . and the size of its hinterland . . . . Before 1717 its trading area included the whole of Manitoba and Saskatchewan. The hinterland of Fort Albany, on the other hand, reached only to the lands lying just to the east of Lake Winnipeg during this period. In 1717, the Hudson's Bay Company opened Fort Prince of Wales (later called Fort Churchill) on the lower Churchill River, and this post siphoned off part of the trade at York Factory. However, . . . the new post never rivalled York Factory as a trading centre, and it drew in the trade of relatively few

Indian groups living to the south of the Churchill River basin. The few who did come were chiefly Woodland Assiniboine and Cree groups who inhabited the North Saskatchewan River region.

Having been blocked from the Bay, the French redoubled their efforts to cut the Hudson's Bay Company off from its hinterland. Although this effort had begun as early as 1680 when Du Lhut built his post on Lake Nipigon to intercept the Assiniboine and Cree on their way to Fort Albany, it had had little effect on the English trade except at the latter post. Beginning in the 1730s, however, the French began to penetrate into the hinterland of York Factory, as La Vérendrye built a string of posts at strategic points in southern Manitoba and Saskatchewan . . . , and these posts began to draw off a portion of York Factory's trade. . . . [T]he volumes of furs and of goods traded were increasing until the early 1730s; thereafter they began an erratic decline reaching their lowest levels in the 1750s when competition was sharpest; and in the late 1750s they began to rise again as the French were forced to withdraw. The values for the *overplus*, which will be explained below, are even more sensitive to changing levels of competition and exhibit the same trends.

While the French and English vied with each other for the trade of the Indians inhabiting the Western Interior, the various Indian groups competed with each other for control of the carrying trade to and from the European posts, particularly that of York Factory.

Unfortunately, very little information is available regarding this aspect of the trade at York Factory until 1714, when the Hudson's Bay Company regained control of the post for the last time. Thereafter, the record becomes increasingly voluminous. James Knight was placed in command of the post in 1714, and he began a concerted effort to re-establish company contacts with the Indians in the interior. In the summer of 1715, 172 canoes came down to the post manned by Misshenipee, Sturgeon, Stone, Upland, Muscotay, Mountain, and Strange Indians.

The first four of these groups were regular visitors at the post and can be readily identified. The Misshenipee, also listed as the Misshenepih and Michinipi, were Cree bands who came from the upper Churchill River region between Reindeer Lake and the Athabasca River.[1] The Sturgeon Indians were another band of Cree who lived in southeastern Manitoba where they were met by La Vérendrye in the 1730s.[2] The Stone Indians were Assiniboine, and were also identified as the Northern Sinepoetts (Woodland Assiniboine) and Southern Sinepoetts (Parkland-Grassland Assiniboine)—and Sinepoets is one of many variant spellings. The Upland Indians included both Assiniboine and Cree, particularly the Woodland Assiniboine and Cree bands living to the west of York Factory between the Saskatchewan and Churchill rivers. The term Southern Indians was also applied to the Cree coming from that quarter, but more often to those coming from southern Manitoba and northern Ontario. Immediately upon the resumption of trade by the Hudson's Bay Company, these four groups accounted for most of the canoes coming down to York Factory.

The other trading parties that arrived at the post were fewer in number and generally came from much greater distances.[3] One of these groups were the Muscotay (as noted earlier, Muscotay was a geographic term referring in this instance to the grasslands between the forks of the Saskatchewan River).[4] The ethnic identity of the Muscotay will, therefore, never be known precisely, but they were, in all probability, either Blood, Blackfoot, or perhaps Gros Ventre, although the latter seems unlikely in this instance since the term Ashkee Indians seems to have been applied to the Gros Ventre at that time.[5] All of the above tribes were known to have traded at the post in later years. For instance, as late as 1758 James Isham, then in charge of York Factory, wrote to Ferdinand Jacobs at Fort Churchill and informed him that five canoes of 'Bloody Indians (or Mithcoo Ethenue) [his parentheses] came down to trade.'[6] Significantly, he added, 'none of the tribe has been here since 1733.'[7] This remark clearly implies that some of the Blood had the practice of coming down to the Bay during the early decades of the eighteenth century. Similarly, in 1757, the 'Earchithinues' came to York Factory in company with a large party of Assiniboine and Cree from the Saskatchewan River area.[8] The term 'Earchithinue' and its more commonly used variant, 'Archithinue,' was a Cree word that applied to the Blackfoot and the Gros Ventre.[9] Precise ethnic identification is therefore not possible, but both groups came from the same general region—the Muscotay Plains.

Of all of the Indians who came to York Factory in 1715, the Mountain Indians were said to have travelled the greatest distance. Knight reported that it took them thirty-nine days to make the trip downstream and three months to return. In 1715, thirty canoes of these Indians arrived at the post. Included in the trading party was an old chief who informed Knight that he had been at Fort Albany sixteen years earlier. In an effort to obtain as much information as he could regarding the Mountain Indian country, Knight held long discussion with this chief as well as with two Upland Indian leaders in the following year. The latter had apparently been to the region. According to Knight:

> Both agreed in one thing they Say the Country is very Mountainious and of [such] a Prodigious height . . . they can not see the capp without it be Clear Weather[.] [T]hey tell me their is abundance of Natives and . . . Sev'll Nations of them and their grows a great deal of Indian Corn Plumbs Hazle Nutts and they have not much Beavor, but abundance of Moose, Buffolo, Wascashus [red deer] and Small Furrs . . . all of them Mountain Indians Garnish themselves with a White Mettle . . . they [also] have a Yellow Mettle Amongst them.[10]

Although this description contains elements of exaggeration and pure fabrication to please the English traders, such as the allusions to silver

and gold, it is significant that reference is made to agriculture, bison, red deer, and mountainous terrain. The only region that could have included this combination of elements is the plains region stretching from the Upper Missouri River to the Rocky Mountains. The Mountain Indians were therefore either Mandan or Hidatsa, and the scraps of information in Knight's journal suggest that the term may have been applied indiscriminately to both groups. For instance, the Mountain Indians were said to live next to the Crow with whom they were at war. When the Mountain Indians arrived at York Factory in 1716, they brought some Crow slaves along with them. In order to extend his trade to the latter tribe, Knight attempted to use these slaves to conclude a peace between the Crow and Mountain Indians. Thus, he wrote that the Mountain Indians returned home with a 'leading Indian his Brother & Wife wch I had Employ'd to go Amongst ye Cocauchee or Crow Indians wch was a Slave Woman of yt Country yt had Undertaken to go into her Country again with her husband and a great many more Indians and make a peace and bring me down a great deal of the Yellow Mettle wch she told me, it was so plenty.'[11]

Considering that it is generally believed that the Crow separated from the Hidatsa sometime during the early eighteenth century due to a feud, it seems likely that the Mountain Indians to whom Knight was referring were Hidatsa.[12] However, in 1721, the Mandan arrived at York Factory to trade. Henry Kelsey was then in charge of the post and referred to them as the Mai-tain-ai-thi-nish.[13] It is distinctly possible, therefore, that Knight's early use of the term Mountain Indian was a corruption of this word. However, the Mandan did not live next to the Crow. For these reasons, it seems likely that the name was applied rather loosely to both the Mandan and Hidatsa at different times at York Factory.

The 'Strange' Indians who arrived at York Factory between 1715 and 1720 are difficult to identify since this term was generally applied to newcomers at the post. In all probability they came from the far west, and they may have been Sarsi Indians. Journal entries in later years suggest that this group did, in fact, visit the post. In 1728–9, 1729–30, 1730–1, and 1740–1, a group variously called the Shussuanna, Shusuanna, Su Hannah, and Susuhannah came to York Factory, usually in company with the Assiniboine and Western Cree (then listed as Keskatchewan Indians).[14] Although they cannot be identified positively, considering that they came from the Saskatchewan region but were not listed as either a band of Assiniboine or Cree according to Andrew Graham, a trader at York Factory, they may well have been the Sarsi.[15] Graham reported that this tribe was known as the Sussou in the late eighteenth century.[16]

In addition to the various Indian trade parties who arrived by canoe, the Northern Indians were also frequent visitors at York Factory before 1717. This group consisted largely of the Athabascan-speaking Chipewyan who arrived on foot in these early years.[17] Included among these parties were Northern Indian Strangers who came from beyond Lake Athabasca toward Great Slave Lake. They were said to live next to the Yellow Mettle Indians (Yellow Knives) with whom they had recently been at war.[18]

. . . [I]n the unsettled period immediately following the resumption of English control at York Factory the post was drawing Indian trading parties from a vast territory reaching from the Missouri River on the southwest to at least Great Slave Lake on the northwest. However, this pattern of trade was relatively short lived. In 1717, when Fort Churchill was opened, the latter post took over nearly all of the trade with the Chipewyan and most of that of the Michinipi Cree.

A small trade was carried on with the Northern Assiniboine as well.

More importantly, through the use of force the various Assiniboine and Cree bands increasingly took over control of the inland trade of York Factory. Although Knight attempted to arrange peace treaties between the Upland Assiniboine and Cree and the Northern,

Western, and Muscotay Indians in the hopes of increasing trade, his efforts largely failed. Most of the treaties that he did manage to arrange were quickly broken. Consequently, after 1720 very few of the more distant tribes appear at York Factory. For example, there are no further references to the Mountain Indians after 1721.[19]

Those that did occasionally make the voyage such as the Shussuanna, Blood, and Archithinue, always arrived in company with the Assiniboine and Cree, suggesting that perhaps they were not permitted to do so without the escort of the latter groups. Individual Cree and Assiniboine may also have travelled as envoys with these parties. For instance, one of the leading Bloody Indian Captains (Trading Leaders) who regularly visited York Factory was an Assiniboine.[20] He may have served in some essentially diplomatic fashion that enabled the Bloody Indians to pass peacefully through Assiniboine and Cree territory.

Besides the Assiniboine and Cree trading blockade, other factors tended to discourage the Plains Indians from continuing to trade directly with York Factory. By 1740 the use of horses had spread northward as far as the parkland belt in Alberta and the Missouri River in the Dakota region. This development, along with an increasingly grassland economic orientation which became characteristic of such groups as the Blood and Blackfoot, meant that many bands of these tribes no longer would have been able to make the journey to the Bay, since they abandoned the use of canoes. This may have been an additional reason why the few who continued to do so travelled with Assiniboine and Cree in the later years on their trips down to York Factory. The Assiniboine and Cree could have served as helmsmen in the Blackfoot and Blood canoes though there is no evidence that this was the case.

In addition, because the Mountain, Blood, and Archithinue had to travel such great distances, they were unable to carry enough provisions in their canoes to supply themselves on the voyage down and back from the Bay. As European traders were to learn in later years, hunting en route was difficult because of the time factor and meagre nature of the forest-resource base. These problems were further aggravated by the occasionally late arrivals of the ships from England. These late arrivals delayed the departure of the Indians from the post and meant that in the cases of these distant tribes, it was impossible to return home before the arrival of winter. Consequently, they ran a considerable risk of facing starvation when undertaking their trading expeditions to York Factory. For instance, the failure of the ships to arrive on time in the summer of 1716 was said to have caused many deaths from starvation of the Mountain, Ashkee, and some of the Northern Sinepoett on their return home. Such losses were very upsetting to James Knight because he believed they could be avoided if more forethought were given to the time ships were dispatched from England. When the Mountain Indians returned next summer on 10 June 1717, he took the opportunity to stress the gravity of the problem and to vent his feelings writing:

> here is 22 Canoes of the Mountain Indians Come & some others as border upon them Says that most of all the Indians as went away from here so Late last fall was Starv'd & Died not being Able to gett home to their Own Country & here is not above 1/3 part of them Indians as came down here Last Year. It Grieves Me to the very heart to think how a Country is Ruin'd by a Senseless Blockhead not having thought care nor consideration.[21]

Unfortunately, the Indians were to experience similar hardships later on. In 1763, Ferdinand Jacobs sent a letter from York Factory to Moses Norton at Fort Churchill, informing him that 'the Bloody Indians were, Some of them, Starved to Death Last year going Back which So intimidated them that I am afraid we Shall never have any more of them Come to Trade.'[22] Jacobs' fears proved to be well founded and the Blood Indians do not appear to have returned to the Bay afterwards.

It is not surprising, therefore, that in 1772 when the Hudson's Bay Company sent Mathew Cocking inland in an attempt to encourage the Archithinue Indians to bypass the Assiniboine and Cree middlemen and come down to York Factory, they refused. According to Cocking 'they said that they would be starved & were unacquainted with Canoes & mentioned the long distance.'[23] It was this combination of distance, hardships experienced in the past, and the abandonment of canoes by many inland bands that played into the hands of the Assiniboine and Cree middlemen. By playing them up, and using intimidation as necessary, they were able to hold a virtual monopoly on the trade at York Factory during most of the eighteenth century. Reflecting this, the canoe tallies that were kept at the post in 1757, 1758, 1759, and 1761, indicate that nearly all of the Indians coming to the post were either Cree or Assiniboine. The only other group that brought a significant portion of the trade were the Ojibwa who accounted for about 12 per cent of the canoe traffic. Of the Assiniboine and Cree canoes, roughly 50 per cent came from the Saskatchewan River Valley, 18 per cent from the Churchill River, and approximately 20 per cent from the area close to the Bay. The latter were the Home Guard Indians, who were later to be known as the Swampy Cree . . . .[24]

In order for the vast York Factory trading system to operate smoothly, a set of complex relationships had to be worked out between the participating groups. This involved the development of a series of devices whereby the barter economy of the Indians could be tied in with the market-oriented enterprise of the Hudson's Bay Company. Throughout the seventeenth and eighteenth centuries, the Indians, especially the Assiniboine and Cree middlemen, held the upper hand in the fur trade at York Factory, and to a considerable extent they dictated the terms of trade. Thus, the company was forced to make most of the adjustments during this period.

Since the Indians lacked any concept of

money, the Hudson's Bay Company was forced to devise a scheme which would allow them to keep records of their barter trade. To achieve this end, the company employed the *made beaver* (MB) as its standard unit of evaluation. It was equivalent to the value of a prime beaver skin and the prices of all trade goods, other furs, and country produce were expressed in terms of MB. . . . [T]rade goods coming from Europe were assigned these values according to the *official standard of trade*, while the furs received from the Indians were evaluated according to the *comparative standard of trade*. One of the primary problems that the company faced was that once the Indians agreed to a standard rate, they were resistant to changes. This often meant that the company was placed in a very difficult position. For example, between 1689 and 1697, while England was engaged in war with France, the prices of goods and seamen's wages were inflating rapidly. The company, therefore, wanted to raise the standard of trade to offset its rising costs. Numerous letters were sent to the Bay from London advocating this measure. Typical of these dispatches was the one that the company sent to Governor Geyer at Port Nelson (York Factory) on 13 July 1689. Regarding the standard of trade, Geyer was instructed:

> To Consider the great Losses wee have of Late sustained, the many hazards wee Run through in these times of danger, Besides the extrordinary expence wee are now at in sending suplies, which Tribles the Charge of former years; from hence you may urge the natives the great difficulties wee undergoe to come to them, and that theirfore they ought now allow more beaver in Truck for our goods then heretofore, but this also is Left to your wise Conduct, for our benefitt the best you can, Carefully avoiding any measures which may disgust them.[25]

In short, it was left to Geyer's judgment as to what should be done as long as he was careful not to alienate the Indians. The note of caution was stressed in nearly all of the letters that the company sent. An examination of the account books for York Factory in subsequent years reveals that only minor changes were made in the official standard of trade . . . . The same was true for the comparative standard.

Because of the relatively inflexible attitudes of the Indians towards these two standards, the company had to find some other way of adjusting prices as European market conditions and local levels of competition varied. As the letter cited above shows, the company left it up to its chief traders or factors to come up with a solution. They responded by employing their own standard, the *factor's* or *double standard* as it was called. This involved raising the values of goods above that which was stated in the official standard of trade. They did this by simply asking for more beaver per item whenever they could or, more commonly, by giving short measures to the Indians of those commodities such as cloth, powder, beads, and so forth that were measured out at the time of trade. However, the Indians also understood this system and again would not tolerate radical departures from accepted norms, though they did permit some adjustments.

Their seemingly greater tolerance for changes in the double standard was undoubtedly a consequence of the fact that they could better understand them and bargain more effectively over the amounts involved. Changes in the official standard of trade quite often would have involved changes in volumetric, linear, or weight measurements which meant little to the Indians who were more accustomed to bartering objects—in other words, discrete units. On the other hand, if a trader tried to give them only one-half a horn of powder for a beaver skin after they had become accustomed to obtaining a full one, they could readily perceive the change and make an attempt to haggle over it and arrive at a compromise. In this way the Indians forced the traders to bargain within their own terms of reference. The official standard of trade thus appears to have served more as a base guideline to the traders themselves. It was essentially their minimum price or exchange level.[26]

At York Factory, as at the other posts, the traders invariably exceeded this base level and the gain which they made was reported as *overplus*. They obtained this figure by subtracting the value of goods traded, in terms of the standard of trade, from the values of all the furs received priced in reference to the comparative standard. If the exchange at the post had been conducted according to these two standards, then the result would have been zero. . . . [T]his was never the case. The value of the goods traded was always less than that of the furs due to the application of the double standard. The magnitude of this difference, or the value of the overplus, depended on competitive conditions. While the Hudson's Bay Company held a monopoly in the Western Interior, the factors were able to drive hard bargains and steadily push the value of the overplus upwards. However, as the French moved into the Manitoba area and consolidated their position, they were able to offer enough opposition to force the York Factory traders to relax their stan-dard or lose an increasingly large portion of the fur trade. The latter traders responded to this threat, and . . . the overplus totals began falling, reaching their lowest point during the 1750s at the height of French competition.

Much of the gain that the traders obtained by applying the double standard was re-invested in the fur trade. To a considerable extent, the traders at York Factory drew upon the overplus account to finance gifts which were given to Indians . . . . These presents were given to band leaders a day or two before actual trading began. The leaders would distribute the gifts to other members of their respective bands after having made token presents of furs to the company factor. This reciprocal gift-giving ceremony was an Indian institution which served to affirm friendship. Had the company refused to participate, no trade would have taken place. In the seventeenth and eighteenth centuries, tobacco, beads, and brandy were some of the items that were given most frequently on those occasions.

NOTES

1. York Factory Journal, 1715, PAC, HBC B 239/a/1, pp. 39–52. Lake Michinipi, or Great Water Lake, appears to have been the name given to Reindeer Lake during this period. See Arthur J. Ray, 'Early French Mapping of the Western Interior of Canada: A View from the Bay', *Canadian Cartographer* no. 2 (1972): 89–98. The term Michinipi was also a general one for the upper Churchill River upstream from its confluence with the Reindeer River. This is clearly shown on an unpublished map of Alexander Henry the Elder entitled 'The North West Parts of America', dated ca. 1775 (copy in PAC, Ottawa).

2. Also, Joseph La France informed Arthur Dobbs that they were still living in the region around Lake of the Woods as late as 1740. See La France's map (Figure 7).

3. Some groups of the Northern Sinepoets were an exception. According to James Knight, some of them lived near the headwaters of the Port Nelson River (Nelson-Saskatchewan river system) and he reported that these Assiniboine had to travel some of the greatest distances of any Indian groups to reach York Factory. York Factory Journal, 1717, PAC, HBC B 239/a/3, p. 58.

4. A.S. Morton, *A History of the Canadian West to 1870–1871*, 2nd edn (Toronto: University of Toronto Press, 1973), 246.

5. According to the York Factory Account Books of 1718–19, a gift was given to an Ashkee Indian leader called Ashkee Ethinee who was said to live near the 'Mountain' near 'Redd Deer River' (probably the Touchwood Hills near the headwaters of the Red Deer River of Saskatchewan). This is roughly the area which was occupied by the Gros Ventre during the middle of the eighteenth century. It is unlikely that the Ashkee Indians were Assiniboine since the latter were usually identi-

fied as Stone, Northern, or Southern Sinepoetts at that time. York Factory Account Books, 1718–19, PAC, HBC B 239/d/10, p. 3.

6. York Factory Correspondence Books, 17 July 1758, PAC, HBC B 239/b/16, pp. 3–4.

7. Ibid.

8. York Factory Journals, 1756–7, PAC, HBC B 239/a/42, p. 35. This trading party included ninety-nine canoes.

9. Rich identifies the 'Archithinue' as the Blood while G. Williams contends that they were the Gros Ventre. See E.E. Rich, *The Fur Trade and the Northwest to 1857* (Toronto: McClelland & Stewart, 1967), 124, and Glyndwr Williams, ed., *Andrew Graham's Observations on Hudson's Bay, 1767–1791* (London: Hudson's Bay Record Society, 1969), 202. Ewers points out that the term 'Archithinue' was a Cree word which was applied to the Blackfoot and their Sarsi and Gros Ventre allies as well: John C. Ewers, *The Blackfeet* (Norman: University of Oklahoma Press, 1968), 25.

10. York Factory Journal, 1716–17, PAC, HBC B 239/a/2, p. 57.

11. York Factory Journal, 1716–17, PAC, HBC B 239/a/2, p. 58.

12. E. Denig, *Five Indian Tribes of the Upper Missouri*, ed. J.C. Ewers (Norman: University of Oklahoma Press, 1961), 138n. According to Ewers the earliest reference to the Crow in the literature is that of Jean Baptiste Trudeau of 1795. The Hudson's Bay Company archival reference thus precedes it by nearly eighty years. Furthermore, it suggests that the Crow-Hidatsa split may have occurred in the early eighteenth century since the two groups appear to have been at war in 1716.

13. York Factory Journal, 1720–1, PAC, HBC B 239/a/6, p. 19.

14. York Factory Journals, 1728–31 and 1740–1,

PAC, HBC B 239/a/13 and 22.

15. Williams, ed., *Graham's Observations*, 207.

16. Ibid., 6–7. In addition to the Sussou he said that the Mithco (Blood) and Blackfoot lived westsouthwest of York Factory 800 miles and used horses.

17. York Factory Journals, 1714–17, PAC, HBC B 239/a/1–3.

18. York Factory Journals, 1715–16, PAC, HBC B 239/a/2, p. 28. Some of these groups took up to two years to make the trek overland to York Factory.

19. Kelsey's reference to the Mai tain ai thi nishe's visit of 26 May 1721 is the last such reference.

20. York Factory Correspondence Books, 1762, PAC, HBC B 239/b/23 p. 15

21. York Factory Journals, 1716–17 PAC, HBC B 239/a/3, p. 56.

22. York Factory Correspondence Books, 1762–3, 25 July 1763, PAC, HBC B 239/b/24.

23. L.J. Burpee, 'An Adventurer From Hudson Bay: Being the Journal of a Journey Performed by Matthew Cocking, Second Factor at York Fort in Order to Take a View of the Inland Country, and to Promote the Hudson's Bay Company's Interest, Whose Trade is Diminishing by the Canadians Yearly Intercepting Natives on Their Way to the Settlements, 1772–1773', *Transactions Royal Society of Canada* ser. 3, vol. 2 (1908): Section 2, 91–121'.

24. These groups of Cree were known as the Home Guard Indians because they lived near the posts and were employed by the company as hunters, guides, messengers between the posts, canoe builders, and so forth.

25. E.E. Rich, ed., *Hudson's Bay Company Letters Outwards* (London, 1957), 96.

26. Ibid., xlii–xlv.

6 From Sylvia Van Kirk, *Many Tender Ties: Women in Fur-Trade Society in Western Canada, 1670–1870* (Winnipeg: Watson & Dwyer, 1980), 53–73.

The economic role played by Indian women in fur-trade society reflected the extent to which the European traders were compelled to adapt to the native way of life. The all-encompassing work role of Indian women was transferred, in modified form, to the trading post, where their skills not only facilitated the traders' survival in the wilderness but actual fur-trade operations. At the North West Company posts and at Hudson's Bay Company posts especially, native women came to be relied upon as an integral if unofficial part of the labour force. Their economic assistance was a powerful incentive for the traders to take Indian wives; even within their own tribes, the women exercised a role in the functioning of the trade which has been little appreciated by historians of this period.

The Nor'Westers had a first-hand knowledge of the usefulness of Indian wives which they gained from the French, and this was an important reason for the Company allowing its men to intermarry with the natives. Besides familiarizing the Frenchman with the customs and language of her tribe, the Indian woman had performed a wide range of domestic tasks. When the Jesuit Father Carheil castigated the French traders at Michilimackinac for keeping Indian women, the traders argued that their primary motive was economic necessity. Their wives ground the corn to make the staple food known as sagamité, made moccasins and leather garments, and performed other essential services such as washing and chopping firewood for the cabins. Carheil's remonstrance that the carrying out of these duties provided but 'a proximate occasion for sin' was a gross underestimate of the genuine importance of the women's tasks.[1] Given that the Nor'Westers with their large force of skilled engagés still relied upon the services of Indian women, it can be appreciated that the Hudson's Bay Company with its limited and inexperienced personnel had an even greater need for their

assistance. Throughout the eighteenth century, officers on the Bay argued with the London Committee that it was essential to keep Indian women in the posts, as they performed important tasks which the British had not yet mastered. The Council at York Factory even protested to the Committee in 1802 that the women should be regarded as 'Virtually your Honors Servants.'[2]

Perhaps the most important domestic task performed by the women at the fur-trade posts was to provide the men with a steady supply of 'Indian shoes' or moccasins. The men of both companies generally did not dress in Indian style (the buckskinned mountain man was not part of the Canadian scene), but they universally adopted the moccasin as the most practical footwear for the wilderness. The first step in making moccasins or other leather apparel such as leggings and mittens was the laborious process of tanning the moose or deer skins:

> The skin they scrape and . . . take the braines of the animal and rub it upon the skin to make it pliable and soft; afterwards they smoke it well and then soak it in warm water for the night in order to render it easy to work with a piece of iron made for that purpose.[3]

Even Joseph Isbister, a stern disciplinarian, stressed the necessity of admitting women into the Bayside forts to provide a constant supply of shoes for the men. Large quantities were needed, for moccasins wore out quickly; at York Factory in 1800, the women made 650 pairs for the men's use in the summer season.[4] On his 1789 expedition, Alexander Mackenzie depended upon the wives of his two French-Canadian voyageurs to keep his party in footwear. The women scarcely ever left the canoes, being 'continually employ'd making shoes of moose skin as a pair does not last us above one Day.'[5]

Closely related to the manufacture of moccasins was the Indian woman's role in making the snowshoes which made winter travel possible. Although the men usually made the frames, the women prepared the sinews and netted the intricate webbing which provided the support. When Samuel Hearne and his small party went inland in 1774 to establish Cumberland House, the first Hudson's Bay Company post inland, they looked to Indian women for assistance. On October 21, Hearne recorded that all the Indians had gone away 'Except 2 or 3 Women who Stays to Make, Mend, Knitt Snowshoes &c for us dureing the Winter.'[6] A man could not even venture outside the post to collect firewood or hunt small game in winter without snowshoes. To be without women to make them was to invite disaster, as Alexander Mackenzie's well-known lament to his cousin Roderic at Fort Chipewyan in 1786 indicates:

> I have not a single one in my fort that can make Rackets [racquettes]. I do not know what to do without these articles see what it is to have no wives. Try and get Rackets—there is no stirring without them.[7]

Without women to provide them with moccasins and snowshoes, Hudson's Bay Company officers stressed, the Company would be seriously restricted in its efforts to compete with its rivals.[8]

In the provision and preservation of food, always a serious concern to the fur traders, Indian women also made an important contribution. For the North West Company, the expense of importing foodstuffs was prohibitive. The problem of supplying its canoe brigades was ideally solved by the use of the Indian food, pemmican—a nutritious, compact mixture of pounded buffalo meat and fat which kept well and took up relatively little space. Pemmican became the staple food of the fur trade, and Indian women performed most of the steps required in its preparation. At posts on the plains, buffalo hunting and pemmican making formed an essential part of the yearly routine,

each post being required to furnish an annual quota for the support of the brigades. In accordance with Indian custom, once the hunters had killed the buffalo, the women's work began. They skinned the animals, cut the meat off the carcasses and collected the marrow and fat for rendering. After the meat was sliced into thin strips, it was dried on racks in the sun or over a slow fire. 'The women employed all day Slicing and drying the meat' was a typical diary entry in the early summer months.[9] When the meat was dry, the women pounded it into a thick flaky mass. About fifty pounds of this meat would then be mixed with forty pounds of melted fat and packed in a *taureau* to make up the standard ninety-pound lot of pemmican. Previously, during the winter, the women had been kept busy making the *taureaux* which were flattish sacks of buffalo hide with the hair on the outside. 'Women all busy stretching buffalo hides to make pemmican bags'; 'All the women at work sewing Bags' were common remarks in many fort journals.[10]

Although pemmican was the staple food of the transport brigades, it was too precious a commodity to form the chief diet at the posts themselves. Fresh meat could be kept in the ice-houses at most of the posts on the plains, but to the north, where game was scarce, the people subsisted mainly on fish and fowl. The women at the posts of both companies on Lake Athabasca were adept fisherwomen, since tending the nets was part of a woman's role in more northerly tribes. After a successful fall fishery, the women were busily occupied splitting and drying hundreds of whitefish for the winter.[11] Across the Rockies, the women preserved vast quantities of salmon, the basic food for the districts of the Columbia and New Caledonia.[12] At the posts around Hudson Bay, geese, either dried or salted by the Indian women, formed an important part of the 'country provisions'.[13]

Apart from curing the produce of the hunt, Indian women were also responsible for collecting auxiliary food supplies which, besides adding variety to the diet, could sometimes mean the difference between life and death. In the area to the west and southwest of Lake Superior, wild rice was a staple food of the Ojibwa. The women harvested the rice from the marshy shores of the lakes and rivers by shaking the ripe heads into the bottom of their small canoes. The rice was then parched and stored in fawn skins. The traders in the area were frequently grateful for such food,[14] and for maple sugar which constituted an important addition to the diet in the Shield area. The spring trip to the sugar bush provided a welcome release from the monotony of the winter routine, and the voyageurs with their families and Indian relatives all enjoyed the annual event. In April 1805, as a typical instance, all the women from the Nor'Westers' post on Rainy Lake were out making sugar. 'Mr. Grant's Girl' seems to have been especially expert at the job and on one occasion traded about thirty pounds of sugar for rum.[15] A kind of sugar could also be made from the Manitoba maple which grew as far west as Fort Carlton. Chief Factor John Stuart noted in April 1825 that the only subject of interest was that all the women were busy making sugar, 'some of it very fine.'[16]

The entire Indian Country teemed with many varieties of berries which the women looked forward to collecting annually. When the Nor'Westers were tracking up the higher reaches of the Saskatchewan, the younger Henry observed: 'the women generally keep on by land, during the use of the line, to gather fruit, which alleviates the labor and revives the spirits of the men.'[17] Later at Rocky Mountain House, he reported that the women would all go off on horseback and return with great quantities of poires, raspberries and strawberries. Dried berries, especially saskatoons, were added to the high-grade pemmican made for the officers. But berries were more than a luxury item. David Thompson declared that berries had kept him alive after he became incapacitated by breaking his leg in 1788:

> I became emaciated till the berries became ripe
> and the kind hearted Indian women brought me

plenty . . . for my support. This was pure charity for I had nothing to give them and I was much relieved.[18]

In New Caledonia and the Columbia, berries and 'wappitoo root' gathered by the women were necessary to alleviate hunger in the spring when supplies of salmon invariably ran low.[19]

Although the wilds of Western Canada gave the appearance of providing abundant sustenance, all regions suffered from seasonal fluctuations and poorer areas faced frequent starvation. In times of scarcity, an Indian woman's skill and resourcefulness came into their own. At Lake Athabasca, it was common for the women to be sent away to the fishery to support themselves and their children when provisions ran low.[20] After his fisherman deserted to the Nor'Westers at Île à la Crosse in 1810, Peter Fidler's Cree wife Mary virtually saved the English from starvation since she was the only one who knew how to mend and set the nets.[21]

The fact that it was also the woman's role in Indian society to snare small game served the traders well. On one occasion, the Indian wife of the bourgeois John Dugald Cameron reputedly kept the people at her husband's post alive with the catch from her snares.[22] The young Nor'Wester George Nelson was certainly grateful for his Ojibwa wife when he found himself in dire straits at a small outpost north of Lake Superior in 1815.[23] After provisions became almost exhausted in February, Nelson's wife set out, well equipped with snares of wire and twine, to catch small game. At first, she had little success because wild animals were devouring her catch before she could return to the snares. After about a week, however, she came in with sixteen partridges and went off with one of the men next day to bring home the thirty hares which she had cached. Nelson's wife had been accompanied by the wife of one of his Hudson's Bay Company competitors, but although the Nor'Wester knew he might be censured for allowing this, he felt his wife's welfare must come before commercial rivalry:

I am happy of it because it is company, she will have less trouble to chop wood & if misfortunately she cuts herself or gets otherwise sick, the others will help her.

The 'she-hunters' returned with all their equipment after about three weeks, having added much to the kettles of both companies. 'My woman brings home 8 hares & 14 Partridges' wrote Nelson with satisfaction on March 3, 'making in all 58 hares and 34 Partridges. Good.' Occasionally even the well-established post of York Factory could run out of fresh provisions, so essential for the prevention of scurvy. In December 1818, Chief Factor James Swain was forced to send his wife and one of his daughters out to try to catch fish or rabbits. They returned a fortnight later in bitterly cold weather with grim news: there were no fish and they had had to walk many miles to secure a few rabbits.[24]

Although Indian women played an important part in preserving and procuring country provisions, they did not take over the official role of cook at the fur-trade posts as might be expected. Usually an Orkneyman or a French Canadian was specifically designated to serve as cook for the officers' mess. At some posts the servants took their meals in a military-type mess, but as families increased it became common for the women to prepare their families' daily rations in the servants' quarters.[25]

Apart from domestic duties relating to the traditional female roles of making clothes and preparing food, the Indian woman was also involved in specific fur-trade operations. Of particular importance to the inexperienced Hudson's Bay Company men was the women's knowledge of dressing furs. As the York Council emphasized to its London superiors, the Indian women 'clean and put into a state of preservation all Beaver and Otter skins brought by the Indians undried and in bad Condition.'[26] Since the North West Company had adopted the birch-bark canoe as the basis of its transport system, Indian women continued in their traditional role of helping in its

manufacture. It was the women's job to collect wattappe (wattap), roots from the spruce tree, which they split fine for sewing the seams of the canoe. The numerous references in the journals testify to the vast quantities needed: 'Women raising wattap—33 women, 8 bundles each'— 'Mr. Grant's Girl brought us 75 Bundles Wattap to day.' On Lake Athabasca, the women at the Hudson's Bay Company post were expected to provide an annual quota of fifty bundles of wattappe each.[27] Having collected the wattappe, the women helped to sew the seams of the canoes and then caulk them with spruce gum which they also collected. At Rocky Mountain House in 1810, Alexander Henry observed the voyageurs' wives busy gathering gum for the Columbia canoes; a brigade which departed without adequate supplies of bark, wattappe and gum for repairs could find itself in dire straits.[28] At York Factory, the women helped to pay for their keep during the winter by making canoe sails.[29]

Besides assisting in the making of canoes, Indian women, because of their traditional training, could readily lend a hand to help man them. Two women assisted in paddling the canoes on Mackenzie's voyage in 1789,[30] but with a large force of voyageurs, it was seldom necessary for the North West Company to call upon this reserve. This was not the case with the Hudson's Bay Company in the early stages of its moving inland. With few experienced canoemen, the Hudson's Bay Company turned to women, who often rendered valuable assistance. John Thomas, on his return to Moose Factory in 1779, told of meeting another officer in charge of three small canoes loaded with provisions for a new inland post; each canoe was manned by an Englishman and an Indian woman, the woman acting as steersman.[31] In the 1790s Chief Factor Joseph Colen declared that one of the reasons for the declining number of canoes coming down to York Factory was that the women were no longer allowed to accompany their husbands and help paddle the canoes.[32] . . .

Altogether, the multi-faceted work role of

Indian women in the fur trade merits their description as 'Your Honors Servants'. But they were servants who never received wages in any real sense and undoubtedly both companies profited by this source of cheap labour. Signifi-

cantly, in fur-trade society, it was the Indian woman's traditional skills which made her a valuable economic partner, a fact which serves to underscore the initial dependence of the traders upon the Indians. . . .

NOTES

1. Jesuits. Letters from Missions. *Black gown and redskins; adventures and travels of the early Jesuit missionaries in North America, 1610–1791*, edited by Edna Kenton (New York, 1956), 401–2.

2. H.B.C.A., B.239/b/79, fos. 40d–41; see also J.B. Tyrrell, ed., *Journals of Samuel Hearne and Philip Turnor, 1774–1792* (Toronto: Champlain Society, XXI), 327, n.6; H.B.C.A., A. 11/116, fo. 77d.

3. P.A.C., Masson Collection, No. 3, 'An Account of the Chipwean Indians', 22.

4. H.B.C.A., B.239/a/105, fo. 11; B.42/a/36, fo. 23; B.42/a/5, fo. 7.

5. W. Kaye Lamb, ed., *The Journals and Letters of Sir Alexander Mackenzie* (Cambridge, England, 1970), 220.

6. Tyrrell, *Journals of Hearne and Turnor*, 125.

7. Lamb, *Journals of Mackenzie*, 424.

8. H.B.C.A., B.239/b/79, fo. 41.

9. P.A.C., Masson Collection, No. 6, John Porter's Journal, 29; H.B.C.A., B.121/a/4, fo. 48d.

10. Elliott Coues, ed., *New Light on the Early History of the Greater Northwest: The Manuscript Journals of Alexander Henry and of David Thompson, 1799–1814* (Minneapolis, 1965), 582–3; Charles M. Gates, ed., *Five Fur Traders of the Northwest* (St Paul, Minn., 1965), 161; L.R.F. Masson, *Les Bourgeois de la Compagnie du Nord-Ouest* (New York, 1960), I: 288.

11. H.B.C.A., B.39/a/16, fo. 21.

12. Gabriel Franchère, *Narrative of a Voyage to the Northwest Coast of America, 1811–1814*, edited by R.G. Thwaites (Cleveland, 1904), 5.

13. H.B.C.A., B.239/a/131–3 passim.

14. Michel Curot, 'A Wisconsin Fur-Trader's Journal, 1803–04', *Wisconsin Historical Collections* 20: 442–3.

15. Gates, *Five Fur Traders*, 237; Curot, 'Journal, 1803–04', 441.

16. H.B.C.A., B.27/a/14, fo. 98.

17. Coues, *New Light on Greater Northwest*, 485.

18. Richard Glover, ed., *David Thompson's Narrative, 1784–1812* (Toronto: Champlain Society, 1962), 55.

19. Coues, *New Light on Greater Northwest*, 859; Ross Cox, *The Columbia River*, edited by Edgar and Jane Stewart (Norman, Okla., 1957), 266.

20. H.B.C.A., B.39/a/16, fos. 4d–13 passim.

21. H.B.C.A., B.89/a/2, los. 7, 10d.

22. Margaret A. MacLeod, ed., *The Letters of Letitia Hargrave* (Toronto: Champlain Society, XXVIII), lii.

23. The following account is taken from the George Nelson Papers, Journal, 29 Jan.–23 June 1815.

24. H.B.C.A., B.239/a/126, fo. 14.

25. MacLeod, *Letitia's Letters*, 85.

26. H.B.C.A., B.239/b/79, fo. 40d; see also Tyrrell, *Journals of Hearne and Turnor*, 237, n.6.

27. Coues, *New Light on Greater Northwest*, 615; Gates, *Five Fur Traders*, 217; E.E. Rich, ed., *Simpson's Athabasca Journal and Report, 1820–21* (London: H.B.R.S., I), 342.

28. Coues, *New Light on Greater Northwest*, 622; Gates, *Five Fur Traders*, 250–2; Curot, 'Journal, 1803–04', 460.

29. H.B.C.A., B.239/a/130, fos. 22d–28 passim.

30. Lamb, *Journals of Mackenzie*, 165.

31. H.B.C.A., A. 11/44, fo. 95.

32. H.B.C.A., B.239/a/99, fo. 18d: Colen further adds that 'this occasions much murmuring among the Men and forces many to leave the Service sooner than they wished to'. Unfortunately, no further information has been found to explain either the cause or ultimate outcome of this action.

EIGHT

☐ Rebellions in Lower Canada, 1837–1838

Readings

PRIMARY DOCUMENTS

HISTORICAL INTERPRETATIONS

INTRODUCTION

■ The principal historical landmarks in the history of the Canadas in the first half of the nineteenth century have always been the rebellions of 1837 (and in Lower Canada, again in 1838), where men in both provinces rose in opposition to their governments. The traditional view has been to see the events of 1837 and 1838 as evidence of constitutional inadequacies connected to imperial administration, eventually corrected by the Union of the Canadas and the achievement of responsible government in the 1840s. In both provinces an entrenched oligarchy, the Family Compact in Upper Canada and the Château Clique in Lower Canada, refused to give way to new political demands from the elected houses of assembly, producing a sense of frustration that resulted in armed uprisings. The rebellions were easily put down by the local authorities with the support of the British military, and they led in the short run to an investigation of the colonial situation by Lord Durham and in the long run to responsible government.

Although loosely related by chronology, common complaints, and the correspondence of rebel leaders such as William Lyon Mackenzie and Louis-Joseph Papineau, the two rebellions were quite distinct. Both rebellions have in recent years received considerably more attention apart from their place in Canadian constitutional development. Certainly the uprising in Lower Canada was far more complex in its origins and more widespread in its popular impact and repercussions. Lower Canada constituted an embattled community with cultural, linguistic, and religious differences. A number of interesting questions have emerged.

Questions for consideration

1. To what extent were the uprisings a logical outgrowth of long-standing structural problems within the province?
2. Were the rebellions produced by the dissatisfaction of a handful of leaders or were they a broadly based political movement?
3. Did the unleashing of discontent allow other less obvious issues to surface?
4. What does the response of the authorities to the uprisings tell us about ultimate political power and its deployment in British North America?
5. Was the British Empire truly a benign and benevolent liberal institution?

Suggestions for further reading

Donald Grant Creighton, *The Empire of the St. Lawrence* (Toronto: Macmillan of Canada, 1956). A classic analysis that sees the problem more in mercantile than in cultural terms.

Helen Taft Manning, *The Revolt of French Canada 1800–1835: A Chapter in the History of the British Commonwealth* (Toronto: Macmillan of Canada, 1962). Still the standard account of the imperial background of French Canada's discontents.

Fernand Ouellet, *Economic and Social History of Quebec, 1760–1850: 'Structures' and 'Conjunctures'* (Toronto: Macmillan of Canada, 1980). A revisionist account by a historian pioneering in quantitative history in the global context.

Elinor Kyte Senior, *Redcoats and Patriotes: The Rebellions in Lower Canada, 1837–38* (Stittsville, Ont.: Canada's Wings/National Museums of Canada, 1985). A balanced study with a heavy emphasis on the military side.

PRIMARY DOCUMENTS

1 From The 92 Resolutions, in Michael Bliss, ed., *Canadian History in Documents* (Toronto, 1967), 26–31.

1. Resolved, That His Majesty's loyal subjects, the people of this province of Lower Canada, have shown the strongest attachment to the British Empire, of which they are a portion; that they have repeatedly defended it with courage in time of war; that at the period which preceded the Independence of the late British Colonies on this continent, they resisted the appeal made to them by those colonies to join their confederation.

9. Resolved, That the most serious defect in the Constitutional Act, its radical fault, the most active principle of evil and discontent in the province; the most powerful and most frequent cause of abuses of power; of the infraction of the laws; of the waste of the public revenue and property, accompanied by impunity to the governing party, and the oppression and consequent resentment of the governed, is that injudicious enactment, . . . which invests the Crown with that exorbitant power (incompatible with any government duly balanced, and founded on law and justice, and not on force and coercion) of selecting and composing without any rule or limitation, or any predetermined qualification, an entire branch of the legislature, supposed from the nature of its attributes to be independent, but inevitably the servile tool of the authority which creates, composes and decomposes it, and can on any day modify it to suit the interests or the passions of the moment.

17. Resolved, That . . . the principal Agent of His Majesty's Government in this Province . . . . has destroyed the hope which His Majesty's faithful subjects had conceived of seeing the Legislative Council reformed and ameliorated, and has confirmed them in the opinion that the only possible mode of giving to that body the weight and respectability which it ought to possess, is to introduce into it the principle of election.

41. Resolved, . . . that the neighbouring States have a form of government very fit to prevent abuses of power, and very effective in repressing them; that the reverse of this order of things has always prevailed in Canada under the present form of government; that there exists in the neighbouring States a stronger and more general attachment to the national institutions than in any other country, and that there exists also in those States a guarantee for the progressive advance of their political institutions towards perfection, in the revision of the same at short and determinate intervals, by conventions of the people, in order that they may without any shock or violence be adapted to the actual state of things.

44. Resolved, That the unanimous consent with which all the American States have adopted and extended the elective system, shows that it is adapted to the wishes, manners and social state of the inhabitants of this continent; . . . and that we do not hesitate to ask from a Prince of the House of Brunswick, and a reformed Parliament, all the freedom and political powers which the Princes of the House of Stuart and their Parliaments granted to the most favoured of the plantations formed at a period when such grants must have been less favourably regarded than they would now be.

49. Resolved, That this House and the people whom it represents do not wish or intend to convey any threat; but that, relying as they do upon the principles of law and justice, they are and ought to be politically strong enough not to be exposed to receive insult from any man whomsoever, or bound to suffer it in silence; that the style of the said extracts from the despatches of the Colonial Secretary, as communicated to this House, is insulting and inconsiderate to such a degree that no legally constituted body, although its functions were infinitely subordinate to those of legislation, could or ought to tolerate them; . . .

52. Resolved, . . . That the majority of the inhabitants of this country are in nowise disposed to repudiate any one of the advantages they derive from their origin and from their descent from the French nation, which, with regard to the progress of which it has been the cause in civilization, in the sciences, in letters, and the arts, has never been behind the British nation, and is now the worthy rival of the latter in the advancement of the cause of liberty and of the science of Government; from which this country derives the greater portion of its civil and ecclesiastical law, and of its scholastic and charitable institutions, and of the religion, language, habits, manners and customs of the great majority of its inhabitants.

64. Resolved, That the claims which have for many years been set up by the Executive Government to that control over and power of appropriating a great portion of the revenues levied in this province, which belong of right to this House, are contrary to the rights and to the constitution of the country; and that with regard to the said claims, this House persists in the declarations it has heretofore made.

73. Resolved, That it was anciently the practice of the House of Commons to withhold supplies until grievances were redressed; and that in following this course in the present conjuncture, we are warranted in our proceeding, as well by the most approved precedents, as by the spirit of the constitution itself.

75. Resolved, That the number of the inhabitants of the country being about 600,000, those of French origin are about 525,000, and those of British or other origin 75,000; and that the establishment of the civil government of Lower Canada for the year 1832, according to the yearly returns made by the Provincial Administration, for the information of the British Parliament, contained the names of 157 officers and others receiving salaries, who are apparently of British or foreign origin, and the names of 47 who are apparently natives of the country, of French origin: that this statement does not exhibit the whole disproportion which exists in the distribution of the public money and power, the latter class being for the most part appointed to the inferior and less lucrative offices, and most frequently only obtaining even these by becoming the dependents of those who hold the higher and more lucrative offices; . . .

79. Resolved, That this House, as representing the people of this province, possesses of right, and has exercised within this province when occasion has required it, all the powers, privileges and immunities claimed and possessed by the Commons House of Parliament in the kingdom of Great Britain and Ireland. . . .

84. Resolved, That besides the grievances and abuses before mentioned, there exist in this province a great number of others (a part of which existed before the commencement of the present administration, which has maintained them, and is the author of a portion of them), with regard to which this House reserves to itself the right of complaining and demanding reparation, and the number of which is too great to allow of their being enumerated here: that this House points out, as among that number,

1stly. The vicious composition and the irresponsibility of the Executive Council, . . . and the secrecy with which not only the functions, but even the names of the members of that body have been kept from the knowledge of this House, . . .

2dly. The exorbitant fees illegally exacted in certain of the public offices, and in others connected with the judicial department, under regulations made by the Executive Council, by the judges, and by other functionaries usurping the powers of the legislature. . . .

4thly. The cumulation of public places and offices in the same persons, and the efforts made by a number of families connected with the administration, to perpetuate this state of things for their own advantage, . . .

5thly. The intermeddling of members of the Legislative Councils in the election of the representatives of the people, for the purpose of influencing and controlling them by force, and the selection frequently made of returning officers for the purpose of securing the same partial and corrupt ends; the interference of the present Governor-in-chief himself in the said elections; his approval of the intermeddling of the said legislative councillors in the said elections; . . .

6thly. The interference of the armed military force at such elections, through which three peaceable citizens, whose exertions were necessary to the support of their families, and who were strangers to the agitation of the election, were shot dead in the streets, . . .

7thly. The various faulty and partial systems which have been followed ever since the passing of the Constitutional Act, with regard to the management of the waste lands in this province, and have rendered it impossible for the great majority of the people of the country to settle on the said lands; the fraudulent and illegal manner in which, contrary to His Majesty's instructions, Governors, Legislative and Executive Councillors, Judges and subordinate officers have appropriated to themselves large tracts of the said lands; . . .

85. Resolved, . . . that this House expects from the honour, patriotism and justice of the reformed Parliament of the United Kingdom, that the Commons of the said Parliament will bring impeachments, and will support such impeachments before the House of Lords against the said Matthew Lord Aylmer, for his illegal, unjust and unconstitutional administration of the government of this province; and against such of the wicked and perverse advisers who have misled him, as this House may hereafter accuse, . . .

86. Resolved, That this House hopes and believes, that the independent members of both Houses of the Parliament of the United Kingdom will be disposed, both from inclination and from a sense of duty, to support the accusations brought by this House, to watch over the preservation of its rights and privileges which have been so frequently and violently attacked, more especially by the present administration; and so to act, that the people of this province may not be forced by oppression to regret their dependence on the British Empire, and to seek elsewhere a remedy for their afflictions. . . .

2   From a despatch from Lord Durham to Lord Glenelg, 9 August 1838, in *The Report and Despatches of the Earl of Durham Her Majesty's High Commissioner and Governor-General of British North America* (London: Ridgways, 1839), 305–9.

Castle of St. Lewis, Quebec, 9 August 1838.

My Lord,

The information which my residence here has enabled me to obtain as to the condition of the two Canadas is of such a nature as to make me doubt whether, if I had been fully aware of the real state of affairs in this part of the world, any considerations would have induced me to undertake so very difficult a task as is involved in my mission. I do not, however, wish it to be understood that I consider success impossible. On the contrary, I indulge a hope that if the difficulties and dangers that are now so apparent to me are appreciated by Her Majesty's Government, so as to lead to their adoption of measures sufficiently comprehensive and decided to meet the emergency, the objects of my mission may be accomplished. My sole purpose, therefore, in adverting to circumstances which threaten a different result is to impress upon your Lordship my own conviction, which has been formed by personal experience, that even the best informed persons in England can hardly conceive the disorder or disorganization which, to the careful inquirer on the spot, is manifest in all things pertaining to Government in these colonies. Such words scarcely express the whole truth: not Government merely, but society itself seems to be almost dissolved; the vessel of the State is not in great danger only, as I had been previously led to suppose, but looks like a complete wreck. It is needless to point out the wide difference between this representation and the opinions on the subject which were, and probably still are, held by Her Majesty's Ministers; but since one who had the benefit of whatever information they possessed is nevertheless compelled to acknowledge that the truth, as it now appears to him, differs so much from his previous conceptions of it, what can he infer but that distance has precluded them from acquiring an accurate knowledge of the whole subject? This is my belief, and it becomes, therefore, an imperative duty on my part to convey to your Lordship the exact impressions which I have derived from personal inquiry and observation. I will not shrink from the performance of that duty.

On the present occasion, however, I propose to confine myself to a particular class of circumstances; that is, to those which relate to the Lower Province, and are of the most unfavourable character; my object in making such a selection being to state without reserve, in a separate despatch, certain facts and opinions, to which, as coming from me, it is most inexpedient that any publicity should be given for the present; this despatch will therefore be marked 'Secret.'

The first point to which I would draw your attention, being one with which all others are more or less connected, is the existence of a most bitter animosity between the Canadians and the British, not as two parties holding different opinions and seeking different objects in respect to Government, but as different races engaged in a national contest.

This hatred of races is not publicly avowed on either side; on the contrary, both sides profess to be moved by any other feelings than such as belong to difference of origin; but the fact is, I think, proved by an accumulation of circumstantial evidence more conclusive than any direct testimony would be, and far more than sufficient to rebut all mere assertions to the contrary.

If the difference between the two classes were one of party or principles only, we should find on each side a mixture of persons of both races, whereas the truth is that, with exceptions which tend to prove the rule, all the British are on one side, and all the Canadians are on the other. What may be the immediate subject of dispute seems to be of no consequence; so surely as there is a dispute on any subject, the great bulk of the Canadians and the great bulk of the British appear ranged against each other. In the next place, the mutual dislike of the two classes extends beyond politics into social life, where, with some trifling exceptions again, all intercourse is confined to persons of the same origin. Grownup persons of a different origin seldom or never meet in private society; and even the children, when they quarrel, divide themselves into French and English like their parents. In the schools and the streets of Montreal, the real capital of the province, this is commonly the case. The station in life, moreover, of an individual of either race seems to have no influence on his real disposition towards the other race: high and low, rich and poor, on both sides—the merchant and the porter, the seigneur and the habitant—though they use different language to express themselves, yet exhibit the very same feeling of national jealousy and hatred. Such a sentiment is naturally evinced rather by trifles than by acts of intrinsic importance. There has been no solemn or formal declaration of national hostility, but not a day nor scarcely an hour passes without some petty insult, some provoking language, or even some serious mutual affront, occurring between persons of British and French descent. Lastly, it appears, upon a careful review of the political struggle between those who have termed themselves the loyal party and the popular party, that the subject of dissension has been, not the connection with England, nor the form of the constitution, nor any of the practical abuses which have affected all classes of the people, but simply such institutions, laws, and customs as are of French origin, which the British have sought to overthrow and the Canadians have struggled to preserve, each class assuming false designations and fighting under false colours—the British professing exclusive loyalty to the Crown of England, and the Canadians pretending to the character of reformers. Nay, I am inclined to think that the true principles and ultimate objects of both parties, taken apart from the question of race, are exactly the reverse of what each of them professes, or, in other words, that the British (always excluding the body of officials) are really desirous of a more responsible Government, while the Canadians would prefer the present form of Government, or even one of a less democratic character. I shall have more to say on this head presently, having mentioned the subject here only for the purpose of citing another fact which tends to prove the existence of a deep-rooted national sentiment on both sides. Such a contradiction between the real and avowed principles of each party, could not have occurred if all the people had been of one race, or if every other consideration had not given way to the sentiment of nationality.

This general antipathy of the Canadians towards the British, and of the British towards the Canadians, appears to have been, as it were, provided for at the conquest of the province, and by subsequent measures of the British Government. If Lower Canada had been isolated from other colonies, and so well peopled as to leave little room for emigration from Britain, it might have been right at the conquest to engage for the preservation of French institutions, for the existence of a 'Nation Canadienne;' but, considering how certain it was that, sooner or later, the British race would predominate in the country, that engagement seems to have been most unwise. It ensured such a strife as has actually taken place; for, notwithstanding the division of Canada into two provinces, for the purpose of isolating the French, the British already predominate in French Canada, not numerically of course, but by means of their superior energy and wealth, and of their natural relationship to the powers of Government. It was long before the Canadians perceived that their nationality was in the course of being overridden by a British nationality. When the Constitutional Act bestowed on them a representative system, they were so little conversant with its nature, and so blind to the probable results of British emigration, that they described the constitution as a 'machine Anglaise pour nous taxer,' and elected to the House of Assembly almost a majority of Englishmen. But with the progress of British intrusion, they at length discovered, not only the uses of a representative system, but also that their nationality was in danger; and I have no hesitation in asserting, that of late years they have used the representative system for the single purpose of maintaining their nationality against the progressive intrusion of the British race. They have found the British pressing upon them at every turn, in the possession of land, in commerce, in the retail trade, in all kinds of industrious enterprize, in religion, in the whole administration of government, and though they are a stagnant people, easily satisfied and disinclined to exertion, they have naturally resisted an invasion which was so offensive to their national pride. The British, on the other hand, impeded in the pursuit of all their objects, partly by the ancient and barbarous civil law of the country, and partly by the systematic opposition of the Canadians to the progress of British enterprize, have naturally sought to remove those impediments, and to conquer, without much regard to the means employed, that very mischievous opposition. The actual result should have seemed inevitable. The struggle between the two races, conducted as long as possible according to the forms of the constitution, became too violent to be kept within those bounds. In order to preserve some sort of government, the public revenue was disposed of against the will of the Canadian people represented by their Assembly. The consequent rebellion, although precipitated by the British from an instinctive sense of the danger of allowing the Canadians full time for preparation, could not, perhaps, have been avoided; and the sentiment of national hostility has been aggravated to the uttermost, on both sides, by that excessive inflammation of the passions which always attends upon bloodshed for such a cause, and still more by this unusual circumstance,—that the victorious minority suffered extreme fear at the beginning of the contest, and that the now subdued majority had been led to hope every thing from an appeal to force.

There seems to me only one modification of this view of the subject. The employment by the Canadians of constitutional and popular means for their national purpose, has taught some of them, consisting chiefly of the most active and able, higher political views than such as belong to the question of nationality. These men are not at heart friendly to the barbarous institutions of their ancestors, but would readily adopt a more enlightened system, if they could do so without losing their own importance. Their necessary dependence on the prejudiced mass has alone restrained them from joining in many of the views for the improvement of the country which are entertained by the British. They have also learned to estimate the practical abuses of Government which affect all classes, and to wish for many reforms without reference to Canadian nationality. They even had, to some extent, succeeded in disseminating their opinions amongst the mass of their countrymen, and they are not unlikely to play a valuable and distinguished part under any new system of government that may put an end to the strife between hostile races.

HISTORICAL INTERPRETATIONS

3   From Alfred G. DeCelles, *The 'Patriotes' of 1837* (Toronto: Glasgow, Brook & Company, 1915), 69–78.

As the autumn of 1837 wore on, the situation in Lower Canada began to assume an aspect more and more threatening. In spite of a proclamation from the governor forbidding such meetings, the *Patriotes* continued to gather for military drill and musketry exercises. (Armed bands went about the countryside, in many places intimidating the loyalists and forcing loyal magistrates and militia officers to send in their resignations to the governor.) As early as July some of the Scottish settlers at Côte St Joseph, near St Eustache, had fled from their homes, leaving their property to its fate. Several houses at Côte St Mary had been fired upon or broken into. A letter of Sir John Colborne, the commander of the forces in British North America, written on October 6, shows what the state of affairs was at that time:

> In my correspondence with Col. Eden I have had occasion to refer to the facts and reports that establish the decided character which the agitators have lately assumed. The people have elected the dismissed officers of the militia to command them. At St Ours a pole has been erected in favour of a dismissed captain with this inscription on it, 'Elu par le peuple.' At St Hyacinthe the tri-coloured flag was displayed for several days. Two families have quitted the town in consequence of the annoyance they received from the patriots. Wolfred Nelson warned the patriots at a public meeting to be ready to arm. The tri-coloured flag is to be seen at two taverns between St Denis and St Charles. Many of the tavern-keepers have discontinued their signs and substituted for them an eagle. The bank notes or promissory notes issued at Yamaska have also the same emblem marked on them. Mr Papineau was escorted from Yamaska to St Denis by a numerous retinue, and it is said that 200 or 300 carriages accompanied him on his route. He has attended five public meetings lately; and at one of them La Valtrie, a priest, was insulted in his presence. The occurrence at St Denis was certainly a political affair, a family at St Antoine opposed to the proceedings of W. Nelson, having been annoyed by the same mob that destroyed the house of Madame St Jacques a few hours before the shot was fired from her window.

Special animosity was shown toward the *Chouayens*, those French Canadians who had refused to follow Papineau's lead. P.D. Debartzch, a legislative councillor and a former supporter of Papineau, who had withdrawn his support after the passing of the Ninety-Two Resolutions, was obliged to flee from his home at St Charles; and Dr Quesnel, one of the magistrates of L'Acadie, had his house broken into by a mob that demanded his resignation as magistrate.

On November 6 rioting broke out in Montreal. The Doric Club, an organization of the young men of English blood in the city, came into conflict with the French-Canadian *Fils de la Liberté*. Which side provoked the hostilities, it is now difficult to say. Certainly, both sides were to blame for their behaviour during the day. The sons of liberty broke the windows of prominent loyalists; and the members of the Doric Club completely wrecked the office of the *Vindicator* newspaper. It was only when the Riot Act was read, and the troops were called out, that the rioting ceased.

Up to this point the *Patriotes* had not indulged in any overt acts of armed rebellion. Some of their leaders, it is true, had been laying plans for a revolt. So much is known from the correspondence which passed between the leading *Patriotes* in Lower Canada and William Lyon Mackenzie, the leader of the rebellion in Upper

Canada. Thomas Storrow Brown, one of Papineau's lieutenants, wrote to Mackenzie asking him to start the ball rolling in Upper Canada first, in order to draw off some of the troops which Sir John Colborne had massed in Lower Canada. But all calculations were now upset by events which rapidly precipitated the crisis in the lower province.

Soon after the fracas in the streets of Montreal between the Doric Club and *the Fils de la Liberté*, a priest named Quiblier waited on Papineau, and advised him, since his presence in Montreal had become a source of disturbance, to leave the city. Whether he came as an emissary from the ecclesiastical authorities or merely as a friend is not clear. At any rate, Papineau accepted his advice, and immediately set out for St Hyacinthe. The result was most unfortunate. The government, thinking that Papineau had left the city for the purpose of stirring up trouble in the Richelieu district, promptly issued warrants for the arrest of Papineau and some of his chief lieutenants, Dr Wolfred Nelson, Thomas Storrow Brown, Edmund Bailey O'Callaghan, and several others.

Meanwhile, on the day that these warrants for arrest were being issued (November 16), a skirmish took place between a small party of British troopers and a band of *Patriotes* on the road between Chambly and Longueuil—a skirmish which may be described as the Lexington of the Lower Canada rebellion. The troopers, under Lieutenant Ermatinger, had been sent to St Johns to arrest two French Canadians, named Demaray and Davignon, who had been intimidating the magistrates. The arrest had been effected, and the party were on their way back to Montreal, when they were confronted by an armed company of *Patriotes*, under the command of Bonaventure Viger, who demanded the release of the prisoners. A brisk skirmish ensued, in which several on both sides were wounded. The troopers, outnumbered by at least five to one, and having nothing but pistols with which to respond to the fire of muskets and fowling-pieces, were easily routed; and the two prisoners were liberated.

The news of this affair spread rapidly through the parishes, and greatly encouraged the *Patriotes* to resist the arrest of Papineau and his lieutenants. Papineau, Nelson, Brown, and O'Callaghan had all evaded the sheriff's officer, and had taken refuge in the country about the Richelieu, the heart of the revolutionary district. In a day or two word came to Montreal that considerable numbers of armed habitants had gathered at the villages of St Denis and St Charles, evidently with the intention of preventing the arrest of their leaders. The force at St Denis was under the command of Wolfred Nelson, and that at St Charles was under the command of Thomas Storrow Brown. How these self-styled 'generals' came to be appointed is somewhat of a mystery. Brown, at any rate, seems to have been chosen for the position on the spur of the moment. 'A mere accident took me to St Charles,' he wrote afterwards, 'and put me at the head of a revolting force.'

Sir John Colborne, who was in command of the British military forces, immediately determined to disperse these gatherings by force and to arrest their leaders. His plan of campaign was as follows. A force consisting of one regiment of infantry, a troop of the Montreal Volunteer Cavalry, and two light field-guns, under the command of Lieutenant-Colonel Wetherall, had already been dispatched to Chambly by way of the road on which the rescue of Demaray and Davignon had taken place. This force would advance on St Charles. Another force, consisting of five companies of the 24th regiment, with a twelve-pounder, under Colonel Charles Gore, a Waterloo veteran, would proceed by boat to Sorel. There it was to be joined by one company of the 66th regiment, then in garrison at Sorel, and the combined force would march on St Denis. After having dispersed the rebels at St Denis, which was thought not to be strongly held, the little army was to proceed to St Charles, where it would be joined by the force under Wetherall.

At eight o'clock on the evening of November 22, Colonel Gore set out with his men from the barrack-square at Sorel for St Denis. The journey was one of eighteen miles; and in order to avoid St Ours, which was held by the *Patriotes*, Gore turned away from the main road along the Richelieu to make a detour. This led his troops over very bad roads. The night was dark and rain poured down in torrents. 'I got a lantern,' wrote one of Gore's aides-de-camp afterwards, 'fastened it to the top of a pole, and had it carried in front of the column; but what with horses and men sinking in the mud, harness breaking, wading through water and winding through woods, the little force soon got separated, those in the rear lost sight of the light, and great delays and difficulties were experienced. Towards morning the rain changed to snow, it became very cold, and daybreak found the unfortunate column still floundering in the half-frozen mud four miles from St Denis.'

Meanwhile word had reached the rebels of the coming of the soldiers. At daybreak Dr Wolfred Nelson had ridden out to reconnoitre, and had succeeded in destroying several bridges. As the soldiers approached St Denis they heard the church bells ringing the alarm; and it was not long before they found that the village was strongly defended. After capturing some of the houses on the outskirts of the village, they were halted by a stockade built across the road covered by a large brick house, well fortified on all sides. The commander of the troops brought reinforcements up to the firing line, and the twelve-pounder came into action. But the assailants made very little impression on the defence. Although the engagement lasted for more than five hours, the troops succeeded in capturing nothing more than one of the flanking houses. The ammunition of the British was running low, and the numbers of the insurgents seemed to be increasing. Colonel Gore therefore deemed it advisable to retire. By some strange oversight the British were without any ambulance or transport of any kind; and they were compelled to leave their dead and wounded behind them. Their casualties were six killed and eighteen wounded. The wounded, it is a pleasure to be able to say, were well looked after by the victorious *Patriotes*.

The British effected their retreat with great steadiness, despite the fact that the men had had no food since the previous day and had been marching all night. They were compelled to abandon their twelve-pounder in the mud; but they reached St Ours that night without further loss. The next day they were back at Sorel.

The number of the insurgents at St Denis has never been accurately ascertained; probably they were considerably in excess of the troops. Their position was one of great strength, and good judgment had been shown in fortifying it. On the other hand, with the exception of a few veterans of Major de Salaberry's Voltigeurs, they were untrained in war; and their muskets and fowling-pieces were much inferior to the rifles of the regulars. Their victory, it must be said, reflected great credit upon them; although their losses had been twice as great as those of the soldiers,[1] these peasants in homespun had stood their ground with a courage and steadiness which would have honoured old campaigners. The same, unfortunately, cannot be said about some of their leaders. Papineau and O'Callaghan were present in St Denis when the attack began; but before the morning was well advanced, they had departed for St Hyacinthe, whence they later fled to the United States. Papineau always declared that he had taken this action at the solicitation of Wolfred Nelson, who had said to him: 'Do not expose yourself uselessly: you will be of more service to us after the fight than here.' In later days, however, when political differences had arisen between the two men, Nelson denied having given Papineau any such advice. It is very difficult to know the truth. But even if Nelson did advise Papineau to leave, it cannot be said that Papineau consulted his own reputation in accepting the advice. He was not a person without military experience: he had been a major in the militia, and was probably superior in rank to any one in the village. His place was

with the brave farmers who had taken up arms on his behalf.

NOTE

1. According to a report twelve *Patriotes* lost their lives during the engagement. Among them was Charles Ovide Perrault, member of the Assembly for Vaudreuil, a young barrister of considerable promise. He seems to have been Papineau's closest follower and confidant. During the last sessions of the Lower Canada legislature Perrault contributed many letters to *La Minerve*.

4   From Fernand Ouellet, 'The 1837/8 Rebellion in Lower Canada as a Social Phenomenon', *Histoire sociale/Social History* 2(1968).

In his book on the popular uprisings in France in the seventeenth century, Boris Porchnev throws light on a series of spontaneous mass insurrections, spread by contagion and the establishment of popular leadership. To this description Porchnev adds an observation directly relevant to my purpose:

> As long as it kept its exclusively popular character, the movement suffered from bad organization and remained blindly impulsive. When its leadership was entrusted to representatives of another social class, they distorted the movement and its essential aims. . . . They contributed to its social blindness: by confining the platform of the uprising to a fight against taxation, they prevented it from developing into a revolutionary anti-feudal, anti-absolutist movement.[1]

Reading Canon Groulx might tempt us to draw a comparison between the Lower Canadian movement and its seventeenth-century French counterpart. The former is described by Groulx as 'an improvised movement, spontaneous in its outbreaks of violence; beyond that, a popular movement, a fairly broad and deep rural phenomenon'.[2] Unfortunately, Groulx's reliance on the somewhat inconsistent statements made by Papineau after his defeat seems to have misled him about the social origin of the revolutionary

movement. By denying any premeditation on the part of the revolutionary leaders, Papineau absolved them—and especially himself—of all responsibility, and incriminated the government against which popular anger was directed. Fair enough, perhaps; but I remain very skeptical. As Wolfred Nelson said, commenting on certain admissions of Papineau's:

> You have to fight liars, whether with their own weapons or with trickery. Frankness is a fine thing among honest men and in private life; in public, it leaves us too exposed. I am annoyed by Mr Papineau's and Mackenzie's admission that we had decided to rebel. That is to justify our opponents and to deprive us of any right to complain that we were attacked.[3]

In fact, the risings of 1837–8, just like the nationalism from which they sprang, started among the upper classes and spread downwards from them. Here is the first variation from the process outlined by Porchnev.

Since 1830 the idea of revolution had gained ground among a section of the militant Patriotes. Some leaders spoke of it as a possibility; others thought it inevitable. However, there was no systematic effort to create a revolutionary organization. It was after the Russell Resolutions in the spring of 1837, which deprived the Patriotes of all hope of success by peaceful means, that the leaders of the party felt bound to change their strategy and consider revolutionary action. It was the leaders of the Montréal region, recruited from the professional class and the merchants, who took on the task of redirecting the Patriote movement. Even though they were careful to destroy the compromising documents—Papineau admitted this himself—there is a mass of corroborative evidence showing precisely what the main lines of the revolutionary strategy were. It consisted of two stages: the first, the so-called 'legal' agitation, was aimed chiefly at forcing the government to modify its position; the second involved (in the event that the first one failed) launching a revolution 'after freeze-up'.[4] This was a compromise between the moderate and extremist elements of the party, the latter leaning more to immediate actions. Besides, how was it possible to intimidate the government without preparing the populace for a possible rebellion? The radical leaders never bothered to make this distinction. From the spring of 1837 they were openly preaching revolt. In June, Léon Charlebois, a Montréal tavern-keeper, declared 'that it was necessary to help the revolutionary party that was then in existence'.[5] At Chambly the Pacauds, who were shipowners, said they 'would be happy if the Patriotes could succeed in their plan for independence from the British government'.[6] Papineau himself did not escape the revolutionary atmosphere, which was spreading rapidly. At several meetings he even went so far as to make seditious remarks, though without refraining from ambiguity. Thus, when he warned the farmers that when the plums were ripe it was time to pick them, he was using language that was perfectly clear to them. Several witnesses testified that on the sixth of August, at a meeting at Saint-Constant, Côme Cherrier and Toussaint Peltier, two Montréal lawyers from the more moderate side of the revolutionary camp, were to make speeches 'tending to incite the local people to rebel if the English government failed to grant them what they had demanded in the Ninety-

two Resolutions'.[7] These are just a few examples from a mass of evidence indicating that 'legal' opposition was more a front than a practical objective: it was a screen behind which an armed uprising could be organized—because it was illusory to think the government would yield to blackmail. If there is no doubt about the premeditation, it is also clear that the movement was not of popular origin. It germinated within the top leadership of the *parti patriote*.

The revolutionary organization, whose centre was Montréal and whose principal body was the Permanent Central Committee, relied for its support not only on the suburbs but mainly on the country districts. Members of the local elites—those who had lined up with the *parti patriote*—formed the local leadership of the movement. It was they who planned the country meetings where the 'big men from the city' appeared, held small parish meetings on Sundays after Mass, and in some cases took up collections. Not only was there large attendance at these meetings, but in some places groups of armed farmers gathered to attack local inhabitants of British origin and 'known bureaucrats'.[8] The response of the rural populace was immediate, all the more since the rebellion was the climax of over thirty years of political conflict. Throughout the summer of 1837 tension and agitation increased in the country parishes surrounding Montréal. In October Montréal acquired its own revolutionary association aimed at reorganizing the populace. The *Fils de la liberté*, with its military and civil sections (the latter a screen for the former), held meetings at which some leaders gave commentaries on books about the French and American revolutions. Thomas Storrow Brown went so far as to declare that it was time 'to arm ourselves, since the country was moving quickly along the road to independence'.[9] The *Fils de la liberté*, sometimes numbering as many as a thousand, did not hesitate to hold military exercises. For this purpose they used one of the properties, in a suburb of Montréal, of Denis-Benjamin Viger, a cousin of

Papineau. This outbreak of agitation, both rural and urban, came to a head at the Six Counties rally, held at Saint-Charles on 23 October—a massive demonstration that marked a real turning point. As Nelson and Côté put it, the time for speeches was over. Papineau arrived at Saint-Charles with an armed escort of some fifteen though he later claimed 'to have come to this meeting only because he happened to be passing'.[10]

At the Saint-Charles rally the Patriote leaders went beyond mere violent words. They issued a declaration on the rights of man, modelled on the American declaration of 1776, and decided to get rid of all the militia officers, justices of the peace, and small-claims commissioners appointed by the government. All these officials, they declared, must be replaced by men elected by the people. This revolutionary action, openly supported by Papineau, meant the overthrow of all opponents of the movement. The Patriotes were trying to gain control of the militia and the judiciary. It was on this occasion, too, that plans for an open rebellion were again laid out by the leaders. A date was set for the beginning of December. The day after the meeting Dr Kimber, one of the leaders, would say:

> The moment the river is frozen up, we shall go with forty or fifty thousand armed men to seize Montréal; the local people are all well armed, well supplied with ammunition, and firmly resolved, and after Montréal we shall take Québec. I was at Saint-Charles and never in any country has there been seen such a rally, so determined to rid itself of the English government.[11]

Even though Kimber could have been tipsy when he made this revelation, his statement nevertheless contained a basis of truth. A letter from Papineau to Mackenzie in February 1838 confirms this:

> If navigation had been closed down as usual about 20 November, if the election of the magistrates

had taken place without violence, and only in December, as had been recommended, so that communication would be cut off between the north and south shores of the St Lawrence, the chances of success would have been better.[12]

On 23 October 1837, the day of the Saint-Charles rally, a Pointe-Claire farmer said 'that the damned *chouaguins* [cabbage-heads, or *Canadiens* who had sold out to the English] were going to be whipped now that everybody in the south and the north was armed, that there was no more law . . . and you could do what you liked . . . Mr Papineau knew that he had to start the revolution at this time, when no help could come from England.'[13] It is not surprising that acts of violence increased after the Saint-Charles rally. In most parishes Patriotes held 'charivaris', demanding the dismissal of militia officers and other government officials. Verbal violence reached something of a peak. A Henryville merchant, Joseph Gariépy, declared that he 'wouldn't rest until all the bureaucrats' heads were cut off'.[14] On 4 November 1837 Jacques Surprenant, innkeeper at Blairfindie, shouted at an opponent that he 'had a good mind to smash him over the head with a bottle because he, the deponent, was a bureaucrat and all bureaucrats had better get out of the country before their brains were blown out, and the said Surprenant said that he would do his utmost to help chop him into pieces.'[15]

At the beginning of November 1837 neither the government, nor members of the clergy who felt a need for strong intervention, could remain passive. Warrants were prepared for the arrest of the principal Patriote leaders. Informed by D.-B. Viger that he was in imminent danger of imprisonment, Papineau had some tense and anxious hours before he finally decided to flee Montréal. A witness to the conversation from the next room, Angélique Labadie, would later report:

> I also heard Mr Papineau say that he would never be satisfied until he was president in this country, and that he would be soon, and that if the gov-

ernment seized this country from him he would snatch it back. Mr Viger then told Mr Papineau that he should keep calm and wait for freeze-up and then he would just have to whistle and all the habitants and thousands of Americans would espouse their cause and they would soon be masters of this country.[16]

This first act of the government—the preparation of the warrants—had a magical effect. It prompted the hasty departure of the chief Montréal leaders, who took refuge in the countryside, where they prepared themselves for any emergency. Deprived of its leaders, the urban populace made no move. At Vaudreuil the situation bordered on comedy. The local leaders, fearing imprisonment, begged the people to protect them, on the grounds that they had incited them to revolt from altruistic motives.[17] Camps were formed at Saint-Denis, Saint-Charles, Saint-Mathias, Saint-Eustache, and Saint-Benôit. Intervention by government troops was then unavoidable, and between 17 November and 15 December 1837 military confrontation occurred. In short the government, sensing that matters were coming to a head, forestalled the Patriotes. Apart from this early intervention by government forces, the second rebellion, which took place during the first two weeks of November 1838, was an exact replica of the preceding one. Devised by the elite, especially refugees in the United States, it would spread to the masses through the intervention of the *Société des Frères Chasseurs*, said to have ten thousand members. Once again, lack of leadership on the spot prevented the fourteen hundred *chasseurs* in Montréal from stirring. In Québec City, where the association was supposed to have two thousand adherents, 'they are more cautious than in Montreal,'[18] according to an informed witness. On the whole, the two rebellions leave an identical impression: anarchy, disorganization, weak leadership, and paralysis. Are those not the characteristics of purely peasant uprisings, at least as Porchnev understands them? In this regard he writes:

These outside elements in the masses certainly left their stamp on the Nu-Pied movement. . . . There is no doubt that these elements helped the insurgents to organize, to follow a more or less systematic policy, to become a large armed force—in a word, to overcome the movement's purely impulsive and spontaneous character.[19]

This outline is interesting, but to what extent does it apply to the Lower Canadian movements? Several hypotheses are possible: superficiality of popular support, a marked persistence of the peasant mentality among the elite, or—what is simpler—betrayal by the elite.

Though fomented by the elite, these uprisings nevertheless had a broadly popular character. The rural and urban masses, which provided ninety-five per cent of the actual revolutionaries, made up the movement's striking force. The excuse so often put forward by the *habitants* and many others, that they gave in to the threats of the leaders, must be largely rejected. In my view fear is an extremely far-reaching and subtle phenomenon but it does not by itself account for participation by the lower classes in revolutionary events. Because its range is more general and more varied, the phenomenon of fear is also more complex in its ramifications. On the other hand, different excuses given by the common people merit even less attention: for example, it is easy to assess the origin of one farmer's tale, when arrested on the road early in the morning, that he was on his way to ask his mother (who lived in the home of a top rebel leader) to knit him a tuque; or that of another farmer, arrested after the battle of Saint-Eustache, who said he was about to drive his wife to confession. Where political vows are concerned, it is so often a matter of 'swearing with the mouth, not with the heart' that we can delude ourselves about them.

After analyzing the files on the rebels of 1837–8, I find it impossible not to perceive a genuine popular phenomenon, widespread and deep-rooted, prompted in large measure by specific, and different, motives than those of the elites who controlled the movement. I reckon that, not counting the sympathizers in Montréal, at least five thousand people were directly involved in the first venture. The following year the number exceeded five thousand, but the incidents took place in a much more limited area. In 1838 the populous parishes north of Montréal made no move. Glancing at the other regions in the province, we find an air of expectation among the people in the Beauce, and in Kamouraska and Charlevoix. Inquiries made at Saint-Joseph de la Beauce in the spring of 1838,

after the failure of the first rebellion, revealed that 260 inhabitants were still in favour of the Patriotes. Even if we allow for regional variations that could have a negative effect on popular attitudes, we still find a psychological receptiveness throughout seigneurial Lower Canada. In short, the motives that spurred farmers, craftsmen, and labourers in the Montréal region to revolutionary action operated elsewhere in varying degrees. The myth of the saviour was too widespread for the popular response not to have had firm roots—both at the time and in the past.

NOTES

1. Boris Porchnev, *Les Soulèvements populaires en France de 1623 à 1648*, pp. 325, 327. Even if one rejects Porchnev's concept of class, his study remains extremely significant.
2. Lionel Groulx, *Histoire du Canada français*, vol. III, p. 235.
3. Quoted in my 'Papineau dans la révolution de 1837–38', *CHAR*, 1958, p. 13. This essay analyzes the ambiguous behaviour of the revolutionary leader.
4. This phrase ('la prise des glaces') recurs frequently in the documents, in reference to the plans of the rebels. My analysis is based mainly on a wealth of archival materials, preserved in 'Les Événements 1837–38' in the Archives of the Province of Quebec, and in the Public Archives of Canada. These documents make possible an understanding of the social aspects of the movement.
5. Deposition of A. Brisebois, Pointe-Claire. It goes on: 'by supplying and contributing with other men of goodwill to supply all the money necessary to buy powder, balls, guns, and other things necessary to put the said rebel party in a position to set forth at the first opportunity to fight against the British government'.
6. Deposition of J. Trudel. See also those of P. Martin and N. Berthiaume. On 18 June 1837, A. Archambault, notary's clerk of Varennes, declared 'that he was working to overthrow the govern-

ment of this province to establish it as a republic and unite it to the United States or make it an independent government, whichever would be judged the more advantageous, and to have free trade with the United States and to stop trade with England'. Deposition of P. Nichols of Varennes.
7. Deposition of H. Guérin of Laprairie. Towards the end of the summer, at Saint-Eustache, Saint Benoit, and Sainte-Scholastique, Chénier, Girouard, and Scott spoke of arming themselves and setting up a provisional government. See the depositions of A. Denis and E. Sabourin.
8. Duncan McColl of Saint-Benoit related that after June 1837 the French Canadians had broken off contacts with the inhabitants of English origin. He and his brothers, one a blacksmith and the other a shopkeeper, had lost all their customers. After 3 July, the patriots had even decided to drive the British out of the parish. There are many such examples.
9. Deposition of Weidenbacker. On 1 November 1837, R. Bélair of Montréal was said to have been present at a rally: 'that the principal object of such meeting . . . was to attack and destroy the city of Montreal.' Deposition of A. Leggo.
10. Ouellet, 'Papineau dans la révolution de 1837–8', p. 20.
11. Ibid., p. 20.
12. Ibid., p. 15

13. Deposition of H. Macdonald.
14. Deposition of L. Holmes. In 1838 there continued to be many such declarations. H. Lefèbvre stated his intention to 'murder all Bureaucrats as they called the English population and destroy their properties'. Deposition of T. Legrand, known as Dufresne.

15. Les Événements 1837–38', p. 513.
16. Deposition of A. Labadie.
17. Deposition of W. Kell.
18. Deposition of Fratelin.
19. Porchnev, p. 327.

5 From Allan Greer, *The Patriots and the People: The Rebellion of 1837 in Rural Lower Canada* (Toronto: University of Toronto Press, 1993), 189–208.

Queen Victoria ascended the throne of England in August 1837, just as tensions in Lower Canada were reaching a boiling point. There is no indication that the seventeen-year-old monarch gave much immediate thought to the political squabbles wracking her North American possessions, but her coronation provided Canadians with an occasion for further reflections on sovereign authority and state forms. 'Loyal' Montreal managed to mount a parade to celebrate the happy event, and at Sorel the little garrison fired off a salute. A tavern-keeper's wife remarked to onlookers at the latter, 'There you are, celebrations for the coronation of the queen; she had better watch out or she'll be decrowned.'[1] It was the Te Deum ordered for the middle of August by the bishop of Montreal, the usual service on such occasions, that aroused the greatest controversy. At Saint-Polycarpe, where the curé dared to say a few words in praise of the new monarch, local Patriots managed to stop the ceremony. 'No sooner did the *Te Deum* commence, than the people quitted the church bodily, leaving the women and *marguilliers* (churchwardens) to keep his Reverence company. The deputy beadle was beginning to ring the bell when the people got out, but the parishioners stopped him, telling him that the bell belonged to them, and not the Queen of England, and that it should not be rung.'[2] Note the language used by the *Vindicator* to describe this incident: the counterposing of 'the *people*' and 'the *women*'. Half the population of the province might well have viewed these words as ominous signals, emanating

as they did from the presses of a journal dedicated to the principle of popular sovereignty!

That this was no accidental slip is underlined by the sexual references in protests against the coronation Te Deum. In the parish of Contrecoeur, a radical merchant led an exodus from the church, shouting, 'It is painful to have to sing the Te Deum for the damn queen, damned whore with her legs in the air.' A Patriot orator addressing the people of Nicolet from the church porch was reported to have said, 'As for the king, he is nothing but a big zero to whom Canadians pay a pension. . . . The proof that kings are nothing but zeros is that we are now governed by a young queen seventeen years of age.' Later, at the time of the battles of November and December, an American Patriot sympathizer got into trouble at Saint-Athanase by throwing 'ridicule on the person of the sovereign by saying the loyalists were governed by a little girl, that they were governed by petticoats.'[3] Such language would certainly have shocked English radicals; they were well disposed towards the young queen, who seemed to them a much more sympathetic figure than her notorious uncle, William IV.[4] At the same time, it directs our attention to some important characteristics of the Patriot movement as regards both gender and concepts of legitimate political authority.

Monarchy or Republic

All the abuse of poor Victoria indicates that of course the queen and the monarchy were not 'a zero' in the French-Canadian countryside. For all that the habitants took for granted a certain popular sovereignty within the local community, their concept of the state and the empire was highly personalized, focusing on the reigning king or queen. . . .

Canadians of course lived far from any flesh-and-blood monarch, although governors under the French and British regimes did do their best to put on a display of viceregal pomp and ceremony in the colony. More generally, political authority in this period did manifest itself in personal terms that reinforced monarchical habits of thought, no doubt accentuated by the strong military presence in Canada. Moreover, the Church did its utmost to impress on the faithful their duty to the king, not only in Te Deum services for coronations and royal births but also in sermons from the pulpit. Political leaders added their voices in support, including the Patriots, who until the eve of the Rebellion always protested their loyalty to the crown even as they denounced colonial Tories and wicked British ministers.[5]

A basically royalist political vocabulary does not imply a docile acceptance of authority. People who have been taught to regard the distant king as a father-figure who has the best interests of his subjects at heart often tend to conclude, when things go badly, that exploitative officials, merchants, or aristocrats are the monarch's enemies as well as their own. In this way royalism can become a revolutionary ideology (though one with built-in limitations inhibiting the development of popular democracy), as it was indeed in countless plebeian risings, such as the one that shook rural France in the summer of 1789, when thousands of peasants attacked seigneurial chateaux, acting, so they thought, 'on orders from the king.'[6] It should be noted that the peasant class is not the only one that tends to venerate the king while blaming his advisers. The American and French revolutions were already well under way before their bourgeois leaders began to attack George III, Louis XVI, and the

institution of monarchy.[7] (Tom Paine's *Common Sense* caused a sensation early in 1776 when it called for an independent American republic.) Yet the dynamic of the revolutions eventually broke the spell of royalty and led to the full development of a republican political discourse, one that had often been there all along in embryonic form. So it was in Lower Canada, where the crisis of the 1830s moved the bourgeois Patriots to an entirely republican outlook. Hence their determination to discredit the monarch as the personal symbol of government authority and metropolitan rule. . . .

The spell of traditional authority, as represented by priest and bishop, governor and queen, was giving way. People of different classes and levels of education were considering new ways of constituting a state and governing a human community. Could Canadians rule themselves? Could government derive its legitimacy from the people rather than historic rights of conquest and religious sanction? Patriot leaders answered these questions in the positive, and they drove home the point explicitly in speeches and newspaper articles, while expressing the same message in symbolic forms as well, notably through the use of flags and banners. Long before he began to take the movement seriously as a military threat, the commander of British forces in Lower Canada fretted over the emblems of popular sovereignty sprouting up in the Richelieu valley 'The tri coloured flag has been displayed at two taverns between St Denis and St Charles,' wrote Sir John Colborne in October 1837. 'Many of the taverns have discontinued their signs and substituted for them an Eagle.'[8] . . .

Masculine Politics

Granted that the Patriots objected to the institution of monarchy and to the fact of British rule; but why did they have to make an issue—and in such a cruel and personal way—of Queen Victoria's sex? Well, certainly their sensitivity was not unique in the international republican community of the period. Recent scholarship has demonstrated that considerations of sexual difference were of central concern to political writers and revolutionaries of the late eighteenth-early nineteenth-century period. To the degree that they challenged existing hierarchies on egalitarian grounds and insisted that 'the people' ought to rule, philosophers, Jacobins, and American patriots had to grapple with the question of what 'the people' was. It certainly was not all human beings resident in a given territory: not everyone was to participate equally and in the same way in sovereign authority. Women in particular tended to be excluded from direct political participation in the republican city. Pronouncements may have been cryptic and susceptible to multiple interpretations, with much assumed and little expressed; the effect was nonetheless for sex to become increasingly the primary dividing line between rulers and ruled in the age of the great bourgeois revolutions. Partly this exclusion arose by default, as older conceptions of political privilege based on birth, sacerdotal status, and so on came under attack, but also it derived from a profoundly gendered republican concept of citizenship.

Inspired by a particular reading of the history of ancient Greece and Rome, modern republicans such as Jean-Jacques Rousseau believed that men were uniquely qualified for the responsibilities of citizenship.[9] They were better suited for military combat, and, it was felt, all good citizens had to be prepared to defend their country on the battlefield. More fundamentally, Rousseau thought that males were by nature more apt to subordinate selfish and sectional interests for the good of the whole community. Women, by contrast, were necessarily associated with childbirth and nurturing; consequently, their orientation was to the family, a particularistic allegiance which they could not fully transcend without denying their nature. Thanks to their looser attachment to specific loved ones, men had the potential to develop the civic virtue—the dedication to the common good—required in any

healthy republic. It is important to note, however, that Rousseau did not consider women inferior to men. On the contrary, he attached great value to the loving and nurturing domestic sphere where women found their true calling. His effusions over motherhood and conjugal bliss underline the fact that for Rousseau women's familial role was the essential complement of active male citizenship. Domestic life and public life, he implied, were equally important elements of civilized existence. In order to discharge her duty, the republican woman needed to exercise a special sort of virtue: not public-spirited courage, but 'sexual innocence and chastity' were her distinguishing characteristics, and as an outward guarantee of monogamous behaviour, she had to confine herself to the private realm.[10]

Rousseau was in no simple sense a male supremacist; indeed his contemporary defenders insist that he accorded a great deal of legitimate power to women, though it was covert power, exercised through their sexual influence over particular men.[11] Moreover, with his emphasis on liberty and on the cultivation of the individual personality, he can plausibly be seen as the intellectual ancestor of modern women's liberation. One need only extend to females the reasoning that the philosopher applies to 'Man' and unsettling conclusions soon follow. . . . The fact remains that Rousseau himself did not present a feminist reading of Jean-Jacques. Everywhere one turns in his writings, the needs of men take precedence, and women appear in a positive light to the degree that they are helpful to men.

I have dwelt on Rousseau not because his works provided an instruction manual for Lower Canadian Patriots, but because he was one of the few writers of the period who gave sustained and explicit attention to the gender dimension of politics. Without denying the originality of his genius, I think it is fair to suggest that many of the essential features of Rousseau's thought in this area were characteristic of the international republican movement. Certainly echoes can be detected in the Patriot press of the notion that men and women possessed complementary but fundamentally different moral natures. An article published in *La Minerve* under the title 'The Two Republics' makes this point quite explicitly:

> The moral world is a mixture composed of men and women and it owes to this combination the greatest part of its customs, usages and ceremonies; if there were no more women in the human race, men would be unrecognizable. It is only in seeking to please the opposite sex that they manage to refine themselves. . . . Women, for their part, owe everything to that other half of the human race, to which they find themselves joined. . . . It is to the desire to please him [man] that they owe that gracious air, those eyes which say so many things, that modest blush which embellishes their complexion, that voice so soft and touching. This reciprocal desire is indeed a precious instinct in both sexes, one which tends towards the perfection of each of them. Thus a man with no interest in women will ordinarily become a savage; by the same token, a woman, intended by nature to get along with and to appear with man, can scarcely hate or despise him without becoming a ferocious and unbearable creature.[12]

Such sentiments were by no means limited to republican circles. Indeed, the basic notion that women belonged in a (valorized) domestic setting while men should run the state and the community became widely prevalent everywhere the bourgeoisie gained the ascendancy throughout the eighteenth century and well into the nineteenth. During the French Revolution, for example, there was some initial encouragement for the politicization of women, but it was soon followed by a policy of rigid exclusion from public life on the grounds that both the polity and the family suffered when women strayed into the male realm of active citizenship. Such treatment at the hands of the Jacobins led the feminist/ royalist Olympe de Gouges to protest that 'Women

are now respected and excluded, under the Old Régime they were despised and powerful.'[13] Earlier, American women had been treated similarly during 'their' revolutionary war.[14]

Women were not always 'respected' under the new order: witness the Patriots' misogynous and obscene verbal assault on Queen Victoria. In this respect, too, Lower Canadian behaviour seems to reflect widespread attitudes of the period, attitudes particularly characteristic of republicanism. What one might call the 'vulgar Rousseauian' outlook venerated the virtuous woman who kept to the domestic sphere, and was profoundly suspicious of any woman who ventured into the political realm. Quite apart from the fact that women were not by nature equipped to cope with public affairs, their attempts to take part in politics posed a direct danger to the hallowed conjugal family, because public life was conceived of in republican discourse as entailing a literally public performance open to the gaze of the community. Whereas for men publicity was the guarantee of virtue, the opposite applied for women. Self-display was repugnant to good women because it signified sexual immorality, just as surely as female confinement to private pursuits indicated chastity. In Rousseau's words, 'A woman's audacity is the sure sign of her shame.' Thus were the two meanings of the phrase 'public woman'—that is, politically prominent individual and prostitute— elided in the republican mind of the period.[15]

Sexual disorder on the part of women, as evidenced by political self-assertion, was considered deplorable for all sorts of reasons, but it is important to note that it posed specifically *political* dangers from the republican point of view. When women forsook the family hearth, they could not support their husbands or raise their sons as good future citizens. More fundamentally, they acted against their chaste and modest nature; the result, since women are so important and men so highly dependent on them, was to denature men, to make them effeminate and therefore susceptible to tyranny. Thus it was that republicans tended to associate political corruption among males—and this of course was the primary threat to liberty—with sexual corruption among females.[16] It is when we recognize this linkage between public roles for women, sexual disorder, and political corruption and tyranny that we begin to understand why the Patriots could even conceive of accusing Victoria Regina—innocent, young, but undeniably a prominent public figure—of being a 'whore.' . . .

In the context of the 1830s the Patriot movement certainly had no monopoly on patriarchy, and their defeat in the course of the Rebellion certainly did not signal the liberation of Lower Canada's women. Indeed, the state structure and political order instituted after 1838 was, if anything, more thoroughly masculine than anything the Patriots seem to have contemplated.[17] The

ideology of 'separate spheres' was gaining strength throughout the Euro-Atlantic world at this time, and influential men of virtually all shades on the political spectrum were affected. One can nevertheless see the Patriot party as the Lower Canadian spearhead of this wider shift in the politico-sexual order. It was within its ranks that the democratic conception of a 'public sphere' open to every citizen without privilege or distinction was enunciated most clearly and forcefully. Since the Patriots' definition of citizenship excluded women, their discourse of liberation was as much about sex as it was about politics. Accordingly, one might well regard the Rebellion of 1837–8 as constituting, among other things, a significant moment in the process of gender formation in French Canada.

NOTES

1. Bibliothèque nationale, Montreal, journal of Romuald Trudeau, 12: 25; ANQ, 1837, no. 1698, Welles to Goldie, 19 November 1838 (author's translation).

2. *Vindicator*, 1 September 1837.

3. ANQ, 1837, no. 324, déposition du Baron Augustin de Diemar, 21 December 1837 (author's translation); ibid., no. 242, déposition de Joseph-Louis Pinard, 1 February 1838; ibid., deposition of Thomas Casson, 31 December 1838 (cf. ibid., no. 1483, Lacombe to Walcott, 23 August 1837). The loyalists, for their part, struck a chivalrous posture, vowing to 'make any sacrifice in maintaining the legitimate authority of our young and beauteous Queen.' Speech by the Hon. Mr McGill, Montreal, 23 October 1837, in *Assemblées publiques, résolutions et déclarations de 1837–1838*, ed. Jean-Paul Bernard (Montreal: VLB éditeur, 1988), 239.

4. Dorothy Thompson, personal communication.

5. See, for example, Papineau's speech on the occasion of the death of George III, in *Papineau: textes choisis*, ed. Fernand Ouellet (Quebec: Presses de l'Université Laval, 1970), 21–2.

6. Georges Lefebvre, *The Great Fear: Rural Panic in Revolutionary France*, trans. Joan White (Princeton, NJ: Princeton University Press, 1973).

7. Pauline Maier, *From Resistance to Revolution: Colonial Radicals and the Development of American Opposition to Britain, 1765–1776* (New York: Knopf, 1972).

8. NA, British Military Records, C1272: 8, Colborne to Gosford, 6 October 1837.

9. This point is made in several studies, but I found particularly useful Joel Schwartz, *The Sexual Politics of Jean-Jacques Rousseau* (Chicago: University of Chicago Press, 1984). The basic texts are the *Discourse on the Origins of Inequality*, the *Social Contract, Letter to M. d'Alembert*, and *Emile*.

10. Joan B. Landes, *Women and the Public Sphere in the Age of the French Revolution* (Ithaca, NY: Cornell University Press, 1988).

11. Schwartz, *Sexual Politics*.

12. *La Minerve*, 28 July 1836 (author's translation).

13. Darline Gay Levy, Harriet Branson Applewhite, and Mary Durham Johnson, eds, *Women in*

Revolutionary Paris, 1789–1795 (Urbana: University of Illinois Press, 1979); Sîan Reynolds, 'Marianne's Citizens? Women, the Republic and Universal Suffrage in France', in *Women, State and Revolution: Essays on Power and Gender in Europe since 1789* (Amherst: University of Massachusetts Press, 1987), 101–22; Landes, *Women and the Public Sphere*. The de Gouges quotation is from Dorinda Outram, 'Le langage mâle de la vertu: Women and the Discourse of the French Revolution', in *The Social History of Language*, ed. Peter Burke and Roy Porter (Cambridge: Cambridge University Press, 1987), 126.

14. Linda Kerber, *Women of the Republic: Intellect and Ideology in Revolutionary America* (Chapel Hill: University of North Carolina Press, 1980).

15. Landes, *Women and the Public Sphere*. Rousseau quotation, 75.

16. Outram, 'Le langage mâle'. A wonderful illustration of this outlook can be found in the work of Rousseau's English contemporary and fellow republican, Edward Gibbon. Gibbon devotes several long and salacious pages in chapter 20 of The *Decline and Fall of the Roman Empire* to the misdeeds of the sixth-century empress, Theodora, whose fond husband, Justinian, committed the fundamental error of making his wife not a consort but a co-ruler. Long before she managed to seduce Justinian, Gibbon explains, Theodora was renowned in Constantinople and beyond for her beautiful face and figure: 'But this form was degraded by the facility with which it was exposed to the public eye, and prostituted to licentious desire. Her venal charms were abandoned to a promiscuous crowd of citizens and strangers, of every rank and of every profession: the fortunate lover who had been promised a night of enjoyment was often driven from her bed by a stronger or more wealthy favourite.' And so on.

17. See Lykke de la Cour, Cecilia Morgan, and Mariana Valverde, 'Gender and State Formation in Nineteenth-Century Canada', in *Colonial Leviathan: State Formation in Mid-Nineteenth-Century Canada*, ed. Allan Greer and Ian Radforth (Toronto: University of Toronto Press, 1992), 163–91.

6   From Jean-Marie Fecteau, '"This Ultimate Resource": Martial Law and State Repression in Lower Canada, 1837–1838', in F. Murray Greenwood and Barry Wright, eds, *Rebellion and Invasion in the Canadas, 1837–1839* (Toronto: University of Toronto Press, 1996), 215–21.

In reality, the events commonly referred to as the 'rebellion' of 1837 consisted of the brutal military repression of the major centres of political and legal dissent which had developed in the countryside surrounding Montreal. In essence, there were a series of pre-emptive strikes designed to nip an anticipated insurrection in the bud. The armed resistance of peasant militias in response to military invasion ultimately provided the justification for the imposition of martial law.

To a great extent, martial law was not a response to a real military threat. Rather, it proved a convenient means of dealing with political deadlock in the short term. When Governor Gosford proclaimed martial law on 5 December 1837, two weeks had already passed since the 'rebels' had been crushed at Saint Charles. The combined forces of the regular army and loyalist volunteer militias ensured that the remaining *patriote* stronghold at Saint-Eustache would meet the same fate on 14 December.

Lacking organization, leadership, and arms, the *patriotes* never posed a serious military challenge. However, in the countryside surrounding Montreal, they did succeed in establishing a widespread system of civil disobedience. The *patriote* strategy, beginning in the summer of 1837, was clear and remarkably effective: mobilize the peasant masses with local assemblies, culminating in the 'Assemblée des Six-Comtés' held at Saint-Charles on 23–24 October 1837, which in turn was to lead to a national convention.[1] Meanwhile, in several counties, militia captains and justices of the peace opposed to the *patriotes* were replaced by individuals more sympathetic to popular demands. It was this loss of political and judicial control, potentially leading to open violence, which forced a hesitant Gosford to turn to martial law. From the end of October, the governor recognized the efficiency of the Patriots' actions: 'Having for their object the superseding of the ordinary administration of justice, by the establishment of a species of tribunal over which magistrates elected by the people are to preside, for the adjustment of differences and the trial of causes, and the organization of volunteer companies of militia, under the command of officers elected by militia men, who are to be drilled in the management of fire-arms, which, with the other accoutrements, the permanent committee pledges itself to provide for those corps that distinguish themselves by their good order and discipline.'[2]

These mobilization tactics rendered irrelevant the judicial apparatus in the countryside, a fact that Gosford had begun to recognize in September.[3] With no hope of cooperation from the House of Assembly, which had been dissolved in August, the executive had few legal means at its disposal for dealing with the situation.[4] Faced with this state of political and legal deadlock, Gosford quickly turned to considering more extreme measures: 'Unless some extraordinary powers be immediately placed in the hands of the local Executive, such as that of suspending the *habeas corpus*, and declaring martial law over the whole or parts of the province, the tide of sedition cannot be stemmed but by resort to active military operations; an alternative which I cannot contemplate without the most painful reluctance.'[5]

Martial law was endorsed by the Executive Council a few days later . . . . By early December,

the colonial secretary, Lord Glenelg, reluctantly agreed with this solution: 'The first and highest prerogative and duty of the Crown is the protection of those who maintain their allegiance against the enemies of order and peace. To repress by arms any insurrection or rebellion to which the civil power cannot be successfully opposed, is therefore a legitimate exercise of the royal authority; and, in the attainment of this object, the proclamation of martial law may become indispensable.'[6] In fact, what set events in motion were the military engagements at Saint-Denis and Saint-Charles on 23 and 25 November. On 27 November, the Court of Sessions of the Peace for Montreal, in special session, implored Governor Gosford to place the district under martial law.[7]

Unsure of the legality of a proclamation of martial law, Gosford had requested, on 21 November, the opinion of Attorney General Charles Ogden and Solicitor General Michael O'Sullivan. Their answer was received on 30 November . . . . Ogden and O'Sullivan began by referring to the opinion of the first attorney general after the Conquest, George Suckling, who had expressed doubts regarding the governor's right to implement martial law.[8] They put more stress, however, on the Irish laws of 1799 and 1833 whose preambles . . . proclaimed that martial law was a matter of royal prerogative. According to the Lower Canadian jurists, this prerogative was de facto extended to colonial governors. Consequently, they informed Gosford that he was entirely within his legal powers in proclaiming martial law without the approval of the assembly.[9]

Gosford would wait for more than a week after receiving the news. Ultimately, what forced his hand appears to have been an injunction issued by the magistrates of Montreal on 5 December:

> Resolved, that in the opinion of this meeting, the turbulent and disaffected persons who have incited the peasantry to rebel against Her

Majesty's Government have been led on and encouraged in their career of crime by a firm belief that, whatever might be their political offences, they would not be declared guilty by any jury impannelled in the ordinary course of law; that the great mass of the population in this district having been engaged in aiding and abetting the late treasonable attempt, a fair and impartial verdict cannot be expected from a jury taken indiscriminately from the legally-qualified inhabitants . . . Resolved . . . that the only effectual mode of . . . arresting the progress of crime and of social disorganization, is to place this district under martial law.[10]

The magistrates' arguments were essentially about the paralysis of the province's judicial apparatus. Martial law was thus presented as a means of overcoming this problem rather than as a temporary exceptional measure aimed at suppressing an open rebellion. Lacking any alternatives, Gosford resigned himself to the need for martial law and proclaimed the measure that very night.

Gosford's hesitation is revealing. It shows how, in the absence of any political authority capable of legitimizing recourse to exceptional measures, martial law presents itself as a last resort in the face of an impending crisis, ensuring the relative stability of key institutions *while waiting* for an eventual conclusion. Thus, martial law is perceived as an eminently temporary measure, carefully linked to the intensity of the crisis and adjusted to its rhythm. Gosford expressed his views on the matter to Glenelg in the following terms: 'It is with the most painful regret I now acquaint your Lordship that from the aspect of affairs in that district, and the subsequent proceedings of the insurgents, I found that I could no longer abstain from a resort to the only measure left untried of maintaining therein the royal authority, and restoring order. Accordingly I last night issued . . . a Proclamation . . . subjecting the district of Montreal to martial law.'[11]

Gosford's departure and his replacement by Colborne signalled the final defeat of the former's policy of conciliation. It coincided with a troubled period during which authorities in London hesitated to act while exploring different scenarios for resolving the crisis. Ultimately, they decided to name Lord Durham as governor general of the British North American colonies. But, while he was appointed on 15 January 1838, Durham would wait four months before taking up his position in Lower Canada.

Meanwhile, Colborne saw in martial law a convenient means of preventing a resurgence of the rebellion. Once again, the uses of martial law had little to do with an actual emergency. The measure simply ensured that the executive would have the means to intervene rapidly in any future troubles without relying on slow and cumbersome legal procedures. However, in Lower Canada, maintaining such a regime for any considerable length of time faced a major obstacle: there was no political authority ready to sanction military intervention in civil affairs, nor even to protect those responsible for implementing martial law from potential legal reprisals. As early as 5 January 1838, Gosford had asked the colonial secretary 'whether whilst legislating for the affairs of the province, it would not be expedient to pass some bill of indemnity to place all recent proceedings beyond the reach of . . . ill-disposed parties.'[12] On 17 March, it was Colborne's turn to show his concern after taking over the reigns of power. An overenthusiastic military regime had arrested, 'beyond the law probably,' the editors of the *Quotidienne* and the *Courrier canadien.* Colborne therefore hoped that 'Her Majesty's Government will think it right to recommend the adoption of measures to prevent my being prosecuted by the factious party, or by individuals who have been checked in their career of mischief, when the Proclamation authorizing Martial Law is withdrawn.'[13]

But it was not merely the arbitrary and exceptional measures taken to maintain order that were poorly protected by a legally fragile system of martial law.[14] Distressed authorities soon realized that the exceptional regime they had hastily put in place could not even guarantee that those implicated in the late rebellion would be punished. As early as 12 March 1838, during the March sessions of the Court of King's Bench in Montreal, Judge Jean-Roch Rolland had sidestepped martial law by issuing a writ of habeas corpus for three individuals imprisoned in September 1837: Toussaint Peltier, Côme-Séraphin Cherrier, and Denis-Benjamin Viger.[15]

An even greater challenge than keeping rebels imprisoned until trial was that of ensuring they would receive an appropriate punishment.[16] As early as 5 January, Gosford had decided that 'some examples, selecting the most notorious and prominent characters in the revolt, must be made.' But since juries were notoriously unreliable when it came to convicting prisoners, 'the only course for effecting this is by trial by Court Martial; I really, at this moment, do not see any other mode by which the ends of justice can be arrived at.'[17] Meanwhile, Lord Glenelg cautioned against resorting 'to this measure without the most conclusive evidence of the inadequacy of any milder remedy to meet the existing evil.'[18]

The future of these initiatives was further placed in doubt by an opinion of the law officers of the crown in Lower Canada, issued on 24 January 1838 ... Ogden and O'Sullivan declared that the establishment of a court martial was illegal since the period of open insurrection had passed and there was no impediment to the operation of the regular courts. They further stated that the Irish precedent of 1799, mentioned above, indicated that the involvement of the House of Assembly was necessary for such a project. As Canadian juries clearly could not be relied upon,[19] and a new session of the Lower Canadian legislature was out of the question, imperial legislative intervention was necessary.[20] On 19 February, Lord Glenelg instructed an uncertain Colborne as to the procedure to follow in the face of what the latter considered to be a 'most embarrassing question'[21]:

With regard to the persons who have been apprehended for political offences and are now in confinement, Her Majesty's Government desire that such of them as you may not think it right at once to liberate should not be brought to trial, unless they can be tried by the ordinary tribunals of the country. In case, therefore, a reference to the ordinary tribunals should not, in your judgment, be yet advisable, a law ought to be passed for the suspension of the *Habeas Corpus* Act, which will enable you to detain such persons in prison till the arrival of Lord Durham. You will propose to the council this measure, if, for the reason I have stated, or for any other reason, you may think it expedient. You will thus be enabled immediately to revoke the proclamation of martial law in the district of Montreal, if still in force.[22]

In the end, the solution to this legal dilemma had to come from the British Parliament. In fact, on 10 February, Parliament had passed a law replacing the Lower Canadian legislature with a Special Council appointed by the governor. . . . [T]he council passed a series of measures from mid-April 1838 onwards shoring up the legality of actions taken since the end of 1837 rebellion, suspending habeas corpus and offering legal protection to anyone who had aided in repressing the rebellion . . . . By 27 April, Colborne felt secure enough to suspend martial law.

The imposition of martial law in 1837 fits perfectly with the pattern of emergency measures taken in British colonies at that time. It had been implemented as a measure of last resort, though not primarily as a response to the threat of an armed uprising. Rather, it met the urgent necessity of overcoming the political and judicial deadlock caused by popular support for the demands of political radicals. Gosford's hesitation and his cautious approach—historians have no reason to suspect his good faith—highlight the specific context in which the loss of political legitimacy on the part of the authorities and the danger it posed for a loyal minority forced ill-prepared authorities to deal with matters one at a time, beginning with the most urgent. In this case, far from constituting the centrepiece of a comprehensive program for relieving the tensions exacerbated by the rebellion, martial law serves to underline the weakness and confusion of the authorities.[23]

The clearly improvised manner in which martial law was imposed, the law officers' rejection of the idea of taking advantage of the state of emergency to dispose of prisoners by means of court martial, the issuing of a writ of habeas corpus by a judge of the Court of King's bench while martial law was supposedly in force: these were all indications of the weak and shaky foundations supporting the regime of martial law in Lower Canada. In fact, the colony needed a political alternative much more than further means of repression. It was precisely as part of this search for a way out of a deep political crisis that imperial authorities placed the fate of Lower Canada in the hands of a liberal and enlightened 'despot': Lord Durham.

NOTES

1. See Jean-Paul Bernard, ed., *Assemblées publiques résolutions et déclarations de 1837–1838* (Montreal: VLB Éditeur, 1988). The mobilization strategy based on large assemblies was directly inspired by the experience of the American Revolution. It was also adopted by the Chartists in England. The best work on the relationship between the peasantry and democracy in Lower Canada is Allan Greer, *The Patriots and the People: The Rebellion of 1837 in Rural Lower Canada* (Toronto: University of Toronto Press, 1993).

2. Gosford to Glenelg, 12 Oct. 1837, *British Parliamentary Papers*, vol. 9, 72.

3. 'The great difficulty of procuring strict trial evidence for bringing home, in a court of justice, to the parties concerned the charges that might be founded on the proceedings had at these meetings, added to the questionable policy of political prosecutions, especially at a time like the present, when the minds of a portion of the jury summoned to try the offence would probably be poisoned by the misrepresentations and efforts of the disaffected, have as yet prevented any resort to the court of law for the punishment of those implicated in such proceedings.' Gosford to Glenelg, 9 Sept. 1837, ibid., 56.

4. A report of the Executive Council from 20 October reflects this feeling of helplessness: 'There is no hope, under existing circumstances, to re-establish the equilibrium between the component parts of the constitution without the intervention of the Imperial Parliament. . . . It becomes absolutely necessary that the Executive Government should be made independent of the house of Assembly, and enabled to carry on the government of the province without the assistance of the legislative body. . . . The commission of the peace is inefficient, inasmuch as several parts of the country are without magistrates and that in the towns there is a general want of that activity which is necessary to meet the emergency of the times.' 'Report of a Committee of the Whole Council', 20 Oct. 1837, ibid., 91.

5. Gosford to Glenelg, 6 Nov. 1837, ibid., 104. See also Report of the Executive Council, 20 November 1837.

6. Glenelg to Colborne, 6 Dec. 1837, ibid., 114.

7. Court of Special Sessions of the Peace, 27 November 1837, ibid., 137. Justice of the peace Denis-Benjamin Viger expressed his dissent, while judges Guy and Castonguay abstained.

8. Suckling's interpretation relies on a strict interpretation of the Petition of Right of 1628: 'There is . . . however after all that has been said a disagreeable kind of obscurity still remaining in the subject which I confess myself unable to remove nor do I think it a matter entirely without doubt that the King can in any case whatever, even in case of an invasion or a rebellion, establish Martial Law by his single authority in England, or delegate power of doing so to his Governor or Governors in Council in the American Colonies,

seeing that the prohibition of the issuing of Commissions to exercise Martial Law in the famous Petition of Right above mentioned is expressed in these very general words which contain no exception whatever.' Cited in Ogden and O'Sullivan to Civil Secretary S. Walcott, 30 Nov. 1837, *RPAC*, CO 42/274/147.

9. Ibid., 147–53. Note how the articles of the imperial acts cited in support of their legal opinion are declaratory. That is to say, they preserve a prerogative believed to exist *already*. Also, the principle that, for any proclamation of martial law, a state of war must be such that the regular courts cannot sit, was interpreted very loosely by Lower Canadian jurists. The mere incapacity to deliver the court's warrants was deemed sufficient to meet this requirement: 'The functions of the ordinary legal tribunals may be considered as having virtually ceased. For although the Courts of Justice may sit with perfect security in the city of Montreal, we can hardly name any part of this district in which process of any description could be served or writs executed by the ministry of Civil Officer.' Ibid., 153.

10. Court of Special Sessions of the Peace, 5 Dec. 1837, in *Parliamentary Papers*, vol. 9, 141. The justices of the peace also cited the danger of an invasion by rebels who had taken refuge in the United States. In fact, the next day, eighty *patriotes* attempted an invasion from the United States, but they were intercepted at Moore's Corner, near the border, by volunteer militiamen.

11. Gosford to Glenelg, 6 Dec. 1837, ibid., 140. The instructions to Colborne, who was charged with putting martial law into effect, were also explicit as to the need to do so with prudence and discretion: '. . . In all cases wherein the unlimited power with which you are now invested can be exercised in cooperation with, or in subordination to, the ordinary laws of the land, and that in all cases where from local circumstances, or from a prompt return to their allegiance, the deluded inhabitants of any part of that district display an honest contrition for their past offences, you will revert at once to the assistance of the civil authorities, and

impress upon a misguided people the conviction that Her Majesty's Government in this Province is equally prompt to pardon the repentant and punish the incorrigible.' S. Walcott, civil secretary, to Colborne, 5 December 1837, ibid., 140–1.

12. Gosford to Glenelg, 5 Jan. 1838, *RPAC*, CO 42/279/18. Glenelg had also already considered granting retroactive legal protection for all acts committed under this special regime: 'Reposing the utmost confidence in your prudence, Her Majesty's Government are fully prepared to assume to themselves the responsibility of instructing you to employ it, should you be deliberately convinced that the occasion imperatively demands it. They will, with confidence look to Parliament for your indemnity and their own.' Glenelg to Colborne, 6 Dec. 1837, *Parliamentary Papers*, vol. 9, 114.

13. Colborne to Glenelg, 17 March 1838, *RPAC*, CO 42/280/196.

14. A curious incident from February 1838 highlights the fragility of arguments justifying martial law in Lower Canada. Governor Colborne issued a proclamation declaring a day of prayers and thanksgiving in honour of the ascension of Queen Victoria. Notably, the proclamation celebrated the fact that the rebellion had been brought under control, 'thus virtually, as it may be supposed, discontinuing the Act declaring Martial law.' However, Colborne had to issue another proclamation on 27 February, announcing the continuation of martial law! On this strange series of events, see the letter from Colborne to Glenelg, 28 Feb. 1838, and the proclamation of 27 Feb. 1838, in *Parliamentary Papers*, vol. 9 (1838), 200.

15. For the story of these legal procedures, see O'Sullivan's letter to Civil Secretary Rowan on 27 March 1838, ibid., 198–9. The prisoners had requested that their trial be held during the session. O'Sullivan noted that, 'if the judges should decide that martial law, as declared by the last mentioned proclamation, is not in force, I cannot help reflecting upon the disagreeable situation in which His Excellency may be placed.' On this

subject, see also *Le Canadien*, 30 April 1838.

16. While martial law was in force, 515 suspects were arrested, of whom 340 were released on bail before 5 April, and about thirty others after that date. See Gérard Filteau, *Histoire des patriotes* (Montreal: Aurore, 1975), 389.

17. See Gosford to Glenelg, 5 January 1838, *RPAC*, CO 42/279/17.

18. Glenelg to Colborne, 6 Jan. 1838, *Parliamentary Papers*, vol. 10, 20.

19. The crown law officers deplored the excessive democratization of the procedure for nominating juries under the law of 1832: 'This change let in upon the administration of criminal justice, an honest but illiterate peasantry. This was found to conduce materially to the increase of popular power and to further the ends of the disaffected. . . . It must be obvious considering the widespread of the recent Rebellion whose ramifications have extended throughout the whole Province, that every person accused of political offence could only be brought to trial with the certainty of an anticipated acquittal.' Ogden and O'Sullivan to Captain Goldie, 24 Jan. 1838, *RPAC*, CO 42/280/67.

20. Ibid., 62. Note how, for the authors of this report, the uprising was not the act of a few agitators but that of an entire population. Their angry description of the influence of the *patriote* leadership is revealing: 'These men have for years past ruled the peasantry of the country as they pleased, and still possess the confidence of their deluded constituents and of several of their fellow members.' Ibid., 68.

21. Colborne to Gosford, 24 Jan. 1838, *RPAC*, CO 42/280/67.

22. Glenelg to Colborne, 19 Feb. 1838, *Parliamentary Papers*, vol. 10, 1–2.

23. Hesitant British authorities would wait four months after the first rebellion to suspend the constitution. This highlights a situation where the *patriotes* had the initiative and where the social forces likely to offer resistance to them—poorly supported by a governor (Gosford) dedicated to conciliation—did not have the political means to react. On this point, see Philip A. Buckner, *The Transition to Responsible Government: British Policy in British North America, 1815–1850* (Westport, Conn.: Greenwood Press, 1985).

□ Assisted Immigration to Upper Canada in the 1820s

INTRODUCTION

■ Between 1815 and the early 1860s, the population of the British colonies in North America grew from 600,000 to over 3,500,000. This sixfold population expansion contributed to the beginning of serious discussions over the unification of British North America, as well as to a growing interest in westward expansion from coast to coast on the northern half of the continent. While much of the growth in numbers of people resulted from natural increase, especially in French Canada, a good deal was also the product of a substantial movement of people, mainly from Europe—and particularly from the British Isles—to British North America in these years. The immigrants helped transform British North America from a collection of colonies in which more than half of the population of European origin spoke French to one in which English predominated in all provinces, including United Canada by 1850. Nearly two million residents of the British Isles sailed westward to destinations in British North America between 1815 and the 1860s as part of a larger exodus of people from the British Isles to the United States and other British settlement colonies (in South Africa, Australia, and New Zealand). After 1849 some even entered the Pacific Ocean to settle on the west coast of British America. While not all of the two million coming to British North America settled permanently there—perhaps as many as half moved on to the United States and some unknown number returned to Britain—the traffic was not solely in one direction, to the United States through British North America. In 1853, for example, Canada West was the seventh most popular destination of immigrants arriving at New York.

In any event, a good many immigrants did put down new roots in British North America during this period. Most of these people financed their own relocation, but between the end of the Napoleonic Wars and 1830 the British government and the British ruling/landlord classes became convinced that the British Isles were overpopulated. They increasingly saw emigration as a preferable alternative to public assistance for the poor and underemployed, as well as an outlet for superfluous farmers in an era of agricultural transformation. The result was a period in which the British government sponsored various programs of assisted immigration, particularly to Upper Canada. These programs proved very expensive and difficult to control, and were eventually abandoned.

Questions for consideration

1. What were the major obstacles to successful immigration?
2. Could the assistance programs have been restructured to become more effective?
3. What are the major differences in the four accounts of the Robinson emigration?
4. How would you account for those differences?

Suggestions for further reading

D.H. Akenson, *The Irish in Ontario: A Study in Rural History* (Montreal and Kingston: McGill-Queen's University Press, 1984). A study of the Irish in two townships of Upper Canada.

Bruce Elliott, *Irish Migrants in the Canadas: A New Approach* (Montreal and Kingston: McGill-Queen's University Press, 1988). This work focuses on the phenomenon of 'chain migration'.

E.C. Guillet, *The Great Migration: The Atlantic Crossing by Sailing-Ship since 1770*, 2nd edn (Toronto: University of Toronto Press, 1963). Often criticized for its scholarship, this work remains the basic source for the Atlantic crossing to British North America.

Cecil Houston and W.J. Smyth, *Irish Emigration and Canadian Settlement: Patterns, Links, and Letters* (Toronto: University of Toronto Press, 1990). A geographical approach, strong on maps, that includes a number of fascinating letters from emigrants.

PRIMARY DOCUMENTS

1 From Alexander Buchanan to Wilmot Horton, 19 May 1827, *Appendix to Third Report of the Select Committee on Emigration from the United Kingdom* (London, 1827), 550–5.

QUERY?

Thirdly:—Do you consider that any sort of practical difficulty will exist in taking an unexpensive and simple security from the Emigrant, both personal as well as a lien upon his land, for the payment of £. 4. per annum interest, being at the rate of 5 per cent upon the sum of £. 80., or in other words upon the sum of £. 60. improved by deferred interest for seven years to the sum of £. 80., interest being only calculated in that instance at £. 4. per cent?

Note:—Every pains must be taken to explain to the Emigrant, that the acceptance of the loan is to be entirely voluntary on his part, precisely the same as if any individual in his own country had proposed, from motives of charity, to advance him a loan of equal amount, upon the same principle of repayment.

ANSWER:

I do not apprehend that any practical difficulty will arise in taking a sufficient security, personal and by mortgage on the land and implements, for the payment of the interest on the principal advanced. I would, however, recommend if practicable the joint security of two or more heads of families for the individual liability of each other; and which would be found more particularly requisite in the case of Query, N° 6.

QUERY?

Secondly:—Do you mainly concur in the necessity of assistance, more or less in these proportions, to the value of £60. furnished to the Emigrant in the following proportions?

Average Estimate of the Expense of settling a Family, consisting of one Man, one Woman, and three Children, in the British North American Provinces; distinguishing the various items of Expenditure.

Expenses of conveyance from the port of disembarkation to place of location—£.10 – –
Provisions, viz. rations for 15 months for 1 man, 1 woman and 3 children, at 1 lb. of flour and 1 lb. of pork for each adult, and half that quantity for each child, making 3½ rations per diem, pork being at £.4. per barrel and flour at £.1. 5s. per barrel

	–	–	–	40	6	10
Freight of provisions to place of settlement	–	–	–	1	10	10
House for each family	–	–	–	2	–	–

Implements, &c.

4 Blankets	–	–	–	£	–	14	–
1 Kettle	–	–	–	–	–	5	10
1 Frying-pan	–	–	–	–	–	1	3
3 Hoes	–	–	–	–	–	4	6

1 Spade	– – – – –	2	9		
1 Wedge	– – – – –	1	4		
1 Auger	– – – – –	2	2		
1 Pick-axe	– – – – –	2	–		
2 Axes	– – – – 1	–	–		
Proportion of grindstone,					
whipsaw and cross-cut saw–	–	14	–		
Freight and charges on					
ditto, 15 per cent	–	–	10	2	

£. 3 18 – (equal to currency) £.4 6 8

Cow	– – – – – – – – – – –	4	10	–
Medicines and medical attendance	– – – – –	1	–	–
Seed corn	– – – – – – –	1	6	
Potatoes, 5 bush. at 2s. 6d	– – – –	12	6	

	–	14	–
Proportion of the expense of building for the depôt	1	–	–
Ditto for clerks, issuers, and surveyors to show the lots	1	5	–
£.60 sterling is equal to	£.66	13	4

ANSWER:

 I do not generally concur in the appropriation of the Sixty pounds, even supposing that sum to be necessary as applicable *to the range of our North American Colonies*; and my conclusions in omitting some items are strengthened by the concurrent opinion of other colonial gentlemen's experience in such matters, including Mr. Robinson and Col. Marshall. The item of Transport to place of location after landing, I think rather embraces the most distant and expensive points that might be selected; and I should suppose that, taking the range of our colonies, *as well below Montreal as above, and up the Ottawa river*, that from five to six pounds per family* would be a fair calculation; and if confined to the Lower provinces alone, I should say *much less*. And I would be strongly inclined to introduce a different ration of food, not only for economy, but I consider the health of the Emigrant a material point in our calculations; and the natural result to an Irish or Scotch Settler, by the transition from his accustomed food, of *potatoes, milk, and oatmeal*, to SALT PORK AND FLOUR, must inevitably bring with it DISEASE and impurity of the blood, *particularly among children*: and bearing strongly in mind that *the system of repayment* will be the *basis* of any future Emigration. The Emigrant will be anxious to keep down any expense that can possibly be avoided; consequently I would suggest, that he provides himself in the first instance *with not less than one pair of blankets, a camp kettle, a frying-pan and spade* (for even a perfect *pauper emigrant* will have no difficulty in collecting those items,) and that no Emigrant be received on board ship without them. The other indispensable implements to be furnished at the settlement, agreeable to the Schedule marked (A.)

 I do not think that any material difference would accrue in the calculation of the expense of the family, whether the number of children should exceed the average adults or not; in fact, the greater the number of children, the more certainty of success the Emigrant would have from the help of labour he could command in his own family.

 I beg to submit the Comparative Expense of transporting a family *from New York to Upper Canada*, by Mr. Charles Smyth, of New York and Albany, general transport agent and carrier; by which you will see with what economy those things are done in the States; and I am disposed to think, from conversation I had lately with a proprietor of the St. Lawrence Steam Boat Company, that arrangements something similar might be made in Canada.

N.B. *I am convinced* contracts can be made for the conveyance of a family from Quebec to Montreal for *about 4 dollars*, or 18s. sterling.

---

* I do not think that free transport, after landing, should be given to any pauper emigrant family, for more baggage than 2 cwt. Over and above the conveyance of women and children; the men and such others of the family capable of walking, should do so.

Note:—Something in the nature of this Schedule, applicable to the special circumstances of the location of each particular Emigrant, would be delivered to him upon his landing; and upon his presenting a voucher to the Emigration Agent at the Colonial Port, showing that he had been approved as an Emigrant, and upon his expressing his wish to receive this sort of loan in kind. In case of this occurring, he would be called upon to sign the security adverted to in the next query, and then conveyed to his location at the Government expense. As two children are considered equal to the expense of an adult, if the family consisted of a widower and five children, or in any other variety of proportion, regulated by this principle of equivalent, would not the £.60. be equally necessary? Every lot must have a working head of a family upon it, who must become responsible for the interest.

Passage of an Adult from New York to Albany	$1
Albany to Rochester	3
Rochester to Upper Canada	1
	$5

Children under 12 years half price, and young children gratis. Baggage per hundred weight, from New York to Canada, one dollar: thus—

Man and Wife, New York to Canada	$10
2 Children	5
Average of one Child	1
2 cwt. Baggage	2
10 days Provisions, at 37½ cents, per day	3 75
at 4s. 4d.	$21 75
is £.4. 14. 3.	

Or we will say Five Pounds sterling for the transport of a Family from NEW YORK to YORK in UPPER CANADA.

N.B. I have no hesitation that a considerable abatement would be made for a large number.

I subjoin a Schedule of Provisions, and other articles that I consider adequate for the location of an Emigrant family, particularly *in the Lower Provinces*; the same facilities, as to variety of food and probable transport to location, would not be generally experienced *in the Upper Provinces*.

SCHEDULE (A.)

The following Rations I would recommend Emigrants, and which might be obtained in any of the provinces below Montreal:—Each family, of man, wife and three children, 3½ full rations for 450 days after arrival on their lands:

		d.
2½ lb. Pork (Irish)		8¾
¼ lb. Molasses		1½
4½ lb. Oatmeal and flour		7
		17¼ per day.

For 260 days, is £.18 13 9

N.B. This Ration 4 days in the week.

	d.
2½ lb. Oatmeal and flour	4
¼ lb. Molasses	1½
10 lb. Potatoes	3
4 Herrings	4
	12½ 9 17 11

For Lower Provinces   Sterling £.28 11   8

For Upper Canada, Pork would cost ½ d. per lb. higher, which would bring the ration per day to about 18¾ d. or 19d. per day for Upper Canada 3 5 10   –

£.64   1   8

Average of each Family will be   £.32   –   10

(carried forward)

N° 7.

Downing-street, 19th May 1827.

Mr. WILMOT HORTON would be much obliged to Mr. *Buchanan*, notwithstanding the Evidence which he has already given before the Emigration Committee, if he would be good enough to furnish him with written and specific Answers to the following Queries:

QUERY?

First:—Taking the whole range of the North American Colonies, and reducing them to one common average, do you think it would be safe to estimate the expense necessary for the satisfactory location of an Emigrant family, of a man, woman and three children, at less than £.60. per family, such expense to be incurred after their landing at a colonial port?

Note:—This query involves the supposition, that the expense of passage is never to be incurred by Government, but is, *in all cases*, to be paid by the parties interested in the removal of a superabundant population, and that the Emigrant's family have been *approved of* by an Agent appointed by Government to examine all proposed Emigrants. All the expenses and circumstances of the passage to be entirely independent of Government assistance or responsibility. No Emigrant would be entitled to Government assistance in the Colonies, who had not received a voucher from a Government agent at home, that such Emigrant and family were proper subjects for receiving Government assistance.

ANSWER:

Taking into calculation the information we have received from Mr. Robinson, who has hitherto been the medium of carrying the intentions of His Majesty's Government into effect most successfully in the experiment of Emigration to Upper Canada, and to whose exertion the favourable result of same is in a great degree owing; yet, as the premises on which *any future Emigration* is to take place embraces the obligation of repayment, and keeping in mind *those points*, and the advantages that may arise by experience from a more *simple plan of economy*, and from the views I have hitherto entertained on the subject of Emigration, and from which subsequent information does not warrant me to vary in any material degree from my hasty Sketch or estimate formerly submitted to the Committee,—I am decidedly of opinion that the sum of *Fifty Pounds sterling*, to be expended *after arrival in the Colonies*, would be sufficient to locate a family; presuming that previous arrangements are made, and such suitable situations *as now present themselves*, and that are well adapted for settlement, would be selected, *without seeking those more distant districts, which, from the difficulty of access alone, renders a very heavy expense unavoidable.*

2   Testimony of Alexander Buchanan, *Third Report of the Select Committee on Emigration from the United Kingdom* (London, 1827), 106–13.

Sabbati, 3° die Martii, 1827.
Alexander Carlisle Buchanan, Esq. called in; and Examined.

815. YOU are generally acquainted with the circumstances of the trade in the carrying of passengers between this country and the United States, as well as between this country and Canada?—From Ireland I am perfectly.

816. Have you made any comparison between the expense that will be occasioned by the restraints proposed in this Act, which has been laid before the Committee as a substitution for a former Act, and the expense occasioned by the Act of the year 1825?—I have.

817. What would be the difference of expense between the two Acts?—About 12 *s.* 6 *d.* for each passenger.

818. What do you consider would be the expense at present?—It is now perhaps 40 *s.* for an adult, or 3 *l.*

819. From what port to what port?—From Londonderry and Belfast, which are the great ports of emigration to our colonies; to the United States it is about 5 *l.* or 6 *l.*

820. What would be the expense of the poorest class of passengers from Belfast to Quebec?—About 50 *s.*, finding their own provisions.

821. By this Act, a certain quantity of provisions is necessary?—They are; but the representations were so numerous from the poor people, that the provisions prescribed by the Act were so expensive, that the officers of His Majesty's Customs saw that it would in effect almost prohibit emigration if it were enforced, and they took upon themselves, I believe, to wave that part of the Act.

822. Do you consider that in point of fact, with respect to emigrants going from Ireland generally, the provisions of that Act have virtually been waved?—Not generally; the restriction as to numbers, and a proper supply of water, surgeon, &c. was particularly attended to

by the officers of Customs, and although they waved that clause respecting a certain description of provisions, they generally made inquiry into the supply the passengers had.

823. Have you an opportunity of knowing that to be the case with respect to the south of Ireland as well as the north?—I have not.

824. Is it your impression that it has been so in the south?—I should think it has been. I dare say I have accompanied 6,000 emigrants to America myself, within the last ten years.

825. In those cases, the provisions of that Act were not enforced?—Not to any great extent; it has been the custom, for the last six or seven years, for the passengers to find their own provisions; formerly the ships found them.

826. Then in point of fact, the passengers themselves took that quantity of provisions which they thought necessary?—They did.

827. Do you imagine that the amount of provisions proposed to be required by this new Act, is greater than what is taken by the poorest of the emigrants who provide for themselves?—I do not think it is near so much.

828. The question applies to the quality as well as the quantity?—I understand it so.

829. Do the emigrants take pork or meat, for instance?—Very seldom; they take a little bacon.

830. Have the provisions which the Act prescribed with respect to tonnage, been actually observed?—They have.

831. The Custom-house officers have uniformly taken care, although they have relaxed with respect to provisions, to have the proportions of passengers to tonnage preserved?—They examine the list of passengers going out, to see that it corresponds with the licence; the licence is granted in proportion to the registered tonnage.

832. Is it the custom after the Customhouse-officer has examined the list, that passengers are taken off the coast?—I do not think it is; I have heard of trifling instances of the kind; the price paid for passage to our own colonies is so trifling, that a captain of a ship would hardly take the trouble.

833. Did you ever know it to happen in any vessel which you yourself were on board?—Never; I have repeatedly seen some relanded that have hid away on board; on the captain examining on leaving port, if he found he had any above his number, he would hove to, and put them on shore.

834. What practical inconvenience do you anticipate from allowing passengers to take with them such provisions as they may think fit, without any legislative enactment on the subject?—I think that the description of emigrants from Ireland particularly are very ignorant, and they have latterly got such an idea of the quick dispatch to America, that they would take a very short supply; they hear of packets coming over from New York to Liverpool in twenty or twenty-five days, and many of them come into Derry, calculating upon a twenty days passage, and without a quantity of oatmeal and other necessaries in proportion, and they are obliged to provide themselves with a larger quantity before they go on board.

835. Have you ever known any inconvenience actually to arise in consequence of a deficiency of provisions?—I have not known any myself, but formerly I have understood there were very great privations suffered, and a great many lives lost, before the Passengers Act passed.

836. Is that an opinion which you have heard from so many quarters as to leave no doubt in your mind of it being the fact?—I am perfectly satisfied of it.

837. Have you not stated that these legislative regulations have, in point of fact, not been adhered to?—They have not, as regards provisions.

838. But although they were not adhered to, they were not so entirely evaded as not to leave them in considerable operation?—Decidedly not.

839. Supposing a passenger, under the expectation of a quick passage, had brought only half the food which this new Act contemplates, what would have taken place in that instance; is any inquiry made by the captain of the passenger, as to the quantity of provision he has?—Always.

840. If the quantity of provisions he had brought was manifestly under what was necessary for an average voyage, would not the captain insist on his taking more?—Decidedly, he would not receive him without.

841. With respect to the tonnage, will you state to the Committee the reason why you are of opinion that there is a necessity for requiring the height of five feet six inches between the decks, and for prohibiting all stores from being placed between the decks?—I consider it indispensable in a ship carrying at the rate of one passenger to every two tons, to reserve the entire space between decks for their accommodation, and the deck of the ship not being at least five feet and a half, it would not be proper to have it double birthed; and a ship carrying at the rate of one passenger to every two tons, will require to be double birthed, and to have six persons in each birth.

842. Are the double-decked merchant vessels usually of that height between the decks?—Generally more; there are very few that are not.

843. Then have you any reason to anticipate that ships would be built for the express purpose of carrying out emigrants, which would be of a less height between decks than the ordinary merchant vessels, or that the vessels that would be used for that purpose would probably be old merchant vessels?—Not at all; there are very few ships that trade to America that are not five feet and a half high between decks, and over.

844. Then do you conceive that there is any necessity for any regulation enforcing that which actually exists without any regulation?—The reason of that clause is, that ships carrying one to every five tons would be saved the necessity of any delay in making an application for a licence; they could take their one to five tons, and proceed on their voyage in the ordinary way; whereas if they take in a greater number than that, some restriction should be imposed.

845. Do you imagine that there will be any practical inconvenience in these regulations being enforced, either at the Custom-house at the port from which they go in England, or at the Custom-house at the port at which they land in the colony?—None whatever.

846. Do you consider that any expense would be incurred in consequence of those regulations, which would of necessity add to the expense of the passage?—None whatever.

847. Then you are of opinion, that if those regulations were considered to be necessary, there would be no objection against them upon the ground of any real inconvenience being sustained by the trade in consequence of them?—None whatever; I am satisfied they would be approved of, both by the emigrants and the shipowners.

848. Do you entertain the opinion, that the parties going out would rather be protected by legislation to the extent proposed, than to have no legislation upon the subject?—I am perfectly satisfied they would.

849. Are the Committee to understand that they object very much to those extreme regulations, which make the expense of the passage beyond their means?—They have a great

objection to being obliged to have a particular description of provisions, but that has been latterly dispensed with.

850. Then, in point of fact, has emigration from Ireland been prevented, in consequence of that part of the Act which relates to provisions?—I do not think it has.

851. As you have stated that the restrictions of this Act with respect to provisions have been virtually superseded in practice, it is presumed that emigration from Ireland cannot have been prevented by the operation of this Act?—To a very small extent; perhaps to the amount of 100 a year or 200 a year more at the outside might have gone; the difference can only be about 10 or 12 shillings in the expense. I have heard a great many statements made about the Passengers Act; as to the Act increasing the expense of passage to the United States, and amounting to a prohibition of emigration, I am satisfied that if the Act were repealed the price would not be diminished one farthing, as the American law imposes a greater limitation as to number than the British and other local regulations.

852. Supposing this Act were not to be passed, requiring the emigrant to take with him a certain specified quantity of food for 75 days, do you imagine that the emigrant could in prudence take a less quantity?—I do not think he could, for I have known instances of very fast sailing ships from Liverpool being 75, 80 or 90 days going out to New York, and frequent instances occur of ships being 60, 70 and 80 days going to Quebec.

853. You say, that you think the emigrants would not take a less quantity of provisions than that which is prescribed by the Act?—I do not think they would; they generally consult the captain; they tell the captain of the ship what quantity they have got, and if he thinks they have not got enough, they put on board more.

854. That Act provides for a certain quantity of bread, meal and flour; is that the species of provision upon which the lower Classes in Ireland live, either entirely or in a great measure?—It is generally their chief support.

855. You are not much acquainted with the south of Ireland?—Not particularly; I consider that oatmeal and potatoes form the principal food of the Irish peasantry generally; I include potatoes when in proper season, say in the spring of the year, very necessary, but in case of bad weather or other casualty, oatmeal, flour or biscuit can only be depended on.

856. You are not aware that in the south of Ireland the peasantry never taste bread from one year's end to another?—I am not aware that they never taste bread, they chiefly live on potatoes; but this Act merely says, that there shall be that quantity of that or any other wholesome food equivalent thereto; I only submit that there should be a certain quantity of something on board, enough to keep them in life for 75 days.

857. If there were no restriction whatever by law as to the food to be taken by the passengers, do not you think that the captain of every ship carrying out passengers would for his own sake take care that no person should be taken on board who had not a proper quantity of provisions?—I think he would, or ought to do.

858. Have not you stated that that is the habit?—They generally inquire what quantity of provisions the passengers have brought; the ship is under a very heavy responsibility; I have known instances where the ship has taken on board a quantity of meal to guard against the possibility of the passengers falling short; I have done so myself, I have taken in a few tons of oatmeal, at the expense of the ship, to prevent any accident.

859. In case of a passenger falling short of provisions, would not the captain have to supply that deficiency?—Perhaps the captain might not have any to spare.

860. Does the captain generally go to sea so short of provisions?—A ship going to sea in the North American trade, if she victuals at home, may take in three or four months provisions, but what would a redundancy of a barrel of biscuit or a barrel of meal be among 300 emigrants.

861. What is the general burthen of those ships that carry 300 persons?—From 300 to 400 tons.

862. How many emigrants, according to the regulations of this Act, would be shipped on board a vessel of 350 tons?—I have put on paper a few observations with respect to the points of difference between the proposed Act and the former Act, which I will read to the Committee. In the first place, the proposed Act permits the ship to carry her full number, say one to two tons register, children in proportion, exclusive of the crew; the former Act included the crew. Secondly, it dispenses with carrying a doctor; the former Act imposed that necessity. Thirdly, it permits the ship carrying cargo, reserving a sufficiency of space, with the whole of the between-decks, for passengers, provisions, water, &c.; the former Act prohibited carrying cargo, or it was so construed by the Irish Board of Customs. Fourthly, it relieves the shipowner and captain from obnoxious and frivolous clauses and expenses that never perhaps would be resorted to, but operated in the calculation of a conscientious shipowner, not to permit his ship to embark in such trade. Fifthly, it permits the passenger or emigrant to lay in his own provisions, or to make any contract they think fit with the captain for that purpose, the captain being responsible that a sufficiency of wholesome food for 75 days of some kind is on board for each adult passenger; the former Act obliged the ship to have on board a particular description of provisions, not suited to the habits of emigrants, and of increased expense. And the proposed amended Act gives every protection to the emigrant, at the same time removing many absurd difficulties to the ship, and permits as many passengers to be put on board as could possibly be justified with any due regard to their health and lives. I shall state in my humble opinion how it operates in a pecuniary way: first, a ship 400 tons by the former Act could only carry, deducting crew, about 180 adults; now 200; difference 20, at 40 s. per head, deducting expense of water, &c. 40 l.: secondly, free from expense of doctor, at least 50 l.: thirdly, giving liberty to carry cargo, is at least worth equal to 25 l.: fourthly, I consider that dispensing with the obligation that many ships are under, to put salt provisions on board to conform to old Act, although not used equal with other matters, to 25 l.; making a total of 140 l., which on two hundred emigrants would be equal to 12 s. or 14 s. per adult; and supposing that a ship was taking in emigrants, and that plenty were offering, it would enable the ship to carry them for so much less than under the former Act, and form as much actual gain on the passage as charging so much higher, so that in fact the emigrant gets his passage for so much less, and without any loss to the ship. A ship of four hundred tons has about seventy-five feet in length of space, and twenty-six feet wide between decks; so, to have her doubled birthed, would give you about twenty-six births aside, or fifty-two in all; and allowing six persons to each birth, would accommodate three hundred and twelve persons, which a ship of four hundred tons is permitted to carry; say two hundred adults, with average proportion of children, would at least make (if not more) the number stated, and with twenty of crew, would give on board altogether 332 persons in a space about 95 feet long, 25 to 26 feet wide, and 5½ or 6 feet high.

863. If there were no responsibility imposed upon the captains of vessels, either with respect to provisions or with respect to tonnage, are you apprehensive that captains might

be found who would be willing to incur risks from which great evils might occur to the passengers?—I am afraid many instances might occur, and unless some legislative regulation existed, I fear captains and shipbrokers would be found that would cram them into any extent, and great hardship would be likely to follow.

864. Do you know of any serious consequences that did arise previous to the passing of the Passengers Act?—I know instances where passengers were carried a thousand miles from the place they contracted for.

HISTORICAL INTERPRETATIONS

3   From Norman Macdonald, *Canada 1763–1841: Immigration and Settlement: The Administration of the Imperial Land Regulations* (London: Longmans, 1939), 255–8.

It was with the evident idea of carrying out a national scheme of emigration that the Imperial Government, in 1823, removed five hundred and sixty-eight persons from disaffected areas in Ireland to Canada, under the personal direction of Peter Robinson, at a cost of £12,538/12/–, or £22/1/6 *per capita*.[1] The reasons were found in the desire to test Horton's plan of pauper colonization, originally intended to be applied to English parishes, but extended to include Ireland where unemployment and disorder, starvation and disease were rampant. Subdivision of the land, early marriages, over-population and corn laws were fast reducing Ireland to a nation of beggars, and neither charity, parliamentary commissioners nor Insurrection Acts were able to stamp out the evils already spreading to Scotland and England, due to the flooding of the labour market by cheap Irish labour. In 1823, a Parliamentary Committee recommended emigration as a possible relief.

The emigrants were chosen from the most disturbed areas of Fermoy, Balhooly and Mallow, and conveyed free to their destination in Packenham township, Rideau Settlement, where the intemperate habits of some of them endangered public peace. As in other instances, one year's provision was supplied to each settler with seed-corn and the necessary implements of husbandry, together with 70 acres of land on condition of cultivation and the usual quit rent after five years of occupation. A reserve of 30 acres was made adjoining each lot which the holder could purchase for £10 within ten years.[2] In 1825, under the same regulations and direction 2,024 additional Irishmen were settled on the Trent River, near Rice Lake, in the district of Newcastle, at a cost of about £43,000, or £21/6/4 *per capita*.[3] An attempt to organize a third party was prevented by the refusal of Parliament to vote the necessary funds until the results of the other experiments had been satisfactorily investigated. The investigation was carried out by the Emigration Commission of 1826–27.

Very conflicting reports have been given regarding the results of these experiments.[4] The Irish settlers were less tractable than the persevering, law-abiding Scot, and the possibilities of failure were therefore greater. By striking a balance, however, between official and non-official opinions, one arrives at an approximation of the truth, and finds the history of these Irish Settlements very similar to many others in the backwoods of Canada. Lieutenant-Governor Maitland, John B. Robinson, and Dr. Strachan spoke in flattering terms of the zeal of the Superintendent on behalf of the settlers, and of the 'industry and rapid advancement so very conspicuous in both his settlements.'[5] Cockburn was skeptical; Talbot and the Emigration

Commissioners of 1832 favoured the scheme because it promoted the happiness of so many poor settlers. MacKenzie, in the *Colonial Advocate*, was severely critical. Dr. Rolph approved a policy that attempted to transform poor settlers into successful farmers.[6] But the credibility of these witnesses is affected by their political and religious bias. Dr. Strachan was too violent a partisan, John B. Robinson was the Attorney-General, a member of the Family Compact, and the brother of the Superintendent, Cockburn was a rival Superintendent, Talbot favoured systematic colonization, MacKenzie opposed the whole policy of the administration, and Rolph favoured a policy that would flood Canada with the unemployed of Great Britain. According to the cold, impersonal evidence of statistics, however, the emigration of 1823 was not a success. At the end of three years only one hundred and twenty out of one hundred and eighty-two heads of families remained on their lands; forty-four had surrendered possession, eight were dead, nine strayed across the international frontier, one returned to Ireland, and at the end of the five years' tenancy others left for the United States. Of those who remained, some were in arrears, and others refused absolutely to pay any rent. As in the case of the Lanark settlers, the Government was at a serious financial loss over the scheme.[7]

The emigrants of 1825, like the Perth settlers ten years earlier, arrived late in the season and had to cut their way to their new home. Some died on the way; the remainder transformed the Rice Lake region, where voluntary emigration had been vainly struggling for years to develop the country. In one year they cleared 1,386 acres, raised 67,799 bushels of potatoes, 25,633 of turnips, 10,428 of maize, sowed 363 bushels of wheat and made 9,067 lbs. of maple sugar, besides purchasing independently forty oxen, eighty cows, and one hundred and sixty-six pigs.[8] They established the now flourishing town of Peterboro, opened roads, built mills, and created new industries. In 1830, Richards was very favourably impressed by the general state of prosperity he met there, which to some people substantiated the truth of the assertion that emigrants fostered and encouraged at the beginning of settlement nearly always succeeded.[9]

In comparison with New Lanark, the Rice Lake Settlement has much in common. The *per capita* cost to Government was about the same; in neither case were these heavy expenses repaid. The initial difficulties were very similar, though the Irish were placed on better lands. Both imposed a heavy financial burden for a problematical future benefit. The removal of a few thousands of starving families, victims of a bad agrarian and industrial system, was simply playing with a serious social evil. Horton's scheme of 'shovelling out paupers' was too theoretical, visionary and expensive.[10] The difficulty remained unsolved since the place of those withdrawn was soon filled up by the natural increase of population. The remedy was to be found in an improved labour market and in the expanding opportunities offered to emigrants in the Colonies and United States, which made Government help unnecessary, except during unusually grave crises, as was found in the Scottish Highlands about the middle of the nineteenth century, and in the post-war industrial depression which in intensity and difficulty of solution offers such striking comparisons and contrasts with the economic and social conditions of a century ago. But a century ago, unlike the present situation, the Imperial Government could secure a measure of financial relief, even though a temporary expedient, by disposing of the waste lands to chartered companies and adopting a general policy of sale as distinct from that of free grant. Both of these measures were forced upon the Government by the results of experience, the recommendations of harassed colonial Governors, and by the cumulative pressure of criticism, both at home and in the Colonies, of a land policy whose only friends were political sycophants, monopolists, and officials whose salaries were augmented by fees upon grants and patent deeds.

NOTES

1. C.O. [Colonial Office Series, British Museum] 324/95, pp. 123 ff., Horton to Horace Townsend, June 6, 1825; J. Bouchette, *British Dominions*, vol. ii, pp. 205 ff.; S.C. Johnson, *History of Emigration*, p. 230; Helen Cowan, *British Emigration to British North America*, chapter 9 gives a detailed account; 1826 (404), vol. iv, *Report from the Committee on Emigration—Cockburn's Evidence*. Horton says the cost amounted to £11,202/9/4; R.C. Mills, *The Colonization of Australia*, pp. 37 ff.

2. Q, vol. 334, pp. 78–125, *A Plan for Settling British and Irish Unemployed in Canada* (London, 1822); ibid., pp. 280 ff.; *Accounts and Papers*, 1823, vol. vi, p. 331; Upper Canada, *Land Book L*, pp. 445–50, July 18, 1825, a plan by J.B. Robinson for Irish Emigration to Upper Canada; Parl. Papers, 1831–32 (334), vol. xxxii, pp. 21–48, *John Richard's Report*; Hansard, N.S., vol. xiv, p. 1361, *Evidence before the Commission of 1823 on Irish Affairs*.

3. C.O. 324/97, pp. 96 ff., Horton to F. Lewis, Oct. 13, 1827; *Accounts and Papers*, 1826–27, vol. v, Robinson's evidence before the Emigration Commission of 1827; ibid., vol. xv, p. 277; C.O. 324/95, p. 123, Horton to Townsend, June 6, 1825.

4. R.C. Mills, *The Colonization of Australia*, p. 39;

Accounts and Papers, 1825, vol. xviii, p. 358, Robinson's Report; ibid., 1831–32, vol. xxxiii, p. 209; 1831–32 (724), vol. xxxii, pp. 209–40, *Report of Commissioners for Emigration*.

5. Q, vol. 343, pp. 241 ff., J.B. Robinson, Jan. 23, 1826; ibid., p. 551, Rev. John Strachan to Horton, July 5, 1826; Q, vol. 345, p. 388, Bishop Macdonell to Bathurst, Feb. 12, 1827; Q, vol. 240, pp. 412 ff., Maitland to Bathurst, March 31, 1826.

6. T. Rolph, *Statistical Account of Upper Canada*, p. 31.

7. C.O. 324/96, Horton to Peter Robinson, May 17; ibid., p. 134 ff., same to same, June 20, 1826, concerning discrepancies in his Reports; C.O. 324/95, pp. 285–7, Horton to Peter Robinson, Dec. 17, 1825, concerning 'Melancholy' reports; C.O. 324/97, p. 99, Peter Robinson was paid an annual salary of £1,000 for the four years, 1823–27.

8. J. Bouchette, *British Dominions*, vol. ii, pp. 205 ff.

9. Parl. Papers, 1831–32 (334), vol. xxxii, pp. 21–48, *Report of John Richards*, p. 7.

10. *Enquiries into the Causes and Remedies of Pauperism*, 1830, 3rd series, p. 22, and 4th series, pp. iii–iv.

---

4 From Helen Cowan, *British Emigration to British North America: The First Hundred Years*, rev. edn (Toronto: University of Toronto Press, 1961), 69–73.

[By 1823] Goulburn and Horton had a scheme in progress for assisting Irish emigration. Wilmot Horton who had developed his emigration theories for the relief of English parishes spoke of the undertaking as an experiment financed by the government for the purpose of planning a great system of emigration for England.[1] In the light of contemporary evidence it is difficult to consider the Irish emigration which followed in 1823 and 1825 as the mere experiments here represented.

Reference has already been made to the attitude and experience of Peel and Goulburn on Irish emigration. Early in 1822 the Secretary for War and the Colonies, Lord Bathurst, had been approached by Irish landlords who desired the encouragement of emigration from overpopulated districts.[2] Before parliamentary committees the same gentlemen gave evidence in favour of emigration. Presently at Goulburn's they were read a plan, adapted or drawn up by Horton, for government-aided emigration. Finally, if the motive stated by Horton were the only one, it is inexplicable why an emigration scheme planned for English parishes should have been hastily arranged for Ireland and tried out with emigrants from the 'most disturbed district,' when upon the success of the venture depended the future policy of Parliament towards the whole problem of relief by emigration. It would seem therefore that whatever the ideals of Horton, the motives of the government officials above him were not entirely those of experimentation but that, as in the case of the northern weavers, it was found expedient to offer a means of partial relief to a district where severe political danger was imminent.

The plan given to the Irish gentlemen at Goulburn's stated as a premise that 'Government desirous of alleviating the inconveniences of excessive population in Ireland, and at the same time of giving the Provinces of Canada an accession of Emigrants capable of improving the advantages afforded by those Colonies to active and industrious men, has taken into consideration the expediency of providing for the transport and location of a certain number of Settlers on a system which will best insure their immediate comfort, and their future prosperity.' To those disposed to emigrate from the south, who were under forty-five years of age and acceptable to the superintendent of emigration, the government promised to the number of 500 passage to Canada and conveyance to their lands free of expense, provisions and medical attendance on their journey and for one year after their arrival on their land; also, seventy acres of land subject to the usual conditions of fee and residence, with a 30-acre pre-emption reserved adjoining, and utensils necessary for a new settler, all furnished at the public expense. The advantages to be gained by one proceeding under these terms rather than as a casual emigrant were emphasized. Finally, as it was the desire of the government that this system should prove satisfactory to the emigrant and beneficial to the public, the terms concluded with the warning that the continuance of assistance must depend upon the 'good conduct in the colony' of those who availed themselves of the offer as well as upon that of future claimants for similar assistance whom it was out of the power of the government to remove the first year.[3]

Towards the end of May Peter Robinson, brother of Attorney-General John B. Robinson of Upper Canada, who was selected by the Colonial Office to superintend the emigration and settlement in Canada, proceeded to Fermoy, Cork. There he was introduced by Lord Kingston, Lord Doneraile, and other proprietors. The greatest objection these gentlemen made to the emigration plan was that 'the most industrious and best disposed' would be most likely to take up the offer. They believed however that the magistrates and landowners could guard against this 'by recommending only those who, if not actually connected with the disturbances,' were almost sure to be so from their situation and lack of employment.[4] Robinson was advised therefore to take as many persons as possible from the worst district, the barony of Fermoy. Accordingly Fermoy, Ballyhooly, Mallow, Newmarket, Charleville, Killdorrery, Doneraile, Killworth, and nearby villages were visited, the terms of the emigration made public, and a list opened from which Robinson and the magistrates would later select the emigrants to receive aid.[5]

The scheme was not at first well received by the Irish. Though they willingly approached Robinson, they would not place their names on the magistrates' lists. This was due, Robinson wrote, to the necessity for 'the Magistrates to be almost daily sitting as judges to enforce the law.'[6] Stories respecting the government's intention were soon widespread: 'It was a *gental* way of transporting them. . . . Government found they could not get rid of them fast enough by the Insurrection Act.' As Robinson stated, the good to be effected by exporting five hundred would depend entirely upon their description; he felt it would be wrong 'openly to hold out a bounty to persons of bad character,' but since he had to procure candidates he was forced to expedients. He told applicants that as for character no questions would be asked; and with the consent of Thomas Arbuthnot, commanding officer of the district, he accepted a few persons of means in order to show the others that it was not a trick to get them out of the country.[7]

Within two weeks, in which Robinson had the assistance of the landlords and the priests, the people evinced 'a perfect mania for going to Canada.' 'All so many questions to ask.' Was Mr. Robinson an American? Was he quite sure there was no catch in it? Were there potatoes, priests, etc.? In Fermoy in one day there were two hundred applicants, some of whom had come fifty miles. The whole number desired might have been enlisted without going over half the territory Robinson visited in order to spread the opportunity throughout a wide district. Even in Buttevant and Doneraile—decidely the most disturbed regions—the full quota was obtained. Most encouraging of all, it appeared that the few taken in 1823 would do 'a great deal of good in relieving the small towns.' For ten days there had been neither fire nor murders in the barony of Fermoy.[8]

So the *Hebe* and the *Stakesby* were enabled to sail on July 8 with all accommodations filled. Some who had promised failed to arrive at the port, it is true, but Robinson had prepared for this contingency by accepting more than he could carry. Though many came on board in dread and terror, other applicants crowded around the vessels in boats offering to go to Canada until the anchors were up and the ships put to sea. After an average crossing on which eight children and one woman were lost by death, the two vessels reached Quebec on the last day of September.[9] Conveyances ordered by the Quebec officials on instructions from Lord Bathurst were ready and the emigrants transferred directly from the *Hebe* and the *Stakesby* to the river steamboats and travelled at once to Montreal. From that port they went forward without stop, now on foot and in wagons to Lachine; here only two days were spent in rest

and loading. Again the party set out, this time in large river boats the crews of which consisted of the Irish emigrants and two Canadians to guide and steer. Notwithstanding the rapidity of the river and the unskilfulness of the men, few of whom had ever been in a boat, Prescott was reached on October 15, two weeks after the emigrants had entered Quebec harbour.[10]

At Prescott one month's provisions were taken over from the representatives of the quarter-master general's department who were waiting there. On October 18 the journey across country to Ramsay and Packenham townships in the Rideau settlements was begun. Four days later Robinson reported his arrival. A few settlers from Glasgow with a party of discharged soldiers had cleared the first land in Ramsay in 1820 and Sir Peregrine Maitland had given orders that Robinson use the remainder of their old stores.[11] There were neither barracks nor government buildings in the neighbourhood and the party was without shelter of any sort until log huts were put up, first in the central encampment and gradually on the various lots. As the Irish were unskilled in the use of the axe, it was necessary to pay old settlers to perform this work. The experience of choosing land upon which the home was to be reared, of receiving tools for work, and of being free men appears to have been fully appreciated. John Mara wrote of his land grant: 'to my judgment [it] was as good land as any in the Country.' As for Robinson, the superintendent, 'he has served us out with Beds and Blankets, all kinds of Carpenter's Tools, Farming Utensils and a Cow to the head of every Family next Spring.' Writing home the same year, Carrol O'Sullivan extended the customary invitation for others to emigrate and added that even the cold Canadian winter was easier 'to put up with' than 'the rebuke of a landlord and the frown of a proctor at home.'[12]

From the success of this pioneering in the Canadian woods, it had been said, would be decided the government's policy towards expenditure on emigration. Horton wrote of the Irish settlers:

If the accounts of them continue favourable, if instead of verifying the predictions which proceed from very high Canadian authority now in England that these men all run away from their Grants as soon as they cease to be provisioned by Government, the Settlers betake themselves to regular industry and proceed with the cultivation of their Grants, North American Emigrants will become a part of our National Policy. If the contrary event take place we shall be brought to disgrace, and as far as any individual will suffer, I am sorry to say that I shall be the most prominent one.[13]

The adoption of a large emigration scheme, however, depended upon Parliament and Parliament was interested, as it turned out, not in any colonial experiment but in conditions and opinions at home. Nevertheless it rested with the Colonial Office to justify its experiment.

From the first, contradictory reports regarding its success were spread. Lord Dalhousie, the high Canadian authority referred to above, had believed that such an addition of poor settlers at a time when the Canadas were already 'overwhelmed by a Voluntary Emigration' would enlarge seriously the difficulties consequent upon all sudden, great increases of population. He objected particularly to the expense and when in the spring of 1824 quarrels arose between the neighbouring Scottish settlers and the Irish newcomers, he felt his fears had been fully realized. He and Captain Marshall, the former local superintendent of the Lanark settlers, were convinced that the Irish were little less than banditti. They advised that the scheme under Peter Robinson 'be stopped at once as a Waste of Public Monies, and a most serious mischief done to the Canadas.'[14]

The reports of Sir Peregrine Maitland, lieutenant-governor of Upper Canada, were as glowing as those of Lord Dalhousie had been gloomy. Although the rationing had been done by the commissariat, the management of the Irish settlement had been very much more in the hands of Upper Canadian officials than that of the military settlements. Maitland commended Robinson's efforts and the industry of the Irish. When in the spring the magistrates of Bathurst sent in protests against the habits of the newcomers in quarrelling with the early Scottish settlers, Maitland pointed out that there had been great jealousy of the Irish because they were assisted more liberally by the government than were the first settlers.[15]

Bare statistics of this venture in government colonization are inconclusive. Of the 567 souls brought out from Ireland only 477, of whom 63 were newly born, were on land in the Bathurst district in 1825; in other words, of the 182 heads of families located in 1823 only 120 were living on their farms in 1825. Eight of the 62 deserted farms had been vacated by death, 9 by departure to the United States, 12 by departure without leave, and 32 by departure of men to work for other settlers, a practice almost universal among penniless settlers.[16] Had the 567 emigrants remained effective settlers, the cost of the emigration would have fallen within the sum estimated, £13,974, or an average of £22 1s. 6d. Allowing for the expenditure on the emigration to the Cape and for the failure of the Navy Board to call for a full account for conveyance, Robinson's outlay was only £750 beyond the sum available from the vote, since his total expense for transporting, locating, equipping, and rationing the emigrants for one year had been £12,539 3s.[17] But if only 477 of the 567 became settlers on the land the whole calculation was altered and the average expense of settling one emigrant rose to something over £26.

NOTES

1. *Parliamentary Papers*, 1825, VIII (129), 5.
2. C.O. 43/62, Bathurst to Lord Kingston, June 29, 1822.
3. C.O. 42/371, statement of terms; C. 628, enclosure in Bathurst to Dalhousie, June 5, 1823.
4. *Parl. Pap.*, 1825, VII (200), 249; C.O. 384/12,

Ennismore to Horton, May 30, 1823, Robinson to Horton, April 2, 1824.

5. C.O. 384/12, Robinson to Horton, June 9; *Parl. Pap.*, 1823, VI (561), 178.

6. C.O. 384/12, Robinson to Horton. This part of the correspondence was omitted from *Parl. Pap.*, 1825, VII (200).

7. C.O. 384/12, Robinson to Horton, June 14, 9, 29, July 1, 1823.

8. Ibid., June 19, July 8, 1823.

9. C.O. 42/197, Robinson to Horton, Sept. 2.

10. C.O. 43/25, Bathurst to Dalhousie, June 5, 1823.

11. C. 629, Commissary of Accounts Office, Quebec, to Colonel Darling, May 10, 21, 1824; N. Macdonald, *Canada, 1763–1841: Immigration and Settlement* (London, 1939), 255.

12. C.O. 384/12, Robinson to Horton, July 20, 1824, stating that the issue of blankets was absolutely

necessary as the settlers were quite uncovered; Feb. 19, 1824.

13. C.O. 324/95, Horton's private correspondence, 1824.

14. C.O. 42/196, Dalhousie to Bathurst, Dec. 20, 1823; C.O. 42/200, Dalhousie to Bathurst, May 18, 1824, with enclosure of Marshall, May 5, 1824.

15. C.O. 42/372, Maitland to Bathurst, Feb. 23, 1824; C.O. 42/373, enclosure in Maitland to Bathurst, July 27.

16. C.O. 42/377, enclosure in Maitland to Bathurst, May 12; C.O. 384/87, Robinson's report to Horton on limited emigration in 1823.

17. C.O. 384/12, from statement of expenditure which was later than that given in *Parl. Pap.*, 1825, VII (200); Robinson to Horton, Jan. 1, 1825.

---

5 From Hugh Johnston, *British Emigration Policy, 1815–1830: 'Shovelling Out Paupers'* (Oxford: Clarendon Press, 1972), 75–90.

In 1822 Peter Robinson, an honorary member of the executive council of Upper Canada and a member of the legislative assembly, had come to London with his brother John Beverley Robinson, Attorney-General of that province. The Robinsons were central figures in the Family Compact, the Upper Canadian ruling clique. They were the sons of an aristocratic Virginia family which had chosen the wrong side in 1776; they had been raised in the home of the first Anglican missionary in Upper Canada; and John Beverley had received his grammar-school education from Dr. John Strachan who was, in many respects, the architect of the Family Compact.[1] This background was reflected in an attitude of conservative and unapologetic intolerance. Few English statesmen defended the Church of England so resolutely or looked upon democracy with such distaste. John Beverley, the younger but abler brother, was first appointed Attorney-General at the age of eighteen before he was

called to the bar; eventually, in 1829, he became Chief Justice, a position which he held in addition to membership in the executive council and speakership of the legislative council. His influence in the government of Upper Canada was already considerable in 1822.

John Beverley Robinson had been sent to London to represent the interests of his province in a dispute with Lower Canada over the division of customs duties collected at Quebec. After his arrival he became involved in an abortive effort by Horton to legislate a union of the two Canadas; this business kept Robinson in London through the winter of 1822–3. He was available for consultation by Horton when the experiment in Irish emigration was launched. At first thought the idea was repugnant. He knew that the Irish gentry wanted to get rid of the young and unemployed who 'hung loose upon society' and were 'the ready actors in all disturbances'.[2] Violence and religious bigotry were native products of

Ireland which Robinson did not wish to import to Upper Canada. Yet he was prepared to believe that the behaviour of the Irish was not ingrained and that, in the calmer atmosphere of a colony in which they were given equal footing with their neighbours, old quarrels could be forgotten. He decided that he would be happier to accept Catholics from the South of Ireland than Protestants from the North; Ulstermen might be more intelligent and less violent, but they were also more republican. Robinson preferred the 'ignorant, poor and priest ridden' to those 'who think for themselves in matters of Government and religion, and too often think wrong'.[3] The desirability of a scheme of government colonization for sparsely populated, land-rich Upper Canada was manifest and nothing could be more welcome to an Upper Canadian than the spending that such a program would entail. Robinson favoured Irish immigration, but not at such a rate than they might become a majority in the province; 'then they would have the law in their own hands' and there would be no stopping their shooting and burning.

On Tuesday 29 April Peel opened the question of Irish emigration; on Saturday 10 May the Robinsons intended to embark for Canada. In that short period Peter Robinson was persuaded to stay behind to superintend the project. It was through John Beverley that Horton approached Peter; John Beverley could think of no one 'more likely to do justice to such a trust than my brother'.[4] Moreover, Peter was there, in Britain, and available. Colonel Thomas Talbot, who knew Ireland as Robinson did not, and who possessed long experience in colonization, would have been an obvious and willing candidate; but Talbot was in Canada and Horton needed a man immediately.[5] Peter Robinson was ready to take the job. He saw an opportunity to gain credit by carrying out a measure of importance both to Britain and the colony; but he was afraid that this credit would be tarnished unless the entire management on both sides of the Atlantic were placed in his hands. He insisted on an overall superintendence in which he would be held directly accountable only to the British government. This condition was acceptable to Horton; Robinson undertook a task singlehandedly which would have been accomplished with greater efficiency if he had been assisted by the authorities in Canada.

At the end of May 1823 Peter Robinson found himself crossing the Irish Sea instead of returning to Upper Canada with his brother. During the first week of June he visited all of the principal towns in the northern part of Cork, appointing in each a person to make a list of those who wished to emigrate.[6] These lists were subsequently combed by magistrates who marked the names of suspected troublemakers who were most eligible to go. The Irish peasants were understandably suspicious of an invitation that smacked so much of deportation. Like Lord Wellesley, they could not appreciate the subtle difference between transporting the convicted for their crimes and the unconvicted for their poverty.

In this respect, the appointment of a foreigner as a recruiting agent in Ireland was fortunate. While local magistrates were not trusted, Robinson himself was very successful in encouraging volunteers.[7] By the end of June he had distributed embarkation tickets to 600 persons. During the first two days of July 571 boarded two vessels provided by the Transport Office. A majority of the men were labourers; a few were unemployed and homeless; a small number were landless farmers. To the best of Robinson's knowledge, which under the circumstances could not be perfect, all were penniless. Robinson asked no questions of the past conduct of his passengers. Although he allowed the magistrates to pick out their least wanted citizens, no man was sent against his will. The law-abiding went with the lawless. As an Upper Canadian Robinson might have been expected to give preference to those who had no criminal background. His impartiality was based on a belief that if men were given the responsibility of owning land, they would become peaceful citizens. This belief was not held universally; the project was a social experiment and something of a gamble.

In the course of an eight-week crossing Robinson discovered that the Irish stomach tolerated a very restricted diet. The emigrants were issued with a minimum allowance of navy rations. Men received a pound of salt pork, a pound of ship's biscuit, and almost half a pint of spirits daily; women were given half a pound of salt pork, a pound of biscuit, and tea and sugar. Cocoa was provided for breakfast and plum pudding for Sunday dinner. The Irish were used to eating potatoes and herring; they normally had meat once in a season. When faced with inferior pork and alien food they lost appetite.[8] Meat was thrown overboard by the hundredweight, plum pudding refused by every man, woman, and child; only a few individuals would touch the cheese, and cocoa was turned aside until the ship's officers proved it could be taken safely. Robinson was amazed to hear sick children crying for potatoes when they were offered arrowroot as a medicament. Yet he learned nothing from his observations. The emigrants were kept on similar rations for fifteen months after they arrived in Canada. Rather than eat food that they found disgusting, they traded a large part of it for whiskey, potatoes, and cows. If he had been more imaginative, Robinson might have provided the head of each family with a small sum and allowed him to make his own purchases.

In spite of the diet and the relatively slow crossing, the health of the emigrants was generally good. One woman and eight children died of smallpox, but these losses could not be blamed on the conditions on board ship.[9] The journey from Cork in Ireland to Prescott in Upper Canada was managed with admirable timing. At Quebec Robinson found steamboats waiting for him and was able to transfer his people to these vessels without landing. Conveyance was also ready for him at Montreal; with a minimum of delay he brought his party to Prescott on 15 September. Nearly 600 men, women, and children, travelling by steamboat,

wagon, and bateaux, had been moved 320 miles in thirteen days.

The season was, nevertheless, advanced, and Robinson had not yet selected a tract of land. On 18 September he left the emigrants in Prescott while he surveyed half a dozen townships in or adjacent to the Rideau Military Settlement. After an absence of several days he returned to Prescott to move the Irish the last 60 miles to their destination. A majority were located in Ramsay Township behind concession lines occupied by some of the Glasgow weavers. The others were placed in adjacent townships which were partially occupied by military men and Scottish assisted emigrants of 1815 and 1820–1. From the beginning the Irish found themselves on poor terms with their neighbours. They were disliked equally for their Catholicism and their reputed lawlessness. Inevitably, the Scottish weavers compared the liberal assistance that the Irish were receiving with the help that they themselves had been given.[10] The weavers were required to repay £10 per head; but each Irish family received a log house, cow, blankets, farming implements, and provisions as outright gifts. Knowledge of this was a factor in the eventual failure of the Scots to return one farthing of their debt. In the meantime they and the other established settlers complained bitterly amongst themselves that so much should be given to such inferior people.

The annual muster of the local militia regiment in the following April sparked a brawl which roused the Irish to commit a subsequent act of vandalism.[11] A party led by the local deputy-sheriff, an Orangeman, marched out to the settlement to make arrests and fired on a building in which the men had gathered. One Irishman was killed and two were wounded. The exaggerated first reports of this incident alarmed authorities at York. John Beverley Robinson was ready to believe the worst; 'I am something staggered in my opinion of Irish Emigration,' he told Horton.[12] After reflection, and with more evidence before him, he took a saner view. It was evident that the Irish had received some provocation before their original outburst; an investigating officer charged the deputy-sheriff's party with a 'wanton and outrageous attack upon the lives of the new settlers'.[13] Any desire to seek blood for blood was checked by the restraint of the Irish in the ensuing months; this was the only occasion on which they were collectively on the wrong side of the law in Upper Canada.

Corrections were slow to catch up with first judgements. Long after J.B. Robinson had qualified his initial statement, he was quoted in the House of Commons in proof of a claim that attitudes in Upper Canada had hardened against further Irish immigration.[14] Although Robinson assured Horton that the provincial legislative assembly would welcome 100,000 Irish paupers if the Imperial government chose to send them, the unfavourable stories were never completely silenced. Prominent among those giving publicity to these stories was the Governor-General of Canada, Lord Dalhousie. His principal source of information was Lieutenant-Colonel William Marshall, superintendent of the Lanark and Rideau Settlements, a man prejudiced on the side of his own settlers and disgruntled by the creation of a new settlement under the supervision of a civilian. Dalhousie had predicted failure for Robinson's emigrants from the moment they were placed on the land; the tone of his dispatch enclosing Marshall's version of the disturbances in Ramsay Township was one of satisfaction in having his doubts confirmed. The Irish would never be reconciled to their neighbours, he claimed, not even in small numbers. Most of them would abandon their land and become wandering beggars. Robinson's scheme should be stopped, he told Bathurst; it was 'a waste of Public monies and a most serious mischief done to the Canadas'.[15]

On this issue, Dalhousie and the Lieutenant-Governor of Upper Canada, Sir Peregrine Maitland, were diametrically opposed. Maitland applauded Peter Robinson's efforts and took a personal interest in the success of his experi-

ment. To a certain extent, Maitland and Dalhousie reflected the separate problems of their provinces. Voluntary emigrants continued to arrive at Quebec at a rate of 10,000 a year. The destitute among them were still creating serious difficulties for the government of the Lower Province. Under these circumstances, Dalhousie was apprehensive about the encouragement of further pauper emigration. Quebec served as the principal port for both Canadian provinces, but the care of helpless, sick, and dying emigrants bound for Upper Canada and the United States became the responsibility of the government of Lower Canada alone. Upper Canadians did not entertain misgivings about pauper emigration because the worst of the human wreckage did not reach them.

An element of vanity influenced Dalhousie's opposition to the emigration conducted by Peter Robinson. The Governor-General had not been consulted, but had simply been informed after all of the arrangements had been made. He objected not so much to the principle involved as to the actual system that had been adopted.[16] First, he argued that the expense of transporting emigrants inland to Upper Canada was too great and that it would be impossible to prevent desertion from that province to the United States. Second, he did not think that Upper Canada required assisted emigration because considerable numbers went there at their own expense. Third, he thought that the Irish emigrants should be placed under strict control to make them work; he asserted that Peter Robinson and his subordinates were not competent to do this. As an alternative, Dalhousie favoured a settlement in his province, in the Gaspé, under the rigid supervision of military personnel.

In November 1825 Dalhousie reported to Horton on Lieutenant-Colonel Marshall's authority that half of the settlers who had come out in 1823 had run away. Maitland replied that this estimate was far from the truth. 'I cannot but regret,' he wrote to Horton, 'that Lord Dalhousie . . . should not have thought it a safer and better course, to have consulted the Government of this Province, as to the real situation of the Emigrants before he transmitted to you such erroneous and discouraging information.'[17] In May 1826 Maitland sent the results of an on-the-spot count. Of 182 heads of families brought out by Peter Robinson, eight had died; 121 were on their land; nine were known to have gone to the United States and one had returned to Ireland. Of the remaining forty-three, at least twenty-two

were working in the immediate vicinity as farm labourers and tradesmen. Many of the others had found jobs in Kingston, Prescott, and Montreal, as rafters on the St Lawrence, or as labourers on the Welland Canal. Some of them could be expected to return to their land after they had earned enough money to buy some stock. Predictions that a majority would slip over the American border at the first opportunity had proved to be without basis.

NOTES

1. C.W. Robinson, *The Life of Sir John Beverley Robinson* (Edinburgh, 1904), p. x.
2. C.O. 384/12, J. Robinson to Horton, 14 June 1825; Add. MSS. 38294, J. Robinson to Horton 5 May 1823.
3. C.O. 384/12, J. Robinson to Horton, 19 Feb. 1824.
4. J. Robinson to Horton, 5 May 1823.
5. On 14 Feb. 1823, Talbot wrote to Horton: 'I . . . hope that you have not abandoned your scheme for encouraging Emigration . . . should a Bill on your plan be carried into operation I offer my humble services . . . in undertaking any portion of the superintendence.' See Wilmot Horton Papers.
6. C.O. 384/12, P. Robinson to Horton, 2 and 9 June 1823; Helen I. Cowan, *British Emigration to British North America: The First Hundred Years*, rev. edn (Toronto, 1961), p. 70.
7. C.O. 384/12, P. Robinson to Horton, 9 June 1823 and 2 Apr. 1824, Becher to Horton, 1 July 1823; *Parl. Pap.* 1825, VII (200), 258.
8. P. Robinson to Horton, 2 Apr. 1824; H.T. Pammett, 'Assisted Emigration from Ireland to

Upper Canada under Peter Robinson in 1825', *O.H.S.P.R.*, 1936, p. 179; *Parl. Pap.* 1826–7, V (550), 347.
9. P. Robinson to Horton, 2 Apr. 1824; Cowan, p. 71.
10. C.O. 42/373, FitzGibbon to Hillier, 10 June 1824.
11. J.K. Johnson, 'Colonel James FitzGibbon and the Suppression of Irish Riots in Upper Canada', *Ontario History*, Sept. 1966, p. 142.
12. C.O. 384/12, J. Robinson to Horton, 10 May 1824.
13. C.O. 42/373, FitzGibbon to Hillier, 10 June 1824. See also C.O. 384/12, J. Robinson to Horton, 14 June 1825.
14. C.O. 384/12, Horton to J. Robinson, 14 June 1825. See also W.H.P., J. Robinson to Horton, 6 July 1830.
15. C.O. 42/200, Dalhousie to Bathurst, 18 May 1824.
16. C.O. 42/204, Dalhousie to Horton, 12 Nov. 1825.
17. W.H.P., Maitland to Horton, 9 Mar. 1826; C.O. 42/377, Maitland to Bathurst, 1 May 1826.

6 From Wendy Cameron, 'Selecting Peter Robinson's Irish Emigrants', *Histoire Sociale/Social History* 9/17 (May 1976): 29–35.

Peter Robinson[1] sailed from Cork with 568 emigrants in 1823 and 2,024 in 1825. He formed

two settlements with them in Upper Canada. The first was based on a depot at Shipman's Mills

(Almonte) in the Bathurst district, and the centre of the second settlement was the future site of Peterborough in the Newcastle district. Robinson's emigrations are usually considered as examples of the kind of colonization advocated by R.J. Wilmot Horton,[2] Robinson's immediate superior, or else, in the context of the history of settlement in Upper Canada.[3] A full investigation from either point of view precludes paying much attention to Robinson's three visits to Ireland in the spring of 1823, the late summer of 1824 and the spring of 1825. During these visits Robinson created an organization for selecting emigrants which is of considerable interest in itself. In addition, a detailed analysis of his selection adds a new dimension to the practical application of Horton's plan and offers a firm base from which to assess the performance of Robinson's emigrants in terms of their origins.

Robinson's emigrations had a varied background. They were marked by the literary sources which had influenced Horton, the writings of Malthus and other political economists, and they owed something to the approximately 10,000 settlers who were located in the government supervised military and Lanark settlements by 1822.[4] Although different settlers had been treated very differently, examples could be found in these settlements of all the kinds of assistance Robinson's settlers received: a passage, a grant of land, superintendence and medical attention, and the distribution of rations, tools and other necessities for the period, Horton set it at one year, until the emigrant became self-sufficient.

The alarming state of Ireland in the early 1820s proved to be the catalyst which enabled Horton to combine previous Colonial Office experience in Upper Canada with his belief in the effectiveness of emigration as a form of pauper relief. In northern county Cork, for instance, armed bands of men retreated to the hills and, by 1820, that part of the country was in a state bordering on 'a miniature civil war.'[5] Historians have since concluded that the wet autumn of 1821 and the resulting loss of much of the potato crop

did more to interrupt the momentum of this movement than the authorities.[6] However this may be, the effect on the population of the partial famine of 1822 and of the continuing unrest made it easy to argue a case for any form of relief in the south of Ireland.

From the beginning, there were two views of Robinson's emigrations current among Horton's contemporaries. Those concerned only with relieving the immediate situation, and they probably included most members of Parliament who voted to finance Horton's emigrations,[7] did not expect to make a noticeable impact on unemployment by sending so few. Their object was accomplished if the hope of being included convinced people to remain quiet through a difficult time. 'Quiet' in Ireland was a relative term, but some of the magistrates directly involved with Robinson did inform Horton that the government emigrations had had a pacifying effect on their immediate neighbourhoods.[8]

The second view of the emigrations was as pilot studies for a scheme of Horton's. He saw them as experiments which would establish an alternative to eviction in clearing estates. At his most optimistic, he considered removing as many as 900,000 rural paupers from the south of Ireland to government supervised settlements in the North American colonies. Despite initial interest from cabinet members such as Sir Robert Peel and Sir Frederick Robinson, Chancellor of the Exchequer, he failed to take his scheme beyond the stages of experiment and discussion in two Select Committees on Emigration in 1826 and 1827.[9] Horton asked too much. As a Malthusian, he insisted that his emigrants be 'redundant' paupers with no productive work and no means of paying their passage, while, as a colonizer, he refused to budge from the estimate of £20 per head which he believed necessary to ensure that they did not become a burden on the colony. In the long run, none of his arguments from the political economy of his time were sufficient to convince either Irish landlords or his cabinet colleagues that his plan was in their interest. They drew back from incurring such a large, immediate expense in the hope of future benefits of which they were far less certain than he.

Horton sent Robinson to Ireland in 1823 with introductions and instructions. Apart from a general letter from Horton, Robinson was introduced to the gentry of county Cork by Lord Ennismore and William Wrixon Becher, two Irish members of Parliament who had taken an early interest in Horton's plan.[10] As Ennismore and Becher represented Cork County and Mallow repectively and as they came from the Blackwater valley, they offered Robinson support in a rural area which had access to the port at the Cove of Cork and which met all Horton's criteria in the way of poverty and unrest. Horton needed nothing more, and he ignored the Irish government so completely that Robinson was at work before Lord Wellesley, the lieutenant governor, or Lord Kingston, the 'principal person of the county'[11] of Cork, had heard of the project. Both men were initially annoyed, but Horton's colleagues mollified Wellesley, and Robinson himself talked Kingston into becoming one of his principal supporters.

Horton's instructions to Robinson set out guidelines for choosing emigrants. Robinson had complete discretion in individual cases, but Horton insisted on several occasions that he must be able to justify each separate exception. No one Robinson took should be able to pay his own way and the heads of families were to be able-bodied, not over 45 and not encumbered by more than three children under 14. Although Horton disliked discriminating on religious grounds, it was 'infinitely more desireable'[12] to take Roman Catholics, an instruction which Robinson heeded. A list of 177 settlers located in 1823 showed only 14 Protestants.[13]

These criteria did no more than establish a body of people from whom a selection might be made. They were intended as both a support and a reminder to Robinson as he negotiated with the local authorities on behalf of the government and Horton's plan. At the same time, Horton was careful to leave Robinson as free a hand as possible. For, while Horton recorded Robinson's selections as though they were pilot studies to be repeated as part of a grand scheme, the actual means at Robinson's disposal were those of a temporary measure of local relief. As a result, we have an unusually well-documented example of the kind of program which depended for its success on a class understanding between government officials and the local gentry. All concerned assumed that the reward for co-operation would be a share in the distribution of the patronage involved. But, it was only because Horton questioned his actions so frequently, that Robinson actually wrote of the need to meet the 'reasonable expectations' of those 'zealously anxious' for the success of the emigrations.[14] This example can be expanded to trace the evolution of the venture until, by the summer of 1825, the selection of emigrants in Fermoy and three neighbouring baronies had acquired an administrative life of its own.

Robinson spent the month of June 1823 selecting emigrants. His official instructions did not reach him until June 2, and he could not take longer because he was anxious to have his emigrants housed before winter. His time in Ireland was divided roughly in half. For the first two weeks he concentrated on selling the idea of assisted emigration to key members of the nobility and magistracy and to potential emigrants. The turning point in the fortunes of the emigration came at about the middle of the month. By this time, both Robinson and Ennismore were certain of the popularity of the measure.[15] Robinson then turned his attention to consolidating his selection and to arrangements for the emigrants' departure.

All of the region from which Robinson drew emigrants, including parts of the counties of Cork, Limerick, Tipperary, Waterford and Kerry, were under the Insurrection Act in the spring of 1823. Within his area of concentration, Ennismore and Becher identified the barony of Fermoy as the most disturbed and, on their advice, Robinson made his headquarters in the town of Fermoy.[16] From Fermoy he branched out into the adjoining baronies of Condons and Glangibbon, Orrery and Kilmore, and Duhallow.

In his official report for 1823 Robinson stated that he had worked in a rough circle. He had first distributed a printed memorandum of the terms of emigration, and then he had visited the towns of Fermoy, Mitchelstown, Doneraile, Charleville, Newmarket, Kanturk and Mallow.[17] The ships lists of the *Hebe* and *Stakesby* recorded the places of origin of the emigrants on board and provided further evidence.[18] With a few exceptions, such as the families who came from Sixmilebridge in county Clare, most of Robinson's emigrants were from the towns named; from places within the 'circle' such as Ballyhooly, Castletownroche, Liscarroll, or Churchtown; or from places within a perimeter of about 15 miles (the distance he estimated people would walk to see him) and on roads leading into the towns where Robinson had lists open. For example, there were families who must have come from Croom and Newmarket, Limerick to Charleville in the northwest, from Rathcormic to Fermoy in the south, and from Clogheen, Tipperary to Mitchelstown in the east.

The letters Robinson wrote to Horton during June 1823 were particularly interesting because they recorded his first impressions. He was shocked at first, not by the poverty and outrages which he expected, but by the lack of trust and communication between classes. He had expected to rely on the magistracy to find him candidates, but he soon discovered that the 'temper and disposition of the lower order of people' could not easily be judged by 'what you hear' and that, on the other side: 'It is not here as in other countries. The noblemen and gentlemen have not in the least the confidence of the lower order. They are governed entirely by appearances.'[19] In terms of Robinson's emigration, the lack of confidence took the form of deep distrust of an offer which landlords seemed to press hardest on

unwanted tenants, and the 'appearance' they picked up was the resemblance between assisted emigration or 'genteel transportation' and the real thing.[20]

As soon as he rode out into the countryside to see the state of the people for himself, Robinson had no doubt that suitable candidates existed. He saw hundreds of men of a 'good sort,' 'bred to farming' and 'completely without work.'[21] In order to reach these people, he introduced a new element into Horton's scheme by approaching people in the middle range of society. Despite what he had been told to the contrary, he found that the Roman Catholic priests were often willing to give him active support and that their relations with their Church of England counterparts were generally amiable. On the first point, he cited the case of the priest at Newmarket who read his memorandum in church and gave a favourable explanation of the terms of assistance.[22] The fuller records of the 1825 emigration provided evidence for this second point: a surprising number of emigrants had character references or recommendations signed by both a Protestant clergyman and a Roman Catholic priest and, in the case of four families from Cape Clear Island, the curate and parish priest were accepted as their only sponsors.[23] Robinson also spent some time discussing emigration with 'respectable people' who came to inquire, a move which alarmed Horton considerably when he heard of it. Robinson, however, defended himself by pointing out that he must consider people's feelings if he was to find candidates. He believed that the presence of these people did more to reassure real paupers than any number of promises.[24]

Robinson could only do so much working through more popular members of the nobility such as Ennismore or the acquaintance he built up as he rode around. In the end, his own personality seems to have been a deciding factor. When he found that candidates regarded their local magistrates only as judges and came more readily to him, he devoted long hours to interviews and to discussing North America: 'Was I [Robinson] an American. Did I live there. Should I go back again. Was I quite sure there was no catch in it. Were there any pigs, potatoes, priests, wild men, beasts.'[25] These measures provided enough evidence of good faith for Robinson to find that by the halfway point he was drawing four times as many candidates as he could handle. As he intended to spread the benefits of the emigration through the district, he adopted a policy, which he followed again in 1825, of taking a proportion of the people who applied at each centre.

By the end of June 1823, Robinson had chosen 600 candidates of whom only 460 responded to his messengers and came to Cork in time for his July 1 deadline. This discrepancy in the numbers may have been some indication of the strength of lingering fears and suspicions, though Robinson attributed it to 'how tardy they are in their movements' and 'the dread the women have of the sea.'[26] He had made some allowance for attrition due to sickness and other causes when he accepted 600, and he made up the remaining numbers in time to sail on July 8 with a full complement of 568 emigrants. Those he took were probably rejected candidates who had followed him anyway; on July 6 he wrote that even as the ships prepared to sail, friends of his emigrants were still coming alongside in boats and offering themselves to go to Upper Canada.

The unrest in the district was outwardly of no concern in the selection. Robinson deliberately avoided, and had his Irish associates avoid, asking candidates any questions about their conduct during the recent disturbances. Nevertheless, the issue dominated the 1823 selection. At one level of society, it was the reason for the candidates' fears of government motives. At another, it supplied the basis of Robinson's understanding with the magistrates. Ennismore spelled out their thinking in a private letter to Horton. He and other landowners had feared the emigration would attract 'the most industrious and best dis-

posed' of their tenants. They could overcome this objection by 'recommending only those who, if not actually connected with the disturbances, are likely to be so from their situation, connexions and want of employment.'[27] The key to Robinson's side of the understanding was Horton's belief that the opportunity to own land, and to support his family honestly in Upper Canada, would be enough to transform a potential troublemaker into a useful citizen. On the strength of this opinion, which he stated as his own in his report, Robinson went over his lists of suitable families with the magistrates in each centre and allowed them to single out those they were 'most desirous to get rid of.'[28] He required a character reference so as not to hold out 'a bounty to bad characters.'[29] With these in hand, he could say that he had not knowingly taken anyone convicted under either the Peace Preservation or Insurrection Acts, but he had no illusions. He knew that some of his emigrants had probably been involved in the disturbances and that he had others who, if the magistrates' fears were justified, might take part in the future.[30]

The reputation of the Irish was such that exaggerations were inevitable when trouble broke out in the Bathurst district settlement. Feuds which had built up through the winter erupted into a riot in April, followed a few days later by a fatal shooting and several arrests. An official investigation proved that Robinson's settlers were by no means solely responsible and gave grounds for modifying the reports which had alarmed Horton and, through the medium of the Irish papers, relatives of the emigrants.[31] Robinson identified the sources of conflict for a committee of the House of Lords. They were religious differences, conflict between Scots and Irish, and resentment that his settlers had received more than disbanded soldiers. He believed that only time was needed, and he cited the example of Protestant Irish settlers in Cavan and Monaghan townships who had settled down quietly after a turbulent beginning in the community. Even so, there remained a parallel between the 'turbulent characters' among the 'young unmarried men' who were described as the instigators on the Irish side, and the 'idle unmarried individuals' Becher would like to have sent in 1825 in place of the 'steady men with families' he knew Robinson wanted.[32] Difficulties might be explained away, but Horton, Robinson and the Upper Canadian authorities all made changes when the Colonial Office sent a second party of emigrants in 1825.

Notes

1. Peter Robinson, 1785–1838. In 1823 he was a member of the Legislative Assembly of Upper Canada and an honorary member of the Executive Council. He was in England on a private visit and was recommended to Horton by his brother, John Robinson.

2. Robert John Wilmot, 1784–1841. He took his wife's surname of Horton in 1823 in fulfillment of her father's will. Under Secretary of State for the Colonies 1822–8.

3. See among others: H.J.M. Johnston, *British Emigration Policy 1815–1830: 'Shovelling out Paupers'* (Oxford, 1972); Helen I. Cowan, *British Emigration to British North America: the First Hundred Years*, revised and enlarged edn (Toronto, 1961); Lillian F. Gates, *Land Policies of Upper Canada*, Canadian Studies in History and Government no. 9 (Toronto, 1968); Jean S. McGill, *A Pioneer History of the County of Lanark* (Toronto, 1968). For a new departure based on a field study of material culture see: John J. Mannion, *Irish Settlements in Eastern Canada: A Study of Cultural Transfer and Adaptation*, University of Toronto Dept. of Geography, Research publication no. 12 (Toronto, 1974).

4. Gates, *Land Policies of Upper Canada*, p. 92.

5. R.B. McDowell, *Public Opinion and Government Policy in Ireland, 1801–1846*, Studies in Irish History, Vol. V (London, 1952), p. 59.

6. Galen Broeker, *Rural Disorders and Police Reform in Ireland 1812–36*, Studies in Irish History, Second series, no. VIII (London, 1970).

7. Parliamentary Papers, House of Commons, XIII (401), Estimates and Accounts, p. 301, item 72; Parl. Papers, 1825, XVIII (131), p. 357, item 3; Parl. Papers, 1836–7, XV (160), p. 267, item 16. Parliament voted £15,000 for assisted emigration in 1823 of which about £10,000 went to Robinson. The vote for the 1825 emigration was £30,000 and it was supplemented in 1827 by an additional £10,480 to cover spending beyond the estimate.

8. C.O. 384/12, First Emigration to Canada 1823, f. 272, Ennismore to Horton, 29 June 1823; Ontario Archives, Peter Robinson Papers, MS 12, series 1, Kingston to Robinson, 19 Dec. 1824.

9. Parl. Papers, 1826, IV (404), First Report of the Select Committee on Emigration from the United Kingdom . . . .; and 1827, V (550), Third Report . . . . As chairman, Horton wrote the reports.

10. C.O. 384/12, f. 11, Minute Readat Mr. Goulburn'sto . . . /f. 16v./ Lord Ennismore, Mr. Becher, Sir N. Colthurst etc., n.d. Irish Emigration 1823. Ennismore was M.P. for Cork County 1812–27 and Becher represented Mallow 1818–26.

11. C.O. 384/12, f. 25, Robinson to Horton, 9 June 1823.

12. C.O. 324/95, Private Letters: Mr. Horton, p. 63, Horton to Robinson, 16 April 1825.

13. C.O. 384/12, f. 93, 'Emigrants from the South of Ireland located in Canada by Mr. Robinson'.

14. C.O. 384/13, 1824–25 Second Emigration to Canada, f. 245, Robinson to Horton, 31 May 1825, query 2.

15. C.O. 384/12, f. 25, Robinson to Horton, 14 June 1823; and f. 270, Ennismore to Horton, 15 June 1823.

16. C.O. 384/12, f. 21, Robinson to Horton, 9 June 1823.

17. P.R. Papers, 1, Report on the 1823 Emigration [2 April 1824], printed in Parl. Papers, 1825, VII (200), p. 249, and 1825, XVIII (131), p. 359. For the state of these towns and of the district at the time of the 1841 census, see T.W. Freeman, *Pre-*

Famine Ireland: A Study in Historical Geography (Manchester, 1957), esp. pp. 230–3.

18. P.R. Papers, 3.

19. C.O. 384/12, f. 23, Robinson to Horton, 12 June 1823; and f. 35 v. 29 June 1823.

20. C.O. 384/12, f. 25 v. 14 June 1823.

21. Ibid., f. 26.

22. C.O. 384/12, f. 21, 9 June 1823; and f. 23, 12 June 1823; P.R. Papers, I, Report on the 1823 Emigration.

23. P.R. Papers, 2, Applications; for the families from Cape Clear see P.R. papers, I, Certificate of character . . . and 8 and 9, Emigrants embarked at Cork.

24. C.O. 384/12, f. 35, Robinson to Horton, 29 June 1823.

25. C.O. 384/12, f. 26, 14 June 1823.

26. C.O. 384/12, f. 46, 1 July 1823.

27. C.O. 284/12, f. 267, Ennismore to Horton, 30 May 1823, private.

28. C.O. 384/12, f. 21, Robinson to Horton, 9 June 1823.

29. Ibid., f. 22.

30. Parl. Papers, House of Lords, 1825, VII (200), Minutes of Evidence of the Select Committee [on] . . . Disturbances . . . in those Districts of Ireland which are now subject to the Insurrection Act . . . , p. 249, Robinson, 23 June 1824.

31. J.K. Johnson, 'Colonel James Fitzgibbon and the Suppression of Irish Riots in Upper Canada', *Ontario History* 58 (1966): 139.

32. C.O. 42/377, Upper Canada 1826, f. 171, Maitland to Bathurst, 31 March 1826; P.R. papers, 1, Becher to Robinson, 3 Oct. 1824, extract.

☐ Women and Politics in British North America

Readings

PRIMARY DOCUMENTS

1   'To the Electors of Quebec County', *Le Canadien*, 21 May 1808.
2   Petitions to House of Assembly, Lower Canada, 4 Dec. 1828, in *Documents Relating to the Constitutional History of Canada 1819–1828*, Arthur G. Doughty and Norah Story

HISTORICAL INTERPRETATIONS

3   From *The Franchise and Politics in British North America 1755–1867*, John Garner
4   From 'Women and the Escheat Movement: The Politics of Everyday Life on Prince Edward Island', Rusty Bittermann
5   From 'Disenfranchised But Not Quiescent: Women Petitioners in New Brunswick in the Mid-19th Century', Gail C. Campbell
6   From 'A "Petticoat Polity"? Women Voters in New Brunswick before Confederation', Kim Klein

INTRODUCTION

■ One of the realities of political life in British North America in the first two-thirds of the nineteenth century—a period that saw profound constitutional changes and the creation of a new North American nation—was that active participation existed on the extremely narrow base of European males over the age of 21. The law in nineteenth-century Canada reflected Canadian society both in theory and practice. It was quite different for men than for women. Women were citizens only in that they were inhabitants of British North America/Canada whose civil rights had yet to be ultimately decided. They were for the most part 'non-legal entities'. Women were more than merely discriminated against or ignored. In a continuation of the patriarchal principles of the English common law and the French *Coutume de Paris*, they were often subsumed under their father's or husband's legal standing because only the males had full membership in the judicial and political community.

Under the common-law doctrine of coverture, married women began the century prevented from acting as their own agents at law or possessing independent property rights. As Sir William Blackstone put it, 'In law husband and wife are one person, and the husband is that person.' A variety of other disabilities operated against the woman. Women were denied any right of participation in either the law's creation or its administration. They could not vote for or be legislators. They could not be lawyers, judges or magistrates, or members of juries that decided the fate of many women in both civil and criminal actions. Nevertheless, the situation for women before the law did gradually improve over the course of the century. There is no point in being either astounded or offended by the blatantly discriminatory nature of the law. What is more important is that we appreciate how it operated and why.

Questions for consideration

1. What sorts of women sometimes voted in the nineteenth century?
2. In what other ways could women exercise political power?
3. Are you persuaded by this material that the generalization about women's political impotence in British North America is inaccurate? If so, how would you alter the generalization? If not, why not?

Suggestions for further reading

Anita Fellman et al., eds, *Rethinking Canada: The Promise of Women's History*, 3rd edn (Toronto: Oxford University Press, 1997). A collection of recent writing on the history of Canadian women.

Alison Prentice et al., *Canadian Women: A History*, 2nd edn (Toronto: Harcourt Brace, 1996). The most thorough overview of the history of women in Canada.

Carol Wilton, *Popular Politics and Political Culture in Upper Canada, 1800–1850* (Montreal and Kingston: McGill-Queen's University Press, 2000). Provides a broad context for understanding early politics in Canada.

PRIMARY DOCUMENTS

1 'To the Electors of Quebec County', *Le Canadien*, 21 May 1808.

TO THE ELECTORS OF QUEBEC COUNTY
Gentlemen,

Although it is not customary for women to address you at election time, I hope you will forgive the liberty of an unfortunate soul who has no other resource than to appeal to your sense of justice. To whom else could I appeal? The ungrateful wretch I complain of is the Judge himself.

You know well enough, Gentlemen, the trouble I went to in working for him during the election campaign at Charlesbourg four years ago; he had suffered badly in the election in the Upper Town; and out of pity, as many of you did, I worked as hard as I could to assure his triumph. Gentlemen, you witnessed this triumph of which he boasted so much. Yet, no sooner had he won than he forgot all I had done for him, and, coward that he is, abandoned me. He had the insolence to tell me that it was I who was harming his reputation among you. Gentlemen, will you let this kind of treachery go unpunished? Will your votes in his favour reward his betrayal? Will you elect him for having broken faith with me?

The ingrate even got married, and began to frequent the Church; this was to obtain your votes. He is inconstant I assure you; I know him, he will use any means to achieve his end.

He makes promises to you, but how many promises did he make to me? He will deceive you as he deceived me. He will deceive you as he deceived the Lower Town. How many promises did he not make to the voters on the day of his triumph four years ago?

This false man has never been able to win an election except in Three Rivers. . . . What honour will you gain in electing him? The Upper Town scorned him four years ago, Deschambault had driven him out, Nicolet had driven him out. Will it be that Charlesbourg will join Three Rivers in electing him!

What will be said of Charlesbourg? What will be said of Beauport, where he is so well known? People will say that it was because he was a Judge, that it was out of fear of losing their cases in court that voters elected him. Did the Upper Town succomb to such fears? Did Deschambault and Nicolet? What now! Canadiens who never feared enemy fire in battle will become cowards for fear of losing a court case!

What an honour for Canadiens to see *their judge* running for election, to see him profane the image of the King whom he represents so unworthily? Do English judges run in elections? . . . Only Canadiens so dishonour themselves. I am a Canadienne, Gentlemen, and I would die rather than consent to such dishonour.

The Unfortunate Jeannette

2 Petitions to House of Assembly, Lower Canada, 4 Dec. 1828, in Arthur G. Doughty and Norah Story, eds, *Documents Relating to the Constitutional History of Canada 1819–1828* (Ottawa, King's Printer, 1935), 519–23.

PETITIONS TO HOUSE OF ASSEMBLY, LOWER CANADA, 4 DEC. 1828.

A Petition of divers Electors of the Upper Town of Quebec, whose names are thereunto subscribed, was presented to the House by Mr. *Clouet*, and the same was received and read; setting forth: That in July One thousand eight hundred and twenty-seven, *William Fisher Scott* was appointed Returning Officer for the election of two Citizens to represent in Parliament the Upper Town of Quebec, and that on the seventh of August a Poll was opened for that purpose near the Bishop's Palace: That the Candidates were Messrs. *Joseph Remy Vallières de St. Réal, Andrew Stuart, George Vanfelson* and *Amable Berthelot*: That the Polling was continued to the fifteenth August, when Messrs. *Joseph Remy Vallières de St. Réal* and *Andrew Stuart* were returned as duly elected: That, however, on the fourteenth, Mrs. Widow *Laperrière* did tender to Mr. *Scott*, the aforesaid Returning Officer, her vote, under oath, which Mr. *Scott* did refuse to take and enregister, whereupon a protest against such refusal was served. That the Petitioners allege that the following conclusions are to be drawn from this refusal: 1. That Mr. *Scott* acted contrary to law; 2. That the election of Mr. *Stuart* is void. That the Petitioners saw with extreme concern and alarm this refusal to take a vote tendered under oath, in the terms of the law; and they allege that Mr. *Scott* had no discretion to exercise, that he was bound to follow the letter of the law, that he was not to sit as a judge of the law. That the Petitioners need hardly avert to the danger of such a power as Mr. *Scott* has exercised. They will not place their dearest right, their elective franchise, in the hands of any one man, but especially they will not place it in the hands of an officer appointed by the Executive, and whose opinions and feelings under almost every circumstances must endanger the free choice of the people, and thus strike at the root of their liberties. That the Petitioners. therefore, deem this refusal to take a vote offered in the terms of the law, a most dangerous precedent, contrary to law, and tending to subvert their rights and constitutional privileges. That the Petitioners represent on the second head, that, as the votes of the Widows were not taken, the return of Mr. *Stuart* is void, inasmuch as the free choice of all the electors was not made known. That the Petitioners may presume to trouble the House with the reasons which they deem conclusive as to the right of Widows to vote; neither in men nor women can the right to vote be a natural right: it is given by enactment. The only questions are, whether women could exercise that right well and advantageously for the State, and whether they are entitled to it. That the Petitioners have not learned that there exist any imperfections in the minds of women which place them lower than men in intellectual power, or which would make it more dangerous to entrust them with the exercise of the elective franchise than with the exercise of the numerous other rights which the law has already given them. That, in point of fact, women duly qualified have hitherto been allowed to exercise the right in question. That the Petitioners conceive that women are fairly entitled to the right, if they can exercise it well. That property and not persons is the basis of representation in the English Government. That the qualifications required by the Election Laws sufficiently shew this. That the same principle is carried into our own constitution. That the paying certain taxes to the State is also a basis of representation; for it is a principal contended for by the best Statesmen of England, that there can be 'no taxation without representation.' That the duties to be performed to the State may also give a right to representation. That in respect of property, taxation and duties to the State, the Widow, duly qualified by our Election Laws, is in every essential respect similarly situated with the man: her property is taxed alike with that of the man: she certainly is not liable to Militia duties, nor is the man above forty-five: she is not called to serve on a jury, nor is a physician: she cannot be elected to the Assembly, nor can a Judge or Minister of the Gospel. It may be alleged that nature has only fitted her for domestic life, yet the English Constitution allows a woman to sit on the Throne, and one of its brightest ornaments has been a woman. That it would be impolitic and tyrannical to circumscribe her efforts in society,—to say that she shall not have the strongest interest in the fate of her country, and the security of her common rights: It is she who breathes into man with eloquent tenderness his earliest lessons of religion and of morals; and shall it be said that his country shall be forgotten, or that she shall mould his feelings while smarting under hateful laws. That the Petitioners allege that Widows exercise, generally, all the rights of men, are liable to most of the same duties towards the State, and can execute them as well. And they pray from the premises: 1. That the House declare Mr. *Scott*, the Returning Officer, guilty of malversation in office, and take measures to enforce the law in such case provided. 2. That the proceedings at the late Election for the Upper Town of Quebec, concluded on the fifteenth August One thousand eight hundred and twenty-seven, by the Return of Mr. *Stuart*, be declared void. The Petitioners further represent, that the Return of Mr. *Stuart* was made after a contestation of seven days, when all the votes, with a few exceptions, had been polled, and the Return was made in consequence of the small majority of nine votes. That the Petitioners are satisfied in their own minds, that Mr. *Berthelot* had a considerable majority of legal votes. That the Petitioners would also represent, that extraordinary means of corruption by threats and actual dismission from employment, were used by the partizans of Mr. *Stuart*, both on the part of private individuals and on the part of Officers holding civil and military appointments; and they wish particularly to call the attention of the House to the fact, that it has come to their knowledge, that, in effect, owing to the interference of authorized overseers, the numerous class of voters labouring on His Majesty's works on the Cape, came forward under the impression that they risked their employment if they did not vote for Mr. *Stuart*. That the Petitioners also beg leave to state, that the Records of the King's Bench, *Quebec*, will shew the conviction of one person, for voting without a right, whom some public-spirited individuals got punished as an example: they did not choose to prosecute about thirty more, of whom they still retain a list taken during the election. That the Petitioners also represent that, in their opinion, a fatal irregularity in keeping the Poll-book was practised when the votes were taken in another Poll-book than that of the Returning Office, by a Clerk not duly sworn. That the Petitioners, in conclusion, pray that the House may act upon the premises as it may deem fitting, and do as to justice appertaineth, in a case which the Petitioners conceive affect their liberties and dearest rights.

Mr. *Clouet* moved to resolve, seconded by Mr. *Labrie*, That the grounds and reasons of complaint set forth in the said Petition, if true, are sufficient to make void the election of the said *Andrew Stuart*, Esquire.

Ordered, That the consideration of the said motion be postponed till Tuesday next.

HISTORICAL INTERPRETATIONS

3 From John Garner, *The Franchise and Politics in British North America 1755–1867* (Toronto: University of Toronto Press, 1969), 155–9.

There was one substantial group of adult British subjects who were universally disfranchised by law at the end of the colonial period, namely women. Women were first disqualified by law in Lower Canada, where the abortive controverted election act of 1834 specifically disqualified them. They were disfranchised by law in Prince Edward Island in 1836, in New Brunswick in 1843, in the Province of Canada in 1849, in Nova Scotia in 1851.[1] In one colony only, Upper Canada, was the franchise never legally closed to women. The spate of legal restrictions which followed the Lower Canada controverted election act of 1834 was occasioned, firstly, by the appearance of women at the polls, and secondly, by the Imperial Reform Act of 1832. This act had for the first time formally restricted the Imperial franchise to males, although it must be mentioned that the denial of the vote to women was extended only to the classes newly enfranchised by the act, and did not technically extend to those formerly privileged to vote.[2]

The above omission was not an oversight nor had the Reform Bill established any new restraint on the franchise, for women had not exercised the franchise in Great Britain for centuries despite the lack of a formal legal restraint. Edward Coke, the famous seventeenth-century jurist, states that already in his day women were not entitled to vote, irrespective of their propertied status.[3] In 1868 a test case before the Court of Common Pleas was to confirm this convention when a Mr. Justice Byles declared that 'Women for centuries have always been considered legally incapable of voting for members of Parliament; as much so as of being themselves elected to serve as members.'[4] The disfranchisement of women in England by convention and the Common Law had been accepted by the colonies as part of their legal heritage. Even the Thirteen Colonies had accepted this restraint as an integral part of their franchise and where convention proved an insufficient barrier against the drive of the frontier woman, they had supplemented the convention by statute as in Virginia in 1699.[5]

The British North American colonies of the Second Empire did not depart from this precedent. Women were not allowed to vote although they were disfranchised neither by statute nor executive decree. New Brunswick alone of the colonies specifically disfranchised women. The Executive Council at the inaugural election restricted the franchise to 'all males of full age' but the ban was not incorporated in New Brunswick's first franchise law of 1791.[6]

New Brunswick and Prince Edward Island, the first of the Maritime colonies to disfranchise women by statute, provide no record of women voting; whereas Nova Scotia, the last Maritime colony to disfranchise them, provides two recorded incidents. The first incident involved a disputed election for Amherst Township where the defeated candidate refused to press his petition when the Assembly decided to test the validity of the election on the property qualification of the member-elect and not on the women voters polled.[7] The second incident is amusingly recorded in the *Novascotian* of December 3, 1840, where a contemporary relates his experience in Annapolis County during the general election of that year.

I rode down to Annapolis Town to see what was going forward in the enemy's camp, and lo and behold, what did I find the Tories there up to. Getting all the old women and old maids, and everything in the shape of petticoats to be carried up to the hustings the next and last day to vote for Whitman. As it was 9 o'clock in the evening no time was to be lost. I gave my horse an extra feed of oats, and after a long, cold and muddy ride and weary from fatigue, and had only eaten one dinner in seven days, I had to post off through the country to inform our good folks what was to be expected. I rode all Tuesday night, and roused up every farmer; and what was the result, they harnessed up their horses, went off, and each one by 10 of the clock, was back with a widow or a fair young fatherless maid, to vote against the Tory women from Annapolis Royal. We mustered by women more than the Tories. They found out we should outnumber them, and at last we had the satisfaction of seeing them return to Annapolis without voting. I believe they numbered twenty-six and our party nearly forty. This manoeuvre on their side was kept very sly but am happy to say we outgeneralled them.

The heat of partisan warfare and a desire to save a Tory riding from a Reform landslide doubtless inspired the Tory politicians to gamble on the vote of their womenfolk. The inspiration for this desperate toss of the political dice they may have gleaned from Lower Canada, for in Nova Scotia itself, Murdoch says, it had never 'been agitated whether females may vote or sit.'[8]

It was in Lower Canada that women exercised the right to vote most widely. The Constitutional Act had made no specific mention of the sex of the electors although it had been inspired by petitions from the inhabitants of Quebec, at least one of which was accompanied by a plan for an Assembly to be elected by 'none but males.'[9] In face of the silence of the Constitutional Act and the lesser influence of convention and the Common Law, it is not surprising that this colony gives repeated examples of women voting. The first recorded incident occurred in the bitter general election of 1809 when Joseph Papineau came out of retirement to lead the French Canadian radicals against the tyranny of Sir James Craig. In the East Ward of Montreal Mme Papineau came forward to the poll and when asked for whom she wished to vote replied: 'For my son M. Joseph Papineau, for I believe that he is a good and faithful subject.'[10] Practised by such a respected personage as Mme Papineau, female voting spread and in the general election of 1820 women voted in Bedford County and in the borough of Three Rivers. Of the latter election Judge Pierre Bedard writing to John Neilson stated that 'Mr. Ogden et M. Badeau ont été élu par les hommes et les femmes des T. Rivieres. Car il faut que vous sachez qu'ici les femmes votent comme les hommes indistinctement. Il n'y a que le cas ou elles sont mariées et ou le mari est vivant; alors c'est lui qui parte la voie comme chef de la communauté. Lorsque le mari n'a pas de bien et qui la femme en a eut le femme qui vote.'[11] This letter explains why in Lower Canada the emphasis was on widows voting. It was not because widows were favoured with the franchise over married or unmarried women, it was rather because they were more likely to possess the necessary property qualifications for exercising the franchise.

It was the election for Bedford County that first brought the issue of women voting before the Assembly. The elections in Bedford were especially bitter because it was a marginal county in which the races were evenly matched. The victorious candidate on this occasion was charged by his opponent with the receipt of many illegal votes based on Crown and Clergy Reserves to which the electors did not have title and with receiving the votes of 'Femes Covert' (*sic*).[12] The evidence produced before the House revealed that twenty-two married women had voted on the same properties for which their husbands had exercised their right to vote.[13] The Assembly thereupon voided the election and at the same time resolved 'that married women voted at the said election and that in the opinion of this House, such votes are illegal.'[14] A suspicion, however, exists that the resolution was prompted less by a hostility to women voting than by racial antagonism, for the women's votes had returned the English-speaking candidate at the expense of the French-speaking former representative.

The suspicion that there was no strong antipathy to women voting is borne out by a petition that was forwarded to the Assembly some eight years later protesting the refusal of the returning officer for Quebec Upper Town to accept the vote of a widow.[15] The returning officer, an English-speaking Canadian, had refused to accept a widow's vote for Amable Berthelot, the vindictive deputy leader of the radical party, and upon this as well as other points the re-election of Andrew Stuart was disputed. The petitioners, after claiming that the returning officer 'had no discretion to exercise, that he was bound to follow the letter of the law [and] that he was not to sit as judge of the law,' declared that women were not disfranchised by law and were therefore entitled to exercise the right to vote. For

the only questions are whether women could exercise that right well and advantageously for the state, and whether they are entitled to it. That the petitioners have not learned that there exist any imperfections in the minds of women which place them lower than men in intellectual power, or which would make it more dangerous to entrust them with the exercise of the elective franchise than with the exercise of the numerous other rights which the law has already given them. That, in point of fact, women duly qualified have hitherto been allowed to exercise the right in question. That the petitioners conceive that women are fairly entitled to the right, if they can exercise it well. That property and not persons is the basis of representation in the English government. . . . It may be alleged that nature has only fitted her for domestic life, yet the English constitution allows a woman to set on the Throne, and one of its brightest ornaments has been a woman. That it would be impolitic and tyrannical to circumscribe her efforts in society, to say that she shall not have the strongest interest in the fate of her country, and the security of her common rights.

The French Canadian party was in a position to benefit from sustaining the theme of the above petition, for in addition to Quebec Upper Town, there was the disputed return of Wolfred Nelson from the borough of William Henry. Nelson, an English supporter of the French Canadian party, had defeated the Attorney General by four votes but had had his election protested on the grounds that he had received 'the votes of women, married, unmarried, and in a state of widowhood.'[16] Should the Assembly have decided to stand by the resolution of 1820, the French Canadian party would have lost two seats. They would have had to unseat Nelson for William Henry and to confirm Berthelot's defeat in Quebec Upper Town. Unable to make up their minds to stand by precedent and lose seats or reverse themselves and gain seats, they made no decision at all. The two election cases were adjourned repeatedly until the end of the session, and although referred to the next they were never taken up again. The procrastination reflected a division of opinion among the French Canadian majority. The more radical leaders such as Louis J. Papineau, Denis Viger, and Louis Bourdages were favourable to women voting, but the traditionalists led by Vallières de St Real were hostile.[17] The future was to be with the traditionalists, for Lower Canadian opinion was soon to be subjected to the orthodoxy of ultramontanism.

In 1832 a violent by-election in Montreal West, Papineau's riding, decided the question. In this election which lasted over three weeks and which ended with a riot and the deaths of three

citizens, men and women had been equally subjected to bribery and intimidation. This venal display so changed Papineau's views that, when John Neilson towards the end of the same Parliament moved to consider the expediency of amending the election law and of settling the question of women voting, Papineau was vehemently in favour of their disfranchisement. 'As to allowing women to vote,' he stated, 'it was just that it should be annulled, it was ridiculous and odious to see them drawn to the hustings by their husbands or their guardians, often against their wills. The public interest, decency, and the natural modesty of the sex required that such scenes should not be again witnessed.'[18] The upshot was the addition of a rider to an act on controverted elections which denied the franchise to women for all future elections.[19] The act received the assent of the Governor General and in the ensuing general election women were for the first time excluded by law from the Lower Canada franchise.

The statutory disfranchisement of Lower Canadian women did not last long. The Colonial Office objected to a clause in the act which allowed select committees on controverted elections to continue beyond the prorogation of the Assembly. The Governor General was ordered to have the offending clause repealed or the act would be disallowed.[20] The Assembly complied with the request of the Colonial Office, but the Legislative Council disarranged their compliance by the addition of an amendment to which the Assembly refused to agree and the Colonial Office was obliged to disallow the act.[21] The disappearance of the brief statutory prohibition against women voting was of little moment. There was to be no recorded recurrence of women voting, for the destruction of the radical leaders in the rebellion of 1837 and the triumph of ultramontanism, as evidenced in Bourget's elevation to the episcopate of Montreal in the same year, effectively ended the practice. Social disapproval was to render statutory prohibition unnecessary.

In 1840 the Act of Union found both Lower and Upper Canada without any legislative enactment against women voting. Upper Canada had never enacted such a restraint and as no complaint of such voting ever reached its Assembly, we may conclude that the acceptance of the Common Law prohibition was sufficiently widespread that few if any women ever voted in that colony. Yet after union the first violation of the Common Law practice occurred in Canada West and not, as precedent might have suggested, in Canada East. In the general election of 1844 in the west riding of Halton County, the defeated Reform candidate, Durand, protested the receipt of the votes of seven women for his Tory opponent, Webster. The deputy returning officer, partial to Webster, had accepted these votes despite the objection of Durand, and Webster had thereby secured his return by a majority of four votes.[22] The Reformers were not to forget this incident. When they returned to power they took advantage of the opportunity to consolidate the election laws and to insert a clause excluding women from the franchise.[23] The Province of Canada thereby joined the colonies of Prince Edward Island and New Brunswick in debarring women from the vote by statute. The social reaction that had set in in the Canadas was to deny women political emancipation long after it had been conceded in most states of the United States. And that denial was to be most prolonged in the province of Quebec where the voting of women of property had in its colonial era reached the widest proportion of any of the colonies.

The confinement of women to the drawing room in England is less surprising than their confinement to the kitchen in the British North American colonies. The colonial women were as important economic units as their husbands or sons. The clearing, building, and establishment of farms and homes on the unfriendly frontier found the women full partners with their menfolk. It is this full partnership in every aspect of frontier life that makes it surprising that women were not granted and did not demand political equality. The activities of John Stuart Mill in favour of their political emancipation drew no response from the colonial women. They saw no 'great improvement in the moral position of women to be no longer declared by law incapable of an opinion,' nor any virtue in the claim that to 'give the woman a vote [would bring her] under the operation of the political point of honour.'[24] Editorializing on Mill's campaign, the *Acadian Recorder* of October 28, 1867, found no moral elevation likely to accrue from the political emancipation of women; it was rather of the contrary opinion, for 'if women are to have votes we can never ask them to go to the poll in person or to mingle in the unavoidable strife of political contests. They must vote by proxy or by paper. . . .'

The general attitude towards women suffrage seems to have been more akin to the opinions of John Stuart Mill's father, who believed the close unity of interest within the family could allow the franchise to be confined to the heads of families and still achieve universality. To James Mill the best interests of the wife, sons, and daughters would be as wisely expressed in the composite vote of the father as by the vote of each individual.[25] The close unity of the frontier family, forged by isolation and economic necessity, made political unity a reality and few men or women looked upon the drive for women suffrage with anything but quiet amusement.

NOTES

1. L.C., *Stat.*, 4 Wm. IV, c. 28 (1834); P.E.I., *Stat.*, 6 Wm. IV, c. 24 (1836); N.B., *Stat.,* 6 Vic., c. 44 (1843); Can., *Stat.*, 12 Vic., c. 27, s. 46 (1849); N.S., *Stat.*, 14 Vic., c. 2 (1851).

2. Br., *Stat.*, 2 Wm. IV, c. 45, ss. 19, 20, 27 (1832).
3. Edward Coke, *Institutes of the Laws of England* (London, 1817), part IV, 5.
4. *Chorlton v. Lings*, 4 C.P., 394 (1868).

5. A.E. McKinley, *The Suffrage Franchise in the Thirteen English Colonies in America* (Philadelphia, 1905), 473f.

6. N.B., *Ex. Co. Min.*, Oct. 11, 1785.

7. N.S., *Ass. J.*, Nov. 20, 24, 1806.

8. B. Murdoch, *Epitome of the Laws of Nova Scotia* (Halifax, 1832), I, 68.

9. 'Plan for a House of Assembly Nov. 1784', in A. Shortt and A.G. Doughty, *Documents Relating to the Constitutional History of Canada 1759–1791* (Ottawa, 1918), II, 754.

10. 'Les Femmes electeurs', *Bulletin des Recherches historiques* 11 (1905): 222.

11. Bedard to Neilson, July 1, 1820, P.A.C., John Neilson Collection, III, 412.

12. L.C., *Ass. J.*, Dec. 30, 1820.

13. Ibid., 1820–1, App. W.

14. Ibid., Dec. 31, 1821.

15. Ibid., Dec. 4, 1828.

16. Ibid.

17. W.R. Riddell, 'Woman Franchise in Quebec, a Century Ago', *Royal Society of Canada, Transactions* Ser. 3, 22 (1928): 93.

18. *Quebec Gazette*, Jan. 29, 1834.

19. L.C., *Stat.*, 4 Wm. IV, c. 28, s. 27 (1834).

20. Glenelg to Aylmer, June 29, 1835, P.A.C., G29.2, 609.

21. Glenelg to Gosford, July 20, 1836, G32.1, 35.

22. Can., *Ass. J.*, Dec. 2, 1844. A partisan select committee, appointed to investigate the disputed return, threw the protest out after two sessions. See ibid., April 30, May 6, 1846.

23. Can., *Stat.*, 12 Vic., c. 27 (1849).

24. J.S. Mill, *On Representative Government* (Oxford, 1947), 223f.

25. James Mill, *An Essay on Government* (Cambridge, 1937), 45.

4 From Rusty Bittermann, 'Women and the Escheat Movement: The Politics of Everyday Life on Prince Edward Island', in Janet Guildford and Suzanne Morton, eds, *Separate Spheres: Women's Worlds in the 19th-century Maritimes* (Fredericton, NB: Acadiensis Press, 1994), 23–30.

In September of 1833, Constable Donald McVarish, acting on behalf of Flora Townshend, the resident owner of an estate in eastern Prince Edward Island, made his way to her property with a bundle of papers in hand. These were warrants of distress, legal documents which permitted Townshend to seize the goods of her tenants for back rents which she claimed were due. It was not to be a pleasant day for McVarish. Rents were going unpaid, as always, because tenants found it difficult to meet these costs, but growing militant resistance to the entire structure of landlordism made rent resistance a political act, too. In the wake of political initiatives begun earlier in the decade, the dream of an escheat was the talk of the countryside. Members of the House of Assembly and the rural population alike were discussing the legitimacy of proprieto-rial claims to the colony's land and arguing that because landlords had never fulfilled the settlement obligations of the original grants of 1767 they did not in fact have valid deeds; their grants had reverted to the Crown by default. Establishment of a court of escheat, it was contended, would expose the fraudulence of landlords' claims on the Island's tenantry and permit them to gain title to the farms they had made productive. McVarish, acting for the landlords, could no longer count on deference to law officers in the rural regions in the fall of 1833. Believing that the existing land system was fundamentally flawed because the titles that supported it were invalid, rural residents balked at complying with the laws pertaining to rents.

McVarish's mission to the Naufrage region of northern Kings County took him into a region that was known for the strength of its anti-land-lord sentiments—arguably, the heartland of agrarian radicalism on the Island. William Cooper, the leading advocate of the idea of an escheat, had propounded his ideas on the flaws of proprietorial title and the rights of tenants in Kings County during the general election of 1830 and then again in a by-election in 1831. The support he received ultimately permitted him to promote these ideas from the House of Assembly. The enthusiastic response from country people in Kings County and elsewhere, expressed in public meetings, petitions and rent resistance, marked the beginning of what came to be known as the Escheat movement. The loaded pistol that McVarish had tucked in his pocket before leaving home probably reflected his understanding of rural sentiments in the region, as did his attempts to hide his mission from those he met and his decision to sometimes travel through fields rather than on the road. McVarish's precautions notwithstanding, he was seen and confronted by a cluster of the tenants for whom his warrants were intended. Hard words were spoken and McVarish drew his pistol. He was, nonetheless, knocked to the ground, disarmed and conveyed to the main road. Having promised he would never return, he was released and helped on his way with a blow from a board.[1]

The person wielding the board was Isabella MacDonald, then well advanced in a pregnancy. Judging from testimony from a subsequent trial, Isabella was the most vociferous party in the altercation. McVarish claimed that the three male and two female tenants who confronted him 'were all alike active and threatening', but when he pulled his pistol he aimed it at Isabella. It would seem that he perceived her as the most violent of the group. This move allowed men who were not receiving McVarish's primary attention to pull him down from behind and disarm him, in turn exposing him to Isabella's wrath. Her blow with the board was the only gratuitous violence McVarish received. Perhaps she

was settling scores for his aiming his pistol at her, perhaps fulfilling the promise of violence which had prompted McVarish's move in the first place.

McVarish's discomfiture at the hands of Isabella and her companions was not an isolated incident. It cannot be explained simply as the act of a particularly forceful female tenant, a matter of personality. Again and again over the course of the Escheat movement, women assumed prominent roles in physically resisting the enforcement of landlords' claims in the countryside. This paper examines these women's behaviour and argues that the modes of resistance they employed had roots in, and were extensions of, the conditions of their daily lives. To discern this, however, it is necessary to move away from the image of rural women most commonly found in North American literature on the pre-industrial countryside. The conception of the rural woman's sphere that dominates this literature draws too heavily from middle-class experiences and sentiments and does not provide an appropriate starting place for understanding the actions of women such as Isabella MacDonald. Attentiveness to the early nineteenth-century perceptions that gave birth to these pervasive images may, however, help us to better understand the roles rural women assumed in violent confrontations. Upper-class beliefs concerning women's sphere shaped the context in which Escheat activism unfolded. Being perceived as the weaker sex and the guardians of domesticity may have permitted women more latitude than men in their use of violence.

While it is important to recognize the significant part that women played in direct action, their participation in this form of popular politics needs to be set in the broader context of the Escheat struggle of the 1830s and early 1840s and the political changes which were occurring during this period. Direct action was not Escheat's main focus. The Escheat challenge was primarily grounded in the development of a new mass politics in the formal political arena. Formal politics, unlike community-level direct action, excluded women. To examine the role of women in the Escheat movement is to be reminded that the changes associated with the rise of bourgeois democracy included the decline of an older popular politics which once afforded women a substantial place.

Direct resistance to the claims of landlords, the area of Escheat activism in which women were most prominent, occurred in two forms. There were household-level defences, such as that Isabella MacDonald engaged in, and there was a larger community-organized resistance. Women were active at both levels. In the first, the members of a single household, or perhaps adjoining households, responded defensively to the arrival of law officers. When officials attempted to serve legal papers, remove possessions or arrest members of the household, those directly involved resisted. Women took part in such protective actions on their own and in the company of men. Catherine Renahau and her husband John acted together to resist the enforcement of their landlord's claims against their premises in southern Kings County in the spring of 1834. In this case, the wife and the husband were both indicted and found guilty of assaulting and wounding the constable who had arrived at their door.[2] The actions of Mrs. McLeod and her husband Hugh fit the same pattern. When a constable and a sheriff's bailiff came to seize their cattle in the summer of 1839, Mrs. MacLeod took up a pike and Hugh an axe. Together they rebuffed the law officers. When a posse was subsequently sent to arrest the two, the entire family took a hand in attempting to prevent the high sheriff and his deputies from invading their house.[3] Charges laid against Mary and Margaret Campbell for assaulting constable William Duncan in 1834 provide some evidence that women also acted without men in farm-level defences.[4]

In addition to these sorts of spontaneous farm-level defences, tenants were involved in more broadly organized actions aimed at securing entire communities or regions from the enforcement of landlords' claims. Women figured prominently in many of these actions. Attempts to arrest the five tenants charged with repelling McVarish provoked two major community-level confrontations. In the spring of 1834, a posse was dispatched from Charlottetown to Naufrage to arrest the miscreants. They were turned back at the Naufrage bridge by a crowd, said to include 'a large number of women', which had assembled in anticipation of their arrival.[5] Armed with muskets, pikes and pitchforks, the assembly informed the deputy sheriff that they were prepared to fight and die before they would permit him to arrest the five tenants he sought. When yet another posse led by the sheriff himself attempted a similar mission the following year, women were said to make up more than one-third of the armed crowd that waited for the posse in the predawn darkness and again blocked the sheriff.[6]

Women were active as well in a series of major community-level confrontations in the fall and winter of 1837–38 that, with the mass meetings being held in support of Escheat, prompted some observers to believe that the Island, like the Canadas, was on the verge of civil war. The first of these confrontations concerning land title was on Thomas Sorell's estate in northern Kings County. In September 1837, when the sheriff and his deputies attempted to enforce court orders Sorell had obtained against John Robertson, a long-time resident on the estate, they were repulsed by a crowd wielding sticks and throwing stones. As well, one ear was removed from each of the law officers' horses, which had been left at a distance from the farm.[7] Women were part of the crowd that blocked the sheriff, and they were reputed to be the primary actors in the violence.[8] Later that winter, women made up part of an armed party which assembled near Wood Islands to repel people whom they believed to be law officers initiating rent actions in that district. In a case of mistaken identity, shots were fired over the head of the rector of Charlottetown and his elite friends, who were on a baptismal mission on behalf of a spiritual lord rather than a rental mission on behalf of a secular one.[9] While the actions of the tenant group were misdirected, they nonetheless served notice that those who might attempt to enforce rent collection in the region were not welcome. On the Selkirk estate the following month, women again were active in co-ordinated crowd actions which blocked the enforcement of rental claims. In several locales, bailiffs attempting to seize farm goods were confronted by tenants armed with pitchforks and sticks. Men and women alike took a hand in resisting the seizure of goods and driving law officers from the communities they had attempted to enter.[10] The cumulative effect of these actions was, for a time, to bring the enforcement of rental payments to a halt across much of the Island and to force the government to consider whether it was willing to hazard deploying troops—then in short supply due to the demands made by the risings in the Canadas—in order to uphold the claims of the Island's landlords.

That rural women would be active in household defences and collective action of this sort would come as no surprise to the student of Old World popular protest. In locations on the eastern side of the Atlantic, a rich array of research has pointed to the importance of women in protest actions and has suggested ways of understanding this activity in terms of their everyday lives.[11] The evidence of female involvement in the popular resistance associated with the Escheat movement fits less easily within North American historiography and its portrayal of rural women. To be sure, the literature is broad and varied and blanket descriptions are misleading. Nonetheless, what emerges again and again in North American descriptions of women in northern pre-industrial rural settings is the image of the farm woman as nurturing caretaker of the

domestic sphere. Though her work was tiring and she was often incessantly busy, hers was an existence bounded by walls and sheltered from the coarser aspects of life. Women looked after the household and, perhaps, the adjacent garden and barns, while the men tended to rough work and public affairs. . . .

The dominant image of the daily lives of rural women is inadequate not only because women's work could be much broader than it depicts, but also because the domestic sphere of work was often much narrower, too. Again and again the existing literature emphasizes the long hours that women spent cleaning house, washing clothes, preparing meals and spinning and weaving. No doubt long hours were spent in this work by those who possessed frame houses and ample wardrobes, ate a varied diet, kept sheep and had spinning wheels and looms. We need to recognize, though, that many did not. In the Maritimes of the early nineteenth century, this picture of the woman's sphere pertains to the rural middle class and does not reflect the circumstances of the whole of the rural population. Indeed, for many, the physical requirements for the woman's separate sphere—multi-roomed house, kitchen and pantry, area for textile manufacture, adjoining dairy and poultry shelters— quite simply did not exist. It did not take long to clean a one-room dwelling, assuming that this was even an objective, nor did cooking and washing absorb a day's labour when household members ate boiled potatoes and oatmeal and possessed little clothing beyond what they were wearing. We need not paint the picture this starkly, however, no matter how real it was for many, to point out that much of the existing view of the rural woman's sphere assumes material circumstances that were far more comfortable than those of much of the rural population.

NOTES

1. Minutes of Naufrage Trial, Colonial Office Records [CO] 226, vol. 52, pp. 91–4, Public Record Office, Great Britain [microfilm copies in Harriet Irving Library, University of New

Brunswick]. I would like to gratefully acknowledge the assistance of the Social Sciences and Humanities Research Council of Canada, whose financial support aided this research. Many thanks are due as well to Margaret McCallum for her comments on an earlier version of this paper.

2. *Royal Gazette* (Charlottetown), 24 June 1834, p. 3; Supreme Court Minutes, 25 June 1834; Indictments, 1834, RG 6, Public Archives of Prince Edward Island [PAPEI]

3. *Royal Gazette*, 23 July 1839, p. 3.

4. *Royal Gazette*, 16 December 1834, p. 3

5. *Royal Gazette*, 17 June 1834, p. 3.

6. *Royal Gazette*, 6 January 1835, p. 3; 'Council Minutes', 7 January 1835, CO 226, vol. 52, pp. 330–2.

7. Executive Council Minutes, 5 September 1837, RG 5, PAPEI; *Royal Gazette*, 5 September 1837, p. 3.

8. Hodgson to Owen, 30 September 1837, MS 3744, vol. 26, PAPEI.

9. George R. Young, *A Statement of the 'Escheat Question' in the Island of Prince Edward: Together with the Causes of the Late Agitation and the Remedies Proposed* (London, 1838), p. 2; 'One of the Party' to the editor, *Colonial Herald* (Charlottetown), 27 June 1838, p. 3; 'O.P.O.' to the editor, *Colonial Herald*, 23 January 1841, p 3; 'Plain Common Sense' to the editor, *Colonial Herald*, 6 February 1841, pp. 2–3; John Myrie Hall to the editor, *Colonial Herald*, 20 February 1841, p. 2; 'The only clergyman resident within the bounds of the district' to the editor, *Colonial Herald*, 20 March 1841, p. 3; Charles Stewart and W.P. Grossard to the editor, *Colonial Herald*, 27 March 1841, p. 3.

10. Statement of Angus McPhee, George Farmer and Robert Bell, 27 February 1838, CO 226, vol. 55, pp. 176–80.

11. John Bohstedt, 'Gender, Household and Community Politics: Women in English Riots, 1790–1810', *Past and Present* 120 (August 1988): 88–122; Rudolf Dekker, 'Women in Revolt: Collective Protest and its Social Setting in Holland in the Seventeenth and Eighteenth Centuries', *Theory and Society* 16 (1987): 337–62; E.I Thompson, 'The Moral Economy of the English Crowd in the Eighteenth Century', *Past and Present* 50 (1971): 76–136; George Rudé, *The Crowd in the French Revolution* (Oxford, 1959); George Rudé, *The Crowd in History: A Study of Popular Disturbances in France and England, 1730–1848* (London, 1964); Olwen Hufton, 'Women in Revolution', *Past and Present* 53 (1971): 90–108; John Stevenson and Roland Quinault, eds, 'Food Riots in England, 1792–1818', in *Popular Protest and Public Order: Six Studies in British History, 1790-1920* (London, 1974), pp. 33–74; Natalie Zemon Davis, *Society and Culture in Early Modern France* (Stanford, 1975), pp. 124–87; Kenneth J. Logue, *Popular Disturbances in Scotland, 1780–1815* (Edinburgh, 1979); Malcolm I. Thomas and Jennifer Grimmet, *Women in Protest 1800–1850* (London, 1982). A useful Canadian extension of this rich literature is Terence Crowley, '"Thunder Gusts": Popular Disturbances in Early French Canada', in Michael Cross and Gregory Kealey, eds, *Readings in Canadian Social History*, vol. 1, *Economy and Society During the French Regime* (Toronto, 1983), pp. 122–51.

5   From Gail C. Campbell, 'Disenfranchised But Not Quiescent: Women Petitioners in New Brunswick in the Mid-19th Century', *Acadiensis* 18, 2 (Spring 1989): 22-6, 35-8.

Canadian women's participation in the political life of their society usually dated from their struggle for and achievement of the vote.[1] Yet denial of the franchise had not prevented women from being actively involved in the political life of their communities. Indeed, from the earliest times, women found ways to influence their government.[2] In the period prior to the introduction of manhood suffrage—a period characterized by deferential politics—distinctions between men's and women's political behaviour were often blurred. Women, as well as men, regularly participated in politics by petitioning legislatures to achieve specific political goals.[3] Women, like men, were involved in creating the political culture of their society.

Political culture, which involves much more than participation in the formal political system, is shaped by those values and attitudes that are so widely accepted they are taken for granted. Such values provide the underpinnings for the development of formal political institutions and structures.[4] The role of women both in maintaining and in shaping societal values requires further investigation. While women undoubtedly had a significant indirect impact on government and politics through their influence within their own families and as members of voluntary groups and organizations within their communities, this paper will focus on women's direct political participation by analyzing the nature and extent of political lobbying by women from three New Brunswick counties, as measured by the number and content of their petitions to the Legislative Assembly during the mid-nineteenth century. In political terms, the decade elected for analysis—1846 through 1857—was a highly significant one. Political parties emerged during this period. Those great moral questions, temperance, and then prohibition, became, for a time at least, the major political issue. And it was on the moral issue that women began to petition the Legislature in numbers during the decade.

While petitions do not represent a new source for the historian, researchers have not normally attempted to identify petition signatories unless they happen to be active members of a specific organization. Often researchers have been satisfied to count the number of petitions, identify the specific sponsoring group and note the number of signatories.[5] In the past, then, petitions have been used only as supplementary evidence. Yet for those who wish to analyze the nature and significance of women's political role in the nineteenth century, petitions provide the key. Only through the medium of petition could a woman gain official access to her government or express her views about policy to the legislators. Thus, the petition provides a useful measure of the signatory's knowledge of the way government worked, her degree of interest in the issues of the day, and her attitudes concerning those issues.

Petitions and petitioners can be divided into two discrete categories. The first category includes petitioners seeking to use the law in some way: to apply for a government subsidy to which they were legally entitled, to redress a grievance, to appeal for aid at a time of personal distress, or to request a grant from public monies to carry out a worthy public project. Individual petitioners normally fall into this first category, and while such petitions do not reveal the petitioner's opinions on the issues of the day, they do suggest the extent to which she both understood the system and was able to use it to her advantage. The second category includes petitioners seeking to change the law in some way. Through the medium of the petition, they sought to influence their government, to persuade the legislators to accept their view. Occasionally such people petitioned as individuals, but usually they petitioned in concert with others. Legislators would, after all, be more inclined to take a petition seriously if they could be persuaded that a majority of their constituents supported it. Regardless of the success or failure of the petition, such documents can provide important insights concerning societal attitudes. Whether the signatories were members of an organized group with a specific platform and goals, or a group of unorganized individuals who coalesced around a specific issue, an analysis of the demographic characteristics of the supporters of the issue can enhance our understanding of political attitudes and political culture.

The petition process was a popular political strategy used by men as well as women. During the ten-year period from 1846 through 1857, between 400 and 500 petitions to the New Brunswick Legislature were received annually. On average, between 25 per cent and 30 per cent of these were rejected and approximately 50 per cent were granted, while the remainder were tabled or sent to Committee. However, if they persisted in their petitions, even those who had initially been rejected could eventually achieve their goals. Moreover, legislators did not prove more responsive to petitions from men whose votes they might risk losing at the next election.[6] Although a minority among petitioners, women demonstrated their ability to use the strategy effectively.

This study is concerned with the women petitioners of the counties of Charlotte, Sunbury and Albert in the mid-nineteenth century. All three counties are in the southern half of the province. Charlotte is a large, economically diverse county in the southwest corner. Sunbury is an agricultural county in the central region, just east of Fredericton; and Albert is in the southeast region between Saint John and Moncton, on the Bay of Fundy. Although originally selected because of the richness of their sources for the study of political history, Albert, Charlotte and Sunbury proved typical in many ways. Thus, while these three counties cannot be considered a microcosm of the province as a whole, they did encompass a broad spectrum of nineteenth-century anglophone New Brunswick society, including areas of pre-Loyalist, Loyalist and post-Loyalist settlement and encompassing rural communities, villages and even large towns. Moreover, one-fifth of New Brunswick's petitioners came from one of these three counties.[7]

Together the three counties included over 30,000 people at mid-century, nearly half of them female. A large majority of those people (over 80 per cent) lived in nuclear families, although a small minority of such families (perhaps as many as 10 per cent) included one or more single or widowed relations, apprentices, boarders or servants. Over 80 per cent of the inhabitants had been born in New Brunswick of American or British stock. Of the immigrant population, nearly 70 per cent had been born in Ireland. Although the three counties included substantial numbers of Episcopalians, Baptists, Presbyterians, Roman Catholics and Methodists as well as a few Universalists and Congregationalists, among others, in both Albert and Sunbury the Baptists were stronger by far than any other denomination, comprising almost 62 per cent of Albert's population and one half of Sunbury's population in 1861.[8]

In both Albert and Sunbury counties, the farm sector accounted for more than half the workers. Even in Charlotte County, which contained very little good agricultural land, over one-third of the population were engaged in agriculture, providing for the needs of the fishery and the lumbering industry. Fifteen per cent of Charlotte's families were employed in the fishery while one-quarter of that county's population depended on the lumbering industry for their livelihood. In each of the three counties 17 per cent of those whose occupation was listed were skilled artisans; a further 15 per cent listed their occupation merely as labourer; and approximately four per cent of all families were headed by merchants and professional men.[9] While the men were occupied in the farming, fishing, and lumbering industries, or as skilled artisans or professionals, the women were scarcely idle. Approximately one in every four women of child-bearing age actually bore a child in 1851 and, aside from running their households and caring for the needs of their 14,600 children, the 6,289 women of the three counties churned 689,363 pounds of butter and wove 94,019 yards of cloth on their hand looms.[10] Yet, despite the demands of their busy and productive lives, hundreds of women in the three counties found the time to petition their government.

A wide variety of motives persuaded these women to put their names to petitions. Many of the women in the first category of petitioners—those who sought to use the law in some way—were widows seeking financial compensation or support which they knew was their due. A cursory examination of their petitions would seem to give credence to the common notion that women were 'forever dependent' on men, and that women who lost their husbands were left destitute, dependent on their sons, family or the charity of the public for support.[11] A more careful reading of the individual petitions leads to quite a different interpretation. Unless their husbands had been soldiers, widows did not generally petition Legislature for support and those rare women who did appeal to their government for aid at a time of personal distress were not begging for charity or long-term support. In fact, most such petitioners were following an accepted and established formula used by men as well as women, to request compensation for the sacrifices they had made for their country and community. . . .

Custom—and perhaps some husbands—prevented married women from signing more petitions dealing with individual and family affairs, but one should not assume either a lack of knowledge about or a lack of interest in the political system and the way it worked, on the part of such women. Moreover, starting in 1853, married women began to sign petitions in numbers. The petitions they signed were qualitatively different from the petitions women had signed up to that time. Such women fell into the second category of petitioners: those who sought to change the law. The issue that finally mobilized them to take up their pens was, not surprisingly, a reform issue. By the final decades of the century it would be an issue closely associated with the organized women's movement. The issue was temperance.

The temperance movement was well entrenched in New Brunswick by 1853, the first formal temperance organization having been established in 1830. Drawing inspiration and encouragement from both Great Britain and the United States, the New Brunswick movement had gained ground throughout the 1830s and 1840s.[12] Temperance societies were established in Fredericton, Saint John, Dorchester, Chatham, St Stephen and St Andrew and temperance *soirées* and teas were very popular.[13] During the early years, the goal had been to encourage moderation and sobriety but by the mid-1840s many temperance activists were advocating total abstinence.[14] As the depression of the late 1840s began, temperance advocates, in their search for explanations, increasingly associated drinking with the broad social problems of crime and poverty.[15] In 1847, the Sons of Temperance, the most successful of the American total-abstinence organizations, established its first division in British North America at St Stephen, New Brunswick. The Sons of Temperance and its affiliates, the Daughters of Temperance and the Cadets of Temperance, had widespread appeal. Teas, picnics, and steamer excursions provided family diversions and attracted many to the great crusade.[16] By 1850 there were branches all over the southern part of the province.[17]

For many years temperance advocates sought to achieve their goals by moral suasion, but by the late 1840s some had become convinced that moral suasion alone was not enough. For a time, they focused their efforts on gaining control of liquor consumption within their own communities through attempts to secure limitations on the number of tavern licences issued by county and city councils.[18] But such efforts proved unsuccessful. In Maine, temperance crusaders facing a similar failure had appealed to a higher authority. By 1851 they had gained enough support in the Legislature there to achieve an effective prohibition law. The 'Maine Law', which was the first prohibitory liquor law in North America, had a significant effect on the New Brunswick temperance movement. In 1852, a so-called 'monster petition' calling for the prohibition of the importation of alcoholic beverages was presented to the House of Assembly.[19] The 9,000 signatures on the petition so impressed the province's legislators that they were persuaded to pass 'An Act to Prevent the Traffic in Intoxicating Liquors'. This act 'forbade the manufacture within New Brunswick of any alcoholic or intox-icating liquors except for religious, medicinal or chemical purposes. Beer, ale, porter and cider were excepted.'[20]

Women had, of course, been involved in the temperance cause from the time of its first appearance in New Brunswick in 1830. But men had always outnumbered women in temperance organizations and until 1853 the vast majority of temperance petitions were submitted by and signed by men.[21] Urban women were the first to take up their pens in the temperance cause: the 'Ladies' Total Abstinence Society for the City and County of Saint John' submitted the first recorded petition from women on the issue to the Legislature in 1847. Three years later Woodstock's Victoria Union No. 4 of the Daughters of Temperance submitted a petition opposing the granting of tavern licences. The fol-lowing year the 'Ladies of Woodstock' went even further, calling for 'an act to prevent the sale of spiritous liquors'. In 1852, the Daughters of Temperance from Woodstock were joined in the campaign by women from Fredericton and the surrounding area. Rural women, including the subjects of this article, in contrast, did not sign temperance petitions to the Legislature before 1853. Yet this cannot be taken as an indication of either a lack of knowledge or a lack of interest. Some, like the women of Albert County, had, for several years, regularly signed petitions addressed to their local county councils oppos-ing the issuance of tavern licences. Such women signed petitions not as members of any organized temperance group, but rather as members of their local community; and this pattern was to continue when they turned their attention to the Legislative Assembly in 1853. Rural women had not participated in the legislative lobbying cam-paign that had culminated in the drafting of the Liquor Bill. Yet they were very much in the main-stream of the temperance movement as it gath-ered force, attempting first to achieve sobriety through moral suasion, then seeking local solu-tions through licensing campaigns.

NOTES

1. Although New Brunswick women were not dis-franchised by statute until 1843, historians have found no record of even propertied women in the colony voting before that time. John Garner, *The Franchise and Politics in British North America, 1755–1867* (Toronto, 1969), pp. 155–6. While it is true that in debates on franchise extension in later years politicians claimed that women of the province had voted before their specific exclusion in 1843, the only evidence that has been found to support their claims is a single letter to the editor that appeared in the *Gleaner and Northumberland Shediasma* in 1830, cited in Elspeth Tulloch, *We, the undersigned: A Historical Overview of New Brunswick Women's Political and Legal Status, 1784–1984* (Moncton, 1985), pp. 3–4. Garner argues that exclusion by statute did not represent a new restraint on the franchise. For centuries, women in Great Britain had not exercised the franchise despite the lack of a formal legal restraint, having, as one judge argued, 'always been considered legally incapable of voting for members of Parliament'. This exclusion by con-vention had been accepted in the colonies as part of their legal heritage. Garner, *The Franchise and Politics*, p. 156. Indeed, evidence from extant newspapers suggests that the purpose of the 1843 statute was mainly to clarify the law in order to 'promote the public peace at elections'. By giving convention the weight of law, the revised statute provided county sheriffs with clear guidance in deciding whether a demanded scrutiny should be carried out. The disfranchisement of women was quite incidental to the amendments and went unnoticed by the newspapers of the day and, apparently, by their readers as well. See 'The

Election Law—The Loan Bill—And the Legislative Council in a Ferment', *The Standard or Frontier Gazette* (St Andrews), 6 April 1843, 'Prorogation of the Legislature', ibid., 20 April 1843, and 'House of Assembly', ibid., 14 April 1843; 'Provincial Legislature', *The Gleaner and Northumberland, Kent, Gloucester and Restigouche Commercial and Agricultural Journal* (Miramichi), 14 February 1843, and 'Editor's Department', ibid., 13 March 1843; 'The New Election Law', *The Loyalist* (Saint John), 23 March 1843; and 'Parliamentary', *St. John Morning News and General Advertising Newspaper*, 31 March 1843.

2. For example, following a long-established European tradition, the women of New France took to the streets during the late 1750s to protest food shortages. Terence Crowley, 'Thunder Gusts: Popular Disturbances in Early French Canada', Canadian Historical Association, *Historical Papers* (1979): 19–20. And evidence from the pre-history period strongly suggests that Iroquois women, at least, had enormous political influence in their society. See especially Judith K. Brown, 'Economic Organization and the Position of Women Among the Iroquois', *Ethnohistory* 17 (1970): 153–6.

3. In an article discussing the role of women in American political society, Paula Baker has made this argument very effectively. Of course, the political transition which separated male and female politics occurred much earlier in the United States where the introduction of manhood suffrage (demonstrating definitively to women that their disfranchisement was based solely on sex) and the rise of mass political parties dated from the early nineteenth century. Paul Baker, 'The Domestication of Politics: Women and American Political Society, 1780–1920', *American Historical Review* 89 (1984): 620–47. For a review of the literature concerning the role of deference in male political behaviour during the antebellum period, see Ronald P. Formisano, 'Deferential-Participant Politics: The Early Republic's Political Culture', *American Political Science Review* 68 (1974): 473–87.

4. For similar definitions of political culture, see Robert R. Alford, *Party and Society: The Anglo-American Democracies* (Chicago, 1963), pp. 2–6; Gabriel A. Almond and G. Bingham Powell Jr, *Comparative Politics: System, Process, and Policy*, 2nd edn (Boston, 1978), ch. II, pp. 25–30; Ronald P. Formisano, *The Transformation of Political Culture: Massachusetts Parties, 1790s–1840s* (New York, 1983), p. 4.

5. See, for example, Carol Lee Bacchi, *Liberation Deferred? The Ideas of the English-Canadian Suffragists, 1877–1918* (Toronto, 1982), pp. 34, 38, 75, 82, 143; Catherine Cleverdon, *The Woman Suffrage Movement in Canada* (Toronto, 1970), pp. 23–110, 160–220; Wendy Mitchinson, 'The WCTU: "For God, Home and Native Land": A Study in Nineteenth Century Feminism', in Linda Kealey, ed., *A Not Unreasonable Claim: Women and Reform in Canada, 1880–1920s* (Toronto, 1979), pp. 155–6.

6. Although these figures represent the average yearly percentages, the success rate varied significantly from year to year, with legislators proving decidedly more sympathetic some years than others. But in no case did male petitioners prove more successful than their female counterparts. Even election years did not necessarily bring a greater likelihood of success than other years. Petitions to the New Brunswick legislature are located in Record Group 4, Record Series 24, 1846–57/Petitions [RG4, RS24, 1846–57/Pe], Provincial Archives of New Brunswick [PANB]. It is also possible that the success rate of certain types of petitions varied over time. In her analysis of the WCTU and its impact, for example, Wendy Mitchinson has suggested that the petition campaign was not a particularly effective strategy and that women were naive in their belief that they could achieve legislative change through the medium of petition. Mitchinson, 'The WCTU', p. 156. If women were naive in this belief, however, they were certainly not alone, for the majority of petitioners were men.

7. Of the 5,081 petitions considered, 1,029 originated in one of the three counties. This suggests

that the people of Albert, Charlotte and Sunbury were slightly over-represented among the colony's petitioners, comprising 20.25 per cent of petitioners as compared to 16.3 per cent of the total population of the province. (The discrepancy is not statistically significant, however, as differences of plus or minus 5 per cent could occur entirely by chance.)

8. Information on denominational affiliation is not available for 1851 and therefore the 1861 census was used in this case. See *The Census of the Province of New Brunswick, 1861* (Saint John, 1862).

9. Unless otherwise noted, all information contained in the demographic profiles provided for the three counties under study is drawn from *The Census of the Province of New Brunswick, 1851* (Saint John, 1852).

10. The 6,289 figure refers only to women over the age of 20. For a discussion of women's role in the dairying industry in British North America during this period, see Marjorie Griffin Cohen, 'The Decline of Women in Canadian Dairying', in Alison Prentice and Susan Mann Trofimenkoff, eds, *The Neglected Majority: Essays in Canadian Women's History*, vol. 2 (Toronto, 1985), pp. 61–70, and *Women's Work, Markets, and Economic Development in Nineteenth-Century Ontario* (Toronto, 1988), pp. 59–117. While the 1851 census does not specify who the weavers are, the manuscript census of manufacturing for 1861 indicates that virtually all of the hand loom weavers engaged in this cottage industry were women. The manuscript census of manufacturing for 1871 also supports this assumption. See Manuscript Census for Charlotte County, 1861 and 1871, PANB.

11. This view of women as forever dependent on men is argued by Rosemary Ball, '"A Perfect Farmer's Wife": Women in 19th Century Rural Ontario', *Canada: An Historical Magazine* (December 1975): 2–21. And even historians like David Gagan, who recognize that 'the fact of subordination was partially, if not wholly, mitigated by environment which cast women in a central

role in the farm family's struggle to improve, and endure' often conclude that 'for those women who outlived their partners, widowhood . . . was a calamity the consequence of which clearly troubled even the stoutest hearts'. David Gagan, *Hopeful Travellers: Families, Land, and Social Change in Mid-Victorian Peel County, Canada West* (Toronto, 1981), pp. 89–90.

12. For evidence of British and American influences, see J.K. Chapman, 'The Mid-Nineteenth Century Temperance Movement in New Brunswick and Maine', *Canadian Historical Review* 35 (1954): pp. 43, 48–50 and T.W. Acheson, *Saint John: The Making of a Colonial Urban Community* (Toronto, 1985), pp. 140–50. Analysts of the nineteenth-century temperance movements in Great Britain and the United States tend to characterize the movement as an Anglo-American crusade. The American and British campaigns began at the same time and nourished each other. See, for example, Brian Harrison, *Drink and the Victorians: The Temperance Question in England, 1815–1872* (Pittsburgh, 1971), pp. 99–103; W.R. Lambert, *Drink and Sobriety in Victorian Wales, c.1820–c.1895* (Cardiff, 1983), pp. 59–61; and Ian R. Tyrell, *Sobering Up: From Temperance to Prohibition in Antebellum America, 1800–1860* (Westport, Conn., 1979), pp. 135, 299.

13. Chapman, 'The Mid-Nineteenth Century Temperance Movement', p. 48.

14. Acheson, *Saint John*, p. 138. The British and American movements had made this shift somewhat earlier. Teetotalism had gained popularity in Britain by the late 1830s while the 'Washingtonians' popularized teetotalism in the United States after their inception in 1840. Lambert, *Drink and Sobriety*, p. 59; Tyrell, *Sobering Up*, pp. 135–90.

15. While the prohibition advocates of a later period would focus on the effects of drinking on individual families, the women petitioners of this early period, like their male counterparts, regarded drinking as a community rather than a family problem. The petitions that went beyond a formulaic request for the enactment of 'a Law to

prevent the importation, manufacture and sale of all intoxicating Liquors within this Province', generally decried intemperance as 'a great public evil'. As the authors of one 1851 petition succinctly put it, 'your petitioners are convinced that crime, pauperism and lunacy in nine cases out of ten are the direct result of drinking habits'. See RG4, RS24, 1846/Pe 45; 1848/Pe 270; 1849/Pe 87; 1849/Pe 151; 1849/Pe 363; 1851/Pe 228; 1854/Pe 220; 1854/Pe 394; 1854/Pe 395; 1854/Pe 404; 1854/Pe 465.

16. Acheson, *Saint John*, p. 149; Chapman, 'The Mid-Nineteenth Century Temperance Movement', p. 50.

17. W.S. MacNutt, *New Brunswick. A History: 1784–1867* (Toronto, 1963, 1984), p. 350.

18. Acheson, *Saint John*, p. 141. Similar attempts were made in New England to control licensing at the local level. Tyrrell, *Sobering Up*, pp. 9l, 242–3.

19. RG4, RS24, 1852/Pe 406, PANB. The Maine Law also had a significant impact in England and within the United States. See Harrison, *Drink and the Victorians*, p. 196; Tyrrell, *Sobering Up*, p. 260.

20. Chapman, 'The Mid-Nineteenth Century Temperance Movement', p. 53.

21. New Brunswick women were by no means atypical in this regard. Barbara Epstein argues, for example, that during this period American women in the temperance movement were generally relegated to subsidiary roles—influencing sons and husbands. Barbara Leslie Epstein, *The Politics of Domesticity: Women, Evangelism, and Temperance in Nineteenth-Century America* (Middletown, Conn., 1981), p. 91.

6 From Kim Klein, 'A "Petticoat Polity"? Women Voters in New Brunswick before Confederation', *Acadiensis*, 26, 1 (Autumn 1996): 71–5.

On 20 June 1820, the New Brunswick *Royal Gazette* printed an editorial written in Montreal about the recent elections in Lower Canada. The writer of the editorial complained that at the elections, 'an absurd and unconstitutional practice [had] crept in', whereby women were allowed to participate as voters. The writer denounced the spiralling influence of women in Lower Canadian politics, concluding that if women continued to vote, they might, in time, acquire greater power, becoming judges, magistrates, even members of Parliament. The unhappy result would be the creation of a 'petticoat polity'.[1]

There are numerous documented episodes of women voting in Lower Canadian elections.[2] As the Lower Canadian writer noted, the colony's election law did not specifically exclude women from voting. A similar situation existed in colonial New Brunswick. Although the instructions that guided the conduct of New Brunswick's earliest assembly elections stipulated that voters must be male, the election statute that was in force from 1795 until 1843 did not specify the gender of eligible voters.[3]

Despite the lack of an explicit legal restriction, historians have uncovered little evidence that New Brunswick women, like their counterparts in Lower Canada, exercised the franchise. No women's names appear in the colony's extant pollbooks. Yet several sources suggest that some women in New Brunswick did cast votes in provincial elections before their formal disenfranchisement in 1843. A writer in *The Gleaner and Northumberland Schediasma* testified that four women voted in the October 1830 election in Kent County. In late nineteenth-century debates, several New Brunswick assemblymen justified their support for women's suffrage by noting that women had occasionally voted before the 1843 regulation came into force.[4] These sources, however, provide no substantive evidence that women voted in colonial New Brunswick.

Tucked among the House of Assembly papers on controverted elections are three documents that confirm that dozens of women voted in provincial elections in New Brunswick before 1843. One document notes simply that the votes of 39 women were among those struck off the pollbook of the controverted Sunbury County election of 1839.[5] The other two documents offer more detailed information. One document lists the names of 43 women who voted in the Kings County election of 1827. The other document provides evidence that another Kings County woman, Tamzen Oram, voted in the 1827 election. The list of Kings County voters provides unique opportunity to learn about the women who occasionally exercised the franchise in colonial New Brunswick and the nature of the elections in which they participated.[6]

Electoral politics in Kings County, especially during the 1820s and 1830s, was highly competitive and the election of 1827 was no exception.[7] Shortly after Lieutenant Governor Howard Douglas dissolved the House of Assembly on 24 May 1827 and issued writs for the election of a new house, six Kings County residents declared their intention to compete for the county's two seats in the Assembly. When the polls opened in Kings County on 15 June 1827, the candidates included the county's two sitting members, David B. Wetmore and John C. Vail; one former assemblyman, Samuel Freeze; the son of a former Kings County assemblyman, James Britain, Jr; and two newcomers to county electoral politics, John Humbert and William McLeod. During the election, nearly one thousand people cast votes. When the election concluded on 2 July 1827, both incumbent assemblymen had been defeated. In their places, the people of Kings County had elected Samuel Freeze and John Humbert. Freeze had a comfortable margin of victory, polling 62 more votes than Humbert, the second-place finisher. John Humbert's edge over his opponents was much narrower. He received only 15 more votes than the third-place candidate, John C. Vail, and only 29 more votes than David B. Wetmore, who finished fourth.[8]

John C. Vail's slender margin of defeat probably encouraged him to challenge the election results in an attempt to regain his assembly seat. After the poll closed, Vail demanded a scrutiny of the votes cast, claiming that he had more good votes than John Humbert. When Vail's effort to have the election results overturned at the poll failed, he petitioned the Assembly, protesting the outcome of the election. After receiving Vail's petition, the Assembly appointed a select committee to review the qualifications of those who voted in the election. The committee made a list of voters whose qualifications to vote were doubtful. On that list were the names of 44 women, 25 of whom had voted for John Humbert and 19 of whom had voted for John C. Vail.[9]

An examination of the backgrounds of the women who voted in the election reveals that most met the legal requirements for voting.[10] To be eligible to participate in provincial elections in New Brunswick in 1827, voters had to fulfill age and property requirements. First, potential electors had to be at least 21 years old. As far as can be determined, all of the women voters were over 21 years of age. Second, potential voters had to own real estate in the county in which they intended to vote. County residents were required to own £25 of real estate and non-residents were required to own £50 of real estate. Freeholders had to have their property registered at least six months before the election writs were issued.[11] At least 34 of the 44 women voters owned sufficient real estate to fulfill the property qualification for voting.[12]

In addition to meeting the age and property requirements, the women of Kings County who voted had another characteristic in common. They could all be described as 'femes soles'. That is, they were probably all independent women, either widows or women who had never been married.[13] Of the 44 women who voted, at least 31 were widows and seven had never married. These women were heads of households and this status was probably a decisive factor when the Kings County sheriff was deciding whether they should be allowed to vote.

Under the letter of the law, the women who voted in the Kings County election of 1827 were qualified to vote. Ultimately, their qualification to vote did not sway the members of the Assembly's committee. In the course of its investigation, the committee determined that ineligible voters cast 93 of Humbert's votes and 83 of Vail's votes. The 44 women were among those deemed ineligible to vote. Next to each ineligible male voter's name, the committee listed the reason for his disqualification. In contrast, the women's names were lumped together on one page under the heading, 'Women's Votes Struck off from Poll Book'. Apparently, the committee disqualified the women who voted in the election solely because of their gender.[14]

Even though their votes did not stand, the question remains, why were they allowed to vote? A review of the other elections in which women voted in British North America and the United States during the eighteenth and early nineteenth centuries reveals that all were, like the 1827 election in Kings County, highly competitive contests. In situations in which every vote was needed, candidates were willing to ignore convention to secure as many supporters as they could.[15]

But how did they secure that support? The reasons why Kings County women chose to vote for either John Humbert or John C. Vail are largely inexplicable. Both Humbert and Vail were well-qualified, by the standards of the time, to serve in the House of Assembly. John Humbert was a native of Saint John who moved to Hampton to set up a mercantile business. John C. Vail, a farmer in Sussex, was a life-long resident of the county. Both were members of prominent families with long records of public service and had themselves served in numerous local offices, thereby proving their fitness for holding provincial office.[16] Shedding light on the candidates' personal and political backgrounds also

serves to shed light on some of the women's electoral choices. John C. Vail had extensive family networks in the county and, in the election of 1827, his mother, Mary Vail; aunt, Mary Ann Barbarie; and sister-in-law, Susan Hallett, voted for him. As a life-long resident of Sussex parish, Vail also won the votes of six of the seven Sussex women who voted in the election. In contrast, John Humbert received only half of the votes of the women of his adopted parish, Hampton.[17]

Although some women in New Brunswick were allowed to vote in provincial elections during the 1820s and 1830s, in the 1840s the Assembly curtailed their participation as electors. In 1843, the Assembly passed a law that clarified the province's statute regulating elections by specifying the gender of eligible voters. Section XVI of the revised law specified that 'male voters' were to choose the members of the Assembly.[18] Transcripts of the debates surrounding the amendment of the election law in 1843 do not survive so we can only speculate about what triggered the legislators' action. The legislators' desire to amend the election law to prohibit women from voting may, however, have reflected broader social and economic changes that were occurring in the mid-nineteenth-century British-American world. In the re-ordering of social relationships that occurred in the transformation from rural, agrarian societies to urban, commercial and industrial societies, appropriate roles for women were being redefined. Increasingly, men and women were supposed to inhabit two separate spheres, the public sphere and the private, or domestic, sphere. Ideally, women confined their activities to the domestic sphere. Formally prohibiting women from voting in New Brunswick may have been part of a broader movement to limit women's activities in the public sphere. By enacting legislation that excluded women from voting in provincial elections, legislators tacitly recognized that some New Brunswick women had participated as electors and sought to circumscribe their political activity and more firmly confine them to domestic roles.

The episode of women voting in the Kings County election of 1827 is more than an interesting footnote to New Brunswick history. New Brunswick was not a 'petticoat polity', but this episode emphasizes that women were active participants in the creation of the colony's political culture. Even though women rarely exercised the franchise, as historians of colonial British America have pointed out, the disenfranchised influenced colonial politics in numerous ways, formal and informal, legal and illegal. Disenfranchised women could not vote but they could, for example, campaign for their favoured candidates, participate in election crowds and petition the government to address their concerns. These activities were undoubtedly more influential in the long run than the isolated episodes in which women were allowed to vote.[19]

NOTES

1. Montreal, 25 April 1820, printed in the New Brunswick *Royal Gazette*, 20 June 1820.

2. John Garner, *The Franchise and Politics in British North America, 1755–1867* (Toronto, 1969), pp. 156–9.

3. The Lower Canada and New Brunswick election statutes were not exceptional in this oversight. Until the mid-nineteenth century, the disenfranchisement of women in colonial British America was customary, and rarely written into election laws. Robert J. Dinkin, *Voting in Provincial America: A Study of Elections in the Thirteen Colonies, 1689–1776* (Westport, Conn., 1977), pp. 29–30; and Garner, *The Franchise and Politics*, pp. 155–6.

4. 'One who Voted for Mr. Jardine', *The Gleaner and Northumberland Schediasma*, 26 October 1830. Elspeth Tulloch notes this letter and legislators' comments regarding episodes of women voting in *We, the Undersigned: A Historical Overview of New Brunswick Women's Political and Legal Status, 1784–1984* (Moncton, NB, 1985), pp. 3–4. Note that the date in Tulloch's citation of the *Gleaner* letter (30 October 1830) is incorrect.

5. In the Case of . . ., Sunbury County, 1839, Controverted Elections Court Cases, RS 60C, Provincial Archives of New Brunswick [PANB].

6. In the Case of John Humbert, 1827, Controverted Elections Court Cases, RS 60C, PANB.

7. In his master's thesis, Raymond G. Watson contended that between 1785 and 1850 Kings County was remarkable for its 'sobriety, stability and solidarity'. He argues that Kings County was so orderly because a conservative Loyalist elite dominated county politics. Evidence gathered from Kings County elections, however, suggests that competition for political power was intense and frequent turnover of the political elite was common. See Raymond G. Watson, 'Local Government in a New Brunswick County: Kings County, 1784–1850', MA thesis, University of New Brunswick, 1967.

8. The Petition of John C. Vail of the Parrish of Sussex, County of Kings, Esquire, to the House of Assembly, 7 February 1828, Legislative Assembly Sessional Papers, RS 24, Session 36, Petition 7, PANB.

9. I must emphasize that at least 44 women voted in the election. Because the committee scrutinized only the votes cast for Humbert and Vail, it is possible that some of the other four candidates may also have received votes from women and that these votes were counted.

10. Biographical information on the women voters, including age, marital status and place of residence, was collected from the following sources: R. Wallace Hale, *Early New Brunswick Probate Records, 1785–1835* (Bowie, Md, 1989); Daniel F. Johnson, comp., *Vital Statistics from New Brunswick Newspapers* (Saint John, 1982–96); and Julia M. Walker and Margaret Duplisea, comps., *The 1851 Census for Kings County New Brunswick, Canada* (Fredericton, 1979).

11. An Act for Regulating Elections, of Representatives in General Assembly, and, for limiting the duration of Assemblies, in this Province. Passed by the General Assembly in 1791 and confirmed by an Order of His Majesty in Council, 3 June 1795. *The Acts of the General Assembly of Her Majesty's Province of New Brunswick From the Twenty-Sixth Year of the Reign of King George the Third to the Sixth Year of the Reign of King William The Fourth* (Fredericton, 1838), pp. 86–93.

12. To determine whether the women owned sufficient property to meet the voting qualification, three sets of sources were consulted. New Brunswickers could acquire real property through government grants, purchase, or inheritance. Government grants are listed in RS 686, records of Kings County land transactions are located in RS 91, Kings County Registry Office Records, and wills are located in RS 66, Kings County Probate Court Files. All of these records are located at the PANB.

13. The marital status of six women is uncertain.

14. Report of the Committee, Legislative Assembly Sessional Papers, RS 24, Session 36, Report 20; and In the Case of John Humbert, 1827, Controverted Elections Court Cases, RS 60C, PANB.

15. See the examples cited in Garner, *The Franchise and Politics*, pp. 155–60; and Edward Raymond Turner, 'Women's Suffrage in New Jersey: 1790–1807', *Smith College Studies* 4 (July 1916): 165–87.

16. Humbert and Vail served as highway commissioners and school trustees for their parishes. Vail and Humbert were appointed justices of the peace in 1826 and 1827, respectively. Both also served as officers (Humbert as a vestryman and Vail as a warden) of their local Anglican parishes. The following sources provided biographical information about Humbert and Vail: Minutes of General Sessions, Kings County Council Records, RS 151/Al, 1815–1828; Vestry Minutes, Trinity Anglican Church, Sussex, MC 223/SI5–1A3; Lists of Church Officers, St. Paul's Anglican Church, Hampton, F1087, PANB.

17. Women resident in every Kings County parish voted in the election. Twelve women voters were residents of Kingston; nine were from Hampton; seven from Sussex; six from Greenwich; three from Westfield; two from Springfield; and one from Norton. The residence of four of the women who voted could not be ascertained although it is likely that at least some of them were residents of Saint John County who owned property in Kings County.

18. An Act to improve the Law relating to the Election of Representatives to serve in the General Assembly, passed 11 April 1843.

19. See, for example, Gail G. Campbell, 'Disfranchised but not Quiescent: Women Petitioners in New Brunswick in the Mid-19th Century', *Acadiensis* 18, 2 (Spring 1989): 22–54; and Carol Wilton, '"A Firebrand amongst the People": The Durham Meetings and Popular Politics in Upper Canada', *Canadian Historical Review* 75, 3 (September 1994): 346–75.

□ Science and the Canadian Prairies

INTRODUCTION

■ In 1850 John McLean (the author of *Twenty-five Years' Service in the Hudson's Bay Territories,* published in 1848 and highly critical of the HBC) wrote to George Brown, the editor of the *Globe* in Toronto, that 'the interior of Rupert's Land belongs to the people of Canada both by right of discovery and settlement and it is therefore *our business* more than that of the people of England to claim the *restoration* of rights of which we have been so unjustly deprived.' These arguments had little effect at the time, but by the middle of the 1850s a small cadre of about 15 individuals had joined McLean to spearhead the movement for Canadian control of the western region.

As so often happened, a variety of unfolding disparate events began to form a pattern. Men became aware that the buffalo were disappearing; the Americans began looking northwest; and in February of 1857 a select committee of the British Parliament began holding hearings and collecting testimony into the licence of trade held by the Hudson's Bay Company. This inquiry was a logical consequence of the impending expiration of the Company's monopoly awarded by the Crown, but it recognized other factors, including the ambitions of the colonies to the east to extend settlement into the region of the monopoly, the need to deal with Vancouver Island, and 'the present condition of the settlement which has been formed on the Red River'. An expedition to learn more of the West, sponsored by the Royal Geographical Society under the auspices of the British government and headed by John Palliser, departed from Liverpool for Red River on 14 May 1857. On 23 July 1857 another expedition—led by Henry Youle Hind and organized by the government of United Canada to investigate the western country and to determine the best route for communication with the region—left Toronto. The findings of these two expeditions, which were not published immediately, served their purpose in expanding geographical knowledge of the West and in helping to end the public perception of this vast region as unfit for human habitation.

The final reports from these expeditions, besides containing much scientific observation, acknowledged the great potentiality of the West. Indeed, the aura of 'impartial science' that surrounded their bulky and stodgy documents gave their findings, in the eyes of enthusiasts for western expansion, greater cachet. Those in the Province of Canada who were interested in expansion found enough support in the work of these expeditions to document their case. Science had now confirmed what continental expansionists had long known instinctively: the Northwest could not only be settled but, as the United Canada government would insist in 1864, was 'capable of sustaining a vast population'.

Questions for consideration

1. What made the reports of the scientific expeditions so exciting?
2. How did their findings fit with other developments of the period?
3. What sort of role would western expansion play in the coming of Canadian Confederation?

Suggestions for further reading

Henry Youle Hind, *Narrative of the Canadian Red River Exploring Expedition of 1857 and of the Assiniboine and Saskatchewan Exploring Expedition of 1858* (London: Longman, Green, 1860). The complete reports of the Canadian expeditions.

Doug Owram, *Promise of Eden: The Canadian Expansionist Movement and the Idea of the West, 1856–1900* (Toronto: University of Toronto Press, 1980). An interpretation of Canadian expansionism.

Irene Spry, ed., *The Papers of the Palliser Expedition, 1857–1860* (Toronto: Champlain Society, 1968). A collection of documents about the Palliser expedition.

Susanne Zeller, *Inventing Canada: Early Victorian Science and the Idea of a Transcontinental Nation* (Toronto: University of Toronto Press, 1987). Argues the importance of science for creating the backdrop for Canadian unification.

PRIMARY DOCUMENTS

1 From John Palliser, *Journals, Detailed Reports and Observations Relative to the Exploration, by Captain Palliser* (London: Eyre & Spottiswoode, 1863), 7, 10–11, 16–18.

The existence of a general law regulating the distribution of the woods in this portion of the continent suggested itself to us during our first summer's explorations, and subsequent experience during the seasons of 1858–9 fully confirmed it.

The fertile savannahs and valuable woodlands of the Atlantic United States are succeeded, as has been previously alluded to, on the west by a more or less arid desert, occupying a region on both sides of the Rocky Mountains, which presents a barrier to the continuous growth of settlements between the Mississippi Valley and the States on the Pacific coast. This central desert extends, however, but a short way into the British territory, forming a triangle, having for its base the 49th parallel from longitude 100° to 114° W., with its apex reaching to the 52nd parallel of latitude.

The northern forests, which in former times descended more nearly to the frontier of this central desert, have been greatly encroached upon and, as it were, pushed backwards to the north through the effect of frequent fires.

Thus a large portion of fertile country, denuded of timber, separates the arid region from the forest lands to the north, and the habit which the Indian tribes have of burning the vegetation has, in fact, gradually improved the country for the purpose of settlement by clearing off the heavy timber, to remove which is generally the first and most arduous labour of the colonist.

The richness of the natural pasture in many places on the prairies of the second level along the North Saskatchewan and its tributary, Battle River, can hardly be exaggerated. Its value does not consist in its being rank or in great quantity, but from its fine quality, comprising nutritious species of grasses and carices, along with natural vetches in great variety, which remain throughout the winter sound, juicy, and fit for the nourishment of stock.

Almost everywhere along the course of the North Saskatchewan are to be found simply, it would be natural to infer their existence along the whole line where the Rocky Mountains run parallel and retain their altitude; but the dry areas are evidently due to other causes primarily, and they are not found above the 47th parallel in fact. It is decisive of the general question of sufficiency of rain to find the entire surface of the upper plains either well grassed or well wooded, and recent information on these points almost warrants the assertion that there are no barren tracts of consequence after we pass the Bad Lands, and the *Coteaus* of the Missouri. Many portions of these plains are known to be peculiarly rich in grasses, and probably the finest tracts lie along the eastern base of the mountains, in positions corresponding to the most desert-like of the plains at the south. The higher latitudes certainly differ widely from the plains which stretch from the Platte southward to the Llano Estacado of Texas, and none of the references made to them by residents or travellers indicate desert characteristics. Buffalo are far more abundant on the northern plains, and they remain through the winter at their extreme border, taking shelter in the belts of woodland on the upper Athabasca and Peace rivers. Grassy savannas like these necessarily imply an adequate supply of rain, and there can be no doubt that the correspondence with the European plains in like geographical position—those of eastern Germany and Russia—is quite complete in this respect. If a difference exists it is in favor of the American plains, which have a greater proportion of surface waters, both as lakes and rivers.

2   From *Reports of Progress; Together with a Preliminary and General Report on the Assiniboine and Saskatchewan Exploring Expedition of 1858* (Toronto: King's Printer, 1859), 131.

If we assume that the prairies of Red River and the Assiniboine east of Prairie Portage, contain an available area of 1,500,000 acres of fertile soil, the total quantity of arable land included between Red River and the Moose Woods on the South Branch of the Saskatchewan will be as follows:

	Acres
Red River and the Assiniboine Prairies east of Prairie Portage	1,500,000
Eastern water-shed of the Assiniboine and La Rivière Salè	3,500,000
Long Creek and the Forks of the Saskatchewan	600,000
Between Carrot River and the Main Saskatchewan	3,000,000
The Touchwood Hill range, the Moose Woods, &c., &c.	500,000
Mouse River, Qu'Appelle River, White Sand River	1,000,000
The region about the head-waters of the Assiniboine, including the valley of Swan River	1,000,000
Total area of arable land of first quality	11,100,000

or eleven million, one hundred thousand acres.

Of land fit for grazing purposes, the area is much more considerable, and may with propriety be assumed as fully equal in extent to the above estimate of the area of arable land.

3   From James Hector, 'On the Capabilities for Settlement of the Central Part of British North America', *Edinburgh New Philosophical Journal*, new series, 4 (1861): 264–7.

These remarks apply to what has been termed the 'Fertile Belt,' and the nature of which I will endeavour to explain.

The wonderfully fertile savannahs and valuable woodlands of the eastern United States are succeeded to the west by a more or less arid desert, which occupies a region on both sides of the Rocky Mountains, and presents a barrier to the continuous growth of settlements between the valley of the Mississippi and the rich states of the Pacific coast, and at present only occupied by one spot of civilization, the Mormon city at the Great Salt Lake.

Under such disadvantageous physical conditions, it is not likely that any line of route for rapid or heavy transport across this desert will be remunerative, while its construction, in the present disturbed state of American politics, may be indefinitely delayed. Nevertheless, during the last seven years our sharp-witted and prompt-acting cousins have been spending much money in having every possible route thoroughly explored and surveyed; and were their domestic troubles over, there is no doubt that they would revert to their attempts to bind together their eastern and western provinces.

It is therefore highly satisfactory for us, as British subjects, to know that the arid region extends but a short way to the north of the 49th parallel of latitude, which is the position of the boundary line, and that even the small area of desert within our territories derives its character more from the nature of the soil than from the general climatic conditions.

The British portion of the arid country is a triangular region, its apex reaching to the 52d parallel, while its base, applied along the 49th, extends between Long. 100° and 114° W. It contains, however, many varieties of land, and some limited areas that are really even good; but, on the whole, it must be described as deficient in wood, water, and grass.

Round the northern border of this arid district sweeps the 'Fertile Belt' of country which I before mentioned. It is nothing more than the ill-defined boundary of the bald plains from the gloomy woodlands of the circum-arctic forests. As it forms the favourite camping grounds of the Indian tribes, the habit which these savages have of burning the vegetation has gradually improved this country for the purposes of settlement, by clearing off the heavy timber, to remove which is always the first and most arduous labour of the colonist. The 'Fertile Belt,' which thus possesses all the good qualities of rich soil and an abundant growth of the nutritious leguminous plants of a woodland country, but associated with open expanses ready for the plough, or for depasturage, stretches from the wooded country at the south end of Lake Winipeg in a northwest direction continuously to the Rocky Mountains, so that the westward progress of settlement will not meet with the same obstacle that checks it within the United States.

We thus perceive that in some respects the Saskatchewan country compares favourably with Canada; but we must not forget that the valuable timber trees, which are such a great source of wealth to that province, totally disappear as we proceed to the west, only very few of them ever reaching the longitude of Lake Winipeg. Beyond that, in the northern thick woods, the coarse and worthless white spruce, with a few small birches, poplars, and willows, compose the forest growth, while in the 'Fertile Belt' almost the only tree is the aspen poplar, which forms very artificial-looking groves and clumps, that add greatly to the beauty of the scenery, but are useless beyond giving shelter and yielding a very inferior quality of firewood.

With all its disadvantages, the Saskatchewan country offers a most desirable field to the settler who is deficient in capital, and who has no desires beyond the easy life and moderate gains of simple agricultural occupations; and it is only the difficulty of access to it that, for the present at all events, prevents its immediate occupation. . . .

If there were a prospect of the western prairies being soon occupied by a producing population, it might in that case be remunerative to have a line of railway constructed entirely within the British territory that would have for its object the connection of Canada with our new colonies on the Pacific coast; but this would justly rank as a great national enterprise, in value much beyond the more western extension of our Canadian provinces.

From the large and flourishing agricultural settlement of whites and half-breeds at Red River, the population of which is now about 8000 souls, such a line of railway might pass westward through the 'Fertile Belt' without encountering any serious engineering difficulties. It has been frequently stated that in the Prairie country nothing would be required but the mere laying of the rails; but this is a total misconception of the physical features of the region. The prairies are very rarely level, except over small areas. They have undulations that often swell to the height of several hundred feet, or for miles the traveller winds among abrupt conical eminences; and it is only the general absence of timber, and the sameness of the scenery, that deceive the eye, and give the appearance of flatness. Moreover, throughout the greater part of the Prairie country, not only all the large rivers, but even small and insignificant streams, flow in valleys, with steep sides, deeply depressed below the general level; and these valleys would require the construction of bridges, and often in districts far distant from a supply of any proper building materials. Nevertheless, I believe I can safely state, that in proportion to the extent of mileage, small engineering expenses would be incurred until the Rocky Mountains are reached.

HISTORICAL INTERPRETATIONS

4   From Irene Spry, 'The Palliser Expedition', in Richard C. Davis, ed., *Rupert's Land: A Cultural Tapestry* (Waterloo, Ont.: Wilfrid Laurier University Press, 1988), 195–202.

John Palliser was the son and heir of a great Irish landowner. The family had originated in Yorkshire. The founder of the Irish branch into which the explorer was born had come to the country in 1660. He studied at Trinity College, Dublin, and became the Most Reverend Archbishop of Cashel. His descendants were among the social elite of the Protestant Ascendancy, with estates in County Tipperary, County Longford, County Waterford, and elsewhere. The explorer's grandfather, another John Palliser, was the guardian of an heiress, Anne Gledstanes, whose property, Annesgift, adjoined the Pallisers' Derryluskan estate. She married the senior John Palliser's heir, Wray Palliser. With their large family they lived, not only on their Irish estates, but in Dublin, London, and Rome.[1]

In the family tradition, young John attended Trinity College, Dublin, though only intermittently. He does not appear to have been an enthusiastic student, but he probably acquired the rudiments of a scientific education before dropping out without taking his degree. He discharged the family and social obligations proper to his class, becoming a captain in the Waterford Artillery Militia, of which regiment his father was colonel and in which he saw only a few scattered months of service (Spry, ed., *Palliser Papers*, xvi–xvii, cxxv, cxxxiii). He may have worked with the Ordinance Survey when it mapped County Waterford.[2] His dominating interests, as with most of his brothers, friends, and relatives, were travel and sport, especially big game hunting. He was also a gifted musician. The whole family travelled widely in Europe. Brothers, brothers-in-law, and close friends ventured to Australia, the China Seas (where Wray Palliser, Jr, rescued a French lady from pirates), Ceylon (now Sri Lanka), Central Africa, and the Arctic, where a brother-in-law was lost with Franklin.

Besides his exploration in what is now western Canada, John Palliser himself made extensive journeys in the United States, crossed the Panama Isthmus, voyaged among the Caribbean Islands, hunted in Spitzbergen and the Kara Sea in the Eastern Arctic, and apparently in emulation of a Scottish friend, William Fairholme, who was to marry his older sister, Grace, spent eleven months (from September 1847 to July 1848) hunting buffalo and grizzly bear in the Missouri country.[3]

This adventure fired him with a resolve to explore the prairies of British North America—and to do some more buffalo hunting, which he considered 'a noble sport.' The Palliser brothers had grown up in the comfortable assurance of family wealth. By mid-century, however, the family fortune was being depleted as a result of the desperate situation created by the Irish potato famine and Colonel Wray Palliser's attempts to help his tenants,[4] as well as by Frederick Palliser's unlucky coffee planting project in Ceylon,[5] which cost Col. Wray some thousands of pounds, to say nothing of the expense of John's American adventures and of other brothers' activities. Evidently the family's private fortune could not stand the strain of another North American expedition for the heir.

John Palliser secured election as a Fellow of the Royal Geographical Society (RGS) in London. To this august body he submitted a plan to explore the country along the as yet unsurveyed and unmarked international boundary between Red River (south of modern Winnipeg) to the Rocky Mountains and possible passes through the southern Rockies in British territory. He intended to get hold of a couple of half-breed guides, with whom he had travelled on the prairies of the Missouri, and to cross the plains directly from east to west, as near to the 49th parallel as possible.

There was good reason to think that a survey of this little-known border country should be undertaken. Even the Hudson's Bay Company had given up any attempt to maintain trading posts on the South Saskatchewan River after the Bow River expedition of 1822–23 and the lack of success of Peigan Post (Old Bow Fort) in the 1840s. The Americans had, in the early 1850s, mounted a series of explorations to find possible routes for transcontinental railroads, and the Russians had been exploring Siberia, but the British knew almost nothing about the country they claimed south of the North Saskatchewan, between Red River and the Rockies, and through and beyond the Rockies to the Pacific Coast along the American boundary.

The RGS was much interested in Palliser's plan but decided that a solitary journey across the plains was too limited a venture. What was needed was a scientific expedition manned by a team of experts and equipped with up-to-date instruments. The Society, therefore, enlarged the scheme and laid it before the Colonial Office with a request for £5,000 to fund it (xxi–xxiii). The under-secretary of state for the colonies was an Irish friend of Palliser's, John Ball. He managed to extract the required sum from a reluctant British Treasury, but added a further responsibility to what the expedition was instructed to do: This was to examine the old North West Company canoe route from the Head of Lake Superior to Red River Colony, to find out whether there was any possibility that it might be developed as a means of communication between the little Colony of the United Canadas and the British prairies. Palliser knew nothing about canoeing and did not want to undertake this extra assignment, but the Colonial Office insisted that it should be carried out.[6]

The help of Sir George Simpson, North American governor of the HBC, was enlisted to give advice and to provide canoes with their crews, as well as to recruit men, carts, and horses for the expedition's overland journey west of Red River. Leading scientists were consulted about what the expedition should try to find out and about possible personnel. Sir Roderick Murchison, president of the RGS and an eminent geologist, recruited Dr. James Hector, a recent medical graduate of the University of Edinburgh, to act as geologist, naturalist, and physician to the expedition. Major-General (later Sir Edward) Sabine of the Royal Society recommended Lieutenant (later Captain) Thomas W. Blakiston, R.A., as a magnetical observer. Sir William Hooker, of the Royal Botanical Gardens at Kew, found a charming, industrious, and experienced little Frenchman, Eugéne Bourgeau, to be the botanical collector. Dr. Edward Purcell of the Royal Naval College at Greenwich nominated John W. Sullivan to be astronomical observer and secretary for the expedition.[7]

Blakiston was to bring the delicate magnetical instruments to the prairies by Hudson Bay and the 'inland navigation' from York Factory to Carlton House on the North Saskatchewan, where he was to meet the other members of the expedition. They crossed the Atlantic to New York, travelling on via Niagara Falls and Detroit to a rendezvous at Sault Ste Marie with the canoes and their crews that were to take them to Red River.[8]

At Red River Settlement the party sought information and advice from old-timers, such as C.F. Edward Harriott, and made preparations for their overland exploration. With the help of Chief Factor Swanston, they hired voyageurs, horses, and carts, though with considerable difficulty, as the twice-yearly buffalo hunt had already left, taking with it most able-bodied men, good horses, and carts.[9]

While the carts carrying the expedition's main supplies set off by the Carlton Trail to Fort Ellice, Palliser, with Hector, Bourgeau, and Sullivan, went south up Red River to the American boundary at Pembina. There they found an American surveyor working for a land company. With him they made observations to discover the exact position of the boundary line on the 49th parallel. They decided that earlier surveys had not been perfectly accurate and left a new marker.

Then they travelled westward along the border, with a digression to St Joe's (now Walhalla, N. Dakota), to Turtle Mountain, noting swarms of grasshoppers and a lack of wood and water when they had ascended 'Pembina Mountain,' the escarpment that took them up to the Second Prairie Level or 'Steppe,' in Hector's alternative term. At the west end of Turtle Mountain they turned northwest to Fort Ellice on Beaver Creek near the junction of the Qu'Appelle River with the Assiniboine. Again, Palliser and Hector, guided by the famous plainsman, James McKay[10] (then in the service of the HBC), made a 'branch expedition' to the southwest via Moose Mountain to La Roche Perée on the Souris River. There Hector had a geological field day, examining the

coal beds and the strange rock formations.

From Fort Ellice, again with McKay as counsellor and guide, they made their way west to the South Branch of the Saskatchewan via Pile of Bones Creek, near modern Regina. They studied the connection of the headwater valley of the Qu'Appelle with the Elbow of the South Saskatchewan, now drowned in Diefenbaker Lake. Having reached the foot of the Missouri Coteau, some sixteen miles upriver from the Elbow, they were now at the eastern limit of the Third Prairie Level. From the Elbow they went northeast to Fort Carlton, where the main party was to winter, while Palliser went back to Montreal and New York in the hope of getting permission from the British Colonial Office to spend more time and more money on what was by then clearly an enormous task.

Blakiston—after a week's magnetical observing at York Factory and the difficult upriver journey—soon arrived at Carlton. He set everyone to work on his meticulous, hourly magnetical observations, but he found time to pursue notable ornithological studies as well as to do some hunting.[11]

Hector was busy with preparations for the coming season of further exploration and with geological investigations. He went to Fort Pitt and Fort Edmonton to recruit men and horses for the projected journey in 1858 through Blackfoot country and across mountain passes. He travelled on to Rocky Mountain House, where he made friends with the Blackfoot, and afterwards to the south of Edmonton, over the Beaver Hills, to find the Lac Ste Anne buffalo hunters, freemen, of whom he engaged twelve, including Gabriel Dumont, senior, uncle of Louis Riel's commander. Hector returned to Carlton by the North Saskatchewan, mapping the whole river from Rocky Mountain House to Carlton. As he travelled, he made geological, meteorological, and geographical observations.

Meanwhile Palliser had made the journey via St Paul to Montreal and New York, returning by St Paul and Red River in the spring to meet the rest of the expedition. He had arranged for men and horses for the 1858 season to go from Red River up to Carlton and had dealt with problems of supplies for the expedition and its accounts with Simpson at Lachine, as well as sending off another letter to the Colonial Office. His journey back down Red River to the Settlement was by canoe. He walked most of the way from Red River Settlement to Carlton, 550 miles or so, hunting as he went to help feed his men.

The united party set out again as soon as there was enough new grass for their horses. The explorers worked their way westward, via the Eagle Hills and Battle River, to the neighbourhood of modern Irricana, Alberta. There, after a splendid buffalo hunt, the party split up. Palliser and Sullivan made a quick dash to the boundary at Chief Mountain and then crossed the Rockies by the North Kananaskis Pass,[12] returning to the prairies by the North Kootenay Pass and then going northward to Edmonton. Blakiston skirted the Rockies to the entrance to the Crow's Nest Pass, which he noted but passed by, as the Indians reported it was a very bad road. He crossed the mountains by the North Kootenay Pass and came back by a route that took him into American territory to reach the South Kootenay (Boundary) Pass, by which he returned to the plains.[13] Hector and Bourgeau probed up the Bow Valley. Bourgeau stayed in the mountains to botanize, delighted to be back in alpine country, like his own Haute Savoie, after what to him were wearisome plains. Hector crossed the Rockies by the Vermilion Pass and returned by the Kicking Horse Pass, from which he found his way to Edmonton by the Bow Pass, the Mistaya Valley, and the North Saskatchewan.

At Edmonton, Blakiston left the expedition in a huff.[14] Hector made further geological and mapping explorations, first to the east and northeast of Edmonton and then along the edge of the Rockies north of the Bow Valley. After that he travelled north to the Athabasca River and the entrance to the traditional fur-trade route over the mountains, the so-called 'Athabasca Portage'

from the headwaters of the Athabasca to the Boat Encampment at the apex of the Big Bend of the Columbia River.

Meanwhile Palliser had been joined by two sporting friends. The three of them spent the winter hunting, examining the country around Edmonton, and making friends with the Blackfoot Indians at Rocky Mountain House.[15] One of the chiefs, Old Swan, named Palliser his grandson (409). With Mrs. Christie, the explorers gave a magnificent Christmas ball at Edmonton House, for which Bourgeau made a splendid lustre and other decorations.[16]

When spring came, Bourgeau (to his colleagues' great regret) had to leave the expedition to keep an earlier engagement in the Caucasus. The party, already reinforced by Palliser's friends, was further strengthened by some American miners who had been delayed by the onset of winter in their journey to the gold diggings on the Fraser River. Hector and Peter Erasmus waited at Edmonton for the expedition's servant, James Beads, who had made a trip to Red River during the winter because his brother had been killed by the Sioux, and who was to bring despatches Palliser was expecting from the Colonial Office. Palliser and the rest of the party travelled southeast by Buffalo Lake to the Sand Hills. There Hector joined them to geologize on the Red Deer River. Sadly, he failed to find any dinosaur remains. The party crossed the Sand Hills, south of the Red Deer, to Bow River. Palliser made a side trip to the junction of the Red Deer with the South Saskatchewan (Bow River) at modern Empress on the Alberta-Saskatchewan border. There, he was satisfied that they were not far from the westernmost point they had reached in their first season and was confident they had achieved a fair idea of the whole spread of prairie country along the South Saskatchewan River.

Now they turned south to the Cypress Hills which they found to be a delightful oasis in the middle of the dry plains, with wood, water, and good pasture. There, they replenished their stocks of food, and their horses ate well. Sullivan made a branch trip to the boundary south of the hills. There, too, Palliser's friends left them to travel home by way of the Missouri. Hector struck off to the northwest, crossing the mountains by Howse Pass to the Columbia Valley. He could not find any practicable way from that valley across the mountains to the west of it and turned up the Columbia to rejoin Palliser.

Palliser and Sullivan had meanwhile travelled westward to the Rockies, which they crossed once more by the North Kootenay Pass to the Tobacco Plains in the Kootenay Valley, a continuation of the Columbia Valley. They struggled with the problem of finding a feasible route to the Pacific Coast from that valley. Like Hector, they were out of food. They went south through American territory, Sullivan taking the men and horses on to Fort Colville, while Palliser traversed Kootenay Lake (in British territory) by canoe to Fort Shepherd. There, he made astronomical observations to establish whether the fort was in British territory. He reported that

> a circle of Scotchmen, Americans, and Indians, surrounded me, anxiously awaiting my decision as to whether the diggings were in the American territory or not; strange to say the Americans were quite as much pleased at my pronouncing in favour of Her Majesty, as the Scotchmen; and the Indians began cheering for King George (478–9).

From Fort Shepherd, Sullivan made a difficult journey through British territory eastward, almost to the Tobacco Plains, while Palliser forced his way westward to Lake Osoyoos. There he met an American party of the Boundary Commission of 1857–60. He had learned from HBC officers and Lieutenant Palmer, R.E., that an all-British trail led from that point to the Pacific.

In their three seasons of work, the explorers had examined the canoe route to Red River Settlement and the route through Minnesota, as well as the river route connecting York Factory and Carlton House. They had zigzagged across the plains from Red River to the mountains, and from the American border to Athabasca River. They had traversed six passes through the southern Rockies. What kind of a report did they bring back to the Imperial Government?

The immensity of the country astonished the explorers, whose members took astronomical observations whenever possible, thereby producing the materials for the great map of 1865, which was published in the fourth of the Blue Books containing their reports. There were errors and gaps in this map, but it was a great improvement on earlier maps, and it served newcomers, such as the NWMP, until new and more accurate maps could be made, based on detailed surveys by the Geological Survey of Canada, the Dominion Land Surveyors, and the Mounties' own observations. The expedition plotted the location of such important geographical features as the North and South branches of the Saskatchewan River, Turtle Mountain, and the Cypress Hills, the latter having been earlier confused with the Porcupine Hills of modern Alberta. They had mapped the basic geographical structure of the vast stretch of country that they traversed.[17]

Besides mapping the country, the expedition described its salient features. Hector noted that there were three Prairie Levels: one at the altitude of Red River and Lake Winnipeg, one stretching from the top of Pembina Mountain to the Missouri Coteau, and one from the summit of the Coteau to the Foothills of the Rockies. The central plains thus rose in a series of three 'Steppes' to the foot of the mountains (cvii–cviii, 8, 20, 104–5, 108). The expedition also described the main river systems and appraised the 'capability' for agriculture and settlement of the country through which they flow.[18]

Hector described its essential geological structure. As well, he identified useful mineral resources, notably coal deposits, such as those on the Souris River and on the Red Deer and North Saskatchewan, and oil, which he called 'black unctuous mud,' that oozed from a round hole so deep that no one had ever found its bottom (199). This was in the Vermilion River area, to the south of the Cold Lake region of modern Alberta. He also identified clay, suitable for making bricks and pottery; rock, useful for building; salt springs; and rock salt. He was, however, unduly optimistic about rich deposits of iron ore.[19]

The explorers kept records of temperature and precipitation (and persuaded local residents to keep additional meteorological records). These records shed new light on the vexed question of whether Rupert's Land was a frozen wilderness, fit for nothing but the fur trade, or a potential Garden of Eden, only awaiting the hands of industrious husbandmen to produce a wealth of agricultural produce.

The expedition made exhaustive lists and collected specimens of the rocks, fossils, fauna and flora, and products of the country. Bourgeau alone collected ten thousand botanical specimens (ciii). Some of these may still be seen in the Royal Botanical Gardens at Kew and elsewhere.

Some new species were discovered that now bear the names of Bourgeau and Blakiston. The party noted a rich variety of game, fur-bearing animals, fish, and wildfowl. The explorers saw immense herds of buffalo, but also recorded that the Indians were beginning 'to apprehend scarcity of buffalo' (137).

The party met and got to know the peoples of the country. They met Governor Sir George Simpson and other HBC officers and missionaries of the Catholic, Anglican, and Methodist persuasions. They established a friendship with the redoubtable mixed-blood guide, James McKay. Earlier, on the Missouri in 1848, Palliser had met the equally redoubtable and 'very intelligent half breed,' James Sinclair. As well, they got to know the Red River voyageurs and the buffalo hunters from Lac Ste Anne. They met a great many Indians, including the Assiniboine encountered in the Souris Valley; many Cree; Blackfoot, Blood, Peigan, and Sarcee; Mountain Stoneys; Kootenay; and Shuswap. . . .

Notes

1. For the sources of data concerning Palliser's family and friends, and social and educational background, see Irene M. Spry, ed., *The Papers of the Palliser Expedition* (Toronto: Champlain Society, 1968), xv–xx. Evidence for most of the statements made in this paper is to be found in this Champlain Society volume, hereafter cited as Spry, ed., *Palliser Papers*. Subsequent page references to this volume are given in parentheses in the text.

2. Local tradition has it that he did so. Though there seems to be no mention of him in the relevant file in the PRO, Kew, England, it does contain a letter that appears to be in Palliser's rather distinctive handwriting.

3. John Palliser, *Solitary Rambles and Adventures of a Hunter in the Prairies* (London: John Murray, 1853 and subsequent editions, including a reprint, Edmonton: Hurtig, 1969); for Palliser's Arctic voyages see Irene M. Spry, 'The Pallisers' Voyage

to the Kara Sea, 1869', *The Musk-Ox* 26 (1980): 13–20.

4. Oral communication by the son of one of those tenants. The County Longford property had to be sold and the entail on the other estates broken to allow them to be mortgaged (cxxxviii).

5. Frederick Palliser's correspondence while he was in Ceylon (now Sri Lanka) in the possession of a granddaughter, Mrs. Anne Gelius of Copenhagen. Copies in the author's possession.

6. Spry, ed., *Palliser Papers*, xxiii–xxv and intermittently thereafter.

7. For preparations for the expedition and its personnel see ibid., xxiv–xli and lvii and Appendix 11.

8. For the explorers' journeys see the expedition's daily journal reprinted from the *Report* of 1863 in Spry, ed., *Palliser Papers*.

9. For the explorers' sojourn in Red River Settlement see, Spry, ed., *Palliser Papers*, 85–94.

10. For a biography of James McKay see Allan Turner, *DCB*, Vol. X, 473–5, and N. Jaye Goossen, '"A wearer of mocassins": The Honourable James McKay of Deer Lodge', *The Beaver* (Autumn 1978): 44–53.

11. See Spry, ed., *Palliser Papers*, Appendix V.

12. For an illustrated discussion of which of the Kananaskis Passes he traversed, see Irene M. Spry, 'Prairies and Passes: Retracing the Route of Palliser's British North American Exploring Expedition 1857–1860', *Journal of the Royal Society for the Encouragement of Arts, Manufactures and Commerce* (September 1965): 807–27.

13. Spry, ed., *Palliser Papers*, Appendix V.

14. For Blakiston's quarrel with Sullivan and Palliser see Spry, ed., *Palliser Papers*, lxxii–lxxv and lxxx–lxxxi.

15. These friends were Captain Arthur Brisco, late of the 11th Hussars, and William Roland Mitchell, who wrote voluminous letters describing this adventure. Copies of these letters are to be found in the Regina holdings of the Saskatchewan Archives Board (SAB(R)). Another set is in the author's possession. The originals are in the possession of the Mitchell family in Dorset, England. See also Spry, ed., *Palliser Papers*, lxxxv–lxxxvi, 502, and 603.

16. Spry, ed., *Palliser Papers*, lxxxviii, and Charles Gay, 'Le Capitaine Palliser et l'Exploration des Montagnes Rocheuses, 1857–1859', *Le Tour du Monde*, 1861, 290.

17. For an analysis of this aspect of the expedition's work see Spry, ed., *Palliser Papers*, xcvi–ci.

18. Spry, ed., *Palliser Papers*, 14–19 and the daily journal.

19. Hector's geological observations are scattered through the journal (see Spry, ed., *Palliser Papers*) and consolidated in his Geological Report in the 1863 *Report*, 210–45. A series of drawings of geological sections is included in the fourth Blue Book of 1865. For Hector's other publications on the structure and geology of the country see the *Palliser Papers*, 617. For a comment on resources of iron ore see, for example, 17.

5   From William L. Morton, *Henry Youle Hind, 1823–1908* (Toronto: University of Toronto Press, 1980), 33–7.

It was with such possibilities brightening the soft glow of Toronto's summer air that Hind began the great adventure of his life. For its sponsors the expedition of 1857 was to be mismanaged and in itself to prove of little value, but for Hind it was to be a chance to prove his quality as explorer and geological observer. It no doubt, therefore, did not greatly trouble him that the expedition began late because of the delay caused by the opposition to it. Not until 18 July was the minute of the Executive Council approving it passed. Preparations must have been going forward in anticipation of approval, as the party left Toronto five days later.

The expedition was a fair sample of the Canadian society which had launched it. The head was George Gladman, born in the Hudson's Bay Company territory and a former chief trader of the company until he retired to settle in Canada. He had been active in arousing the new interest in the Northwest, and had given evidence before the Canadian Select Committee earlier in 1857. Because of his experience, the veteran trader was put in charge of the expedition as a whole and made responsible for carrying out its 'primary object . . . a thorough examination of the tract of country between Lake Superior and Red River.'[1] He, with his son Henry Gladman, his assistant, represented the old skills and interests of the fur trade. Associated with George Gladman, but with special instructions of their own, were Simon J. Dawson, civil engineer, and W.H.E. Napier, public land surveyor, with the joint responsibility for deciding how the old canoe route might be made a passage by road and water transport for settlers in the Northwest. Their assistants were S.L. Russell, C.F. Gaudet, A.M. Wells, J.A. Dickenson, and Robert Wynne, all representatives of the newer class of professional men who from the Eastern Townships of Canada East to Georgian Bay of Canada West were carrying the Canadian frontier forward by land road and railroad surveys. As levellers and chainmen, the engineers and surveyors had young men, like engineering students today, H.H. Killaly, Edward Cayley, J. Cayley, and another called Campbell, whose names gave rise to the *Globe*'s sour comment that the expedition was largely a summer outing for the sons of politicians. Included, perhaps for political reasons and for good relations with the French element in Red River, was Colonel Charles Irumberry de Salaberry, son of the victor of Châteauguay. These were, in the language of the day, 'the gentlemen' of the expedition. With them were, as the man power of the party and representatives of the fur trade, a dozen Iroquois, and later the same number of Ojibwas and several French Canadians, a half breed and a Scot.[2]

Hind himself was designated 'Geologist and Naturalist to the party' under the direction of Gladman. He was to collect information for 'a description of the main geological features of the country' traversed, and to record 'whatever pertains to its natural history' that he might have an opportunity to observe. With reference to geology in particular he was to be guided by the memorandum supplied by Sir William Logan to the government and to give special attention, as far as possible, to

1. The boundaries of formations. 2. The distribution of limestone. 3. The collection of fossils. 4. The occurrence of economic minerals. 5. The exact position of all facts, and the attitude of the rocks.

With respect to natural history, he was to collect what he could and note as minutely as possible in a daily journal 'all leading features of topography, vegetation, and soil' along the line of route, as well as make meteorological observations. Hind was to be paid thirty shillings a day while on the expedition—a princely rate compared with his academic salary—and to have the appointment of one assistant. He chose John Fleming, younger brother of Sandford, another evidence of the friendly relations between the elder Fleming and Hind. John Fleming's particular duties were those of 'draughtsman,' and his pencil drawings and water colours were to prove with Hind's writings among the lasting results of the expedition.[3]

The historic Canada of the partnership of Indian and European and the new Canada of the engineer's and geologist's frontier were thus united in the hastily assembled party. On 23 July 1857 it entrained at the Toronto depot of the Northern Railway for Collingwood. The line, just completed in 1855, was itself an expression of the quest of Toronto for the trade of the upper lakes and the Northwest, and the work of engineers like Sandford Fleming and mining and railway promoters like Allan Macdonell.[4] The still humpy track winding to Barrie and to Collingwood on Georgian Bay had been laid for just such purposes as the party represented: migration, settlement, mining. The expedition, on reconnaissance for the Canadian frontier in the eager expansion of the fifties, was only a larger version of such expeditions as Sandford Fleming and Hind had made to the Saugeen in 1856, or Simon Dawson many times in the valleys of the Ottawa and St Maurice rivers. Like them, it was to look, with the best scientific means available, for routes for road and railway, land for settlement, timber for felling, minerals for mining.

The S.S. *Collingwood*, a squat little paddlewheeler, left her home on 24 July with the party and its canoes brought from Lachine, and reached Sault Ste Marie on the 27th. It had bypassed the falls of St Mary's River by the new American lock opened in 1855, on the significance of which for western expansion Hind was to dilate in his report. The ship entered at once into the storms and fogs of Lake Superior, to run aground that night on an island near Michipicoten harbour, as Fleming's sketch records.[5] When the *Collingwood* was refloated and repaired, the expedition resumed its voyage on 30 July, and the next day entered the grand portals of Thunder Bay. Here at Fort William the work of the expedition began, with the organization of two brigades of three canoes each, the hiring of twelve additional (Ojibwa) canoemen, and the sorting and packing of supplies.

Hind was free to occupy himself with observations of the region and to talk with Chief Trader John McIntyre of the Hudson's Bay Company post at Fort William and Father Jean-Pierre Choné of the Roman Catholic mission. As he had done since the party left Collingwood, he collected material for the journal on which he was to base his official report and ultimately his own *Narrative*. In doing so, he was, of course, following not only his instructions but also the discipline of all serious observers in the field. As surviving notebooks of Hind's in the Manitoba Archives in Winnipeg and in the Saint John Museum show, he was a regular and careful keeper of journals, and his work would always be based, whatever its ultimate form, on his own observations recorded on the spot. On this expedition these were amplified with thermometer readings of air and water temperatures, barometric readings of elevation, the results of the engineers' levellings, and similar scientific data. Hind was taking his duties with the utmost seriousness, the seriousness of a man who had found his calling. It is to be noted also how amply he interpreted his already broad instructions; he would be equipped to write a report of the whole expedition, and even more than a report. . . .

NOTES

1. Province of Canada, *Report on . . . Exploration between . . . Lake Superior and Red River . . . 1857* (Toronto, 1858), p. 5.
2. Public Archives of Canada, RG 5, C1, vol. 523, a list of the names of the members of the expedition. See also Hind's *Narrative of the Canadian Red River Exploring Expedition of 1857 and of the* *Assinniboine* [sic] *and Saskatchewan Exploring Expedition of 1858* (London, 1860), I, 3.
3. *Report . . . 1857*, instructions to Hind, pp. 14–16; also *Narrative*, I, 5–8.
4. D.C. Masters, *Rise of Toronto* (Toronto, 1947), p. 66.
5. *Narrative*, I, 12.

6 Doug Owram, *Promise of Eden: The Canadian Expansionist Movement and the Idea of the West, 1856–1900* (Toronto: University of Toronto Press, 1980), 68–74.

. . . The identification of the prairie with the Great American Desert had existed long before Palliser and Hind made their trek west. If, however, the triangle did little to encourage the expansionists, the same cannot be said of the fertile belt. It was this term that gave the expansionists what they needed, and ultimately it dominated the image of the sterile triangle in determining the Canadian assessment of the value of the North West. The concept of the fertile belt was essential to those who wanted to annex the North West. Presented most dramatically by Hind in a map in his 1860 *Narrative*, the area of fertility was depicted as a vast band of yellow sweeping in a giant arc from the American border at Red River northwest to the forks of the Saskatchewan and from there along the North Saskatchewan to the Rocky Mountains. As it approached the foothills of the Rockies it turned southward until it reached the border at 114 degrees west.[1] Here was scientific and dramatic support for those who would extend the proven fertility of the Red River valley to the west. The settlement was no longer an oasis in a desert but simply the small, easternmost portion of a vast area of land suitable for settlement.

Interestingly, neither the existence of the triangle nor the fertile belt challenged the older traditional relation between the absence of trees and aridity. The line between the fertile belt and the triangle was the region that Palliser and Hind felt divided the natural prairie from those areas that would support trees. Hind, in fact, began his definition of the area which he thought was an extension of the American desert by describing it as a 'vast treeless region.'[2] Equally, both parties went out of their way to explain the absence of trees in some portions in the fertile belt. Palliser dismissed the absence of trees in the Battle River area as artificial, pointing to the 'debris of large trees' as proof that the area could support vegetation. The lack of trees, both felt, was due to prairie fires, often set by Indians.[3] It was still felt necessary, then, to explain why trees did not exist in a supposedly fertile land.

Given the definition of Palliser's triangle and the caution with which both Hind and Palliser approached the prairie, it is perhaps surprising that they played such an important role in changing the image of the West. Their impact came from the fact that, having accepted an extension of the Great American Desert, they then imposed definite limits on it. Furthermore, they inserted between that area and the other region that had tainted the image of the West, the Arctic, an extensive band of fertile land and appropriate climate. The fertile belt provided the agricultural hinterland and path to the Pacific which the expansionists sought. Hind was acutely aware of this and thought it of sufficient importance to set it down in block letters. 'IT IS A PHYSICAL REALITY OF THE HIGHEST IMPORTANCE TO THE INTERESTS OF BRITISH NORTH AMERICA THAT THIS CONTINUOUS BELT CAN BE SETTLED AND CULTIVATED FROM A FEW MILES WEST OF THE LAKE OF THE WOODS TO THE PASSES OF THE ROCKY MOUNTAINS, AND ANY LINE OF COMMUNICATION, WHETHER BY WAGGON ROAD OR RAILROAD, PASSING THROUGH IT, WILL EVENTUALLY ENJOY THE GREAT ADVANTAGE OF BEING FED BY AN AGRICULTURAL POPULATION FROM ONE EXTREMITY TO ANOTHER.'[4] This fact was what mattered to Canadians. The implications of the fertile belt made all the qualifications of both Hind and Palliser seem largely irrelevant. The point had been made that the North West was not a barrier to the Pacific and that it had resources which would allow it to become a valuable hinterland for Canada.

The importance of the two scientific expeditions was probably best summed up by Hind himself when he commented that 'the North-West Territory is no longer a *terra incognita.*'[5] The weakest link in the chain of expansionist arguments had been the lack of knowledge concerning the region in which they placed so much faith. Now, with the results of the expeditions, the expansionist could state with certainty that these reports 'have established the immediate availability for the purposes of Colonization,' of vast portions of the Hudson's Bay territory.[6]

The expansionists had not needed much convincing, of course. They simply found in the efforts of the scientific expeditions confirmation of what they had believed all along. The real importance of the two expeditions lay in the influence they had on those less committed. These people had needed proof, and in the seemingly objective assessments of Palliser and Hind they found strong evidence of the validity of the expansionist position. The work of these two parties provided sufficient material on the potential of the North West to shift the weight of evidence in favour of the expansionist argument. Over the next years it became standard in Canada to accept the conclusion that the North West was suitable for settlement rather than the reverse. By the time the Canadian government, in 1864, talked of the region as being 'fertile and capable of sustaining a vast population,' the comment was so commonplace as to be almost a cliché.[7]

Scientific reports alone were not responsible for the dramatic change in the image of the North West. While the volumes published on the two expeditions provided an essential basis of evidence, they were hardly the sort of material that could, by themselves, have wrought the transformation that took place in the public mind. Toronto scientist, Daniel Wilson, summed up their limitations when he commented: 'it is an old saying that Parliament can print blue books, but it is beyond its power to make people read them.'[8] In order to understand the change that occurred it is necessary to consider all those writings, whether by scientist or layman, that appealed, as one expansionist later put it, to the 'mind and emotion of the great agricultural community.'[9] The experience of the West after 1857 was as much an emotional process as it was intellectual.

Anyone who went west in the later 1850s or 1860s could not escape the feeling that he was entering a distinct environment. The Hudson's Bay territories were still isolated from the rest of British North America in terms of both trade and transportation. Most who journeyed to Red River had to go by way of the United States to St Paul in Minnesota and then northward. By the time they approached Fort Garry they had left behind such symbols of civilization as the railroad and the telegraph. Those who made the journey saw their own movement from civilization to wilderness as significant. Travellers gloried in their ability to return to a basic, primitive mode of existence and to thrive on it. The travellers of the 1860s, especially those tourists who had come to the West specifically for a wilderness adventure, recreated the sense of romance that had long been apparent in the writings of R.M. Ballantyne. The Earl of Southesk, on leaving Crow Wing, Minnesota, in May 1859, exulted: 'at last, I thought, as last the prisoner of civilisation is free.' British tourist, Doctor William Cheadle, was in a long-standing tradition when he concluded after his own trip on the prairies that 'truly the pleasures of eating are utterly unknown in civilised life.'[10]

In spite of the timelessness of such comments, the reaction to the wilderness was changing. In the wake of the expansionist campaign, explorers and travellers approached the wilderness in a manner that differentiated them from both the romantics and those earlier missionaries who had reacted so adversely to a heathen land. Gradually the very idea of the wilderness began to soften and change until it too conformed to the requirements of progress.

The changing approach was typified by the reaction of Henry Youle Hind, one of the first to reconcile the romance of the wilderness with the implications of expansionism. As had many before him, Hind found certain aspects of the wilderness life to be charming. His lengthy description of a camp scene early in the morning, where 'the stars are slightly paling,' and 'the cold yellow light begins to show itself in the east,' reveals that his sensitivity was not constricted by his scientific purpose. It was a description, more than anything else, of a peace inherent in nature, where 'no sound at this season of the year disturbs the silence of the early dawn.'[11] Such scenes and experiences of 'boundless prairies, sweet scented breezes, and gorgeous sunsets,' made a trip to the North West an emotional as well as an intellectual experience for Hind.[12]

If the beauty and peace of the wilderness were impressive, so was its power. The incredible forces that often shattered the peace of nature were awesome to Hind. 'The grandeur of a prairie on fire belongs to itself,' he wrote. Only unchecked nature was capable of creating such an impressive sight, since, 'like a volcano in full activity, you cannot imitate it, because it is impossible to obtain those gigantic elements from which it derives its awful splendour.' Even the tiny grasshoppers, massed in quantities appropriate to the vastness of the West, became an awe-inspiring, if destructive, manifestation of the power of the wilderness: 'Lying on my back and looking upwards as near the sun as the light would permit, I saw the sky continually changing colour from blue to silver to white, ash grey and lead colours, according to the numbers in the passing cloud of insects . . . the aspect of the heavens during the greatest flight was singularly striking. It produced a feeling of uneasiness, amazement and awe in our minds, as if some terrible, unforeseen calamity were about to happen.'[13]

While Hind was awed by the wilderness he felt no temptation to ascribe to it moral attributes superior to civilization. His enthusiasm, for instance, did not extend to the men who lived in the wilderness. His attitude to the Indian, in fact, resembled the disdain and pity of the missionary more that it did the praises of the romantic. The native, he felt, was not in harmony with nature but degraded by it. When Hind visited an Indian village he thought of the comparison 'between the humanizing influence of civilization and the degraded, brutal condition of a barbarous heathen race.' The power and beauty of the wilderness was indeed impressive, but it was too powerful for man to accept unaltered without becoming dominated by it.

Hind's whole reaction to the wilderness and to the North West rested on his awareness and acceptance of Canadian expansionism. The power and beauty of the wilderness were, for him, inseparable from his hopes for the movement. In fact, it simply demonstrated the importance of expansion: 'the vast ocean of level prairie which lies to the West of Red River must be seen in its extraordinary aspects, before it can be rightly valued and understood in reference to its future occupation by an energetic and civilised race, able to improve on its vast capabilities and appreciate its marvellous beauties.'[14] Hind felt none of the conflicts of Alexander Ross, because for him the romance of the wilderness was not in its own intrinsic beauty but in its potential.

In the wake of the expansionist crusade the land began to be viewed in terms of agricultural potential not only in the scientific but in the aesthetic sense. Descriptions of present scenes of beauty became prophecies of future development. 'I stood upon the summit of the bluff' near the Qu'Appelle, wrote James Dickinson, a member of the Hind expedition, 'looking down upon the glittering lake 300 feet below, and across the boundless plains, no living thing in view, no sound of life anywhere.' It was a romantic scene in itself, but for Dickinson the romance was as much in the mind as in the scene, for he 'thought of the time to come when will be seen passing swiftly along the distant horizon the white cloud of the locomotive on its way from Atlantic to Pacific, and when the valley will not resound from the merry voices of those who have come from the busy city on the banks of the Red River to see the beautiful lakes of the Qu'Appelle.'[15] Similarly, while traversing a series of hills the English tourists, Milton and Cheadle, 'remarked to one another what a magnificent site for a house one of the promontories would be, and how happy many a poor farmer who tilled unkindly soil at home would feel in possession of the rich land which lay before us.'[16]

In the later 1850s and 1860s man's reaction to the North West began increasingly to be determined by his sense of its potential, in the same way that, in previous years, the missionary's reaction had been conditioned by the fact that it was a heathen wilderness. The prairie took on a new beauty because of the resources it contained. As S.J. Dawson said of Red River, 'if the scenic beauty which characterizes the region so near it to the eastward is wanting, this country is incomparably superior in all that can minister to the wants of man.'[17] Charles Mair said almost the same thing a decade later when he enthused that 'there is, in truth, a prospective poetry in the soil here—the poetry of comfort and independence.'[18] It is not surprising that expansionists paid little heed to the costs that civilization would impose on the North West, for to them the charm of the wilderness lay mainly in its potential for development.

The expansionists' belief that civilization was, unquestionably, preferable to wilderness placed them closer to the missionary than to the romantic. Even the rhetoric of expansionism often resembled the earlier missionary tracts. Both groups looked forward continually to a time when 'the deserts of the North-West shall blossom as a rose where now a few thousand savages drag out a miserable existence.'[19] The views of the two groups were, however, far from identical. The missionary had found little beauty or romance in the wilderness. Landscape had, for him, been viewed against the heathen and miserable condition of the Indian. The expansionists, on the other hand, enthused over the land and scenery even as they looked to the time when it would be transformed. Whereas the missionary had found the wilderness a reproof to the moral sensibilities of man, the expansionist saw as positive the very fact that the land was still a wilderness.

The fact that vast areas of good and habitable land still existed was in fact providential. The region had been kept isolated from the rest of the world until Canada had been prepared to occupy it.[20] Now, however, its potential was becoming known. As George Brown pointed out, it involved an area 'greater in extent than the whole soil of Russia,' and that vast resource would be 'opened up to civilization under the auspices of the British American Confederation.'[21] The millions of acres available for the farmer were valuable precisely because even after centuries of expansion and settlement they lay 'free and unoccupied.'[22] The missionary had felt blocked and frustrated by the isolation, emptiness, and seeming permanence of the wilderness in which he worked. In contrast the wilderness state added to the expansionist's estimate of the region. 'Man is a grasshopper here,' wrote Charles Mair, 'making his way between the enormous discs of heaven and earth. And yet man is master of all this.'[23]

This reaction to the wilderness was reinforced by the fact that the North West was in a state of flux. The wilderness, as if preparing for things to come, already seemed to be receding.

'The days when it was possible to live in plenty by the gun and the net alone, have already gone by on the North Saskatchewan,' wrote Milton and Cheadle. While the disappearance of game signalled the end of the wilderness, other developments predicted the coming of civilization. 'The river communication has been opened up,' Bishop Anderson noted in 1860; 'the road over the prairie has been traversed; and the appliances of modern science have rendered more easy the production of some necessities of modern life.'[24]

Observations such as these, and the continued orientation towards the potential of the region, began to diminish the image of the wilderness in the minds of those who observed the North West. Wilderness, by definition, implied a region where the natural dominated the works of man, whether those works be put in technological, legal, or spiritual terms. This view was common to Hind, Ross, and the early missionaries. Where earlier observers differed from the expansionists, however, was in the implication they drew from this fact. In various ways both the missionaries and Ross had tended to see the wilderness as irreconcilable with civilization; there was, in a sense, an adversary relationship between the two states. To Hind and the expansionists no such implication was thought to be necessary; rather civilization, the works of man, were a superstructure to be imposed on nature. The only necessary question, therefore, was whether the natural environment was suitable as a base for European society. The re-evaluation of the climate of the North West had, seemingly, answered that question, and thus in a very real sense the distinction between wilderness and civilization was reduced to matter of time. The only difference between the resident of the North West and that of Europe was, 'if the greatness of his country is past or passing, ours is yet to come.'[25]

The more that men viewed the North West in terms of its potential, the more they began to concentrate, either inadvertently or deliberately, on those attributes of the region that reinforced the new image. Those facets of the North West which had previously been used to emphasize its wilderness state—isolation, savagery, harshness—were downplayed and replaced with quite different attributes. Ruggedness of land and climate was scarcely mentioned; instead, the North West began to be described in terms more appropriate to the estate of a well-to-do landowner than to a vast unpeopled land: 'There are many delightful spots in the belts, the herbage is clean as well shaven lawn, the clumps of aspen are neatly rounded as if by art, and where little lakes alive with waterfowl abound, the scenery is very charming, and appears to be artificial, the result of taste and skill, rather than the natural features of a wild, almost uninhabited country.'[26] While the harsh and wild aspects of the North West were not ignored, there was an increased tendency, from the time of Hind on, to look on the North West as a rather tame wilderness.

NOTES

1. Henry Youle Hind, *Narrative of the Canadian Red River Exploring Expedition of 1857 and of the Assiniboine and Saskatchewan Exploring Expedition of 1858* (London, 1860), I, 'Map of the Country from Lake Superior to the Pacific Ocean'.

2. Henry Youle Hind, *North-West Territory, Report on the Assiniboine and Saskatchewan Exploring Expedition* (Toronto, 1859), 124.

3. United Kingdom, *The Journals, Detailed Reports and Observations Relative to the Exploration by Captain Palliser* (London, 1859), 86; Palliser, *Papers Relative to the Exploration of British North America* (London, 1859), 30; Hind, *North-West Territory*, 53.

4. Hind, *Narrative*, II, 234.

5. [Hind], 'North-West British America', *British American Magazine*, May 1863, p. 3.

6. *Nor'Wester*, 'Prospectus', 1859.

7. 'Report of the Committee of the Executive Council', approved 11 Nov. 1864; *Documents Relating to the Opening up of the North West Territories to Settlement and Colonisation* (n.p., 1865), 4.

8. *Canadian Journal*, March 1861, p. 175.

9. Charles Mair, 'The New Canada: Its Natural Features and Climate [Part 1]', *Canadian Monthly and National Review* 8 (July 1875): 1.

10. Earl of Southesk, *Saskatchewan and the Rocky Mountains* (London, 1875), 13; Viscount Milton and W.B. Cheadle, *The North-West Passage by Land* (London, 1865), 98.

11. Hind, *Narrative*, I, 70–2.

12. Hind, T.C. Keefer, J.G. Hodgins, Charles Robb, M.H. Perley, Rev. W. Murray, *Eighty Years' Progress of British North America* (Toronto, 1863), 88.

13. Hind, *North-West Territory*, 52, 44.

14. Hind, *Narrative*, I, 124, 134.

15. Ibid., 373.

16. Milton and Cheadle, *North-West Passage by Land*, 72.

17. *Journals of the Legislative Assembly*, 1859, app. 36.

18. *Globe*, 20 Jan. 1869, letter from Mair.

19. George V. Le Vaux, 'The Great North West—No. II', *New Dominion Monthly*, Jan. 1869, p. 226.

20. Alexander Morris, *The Hudson's Bay and Pacific Territories* (Montreal, 1859), 7–10.

21. Province of Canada, *Parliamentary Debates on the Subject of the Confederation of the British North American Provinces* (Quebec, 1865), 86.

22. Hind, *Narrative*, I, 191.

23. *Globe*, 28 May 1869, letter from Mair.

24. Milton and Cheadle, *North-West Passage by Land*, 160; David Anderson, *A Charge Delivered to the Clergy of the Diocese of Rupert's land at his Triennial Visitation, January 6, 1860* (London, 1860), 8.

25. *Nor'Wester*, 14 Feb. 1860.

26. Hind, *North-West Territory*, 68.

7   From Susanne Zeller, *Inventing Canada: Early Victorian Science and the Idea of a Transcontinental Nation* (Toronto: University of Toronto Press, 1987), 170–3, 176.

By the mid-1850s meteorological data invited attempts at generalization; nowhere was this more true than with regard to the northwestern region of British North America. Only a decade earlier the northwest had been labelled *terra incognita* on Alexander von Humboldt's isothermic maps. On these maps, lines of equal temperature deviated from the latitudinal grid and challenged the long-held assumption that temperature varied inversely and rigidly with latitude. Humboldt's isotherms measured annual as well as seasonal temperature means, facilitating the comparative climatology he pursued as part of his larger study of the *Kosmos*. By 1849 the usefulness of isolines as a climatological research tool was enhanced when Wilhelm Dove at Berlin narrowed their scope from annual to monthly means.[1]

It was not only that these developments challenged some old scientific assumptions; they reshaped still others to lend scientific authority to expansionist ideologies. One example was the idea that climate improves as one proceeds westwards on a large continental mass. This widely held notion was a colloquial version of an eighteenth-century hypothesis formulated by the German naturalist and geographer Georg Forster. Forster (1754–94) accompanied James Cook on his second circumnavigation of the globe from 1772 to 1775. In comparing the European with the North American continent, Forster noted two things. First, considerable temperature and climatic differences separated the west and east coasts of each continent. Second, the west coasts of both resembled each other in the relative mildness of their climates. Forster became Alexander von Humboldt's mentor and prodded him to investigate the significance of these observations.[2]

English immigrants who settled in eastern North America also accepted as self-evident the adage that climate improved 'by westing.' They relied on it to assess the agricultural potential of North America. It surfaced in the well-known and influential 1847 address by Robert Baldwin Sullivan entitled 'Emigration and Colonization,' which inspired a reconsideration of the possibilities of the great northwest:

> Just take the map of Canada—but that will not do—take the map of North America, and look to the westward of that glorious inland sea, Lake Superior. I will say nothing of the mineral treasures of its northern shores, or of those of our own Lake Huron, but I ask you to go with me on to the head of Lake Superior, to the boundary line: you will expect a cold journey, but I tell you the climate still improves as you go westward. At the head of Lake Superior, we ascend to the height of land, and then descend into the real garden of the British possessions, of which so few know anything.[3]

The idea attained its full ideological application in the testimony of convinced expansionists a decade later before the Canadian select committee on the HBC territories. William Logan mentioned it in his GSC report of 1845. It was accepted even by non-expansionist scientists such as J.H. Lefroy and Lt. Thomas Blakiston, the magnetic and meteorological surveyor who accompanied the Palliser expedition in 1857.[4]

Closely related to the idea that climate improves 'by westing' was the theory of climatic amelioration, a phenomenon that as we have seen, was believed to result from clearing and cultivation. Published expressions of this theory date back at least to 1544, and it was taken up again in Pierre François Xavier de Charlevoix's influential *Journal*, published in 1761. When Canada was found by early settlers to deviate from European climatic norms at comparable latitudes, the obvious differences in population and cultivation seemed reasonable explanations. Other eighteenth-century writers, including Abbé J.B. du Bos (*Réflections sur la Poésie et la Peinture* [I719]), Simon Pelloutier (*Histoire des Celtes* [1740]), and David Hume (*The History of England from the Invasion of Julius Caesar* [1754–62]), studied ancient descriptions of the climate in Germany. They theorized—from accounts that the Rhine and the Danube often froze over with ice thick enough to support invading barbarian armies and that reindeer had frequented the forests of Germany and Poland—that Europe had formerly been much colder. It seemed to follow that the cold had been diminished by clearing woods and draining swamps, improvements which permitted the rays of the sun to penetrate and warm the earth. As the soil was cultivated, the earth became more temperate.[5] It did not take long to draw what seemed an obvious analogy with the climate of North America.

The notion that the climate of Canada would be ameliorated with increased deforestation and cultivation received the stamp of authority from Edward Gibbon's *History of the Decline and Fall of the Roman Empire*, first published in 1776. Relying on Charlevoix, Hume, du Bos, and Pelloutier, Gibbon wrote: 'Canada, at this day, is an exact picture of ancient Germany. Although situated in the same parallel with the finest provinces of France and England, that country experiences the most rigorous cold.' Gibbon's *History* became a literary institution even in his own day, and his interpretation of Canadian climate was perpetuated in the minds of generations to come. Nearly every educated person in the English-speaking world read Gibbon's *History*, which fixed a certain impression of the climate of Canada.[6]

The theory of climatic progress helps to explain why early settlers attacked the forest with more than the necessary vigour. Despite William Kelly's protestations, most new settlers resembled Catharine Parr Traill, who believed that the harsh climate of the backwoods would gradually be moderated as the forests were cleared. J.H. Lefroy, as we have seen, induced

Egerton Ryerson in 1850 to organize observations at the grammar school stations with this problem in mind. As late as 1855 the chief clerk in the Crown Lands Department, William Spragge, testified before a select committee of the House of Assembly that the climate of Upper Canada had indeed, 'with the progress of improvement, and of opening up the country become wonderfully ameliorated, and seems to be approaching to the character of the same Latitude in Europe.' He inferred that a milder climate would be felt in Lower Canada under corresponding circumstances.[7]

That same year, first prize was awarded by the Paris Exhibition Committee of Canada to John Sheridan Hogan for his essay on Canada, which included the observation: 'Since 1818 the climate has greatly changed, owing principally, it is supposed, to the large clearings of the primeval forests.' Abbé J.B.A. Ferland addressed the question in his *Cours d'histoire du Canada*, published in 1861, and the Canadian Institute interviewed G.T. Kingston on the matter in 1862. In 1864 the New York *Evening Post* claimed, 'The severity of the cold season has also much abated since the forests have been cut into; the winters of New Brunswick have, it is affirmed, been shortened two months by this one cause.'[8]

Yet enough meteorological data had been accumulated and reduced by the 1850s that some observers doubted the validity of the theory of climatic progress. Ferland, Kingston, and Lefroy joined those who saw little scientific evidence that the climate of Canada had indeed improved with cultivation. When asked outright by the British parliamentary select committee on the HBC in 1857 whether his experiences in British North America could support the impression created by Gibbon, Lefroy replied in the negative.[9] . . .

While developments in the science of meteorology bestowed legitimacy upon a growing Canadian expansionist movement, they also challenged Canadians' views of themselves as a mere colonial people. The optimistic interpretation of the northwest encouraged by Hind and Palliser, combined with growing meteorological evidence by the late 1850s that Canada's climate would never resemble that of western Europe, proved fertile soil for the idea of Canada's 'northernness' as connoting an appealing manliness. As Gibbon wrote, in ancient times the rigorous northern cold of the north and 'the keen air of Germany formed the large and masculine limbs of the natives, who were, in general, of a more lofty stature than the people of the South; gave them a kind of strength better adapted to violent exertion than the patient labourer, and inspired them with constitutional bravery, which is the result of nerves and spirits.' The severity of a winter campaign 'that chilled the courage of the Roman troops, was scarcely felt by these hardy children of the North.'[10]

In 1836 Catharine Parr Traill noted 'the spirit and vigour infused into one's blood by the purity' of the winter air in Canada. Early interpretations of the 'dry, cold and elastic' northwest wind as favourable to health and longevity were borrowed from Hind by both John Sheridan Hogan and Alexander Morris for their prize essays in 1855. By 1858 Morris had constructed a full-blown image of a 'Great Britannic Empire of the North,' with its 'goodly band of Northmen from Acadia, and Canada, and the North-West, and the Columbia, and the Britain of the Pacific.' They constituted 'a noble army of hardy spirits encased in stalwart forms.' He invited Canadian audiences to 'consider the energetic character inherited by our people, which the fusion of races and the conquering from the forest of new territories' had fostered, and which climate had 'rendered hardier.' The result, he predicted, would be one nation, a 'harmonious whole— rendered the more vigorous by our northern position.'[11]

NOTES

1. Alexander von Humboldt, *Kosmos: Entwurf einer physischen Weltbeschreibung* (Stuttgaart, 1845), I: 345–7; F. Model, 'Alexander von Humboldts Isothermen', *Deutsche Hydrographische Zeitschrift* 12 (1859): 29–33; Werner Horn, 'Die Geschichte der Isarithmenkarten', *Petermanns Geographische Mitteilungen* 103/3 (1959): 225–32; A.H. Robinson and Helen M. Wallis, 'Humboldt's Map of Isothermal Lines: A Milestone in Thematic Cartography', *Cartographic Journal* 4, 2 (Dec. 1967): 119–23.

2. Georg Forster, *Kleine Schriften*, III (Leipzig, 1794), 87; von Humboldt, *Kosmos*, 345–6.

3. Toronto *Globe*, 24 Mar. 1847.

4. Province of Canada, House of Assembly, *Journals*, 1857, App. 17. GSC, R of P 1845–6; Great Britain, Parliament, House of Commons, *Report of the Select Committee on the Hudson's Bay Company* (1857), 20. On Blakiston, see 'Report on the Interior of British North America', in John Palliser, *Further Papers Relating to the Exploration of British North America* (London, 1860), 40.

5. Abbé J.B.A. Ferland, *Cours d'Histoire du Canada*, 2nd edn (Quebec, 1882), I: 507–8 and App. B; first published 1861. P.F.X. de Charlevoix, *Journal of a Voyage to North America* (London, 1761), I: 237, 240. Edward Gibbon, *The History of the Decline and Fall of the Roman Empire*, I (London, 1791), 346–7.

6. Gibbon, *Decline and Fall of the Roman Empire*, 346–8. J.B. Black, *The Art of History* (London, 1926), 143; cf. also chap. 8, note 31.

7. Kenneth Kelly, 'The Changing Attitude of Farmers to Forest in 19th-century Ontario', *Ontario Geography* 1, 8 (1974): 64–7. Catharine Parr Traill, *The Backwoods of Canada* (London, 1836), 312. PAO, Crown Lands Department, RG1, Series A14, Vol. 35, 'Statement prepared', 23 Mar. 1855, 97.

8. J. Sheridan Hogan, *Canada: An Essay to which was awarded the First Prize by the Paris Exhibition Committee of Canada* (Montreal, 1855), 53. 'The Climate of Canada', *JEUC* (May 1862): 67. 'British American Confederacy', New York

Evening Post, reprinted in *JEUC* (Dec. 1864): 182.

9. *JEUC* (May 1862): 67. Ferland preferred to believe that Canadian temperatures were linked to terrestrial magnetism and the proximity of the north magnetic pole; see *Cours d'Histoire*, 510. Great Britain, House of Commons, *Report of the Select Committee*, 17, 189.

10. Gibbon, *Decline and Fall of the Roman Empire*, I: 348–9.

11. Traill, *Backwoods of Canada*, 203; Hogan, *Canada*, 53; Alexander Morris, *Canada and Her Resources: An Essay, to which, upon a reference from the Paris Exhibition Committee of Canada, was awarded . . . second prize* (Montreal, 1855), 136–7, 143; Morris, *The Hudson's Bay and Pacific Territories* (Montreal, 1858), 89; Morris, *Nova Britannia* (Montreal, 1858), 49.

☐ The British Columbia Gold Rush

INTRODUCTION

■ The discovery of gold and the subsequent gold rushes into British Columbia starting in 1857 completely altered affairs on the Pacific slope of British North America. Instead of continuing as a fairly staid British colony, British Columbia experienced all sorts of new problems. At the same time, the discovery of gold in the mainland region, along the Thompson and Fraser rivers, produced a sudden ability for the world to connect with the west coast of British America. The California Gold Rush of 1848–9 was still fresh in everyone's mind, although when Governor James Douglas exhibited a few grains of gold from the North Thompson at dinner in the Hudson's Bay Company's mess hall, only he seemed to appreciate its importance as an instrument of 'great change and busy time'.

The amount of gold easily accessible was quite small by California standards, and the ensuing rush was a pale imitation of the American one. In the goldfields of British Columbia, however, where hundreds of American gold miners suddenly joined First Nations people in the 1850s to constitute the bulk of the early population, law and the administration of justice became serious matters. Much energy on the part of the colonial government in Victoria was spent in attempting to regulate and control the gold miners, who were often suspected of being a potential source of American influence. The Americans were more easily regulated than the colonial authorities had anticipated. Not surprisingly, law in British Columbia meant quite different things to different segments of the community. Certainly, the colonial authorities had a quite different view of it than did the miners in the camps.

Although Canadian historians have long been fascinated with political and constitutional history, they have been much slower to show much interest in the history of the law, which has recently become one of the many flourishing subfields in Canada. Despite the increasing interest in the subject of the development of law, it still probably suffers from a common perception of being both arcane and dull.

Questions for consideration

1. Why was the introduction of British justice regarded as a matter of such high priority in British Columbia in the 1850s?
2. To what extent did British justice succeed because it adapted itself to the needs and wishes of the new inhabitants?

Suggestions for further reading

Jean Barman, *The West beyond the West: A History of British Columbia*, rev. edn (Toronto: University of Toronto Press, 1996). A recent survey of the history of the province.

George Fetherling, *The Gold Crusades: A Social History of Gold Rushes, 1849–1929* (Toronto: Macmillan of Canada, 1988). A comparative study of the quest for gold in the nineteenth and early twentieth centuries.

Tina Loo, *Making Law, Order and Authority in British Columbia, 1821–1871* (Toronto: University of Toronto Press, 1994). A study focusing on the administration of justice in British Columbia.

David Williams, *The Man for a New Country: Sir Matthew Baillie Begbie* (Sidney, BC: Gray's Publishing, 1977). A biography of the 'hanging judge'.

PRIMARY DOCUMENTS

1   From Dr Carl Friesach, *Ein Ausflug nach Britisch-Columbien im Jahre 1858*, trans. and reprinted by Robie L. Reid in 'Two Narratives of the Fraser River Gold-Rush', *British Columbia Historical Quarterly* 5 (1941): 224–7.

[July 1858]

We moved at once on board the S.S. *Umatilla*, which was due to sail for Fort Hope in the early hours of the morning. Unfortunately the boat was not comfortably fitted up. It did not contain any cabins and even mattresses and blankets were lacking; the floor of the saloon

was so covered with coal dust that it was impossible to lie down without getting very dirty. Moreover the passengers, who were mostly miners, were so numerous that it was difficult to find sleeping room. Finally two of us lay down on the dining table, another under it. Another, too fastidious in the matter of cleanliness, spent the whole night sitting on a bench.
. . .

The next morning we were awakened early by the noise of the machinery, but our departure was postponed until 8 a.m. by a thick fog which perceptibly lowered the temperature. When the fog lifted we had a wonderful panorama of the Cascade mountains [which appeared to be] scarcely a half mile distant with their strange jagged peaks and the ice-clad Mount Baker. We reached the mountains about ten o'clock, and from that time on we travelled through the most wonderful mountain landscape.

The river runs mostly through a double abrupt wall more than a thousand feet high and follows a tortuous course through the rocks. The mountains covered with tall forests frequently tower up above snowline and on the higher peaks are glaciers, some of which run down in ravines almost to the river. We covered only a small distance during the afternoon on account of the swift current which got stronger as we neared our goal. In the evening we landed at a point where the river runs into a half circle, opposite a magnificent glacier, and made fast for the night.

Some of the passengers had the gold fever so badly that they felt they must search the sands on the shore, but were disappointed when they did not find the smallest dust in their pan. They were still busy washing the sand when a few Indians came down stream in canoes, and in spite of the cold wind their only clothing was a woollen blanket which sometimes fell from their shoulders with the exertion of paddling.

On September 9 we started at dawn. It was a cold and clear morning. Unfortunately we were prevented from enjoying the beautiful landscape by a strong wind, which, blowing in the direction of our course, caused the sparks from the smokestack to fall all about us, burning holes in our hats and clothes.

The shores began to show some animation. Indian wigwams were alternating with the tents of the miners, of whom we encountered quite a number on the sand banks. At 8 a.m. we found ourselves only 200 feet distant from the landing at Fort Hope, but the current was so strong that our ship took a full half hour to reach the landing.

Fort Hope is a tent city sheltering a few hundred on the left bank of the Fraser. . . . The valley is thickly wooded and is watered by two creeks which flow into the Fraser near the village. There is a Hudson Bay Company's Fort near the village. Sir James Douglas, Governor of Vancouver Island, was staying there at the time, during a tour of inspection of the upper Fraser Valley. . . .

As soon as we landed we went to pay our respects to the Governor. When he heard that we could only spend three or four days on our trip, he recommended us to visit Fort Yale and, if possible, to go as far as the Grand Canyon, and he gave us a letter of introduction to the officer commanding at the Fort.

We immediately prepared to proceed on our trip. We had been advised to use an Indian canoe going up-stream, because the Indians were the most reliable guides on account of their knowledge of the river and their experience in canoe work. We were, however, unable to secure Indian guides and had to be satisfied with American rivermen.

The boat could comfortably seat 8–10 people, and there were, including the two boatmen, only six of us, but a forge-bellows, which had to be taken to Fort Yale, took up most of the room in the boat.

At first we rowed along the left bank, where the current was not so strong, and fair progress made during the first hour. . . . We soon reached a bend of the river where the current was so strong that oars were useless, and part of the company were compelled to disembark and tow the canoe by a rope, while others stayed in the canoe to prevent it from being damaged by the submerged rocks. . . .

On arriving at Fort Yale . . . we went to the village to call on the officer in command . . . [who] after perusing the letter of introduction given us by the Governor, promised to let us have some Indian guides as soon as possible who would take us up the river to the Canyon. . . .

Our urgent need for food induced us to cut the interview short. As we wandered among the tents we noticed a large cabin, displaying the sign, 'American Restaurant.' The only table was occupied by three wild-looking men, one of whom was recognized by one of my friends as 'Captain Pocahontas.' In spite of our repugnance, we were compelled to sit at the table, and while awaiting our food, they talked with us and invited us to drink with them, but we refused on the pretext that we drank nothing but water. They were quite insulted at our refusal, and it looked as if we were going to be mixed up in a quarrel; but we remained calm and casually showed our weapons, and perhaps, because they had more enemies than friends among the bystanders, they departed, swearing as they went.

The Gold Rush had attracted a large number of adventurers of the worst kind, and a number of bad characters whom the vigilance committee of San Francisco had sent away were to be found at Fort Yale in 1856 [sic; 1858]. . . .

Though our meal consisted only of old fish, dried salmon, and almost undrinkable coffee, we had to pay several dollars for it; nevertheless we enjoyed it after the hard day's work. We then took a stroll around the camp, in the course of which we noticed a wonderful display of insects which decorated the walls of the tents. The place showed, at that time, great animation and might have contained three thousand inhabitants. The majority of these lived in tents, a few only in frame cabins.

It would have been difficult to find in one place a greater mixture of different nationalities. Americans were undoubtedly in the majority—California, especially had sent a large contingent. Then followed Germans, French, and Chinese. Next came Italians, Spaniards, Poles, etc. The feminine population consisted of only six. Many Indians lived in the neighbourhood, who on the whole were on friendly footing with the Whites. In spite of the rough life and the privations arising from such a life in a new land, almost all had a healthy and happy appearance. The tents stood in groups, partly on the river bank and partly in the bush. The river, which here flows between a double wall of very high and rugged mountains, runs with many windings and whirlpools and makes navigation very dangerous. Hardly a day passes without some life being lost in the strong current. . . . As we waited for the Indian guides we resolved to visit Hill's Bar. A canoe took us across the river, and we reached the camp by a three-quarter hour walk along the bank. We found the river bank covered with miners for the distance of over a mile. Some of them were digging in the sand, others working at their rockers, others at their sluices. A sluice is a trough made of thin boards, a klafter[1] or so long, built on a slight incline; the gold-bearing sand is piled up at the end of the trough and is slowly washed down with the water, and the particles of gold contained in the sand are deposited in the bottom of the trough where they are retained by various devices. These consist mostly of a number of asperities and little hollows, amalgamated copper plates, and little depressions filled with quicksilver. When a certain amount of sand has been washed down the trough the bottom is carefully searched for gold particles, the quicksilver is distilled in iron retorts, the gold remaining in the vessel in the form of a shapeless mass called granulation. Experience has shown that this process derives a much larger quantity of gold than the rocker. However, the establishment of a sluice entails quite an expense; small partnerships, of six or eight partners, being generally formed to put one up. I was astonished at the enormous amount of gold which was found at Hill's Bar. Nearly all of those we spoke to reported very satisfactory results. A large number considered $30 per day an average production and assured us that they had taken as much as $80 to $100 on exceptionally good days. However, there are others who obtain only $4 to $5 a day, a few feet away from the lucky ones. There is hardly a more hazardous form of work than gold washing. The test of the pan often gives a good result when the soil is later on found to be hardly worth working. . . .

NOTE

1. A German measure of 2.07 yards.

2   Letter of Charles Major, 20 Sept. 1859, in *Daily Globe*, Toronto, 2 January 1860, reprinted in Reid, 'Two Narratives', 229-31.

[From *The Daily Globe*, Toronto, Canada West, January 2, 1860.]
NEWS FROM BRITISH COLUMBIA. (From the Sarnia *Observer*.)
The following letter recently received by a person in this neighborhood, from the writer who is at present in British Columbia, was handed to us for perusal. As it contains much valuable and reliable information in reference to the country, we requested permission to publish it, which was at once granted. We therefore lay the most important portions of the letter before our readers, without further apology, satisfied that it will be read with interest by all:—

Fort Hope, Frazer River
Sept. 20th, 1859

Dear Sir:—I am afraid you will think I had forgot my promise,—but I wanted to know something about the country before writing to you. In the first place, do not think that I have taken a dislike to the country because I am not making money; the dislike is general all over the country. To give you anything like a correct idea of it would take more paper than I have small change to purchase, and more time than I could spare, and then it would only be commenced.

The country is not what it was represented to be. There is no farming land in British Columbia, as far as I can learn, except a very small portion joining Washington Territory, and on Vancouver's Island, where there is one valley of 20,000 acres; but that cannot be sold until Col. Moody's friends come out from the old country, and get what they want.

It never can be a *place*, because there is nothing to support it, except the mines, and just as soon as they are done the place goes down completely, for there is absolutely nothing to keep it up; and I tell you the truth the mines are falling off very fast. There is nothing in this country but mines—and very small pay for that; they are you may say, used up. We have been making two, three and four dollars per day, but it would not last more than two or three days; and so you would spend that before you would find more. There has been great excitement about Fort Alexander, three hundred miles above this, and also about Queen Charlotte's Island. They have both turned out another humbug like this place. A party arrived here yesterday from Alexander, and they are a pitiful looking lot. They are what the Yankees call *dead broke*. They have been six hundred miles up the river. When they got down here they had no shoes to their feet. Some had pieces of shirt and trowsers, but even these were pinned together with small sharp sticks; and some had the rim of an old hat, and some the crown. They had nothing to eat for one week, and not one cent in money. This is gold mining for you!

I expect the Frazer River fever has cooled down by this time, at least I hope so; for I do pity the poor wretches that come out here to beg. They can do that at home; as for making money, that is out of the question. Since we came here (to use the miners' term,) we have been making grub; and those who can do that, think they are doing well. If there are any making arrangements to come to this place, let them take a fool's advice *and stay at home*. I would just about as soon hear that anyone belonging to me was dead, as to hear they had started to come here. They say it wants a man with capital to make money here; but a man with money in Canada will double it quicker than he will here. And if I, or any other, was to work as hard and leave [live] as meanly, I could make more money in Canada than I can here. Since we have been on the River we have worked from half-past two and three o'clock in the morning till nine and ten o'clock at night, (you can see the sun twenty hours out of the twenty-four in the summer season.)—and lived on beans! If that is not working, I don't know what it is. Besides this you go home to your shanty at night, tired and wet, and have to cook your beans before you can eat them. And what is this all for? For *gold* of course; but when you wash up at night, you may realize 50 cents, perhaps $1.

There have been some rich spots struck on this river, but they were very scarce, and they are all worked out; and the miners are leaving the river every day, satisfied there is nothing to be made. But now that I am in the country I will remain for a year or so, and if nothing better turns up by that time, I think I will be perfectly satisfied. I have met with some that I was acquainted with, and it is amusing to see those who felt themselves a little better than their neighbors at home, come here and get out of money, and have to take the pick and shovel, perhaps to drag firewood out of the woods and sell it, or make pack-mules of themselves to get a living. I do not mean to say that it is so all over the Colony, but it is from one end of Fraser River to the other. I dare anyone to contradict what I say; and I have good reason to believe it is as bad all over the country. I saw a patch of oats here the other day. They were out in head, only four inches in height, yellow as ochre, and *not thick enough on the ground to be neighbours*. Vegetables and other things are as poor in the proportion; and as for the climate, it is just as changeable as in Canada, if not more so. I can't say much about the climate on Vancouver's Island, but I think it is rather better.

I met T.G., the carpenter, from Sarnia, who left there about a year ago. He went round the Horn, and he was ten months and fifteen days in coming here. He is cutting saw logs making a little over grub. He says he is going to write to the Sarnia *Observer*, and give this place a cutting up! There are a great many Canadians here, and they would be glad to work for their board. A man could not hire out to work a day if he was starving. I have seen some parties from California; they say times are very hard there. There are just three in our party now, H.H., J.R., and myself. There were two of the H's; one was taken sick and had to leave the river; he is in Victoria, and is quite recovered again; has been there two months, and has not got a day's work yet. I was very sick myself when I just came here, but am quite healthy now, and so fat I can hardly see to write. The rest are quite well.

The Indians are not very troublesome at the mines; they are kept down pretty well. They are very numerous here and on the Island, the lowest degraded set of creatures I ever saw.

It is estimated that the number of miners who make over wages, is one in five hundred; and the number that do well in the mines is one in a thousand. So you see it is a very small proportion. If you know anyone that wants to spend money, why, this is just the place. Anyone bringing a family here would require a small fortune to support them in this horrible place, hemmed in by mountains on all sides, and these covered with snow all the year.

I have lived in a tent since I came up the river, and I have to lie on the ground before the fire and write; it gives a very poor light, so excuse the writing. It has been raining here steady one week, and the mountains are all covered with snow; for when it rains here it is snowing upon the mountains. It is a wild looking place. You will please tell our folks you hear from me, and that we are all well. I will write to some of them in about two weeks or so. I have wrote five letters already, but I have not heard from any of them; so many letters go astray in coming here and going from this place, that perhaps they do not get them at all. Give my respects to old friends, and tell them to be contented and stay at home.

I remain, yours truly
CHARLES MAJOR.

HISTORICAL INTERPRETATIONS

3 From T.A. Rickard, 'Indian Participation in the Gold Discoveries', *British Columbia Historical Quarterly* 2 (Jan. 1938), 3–10.

Numerous descriptions of the early gold discoveries in British Columbia have made the story familiar to those interested in the subject. No episode in the history of the American Northwest has been recounted so often, because its romantic aspect has appealed irresistibly to our people. Nevertheless there remains an important feature of the gold-rush in 1858 that has been overlooked, namely, the part played by the indigenes of the region, the Indians, in the discovery of the gold and in the mining operations that ensued.

The search for gold in our Province was incited by the successful exploitation of auriferous river-beds in California. The critical discovery, by James W. Marshall, at Coloma, on January 24, 1848, caused a tremendous rush to the diggings along the western slope of the Sierra Nevada, and aroused the belief that other rich deposits of gravel might be found elsewhere in the region adjacent to the Pacific Coast. It is interesting, therefore, to note how the extensive occurrence of gold-bearing alluvium was signalized by successive discoveries that served to link the productive diggings at Coloma, on the south fork of the American River, with those on the Thompson and Fraser Rivers in British Columbia. The first advance was to Oroville, on the Feather River, in 1848; then to Reading's Bar on the Trinity River in 1849; next came Scott's Bar on the Klamath in 1850. Gold was found in the sea-beach off Gold Bluff in the same year, and in the sand at the mouth of the Coquille River, in southern Oregon, in 1853. Meanwhile the diggings on Jackson Creek, also in Oregon, marked another step northward. In 1853 George McClellan found gold plentifully when engaged in surveying a military road in what is now northern Washington, through the Cascade Mountains from Walla Walla to Fort Steilacoom, on the coast near Admiralty Inlet. Gold was discovered also at that time during the exploration of a route for the Northern Pacific Railway, on the Similkameen River, which rises not far from Hope, on the Fraser River, and joins the Okanagan at the International Boundary. Then, in 1855, gold was found by a 'servant' of the Hudson's Bay Company near Fort Colville,[1] in the valley of the Columbia River, just south of the Canadian border.

James Cooper, testifying before the select committee on the Hudson's Bay Company, in London, in 1857, linked this discovery of gold at Fort Colville with the subsequent finding of it on Thompson's River.[2] George M. Dawson, the distinguished Canadian geologist, was of the same opinion. Writing in 1889, he says: 'It seems certain that the epoch-making discovery of gold in British Columbia, was the direct result of the Colville excitement. Indians from Thompson River, visiting a woman of their tribe who was married to a French Canadian at Walla Walla, spread the report that gold, like that found at Colville occurred also in their country, and in the summer or autumn of 1857, four or five Canadians and half-breeds crossed over to the Thompson, and succeeded in finding workable placers at Nicoamen, on that river, nine miles above its mouth. On the return of these prospectors the news of the discovery of gold spread rapidly.'[3]

Thus it is evident that information derived from the Indians lured the prospectors northward into British Columbia; but before proceeding with the sequential story of gold discovery in our Province it must be noted that an unheralded find of gold was made by the famous botanist, David Douglas, at a date long precedent to the epochal discoveries in California and Australia, in 1848 and 1851, respectively. Captain W. Colquhoun Grant, of Sooke, in a paper presented to the Royal Geographical Society in 1859, says: 'There can be little doubt that it [gold] exists in the mountains of New Caledonia, to the northward of where men are now looking for it, and also a little to the southward, where several years ago David Douglass [sic], the eminent botanist, found enough whereof to make a seal. This occurred on the shores of Lake Okanagan. . . .'[4] No doubt the discovery was made at the mouth of a creek that entered the lake. Douglas was there in 1833.[5] He was killed in July of 1834, when in the Hawaiian Islands, and, as he did not go to England during the interval, no word of the discovery reached the outside world. At that date, moreover, even to a scientist such as Douglas, the finding of gold would not suggest the portentous consequences that might ensue from the successful development of profitable mines. The same inability to foresee such consequences was shown by officials in California and Australia when the finding of gold was made known in those regions several years before the discoveries that started the world-wide stampedes to the diggings.

The earliest gold discovery in British Columbia that aroused public interest was made by an Indian on one of the Queen Charlotte Islands. Richard Blanshard, the first Governor of Vancouver Island, reported to Earl Grey, the Colonial Secretary, in August of 1850, that he had seen 'a very rich specimen of gold ore, said to have been brought by the Indians of Queen Charlotte's Island.'[6] In the following year, 1851, an Indian woman found a nugget on the beach of Moresby Island. After a part of it had been cut off, it was taken to Fort Simpson, where it passed by trade into the hands of the Hudson's Bay factor at that place. The nugget, as received, weighed about 5 ounces. Later it was sent to the headquarters of the Hudson's Bay Company at Fort Victoria. On March 29, 1851, Governor Blanshard informed Earl Grey: 'I have heard that fresh specimens of gold have been obtained from the Queen Charlotte islanders; I have not seen them myself, but they are reported to be very rich.'[7] The Hudson's Bay Company sent the ship *Huron* to Mitchell Harbour for the purpose of investigation. Some gold-quartz was brought back to Fort Victoria and stimulated further interest in the discovery. In July and again in October, 1851, the brigantine *Una* was sent thither by the Hudson's Bay Company and returned with information concerning a quartz vein that was 7 inches wide and traceable for 80 feet. It was reported to contain 'twenty-five per cent of gold in some places,'[8] which indicates specimen stuff, goodly to look upon. Some of this quartz was blasted and then shipped, despite the interference of the Indians. The *Una* was lost on her second return voyage. Then the *Orbit*, an American ship, which was on the rocks off Esquimalt, was bought by the Company, repaired, and renamed the *Recovery*. She was sent north with thirty miners in addition to her crew, these miners having agreed to share their luck. Three months were spent in getting a cargo of ore, which was taken to England and eventually yielded a sum of money giving the miners $30 per month for their labour.

When these facts were noised abroad, not only at Fort Victoria but at San Francisco, several vessels sailed from that Californian port for Mitchell Harbour. The deposit had been nearly exhausted and the Americans soon left, disappointed. Later the American ship *Susan Sturges* arrived and the captain collected some of the ore discarded by the *Una* expedition. This shipment was sold for $1,400 at San Francisco. A second voyage by the same ship ended in disaster, for she was captured and the crew made prisoners

by the Indians at Masset, on Graham Island. The American gold-seekers were rescued by a party sent thither on the Hudson's Bay Company's steamer *Beaver*. Altogether about $20,000 was taken from the little quartz vein at Mitchell Harbour, known also as Gold Harbour and Mitchell Inlet.[9]

We have seen how soon the miniature rush to these northern islands came to a dismal end, because but little gold was found and the occurrence of the precious metal proved to be extremely patchy; nevertheless, the event is of historic importance because it made the few people then on our western coast aware of the possibility of developing profitable mines. It made them gold-conscious. Moreover, it was the means of establishing an important precedent, for, in 1853, James Douglas, the second Governor of Vancouver Island, asserted the regalian right to any gold deposits that might be discovered. This action on his part proved deeply significant.

The regalian right, or royal claim, to deposits of precious metal is traditional; it is a kingly perquisite that comes from the days of the Roman emperors. In the sixteenth century the Spanish king's share was fixed at a fifth of the gold or silver obtained by his subjects, chiefly in Mexico and Peru. In England the doctrine of *fodinae regales*, or mines royal, was revived by Henry III (1216–1272) and was well established in the reign of Queen Elizabeth. It is sustained by Blackstone in his *Commentaries*, under date of 1765.[10] In modern days, the regalian right was asserted when gold was discovered in Australia, and was therefore well fortified by precedent when invoked by Governor Douglas.

At that time James Douglas had become the Governor of Vancouver Island while still the Chief Factor, at Victoria, of the Hudson's Bay Company. The proclamation in 1853, which asserted the rights of the Crown and exacted a licence fee from the gold-miners, was instigated by Sir John Pakington, the Colonial Secretary in London. He, in September, 1852, instructed Douglas 'to take immediate steps for the protection of British interests against the depredations of Indians, or the unwarranted intrusions of foreigners, on the territory of the Queen,'[11] and forthwith issued a commission making Douglas Lieutenant-Governor of the Queen Charlotte Islands. Whereupon, in March of 1853, Governor Douglas issued the proclamation asserting the right of the Crown to any gold found in 'the Colony of Queen Charlotte's Island,' and followed this action in April by fixing a miner's licence fee of ten shillings per month, payable in advance, and to be obtained only at Fort Victoria.

We may note that the earliest gold to come within the cognizance of the Hudson's Bay officers was brought to them by the Indians. This is not surprising. Gold was usually the first metal to become known to primitive man. He saw the shining substance on the edge of the river-beds that were his highways through the wilderness. Gold does not corrode or tarnish, it is beautiful, and it is so soft as readily to be shaped by hammering with a stone. Primitive man at an early stage of his existence began to use the metal for making ornaments, such as ear-plugs and bangles. When the European came among the Indians on our western coast, he wore rings and watch-chains, his women wore ear-rings and bracelets, all made of gold; the natives therefore saw readily that the white people set a high value on gold, and they inferred correctly that if they brought it to the trader he would be willing to barter his goods for the precious metal. This led the Indians to search for it and to bring it to the Hudson's Bay Company's posts. Moreover, the natives resented the trespass upon their domain, strange as it may seem to some people, and annoyed the gold-seekers that came to the Queen Charlotte discovery; they stole the tools of the miners, and the gold as well. Chief Trader W.H. McNeill, who accompanied the *Una* expedition, reported to Douglas:—

I am sorry to inform you that we were obliged to leave off blasting, and quit the place for Fort Simpson, on account of the annoyance we experienced from the natives. They arrived in large numbers, say 30 canoes, and were much pleased to see us on our first arrival. When they saw us blasting and turning out the gold in such large quantities, they became excited and commenced depredations on us, stealing the tools, and taking at least one-half of the gold that was thrown out by the blast. They would lie concealed until the report was heard, and then make a rush for the gold; a regular scramble between them and our men would then take place; they would take our men by the legs, and hold them away from the gold. Some blows were struck on these occasions. The Indians drew their knives on our men often. The men who were at work at the vein became completely tired and disgusted at their proceedings, and came to me on three different occasions and told me that they would not remain any longer to work the gold; that their time was lost to them, as the natives took one-half of the gold thrown out by the blast, and blood would be shed if they continued to work at the digging; that our force was not strong or large enough to work and fight also. They were aware they could not work on shore after hostility had commenced, therefore I made up my mind to leave the place, and proceed to this place [Fort Simpson].

The natives were very jealous of us when they saw that we could obtain gold by blasting; they had no idea that so much could be found below the surface; they said that it was not good that we should take all the gold away; if we did so, that they would not have anything to trade with other vessels should any arrive. In fact, they told us to be off.[12]

McNeill had with him only eleven men, a force much too small to discipline the Indians; moreover, it was the policy of the Hudson's Bay Company not to antagonize the natives, with whom they traded for furs. Therefore any sort of lethal contest was avoided.

The discoveries of gold on the mainland, like the one made on Moresby Island, must be credited to the Indians; it was they, and not any canny Scot or enterprising American, that first found the gold on the Thompson and Fraser Rivers, or first proceeded to gather it for the purpose of trade. The Hudson's Bay agent at Kamloops, on the Thompson River, obtained gold from the Indians as early as 1852, and similar gold came, in course of trade with the natives, to other posts of the fur company. In the records of the fur trade, as kept at Fort Victoria, it is stated that 3¾ ounces of gold were included in the takings at Fort Kamloops in 1856.[13] 'Gold,' says Douglas in his memoranda under date of 1860, 'was first found on Thompson's River by an Indian, a quarter of a mile below Nicoamen. He is since dead. The Indian was taking a drink out of the river. Having no vessel he was quaffing from the stream when he perceived a shining pebble which he picked up and it proved to be gold. The whole tribe forthwith began to collect the glittering metal.'[14] This probably was in 1852. Roderick Finlayson, Chief Factor at Fort Victoria, says that gold was discovered by the Indians in crevices of the rocks on the banks of the Thompson. Donald McLean, the trader in charge at Kamloops, inspected the gold-bearing ground and then sent down to Victoria for some iron spoons to be used by the Indians for the purpose of extricating the nuggets from the crevices in the rocky beds of the creeks. The spoons were sent, as requested, and McLean was instructed to encourage the natives in searching for gold and using it for trade.[15]

News of the important discovery at Colville reached Douglas in the spring of 1856. He was not at all secretive about the finding of gold, and on April 16 reported to the Colonial Secretary as follows: 'I hasten to communicate for the information of her Majesty's Government a discovery of much importance, made known to me by Mr. Angus McDonald, Clerk in charge of Fort Colville, one of the Hudson's Bay Company's Trading Posts on the Upper Columbia District. That gentleman reports, in a letter dated on the 1st of March last, that gold has been found in considerable quantities within the British territory, on the Upper Columbia, and that he is moreover of opinion that valuable deposits of gold will be found in many other parts of the country; he also states that the *daily earnings* of persons then employed in digging gold were ranging from £2 to £8 [$10 to $40] for each man. . . . Several interesting experiments in gold washing have been lately made in this colony, with a degree of success that will no doubt lead to further attempts for the discovery of the precious metal.'[16] In October, 1856, Douglas reported further that the extent of the gold deposits was as yet undetermined, but that he took a sanguine view of their possible value. The amount of gold produced was not known, but some 220 ounces had been received at Victoria from the Upper Columbia.[17]

NOTES

1. Formerly spelled Colvile, after Andrew Colvile, a Governor of the Hudson's Bay Company.
2. *Report from the Select Committee on the Hudson's Bay Company* (London, 1857), pp. 205, 207.
3. George M. Dawson, *The Mineral Wealth of British Columbia* (Montreal, 1889), p. 18R (Geological Survey of Canada).
4. W.C. Grant, 'Remarks on Vancouver Island', *Journal of the Royal Geographical Society* 31 (1861): 213.
5. *Oregon Historical Quarterly* 6 (1905): 309.
6. *Correspondence relative to the Discovery of Gold in Queen Charlotte's Island* (London, 1853), p. 1. (Cited hereafter as *Queen Charlotte's Island Papers*.)
7. Ibid.
8. Dawson, *The Mineral Wealth of British Columbia*, p. 17R.
9. Ibid., p. 18R.
10. T.A. Rickard, *Man and Metals* (New York, 1932),

pp. 606, 617.

11. *Queen Charlotte's Island Papers*, p. 13.

12. Ibid., second series (London, 1853), p. 8.

13. Columbia District and New Caledonia Fur Trade Returns (MS. in Archives of B.C.).

14. James Douglas, Private Papers, First Series, p. 78 (transcript in Archives of B.C.).

15. Roderick Finlayson, *History of Vancouver Island and the Northwest Coast*, p. 43 (transcript in Archives of B.C.).

16. *Correspondence relative to the Discovery of Gold in the Fraser's River District* (London, 1858), p. 5.

17. Ibid., p. 6.

4   From Margaret Orsmby, *British Columbia: A History* (Toronto: Macmillan of Canada, 1958), 157–61.

. . . For [Governor] Douglas, every day since April, 1858, had been filled with activity: his correspondence with the Colonial Office, as he said, had been carried on in the midst of 'varied cares and anxieties'. For months he was chained to his desk, and only twice did he feel justified in stealing time away from his office to inspect the gold-fields. But both trips were necessary, for many disturbing rumours had reached Victoria concerning conditions at the mines, and he needed first-hand information in order to plan constructively.

From the tour which he made of the mining-fields early in the summer, he obtained the impression that gold had succeeded furs as the new staple and that it would no longer be possible to maintain the Hudson's Bay Company's position on the Mainland. 'Fort Yale', he noted in his journal, 'a great site for a town, yields large sums of Money, probably a million before 6 months are over'.[1] To maintain peace, he appointed both English and Indian magistrates; to ensure the collection of licence fees, he selected local revenue officers; and a little later, he inaugurated the office of gold commissioner.

He returned to Victoria convinced that the problem of transportation and supply would have to be tackled immediately. To provide facilities for the miners and to prevent trade taking the direction of the Columbia River, he modified the offer which the Pacific Mail Steamship Company had declined and extended it to other steamship companies. They found the terms acceptable, and two side-wheel steamers which had been used on the Sacramento River immediately applied for sufferances.

On June 6, one of these, the *Surprise*, made the first steamboat ascent from Fort Langley to Fort Hope. Before the season ended, she made fifteen return trips from Victoria, sometimes carrying a capacity load of 500 passengers. After expending the greatest effort to fight the current, the little *Sea Bird* also reached Fort Hope in June, but her return voyage ended in disaster. Far more suited than either of these for navigating the river was the *Umatilla*, a stern-wheeler from the Columbia River, which on July 21 successfully reached Yale, the head of navigation. In her five-hour struggle against the stream from Fort Hope to Fort Yale, the miners urged her on with shouts of joy and the firing of guns and pistols. At Fort Yale, she received an enthusiastic reception, and then, after her captain had entertained 'a number of the principal inhabitants' at a banquet, commenced her first down trip. Like 'a streak of chain lightning', she returned to Fort Hope in fifty-one minutes.[2]

Almost before Douglas knew it, an American monopoly of transportation on the Fraser River was substituted for the Hudson's Bay Company's control. Although more sufferances were issued to American boats, he put both the *Beaver* and the *Otter* on the run in order to provide sufficient competition to force down freight and passenger rates.

On July 25, the *Umatilla* left Fort Langley with eighty passengers and a special correspondent of the *Victoria Gazette* for a trial run of Harrison River and Harrison Lake. Granular gold had now been found near the Forks (soon to be renamed Lytton) and a few miners were using the overland route by Seton and Anderson Lakes to the upper Fraser which A.C. Anderson had discovered in 1846. After the *Umatilla* established the navigability of this waterway, Douglas laid plans for opening an access route by way of the chain of lakes to Lillooet. When the steamer retraced her route in August, she carried 260 men who had entered into a contract with him to build the Harrison–Lillooet Road.

This, the first highway project in British Columbia, was launched for the dual purpose of solving the problem of communication and easing the burden of unemployment. The waters of the Fraser River had already started to rise in the spring freshet while Douglas was at Fort Yale in early June, but at that time the miners were still working their rockers. The scale gold was almost at the surface; no excavation was deeper than two feet. Throughout June and July, however, and into August, high water put an end to work on the bars; with disgust, 3,900 miners returned to San Francisco in August to denounce 'the Fraser River Humbug'. On their way homeward, they swarmed into Victoria, alarming the inhabitants by their unruly behaviour. On the night of July 31, Douglas was forced to call on the men of the Boundary Commission to provide assistance in putting down a riot. They arrived on H.M.S. *Plumper*, a man-of-war then engaged in a survey of the coast. 'It was very exciting when we came in sight of the town & the order was given to load & the ship's guns run out & cleared for action', one of the officers wrote; 'we had to disembark in boats & if there had been any resistance there would have been very few of us not knocked over. Luckily however we found that after rescuing a prisoner & knocking over the sheriff the mob had dispersed. . . .'[3]

To withdraw a restless element from the Colony and at the same time to improve internal communications on the Mainland, Douglas laid his plans for constructing a road, 'though passable, in the first instance, only for pack horses',[4] through the mountain barrier north of Fort Yale. On hearing of his intention, 500 miners came forward to volunteer their services. The project became a co-operative venture: each of the miners deposited $25 with the Governor as security of good conduct and agreed to work without pay. Douglas promised to supply transportation and food, and to repay the deposit in the form of provisions delivered at Victoria prices at the commencement of the road. On August 5, the first party left Victoria under the command of A.C. Anderson, and the work of cutting the trail commenced on August 9. Two days later, the miners approached Anderson with the request that the southern terminus of the road be named in his honour, but he 'declared that if any compliment were meant, no gentleman was better entitled to it than His Excellency, the Governor; and he named the place Port Douglas, which was responded to by three hearty cheers for Governor Douglas, and three more for himself'.[5] Many things went wrong after this, and it was not until the middle of October that most of the trail was completed; at best, it provided but difficult travel for mule trains. And poor as it was, the cost of providing transportation and supplying food for the workmen had amounted to £14,000.

Douglas's second visit to the mines was as productive of action as his first. When news reached Victoria of an outbreak of serious trouble above Yale, where the Indians were attempting to expel the miners from the diggings, the Governor immediately requisitioned marines and sappers from the Boundary Commission and started out in their company on August 30. By the time he reached Fort Hope, order had been restored by the miners themselves, who had organized themselves into military units, taken some punitive action, and then entered into treaties with the Indians. But it struck Douglas that he 'had never before seen a crowd of more ruffianly looking men'. When he addressed them, however, 'they were profuse in acclamations, and did, at my command, give three cheers for the Queen, but evidently with a bad grace. There is a strong American feeling among them, and they will require constant watching, until the English element preponderates in the Country'.[6]

There were a few California desperadoes in the area, and Douglas decided not only to show them that he represented British authority, but that criminal acts would be punished. To bring a murderer to trial, he set up a temporary court at Fort Hope. George Pearkes, the Crown Solicitor of Vancouver Island, presided over it, American

miners gave testimony, and in the absence of a gaol, the murderer was sentenced to transportation. Douglas then organized a police force, appointed special constables to be stationed at Yale and also set up there a temporary court for trying offences. The miners themselves spoke of the necessity of the appointment of additional magistrates, and he was much gratified to learn that 'the general feeling is in favor of English rule on Fraser's River, the people having a degree of confidence in the sterling uprightness and integrity of Englishmen which they do not entertain for their own countrymen'.[7]

NOTES

1. [James Douglas], Diary of Gold Discovery on Fraser's River in 1858. Entry for June 1, 1858. Provincial Archives of British Columbia (PABC), Private Papers of Sir James Douglas, First series, Transcript, p. 63.

2. Alexander Begg, *History of British Columbia* (Toronto, 1894), p. 282.

3. Wilson Journal. Entry for July 31, 1858.

4. Douglas to Stanley, July 26, 1858. PABC, Van-

couver Island, Governor Douglas, Despatches, 1855–1859.

5. *Victoria Gazette*, August 17, 1858.

6. Douglas to Merivale, private, October 29, 1858. PABC, PRO Transcripts, CO 60, vol. 1, part 1, 1858, pp. 247–8.

7. Douglas to Lytton, September 29, 1858. Ibid., pp. 124–5.

5   From David Ricardo Williams, 'The Administration of Criminal and Civil Justice in the Mining Camps and Frontier Communities of British Columbia', in L. Knafla, ed., *Law and Justice in a New Land: Essays in Western Canadian History* (Toronto: Carswell, 1986), 217-20.

Mining Camp Justice American Style

Although Americans formed the largest fraction of the new arrivals, the population mix was remarkably heterogeneous, many of the Americans themselves possessing varied ethnic backgrounds. Many of these Americans had been through the California gold rush, and their knowledge of mining methods and familiarity with mining regulations lent an element of stability to the shifting population. Their desire to make money at mining by lawful methods was

not understood by many colonial observers, who expressed surprise at the generally peaceable nature of miners and their amenability to constituted authority.[1] The American miners were encouraged to adopt that attitude by their own countryman, John Nugent, who counselled them to show 'a decent conformity with local regulations', and to display both 'obedience to the laws' and a 'proper show of respect for the authorities by whom those laws are administered'.[2]

In each mining camp could be found hard

workers and layabouts, honest men and rogues, Christians and atheists, respectable women and prostitutes. Before a camp developed into a permanent town (if it did at all), the common characteristic was the frenetic activity of the residents. The prospect of gold running out gave an urgency to all activity: one must recover what gold there was as soon as possible. One's living habits had the same urgency. Judge Begbie penned an amusing aphorism about the habits of mind of the miners:

> The miner with gold dust conceals his riches, in order to avoid plunder—the miner who has none pretends to be rich in order to obtain credit.[3]

Like all aphorisms, this one is only partly true. Many successful miners squandered their money publicly, and many failures obtained no credit and left their claims. But the attitudes of the miners, particularly the Californians, became important in the development of both civil and criminal law in the colony. The imposition of English civil law accorded fairly easily with what they had been used to in the informal regulation of mining activity. In California, in the absence of governmental statute (until 1866), self-government was the norm, and making money was dependent upon stable and just self-regulation by the miners. There, as soon as miners established themselves at a gold-bearing site, they enacted rules which were intended to have the force of law. Whether in fact they had the force of law depended upon the integrity and single-minded purpose of those chosen to administer them. The typical California experience was to elect a three-man mining committee in whose hands rested decisions over the ownership and extent of claims. Although there were differences in detail from camp to camp, there were principles recognized by all: ensuring that all claims were of uniform size, laying down the conditions of use or occupation, recording all claims, and insisting that the record was conclusive.[4]

The size of claims was governed by the lev-elness or steepness of the banks of a creek. Regulations were passed to dictate for what period of time a claim could be left unattended without losing entitlement, either through illness or because the claim-holder had gone to the nearest town on a bender; the overt leaving of mining tools for a period of days would ensure continued title. One could stake and have recognized a 10-foot-wide cross-section of an auriferous creek, but how did one determine the reference points? From where did one start? And if there were outcroppings into the bed of the creek, were they to be counted as part of the bed over which the claim extended, or should the 10 feet be extended through the workable sections of the creek to compensate for the unyielding rock intrusion?

These were problems of a civil nature, frequently leading to disputes between individuals, not only in California, but also in British Columbia. But what of behaviour dangerous to the peace of the community? The mining camps in California evolved an efficient system of criminal law which worked, generally speaking, without undue harshness, except perhaps to Indians and Chinese who were considered by the standards of the time as persons not deserving equal protection before the law. In the California mining camps, rules governing potential criminal behaviour were regarded as necessary as those relating to the regulation of mining claims, and they developed as naturally. Because they were so fundamental to the welfare of the community, the entire community, in a sense, formed the tribunal. A large camp would select a presiding judicial officer, a sheriff and a 12-man jury. A member of the camp—perhaps someone with an education—would be appointed to defend a man accused of a serious crime. In smaller camps, votes on guilt or innocence would be restricted to those living in the camp where the alleged crime occurred, unless the crime was murder, in which case members of other camps could appear and cast their vote. This vigilante system of camp criminal justice filled a vacuum. No government body existed to control crime; instead, citizens filled the breach. The phenomenon was wrongly viewed in British Columbia as a form of anarchy—'lynch law'. One reads constantly in the reports of colonial officials in British Columbia of their worry that vigilantism would come to British Columbia, by which they meant that chaos would prevail.[5]

It was worries of that kind which prompted James Douglas late in 1857 to promulgate mining regulations for the mainland over which, as Governor of Vancouver Island only, he had no jurisdiction. On payment of a licence fee of 21 shillings (1 guinea), a person could prospect for gold on the Fraser River within a claim 12 feet square. It was a condition of the licence that the miner give 'due and proper observance of Sundays'.[6] Much more detailed regulations were enacted in 1858, which required a bond of £2,000 (a very large sum of money) and payment of a royalty of 10 per cent before a claim could be worked. The claimholder was required to employ at least 20 persons within six months of being licensed. Claims could also be larger than those authorized the year before.[7] Obviously Douglas, by these stringent measures, hoped to achieve economic stability by encouraging large-scale operations and discouraging the individual miner and riff-raff. Such an attempt, however, was futile, both because the regulations, like their predecessors, were without legal effect, and because they could not withstand the onslaught of hordes of invading miners who imposed on themselves their own regulations which, if not legal, were not demonstrably illegal and were far more practical.

Details of mining regulations in three camps in the pre-colonial period, and another in the immediate post-colonial period, have survived. Two of the former were on the Fraser at Hills Bar and Fort Yale. Each set the claim size at a 25-foot width extending backward from mid-channel to high water mark. The Hills Bar regulations required one working day in three to maintain the claim, but Fort Yale insisted on only one in five; in each case the requirement would be relaxed in cases of sickness or, as at Fort Yale, in the case of discharging 'public business'. In wintertime, however, the severity of the climate often made active work impossible, and all claims were 'laid over' until the return of spring or more clement weather. Recorders registered the claims for a nominal fee, but there were severe limitations upon the number of claims an individual could hold.

These mining regulations were fairly humdrum and were exactly what one would have expected of a Californian gold miner. What sets apart the camp regulations in British Columbia, passed by perhaps some of the same individuals or others like them in California, were those which related to criminal conduct. Theft by a white man at Hills Bar could result in forfeiture of a claim held by him (not a surprising regulation), but the same camp forbade 'molesting' of Indians and prohibited the sale of liquor to them. Punishment for the latter offence could also result in forfeiture of a claim. The camp at Fort Yale went even further: all sales of liquor, to white and Indian alike, were prohibited, and all caches of liquor were to be destroyed. Any member of the mining camp found selling or in possession of liquor would be whipped and expelled. Similarly, if any miner of the camp sold firearms to an Indian, he would be lashed and expelled. These resolutions were not, however, passed in the interest of the Indians, but 'for the better protection of life and property' of the miners themselves. Still, the regulations are illuminating as they reflect the attitudes of a law-abiding community.[8] At Rock Creek in the Similkameen area similar mining regulations were made, but there the miners—true to California mode—forbade Chinese from holding claims.[9]

NOTES

1. See, for example, Begbie's report to the Colonial Secretary (B.C.), 19th January 1863, misc. correspondence inward, Provincial Archives of British Columbia (PABC), file F142-F.

2. See *Report to the thirty-fifth Congress, Second Session of the United States of America by John N. Nugent, a Special Agent of the United States, January 8th, 1859*, Library of Congress, Washington, DC.

3. Begbie, 'Report After Autumn Circuit in British Columbia', 7th November 1859, misc. correspondence inward, PABC, file F142-B 17b.

4. C.H. Shinn, *Mining Camps: A Study in American Frontier Government* (Gloucester, Mass., 1970).

5. See, for example, Arthur Nonus Birch manuscript, Birch Family Papers, PABC, C.4.

6. Quoted in Kinahan Cornwallis, *The New Eldorado* (London, 1858), p. 401.

7. Quoted in *Victoria Daily Gazette*, 5 August 1858.

8. Walter N. Sage, *Sir James Douglas and British Columbia* (Toronto, 1930), p. 223; Cornwallis, *The New Eldorado*, pp. 402–3; Frederick W. Howay and E.O.S. Scholefield, *British Columbia From the Earliest Times to the Present* (Vancouver, 1914), II, pp. 33–4.

9. *Mapping the Frontier: Charles Wilson's Diary of the Survey of the Forty-Ninth Parallel, 1858–1862, while Secretary of the British Boundary Commission*, ed. George F.G. Stanley (Toronto, 1970).

6 From Tina Loo, '"A Delicate Game": The Meaning of Law on Grouse Creek', *BC Studies*, 96 (Winter 1992-3): 41-4.

At the end of June in 1862, one hundred miners returning from the Cariboo boarded the steamer *Henrietta* in Douglas for the trip to New Westminster. They refused to pay for their passage, claiming that their misadventures in the upper country gold fields had left them 'starving and broken,' as well as broke. Despite the obvious illegality of the miners' actions, Douglas magistrate John Boles Gaggin advised the master of *Henrietta* to 'take the men on, and on arrival at New Westminster, apply to the proper authorities for redress.' Gaggin took this course of action believing, as he told the Colonial Secretary, that

> to attempt coercion with a force unable to command it would have weakened the apparent power of the Law; . . . [and] that the getting of these men out of Douglas was in every way desirable, . . . any attempt to arrest would have provoked a riot, perhaps bloodshed, and I believe I acted prudently in avoiding the least risk of this.[1]

In an effort to further justify his actions, Gaggin closed his report on a defiant note with this telling observation:

> Magistrates in these up country towns have a delicate game to play, and I believe we are all of opinion that to avoid provoking resistance to the Law is the manner in which we best serve the interests of His Excellency, the Governor. . . . [A]s it is the matter passed off without riot and without defiance of the Magistrate, though the Master of the steamer . . . was somewhat annoyed—I shall be very sorry if the cautious way I acted, with such quiet results, does not meet His Excellency's approval, but I acted for the best.[2]

The colonial government chastised the magistrate for his 'want of nerve and judgment' in allowing 'the occurrence of so lawless a proceeding.'[3] 'It appears,' noted Colonial Secretary W.A.G. Young,

> that you consider yourself vested with discretionary power to temporize with your duties, and

that you are unaware that, while rigidly dispensing the laws for the protection of life and property, a Magistrate may act with perfect temper and discretion.[4]

This brief episode raises questions about the social meaning of the law which I am concerned to address. Gaggin considered law to be the preservation of order—'quiet results'—and told his superiors so. From his vantage point in Victoria, Governor James Douglas saw things rather differently. The law, through its rigid application, served a more particular end by securing life and property. There was yet another perspective. Both Gaggin and Douglas considered the miners' actions 'lawless,' but those who boarded *Henrietta* likely did not feel the same way. Different people attached different meanings to the law, and when they used the courts to resolve their disputes these differences became apparent. As legal anthropologists argue, courts are forums in which people 'bargain for reality'; not only do they dispute the 'facts'—what happened—but they also dispute what constitutes legal and just action.[5]

From their arrival, British Columbia's miners possessed a reputation as a self-conscious and vocal interest group with a penchant for self-government which they learned in California's gold fields. Despite their impermanent character, California's gold mining camps developed an elaborate system of informal regulation centred on the Miners' Meetings.[6] These were elected tribunals of local miners who drafted the rules which governed behaviour in a specific locale. Their regulations covered a wide range of activities, from claim size, the technicalities of ditch widths and water rights to the use of alcohol and firearms in the camps.[7] This experience instilled the miners with a taste for local government and a certain degree of independence.[8] It was this independence that made those who streamed northward to British Columbia in 1858 to try their luck in the Fraser and Cariboo rushes so dangerous in the eyes of British colonial administrators like James Douglas and Supreme Court Judge Matthew Baillie Begbie.[9] These men considered the miners a lawless bunch and took steps to prevent local government from gaining a foothold on the banks of the Fraser River.

In September 1858, just a month after the mainland colony was formed, James Douglas issued the first Gold Fields Act.[10] It and subsequent Acts created and elaborated formal government institutions and regulations specifically designed to regulate gold mining.[11] An Assistant Gold Commissioner presided over locally based Gold Commissioner's or Mining Courts. He had jurisdiction to hear all mining or mining-related disputes and to dispose of them summarily. By doing so, the Gold Commissioner's Court allowed suitors to avoid the costly delays associated with Supreme Court actions and jury trials. A locally elected Mining Board replaced the Californian Miners' Meetings, drafting bylaws which governed behaviour. Unlike the American institution they replaced, however, the decisions of the Mining Board could be overturned by the Assistant Gold Commissioner, who also possessed the power to dissolve the board at his pleasure.

Despite the early intrusion of this formal regulatory institution into the gold fields, British Columbia's miners retained a sense of themselves and their enterprise as distinct and crucial to the development of the colony. Despite their impermanent character, gold rush communities were localistic, regardless—paradoxically—of their location.[12] Miners were particularly interested in the administration of the law, watching Mining Court decisions with an eye to their own fortunes. Though the law and the courts brought British Columbia's diverse and far-flung miners together in a common process of dispute settlement, they also were the cause of much division, for they resolved differences by creating other ones. The law defined plaintiffs and defendants, assessed guilt and innocence, and ultimately, in the eyes of those involved, determined right and wrong. The potential for conflict was thus inherent in the process of dispute settlement. . . . different concepts of law stood in bold relief against this structured background of formal dispute resolution.

British Columbians understood and meas-

ured their laws with a standard that was rooted in a particular geographic, social, and cultural milieu and that was not always shared by those charged with its administration. . . .

NOTES

1. Gaggin to the Colonial Secretary, Douglas, B.C., 2 July 1862. British Columbia Archives and Records Services (hereafter BCARS), Colonial Correspondence, GR 1372, reel B-1330, file 621/14. For more on this episode and Gaggin see Dorothy Blakey Smith, '"Poor Gaggin": Irish Misfit in the Colonial Service', *BC Studies* 32 (Winter 1976–7): 41–63.

2. Ibid.

3. Cited in Smith '"Poor Gaggin"', 45.

4. Ibid., 47.

5. For instance, see Clifford Geertz, 'Local Knowledge: Fact and Law in Comparative Perspective', in his *Local Knowledge: Further Essays in Interpretive Anthropology* (New York, 1983); John L. Comaroff and Simon Roberts, *Rules and Processes: The Cultural Logic of Dispute in an African Context* (Chicago, 1981); Lawrence Rosen, *Bargaining for Reality: The Construction of Social Relations in a Muslim Community* (Chicago, 1984) and his 'Islamic "Case Law" and the Logic of Consequence', in June Starr and Jane F. Collier, eds, *History and Power in the Study of Law: New Directions in Legal Anthropology* (Ithaca, NY, 1989), 302–19. In the latter essay, Rosen notes 'Law is . . . one domain in which a culture may reveal itself. But like politics, marriage, and exchange, it is an arena in which people must act, and in doing so they must draw on their assumptions, connections, and beliefs to make their acts effective and comprehensible. In the Islamic world, as in many other places, the world of formal courts offers a stage—as intense as ritual, as demonstrative as war—through which a society reveals itself to its own people as much as to the outside world' [318]. This essay shares Rosen's assumptions about the law and what it can reveal about society.

6. See Hubert Howe Bancroft, *Popular Tribunals* (San Francisco, 1887), v. 1, Chapter Ten; Charles Shinn, *Mining Camps: A Study in American Frontier Government*; and on California and British Columbia, David Ricardo Williams, 'The Administration of Civil and Criminal Justice in the Mining Camps and Frontier Communities of British Columbia', in Louis Knafla, ed., *Law and Justice in a New Land: Essays in Western Canadian Legal History* (Calgary, 1986).

7. Williams, 'The Administration of Civil and Criminal Justice', 217–19.

8. See Shinn, *Mining Camps*, Introduction.

9. Morley Arthur Underwood, 'Governor Douglas and the Miners, 1858–1859', University of British Columbia BA Essay, 1974.

10. The Gold Fields Act, 1859 [31 August 1859]; William J. Trimble, *The Mining Advance into the Inland Empire* (Madison, Wisconsin, 1914), 187–214, 336–7.

11. Rules and Regulations for the Working of Gold Mines under the 'Gold Fields Act, 1859' [7 September 1859]; Rules and Regulations for the working of Gold Mines, issued in conformity with the 'Gold Fields Act, 1859' (Bench Diggings) [6 January 1860]; Rules and Regulations under the 'Gold Fields Act, 1859' (Ditches) [29 September 1862]; Further Rules and Regulations under the 'Gold Fields Act, 1859' [24 February 1863]; Proclamation amending the 'Gold Fields Act, 1859' [25 March 1863]; The Mining District Act, 1863 [27 May 1863]; The Mining Drains Act, 1864 [1 February 1864]; An Ordinance to extend and improve the Laws relating to Gold Mining [26 February 1864] and An Ordinance to amend and consolidate the Gold Mining Laws [28 March 1865]; An Ordinance to amend the

Laws relating to Gold Mining, 2 April 1867.

12. On this theme, and more generally, the idea that mining society was not as disorganized as traditionally thought, see Thomas Stone, *Miners' Justice: Migration, Law and Order on the Alaska-Yukon Frontier, 1873–1902* (New York, 1988).

☐ Confederation and the Anti-Confederates

INTRODUCTION

■ Perhaps no group of Canadian politicians has suffered more from the national approach to Canadian history than the Anti-Confederates, those who in the 1860s opposed the passage of the British North America Act and the establishment of the Canadian federation. The opponents of union have been charged with lack of vision, parochialism, negativism, cynicism, and absence of any real theoretical understanding of the meaning of federalism. Their part in the debates over union has not only been misrepresented, but more often almost completely ignored. There is not a single book-length study devoted to analyzing their cause. Particular opponents, such as Joseph Howe and Ike Smith, have been labelled political opportunists, as if those who favoured Confederation were altruists who did not expect to benefit from its achievement. In the context of the 1860s, as well as in the present period after another round of constitutional reform—successful or unsuccessful—the Anti-

Confederate criticisms of the British North America Act resonate a good deal better than they did in the years surrounding the centennial of Confederation, when everyone celebrated the achievement of union.

Though the anti-Confederationist case may have been subsequently disproved by the course of events—at least through 2003—in its own day it was certainly not unreasonable to view the unification of British North America as an impractical visionary scheme, proposed by politicians in the Province of Canada to meet its needs, but not really in the best interests of other and smaller colonies. Even a supporter of union could object to the specific terms of union worked out in 1864. One of the important aspects of the opposition to union that has weakened the force of its case is that the issues were debated in a variety of contexts and venues in the mid-1860s. There was not one movement of anti-Confederation, but several, often not having much in common. Confederation certainly looked quite different to a politician in Canada than it did to one from Nova Scotia or Prince Edward Island, regardless of whether he favoured or opposed it.

Questions for consideration

1. What were some of the major criticisms made of the scheme of union?
2. Under what advantages and disadvantages did the Anti-Confederates operate?
3. Should the opponents of the proposed union have offered an alternative scheme?

Suggestions for further reading

Donald G. Creighton, *The Road to Confederation: The Emergence of Canada, 1863–1867* (Toronto: Macmillan, 1964). A well-written and well-argued account from the nationalist perspective.

Ged Martin, *Britain and the Origins of Canadian Confederation 1837–1867* (Vancouver: University of British Columbia Press, 1995). A series of essays exploring the imperial context of Confederation.

Christopher Moore, *1867: How the Fathers Made a Deal* (Toronto: McClelland & Stewart, 1997). A modern account influenced by the constitutional crises of the 1990s.

W.L. Morton, *The Critical Years: The Union of British North America 1857–1873* (Toronto: McClelland & Stewart, 1964). A balanced account of unification.

PRIMARY DOCUMENTS

1   From a speech by Joseph Howe at Dartmouth, Nova Scotia, 22 May 1867, in Joseph Andrew Chisholm, ed., *The Speeches and Public Letters of Joseph Howe*, vol. 2 (Halifax: Chronicle Publishing Company, 1909), 510–13.

The old men who sit around me, and the men of middle age who hear my voice, know that thirty years ago we engaged in a series of struggles which the growth of population, wealth and intelligence rendered inevitable. For what did we contend? Chiefly for the right of self-government. We won it from Downing Street after many a manly struggle, and we exercised and never abused it for a quarter of a century. Where is it now? Gone from us, and certain persons in Canada are now to exercise over us powers more arbitrary and excessive than any the Colonial Secretaries ever claimed. Our Executive and Legislative Councillors were formerly selected in Downing Street. For more than twenty years we have appointed them ourselves. But the right has been bartered away by those who have betrayed us, and now we must be content with those our Canadian masters give. The batch already announced shows the principles which are to govern the selection.

For many years the Colonial Secretary dispensed our casual and territorial revenues. The sum rarely exceeded £12,000 sterling, but the money was ours, and yielding at last to common sense and rational argument, our claims were allowed. But what do we see now? Almost all our revenues—not twelve thousand but hundreds of thousands—are to be swept away and handed over to the custody and the administration of strangers.

The old men here remember when we had no control over our trade, and when Halifax was the only free port. By slow degrees we pressed for a better system, till, under the enlightened commercial policy of England, we were left untrammelled to levy what duties we pleased and to regulate our trade. Its marvellous development under our independent action astonishes ourselves and is the wonder of strangers. We have fifty seaports carrying on foreign trade. Our shipyards are full of life and our flag floats on every sea. All this is changed: we can regulate our own trade no longer. We must submit to the dictation of those who live above the tide, and who will know little of and care less for our interests or our experience.

The right of self-taxation, the power of the purse, is in every country the true security for freedom. We had it. It is gone, and the Canadians have been invested by this precious batch of worthies, who are now seeking your suffrages, with the right to strip us 'by any and every mode or system of taxation.'

We struggled for years for the control of our Post Office. At that time rates were high, the system contracted; offices had only been established in the shire towns and in the more populous settlements. We gained the control, the rates were lowered and rendered uniform over the Provinces, newspapers were carried free, offices were established in all the thriving settlements and way offices on every road, but now all this comes to an end. Our Post Offices are to be regulated by a distant authority. Every post-master and every way office keeper is to be appointed and controlled by the Canadians.

Since the necessity for a better organization of the militia became apparent, our young men have shown a laudable spirit of emulation and have volunteered cheerfully, formed naval brigades, and shown a desire to acquire discipline and the use of arms. I have viewed these efforts with special interest. There is no period in the history of England when the great body of the people were better fed, better treated, or enjoyed more of the substantial comforts of life, than when every man was trained to the use of arms, and had his long-bow or his cross-bow in his house. The rifle is the modern weapon, and our people have not been slow to learn the use of it. Organized by their own Government, commanded by their friends and neighbours, 50,000 men have been embodied and partially drilled for self-defence. But now strangers are to control this force—to appoint the officers and to direct its movements; and while our own shores may be undefended, the artillery company that trains upon the hills before us may be ordered away to any point of the Canadian frontier.

By the precious instrument by which we are hereafter to be bound, the Canadians are to fix the 'salaries' of our principal public officers. We are to pay, but they can fix the amount, and who doubts but that our money will be squandered to reward the traitors who have betrayed us? Our 'navigation and shipping' pass from our control, and the Canadians, who have not one ship to our three, are already boasting that they are the third maritime power in the world. Our 'sea-coast and inland fisheries' are no longer ours. The shore fisheries have been handed over to the Yankees, and the Canadians can sell or lease to-morrow the fisheries of the Margaree, the Musquodoboit or the La Have.

Our 'currency,' also, is to be regulated by the Canadians, and how they will regulate it we shrewdly suspect. Many of us remember when Nova Scotia was flooded with irresponsible paper, and have not forgotten the commercial crisis that ensued. In one summer thousands of people fled from the country, half the shops in Water Street, Halifax, were closed, and the grass almost grew in the Market Square. The paper was driven in. The banks were restricted to five-pound notes. All paper, under severe penalties, was made convertible. British coins were adopted as the standard of value, and silver has been ever since paid from hand to hand in all the smaller transactions of life. For a quarter of a century we have had free trade in banking, and the soundest currency in the world. Last spring Mr. Galt could not meet the obligations of Canada, and he could only borrow money at ruinous rates of interest. He seized upon the circulation, and partially adopted the greenback system of the United States. The country is now flooded with paper; only, if I am rightly informed, convertible in two places—Toronto and Montreal. The system will soon be extended to Nova Scotia, and the country will presently be flooded with 'shin-plasters,' and the sound specie currency we now use will be driven out.

Our 'savings banks' are also to be handed over. Hitherto the confidence of the people in these banks has been universal. We had the security of our own Government, watched by our own vigilance, and controlled by our own votes, for the sacred care of deposits. What are we to have now? Nobody knows, but we do know that the savings of the poor and the industrious are to be handed over to the Canadians. They also are to regulate the interest of money. The usury laws have never been repealed in Nova Scotia, and yet capital could always be commanded here at six, and often at five per cent. In Canada the rate of interest ranges from eight to ten per cent., and is often much higher. With confederation will come these higher rates of interest, grinding the faces of the poor.

But it is said, why should we complain? we are still to manage our local affairs. I have shown you that self-government, in all that gives dignity and security to a free state, is to be swept away. The Canadians are to appoint our governors, judges and senators. They are to 'tax us by any and every mode' and spend the money. They are to regulate our trade, control our Post Offices, command the militia, fix the salaries, do what they like with our shipping and navigation, with our sea-coast and river fisheries, regulate the currency and the rate of interest, and seize upon our savings banks. What remains? Listen and be comforted. You are to have the privilege of 'imposing direct taxation, within the Province, in order to the raising of revenue for Provincial purposes.' Why do you not go down on your knees and be thankful for this crowning mercy when fifty per cent. has been added to your *ad valorem* duties, and the money has been all swept away to dig canals or fortify Montreal. You are to be kindly permitted to keep up your spirits and internal improvements by direct taxation.

Who does not remember, some years ago, when I proposed to pledge the public revenues of the Province to build our railroads, how Tupper went screaming all over the Province that we should be ruined by the expenditure, and that 'direct taxation' would be the result. He threw me out of my seat in Cumberland by this and other unprincipled war-cries. Well, the roads have been built, and not only were we never compelled to resort to direct taxation, but so great has been the prosperity resulting from those public works that, with the lowest tariff in the world, we have trebled our revenue in ten years, and with a hundred and fifty miles of railroad completed, and nearly as much more under contract, we have had an overflowing treasury, and money enough to meet all our obligations, without having been compelled, like the Canadians, to borrow money at eight per cent. and to manufacture greenbacks.

But if we had been compelled to pay direct taxes for a few years to create a railroad system that by-and-by would be self-sustaining, and that would have been a great blessing in the meantime, the object would have been worth the sacrifice. But we never paid a farthing. What then? The falsehood did its work. Tupper won the seat, and now, after giving our railroads away, and all our general revenues besides, the doctor, after being rejected by Halifax, is trying to make the people of Cumberland believe that to pay 'direct taxes' for all sorts of services is a pleasant and profitable pastime. Cumberland may believe and trust him again, but if it does, the people are not so shrewd or so patriotic as I think they are.

2   From a speech by William Lawrence in Nova Scotia House of Assembly, 1866, in Janet Ajzenstat et al., eds, *Canada's Founding Debates* (Toronto: Stoddart, 1999), 383–5.

There can be no great love of union where the parties to be joined have not the slightest desire to associate with each other. Right or wrong, beneficial or otherwise, it is impossible to persuade the mass of the people that the system which gives to them an equal voice in the government of the country is not the best. How many of the present members would be here if they said to the people, in 1863, that they were going to change the constitution of the country?

A mere politician, thrown up by the dark and turbid waters of party, actuated by self-interest, can have no lasting influence over a question of this sort. This is no party question; it passes beyond all such considerations, and such feelings should be far from every mind. Gentlemen mistake the feeling of the people of this country if they hope to excite their admiration or secure their confidence by displaying such newborn zeal in forcing Confederation on the people. The spirit of liberty will make itself heard wherever it exists. Let us take care of our rights, for political expediency in limiting a people's freedom is a dangerous principle and will never satisfy a free people. I believe one of our great objects, at the present time, should be to foster a spirit of peace and harmony amongst our own people, and harmony can only be maintained by a patriotic, wise, and noble use of power. The people in every part of this country must feel that their rights are protected. So far from lending ourselves to any scheme which would threaten the safety or prosperity of our country, we should not hesitate to plant ourselves in opposition even to our political associates when they seek to promote it.

We are a free people, prosperous beyond doubt, advancing cautiously in wealth, under the protection of our good old flag, the only banner which floats over a limited monarchy and a free people. Under the British Constitution we have far more freedom than any other country on the face of the earth. We have sprung from a nation in whose veins the blood of freedom circulates, and who carry everywhere the deepest attachment to their sovereign. It is the spirit of that constitution which unites and invigorates every part of the empire, down to the lowest member, but to pass Confederation, without asking the voice of the people, will only be sowing the seed of dissatisfaction and contention among a very large portion of our population. A representative of the people is bound by the highest moral obligations to respect their wishes and obey their will, when their sober judgement has been ascertained. . . .

Now I deplore the intolerant spirit which I see every day manifested around these benches; it is utterly inconsistent with the true spirit of freedom. The foundation of free constitutional government is the voice of a majority of the people, and so long as it deserves the name and wins the affection of the people it can never be in any great danger. Now if a question of right arises between the constituent and the representative body, by what authority shall it be decided? If you leave it to the judges, they will tell you that the law of parliament is above them. What then remains but to leave it to the people to decide themselves?

[In] regard to Confederation, I say frankly that whenever a majority of the people speak in favour of union, let them have it; but I will not consent to a change of the constitution without their consent. If the representatives are unfaithful to their trust and abuse their powers by disposing of the birthright of the people, then responsible government is not worthy of the name. We have no right to surrender the liberties and privileges which we were appointed to guard. The multitude, even though they know very little of political science, can form a good practical judgement upon government in general and even a better one than those in office, who cannot see their own defects and errors. . . .

The principle which lies at the foundation of our constitution is that which declares the people to be the source of political power. A constitution written on paper is not a safe one; a constitution to be safe must be written on the hearts of the people. The powerful temptation to betray our trust, held out by the government, to surrender up our own convictions, ought to be resisted; a steady adherence to truth, whether in favour or out of favour, must mark the course of every man who will not lose his own respect. I do not despise popularity, I respect it. But it is that popularity which follows, not that which is sought after; and if there be one quality which a representative of our country ought to cultivate at the present time above all others, it is independence. Not a defiance of the well-understood wishes of the people; his course should be a manly and steady adherence to principle, through good report and evil report; a stout defiance of what he considers right through sunshine and through storm. . . . Our liberty, once taken away, may never return.

3 From a speech by Christopher Dunkin in Canadian House of Parliament, 27 February 1865, in *Parliamentary Debates on the Subject of the Confederation of the British North American Provinces* (Quebec: Hunter, Rose & Co., 1865), 483–5.

Here is a measure proposed for our acceptance, embodied in seventy-two resolutions, and which resolutions affirm a great many more than seventy-two propositions, connected with almost every principle known to have reference to the theory and practice of popular government. I say it is a scheme which is as complex and as vast as one can well imagine, and declamation about first principles can be of no real use in its discussion—can avail only to mislead in reference to it. We have to deal with no mere abstract question of a nationality, or of union or disunion, or of a Federal as opposed to a Legislative union. It is idle to talk vaguely about the maintenance of British connection, or to go into magnificent speculations about the probable results of independence, or blindly to urge this scheme as a sure preventative of annexation to the United States. These cheap and easy generalities are thoroughly unreliable. The only question is, how is this plan, in its entirety, going to work? And this question is one which is not easy to answer; it is one requiring much patience, and a close examination of details. It is the question which, if the House will lend me its attention, I will endeavor to discuss to the extent of my ability. (Hear, hear.) I may further take leave to say at starting, that I do not approach this question from any new point of view whatever. Always I have been, and now I am, a unionist in the strictest and largest sense of the term. I desire to perpetuate the union between Upper and Lower Canada. I desire to see developed, the largest union that can possibly be developed (I care not by what name you call it) between all the colonies, provinces, and dependencies of the British Crown. I desire to maintain that intimate union which ought to subsist, but which unfortunately does not subsist as it ought, between the Imperial Government and all those dependencies. I am a unionist, who especially does not desire to see the provinces of Upper and Lower Canada disunited. To my mind, this scheme does not at all present itself as one of union; and if hon. gentlemen opposite will admit the truth, they will acknowledge that, practically, it amounts to a disunion between Upper and Lower Canada. (Hear, hear.) I confess that I am irreconcilably opposed to that portion of the scheme. I repeat I do not care to see Upper and Lower Canada more dissevered than they are; on the contrary, I wish to see them brought into closer union; and far from regarding this scheme as cementing more closely the connection of these provinces with the British Empire, I look upon it as tending rather towards a not distant disunion of these provinces from the British Empire. (Hear, hear.) My position as regards this scheme is that of one who desires to see this union perpetuated, and not of one who would contemplate a state of disunion between any of the component parts of the British Empire. I hold that proper means ought to be taken to prevent our disunion from the British Empire and absorption into the United States, and that this scheme by no means tends that way. I have no fancy for democratic or republican forms or institutions, or indeed for revolutionary or political novelties of any sort. The phrase of 'political creation' is no phrase of mine. I hold that the power to create is as much a higher attribute than belongs to man, in the political world, as in any other department of the universe. All we can do is to attend to and develop the ordinary growth of our institutions; and this growth, if it is to be healthy at all, must be slow. There must be the same slow, steady change in political matters, which answers to the growth visible in the physical world. I do believe in this gradual development of our institutions, but I do not believe in any of those violent and sudden changes which have for their object the creation of something entirely new. I fear this scheme is just of the character to prevent that slow, gradual, healthy development which I would wish to see steadily carried out. If I could be astonished at anything in politics, Mr. SPEAKER, I should be astonished at the attempt which has been made by some honorable gentlemen on the Treasury benches to represent the state of the public feeling on this subject as not having that mere sudden, sensational, unreliable character which I have ascribed to it. Long forgotten expressions of individual opinion; clauses said to have formed part of bills not to be found, and not known to have been even drawn; motions threatened but never made, the small party fencings of past times, from before the days of the Canada Trade Act downwards, have been pressed into service to meet the exigencies of a hard case. Well, I shall not follow out that line of argument: it is not worth while. We all know that, from the time of the union of Canada, at all events, until very lately indeed, nothing like serious discussion of the propriety or impropriety of a Federal union, or of any union at all, of the aggregate of these British American Provinces, has ever so little occupied the public mind. I will here go back merely to 1858, when the sixth Parliament was elected, and from that time bring under review, as rapidly as I can, such few points of our political history as are relevant to shew that this is the fact; although, indeed, argument to establish it is scarcely necessary. At the election of 1857–'58, what really were the issues before the country? They can be easily stated. I take the *résumé*, in fact, from the announcements of the *Globe*, the organ of the great popular party of Upper Canada at that time; mentioning not everything, but everything at all material. The great demand of the then Upper Canada Opposition, which gave the key-note to the whole political controversies of the time, was representation according to population, irrespectively of the dividing line between Upper and Lower Canada. That was urged as involving everything. It was urged for the sake of all the rest, and as sure to bring about all the rest, that was demanded by the party. It was to enable them to carry out their opposition to what were called sectarian grants, their opposition to the holding of land in mortmain for sectarian uses, their opposition to separate schools on a sectarian basis. It was urged for the avowed purpose of obtaining uniform legislation in the future for the two sections of the province, and also what was spoken of as the assimilation of the existing institutions of the two sections of the province, but which was meant to be an assimilation of those of Lower Canada to those of Upper Canada much more than of those of Upper Canada to those of Lower Canada. (Hear, hear.) It was urged with the view of obtaining what was called free-trade, that is, an anti-Lower Canadian commercial policy. It was urged with the view of obtaining the settlement of the North-West; in other words, the relative aggrandizement of Upper Canada. It was urged, also, no doubt, with the view of obtaining what was called administrative reform—the driving from power of a set of men who were alleged, for various reasons, to be unworthy of holding it. But the great questions of measures above alluded to came first; those as to the mere men, second. (Hear, hear.) The grand object was declared to be to obtain an Upper Canadian preponderance of representation on the floor of this House, in order to put an end to everything like sectarian grants, the holding of lands in mortmain and separate schools, to render uniform our legislation, to assimilate our institutions, to carry out an anti-Lower Canadian commercial policy, and to secure the North-West for the aggrandizement of Upper Canada. In this way the question of Upper Canada against

Lower Canada was unmistakably raised. What must have been, what could not fail to be, the result of an appeal of that kind? It was easy to foresee that there would be returned in Upper Canada a majority in favor of these demands, and in Lower Canada an overwhelming majority against them. I do not go into this to raise the ghost of past animosities; I am merely showing what cannot be denied—that no one at that time spoke of or cared for this magnificent idea of the union of the provinces, by Confederation or otherwise. (Hear, hear.) The session commenced. Those who had the advantage or disadvantage of sitting in that Parliament that session will remember the tremendous contrast there was between all those debates which had reference to this class of subjects, and the one single debate which was attempted, but could not be made to take place, on the question of the Confederation of the Provinces. With all his ability—and there are few abler men than the hon. gentleman who undertook at that time to bring that question before the House—with all his ability, and the most earnest effort on his part to press it on the attention of the House, he could scarcely obtain a hearing. No one cared for the matter; and it was felt by every one that such was the case. Soon after, a ministerial crisis took place. A new government came in for a few hours, and started a policy. But that policy, again, was not this policy. It did not touch this question. (Hear, hear.) It was proposed, indeed, to deal with that question of representation by population by applying some system of checks or guarantees, doing or trying to do something that might lessen the objection of Lower Canada to a change urged forward as that had been. But that was all. That government fell—fell instantly—and another was formed in its place. And the present Finance Minister, the honorable member for Sherbrooke, who, with all his ability, had not been able to obtain a serious hearing for his proposal of Confederation of the provinces, going into the new government, induced his colleagues to come before the House and the country, with that as a professed portion of their policy. I may be pardoned, perhaps, for a single word here of personal reference, for saying, *en passant*, that when that idea was thus broached (as it was by a Government of which I was as firm a supporter as any man in the House), I did not fail to make it known, that if ever it should be presented to the House as a practical measure by that Government, I should cease to be (so far as it was concerned) one of such supporters. (Hear, hear.) That was not the first time I had thought of it. It had long been a matter of study with me; and all the anxious reflection I have ever been able to give it, has only had the result of strengthening my convictions against it every day. But how was this idea then brought forward? Tentatively, and just to neutralize the scheme which the BROWN-DORIAN Administration had hinted to the country. The one fire was to burn out another's burning. (Hear, hear.) The plan of that Government was to make propositions to the Imperial Government and to the governments of the Lower Provinces. But how? If you want to gain an object, you put that object before those to whom you propose it in the way most likely to induce them to say yes. This scheme was suggested to the Imperial Government, and to the people and governments of the Lower Provinces, precisely in the way most calculated to induce them to say no. We went and told them, 'We are in such a state of embarrassment, we have political questions which so trouble and bother us, that we do not know if we can get along at all, unless you will be so kind as to come into this union with us.' (Hear, hear.) It was just as though I were in business, and went round to half a dozen capitalists, telling them, 'I have got into debt; my business is gone to the dogs; I have no business capacity; help me by going into partnership with me, or I am ruined.' (Hear, hear) If the object had been not to carry it, it does appear to me that those gentlemen could not have taken a better method of accomplishing that object. And we saw this—that just so soon as it was found that the Lower Provinces did not, as under the circumstances they could not, say yes to a proposal of this kind, and that the Imperial Government let the matter drop, our Administration let it drop too. We never heard another word about it. The despatches were laid on our table in 1859, but nobody asked a question about them. The child was still-born, and no one troubled himself about its want of baptism. We went on with our old questions—representation by population; Upper Canada against Lower Canada; measures, to a great extent; men also, to a great and increasing extent. And we quarrelled and fought about almost everything, but did not waste a thought or word upon this gigantic question of the Confederation of these provinces. (Hear, hear.)

HISTORICAL INTERPRETATIONS

4   From P.B. Waite, *The Life and Times of Confederation 1864–1867: Politics, Newspapers, and the Union of British North America* (Toronto: University of Toronto Press, 1962), 151–6.

The Confederation debates were remarkable in many ways. That they were recorded at all was an indication of the Canadian government's determination to give them all the weight the occasion demanded. No other Canadian debates were so reported.[1] They also gave an opportunity for every member, if he wanted, to speak for the record, and over a thousand stout, double-columned pages show the advantage that they took of it.[2] The debates were held at a critical time; many of the speakers felt powerfully the circumstances that made vital, perhaps imperative, some change in the isolated helplessness of the North American British colonies. Cartier's remarks were suggestive of many others. 'Confederation was . . . at this moment almost forced upon us. We could not shut our eyes to what was going on beyond the lines. . . . We could not deny that the struggle now in progress must necessarily influence our political existence.'[3] After the ministerial speeches many an aspiring member followed, and ultimately it was the opposition speeches that aroused the most interest. The newspapers liked both Dunkin and J.B.E. Dorion, the former for his comprehensiveness and mastery, the latter for his incisiveness.

Christopher Dunkin was an independent Conservative, the member for Brome County, on the American border in Canada East. On Monday night, February 27, 1865, and the next night, Dunkin delivered a criticism of the Quebec Resolutions that towers over every other. A thin, sick, tired little man, a 'bag of bones' as one correspondent described him,[4] he stood there, for four hours each night. His speech was comprehensive, it was exhaustive, and it showed Confederation as a shambling, illogical mixture of compromises and rule-of-thumb methods. Dunkin could not, did not, believe that in seventeen days thirty-three gentlemen could contrive a constitution that was a judicious blend of the best in the British and American systems. Far from the Quebec Resolutions having taken the best in each, Dunkin maintained they had taken the worst, and this, together with concessions to Lower Canada and compromises for the benefit of the Maritimes, had produced an indescribable jumble. Dunkin's speech was largely devoted to showing what these weaknesses were and what would be their effect in the future. He could not believe either that the haste with which Confederation had been suggested, put together, and brought before the House was justified by the nature of the project or by the circumstances of the time. Nothing good would come from such haste, and much that was anything but good. This provoked McGee to remark, 'If 'twere done, 'twere well 'twere done quickly.' McGee must have realized as soon as he spoke that the allusion was unfortunate. Dunkin retorted that McGee was a good enough scholar to know that it was to something very bad. 'The hon. gentleman is welcome to all he can make of his quotation. . . .'⁵

Even the Montreal *Gazette*, March 6, 1865, although a little pained at Dunkin's desertion of the Conservatives, admitted that Dunkin's speech was a perfect chart of all the shoals and reefs ahead of Confederation. The Oshawa *Vindicator*, March 8, thought it the ablest of all the speeches. So did the St Thomas *Dispatch* (May 18). 'What a pity,' said the *London Free Press* correspondent, 'Mr. Dunkin was not made a Minister . . . and what a vast improvement the scheme of union would have shown upon its present bungling and crude condition if he had been called to aid Her Majesty's Councils. . . .'⁶

By this time almost a month had elapsed, and gradually after Dunkin's speech an air of weariness crept over the debate. It was said that the Opposition were talking against time in order to circulate petitions against Confederation. The Quebec *Chronicle* lamented:

> The Confederation discussion is growing wofully [sic] stale; not a new idea is to be coined and honorable gentlemen are doomed to talk to the clock and empty benches of the Legislative Chambers. . . . In truth the question of the Union of the Provinces . . . is worn threadbare, and no one cares to listen to vain repetitions, worse and worse, presented as each fresh speaker brings the dead carcase of a worn-out argument to fill up the leaden periods he is endeavoring to make acceptable to an unwilling and wearied audience.⁷

This was Monday, March 6. The debate, it is true, was becoming insufferable, dragging its slow

length along at about three hours a day. On February 24 there were only 20 members present—a bare quorum;⁸ and although Dunkin had enlivened things, the debate soon resumed its heavy plodding while the Belleroses and the Fergusons addressed their constituents 'at Buncome town.' On March 7, John A. Macdonald moved the previous question. He did so on grounds of defence; it was desirable that Canadian ministers be in England as soon as possible to discuss defence and Confederation. But there was another reason. The defeat of Tilley in New Brunswick had been revealed over that weekend—gleefully announced to the House at 3 a.m. Saturday, March 4, by Sandfield Macdonald.

The full extent of Tilley's defeat was not yet known, but defeat it was. At one stroke the head-long progress of Confederation was suddenly stopped. Confederation could survive the troubles that were besetting it in Prince Edward Island, the uncertainties that were appearing in Newfoundland—the immediate adhesion of those two colonies was not vital—but in Nova Scotia Tupper could only get Confederation through the House provided New Brunswick passed it.⁹ New Brunswick had in fact torpedoed Confederation. The ship was still afloat, but she could have little steerage way until the damage was rectified.

In Canada, where New Brunswick had been counted for a dead certainty,¹⁰ the Government was staggered and the Opposition much heartened. The defeat of Tilley gave them new hope, and the monotonous tenor of the debate was now enlivened with strong bucking from the Opposition. Sandfield Macdonald, Holton, Dorion, and others sprang into life; Macdonald's moving of the previous question and the New Brunswick defeat gave them a pair of weapons with which to attack the Government. It was in these circumstances that J.B.E. Dorion made his speech, one which even the government press admitted was remarkable.¹¹ Dorion was trenchant and ironic by turns. Paul Denis, who followed him, had to admit his cleverness at agitation and the skilful distortion of the Government's position.[12] 'Could you inform me, Mr. SPEAKER,' Dorion asked, 'what has become of the $100,000 question?'[13] Swallowed up in the scandalous Coalition, was Dorion's own answer. The Canadian constitution had hampered the 'curvetings and prancings of our leading chiefs too much,'[14] and it was therefore abandoned and by a piece of legerdemain that denied every political principle.

None of the Opposition, Dunkin and Dorion included, had much to suggest as a substitute for Confederation. Yet a return to the old state of affairs was probably impossible. The Reform party had come too far. 'He must be a sanguine man,' said the Montreal *Gazette*, March 3, 1865, 'who thinks that, after an acknowledgement that Upper Canada is entitled . . . to seventeen more members than Lower Canada, the agitation can ever again be quelled.' The Opposition that Dunkin and the Dorions offered was criticism, able certainly; but they had little to substitute for the measure they so effectively ridiculed. Their real work was in pointing out the problems that faced Confederation, and to render the supporters of it if possible less complacent. The Confederation debate ended early on Saturday morning, March 11, with recalcitrant desk-rattling, whispering and bird singing from some members when the speaker was not to their taste.[15] A lively account of the last hours of the debate was given by the Parliamentary correspondent of the *Stratford Beacon*:

. . . the House was in an unmistakeably seedy condition, having, as it was positively declared, eaten the saloon keeper clean out, drunk him entirely dry, and got all the fitful naps of sleep that the benches along the passages could be made to yield. For who cared at one, two, three, and four in the morning, to sit in the House, to hear the stale talk of Mr. Ferguson, of South Simcoe, or to listen even to the polished and pointed sentences of Mr. Huntingdon? Men with the strongest constitutions for Parliamentary twaddle were sick of the debate, and the great bulk of the members were scattered about the building, with an up-all-night, get-tight-in-the morning air, impatient for the sound of the division bell. It rang at last, at quarter past four, and the jaded representatives of the people swarmed in to the discharge of the most important duty of all their lives.[16]

At 4:30 a.m. the main motion was agreed to, 91–33.[17] At this the House broke into ringing cheers, and as the Speaker was leaving the Chair the French Canadian members burst out with some old paddling song, the English Canadians following with 'The Queen,' and the whole bawled forth with the same sorry energy characteristic of the fag end of a public dinner. And over by the St Charles River the convent bell was ringing five as the members trooped wearily home to their lodgings.[18]

NOTES

1. Nova Scotia and Prince Edward Island regularly, and New Brunswick intermittently, reported their debates. Note the following from the Saint John *Daily Evening Globe*, Feb. 19, 1864: 'The House of Assembly has resolved not to have any authorized debates published this year. This is quite right. The official debates were always a great humbug. Nobody read them but the reporters who wrote them; the members for whom they were written . . . and the unfortunate proof readers who put the finishing stroke upon them.'

2. The cost of printing them came nearly to the total of the bills for entertaining the Quebec Conference, $14,490.65. (Canada, Assembly, *Journals*, 1865, Appendix 2, 15.)

3. *Confederation Debates*, 55; for Taché on the same thing, ibid., 7; Macdonald, 32; Brown, 114; McGee, 131.

4. London (C.W.) *Canadian Free Press*, March 10, 1865, report of Feb. 28 and March 1 from Quebec, signed 'Fag'. Dunkin lived however until 1881.

5. For Dunkin's speech see *Confederation Debates*, 482–544.

6. *Canadian Free Press*, March 10, 1865, report of March 1 from Quebec, by 'Fag'.

7. Quebec *Morning Chronicle*, March 6, 1865. Cf. also Montreal *Gazette*, March 9, 1865; Barrie *Northern Advance*, March 15, 1865.

8. *Stratford Beacon*, March 3, 1865, report of Feb. 25 from Quebec.

9. So Tupper told Gordon when in Fredericton, in June, 1865. P.R.O., Cardwell Papers, Gordon to Cardwell, June 5, 1865 (private).

10. *Stratford Beacon*, March 10, 1865, report of March 6 from Quebec.

11. Hamilton *Spectator*, March 10, 1865.

12. *Confederation Debates*, 872.

13. This was a reference to the reputedly unautho-

rized advance of this amount to the City of Montreal by the Conservative government, which had caused the defeat of the Government on June 14, 1864.

14. *Confederation Debates*, 857–8.

15. Joseph Cauchon had an irritating habit of imitating bird calls in late sittings of the House. (Oshawa *Vindicator*, March 15, 1865.) In later years he seems to have taken up the Jew's harp. (G.W. Ross, *Getting into Parliament and After* [Toronto, 1913], 82.)

16. *Stratford Beacon*, March 17, 1865, report of March 11 from Quebec.

17. *Confederation Debates*, 962; Canada, Assembly, *Journals*, 1865, 191.

18. *Stratford Beacon*, March 17, 1865, report of March 11 from Quebec.

5   From C.M. Wallace, 'Albert Smith', in *Dictionary of Canadian Biography*, vol. 11 (Toronto: University of Toronto Press, 1982), 829–31.

Negotiations among the British Americans had matured into a full-blown British North American federation movement in 1864, with Tilley its New Brunswick apostle. Gordon had wanted a Maritime union, with himself as governor, but had lost the initiative. Smith was infuriated by the developments, and it was with an eye on Smith that Tilley constructed a coalition to carry the confederation project. Tilley recruited such former opponents as Chandler and Gray as well as discarded colleagues such as Fisher. The exclusion of Smith has never been fully explained. Perhaps he would not have joined. It is more likely that he was not invited because he was so completely opposed to any union scheme as well as to the Intercolonial Railway, which Tilley saw as the prize of negotiations. At any rate, by the time Tilley had returned from the ambulatory conference that had taken him to Charlottetown, Halifax, Quebec, Montreal, Ottawa, Toronto, and Niagara (Niagara-on-the-Lake), he encountered a hostile New Brunswick being

given direction by Albert Smith, 'The Douglas of Dorchester . . . the Lion of Westmorland.' Late in November 1864 Smith published a 'Letter to the Electors of the County of Westmorland,' which was to become the force behind the anti-confederation blast in New Brunswick. The delegates to the conference, with a mandate to discuss only Maritime union, had acted unconstitutionally, he declared, and had placed the interests of Canada ahead of those of New Brunswick. The dominant Canadians would impose prohibitive taxes on the colony to pay for their past extravagances such as canals and railways. There would also be the cost of two governments rather than one and representation by population would place New Brunswick permanently in a subordinate position. When Tilley called an election early in 1865, Smith was ready for him. He stumped the province with a devastating speech in which he said that confederation had been conjured up in the 'oily brains of Canadian politicians' as a solution to their own problems and as a scheme to exploit others. He warned his listeners to examine the two states, 'one [Canada] suffering from anarchy and disquiet . . . [the other] New Brunswick . . . enjoying all the blessings of this life.' The spectre of direct taxation served as a backdrop to the designs of the Canadians, who would increase in dominance as their population and appetite grew, relegating New Brunswick to the status of a 'mere municipality.' As an alternative Smith offered both continued reciprocity with the United States and the Western Extension Railway, part of the European and North American, from Saint John to the American border. But fear of Canada was the essential ingredient in his message. Smith presented his case with 'great force and animation' and the anti-confederates in New Brunswick, with Smith the 'heart and soul of the opposition,' shattered the union movement by carrying 26 of the 41 seats in the assembly. Four independents and 11 unionists were also elected.

After the anti-confederate victory Gordon had the mortifying task of inviting the despised Smith to form the government, though he tempered the chore by asking both Smith and Robert Duncan Wilmot, a Conservative who opposed the Quebec plan, to select the Executive Council. Together they wrestled with the problem of choosing a cabinet from men united only in their opposition to the Quebec Resolutions. Some of the members of the cabinet they chose actually supported a British North American union with either a stronger central government or stronger provincial governments. John Campbell Allen of Fredericton, the attorney general, was a Conservative like Wilmot and like him favoured a legislative union. Smith and George Luther Hatheway, the chief commissioner of public works, wanted greatly increased provincial rights if any union scheme went forward, while Arthur Hill Gillmor, the provincial secretary, and Timothy Warren Anglin were opposed to all union schemes. Anglin, the leader of the Saint John Catholics, was considered an Irish radical and rebel by some and was especially difficult to

work with because he refused to make any concessions or compromises. Since the Roman Catholic vote had been decisive in many constituencies where Smith's supporters won, the Anglin and Catholic position could not be ignored. The general consensus on the cabinet was that it was a 'queer admixture of Tories and Liberals' though Gordon admitted they were 'men of undoubted honesty' and 'an improvement on . . . the previous Council.' Smith, the president of the council, he described as 'a man of some ability & considerable obstinacy. His views are narrow & his temper violent but though very impatient of opposition or control I believe him to possess the merits of honesty of purpose & resolution. He belongs to the radical section of politicians, but, at the same time, is very hostile towards the U.S.'

The mutual distrust that existed between Smith and Gordon was only one of a variety of problems. The members of the council disagreed on most issues and policies, from the militia and railways to external relations and the role of the lieutenant governor. A master manipulator might have manoeuvred among them with dexterity; Smith seemed paralyzed by the situation. Shortly after assuming office in March 1865, Smith was characterized by the Saint John *Morning Telegraph* as the 'ablest and most eloquent apostle of the genus and generation stand-still,' a view proved unfair when the government introduced a new militia bill and a Western Extension Railway bill in the spring session of that year.

The determination of the British government to reverse the New Brunswick decision on confederation was Smith's greatest concern, and for that reason he and Attorney General Allen left for London on 20 June 1865 to counteract imperial pressures. They also sought support for a renewed reciprocity treaty, for a railway link between New Brunswick and Nova Scotia, and for a loan of £25,000 sterling from Baring Brothers to meet provincial fiscal obligations. Though they were successful on the last three, Edward Cardwell, the colonial secretary, made it clear that he was committed to confederation. He may have offered Smith a position such as a colonial governorship to induce his support.

Smith returned to New Brunswick less confident than he had been on leaving it. His council was becoming restless and his policies were in jeopardy. The first sod was turned on the Western Extension Railway on 10 Nov. 1865 but because of financial difficulties construction never proceeded. Anglin, who was strongly committed to the railway, chose to resign from the cabinet. Vacancies on the bench led to the appointment of Allen to the Supreme Court and in a brutally fought by-election in York County Charles Fisher defeated Smith's candidate, John Pickard. Another vacancy on the bench caused more dissension and the defection from the cabinet of Andrew Rainsford Wetmore, whose claims had been ignored. The American rejection of reciprocity early in 1866 left Smith without a program and prompted the resignation of Wilmot, who now openly supported confederation. In the meantime, Gordon, as a dutiful imperial servant under pressure, exerted all the force he dared to achieve a union policy. In February 1866 Smith was compelled to take a hard look at his position. His original council was fragmented beyond recognition and his promises of reciprocity and the Western Extension had proved empty. The independents in the assembly were drifting away and were joined by deserters such as Wilmot and Wetmore. Though Smith was convinced he still had the support of the assembly and the province, he was also aware of his mounting failures and the increase in the pro-union sentiment. Gordon continuously pressed Smith to pursue a union policy that would be acceptable to the imperial authorities, the Canadians, and the majority of New Brunswickers. From late 1865 Smith probably realized he would have to follow such a course, but he vacillated for weeks before deciding to include a vague paragraph in the speech from the throne on 8 March 1866 suggesting that his government would advocate some form of British North American union. Whether Smith had a plan in mind is not known. It may have been no more than a notion to pursue some form of union. Opponents both within and outside his party never let him work out his ideas. Internally, the Acadian and Roman Catholic members would not support any union legislation. Externally, Charles Fisher and the confederates were determined that Smith should not carry confederation and claim the anticipated rewards. To that end they fought him in the assembly with a debate on an amendment to the speech from the throne, accusing him of failing to take adequate steps to protect the province from the threatened Fenian invasion. For four long weeks the debate dragged on and the government was paralyzed. Gordon, convinced that his future in the colonial service depended upon his colony pursuing a union path, became alarmed as Smith appeared to abandon any move towards confederation. By the beginning of April Gordon could no longer tolerate the situation. He decided to force Smith from office by accepting a strongly worded pro-confederation reply to the speech from the throne from the upper house, the Legislative Council. In a colony with responsible government this was a highly irregular procedure for a governor to follow. Smith correctly insisted that it was his right to be consulted and to recommend, but Gordon cared little about the rights and dignity of colonials. Smith resigned. It was his only course. It was also a constitutional crisis of the first order and one that Tilley considered unnecessary since he was convinced Smith would have had to capitulate within a few weeks. Still, the confederates took office when it was offered to them by Gordon and immediately went to the electorate for approval.

6   From J.M. Beck, *Joseph Howe: Anti-Confederate* (Ottawa: Canadian Historical Association, 1968), 11, 14.

Why did Howe turn against the Quebec scheme? The analysis of human behaviour—never easy—presents special difficulties in issues which are as complex as Confederation was in Nova Scotia. The leading public men may actually believe they are acting under one set of motives when another is the real determinant of their conduct: whether this is true or not, their opponents are likely to ascribe the worst possible motives to their actions. . . .

Howe feared, most of all, that the discussion of union would take the minds of both Britons and colonials away from what he deemed was the most vital question of the time, the organization of the Empire, and that the implementation of union would prevent such an organization from being effected for many years to come, if at all. Thus he was not being inconsistent with his basic nature in opposing the Quebec Resolutions. He already had a far-reaching project to which he had committed himself and he could not be enthusiastic about anything which might stand in its way.

The organization of the Empire was not a new theme for Howe. Even before responsible government had been conceded, he was already arguing that colonials ought to have some say in determining the Empire's policies. British subjects everywhere, he maintained, had 'a common right to share in much that our ancestors have bequeathed,' including that of helping to make the decisions which affected them. He thought, too, that the leading colonial minds should be able to aspire to colonial governorships and senior positions at the Colonial Office, or, as he put it, 'to have a fair field of competition on which to illustrate, side by side, with the other branches of the family the heroic or intellectual qualities which "run in the blood".' A stout autonomist like Professor Lower might wonder whether Howe, 'despite his earlier work for Responsible Government was [any] more than a colonial who

preferred the crumbs that fell from the rich man's table in England to the promise of North American nationhood.' But actually Howe's proposals indicated anything but subservience; in his mind they were simply the logical outcome of responsible government.

Professor Creighton calls Howe a liberal imperial federationist born out of his time. 'Even Whigs like Russell and Palmerston,' he says, 'would have thought him comically old-fashioned. Hard-eyed, cost-accounting Liberals like Cardwell and Gladstone would have regarded his imperial dreams as stupid and dangerous. There was not the slightest chance that the Empire for which he hoped could ever come into existence during his lifetime.' Creighton seems to imply a much more complex organization of the Empire than Howe had intended. But in any case Howe could not be expected to possess the hindsight of modern historians. Perhaps he was obtuse; certainly he had not yet realized that none of the British statesmen cared nearly as much for the Empire as he did. That disillusioning experience was to come later. In 1865–66 Howe was not the worn-out, lack-lustre, despairing individual whom Roy portrays, but no less energetic and ebullient than before. And with the same enthusiasm for the Empire. 'Do we want to be part of a great nationality?' he asked the people of Yarmouth in May, 1866. 'We are already a portion of the greatest empire on which the sun has ever shone.' A little later he told the people of Barrington:

> When the Apostle [Paul] claimed his Roman citizenship, he knew what it embraced—the protection of the eagles, the majesty and power of Rome. I am a British subject, and for me that term includes free trade and a common interest with fifty Provinces and two hundred and fifty millions of people, forming an Empire too grand and too extensive for Paul's imagination to conceive. You

go down to the sea in ships, and a flag of old renown floats above them, and the Consuls and Ministers of the Empire are prompt to protect your property and your sons in every part of the world.

Howe had no doubts about the direction in which Nova Scotians ought to look, and it was not westward to the backwoods of Canada. None gloried more than he in the Nova Scotian mercantile marine and the doings of his compatriots upon the high seas. Should they not continue, therefore, to work out their own destiny along these lines 'without running away, above tidewater, after the will-of-the-wisp at Ottawa, which will land us in a Slough of Despond?' What could Ottawa ever be anyway? It was as close to the North Pole as almost any city in the world, and had no attractions other than a waterfall. 'Take a Nova Scotian to Ottawa, away above tidewater, freeze him up for five months, where he cannot view the Atlantic, smell salt water, or see the sail of a ship, and the man will pine and die.'

A union, he admitted, might sometime be practicable. But it had to come by stages, 'by Railroads first, social and commercial intercourse afterwards, and then, when we were prepared for it by a natural development of our system on the model we admire at Home.' To union in general he put forward the same objections as in 1840,— the defenceless state of the frontier of Canada, the mixed and hostile character of the population and so on. Had the French Canadians, by sticking together, not controlled the government of Canada since the Act of Union? 'They will do the

same thing in a larger Union . . . But should a chance combination thwart them, then they will back their Local Legislature against the United Parliament, and, in less than five years, will as assuredly separate from the Confederacy as Belgium did from Holland.'

Of the Quebec scheme in particular Howe was equally critical. The United Kingdom, for its own safety, had repudiated the local legislatures which Scotland and Ireland had once possessed. Yet it would now foist five Parliaments upon four millions of people who had no foreign affairs to manage or colonists to govern. If the Dominion Parliament was to be completely paramount, as it was apparently intended, why have provincial legislatures at all? Would they not be useless, mischievous, perhaps even dangerous? Not only had the Nova Scotian delegates permitted the provincial Assembly to be 'shorn of all dignity and authority,' but in accepting representation by population they had been 'done Brown.' As a result, the Canadians would 'appoint our governors, judges and senators. They are to "tax us by any and every mode" and spend the money. They are to regulate our trade, control our Post Office, command the militia, fix the salaries, do what they like with our shipping and navigation, with our sea-coast and river fisheries, regulate the currency and the rate of interest, and seize upon our savings banks.' All in all, he concluded, that 'where there are no cohesive qualities in the material, no skill in the design, no prudence in the management, unite what you will and there is no strength.'

7 From Ged Martin, 'Painting the Other Picture: The Case against Confederation', in C.C. Eldridge, ed., *From Rebellion to Patriation: Canada and Britain in the Nineteenth and Twentieth Centuries* (Aberystwyth: Canadian Studies Group in Wales, 1989), 55–60.

'I do not know of anyone opposed to union in the abstract', said New Brunswick's Timothy Warren Anglin, 'but my impression is that the

time has not arrived for any kind of union, and I will oppose it to the last.'[1] This was a common theme among the critics: intercolonial union in principle, union one day, but not this union, not now.[2] As Edward Whelan put it, the critics accepted the principle of ploughing the field, but objected to destroying the daisies and field mice.[3] How sincere were these protestations—by some, but by no means all the critics of Confederation—in favour of an eventual British North American union? Perhaps they were gestures of open-mindedness merely to win over waverers: David Reesor found it 'extraordinary' that so many members of the Legislative Council spoke 'strongly and emphatically against many of the resolutions', while declaring their reluctant intention to vote for the package.[4] Yet even Dorion, who went to some lengths to clear his name of the slander of ever having spoken favourably of the idea, could leave open a faint and distant possibility. 'Population may extend over the wilderness that now lies between the Maritime Provinces and ourselves, and commercial intercourse may increase sufficiently to render Confederation desirable.'[5] As late as 1864, admittedly at a social occasion, Joseph Howe proclaimed: 'I have always been in favour of uniting any two, three, four, or the whole five of the provinces.'[6] It is not necessary to follow McGee in the full flight of his oratory, but it may well be that the idea of Confederation had become an autonomous cause of its own happening. 'If we have dreamed a dream of union . . . it is at least worth remarking that a dream which has been dreamed by such wise and good men, may, for aught we know or you know, have been a sort of vision—a vision foreshadowing forthcoming natural events in a clear intelligence.'[7]

If some of the opponents subscribed to the idea of an eventual intercolonial union, most of the critics in the province of Canada argued that Confederation was not a solution to present difficulties, and it would itself require a far greater degree of political wisdom than was necessary to rescue the existing system. Henri Joly felt that the various provinces would meet in a confederated parliament 'as on a field of battle'.[8] Christopher Dunkin referred to the airy dismissals of such warnings by ministerial supporters: 'Oh! there won't be any trouble; men are in the main sensible, and won't try to make trouble.' If public men were so reasonable as to be able to work the new system, why then had the province of Canada had 'four crises in two years'?[9] In any case, even if it were accepted that Upper and Lower Canada were not living together in harmony, the answer was surely for them to work out a new system of government and not to claim that only through a wider union could they get along. Dunkin noted that in the years between the lapsing of Galt's federation initiative in 1859 and the formation of the Grand Coalition of June 1864, 'we quarrelled and fought about almost everything, but did not waste a thought or a word upon this gigantic question of the Confederation of these Provinces.'[10] 'Surely', Thomas Scatcherd argued, 'if parties could unite as they did in June last, they could have united to prevent the difficulty complained of . . . without entering upon a scheme to subvert the Constitution'.[11]

While some critics of Confederation admitted that the Canadian Union had its problems, others felt them to have been exaggerated. Henri Joly contrasted Taché's claim that 'the country was bordering on civil strife', with the ministry's throne speech, which thanked 'a beneficent Providence for the general contentment of the people of this province'.[12] Joseph Perrault asked 'have we not reason to be proud of our growth since 1840, and of the fact that within the past twenty-five years, our progress, both social and material, has kept pace with that of the first nations in the world?'[13] Some Lower Canada members were suspicious of the motives behind the agitation for 'representation by population' in Upper Canada, dismissing it—in Joly's words— as 'one of those political clap-traps which ambitious men, who can catch them in no other way, set to catch the heedless multitude'. Both Joly and Perrault argued that hypocrisy was proved by the alacrity with which Upper Canada Reformers entered the Macdonald-Sicotte administration of 1862, which was bound not to press the issue—proof that 'Upper Canada is much more indifferent, and its leaders much less sincere touching this question of the representation, than they would have us believe.'[14] Perrault, however, went much further. In a speech presumably aimed at stoking every French Canadian fear of assimilation—it ranged from the Acadian deportation, via the history of Mauritius to the francophobia of Lord Durham's Report—Perrault denied that Upper Canada had more people than Lower Canada at all. The 'true total' of the population of Upper Canada had been 'greatly exaggerated. . . . Did not all their journals declare that the census of 1861 *must* indicate a very large total population in favour of Upper Canada over Lower Canada?' The prophecy had been self-fulfilling, 'the number of the living increased and the number of the dead diminished', a fraud revealed when it was noticed that the population under the age of one year exceeded the live births of the previous twelve months by eight thousand. The census had also under-counted the population of Lower Canada, for 'our farmers have always stood in dread of the census, because they have a suspicion that it is taken with the sole object of imposing some tax, or of making some draft of men for the defence of the country.' Confusingly, he also contended that even if Upper Canada's population did exceed that of Lower Canada, it was no more than a temporary blip, caused by Irish famine migration, which had now ceased. So too had the outward flow of French Canadians to New England, with the result that within ten years, the higher birth rate of Lower Canada would bring the two provinces back to equality of population.[15]

The core of the case against Confederation was that there was no crisis sufficient to justify so large a change. Consequently, critics largely refused to enter the trap of offering alternative solutions. 'We are asked, "what are you going to do? You must do something. Are you going to fall back into our old state of dead-lock?"', Dunkin reported, adding that whenever he heard the argument 'that something must be done, I sus-

pect that there is a plan on foot to get something very bad done'.[16] Henri Joly took the same line. 'I am asked: "If you have nothing to do with Confederation, what will you have?" I answer, we would remain as we are.'[17] 'Now my proposition is very simple', Joseph Howe told the people of Nova Scotia. 'It is to let well enough alone.'[18] Not surprisingly, the opponents of Confederation indignantly rejected the argument that they were—wittingly or otherwise—working for annexation to the United States. They replied that the campaign for Confederation itself contained the germ of an annexationist threat. Matthew Cameron, one of the few prominent Upper Canada Conservatives to oppose the scheme, warned that the delusive arguments of material gain from Confederation with the tiny Maritimes 'are arguments tenfold stronger in favour of union with the United States'.[19] Nor did the danger lie simply in encouraging hopes of greater prosperity, as was shown when a moderate Lower Canadian journal could proclaim 'qu'à tous les points du vue, nos institutions, notre langue, et nos lois seront mieux protégées avec la confederation américain qu'avec le projet de conféderation de l'Amérique du Nord'.[20] 'Once destroy public confidence in our institutions', warned T.C. Wallbridge, 'and it is impossible to predict what extremes may be resorted to.'[21] Joseph Howe predicted that the imposition of Confederation on unwilling provinces would lead to 'undying hatreds and ultimate annexation'.[22] . . .

. . . [S]upporters of Confederation had little motive in demanding that its opponents come up with rival schemes, but rather preferred to present the Quebec scheme as an immutable package, agreed behind locked doors as a balanced intercolonial treaty. Critics objected to being faced with the resolutions as a package. 'What is the use of considering them if we cannot come to our conclusions and give them effect in the shape of amendments?', asked James Atkins.[23] At Quebec, Dunkin pointed out, twenty-three men had sat for seventeen working days to produce 'a scheme of a Constitution which they vaunt as being altogether better than that of the model republic of the United States, and even than that of the model kingdom of Great Britain'.[24] William Annand thought that a scheme 'matured in a few weeks, amid exhaustive festivities' could not be the best constitution possible.[25] Joseph Howe noted that the inflexibility of the Quebec scheme would be carried forward to the future. 'No means are provided by which the people, should it be found defective, can improve it from time to time. Whenever a change is required they must come back to the Imperial Parliament.'[26] Let it never be said that Joseph Howe lacked vision for the future.

Coupled with resentment at the rejection of any possibility of amendment was anger at the total refusal of a popular vote on so major a constitutional change. As a Hamilton paper put it, if there was to be no general election on Confederation, the polling booths 'may as well be turned into pigpens, and the voters lists cut up into pipe-lighters'.[27] In Nova Scotia, where peti-tion after petition dwelt on the province's long tradition of representative and responsible government, the people of Shelburne put the issue in more fundamental and sober terms: 'whilst Your Majesty's petitioners freely admit the right of their representatives in Provincial Parliament to legislate for them within reasonable limits, they cannot admit the right of such representatives to effect sudden changes, amounting to an entire subversion of the constitution, without the deliberate sanction of the people expressed at the polls.'[28] As Joseph Howe put it in more succinct and homely terms, the local legislature had 'no right to violate a trust only reposed in them for four years, or in fact to sell the fee simple of a mansion of which they have but a limited lease'.[29] If the scheme were beneficial, which the people of Queen's County flatly doubted, 'the means employed to force it upon the country without an appeal to the people, and with full knowledge of their intense dislike of the measure', were enough to discredit it.[30]

NOTES

1. Speech of 7 April 1866, quoted in William M. Baker, *Timothy Warren Anglin 1822–1896: Irish Catholic Canadian* (Toronto, 1977), 103, and see also 58. Anglin was editor of the Saint John *Morning Freeman*. According to Creighton, Anglin was 'an unsubdued ex-rebel' who 'flung the full force of his abusive and mendacious journalism against Confederation' (D.G. Creighton, *The Road to Confederation: The Emergence of Canada 1863–1867* [Toronto, 1964], 251, and see also 247). It is unlikely that Anglin took part in the Irish rising of 1848 and there is no reason to think that his journalism was unusually mendacious or abusive by contemporary standards, which were admittedly low. Thus have critics of Confederation been dismissed.

2. Similar views were expressed in the Canadian Legislative Council by James G. Currie, Billa Flint and David Reesor and in the Assembly by Christopher Dunkin, Joseph Perrault, Thomas Scatcherd and T.C. Wallbridge. *Parliamentary Debates on the Subject of the Confederation of the British North American Provinces* (3rd Session, 8th Provincial Parliament of Canada, Quebec, 1865), 46, 164, 319, 483, 585, 749, 660 (hereafter CD).

3. Charlottetown *Examiner*, 13 August 1864, 30 January 1865, quoted in P.B. Waite, *The Life and Times of Confederation 1864–1867: Politics, Newspapers, and the Union of British North America* (Toronto, 1962), 186.

4. CD, 328.

5. CD, 248.

6. Speech in Halifax, 13 August 1864, in J.A. Chisholm, ed., *The Speeches and Public Letters of Joseph Howe*, 2 vols (Halifax, 1909), II, 433. A Nova Scotian critic, John Locke (MLA for Shelburne), discounted the fact that 'at different times various politicians have . . . made grand

speeches in favour of Union' because 'it was well understood at that time, that nothing was to come of it.' Quoted by James Sturgis, 'Opposition to Confederation in Nova Scotia, 1864–1 870', work-in-progress paper, 7. However, the statements quoted in this section were all made after the Charlottetown meeting.

7. CD, 126.

8. CD, 352. Henri-Gustave Joly (1829–1908) was an unusual figure. A Protestant, born in France, he represented Lotbinière, which was also the family seigneurie. In 1888, he formally added 'de Lotbinière' to his surname.

9. CD, 508. A Conservative, the MPP for Brome, Christopher Dunkin (1812–81) opposed Confederation, delivering the longest speech of the debates, which stretched over two evenings and lasted for eight hours, despite ill health. As Waite observes, it was 'a criticism of the Quebec Resolutions that towers over all others'. Waite, *Life and Times*, 153. His dry and aloof manner may have undermined the effectiveness of his criticisms. McGee commented: 'we ought to aim at perfection, but who has ever attained it, except perhaps the hon. Member for Brome.' CD, 136. Despite his stand, he joined Macdonald's cabinet in 1869.

10. CD, 485.

11. CD, 747. Thomas Scatcherd (1823–76), a Reformer, was MPP for Middlesex West.

12. CD, 357. Etienne-Paschal Taché (1795–1865) was a Bleu who had retired from active politics in 1858, but was persuaded to return in 1864, and presided over the coalition ministry. On his death, John A. Macdonald called him 'as sincere and truly honorable a gentleman as ever moved in public or private life'. Quoted in Waite, *Life and Times*, 152.

13. CD, 586. Joseph-François (also known as Joseph Xavier) Perrault (1838–1905) was MPP for Richelieu. A Rouge, he delivered a five-hour attack on the Quebec scheme in the Confederation debates.

14. CD, 357 (Joly) and cf. 591 (Perrault).

15. CD, 593–5, 625–6.

16. CD, 543.

17. CD, 356–7.

18. Open letter, 10 April 1866, in Chisholm, ed., *Speeches and Letters of Joseph Howe*, II, 463.

19. CD, 456.

20. *L'Ordre*, 7 June 1865, quoted in Waite, *Life and Times*, 147.

21. CD, 659. Thomas Cambell Wallbridge was a Clear Grit MPP for Hastings North.

22. Howe to Isaac Buchanan, 26 June 1866, in Chisholm, ed., *Speeches and Letters of Joseph Howe*, II, 464. In his 1866 pamphlet, *Confederation Considered in Relation to the Interests of the Empire*, Howe complained that in the New Brunswick election that year, 'one half of an entirely loyal population were taught to brand the other half as disloyal.' Quoted in Chisholm, ed., *Speeches and Letters of Joseph Howe*, II, 484.

23. CD, 155, 158. James Aikins (1823– 1904) was MLC for the Home District. A former Clear Grit, he joined Macdonald's government in 1867.

24. CD, 487.

25. Halifax *Morning Chronicle*, 24 January 1866, quoted in Waite, *Life and Times*, 221. Annand used the argument, not to reject Confederation, but as a device to suggest an alternative approach.

26. *British Parliamentary Papers* (BPP), 1867, xlviii, Correspondence Respecting the Proposed Union of the British North American Provinces, Howe, Annand and McDonald to Carnarvon, 19 January 1867, 13.

27. Hamilton *Times*, November 1864, quoted in Waite, *Life and Times*, 122. See also Bruce W. Hodgins, 'Democracy and the Ontario Fathers of Confederation', in Bruce Hodgins and Robert Page, eds, *Canadian History Since Confederation: Essays and Interpretations*, 2nd edn (Georgetown, Ont., 1979), 19–28.

28. Shelburne Petition, June 1866, in BPP, 1867, xlviii, Correspondence, 70.

29. BPP, 1867, xlviii, Howe et al. to Carnarvon, 19 January 1867, 18.

30. BPP, 1867, xlviii, Correspondence, 75.

by permission of University of Toronto Press Inc.

Gustave Lanctôt, excerpt from *Canada and the American Revolution, 1774–1783*, trans. Margaret M. Cameron. Toronto: Clarke, Irwin, 1967, pp. 30–5.

Philip Lawson, excerpt from *The Imperial Challenge: Quebec and Britain in the Age of the American Revolution*. Montreal and Kingston: McGill-Queen's University Press, 1989, pp. 126–9. Reprinted by permission of McGill-Queen's University Press.

Earl Lockerby, excerpt from 'The Deportation of the Acadians from Ile St-Jean, 1758' *Acadiensis*, XXVII (Spring 1998), pp. 45–6. Reprinted by permission of Acadiensis.

Tina Loo, excerpt from '"A Delicate Game": The Meaning of Law on Grouse Creek', *BC Studies*, 96, Winter 1992–3, pp. 41–4. Reprinted by permission of BC Studies.

Anne McIlroy, 'Who were the first North Americans?' from *The Globe and Mail*, 6 September 2003. Reprinted with permission from The Globe and Mail.

Charles D. Mahaffie, Jr., excerpts from *A Land of Discord Always: Acadia from its Beginning to the Expulsion of its People, 1604–1755* . Camden, ME: Down East Books, 1995, pp. 248–60.

Joyce Marshall, excerpt from *Word from New France: The Selected Letters of Marie de l'Incarnation*, translated and edited by Joyce Marshall. Toronto: Oxford University Press, 1967, pp.75–6. © Joyce Marshall. Reprinted by permission of Joyce Marshall.

Ged Martin, excerpt from 'Painting the Other Picture: The Case Against Confederation' by Ged Martin from *From Rebellion to Patriation: Canada and Britain in the Nineteenth and Twentieth Centuries*, C.C. Eldridge, ed. Aberystwyth: Canadian Studies Group in Wales, 1989, pp. 55–60.

Elaine Allen Mitchell, excerpts from 'The Scot in the Fur Trade' in *The Scottish Tradition in Canada*, W. Stanford Reid, ed. Toronto: McClelland & Stewart, 1976, pp. 31–40.

William L. Morton, excerpt from *Henry Youle Hind, 1823–1908*. Toronto: University of Toronto Press, 1980. Reprinted by permission of University of Toronto Press Inc.

Hilda Neatby , excerpt from *Quebec: The Revolutionary Age, 1760–1791*. Toronto: McClelland & Stewart, 1966, pp. 125–7.

Mary Beth Norton, excerpts from 'Eighteenth-Century American Women in Peace and War: The Case of the Loyalists', *William and Mary Quarterly*, Third Series, 33, 1976, pp. 386–409. Reprinted by permission of the Omohundro Institute of Early American History and Culture.

Maregaret Ormsby, excerpt from *British Columbia: A History*. Toronto: Macmillan of Canada, 1958, pp. 157–61.

Fernand Ouelette, excerpt from 'The 1837/8 Rebellion in Lower Canada as a Social', *Histoire sociale/Social History*, Vol. 2, 1968. Reprinted by permission of Histoire sociale/Social History.

Doug Owram, excerpt from *Promise of Eden: The Canadian Expansionist Movement and the Idea of the West, 1856–1900*. Toronto: University of Toronto Press, 1980. Reprinted by permission of University of Toronto Press Inc.

Arthur J. Ray, excerpt from *Indians in the Fur Trade: Their Role as Trappers, Hunters, and Middlemen in the Lands Southwest of Hudson Bay 1660–1870*. Toronto: University of Toronto Press, 1974. Reprinted by permission of University of Toronto Press Inc.

Irene Spry, excerpt from 'The Palliser Expedition' in *Rupert's Land: A Cultural Tapestry*, Richard C. Davis, ed. Waterloo: Wilfrid Laurier University Press, 1988, pp. 195–202. Reprinted by permission of Wilfrid Laurier University Press.

Marcel Trudel , excerpts from *The Seigneurial Regime*. Ottawa: Canadian Historical Association, 1971, pp. 12–17. Reprinted by permission of the Canadian Historical Association.

Sylvia Van Kirk, excerpt from *"Many Tender Ties": Women in Fur-Trade Society, 1670–1870* . Winnipeg, 1980, pp. 53–73. Reprinted by permission of J. Gordon Shillingford Publishing Inc.

P.B. Waite, excerpt from *The Life and Times of Confederation 1864–1867: Politics, Newspapers, and the Union of British North America*, Third Edition. Toronto: Robin Brass Studio, 2001, pp. 167–72. Reprinted by permission of the author.

James W. St G. Walker. 'The Establishment of a Free Black Community in Nova Scotia, 1783–1840'. Reprinted by permission of the publisher from *The African Diaspora: Interpretive Readings*, edited by Martin L. Kilson and Robert Rotberg, pp. 207–215, Cambridge, Mass.: Harvard University Press. Copyright © 1976 by the President and Fellows of Harvard College.

C.M. Wallace, excerpt from 'Albert Smith' in *Dictionary of Canadian Biography*, Vol. 11. Toronto: University of Toronto Press, 1982. Reprinted by permission of University of Toronto Press Inc.

David Ricardo Williams, 'The Administration of Criminal and Civil Justice in the Mining Camps and Frontier Communities of British Columbia' from *Law & Justice in a New Land: Essays in Western Canadian History*, ed. Louis A. Knafla. Calgary: Carswell, 1986, pp. 217–21. Reprinted by permission of Carswell, a division of Thomson Canada Limited.

Suzanne Zeller, excerpt from *Inventing Canada: Early Victorian Science and the Idea of a Transcontinental Nation*. Toronto: University of Toronto Press, 1987, pp. 170–3, 176. Reprinted by permission of the author.